724 Speedy Recipes At Your Fingertips

IN THE THREE YEARS we've published *Quick Cooking* magazine, we've heard from thousands of readers who enjoy sitting down with their families for hearty, home-cooked meals that don't take long to prepare.

Saving time is the successful premise behind this indispensable cookbook. Whether you have only 10 minutes to get dinner on the table, or you want to make everything ahead of time, we've got you covered.

This *2001 Quick Cooking Annual Recipes* conveniently gathers every rapid recipe published in *Quick Cooking* during the year 2000—that's 724 recipes in all—into one reader-friendly treasury. These recipes were submitted by real home cooks from across the country. The book is filled with large-print recipes and hundreds of photos, so you can see what many of the dishes look like before you prepare them.

Here's what else you'll find inside:

Chapters That Meet Your Needs. With 20 chapters that correspond to popular features in *Quick Cooking* magazine, it's a snap to find a recipe that matches your family's taste and your timetable. (A complete list of chapters can be found on Page 3.)

For example, if you're too busy to prepare a fancy dinner, check out the 12 complete meals in "30 Minutes to Mealtime". Every one will satisfy your family's hunger in a hurry.

Or why not come home to the mouth-watering aroma of Pennsylvania Pot Roast, ready to eat the minute you open the front door? You'll find it plus 42 other slow cooker creations in the "Timeless Recipes with Kitchen Tools" chapter.

Award-Winning Recipes. You'll get all the family-pleasing, quick-to-make recipes that earned prizes in the six national contests we held last year: Easy Chocolate Desserts, Light 'n' Luscious Dishes, Speedy Sandwiches, Summer Salads, Bread Machine Recipes and Slow-Cooker Favorites.

Easy-to-Use Indexes. To make all 724 recipes fast to find, we've listed them in two simple-to-use indexes. (See page 336.) The general index lists every recipe by food category and/or major ingredient. The alphabetical recipe listing is perfect for folks who are looking for a specific family favorite. In both indexes, you'll find a bold red checkmark (✓) in front of all recipes that use less fat, sugar or salt and include Nutritional Analysis and Diabetic Exchanges.

What's on the Menu? To make meal planning simple, our food editors "grouped" several recipes from various chapters to create a host of around-the-clock suggested menus. (This time-saving tool appears on page 4.)

Every recipe and hint in this *2001 Quick Cooking Annual Recipes* cookbook was specifically selected with the busy cook in mind. You're sure to enjoy this collection for years to come...and you'll be able to treat your loved ones to comforting, wholesome home cooking without spending all your precious time in the kitchen.

2001 Quick Cooking Annual Recipes

Editors: Heidi Reuter Lloyd, Julie Schnittka

Art Directors: Nancy Robjohns, Maribeth Greinke

Food Editor: Janaan Cunningham

Associate Editor: Susan Uphill

Assistant Art Director: Nicole Malmberg

Production: Ellen Lloyd, Catherine Fletcher

Cover Photography: Rob Hagen

Food Photography Artist:
Stephanie Marchese

Taste of Home Books
©2000 Reiman Publications, LLC
5400 S. 60th St., Greendale WI 53129

International Standard Book Number:
0-89821-301-0
International Standard Serial Number:
1522-6603

PICTURED ON THE COVER: Ladyfinger Cheesecake
(p. 202), Vegetable Wild Rice (p. 249), Snappy Peas 'n'
Mushrooms (p. 282) and Tangy Pork Tenderloin (p. 282).

To order additional copies of this book or any other
Reiman Publications books, write: *Taste of Home* Books,
P.O. Box 908, Greendale WI 53129; call toll-free 1-
800/344-2560 to order with a credit card or visit our
Web site at **www.reimanpub.com**.

Taste of Home's
QUICK COOKING

Executive Editor: Kathy Pohl
Editor: Julie Kastello
Food Editor: Janaan Cunningham
Associate Food Editors: Coleen Martin, Diane Werner
Senior Recipe Editor: Sue A. Jurack
Recipe Editor: Janet Briggs
Associate Editors: Kristine Krueger, Ann Kaiser,
Faithann Stoner
Test Kitchen Director: Karen Johnson
Test Kitchen Home Economists: Karen Wright,
Julie Herzfeldt, Sue Draheim, Kristin Koepnick,
Pat Schmeling, Wendy Stenman
Test Kitchen Assistants: Rita Krajcir, Megan Taylor
Editorial Assistant: Ursula Maurer
Design Director: Jim Sibilski
Art Director: Julie Wagner
Art Associate: Brian Sienko
Food Photography: Rob Hagen, Dan Roberts
Food Photography Artist: Stephanie Marchese
Photo Studio Manager: Anne Schimmel
Production: Ellen Lloyd, Catherine Fletcher
Publisher: Roy Reiman

⏱ *Contents*

What's on The Menu?

GRAB A MENU from the best "fast food" place in town—your kitchen! The price is right, the atmosphere is relaxing, and the service couldn't be friendlier nor the guests more appreciative. And with the *2001 Quick Cooking Annual Recipes* book in your hands, you've already given yourself a generous tip!

Here's how to use the menu ideas featured here: Our food editors screened all the recipes that appear in this book, then "grouped" several from various chapters to make up menus for everyday and special-occasion family meals. Plus, you can mix and match recipes to make up menus of your own.

For even more complete meals, turn to the following chapters: The Busiest Cooks in the Country (p. 6), 30 Minutes to Mealtime (p. 20), Thinking Up a Theme (p. 34) and Company's Coming! (p. 302).

Six Breakfast Choices

Eighteen Lunch Choices

Thirty-Two Dinner Choices

Chapter 1

⏱ *The Busiest Cooks in the Country*

FROM THE MOMENT the alarm clock goes off in the morning until the sun sets in the evening, your typical day is probably packed with work, school and a host of other activities.

So you likely think there's little time left to prepare a savory sit-down dinner for the whole family. But this chapter can help!

Six fellow frenzied cooks from across the country share family-favorite recipes, timeless kitchen tips and menu-planning pointers that will put you on the fast track for making memorable meals your entire clan will enjoy.

FAMILY FARE. Clockwise from upper left: Roast Beef Quiche, Greek Garden Salad and Chocolate Mallow Pie (all recipes on pp. 12 and 13).

Dishing Up In-a-Dash Dinners

VISIT a tourist attraction called The Big Well in Greensburg, Kansas and you're likely to be greeted by Rhonda McKee. She's one of the friendly folks who staff the world's largest hand-dug well, measuring 32 feet across and 109 feet deep.

Rhonda's a dedicated wife and mother of two. She puts in part-time hours at the gift shop, while husband Chris works at the Greensburg Light Plant. She also keeps son Devin and daughter Kaley on track with their activities.

"I enjoy cooking, but my time in the kitchen is very limited. We try to sit down together for dinner at least 4 days a week. Finding nutritious and tasty recipes can be a challenge," she concedes.

Rhonda doesn't have to dig very deep into her recipe collection to come up with a made-in-minutes menu that will please her on-the-go family.

Fast-to-Fix Fiesta

"Chris loves Mexican food, so I make this meal often. It's easy and very satisfying," she promises.

Rhonda credits a friend with the recipe for Tomato Nacho Dip. The thick and creamy cheese dip gets its zip from convenient canned green chilies. It's a snap to zap in the microwave.

Next, Rhonda stirs up a batch of Cornmeal Drop Biscuits. The light golden biscuits are flecked with cheese and taste delicious spread with butter.

Rhonda then moves on to Taco Casserole, which bakes at the same oven temperature.

The casserole tastes like a taco salad and is a breeze to assemble. Rhonda crushes tortilla chips to form a bottom layer, then spreads on refried beans, a spicy meat mixture and cheese.

While it bakes, she readies chopped tomatoes, lettuce and other toppings. "You can serve helpings with whatever taco fixings your family likes," she notes.

To round out this Mexican meal, Rhonda serves rich Caramelitas. The chewy bars have a tasty oatmeal crust that's covered with gooey caramel ice cream topping, chocolate chips and walnuts.

"These sweet treats can be baked ahead, sealed in a container and kept in the fridge," she advises.

Tomato Nacho Dip

Ready in 15 minutes or less

1 can (4 ounces) chopped green chilies
1/2 cup chopped onion
2 tablespoons butter *or* margarine
2 tablespoons all-purpose flour
1/2 cup milk
1-1/2 cups (6 ounces) cubed process American cheese
1 cup (4 ounces) shredded Monterey Jack cheese
1/2 cup chopped fresh tomato
Tortilla chips

In a 1-1/2-qt. microwave-safe dish, combine chilies, onion and butter. Cover and microwave on high for 1-2 minutes or until butter is melted. Stir in flour until smooth. Gradually stir in milk until blended. Cook, uncovered, on high for 1-2 minutes or until thickened. Add cheeses and tomato. Microwave, uncovered, at 70% power for 2-3 minutes or until cheese is melted. Serve with tortilla chips. **Yield:** 2-2/3 cups. **Editor's Note:** This recipe was tested in an 850-watt microwave.

Cornmeal Drop Biscuits

Ready in 1 hour or less

1-1/3 cups all-purpose flour
1/2 cup cornmeal
2-1/2 teaspoons baking powder
1/2 teaspoon salt
1/2 teaspoon ground mustard
1/2 cup shortening
1/2 cup shredded cheddar cheese
1 cup milk

In a bowl, combine the first five ingredients; cut in shortening until crumbly. Stir in cheese and milk just until moistened. Drop by 1/4 cupfuls 2 in. apart onto a greased baking sheet. Bake at 375° for 26-28 minutes or until golden brown. Serve warm. **Yield:** 10 servings.

Taco Casserole

Ready in 1 hour or less

 Uses less fat, sugar or salt. Includes Nutritional Analysis and Diabetic Exchanges.

1 pound ground beef
1/4 cup chopped onion
1/4 cup chopped green pepper
1 envelope taco seasoning
1/2 cup water
1 cup crushed tortilla chips
1 can (16 ounces) refried beans
1 cup (4 ounces) shredded cheddar cheese
Toppings: chopped lettuce and tomatoes, sliced ripe olives, sour cream and picante sauce

In a skillet, cook beef, onion and green pepper over medium heat until meat is no longer pink; drain. Stir in taco seasoning and water. Cook and stir until thickened, about 3 minutes; set aside. Place chips in a greased 8-in. square baking dish. In a bowl, stir refried beans until smooth; spread over chips. Top with beef mixture and cheese. Bake, uncovered, at 375° for 15-20 minutes or until heated through. Top with lettuce, tomatoes and olives. Serve with sour cream and picante sauce. **Yield:** 4 servings. **Nutritional Analysis:** One serving (prepared with lean ground beef, reduced-sodium taco seasoning, low-fat tortilla chips, fat-free refried beans and reduced-fat cheddar cheese; calculated without toppings) equals 405 calories, 1,181 mg sodium, 47 mg cholesterol, 31 gm carbohydrate, 37 gm protein, 12 gm fat, 6 gm fiber. **Diabetic Exchanges:** 3-1/2 lean meat, 2 starch.

Caramelitas

1 cup plus 1 tablespoon all-purpose flour, *divided*
1 cup quick-cooking oats
3/4 cup packed brown sugar
1/2 teaspoon baking soda
1/4 teaspoon salt
3/4 cup butter *or* margarine, melted

1 cup (6 ounces) semisweet chocolate chips
1 jar (12-1/4 ounces) caramel ice cream topping
1/2 cup chopped walnuts

In a bowl, combine 1 cup of flour, oats, brown sugar, baking soda and salt. Stir in butter; mix well. Press into a greased 13-in. x 9-in. x 2-in. baking pan. Bake at 350° for 10 minutes or until set. Sprinkle with chocolate chips. Combine caramel topping and remaining flour until blended; drizzle over chips. Sprinkle with nuts. Bake 20-22 minutes longer or until bubbly. Cool completely; cut into bars. **Yield:** 3 dozen.

Rhonda's Helpful Hints

- Do anything that you can do ahead of time. Sometimes using a few moments of free time to chop ingredients or make a dessert really helps later.
- Plan a weekly menu, make your grocery list accordingly, then shop once a week using coupons. This takes only a few minutes to plan, yet saves lots of time and money in the long run.
- Get your kids interested in cooking at an early age. Although I do most of the cooking, my kids are learning to prepare some meals themselves.

—*Rhonda McKee*

Teacher Makes The Grade At Mealtime

ALTHOUGH Shelley McKinney traded in her job as a teacher to become a stay-at-home mom, she still has plenty of opportunities to teach.

"I'm proud of the fact that I'm the fourth generation of teachers in my family," Shelley notes. "I taught for 5 years before I had our first baby."

She and husband Brian live in New Castle, Indiana with their two daughters, Megan and Allison.

"Now I have time to be a room mother for Megan's class, listen to her classmates practice reading and go on field trips. I also home-school Allison for preschool," she says.

In addition, Shelley baby-sits regularly for a family with three children, teaches a weekly program for 3- to 5-year-olds at her church and volunteers to staff phones at a crisis center.

Despite her activities and Brian's work schedule, Shelley gathers her family for meals at least three times a week.

"Brian's job as a car salesman keeps him at the dealership until 5 p.m. for 2 weeks a month, then 'til 7 p.m. the other 2 weeks," she explains.

"On evenings he works late, I like to have dinner on the table as soon as he walks in the door. So I rely on one-dish dinners."

Slow-Cooked Specials

"I would have a hard time getting along without my microwave, bread machine or slow cooker," Shelley acknowledges.

Shelley uses her slow cooker to help prepare the mouth-watering meal featured here. In fact, she served this menu—with the addition of homemade bread from her bread machine—to 16 people from her church's Home Fellowship group.

"When we have company, I often serve Slow-Cooked Spaghetti Sauce because it's delicious, inexpensive and easy to prepare," she relates.

"It's wonderful to quickly assemble in the morning and let it simmer all day. Plus, it fills the house with a rich savory aroma," Shelley adds.

"Guests often tell me it's the best sauce they've ever had. The original recipe came from my mother, who cooked it on the stovetop, but I adapted it for the slow cooker," she notes.

For a spicy sauce, Shelley suggests adding 1-1/2 teaspoons of crushed red pepper flakes.

To accompany her main dish, Shelley tosses together Robust Italian Salad, a hearty combination of lettuce, pastrami, tomatoes and mozzarella cheese. Homemade Seasoned Croutons make it outstanding.

Butterscotch Chocolate Cake can be made ahead. A moist cake is covered with rich butterscotch ice cream topping, whipped topping and crushed candy bars.

Slow-Cooked Spaghetti Sauce

Plan ahead...uses slow cooker

1 pound ground beef *or* bulk Italian sausage
1 medium onion, chopped
2 cans (14-1/2 ounces *each*) diced tomatoes, undrained
1 can (8 ounces) tomato sauce
1 can (6 ounces) tomato paste
1 bay leaf
1 tablespoon brown sugar
4 garlic cloves, minced
1 to 2 teaspoons dried basil
1 to 2 teaspoons dried oregano
1 teaspoon salt
1/2 to 1 teaspoon dried thyme
Hot cooked spaghetti

In a skillet, cook beef and onion over medium heat until meat is no longer pink; drain. Transfer to a slow cooker. Add the next 10 ingredients. Cover and cook on low for 7-8 hours or until heated through. Discard bay leaf. Serve over spaghetti. **Yield:** 6-8 servings.

Robust Italian Salad

Ready in 15 minutes or less

 Uses less fat, sugar or salt. Includes Nutritional Analysis and Diabetic Exchanges.

1 package (16 ounces) ready-to-serve salad
1 package (2-1/2 ounces) sliced pastrami, cut into 1/2-inch pieces, optional
1 cup (4 ounces) shredded mozzarella cheese
4 plum tomatoes, chopped
1 teaspoon Italian seasoning
1/3 cup Italian salad dressing
1 cup Seasoned Croutons (recipe on next page)
Sliced ripe olives, optional

In a large salad bowl, combine the first five ingredients. Drizzle with dressing; toss to coat. Top with croutons and olives if desired. **Nutritional Analysis:** One serving (prepared with part-skim mozzarella and fat-free salad dressing and without pastrami and olives) equals 53 calories, 161 mg sodium, 6 mg cholesterol, 5 gm carbohydrate, 3 gm protein, 2 gm fat, 1 gm fiber. **Diabetic Exchanges:** 1 vegetable, 1/2 fat.

Seasoned Croutons

Ready in 30 minutes or less

2 tablespoons butter
1 tablespoon olive *or* vegetable oil
1/4 teaspoon garlic powder
1/4 teaspoon onion powder
1/4 teaspoon dried oregano
1/4 teaspoon dried basil
Pinch salt
6 slices day-old bread, cubed

In an ungreased 13-in. x 9-in. x 2-in. baking pan, combine the first seven ingredients. Place in a 300° oven until butter is melted. Remove from the oven; stir to combine. Add bread cubes and toss to coat. Bake for 10-15 minutes or until lightly browned, stirring frequently. Cool. Store in the refrigerator in an airtight container. **Yield:** 3 cups.

Butterscotch Chocolate Cake

Plan ahead...needs to chill

1 package (18-1/4 ounces) chocolate cake mix
1 jar (17 ounces) butterscotch ice cream topping

1 carton (8 ounces) frozen whipped topping, thawed
3 Butterfinger candy bars (2.1 ounces *each*), coarsely crushed

Prepare and bake cake according to package directions, using a greased 13-in. x 9-in. x 2-in. baking pan. Cool on a wire rack for 30 minutes. Using the end of a wooden spoon handle, poke 12 holes in warm cake. Pour butterscotch topping over cake; cool completely. Spread with whipped topping; sprinkle with candy bars. Refrigerate for at least 2 hours before serving. **Yield:** 12-16 servings.

Shelley's Supper Suggestions

- Get your family involved. My daughters set the table and help me make bread in the bread machine. My husband knows how much I hate doing dishes, so he pitches in and loads the dishwasher.
- Create a relaxing atmosphere. I love to use pretty dishes with matching glasses and cloth napkins at each meal. We have candlelight and classical CDs playing in the background, even if we're just eating soup and sandwiches.
- Make weekend meals special. I often make homemade pizza, allowing a different family member to choose the toppings each time. We've also developed a tradition of having cake for dessert on Friday evenings.
  —*Shelley McKinney*

Satisfying No-Fuss Family Fare

WHILE SOME FOLKS don't like to live in the past, Glenda Parsonage of Maple Creek, Saskatchewan is not one of them. The rancher's wife and mother of two is eager to do her part to keep history alive.

From May to October, Glenda works full-time as a heritage communicator at Fort Walsh National Historic Site in the beautiful Cypress Hills of Saskatchewan. The fort, built in 1875, was the second North West Mounted Police fort in the western part of Canada.

Glenda lives on a cattle ranch about 20 miles from the fort, with her husband, Jim, and their daughters, Abbey and Emilie.

"I'm a bilingual interpreter, and I transport visitors on a 32-seat bus and give tours," she explains. "Since my employment mostly revolves around the tourist season, I have the opportunity to stay at home and spend more time with our children the other 6 months of the year."

In addition to her efforts to preserve history, Glenda makes a point of keeping in touch with happenings at her daughters' school.

"I substitute-teach in the off-season and act as secretary-treasurer for the local school board," she says.

At Home in the Kitchen

Like many country cooks, Glenda finds that the kitchen is the center of activity in her home. "No matter how much work has to be done or how little time there is left in the day, there's always time for a hearty meal spent with family talking around the table," she affirms.

"Every meal I cook is a sit-down affair, just like when I was a child," relates Glenda. "My mother was a great cook, and I often helped her prepare the meat-and-potato fare our whole family enjoyed."

Now Glenda preserves that tradition by serving those same kinds of satisfying suppers to her husband and daughters. The menu she shares here makes the most of items from her freezer, pantry and garden.

"Since our freezer is always full of our own Angus beef, it's a frequent ingredient in many recipes, including Roast Beef Quiche," explains Glenda.

"I took a traditional quiche recipe and adapted it by replacing the ham with beef," she notes. "It's a great way to use up leftover beef roast or steak.

"To further speed the preparation of this hearty main dish, I keep prepared pie crusts or a premeasured portion of homemade pastry on hand," she adds.

"While the quiche is baking, I fix a salad or vegetable so that both are ready at the same time."

During the summer and fall, when vegetables from her garden are in abundance, Glenda might serve Greek Garden Salad. The crisp medley gets its fresh flavor from tomatoes, cucumber and peppers.

"We eat this pretty blend often," Glenda relates. "It's handy to make with convenient bottled Italian dressing. But don't put the dressing on too early or the vegetables will get soggy."

To complete the meal, Glenda serves up slices of not-too-sweet Chocolate Mallow Pie. "This rich and creamy dessert is so easy to assemble," she assures. "To save time, I often prepare and freeze a graham cracker pie crust so all I have to do is thaw and fill it."

Experiment with a variety of pudding mixes depending upon what's in your cupboard.

Roast Beef Quiche

(Also pictured on page 6)

Ready in 1 hour or less

   1 unbaked pastry shell (9 inches)
1-3/4 cups finely chopped cooked roast beef
 1/4 cup chopped green onions
   1 tablespoon all-purpose flour
   4 eggs
 1/2 cup evaporated milk
   1 tablespoon steak sauce
 1/8 teaspoon *each* dill weed, dried basil and dried oregano

Glenda's Guide to Stocking Up

- I have a small white board on the front of our fridge. As soon as an ingredient is low or gone, I write it down so I'm sure to replace it on the next shopping trip. Jim and the girls add to the list as well, and this way I'm seldom wanting for the ingredients I most need and use.

- I stock up as much as possible since we live more than 50 miles from the nearest shopping center. I try not to be without canned soups, canned mushrooms, cheeses, frozen pie crusts, pastas, tortilla shells, instant pudding mixes and envelopes of whipped topping mix.

- When I cook, I often double or triple recipes and freeze the extra for later meals. For example, when I cook long grain rice, I make a big pot of it. I measure out 2-cup portions and freeze them. When we need a side dish to complement a meal, we pull out a bag of rice and warm it in the microwave for 3-5 minutes.
  —*Glenda Parsonage*

Salt and pepper to taste
   2 cups (8 ounces) shredded cheddar cheese
   1/2 cup chopped green pepper

Line unpricked pastry shell with a double thickness of heavy-duty foil. Bake at 450° for 5 minutes; remove foil. Bake 5 minutes longer. Reduce heat to 375°. Sprinkle beef and onions into the crust. In a bowl, beat the flour and eggs until smooth. Add milk, steak sauce and seasonings; beat until smooth. Stir in cheese and green pepper. Pour into crust. Bake for 25 minutes or until center is set. Let stand for 10 minutes before cutting. **Yield:** 6-8 servings.

Greek Garden Salad

(Also pictured on page 7)

Ready in 15 minutes or less

✓ Uses less fat, sugar or salt. Includes Nutritional Analysis and Diabetic Exchanges.

   2 large tomatoes, chopped
   3/4 cup chopped cucumber
   1/2 cup chopped green pepper
   1/2 cup chopped sweet red pepper
   1/2 cup crumbled feta cheese *or* blue cheese
   1/4 cup thinly sliced green onions
   1/4 cup sliced ripe olives

   1/2 cup Italian salad dressing
   1/8 teaspoon dried oregano
Leaf lettuce, optional

In a bowl, combine the first seven ingredients. Just before serving, add salad dressing and oregano; toss to coat. Serve in a lettuce-lined bowl if desired. **Yield:** 6 servings. **Nutritional Analysis:** One serving (prepared with feta cheese and fat-free Italian dressing) equals 69 calories, 389 mg sodium, 11 mg cholesterol, 7 gm carbohydrate, 3 gm protein, 4 gm fat, 2 gm fiber. **Diabetic Exchanges:** 1 vegetable, 1 fat.

Chocolate Mallow Pie

(Also pictured on page 6)

Ready in 30 minutes or less

   1 package (8 ounces) cream cheese, softened
   2 cups cold milk, *divided*
   1 package (3.9 ounces) instant chocolate pudding mix
1-1/2 cups miniature marshmallows
   1 graham cracker crust (9 inches)

In a mixing bowl, beat cream cheese and 1/2 cup milk until smooth. Add pudding mix and remaining milk; mix well. Fold in the marshmallows. Pour into the crust. Refrigerate until serving. **Yield:** 6-8 servings.

A Direct Route to Tasty Menus

CHANGING GEARS on a moment's notice is nothing new to Judy Long of Limestone, Tennessee, a small rural community near Jonesborough.

This mother of two and grandmother of seven works full-time for Quality Transportation Services as a driver, shuttling people to and from their medical appointments.

"My hours vary depending on our clients' needs," she explains. "If someone has a very early appointment, I might be on the road at 3:30 a.m. I'll work just 25 hours some weeks and more than 40 hours other weeks."

Her husband, David, is a maintenance mechanic who covers 12-hour shifts—sometimes days, sometimes nights—at a chemical company. He's also a deacon at their church.

Judy's involved there, too, volunteering as a sign-language interpreter at services and bringing meals to covered-dish dinners.

When she's not fixing fast fare from her collection of cookbooks, you might find her sewing, crocheting tablecloths or spending time with her family.

The couple's son, Earnie, and his wife, Lisa, have four children and live in Mt. Carmel; daughter Judie and her husband, John, have three children and live in Chattanooga.

Family visits will likely become more frequent once Judy and David retire. "We recently built and moved into a small home on 4 acres where we plan to retire," she reports.

Slow Cooking in Fast Lane

To navigate her busy schedule of work, home and social obligations, Judy plans ahead and takes advantage of her slow cooker when preparing meals.

"I use my slow cooker quite a bit when I'm working or expecting company," she relates. "It's easy to assemble a main dish in the morning before work and forget it. Then I don't have to worry about fixing it when I get home."

Besides cooking ham, chicken and prize-winning chili in the slow cooker, Judy usually prepares Cube Steaks with Gravy two or three times a month. But in this hearty entree, taste doesn't take a backseat to convenience.

"Before I tried this recipe, my family did not like this particular cut of beef because it was chewy. But these cube steaks, slow-cooked until they're nice and tender, are now one of our favorites," she reports.

"Since we love mushrooms, I often add a can of them to the gravy," she relates. "The meat and gravy are good served with noodles, but we especially like them over mashed potatoes."

Dad's Favorite Salad is a pleasant complement to Judy's meaty main dish. "My father always liked salads, so I shared this recipe with my mom," Judy recalls with a smile.

"When she first made it for Dad, he enjoyed it so much he told her to be sure to share the recipe with me. I laughed because he didn't know that I had given the recipe to Mom in the first place. I knew he'd like it," she explains.

"Although he loved to try different things, Dad said he could eat this salad every day."

Judy often blends together the pleasant sweet-sour dressing early in the day and keeps it in the refrigerator to chill. When it's time for dinner, she tosses hard-cooked eggs, bacon bits and pretty red onion rings with the greens.

"I usually serve crunchy croutons on the side so they don't get soggy," she recommends.

Judy doesn't have to drive a hard bargain to get her clan to polish off Strawberry Peach Pie, a fruity dessert that's easy as pie to make.

A prepared graham cracker crust features lovely layers of sweetened cream cheese, canned peaches and glazed strawberries.

Cube Steaks with Gravy

Plan ahead...uses slow cooker

1/3 cup all-purpose flour
6 beef cube steaks (1-1/2 pounds)
1 tablespoon vegetable oil
1 large onion, sliced and separated into rings

Judy's Planning Pointers

- Before starting a recipe, check that you have all the ingredients. I always make a grocery list and shop every 2 weeks, so my pantry and freezer are well-stocked. In fact, because I keep extra on hand for our kids and their families, they tease me that the grocery store is in our house!

- If you know time will be tight before dinner, make sure your menu includes items that have make-ahead convenience, like the slow-cooked main dish and refrigerated dessert I share here.

- Don't wait until the last minute. I'll do some of the prep work for a meal, like chopping vegetables or blending salad dressings, early in the day or even the night before. This allows me to spend more quality time with friends and family.
  —Judy Long

3 cups water, *divided*
1 envelope brown gravy mix
1 envelope mushroom gravy mix
1 envelope onion gravy mix
Hot mashed potatoes *or* cooked noodles

Place flour in a large resealable plastic bag. Add the steaks, a few at a time, and shake until completely coated. In a skillet, cook the steaks in oil until lightly browned on each side. Transfer to a slow cooker. Add the onion and 2 cups of water. Cover and cook on low for 8 hours or until meat is tender. In a bowl, whisk together gravy mixes with remaining water. Add to the slow cooker; cook 30 minutes longer. Serve over mashed potatoes or noodles. **Yield:** 6 servings.

Dad's Favorite Salad

Ready in 15 minutes or less

1 cup vegetable oil
1/3 cup sugar
1/3 cup vinegar
1 small onion, quartered
1 tablespoon prepared mustard
1 teaspoon celery seed
1/2 teaspoon salt
1/2 teaspoon pepper
6 cups torn mixed salad greens

1 small red onion, sliced and separated into rings
2 hard-cooked eggs, sliced
8 bacon strips, cooked and crumbled

Combine the first eight ingredients in a blender; cover and process until blended. Arrange greens, onion, eggs and bacon on salad plates; drizzle with desired amount of dressing. Serve immediately. **Yield:** 6 servings.

Strawberry Peach Pie

Plan ahead…needs to chill

1 package (8 ounces) cream cheese, softened
1/4 cup sugar
1 tablespoon milk
1 graham cracker crust (9 inches)
1 can (15-1/4 ounces) sliced peaches, well drained
3 cups sliced fresh strawberries
1 carton (16 ounces) strawberry glaze

In a mixing bowl, beat cream cheese, sugar and milk until smooth. Spread over the bottom and up the sides of the crust. Cut peach slices in half if desired. Arrange over cream cheese. Combine the strawberries and glaze; spoon over peaches. Refrigerate for up to 4 hours before serving. **Yield:** 6-8 servings. **Editor's Note:** This pie is best eaten the same day it's prepared.

You'll Stay in Sync with Snappy Supper

MUSIC TEACHER Jennifer Trenhaile doesn't miss a beat, even when orchestrating a grand undertaking.

One summer, she and her husband, Bill, packed up their belongings and their five children—Heather, Eathan, Emily, Sidney, and Noah—and moved to Emerson, Nebraska, a small rural community about 25 miles southwest of Sioux City, Iowa. Both Bill and Jennifer are teachers who enjoy meeting students and their parents.

Jennifer teaches vocal and instrumental music full-time at the local high school. "I also offer piano lessons at our home 5 nights a week," she adds.

When she's not teaching or tunefully tickling the ivories, Jennifer enjoys walking, reading, counted cross-stitch and baking yeast breads, rolls and cookies. She also volunteers as a Girl Scout leader and keeps in step with her children's other activities.

To band her clan together, Jennifer arranges sit-down meals as often as possible. She drums up the support of the whole family to accomplish this on a regular basis.

"Although I do most of the cooking, everyone pitches in at mealtime," she explains. "Bill is a great cook, and Heather is showing a lot of interest in baking. The younger kids set the table and help with cleanup.

"It's all about planning," Jennifer notes. "If I'm baking cookies, for example, I'll make two or three different kinds and double each batch. They freeze well, so they're perfect for quick snacks, bake sales or whenever I'd like to serve a sweet treat.

"I also make a lot of different casseroles because they're easy to prepare and can often be made ahead of time," she shares. "During the week, all I have to do is pop one in the oven and get everyone to the table at the same time.

"On weekends, I'll serve a special Sunday supper, such as roast with mashed potatoes and gravy," Jennifer reveals. "It's the kind of meat-and-potatoes menu my mom made when I was growing up."

"As a teenager, I liked trying new recipes," recalls Jennifer. "I'd typically make things that Mom didn't care to fix, so we learned a lot from each other."

Stocks Up on Staples

Now that she's cooking for her own family, Jennifer makes sure her pantry shelves hold a variety of every-day ingredients.

"I do the bulk of my shopping once a month, so I try to keep on hand basic ingredients that can be pulled together in various dishes," she says.

"When the weather gets colder, I stock up on plenty of items to make soup," Jennifer adds.

One of the family's favorites is Cheesy Ham Chowder, a tasty blend that's chock-full of potatoes, carrots and ham. "I like to make this comforting soup once or twice a month during the fall and winter," explains Jennifer.

"It's nice because this soup doesn't take hours to simmer. In fact, you can have it on the table in about a half hour if you chop up the veggies ahead of time," she assures.

She serves hearty bowls of it with Basic Biscuits. "The ingredients are very simple, so you're likely to have them on hand," she observes. "They're easy to make, and their from-scratch flavor is wonderful!

"We like these light, tender treats with butter, jelly or honey. Or try them with sausage and gravy for breakfast," she recommends.

To complete the medley, Jennifer serves up sweet Oatmeal Brownies. "The recipe makes the most of a handy packaged brownie mix, so they're fast to fix," she promises.

"If you don't have the mini M&Ms, use chocolate chips instead," she suggests. "Our kids love these rich fudgy squares with a scoop of ice cream."

Cheesy Ham Chowder

Ready in 1 hour or less

- 10 bacon strips, diced
- 1 large onion, chopped
- 1 cup diced carrots
- 3 tablespoons all-purpose flour
- 3 cups milk
- 1-1/2 cups water
- 2-1/2 cups cubed potatoes
- 1 can (15-1/4 ounces) whole kernel corn, drained
- 2 teaspoons chicken bouillon granules
- Pepper to taste
- 3 cups (12 ounces) shredded cheddar cheese
- 2 cups cubed fully cooked ham

In a Dutch oven or large soup kettle, cook the bacon over medium heat until crisp. Remove to paper towels to drain. In the drippings, saute onion and carrots until tender. Stir in flour until blended. Gradually add milk and water. Bring to a boil; cook and stir for 2 minutes or until thickened. Add the potatoes, corn, bouillon and pepper. Reduce heat; simmer, uncovered, for 20 minutes or until potatoes are tender. Add cheese and ham; heat until cheese is melted. Stir in bacon. **Yield:** 10 servings.

Basic Biscuits

Ready in 30 minutes or less

- 2 cups all-purpose flour
- 4 teaspoons baking powder
- 3 teaspoons sugar
- 1/2 teaspoon salt
- 1/2 cup shortening
- 1 egg
- 2/3 cup milk
- 1 tablespoon honey

In a bowl, combine the flour, baking powder, sugar and salt. Cut in shortening until the mixture resembles coarse crumbs. Combine the egg, milk and honey; stir into flour mixture just until combined. Turn onto a floured surface; knead 8-10 times. Roll out to 1/2-in. thickness. Cut with a floured 2-1/2-in. biscuit cutter. Place 1 in. apart on an ungreased baking sheet. Bake at 425° for 10-12 minutes or until golden brown. Serve warm. **Yield:** 10 biscuits.

Oatmeal Brownies

- 1-1/2 cups quick-cooking oats
- 1 cup M&M miniature baking bits
- 1/2 cup all-purpose flour
- 1/2 cup packed brown sugar
- 1/2 chopped walnuts
- 1/2 teaspoon baking soda
- 1/2 cup butter *or* margarine, melted
- 1 package fudge brownie mix (13-inch x 9-inch pan size)

In a bowl, combine the first seven ingredients; mix well. Set aside 1 cup for topping. Pat the remaining mixture into a greased 15-in. x 10-in. x 1-in. baking pan. Prepare brownie batter according to package directions. Spread over the crust. Sprinkle with the reserved oat mixture. Bake at 350° for 25-30 minutes or until a toothpick inserted near the center comes out clean. Cool on a wire rack. Cut into bars. **Yield:** 5 dozen.

Jennifer's Keys to the Kitchen

- Clean your kitchen as you go. I try to get as many dirty dishes as possible out of the way before we sit down to eat. After supper, there's less mess, which means more time to spend with family.
- Make a grocery list and set a budget, then stick to them when shopping. I shop once a month, with the exception of things such as milk and eggs. That way, I don't have to go to the store as often and can keep a closer eye on my spending.
- Don't try to do everything yourself. I let my husband and our children lend a hand whenever possible. The older kids enjoy helping me cook, while the little ones are happy to set and clear off the table.

—Jennifer Trenhaile

Quick Cooking For a Crowd

GETTING HER kids to eat healthy takes on a whole new meaning for Yvonna Nave of Lyons, Kansas.

Not only is she responsible for the nutritional needs of her two children, as director of a local day-care center, she's accountable for the daytime diets of more than 100 other youngsters.

When she's not keeping the center running smoothly, she's managing things at home. She and husband Tony have a daughter, Cheyenne, and a son, Dakota. Tony works for a local feedlot, which prepares livestock for market.

Cooking Is a Joyful Task

"I just love to cook," beams Yvonna. "As a child, I did a lot of from-scratch cooking with my mother and grandmother. And I took every cooking class available at my high school."

These early experiences had a lasting effect on Yvonna. She now involves her kids in the kitchen as often as possible.

Another tradition she's carried on is family mealtime. "My mother insisted on a sit-down dinner with the whole family every night," she recalls. "We want our kids to have that experience, too."

"Because of Tony's job, we eat a lot of beef," Yvonne says. "Foods that can be thrown together with ground beef for a quick meal are mainstays," she adds.

Tried-and-True Recipes

One of her favorites is Barbecued Meatballs. "This recipe came from my home ec teacher in high school," she remembers. "I enjoy making it because you can throw it in the oven and still have time to do other things."

To complement the main dish, Yvonna relies on her mother's recipe for Creamy Hash Brown Bake.

Home-Style White Bread is a frequent addition to the family's meals because it takes advantage of Yvonna's bread machine—a real time-saver when she knows she'll have a busy day.

"I appreciate my bread machine because I can assemble the ingredients in the morning, set the timer and come home to a fresh loaf for supper," she says.

With such filling fare, it's hard to save room for dessert, but few can refuse Yvonna's Apple Crisp.

Barbecued Meatballs

Ready in 1 hour or less

1 egg, lightly beaten
1 can (5 ounces) evaporated milk
1 cup quick-cooking oats
1/2 cup finely chopped onion
1 teaspoon salt
1 teaspoon chili powder
1/4 teaspoon garlic powder
1/4 teaspoon pepper
1-1/2 pounds ground beef
SAUCE:
1 cup ketchup
3/4 cup packed brown sugar
1/4 cup chopped onion
1/2 teaspoon liquid smoke, optional
1/4 teaspoon garlic powder

In a bowl, combine the first eight ingredients. Crumble beef over mixture and mix well. Shape into 1-in. balls; place in a greased 13-in. x 9-in. x 2-in. baking dish. Bake, uncovered, at 350° for 18-20 minutes or until meat is no longer pink. Meanwhile, combine the sauce ingredients in a saucepan. Bring to a boil. Reduce heat and simmer for 2 minutes, stirring frequently. Pour over meatballs. Bake 10-12 minutes longer. **Yield:** about 4 dozen.

Creamy Hash Brown Bake

1 can (10-3/4 ounces) condensed cream of mushroom soup, undiluted
1 can (10-3/4 ounces) condensed cheddar cheese soup, undiluted
1 cup (8 ounces) sour cream
1/2 cup butter or margarine, softened

Yvonna's Tips on Staying Organized

- I plan my menus for 2 weeks at a time and shop accordingly. Because I have the ingredients I need on hand, I eliminate last-minute trips to the store for just an item or two. Having a menu plan also takes the guesswork out of what's for supper when I get home.

- Whenever I can, I double a recipe and freeze half for later use. For example, I double my recipe for Barbecued Meatballs (above) and freeze half for a home-cooked meal later. Or I'll stir up a big batch of cookie dough and keep it in the freezer. When my family craves warm-from-the-oven cookies, I can bake them in a hurry.

- To save money when grocery shopping, I use coupons, take advantage of sales and buy in bulk. It's easy to separate large packages of foods into family-size servings when I get home.

—*Yvonna Nave*

1/4 cup chopped onion
1/2 teaspoon salt
1 package (28 ounces) frozen O'Brien hash brown potatoes
3/4 cup crushed potato chips

In a large bowl, combine the soups, sour cream, butter, onion and salt. Add potatoes; mix well. Pour into a greased 13-in. x 9-in. x 2-in. baking dish. Sprinkle with potato chips. Bake, uncovered, at 350° for 55-60 minutes or until the potatoes are tender. **Yield:** 10-12 servings.

Home-Style White Bread

Plan ahead...uses bread machine

1 cup water (70° to 80°)
2 tablespoons butter *or* margarine, softened
1 teaspoon salt
2 tablespoons sugar
2 tablespoons nonfat dry milk powder
3 cups bread flour
2 teaspoons active dry yeast

In bread machine pan, place all ingredients in order suggested by manufacturer. Select basic bread setting. Choose crust color and loaf size if available. Bake according to bread machine directions (check dough af-ter 5 minutes of mixing; add 1 to 2 tablespoons of water or flour if needed). **Yield:** 1 loaf (about 1-1/2 pounds).

Apple Crisp

8 cups sliced peeled tart apples (about 8 medium)
3/4 cup sugar
1/2 teaspoon ground cinnamon
1/8 teaspoon salt
TOPPING:
1/2 cup quick-cooking oats
1/2 cup all-purpose flour
1/2 cup packed brown sugar
1/4 teaspoon baking powder
1/8 teaspoon baking soda
3 tablespoons cold butter *or* margarine
Vanilla ice cream, optional

In a large bowl, toss the first four ingredients. Pour into a greased 8-in. square baking dish. In a bowl, combine oats, flour, brown sugar, baking powder and baking soda. Cut in butter until mixture resembles coarse crumbs. Sprinkle over apple mixture. Bake at 350° for 55-60 minutes or until apples are tender and topping is golden. Serve warm with ice cream if desired. **Yield:** 10 servings.

Chapter 2

⏱ 30 Minutes to Mealtime

ALTHOUGH you love preparing savory, satisfying meals for your family, spending hours in the kitchen is a luxury that your busy schedule seldom allows.

With your hectic days in mind, this chapter features 12 complete meals that go from start to finish in less than half an hour.

Hurried cooks just like you share rapid recipes and time-saving preparation tips for their family-favorite meal. Each tried-and-true dish will earn you high marks in your kitchen as well.

So turn to this time-saving section the next time your family is eyeing the table...and *you're* eyeing the clock!

QUICK FIXES. Onion Salisbury Steak, Carrots with Raisins and Biscuit Apple Cobbler (all recipes on p. 30).

Chicken Marinara

✓ Uses less fat, sugar or salt. Includes Nutritional Analysis and Diabetic Exchanges.

4 boneless skinless chicken breast
  halves (1 pound)
2 cups sliced fresh mushrooms
3 garlic cloves, minced
1 teaspoon dried basil
1/2 teaspoon Italian seasoning
1 jar (28 ounces) meatless spaghetti
  sauce
1/2 cup red wine *or* chicken broth
Hot cooked angel hair pasta *or* spaghetti

In a nonstick skillet coated with nonstick cooking spray, cook chicken for 6 minutes on each side; remove and keep warm. Add mushrooms, garlic, basil and Italian seasoning to skillet; saute until mushrooms are tender. Stir in spaghetti sauce and wine or broth. Add chicken; cover and simmer for 10 minutes or until heated through. Serve over pasta. **Yield:** 4 servings. **Nutritional Analysis:** One serving (prepared with low-sodium broth and reduced-sodium spaghetti sauce; calculated without pasta) equals 332 calories, 118 mg sodium, 73 mg cholesterol, 20 gm carbohydrate, 31 gm protein, 13 gm fat, 5 gm fiber. **Diabetic Exchanges:** 4 lean meat, 1 vegetable, 1 starch.

Italian Bread Salad

4 slices Italian *or* French bread (1 inch thick)
2 tablespoons olive *or* vegetable oil, *divided*
2 plum tomatoes, halved lengthwise and sliced
1 medium cucumber, seeded and chopped
2 *or* 3 green onions, sliced
2 tablespoons shredded Parmesan cheese
Lettuce leaves
3 tablespoons cider *or* red wine vinegar
1 garlic clove, minced
1/4 teaspoon dried basil

Brush both sides of bread with 1 tablespoon of oil. Place on a baking sheet. Broil 5 in. from the heat for 1-2 minutes on each side or until lightly browned. Cut into 1/2-in. cubes. In a bowl, gently toss the bread cubes, tomatoes, cucumber, onions and Parmesan cheese. Divide among four lettuce-lined salad plates. In a small bowl, whisk vinegar, garlic, basil and remaining oil. Drizzle over salads. Serve immediately. **Yield:** 4 servings.

Lemon Ice

1/4 cup raspberry preserves
2 tablespoons orange juice
1 pint lemon ice *or* sherbet
Chocolate syrup

In a bowl, combine raspberry preserves and orange juice; mix well. Spoon 1 tablespoon each into four dessert dishes. Top each with a scoop of lemon ice. Drizzle with chocolate syrup. Serve immediately. **Yield:** 4 servings.

Tasty Trio Has Italian Touch

"IMAGINE my surprise when I discovered retirement does not necessarily mean you have more time to devote to meal preparation," states Kathleen Williams of St. Albans, West Virginia.

She and her husband, Buddy, are both retired from Columbia Gas Transmission Corp. and have two grown children.

"I love camping, boating and, of course, cooking," Kathleen relates. "I also volunteer 1 day a week at a diabetes education center in the area.

"When time's tight, I fall back on the fast-to-fix recipes that were a staple when I was working, like this Italian meal," she comments.

Garlic and basil flavor the tomato sauce that coats tender Chicken Marinara. "A friend gave me this skillet recipe several years ago," Kathleen says. "It's easy to make using pre-sliced mushrooms, commercial pasta sauce and quick-cooking pasta."

For a fresh-tasting side dish, Kathleen serves Italian Bread Salad. "This pretty blend is a snap to prepare.

"For variety, add whatever veggies you like, such as green or yellow peppers, zucchini, summer squash or sliced olives," she suggests.

Kathleen takes advantage of convenient pantry items to dress up Lemon Ice. "I concocted this refreshing dessert when I wanted to turn plain lemon ice into something more satisfying.

"The raspberry preserves and chocolate syrup reduce the prep time to almost nothing," she adds.

Speedy Supper Will Satisfy

AS THE WIFE of a farmer, Kathy Giesbrecht spends most of her day lending a hand with chores on their acreage near Prespatou, British Columbia.

When she's not outdoors, you might find Kathy visiting with the couple's six grown children and 10 grandchildren, quilting, singing in the church choir, volunteering at Ladies Aid group activities or teaching Sunday school.

"I serve this quick meal often when I'm helping with haying, calving or working the field, or when the kids pop in unexpectedly," she shares.

"Mashed Potatoes with Ham evolved from scalloped potatoes, which are tasty but time-consuming to make," Kathy explains. "I warmed up leftover mashed potatoes, threw in some ham, then added a cheese and crumb topping."

Once it's in the oven, she readies the ingredients for Fruited Cabbage Salad. "The recipe came from a neighbor who invited us over for lunch after church," Kathy recalls.

"You can be creative with this salad. Substitute lettuce for the cabbage and add almost any fruit. Almonds, peanuts or sunflower kernels can be used in place of the pecans," she adds.

You'll need just four ingredients to make the sweet crumb topping for Butter Crunch Pudding.

Mashed Potatoes with Ham

- 1/2 cup finely chopped onion
- 2 tablespoons butter *or* margarine, *divided*
- 3-1/2 to 4 cups hot mashed potatoes (prepared with milk and butter)
- 1-1/2 cups cubed fully cooked ham
- 1/4 teaspoon onion salt
- 1/8 teaspoon pepper
- 1/2 cup shredded cheddar cheese
- 1/3 cup crushed cornflakes

In a large microwave-safe bowl, combine onion and 1 tablespoon of butter. Microwave, uncovered, on high for 2 minutes or until tender, stirring once. Add potatoes, ham, onion salt and pepper; mix well. Transfer to a greased 1-1/2-qt. baking dish. Sprinkle with cheese and cornflakes; dot with remaining butter. Bake, uncovered, at 375° for 15 minutes or until heated through. **Yield:** 4 servings.

Fruited Cabbage Salad

✓ Uses less fat, sugar or salt. Includes Nutritional Analysis and Diabetic Exchanges.

- 4 cups shredded cabbage
- 1 medium red apple, diced
- 1 medium firm banana, sliced
- 1/3 cup chopped pecans
- 2 tablespoons raisins
- 1/2 cup mayonnaise *or* salad dressing
- 2 tablespoons milk
- 2 tablespoons sugar
- 1 tablespoon lemon juice
Salt to taste, optional

In a bowl, combine the first five ingredients; set aside. In a jar with a tight-fitting lid, combine the mayonnaise, milk, sugar, lemon juice and salt if desired; shake well. Pour over cabbage mixture and toss to coat. **Yield:** 4-6 servings. **Nutritional Analysis:** One 3/4-cup serving (prepared with fat-free mayonnaise, skim milk and sugar substitute equivalent to 2 tablespoons sugar and without salt) equals 114 calories, 152 mg sodium, trace cholesterol, 18 gm carbohydrate, 2 gm protein, 5 gm fat, 3 gm fiber. **Diabetic Exchanges:** 1 fruit, 1 fat, 1/2 vegetable.

Butter Crunch Pudding

- 1 cup all-purpose flour
- 1/2 cup flaked coconut
- 1/4 cup packed brown sugar
- 1/2 cup cold butter *or* margarine
- 2 cups cold milk
- 1 package (3.4 ounces) instant lemon pudding mix *or* flavor of your choice

In a bowl, combine flour, coconut and sugar; cut in butter until crumbly. Spread in a 15-in. x 10-in. x 1-in. baking pan. Bake at 375° for 15 minutes, stirring once. Cool slightly. Meanwhile, in a mixing bowl, beat milk and pudding mix for 1 minute or until slightly thickened; chill 5 minutes. Spoon half of crumbs into four bowls. Top with pudding and rest of crumbs. **Yield:** 4 servings.

Fast Fare Fits Busy Schedule

AS A FULL-TIME instructor at Southwest Wisconsin Technical College, Sondra Ostheimer spends her days in the classroom. The Boscobel, Wisconsin woman's evenings are booked, too, because she teaches night classes at the college and at a local university.

She also is an adviser to the college's Business Professionals of America student organization and serves on its executive board.

Sondra has learned to keep pace with her activity-packed calendar by eating healthy foods and running 16 miles a week to reduce stress.

"When planning meals, I look for recipes that are not only nutritious, but easy and great tasting, too," she states.

Because both she and husband Jeff are teachers with busy weekday schedules, they do most of their cooking on weekends. For example, Sondra might prepare a big pot of rice to use in a variety of dishes later in the week.

"Broccoli with Rice is a time-saver, because it takes advantage of cooked rice and convenient canned soup," she explains. "And unlike most side dishes, there are not a lot of vegetables to cut up."

That three-ingredient combination is a nice accompaniment to Crunchy-Coated Walleye.

Potato flakes make a golden coating for these fish fillets, which are a breeze to fry on the stovetop.

For a light ending to the meal, Sondra assembles Banana Yogurt Trifles.

"We try to keep sweets to a minimum, so I don't make this often," she shares. "But it's easy because there's no mixing or fussing, and you can buy prepared angel food cake."

The cool, refreshing dessert is versatile, too. Substitute strawberries or other fresh fruit for the bananas and choose different flavors of yogurt.

Broccoli with Rice

1 package (16 ounces) frozen broccoli cuts
1-1/2 cups cooked rice
1 can (10-3/4 ounces) condensed cream of mushroom soup, undiluted

In a saucepan, cook broccoli according to package directions; drain. Add rice and soup. Cook until heated through. **Yield:** 4 servings.

Crunchy-Coated Walleye

1/3 cup all-purpose flour
1 teaspoon paprika
1/2 teaspoon salt
1/4 teaspoon pepper
1/4 teaspoon onion powder
1/4 teaspoon garlic powder
2 eggs
2-1/4 pounds walleye, perch *or* pike fillets
1-1/2 cups mashed potato flakes
1/3 cup vegetable oil
Tartar sauce and lemon wedges, optional

In a shallow bowl, combine flour, paprika, salt, pepper, onion powder and garlic powder. In another bowl, beat the eggs. Dip both sides of fillets in flour mixture and eggs, then coat with potato flakes. In a skillet, fry fillets in oil for 5 minutes on each side or until fish flakes easily with a fork. Serve with tartar sauce and lemon if desired. **Yield:** 4 servings.

Banana Yogurt Trifles

2 medium ripe bananas, sliced
1/3 cup orange juice
6 slices angel food cake, cubed
2 cartons (8 ounces *each*) strawberry-banana yogurt

In a bowl, toss the bananas with orange juice. Layer half of the cake cubes in four dessert dishes. Top with half of the bananas and yogurt. Repeat the layers. **Yield:** 4 servings.

1-1/2 pounds boneless round steak, thinly
        sliced
    1 tablespoon vegetable oil
    1 can (10-3/4 ounces) condensed cream of
        mushroom soup, undiluted
  1/2 cup water
    1 envelope onion soup mix
  1/2 cup sour cream
Hot cooked noodles
Minced fresh parsley, optional

In a large skillet, stir-fry beef in oil until no longer pink. Stir in soup, water and onion soup mix. Reduce heat; cover and simmer for 20 minutes. Stir in sour cream; heat through (do not boil). Serve over noodles; garnish with parsley if desired. **Yield:** 6 servings. **Nutritional Analysis:** One serving (prepared with low-fat cream of mushroom soup, reduced-sodium onion soup mix and light sour cream; calculated without noodles) equals 250 calories, 521 mg sodium, 81 mg cholesterol, 10 gm carbohydrate, 29 gm protein, 9 gm fat, 0 fiber. **Diabetic Exchanges:** 3-1/2 lean meat, 1 starch.

Orange Lettuce Salad

✓ Uses less fat, sugar or salt. Includes Nutritional Analysis and Diabetic Exchanges.

    8 cups torn Bibb lettuce *or* salad greens of
        your choice
    3 green onions, sliced
    1 can (15 ounces) mandarin oranges, drained
  1/4 cup vegetable oil
    2 tablespoons vinegar
    2 tablespoons sugar
    2 tablespoons minced fresh parsley
  1/2 teaspoon salt, optional
Dash pepper
    4 drops hot pepper sauce
  1/4 cup slivered almonds, toasted, optional

In a salad bowl, toss lettuce, onions and oranges; set aside. In a jar with a tight-fitting lid, combine oil, vinegar, sugar, parsley, salt if desired, pepper and hot pepper sauce; shake well. Drizzle desired amount over salad; toss to coat. Sprinkle with almonds if desired. Refrigerate any remaining dressing. **Yield:** 8 servings. **Nutritional Analysis:** One serving (prepared with artificial sweetener equivalent to 2 tablespoons sugar, and without salt and almonds) equals 104 calories, 7 mg sodium, 0 cholesterol, 11 gm carbohydrate, 1 gm protein, 7 gm fat, 1 gm fiber. **Diabetic Exchanges:** 1 vegetable, 1 fat, 1/2 fruit.

Cream-Topped Grapes

    1 pound seedless grapes
    1 cup (8 ounces) sour cream
  1/4 cup dark brown sugar

Place grapes in six dessert cups. Combine sour cream and brown sugar until smooth. Refrigerate until ready to serve. Spoon over grapes. **Yield:** 6 servings.

Traditional Dish Is Tasty

"SINCE our children are all married now, I usually cook dinner for just my husband, Roy, and me," notes Joyce Key, a retired nurse and nanny from Snellville, Georgia. "But I still think the less time it takes to prepare the better."

With Roy working just 2 days a week, the couple often travel in their motor home. They take short trips to tour Civil War sites and longer cross-country trips to visit family and friends.

Joyce says made-in-minutes menus, like the one she shares here, are especially handy when camping.

An envelope of onion soup mix adds the speedy seasoning to Three-Step Stroganoff, a quick version of the traditional entree.

"This recipe came from a community cookbook that my mother gave me," Joyce says. "The original called for ground beef, but we prefer it with sliced beef."

While her main dish simmers, Joyce prepares Orange Lettuce Salad. A flavorful dressing sparks fresh greens that are tossed with colorful oranges and green onions and sprinkled with toasted almonds.

For dessert, Cream-Topped Grapes look lovely when served in sherbet glasses.

Three-Step Stroganoff

✓ Uses less fat, sugar or salt. Includes Nutritional Analysis and Diabetic Exchanges.

"We like to use hot sausage for a spicy taste that's sure to wake up your taste buds."

While the pizza is baking, LaChelle prepares Fruit Kabobs with Dip. The creamy dipping sauce, sweetened with honey, is easy to make. Its pleasant banana flavor complements fresh fruit.

To complete this meal, you'll need just three ingredients for frosty Pineapple Orange Drink. "This delightful beverage is not too sweet and so easy...just throw it in a blender and it's done."

Brunch Pizza Squares

✓ Uses less fat, sugar or salt. Includes Nutritional Analysis and Diabetic Exchanges.

> 1 pound bulk pork sausage
> 1 tube (8 ounces) refrigerated crescent rolls
> 4 eggs
> 2 tablespoons milk
> 1/8 teaspoon pepper
> 3/4 cup shredded cheddar cheese

In a skillet, cook sausage over medium heat until no longer pink; drain. Unroll crescent dough into a lightly greased 13-in. x 9-in. x 2-in. baking pan. Press dough 1/2 in. up the sides; seal seams. Sprinkle with sausage. In a bowl, beat the eggs, milk and pepper; pour over sausage. Sprinkle with cheese. Bake, uncovered, at 400° for 15 minutes or until the crust is golden brown and the cheese is melted. **Yield:** 8 servings. **Nutritional Analysis:** One serving (prepared with turkey sausage, egg substitute equivalent to 4 eggs, skim milk and reduced-fat crescent rolls and cheese) equals 243 calories, 687 mg sodium, 50 mg cholesterol, 14 gm carbohydrate, 18 gm protein, 13 gm fat, 1 gm fiber. **Diabetic Exchange:** 2 meat, 1 starch, 1/2 fat.

Fruit Kabobs with Dip

Assorted fruit—green grapes, watermelon balls, cantaloupe balls and strawberry halves
> 1 cup (8 ounces) plain yogurt
> 1/2 medium ripe banana
> 4 teaspoons honey
> 1/8 teaspoon ground cinnamon

Thread fruit alternately onto skewers. In a blender, combine remaining ingredients; cover and process until smooth. Serve with kabobs. **Yield:** 1-1/2 cups dip.

Pineapple Orange Drink

> 6 cups orange juice
> 2 cans (8 ounces *each*) crushed unsweetened pineapple, undrained
> 16 ice cubes

Place half of the orange juice, pineapple and ice cubes in a blender; cover and process until smooth. Repeat with remaining ingredients. Pour into chilled glasses. Serve immediately. **Yield:** 8 servings.

Breakfast Has Sunny Flavor

DOES LIVING in the Sunshine State give you a sunny outlook on life? It seems to for LaChelle Olivet, a resident of Pace, a small town just outside Pensacola, Florida.

This radiant stay-at-home mom loves to cook, sew and create scrapbooks. She also sets a shining example as a volunteer at her church.

One of the brightest spots in her and husband Mark's lives is their daughter, McKenna. The couple also has another child on the way.

"As my family continues to grow, I know finding time to make dinner will be my main concern," LaChelle relates. "So 30-minute meals will be particularly useful to me."

Here she shares a menu for a weekend breakfast or weekday lunch.

"I love using convenience items, like the crescent rolls in easy Brunch Pizza Squares," LaChelle notes. "When I serve it to guests, they always ask me for the recipe.

"To hurry along the preparation of this dish, I frequently brown a few pounds of sausage ahead of time and keep it in the freezer," she remarks.

Supper Is a Breeze to Make

FAST-TO-FIX meals are important to Ruth and Severt Andrewson of Peck, Idaho, because less time in the kitchen means more to enjoy the great outdoors.

"We both like to hike, fish and watch the wildlife roam," Ruth explains. "This swift supper suits our active lifestyle."

"I toss together the Summer Veggie Salad, then refrigerate it until serving," Ruth notes.

Raspberry Pudding Parfaits are fast and fuss-free because they take advantage of convenient instant pudding and whipped topping.

With both salad and dessert chilling, Ruth mixes up the filling for Chicken Cheddar Wraps. "I keep cooked chicken in the freezer, so these are simple to assemble in a hurry," she notes.

Summer Veggie Salad

☑ Uses less fat, sugar or salt. Includes Nutritional Analysis and Diabetic Exchanges.

    3 cups cauliflowerets
    3 cups broccoli florets
    1 green pepper, julienned
    1 sweet red pepper, julienned
    1 cup sliced red onion
    1 cup sliced fresh mushrooms, optional
DRESSING:
    1/4 cup olive or vegetable oil
    4-1/2 teaspoons cider or red wine vinegar
    4-1/2 teaspoons lemon juice
    1 teaspoon salt
    1/2 teaspoon dried basil
    1/2 teaspoon sugar
    1/8 teaspoon cayenne pepper

In a large bowl, combine the cauliflower, broccoli, peppers, onion and mushrooms if desired. Combine dressing ingredients in a jar with a tight-fitting lid; shake well. Pour over vegetables and toss to coat. Refrigerate until serving. **Yield:** 12-14 servings. **Nutritional Analysis:** One 1-cup serving equals 53 calories, 177 mg sodium, 0 cholesterol, 4 gm carbohydrate, 1 gm protein, 4 gm fat, 1 gm fiber. **Diabetic Exchanges:** 1 vegetable, 1/2 fat.

Raspberry Pudding Parfaits

    2 cups cold milk
    1 package (3.4 ounces) instant vanilla or
      French vanilla pudding mix
    1 cup whipped topping
    1 pint fresh raspberries

In a mixing bowl, beat milk and pudding mix on low speed for 2 minutes. Fold in 1 cup whipped topping. Spoon a third of the pudding into six parfait glasses. Set aside six raspberries for garnish; divide half of the remaining berries over pudding. Repeat layers. Top with remaining pudding and garnish with the reserved berries. **Yield:** 6 servings.

Chicken Cheddar Wraps

☑ Uses less fat, sugar or salt. Includes Nutritional Analysis and Diabetic Exchanges.

    1 cup (8 ounces) sour cream
    1 cup chunky salsa
    2 tablespoons mayonnaise
    4 cups cubed cooked chicken
    2 cups (8 ounces) shredded cheddar cheese
    1 cup thinly sliced fresh mushrooms
    2 cups shredded lettuce
    1 cup guacamole, optional
    12 flour tortillas (6 or 7 inches)
Tomato wedges and additional guacamole,
    optional

In a bowl, combine the sour cream, salsa and mayonnaise. Stir in chicken, cheese and mushrooms. Divide lettuce and guacamole if desired between tortillas. Place about 1/2 cup chicken mixture on each tortilla. Fold sides over the filling. Garnish with tomato and additional guacamole if desired. **Yield:** 12 wraps. **Nutritional Analysis:** One wrap (prepared with nonfat sour cream and reduced-fat mayonnaise and cheese, and without guacamole and tomato) equals 271 calories, 537 mg sodium, 34 mg cholesterol, 35 gm carbohydrate, 18 gm protein, 6 gm fat, 2 gm fiber. **Diabetic Exchanges:** 2 starch, 2 lean meat, 1 vegetable.

Meal for Busy Moms

DINNERTIME rolls around in a hurry for Renee Endress of Galva, Illinois. When she isn't helping husband Bill around the farm, she's home-schooling and caring for their four children—Andrea, Tyler, Brendan and Mikaela.

"Although time is tight, I think it's very important that we sit down to every supper as a family," she relates.

On action-packed evenings, Renee is likely to turn to the delicious dishes featured here. She works backward, fixing the dessert first so it can chill while she prepares the rest of the meal.

"I created Cookies 'n' Cream Fluff when I had unexpected guests," shares Renee. "I needed something speedy and simple enough to make from ingredients I had in my pantry. It was an instant hit."

Next, Renee mixes up a batch of Creamy Coleslaw. "A package of shredded cabbage and carrots really cuts down on prep time," she explains.

To complete the meal, Renee assembles colorful Pineapple Chicken Stir-Fry. "The frozen veggies and canned pineapple chunks make this tender chicken dish so convenient without sacrificing any flavor," she assures.

Cookies 'n' Cream Fluff

2 cups cold milk
1 package (3.4 ounces) instant vanilla pudding mix
1 carton (8 ounces) frozen whipped topping, thawed
15 chocolate cream-filled sandwich cookies, broken into chunks
Additional broken cookies, optional

In a bowl, whisk the milk and pudding mix for 2 minutes or until slightly thickened. Fold in the whipped topping and cookies. Spoon into dessert dishes. Top with additional cookies if desired. Refrigerate until serving. **Yield:** 6 servings.

Creamy Coleslaw

1 package (16 ounces) coleslaw mix
3/4 cup mayonnaise *or* salad dressing
1/3 cup sour cream
1/4 cup sugar
3/4 teaspoon seasoned salt
1/2 teaspoon ground mustard
1/4 teaspoon celery salt

Place coleslaw mix in a large bowl. In a small bowl, combine the remaining ingredients; stir until blended. Pour over coleslaw mix and toss to coat. Refrigerate until serving. **Yield:** 6 servings.

Pineapple Chicken Stir-Fry

✓ Uses less fat, sugar or salt. Includes Nutritional Analysis and Diabetic Exchanges.

1/4 cup soy sauce
2 tablespoons sugar
1 tablespoon vinegar
1 tablespoon ketchup
1/2 teaspoon ground ginger
2 garlic cloves, minced
1 pound boneless skinless chicken breasts, cut into strips
2 tablespoons vegetable oil
1 package (16 ounces) frozen stir-fry vegetables
1 can (8 ounces) unsweetened pineapple chunks, drained
Hot cooked rice

In a small bowl, combine the first six ingredients; set aside. In a large skillet or wok, stir-fry chicken in oil for 5-6 minutes or until juices run clear. Add the vegetables; stir-fry for 3-4 minutes or until crisp-tender. Stir in pineapple and reserved soy sauce mixture; heat through. Serve over rice. **Yield:** 6 servings. **Nutritional Analysis:** One serving (prepared with light soy sauce; calculated without rice) equals 232 calories, 877 mg sodium, 44 mg cholesterol, 21 gm carbohydrate, 21 gm protein, 7 gm fat, 1 gm fiber. **Diabetic Exchanges:** 2 lean meat, 1 starch, 1 vegetable, 1/2 fat.

Fast Family Feast Fit for All Ages

TWO small children and a husband who works long hours keep Melissa Stevens on her toes. When time is crunched, this active mom flexes her culinary muscle by fixing satisfying yet simple suppers.

They're sometimes a must for Melissa, who spends part of her day caring for children at a local fitness center. She's also full-time mother to daughter Alexandra and son Brayden.

Her husband, Shane, works in construction, which means he often spends evenings away from the family's Elk River, Minnesota home.

"Because Shane eats later, I need quick meals that can be reheated easily," shares Melissa. "I not only look for foods that will pass his taste test, but ones that are healthy and nutritious as well."

This is not surprising, since diet and exercise are very important to Melissa. Her interests include weight lifting, aerobics, walking and marathon running to boot.

"Many of my recipes can be made with low-fat ingredients," says Melissa. "I try to make them kid-friendly as well."

Children of all ages are sure to enjoy Bacon Cheeseburger Pasta, an effortless entree Melissa concocted to duplicate the flavors of her favorite hamburger.

"I start the pasta boiling first," Melissa notes. "While the noodles cook, I brown the ground beef and crisp the bacon. Then I combine the meat, tomato soup and pasta, heat through and sprinkle with cheese for a dish that's a snap to make.

"Meanwhile, I toss together Basil Cherry Tomatoes. I especially like this light, refreshing salad in summer when cherry tomatoes from the garden are in abundance," she reports.

For dessert, Melissa indulges in her love for ice cream by assembling Cookie Ice Cream Sandwiches. The tempting treats take advantage of store-bought oatmeal raisin cookies, ice cream and peanut butter.

Bacon Cheeseburger Pasta

  8 ounces uncooked tube *or* spiral pasta
  1 pound ground beef
  6 bacon strips, diced
  1 can (10-3/4 ounces) condensed tomato soup, undiluted
  1 cup (4 ounces) shredded cheddar cheese
Barbecue sauce and prepared mustard, optional

Cook pasta according to package directions. Meanwhile, in a skillet, cook beef over medium heat until no longer pink; drain and set aside. In the same skillet, cook bacon until crisp; remove with a slotted spoon to paper towels. Discard drippings. Drain pasta; add to the skillet. Add soup, beef and bacon; heat through. Sprinkle with cheese; cover and cook until the cheese is melted. Serve with barbecue sauce and mustard if desired. **Yield:** 4-6 servings.

Basil Cherry Tomatoes

  3 pints cherry tomatoes, halved
  1/2 cup chopped fresh basil
 1-1/2 teaspoons olive *or* vegetable oil
Salt and pepper to taste
Lettuce leaves, optional

In a bowl, combine the tomatoes, basil, oil, salt and pepper. Cover and refrigerate until serving. Serve on lettuce if desired. **Yield:** 4-6 servings.

Cookie Ice Cream Sandwiches

Peanut butter
  12 oatmeal raisin cookies
  1 pint vanilla ice cream *or* flavor of your choice
Miniature chocolate chips

Spread peanut butter over the bottom of six cookies. Top with a scoop of ice cream. Top with another cookie; press down gently. Roll sides of ice cream sandwich in chocolate chips. Wrap in plastic wrap. Freeze until serving. **Yield:** 6 servings.

Cook Cuts Kitchen Time

SHE CALLS herself a silver-haired citizen, but Claudine Moffatt of Manchester, Missouri is much more than that. This mother, grandmother and great-grandmother is a woman with golden memories of an action-packed life.

After raising her family and dedicating years to a career in publishing hobby and craft magazines, Claudine retired. But she didn't slow down.

Instead, she slipped on her traveling shoes and visited Japan, toured Europe and cruised the Nile.

When she wasn't traveling, she devoted much of her energy to senior centers, where she taught crafts and often sat on the board of directors.

These days, Claudine stays closer to home. She enjoys watching cooking shows on television, playing computer games and surfing the Internet.

But she remembers when everyday life didn't include many of today's modern conveniences. "When I was learning to cook, going out for chicken meant going to a poultry yard and picking out a chicken.

"Feeding a family required a lot of preplanning, so I got used to cutting out unnecessary steps," Claudine notes. "Today, most of my meals can be prepared in 15 minutes or less.

"In the time it takes to drive to a fast-food place, wait in line and drive home, I can make a healthier meal that's tastier and less expensive," she assures.

For a stick-to-your-ribs dinner, Claudine might prepare Onion Salisbury Steak. "I've relied on this recipe for as long as I can remember," she shares. Ground beef patties, tender onion slices and a rich gravy top toasted bread to make this Depression-era favorite.

To complement it, Claudine serves Carrots with Raisins. "You can fix this simple side dish in minutes," she says. "Just mix the ingredients, then microwave."

She tops off the meal with comforting Biscuit Apple Cobbler. The sweet treat requires only four ingredients but tastes like you fussed.

Onion Salisbury Steak
(Also pictured on page 20)

  1 **pound lean ground beef**
1/2 **teaspoon salt**
1/8 **to 1/4 teaspoon pepper**
  2 **medium onions, thinly sliced**
  4 **slices bread, toasted**
1/4 **cup all-purpose flour**
1-1/2 **cups water**
  1 **tablespoon beef bouillon granules**

In a bowl, combine beef, salt and pepper; shape into four oval patties. In a skillet, brown patties on one side. Turn and add onions. Cook until meat is no longer pink. Place toast on serving plates. Top each with onions and a beef patty; keep warm. Stir flour into skillet until blended. Gradually add water; stir in bouillon. Bring to a boil; cook and stir for 2 minutes or until thickened and bubbly. Serve over meat and onions. **Yield:** 4 servings.

Carrots with Raisins
(Also pictured on page 20)

  4 **medium carrots, julienned**
1/4 **cup water**
1/4 **cup raisins**
  2 **tablespoons brown sugar**
1/2 **to 1 teaspoon salt**
1/8 **to 1/4 teaspoon pepper**

In a microwave-safe bowl, combine all ingredients. Cover and microwave on high for 2 minutes. Stir; cook 1-2 minutes longer or until carrots are tender. **Yield:** 4 servings. **Editor's Note:** This recipe was tested in an 850-watt microwave.

Biscuit Apple Cobbler
(Also pictured on page 20)

  1 **can (21 ounces) apple pie filling**
1/2 **teaspoon ground cinnamon**
  1 **tube (6 ounces) refrigerated flaky buttermilk biscuits**
Whipped topping and mint, optional

Place pie filling in an ungreased 9-in. pie plate. Sprinkle with cinnamon. Separate each biscuit into three layers and arrange over apples. Bake at 400° for 12-14 minutes or until the biscuits are browned. Garnish with whipped topping and mint if desired. **Yield:** 4-6 servings.

and snow peas, and an easy-to-stir-up soy sauce and ginger dressing.

Baked Shrimp and Asparagus

- 1 package (12 ounces) frozen cut asparagus
- 1 pound medium shrimp, peeled and deveined
- 1 can (10-3/4 ounces) condensed cream of shrimp soup, undiluted
- 1 tablespoon butter *or* margarine, melted
- 1 teaspoon soy sauce
- 1/2 cup salad croutons, optional

Hot cooked rice

Combine the first five ingredients. Spoon into a greased 8-in. square baking dish. Bake, uncovered, at 425° for 20 minutes or until shrimp turn pink. Top with croutons if desired; bake 5 minutes longer. Serve over rice. **Yield:** 4-6 servings.

Oriental Tossed Salad

- 1/2 cup vegetable oil
- 1/3 cup vinegar
- 7-1/2 teaspoons sugar
- 1 tablespoon soy sauce
- 1/4 teaspoon ground ginger
- 1 package (12 ounces) ready-to-serve salad greens
- 1 cup fresh bean sprouts
- 1 cup fresh snow peas

In a jar with a tight-fitting lid, combine oil, vinegar, sugar, soy sauce and ginger; shake well. In a salad bowl, combine greens, bean sprouts and peas. Drizzle with dressing; toss to coat. **Yield:** 6-8 servings.

Pineapple Fluff Pie

 Uses less fat, sugar or salt. Includes Nutritional Analysis and Diabetic Exchanges.

- 1 can (20 ounces) unsweetened crushed pineapple, drained
- 1 package (3.4 ounces) instant lemon pudding mix
- 1 carton (8 ounces) frozen whipped topping, thawed
- 1 graham cracker crust (9 inches)

In a bowl, combine the pineapple and pudding mix until thickened; fold in the whipped topping. Spoon into crust. Refrigerate until serving. **Yield:** 8 servings. **Nutritional Analysis:** One serving (prepared with sugar-free vanilla pudding mix, light whipped topping and a reduced-fat graham cracker crust) equals 190 calories, 125 mg sodium, 0 cholesterol, 28 gm carbohydrate, 2 gm protein, 7 gm fat, 1 gm fiber. **Diabetic Exchanges:** 1-1/2 fat, 1 starch, 1 fruit.

Flavorful Fare Earns Raves

JANE RHODES of Silverdale, Washington has a lot of people counting on her. She's married to Webster and has two grown sons, Rob and Jack.

Besides managing a household, Jane works at a local college, where she teaches early childhood education and provides instructional support.

She also keeps her musical skills in tune for Sunday Mass at Naval Station Bremerton and Jackson Park Naval Housing. "I play the piano, organ and conduct choir practices," she shares.

When she's not on the job or enjoying one of her hobbies, you'll likely find Jane in the kitchen. "I love cooking for others," she enthuses. "Entertaining friends and family is such a joy for me."

One of her favorite company menus starts with Baked Shrimp and Asparagus served over hot rice.

"I invented this casserole when I needed to serve 30 co-workers for a holiday party," Jane recalls. "I knew it was a hit when people asked for the recipe. Now I make it frequently for guests because it tastes special, yet it's fast to fix."

With the main dish in the oven, Jane whips up Pineapple Fluff Pie. "This dessert has been a lifesaver for more than 20 years of entertaining and potlucks," she assures.

That leaves plenty of time to assemble Oriental Tossed Salad. The scrumptious medley takes advantage of a ready-to-serve salad mix, fresh bean sprouts

While dessert chills in the refrigerator, Rhonda prepares Teriyaki Beef Stir-Fry. "I combined slices of steak with sweet red pepper and onion to create it," she says.

To complement the easy entree, Rhonda fixes fast Fried Rice. "I revised this recipe from an old cookbook," she notes. "It's a great way to use up leftover cooked rice, and it can be ready in just a few minutes."

Teriyaki Beef Stir-Fry

1 pound round steak, cut into 1/4-inch strips
2 tablespoons vegetable oil
5 tablespoons teriyaki sauce, *divided*
1/2 teaspoon seasoned salt
1/4 teaspoon pepper
1/2 cup julienned onion
1 medium sweet red *or* green pepper, julienned
1 tablespoon cornstarch
1/2 cup cold water

In a skillet, brown steak in oil; drain. Sprinkle with 3 tablespoons of teriyaki sauce, seasoned salt and pepper. Cover and cook over medium heat for 5 minutes or until meat is almost tender, stirring frequently. Stir in onion and red pepper. Cover and cook for 5-8 minutes or until meat and vegetables are tender. In a bowl, combine cornstarch, water and remaining teriyaki sauce until smooth. Add to skillet. Bring to a boil; cook and stir for 2 minutes or until thickened. **Yield:** 4 servings.

A Swift Skillet Supper

A SPIRITED schedule most every day of the week keeps Rhonda Olivieri of rural East Earl, Pennsylvania on the go. By weekday, she's a full-time agent for a fast-paced insurance company. By weekend, she files her office identity to tend to her spiritual side.

"I'm very involved at my church," says Rhonda. "Besides teaching Sunday school, I'm on several committees and edit a bimonthly newsletter for a mission organization."

When she's not working or volunteering, she enjoys cooking, sewing, taking long walks and clerking for a local auctioneer a few Saturdays a month.

To make the most of her time in the kitchen, Rhonda makes a point of staying organized and planning ahead. One of her favorite tricks is to prepare several dishes on a free evening and then use them as lunches throughout the week.

These cooking marathons sometimes include fixing filling fare, like lasagna or meatballs, that can be frozen to enjoy later as a quick meal anytime.

"I also plan menus a week ahead of time, so I know exactly what I need to do each night when I get home from work," she explains. Most of her meals—including the one she shares here—can be on the table within a half hour.

"I usually begin by assembling refreshing Lime Yogurt Pie," reports Rhonda. It's a breeze to make because it takes advantage of a prepared crust.

Fried Rice

1/3 cup chopped onion
1/4 cup butter *or* margarine
4 cups cooked rice
3 tablespoons teriyaki sauce
2 tablespoons minced fresh parsley
1 teaspoon garlic powder
1/8 teaspoon pepper
1 egg, lightly beaten

In a skillet, saute onion in butter until tender. Stir in the rice, teriyaki sauce, parsley, garlic powder and pepper. Cook over medium-low heat for 5 minutes, stirring occasionally. Add the egg; cook and stir until egg is completely set, about 3 minutes. **Yield:** 4 servings.

Lime Yogurt Pie

1 package (3 ounces) lime gelatin
2 cartons (6 ounces *each*) key lime pie yogurt
1 carton (8 ounces) frozen whipped topping, thawed
1 graham cracker crust (9 inches)

In a bowl, combine gelatin powder and yogurt. Fold in whipped topping. Spread into crust. Refrigerate for at least 20 minutes before serving. **Yield:** 6-8 servings.

Dinner for The Holidays

LONG HOURS and an ever-changing schedule are just part of the bargain for salesperson Virginia Conley of Milwaukee, Wisconsin, who works full-time for a local furniture gallery.

During her free time, Virginia enjoys the outdoors, walking, canoeing, the arts, reading, shopping and relaxing with family and friends over a nice home-cooked meal.

"Cooking is fun when you can look forward to sampling something tasty," she relates. "But it's more fun when you can share that pleasure with others."

When time is tight, this savvy working woman relies on recipes that can be prepared in a hurry. That's why Chicken with Mushroom Sauce is one of Virginia's favorites. The chicken is baked in a flavorful sauce made with canned soup and mushrooms, then served over hot noodles.

While the chicken's in the oven, it takes only moments to boil the noodles.

Next, she tosses Red and Green Salad. "I enjoy cooking with fresh ingredients, and this medley features crisp greens and colorful fruit," she notes. The combination is perfect for a Christmastime meal.

Finally, Virginia gathers the ingredients for Peppermint Ice Cream Dessert. The sundae-like treats are a snap to make with crumbled cookies, minty ice cream and a dollop of chocolate-flavored whipped cream.

Chicken with Mushroom Sauce

4 boneless skinless chicken breast halves
2 tablespoons butter *or* margarine
1 can (10-3/4 ounces) condensed cream of mushroom soup, undiluted
1 cup (8 ounces) sour cream
1 can (4 ounces) mushroom stems and pieces, drained
1/4 cup white wine *or* chicken broth
1/2 teaspoon garlic powder
1/2 teaspoon salt
1/2 teaspoon pepper
Hot cooked noodles *or* rice
Sliced almonds, toasted, optional

In a skillet, brown chicken on both sides in butter; drain. Place in a greased 11-in. x 7-in. x 2-in. baking dish. In a bowl, combine the soup, sour cream, mushrooms, wine or broth, garlic powder, salt and pepper; pour over the chicken. Bake, uncovered, at 375° for 20 minutes or until meat juices run clear. Serve chicken and sauce over noodles or rice. Garnish with almonds if desired. **Yield:** 4 servings.

Red and Green Salad

✓ Uses less fat, sugar or salt. Includes Nutritional Analysis and Diabetic Exchanges.

4 cups torn mixed salad greens
2 tablespoons sliced green onion
2 medium red apples, diced
2 kiwifruit, peeled and sliced
1 cup unsweetened raspberries
1/2 cup poppy seed *or* French salad dressing

In a bowl, toss the salad greens, onion and fruit. Drizzle with dressing. Serve immediately. **Yield:** 4 servings.
Nutritional Analysis: One serving (prepared with fat-free French dressing) equals 131 calories, 314 mg sodium, 0 cholesterol, 34 gm carbohydrate, 8 gm protein, 1 gm fat, 7 gm fiber. **Diabetic Exchanges:** 2 fruit, 1 vegetable.

Peppermint Ice Cream Dessert

4 chocolate cream-filled sandwich cookies, broken
1 quart peppermint stick *or* mint chocolate chip ice cream
1/2 cup whipping cream
1 tablespoon confectioners' sugar
2 teaspoons baking cocoa
Miniature candy canes and additional cookies, optional

Sprinkle the broken cookies into four dessert dishes. Top with scoops of ice cream. In a mixing bowl, beat the cream, confectioners' sugar and cocoa until soft peaks form. Dollop over ice cream. Garnish with candy canes and additional cookies if desired. **Yield:** 4 servings.

Chapter 3

PLANNING A PARTY? Why not add a fun and festive touch to your ordinary get-togethers with friends and family? In this chapter, fellow cooks and the *Quick Cooking* kitchen staff show how a short time in the kitchen can result in memorable occasions. There are six easy theme-related menus that celebrate events throughout the year.

Welcome warm weather with garden-fresh fare, a Memorial Day party and country fair fixin's. Or when cool winds begin to blow, sing the praises of your musically inclined family with a mouthwatering medley, kick off a sensational Super Bowl party and herald the holidays with a "berry" merry menu.

FOOTBALL FUN. Clockwise from upper right: Sideline Snackers, Victory Veggie Pizza, Football Brownies and Quarterback Calzones (all recipes on p. 47).

Garden-Fresh Fare

HERALD spring's arrival with these delightful dishes from our test kitchen.

Raindrop Raspberry Tea

Ready in 15 minutes or less

Serve tall cool glasses of this quick-to-fix raspberry combo.

- 4 cups water
- 6 individual tea bags
- 3/4 to 1 cup sugar
- 4 cups cold water
- 1 cup raspberry juice blend concentrate

In a saucepan, bring 4 cups water to a boil. Remove from heat; add tea bags. Cover; steep 5 minutes. Discard bags. Stir in sugar until dissolved. Add cold water and concentrate; mix well. Serve over ice. **Yield: 2 quarts.**

Umbrella Salads

Ready in 30 minutes or less

It's a snap to shape tortillas into umbrellas when you bake them over custard cups. Or use 4-in. diameter foil balls.

- 6 flour tortillas (8 inches)
- 2 tablespoons butter, *or* margarine melted
- 6 cups torn fresh spinach
- 1-1/2 cups cubed fully cooked ham
- 1-1/2 cups sliced fresh mushrooms
- 1 cup cubed cheddar cheese
- 3 slices red onion, separated into rings
- 6 sweet red pepper slices (1/4 inch thick)
- 6 pitted ripe olives
- Salad dressing of your choice

Place six 10-oz. custard cups upside down in a shallow baking pan; set aside. Brush both sides of tortillas with butter; place in a single layer on ungreased baking sheets. Bake, uncovered, at 400° for 1 minute. Place a tortilla over each custard cup, pinching sides to form a bowl shape. Bake 7-8 minutes or until crisp. Remove tortillas from cups; cool. Combine spinach, ham, mushrooms, cheese and onion; place about 1 cup in each bowl. For umbrella handle, cut off a curved end from each red pepper slice; insert straight end into olive. Place in center of salad; arrange salad ingredients to hold handle upright. Serve with dressing. **Yield:** 6 servings.

Blooming Breadsticks

Ready in 1 hour or less

Convenient refrigerated breadsticks make fuss-free flowers.

- 1 tube (11 ounces) refrigerated breadsticks
- 1/4 cup butter *or* margarine, melted
- 1 teaspoon dried parsley flakes
- 1/2 teaspoon garlic powder
- 1/2 teaspoon Italian seasoning
- Additional parsley flakes
- Sesame seeds

Unroll dough; separate into 12 breadsticks. Adjust length of each breadstick to 6 in. For each flower, cut one breadstick into 1-in. pieces and another breadstick into one 4-in. piece and two 1-in. pieces. For stem, twist 4-in. piece twice and place on a greased baking sheet. For leaves, pinch one end of two 1-in. pieces; place on each side of stem and pinch to seal. Roll one 1-in. piece into a ball; place 1 in. above stem for flower center. For petals, pinch one end of remaining five pieces; position with sides touching flower center and other petals. Combine butter, parsley, garlic powder and Italian seasoning; brush over dough. Sprinkle parsley on stem and leaves. Sprinkle sesame seeds on flower center. Bake at 375° for 10-12 minutes or until golden. **Yield:** 6 servings.

Flower Box Cake

Plan ahead...needs to chill

Store-bought goodies, including a pound cake and cookies, create the planter for these edible hyacinths and tulips.

- 1/4 cup butter *or* margarine
- 1 package (10-1/2 ounces) miniature marshmallows
- Red and blue liquid food coloring
- 4 cups Frosted Cheerios
- 15 leaf-shaped spearmint gumdrops
- 15 wooden skewers (8 inches)
- 3 strawberry-flavored Fruit by the Foot rolls
- 6 large marshmallows
- Colored sugar
- 3/4 cup chocolate frosting
- 1 loaf (10-3/4 ounces) frozen pound cake, thawed
- 12 crisp rectangular cookies (about 3 inches x 1-3/4 inches)

For hyacinths, combine the butter and marshmallows in a saucepan; cook and stir over low heat until melted. Divide into two large bowls. Stir 2-3 drops each of red and blue food coloring into one bowl; stir 1-2 drops red food coloring into other bowl. Add 2 cups cereal to each bowl; stir until well coated. Insert one gumdrop on nine skewers. With greased hands, quickly shape about 1/2 cup cereal mixture into a 3- to 4-in.-long hyacinth shape around gumdrop. Place on waxed paper-lined baking sheets. Loosely cover and chill for 4 hours or until firm.

For each tulip, cut six 2-1/2-in.-long pieces of fruit roll. With kitchen shears, trim one end of each piece into tulip petal shape. Trim 1/4 in. from each corner of opposite end. With a small pastry brush, lightly brush water on one end of marshmallow; dip in sugar. Lightly brush  water on sides and bottom of marshmallow. Gently press a petal onto side of marshmallow so top of petal is 1/2 in. above sugared end (see photo above).

Repeat five times, overlapping the side of each petal by 1/8 in. Fold bottom of petals under marshmallow, overlapping tapered ends. Brush with water if needed to hold petals together. Insert a skewer through petals into center of marshmallow. Insert a gumdrop into the other end of skewer to hold marshmallow in place.

Frost top and sides of cake; place cookies vertically around cake. Just before serving, insert flowers into cake, trimming bottom of skewers to varied lengths. **Yield:** 8 servings of cake plus 9 hyacinths and 6 tulips.

Memorable Menu for Memorial Day

TO MARK festive occasions such as Memorial Day, Flag Day or the Fourth of July, reach for this patriotic menu of show-stopping stars.

Firecracker Roll-Ups

Ready in 1 hour or less

Flour tortillas are filled with crunchy broiled vegetables. For fun presentation, wrap sandwiches in plastic wrap and tie with ribbon to resemble firecrackers.
—Kathleen Tribble, Buellton, California

> 1 medium green pepper, cut into 3/4-inch strips
> 1 medium red onion, cut into 1/2-inch strips
> 1 medium zucchini, cut into 1/4-inch slices
> 2 cups quartered fresh mushrooms
> 3 teaspoons dried basil, *divided*
> 2 teaspoons garlic powder, *divided*
> 1/4 teaspoon salt
> 1/4 teaspoon pepper
> 1/4 cup mayonnaise
> 2 teaspoons dried parsley flakes
> 4 flour tortillas (8 inches)
> 1-1/3 cups shredded lettuce

Place vegetables in a greased 15-in. x 10-in. x 1-in. baking pan. Spritz with nonstick cooking spray. Sprinkle with 2 teaspoons basil, 1 teaspoon garlic powder, salt and pepper. Broil 4-6 in. from the heat for 16 minutes or until vegetables are browned, stirring once. Meanwhile, in a bowl, combine mayonnaise, parsley and remaining basil and garlic powder. Warm the tortillas; spread 1 tablespoon of mayonnaise mixture on each. Spoon 3/4 cup vegetables down the center; top with 1/3 cup lettuce. Fold bottom of tortilla over filling and roll up. **Yield:** 4 servings.

Patriotic Picnic Club

Ready in 15 minutes or less

I used to work in a sandwich and ice cream parlor, and this deli club was one of our most popular. Chili sauce and pickle relish add spark to the special sauce that makes this layered sandwich deliciously different.
—Esther Lehman, Fayetteville, Pennsylvania

> 1/2 cup mayonnaise
> 1 to 2 tablespoons chili sauce
> 1 tablespoon sweet pickle relish
> 9 slices bread, toasted
> 3 thin slices deli ham
> 3 slices Swiss cheese
> 3 thin slices deli turkey
> 6 thin slices tomato
> 3 lettuce leaves

In a bowl, combine mayonnaise, chili sauce and pickle relish. Spread 1 tablespoonful on each slice of bread. Top three slices of bread with a slice of ham and Swiss cheese. Top each with another slice of bread. Layer with turkey, tomato and lettuce. Top with remaining bread. Secure with toothpicks if necessary. Cut into quarters. **Yield:** 3-6 servings.

Starry Fruit Soup

Ready in 1 hour or less

If you want to make a soup that your children will love, try this cool and refreshing summer blend. The impressive star design is simple to create with sweetened sour cream.
—Edie DeSpain, Logan, Utah

> 1 can (15 ounces) sliced pears, undrained
> 1 package (10 ounces) frozen sweetened raspberries, thawed
> 1 can (6 ounces) frozen orange juice concentrate, thawed
> 2 medium ripe bananas, cut into chunks
> 1/4 cup lemon juice
> 1 to 2 teaspoons grated orange peel
> 1/8 to 1/4 teaspoon ground coriander, optional
> 1/2 cup sour cream
> 2 tablespoons confectioners' sugar

In a blender, combine the first seven ingredients; cover and process until smooth. Strain to remove seeds if desired. Chill until serving. Combine sour cream and sugar until smooth; place in a heavy-duty resealable plastic bag. Cut a small hole in a corner of bag. Pipe two thin concentric circles 1/2 in. apart on top of each bowl of soup. Beginning with the center circle, gently pull a toothpick through both circles toward outer edge. Wipe toothpick clean. Draw toothpick from outer edge of bowl back to center. Repeat to complete star pattern (see photo above). **Yield:** 6 servings.

Old Glory Dessert

Ready in 1 hour or less

Our home economists took advantage of convenient refrigerated cookie dough to create the crust for this fresh patriotic fruit pizza.

> 1 tube (18 ounces) refrigerated sugar cookie dough*
> 2 packages (one 8 ounces, one 3 ounces) cream cheese, softened
> 3/4 cup confectioners' sugar
> 4-1/2 teaspoons lemon juice
> 1/2 cup fresh blueberries
> 2 cups quartered fresh strawberries

Press cookie dough into a greased 15-in. x 10-in. x 1-in. baking pan. Bake at 350° for 10-12 minutes or until golden brown. Cool on a wire rack. In a mixing bowl, beat cream cheese, sugar and lemon juice until smooth. Set aside 1/4 cup. Spread remaining cream cheese mixture over crust. Decorate with blueberries and strawberries to resemble a flag. Cut a small hole in a corner of a pastry or plastic bag. Insert star tip #16. Fill with reserved cream cheese mixture. Beginning in one corner, pipe stars in the spaces between the blueberries. **Yield:** 12-15 servings. ***Editor's Note:** 2 cups of any sugar cookie dough can be substituted for the refrigerated dough.

County Fair
Fixin's

IF YOU'RE one of the many folks who just can't wait for the county fair, you'll love this finger-lickin' fare that exhibits plenty of good taste.

Blue-Ribbon Beef Nachos

Ready in 30 minutes or less

Chili powder and sassy salsa season a zesty mixture of ground beef and refried beans that's sprinkled with green onions, tomatoes and ripe olives. It's a tasty topper for tortilla chips.   —Diane Hixon, Niceville, Florida

1 pound ground beef
1 small onion, chopped
1 can (16 ounces) refried beans
1 jar (16 ounces) salsa
1 can (6 ounces) pitted ripe olives, chopped
1/2 cup shredded cheddar cheese
1 green onion, chopped
2 tablespoons chili powder
1 teaspoon salt
Tortilla chips
Sliced ripe olives and chopped green onions and
   tomatoes, optional

In a skillet, cook the beef and onion over medium heat until meat is no longer pink; drain. Stir in the next seven ingredients; heat through. Serve over tortilla chips. Top with olives, onions and tomatoes if desired. **Yield:** 6 servings.

Watermelon Ice

Plan ahead...needs to freeze

This sweet frosty snack is so refreshing on hot summer days. Store it in the freezer, so it's a snap to scoop and serve in snow cone cups.
                                    —Darlene Markel
                                    Mt. Hood, Oregon

1/2 cup sugar
1/4 cup watermelon *or* mixed fruit gelatin
   powder
3/4 cup boiling water
5 cups seeded cubed watermelon

In a bowl, dissolve sugar and gelatin in boiling water; set aside. Place watermelon in a blender; cover and puree. Stir into gelatin mixture. Pour into an ungreased pan. Cover and freeze overnight. Remove from the freezer 1 hour before serving. Spoon into paper cones or serving dishes. **Yield:** 4-6 servings.

Hot Dog Cookies

Plan ahead...needs to chill

These crowd-pleasing cookies, shaped like miniature hot dogs in buns, are plump with possibilities. (The recipe comes from our creative home economists.) Add time-easing toppings such as green-tinted coconut for "relish" and yellow frosting for "mustard".

1 cup butter (no substitutes), softened
1/2 cup confectioners' sugar

2 cups all-purpose flour
1 teaspoon vanilla extract
Red and green liquid food coloring
3 tablespoons flaked coconut
Yellow decorator's frosting

In a mixing bowl, cream butter and sugar. Beat in flour and vanilla. Remove 1 cup dough; add red food coloring and knead until well combined. Cover and refrigerate remaining dough for 1 hour. For hot dogs, divide red dough into 16 portions. Shape into 2-1/2-in. logs and round the ends; set aside. Divide plain dough into 16 portions. Shape into 3-in. logs; make a very deep lengthwise groove in each. Smooth edges to form buns. Place 3 in. apart on an ungreased baking sheet. Place hot dogs in buns. Bake at 350° for 12-15 minutes or until edges are golden brown. Cool. Meanwhile, for pickle relish, combine coconut and green food coloring in a resealable plastic bag; shake well. Sprinkle over hot dogs. For mustard, pipe a stripe of yellow frosting down the center of each. **Yield:** 16 servings.

County Fair Funnel Cakes

Ready in 30 minutes or less

What would the fair be without these delicious deep-fried pastries shared by our home economists? To make these timeless treats, slowly swirl batter into oil, brown it to perfection and lightly dust with confectioners' sugar.

2 eggs, lightly beaten
1-1/2 cups milk
1/4 cup packed brown sugar
2 cups all-purpose flour
1-1/2 teaspoons baking powder
1/4 teaspoon salt
Oil for deep-fat frying
Confectioners' sugar

In a bowl, combine the eggs, milk and brown sugar. Combine flour, baking powder and salt; beat into egg mixture until smooth. In an electric skillet or deep-fat fryer, heat oil to 375°. Cover the bottom of a funnel spout with your finger; ladle 1/2 cup batter into funnel. Holding the funnel several inches above the skillet (see photo at right), release finger and move the funnel in a spiral motion until all of the batter is released (scraping funnel with a rubber spatula if needed). Fry for 2 minutes on each side or until golden brown. Drain on paper towels. Repeat with remaining batter. Dust with confectioners' sugar; serve warm. **Yield:** 6 servings. **Editor's Note:** The batter can also be poured from a liquid measuring cup instead of a funnel.

Musical Medley's a Hit

DO YOU often hear the plink-plunk of piano keys in the parlor? The din of drums in the kitchen? Fiddling in the family room or crooning in the kitchen?

Then this luncheon menu composed by the home economists in our test kitchen will strike a pleasant chord with you.

Even if entertaining isn't your forte, this no-fuss fare will help you celebrate a recital, cap off a choir concert or sing the praises of the musically minded individuals in your family.

The recipes are so simple, you won't find yourself singing the "no time to cook" blues. Plus, guests will find the fabulous flavors worthy of an encore.

Symphony Onion Soup

You won't miss a beat with this savory soup that gets a touch of sweetness from molasses. Tender onions and a beefy broth make it especially noteworthy. You can serve it solo or topped with Quarter Note Croutons.

>   8 cups thinly sliced onions
>   1/4 cup butter *or* margarine
>   2 to 3 teaspoons molasses
>   1 teaspoon sugar
>   3 tablespoons all-purpose flour
>   1/4 cup white wine *or* water
>   5 cans (14-1/2 ounces *each*) beef broth
>   2 bay leaves
>   1 teaspoon salt
>   1/2 teaspoon Worcestershire sauce
>   10 Quarter Note Croutons (recipe below)

In a Dutch oven or soup kettle, saute onions in butter. Cover and cook over medium heat for 15 minutes, stirring occasionally. Stir in the molasses and sugar. Cover and cook for 20 minutes. In a small bowl, combine flour and wine or water until smooth. Add to onion mixture with broth, bay leaves, salt and Worcestershire sauce. Bring to a boil. Reduce heat; simmer, uncovered, for 20 minutes. Discard bay leaves. Ladle into bowls; top with croutons. **Yield:** 10 servings.

Quarter Note Croutons

Ready in 15 minutes or less

A cookie cutter shaped like a musical note is instrumental in making these crunchy croutons from French bread. Slices are topped with a buttery garlic blend, sprinkled with two kinds of cheese and browned to perfection.

>   1 loaf (1 pound) French bread
>   2 tablespoons butter *or* margarine, melted
>   1/4 teaspoon garlic salt
>   1/4 teaspoon dried oregano
>   1/4 cup shredded mozzarella cheese
>   1/4 cup shredded Swiss cheese

Cut bread into 10 diagonal slices (5 in. x 2-1/2 in.). Cut each slice with a 4-in. musical note cookie cutter. (Discard remaining bread or save for another use.) In a bowl, combine the butter, garlic salt and oregano. Brush over one side of each note. Place on a baking sheet; sprinkle with cheeses. Broil 4 in. from the heat for 2-3 minutes or until cheese is melted. **Yield:** 10 croutons.

Jazzy Gelatin

Plan ahead...needs to chill

Chock-full of mandarin oranges and crushed pineapple, this colorful gelatin is so refreshing that guests won't be able to refrain from seconds.

>   1 package (6 ounces) orange gelatin
>   2 cups boiling water
>   1 cup ice cubes
>   1 can (15 ounces) mandarin oranges, drained
>   1 can (8 ounces) unsweetened crushed
>   pineapple, undrained
>   1 can (6 ounces) frozen orange juice
>   concentrate, thawed
> Green grapes and fresh mint, optional

In a bowl, dissolve the gelatin in boiling water. Add the ice cubes, oranges, pineapple and orange juice concentrate. Pour into a 6-cup ring mold coated with nonstick cooking spray. Refrigerate overnight or until firm. Just before serving, unmold onto a serving plate. If desired, fill center with grapes and garnish with mint. **Yield:** 12 servings.

Tune-a-Piano Sandwiches

Ready in 1 hour or less

Slices of pumpernickel and white bread are the key to creating the fun piano shape of these munchable ivories. A tempting tuna filling flecked with cheese is sure to tickle the taste buds.

>   17 slices white bread
>   2 slices pumpernickel bread
>   2 cans (6 ounces *each*) tuna, drained
>   1/2 cup plus 1 tablespoon mayonnaise, *divided*
>   1/3 cup shredded cheddar cheese
>   3 tablespoons chopped onion
>   3 tablespoons diced celery
>   1/2 teaspoon dill weed
> Salt and pepper to taste

Remove crusts from bread. Cut white bread into 1-in. strips. Cut pumpernickel bread into 1/2-in. strips, then cut each in half widthwise. In a bowl, combine tuna, 1/2 cup mayonnaise, cheese, onion, celery, dill, salt and pepper. Spread on half of the white bread strips; top with remaining strips. Place side by side on a 3-ft. covered board for "white keys" of keyboard. Spread the remaining mayonnaise on one side of each pumpernickel bread strip. Place over the white strips, mayonnaise side down, for "black keys". See illustration below for placement of keys, repeating pattern as necessary until all bread strips are used. **Yield:** 8-10 servings.

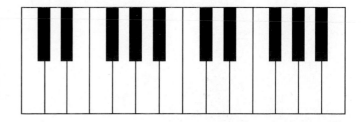

Very Berry Menu

BRING ON THE BERRIES! The rich reds and lush greens of cranberries, raspberries and holly naturally echo the glorious hues of Christmas.

Ripe with flavor, these favorites from our home economists are a great way to greet guests at an open house or welcome carolers after a song-filled evening.

All of the delicious dishes have steps that can be done ahead of time, so you won't get bogged down by last-minute prep work.

Merry Berry Salad

Ready in 30 minutes or less

Dried cranberries, crunchy apple chunks and toasted almonds dress up this crisp green salad. It's drizzled with a sweet-tart dressing that's a snap to blend.

    1 package (10 ounces) mixed salad greens
    1 medium red apple, diced
    1 medium green apple, diced
    1 cup (4 ounces) shredded Parmesan cheese
  1/2 cup dried cranberries
  1/2 cup slivered almonds, toasted
DRESSING:
    1 cup cranberries
  1/2 cup sugar
  1/2 cup cider vinegar
  1/4 cup apple juice concentrate
    1 teaspoon salt
    1 teaspoon ground mustard
    1 teaspoon grated onion
    1 cup vegetable oil

In a large salad bowl, toss first six ingredients. In a blender, combine cranberries, sugar, vinegar, apple juice concentrate, salt, mustard and onion. Cover and process until smooth. While processing, gradually add oil in a steady stream. Drizzle over salad just before serving. Refrigerate any leftover dressing. **Yield:** 10 servings.

Holly Sandwich Wreath

Guests who have sweet expectations are in for a savory surprise when they sample warm slices of this golden wreath. Made with no-fuss pizza crust, the sandwich ring is packed with turkey, cheese, red pepper and green onions.

    2 tubes (10 ounces *each*) refrigerated pizza
      dough
  1/4 cup prepared Italian salad dressing
    1 pound thinly sliced deli turkey
1-1/2 cups (6 ounces) shredded Monterey Jack
      cheese
  1/2 cup chopped sweet red pepper
  1/2 cup sliced green onions
    2 egg yolks, *divided*
Red and green liquid food coloring

Unroll pizza dough. Place dough side by side on a baking sheet with two short sides touching; pinch to seal. Cut a 2-in. strip from one short side; set aside. Brush the remaining dough with salad dressing to within 1/2 in. of edges. Top with turkey, cheese, red pepper and on-

ions. Roll up, jelly-roll style, starting with a long side; pinch seam to seal. Place seam side down on an ungreased baking sheet; form a ring and pinch ends together. Beat one egg yolk; brush over dough. Bake at 350° for 30 minutes. Meanwhile, for glaze, beat remaining egg yolk; divide between two custard cups. Tint one green and one red. On a floured surface, roll out reserved dough to 1/8-in. thickness. Use a small cookie cutter to cut out nine holly leaves, about 2 in. long. Or outline leaf shapes on the dough with a small new paintbrush dipped in green glaze; cut out leaves with a paring knife. Apply green glaze to holly leaves. Shape remaining dough into nine small balls for holly berries; brush with red glaze. Arrange leaves and berries in groups of three on hot dough. Bake 5 minutes longer or until wreath is golden brown. **Yield:** 10 servings.

Cranberry Party Punch

Plan ahead...needs to chill

Cute cranberry-filled ice molds shaped like candy canes float in this refreshing five-ingredient fruit punch. It's easy to stir up and serve right away.

    1 cup cranberries
    1 cup crushed ice
    4 cups cranberry juice, chilled
    4 cups pineapple juice, chilled
1-1/2 cups sugar
    1 tablespoon almond extract
    2 liters ginger ale, chilled

Using three 4-in. candy cane molds or shape of your choice, arrange cranberries and crushed ice alternately in a striped pattern. Add cold water to fill molds. Freeze for 2 hours. To unmold, wrap a hot damp cloth around the bottom of the mold; invert onto a baking sheet. In a punch bowl, combine the juices, sugar and extract; stir until sugar is dissolved. Add ginger ale. Place ice molds in bowl, rounded side up. Serve immediately. **Yield:** 4 quarts (20 servings).

Raspberry Sundaes

Ready in 30 minutes or less

For a fast-to-fix finish, spoon this ruby-red raspberry sauce over individual dishes of vanilla ice cream for a simple yet special dessert.

    2 packages (10 ounces *each*) frozen sweetened
      raspberries, thawed
    2 tablespoons cornstarch
  1/2 teaspoon almond extract
Vanilla ice cream

Drain raspberries, reserving juice; set berries aside. In a bowl, combine cornstarch and 2 tablespoons of juice until smooth. In a saucepan, bring the raspberries and remaining juice to a boil; stir in the cornstarch mixture. Cook for 1-2 minutes or until thickened. Remove from the heat; stir in almond extract. Cool. Serve over ice cream. **Yield:** 1-1/2 cups sauce.

Savory Super Bowl Party

Quarterback Calzones

Select your favorite ingredients to fill these pockets.

    1 package (48 ounces) frozen dinner roll
      dough, thawed
    1 can (15 ounces) pizza sauce
    2 cups (8 ounces) shredded mozzarella cheese
1/2 cup finely chopped green pepper
1/3 cup chopped ripe olives
   32 pepperoni slices
Vegetable oil

For each calzone, press two dinner rolls together. On a lightly floured surface, roll dough into a 6-in. x 3-1/2-in. oval. Spread 1/4 cup sauce to within 1/2 in. of edge. Top with 1/4 cup cheese, 1 tablespoon green pepper, 1 to 2 teaspoons olives and 4 pepperoni slices. Press two more rolls together and roll into a slightly larger oval. Place over filling; firmly press edges to seal. Cut another roll in half and roll out to 1/8-in. thickness. Cut a 3-in. x 1/4-in. strip. Place lengthwise down center of calzone. To form laces, cut four 1-in. x 1/8-in. strips; place across center strip. Cut two 4-in. x 1/4-in. pieces of dough. Place one across each end of calzone, curving to form a crescent shape. Transfer to a greased baking sheet. Lightly brush tops with oil. Cover and let rise in a warm place for 15 minutes. Bake, uncovered, at 375° for 16-17 minutes or until golden brown. Cut calzones in half before serving. **Yield:** 8 calzones (16 servings).

Victory Veggie Pizza

Convenient crescent roll dough is dressed up with vegetables and a tasty cream cheese spread.

    2 tubes (8 ounces *each*) refrigerated
      crescent rolls
    1 package (8 ounces) cream cheese, softened
1/4 cup mayonnaise
    1 teaspoon Worcestershire sauce
1/2 teaspoon garlic powder
   10 to 12 drops hot pepper sauce
3/4 cup shredded cheddar cheese
1/3 cup chopped green pepper
1/3 cup chopped fresh mushrooms
1/4 cup chopped onion
1/4 cup chopped ripe olives
TOPPINGS:
    3 cups chopped fresh broccoli
1/2 cup chopped cherry tomatoes
1/2 cup chopped fresh mushrooms
    1 package (3 ounces) cream cheese,
      softened, *divided*
    7 medium fresh mushroom caps
    7 large cherry tomatoes
    1 slice process American cheese
    1 slice process Swiss cheese
    1 whole pitted ripe olive
    3 to 5 drops food coloring

Unroll crescent roll dough into a greased 15-in. x 10-in. x 1-in. baking pan. Seal seams and perforations; press dough up sides of pan. Prick with fork. Bake at 375° for 11-13 minutes or until golden; cool on a wire rack. In a mixing bowl, beat cream cheese, mayonnaise and seasonings until smooth. Stir in cheddar cheese, green pepper, mushrooms, onion and olives. Spread over crust. Sprinkle broccoli over "field" to within 2 in. of each short side. Sprinkle end zones with tomatoes and mushrooms. Set aside 2 tablespoons cream cheese. Place remaining cream cheese in a small heavy-duty resealable plastic bag; cut 1/4-in. hole in a corner. Pipe yard lines every 2 in. over broccoli. (A small amount will remain in bag; set aside.) For helmets, cut an opening in mushroom caps; carefully clean out. Cut opening in cherry tomatoes; remove pulp and invert tomatoes on paper towels. With 3/4-in. circle cutter, cut seven circles from each slice of cheese. Insert American cheese circles into mushrooms and Swiss circles into tomatoes. Cut a tiny hole in another corner of reserved bag. Pipe cream cheese lines on tomato helmets and laces on olive. In another small bag, combine food coloring and reserved cream cheese. Cut a small hole in a corner; pipe lines on mushroom helmets. Place helmets on field with olive football in middle. **Yield:** 24 servings.

Football Brownies

Homemade chocolate frosting adds a special touch to these moist brownies prepared from a mix.

    1 package fudge brownie mix (13-inch x 9-inch
      pan size)
    6 tablespoons butter *or* margarine, softened
2-3/4 cups confectioners' sugar
1/2 cup baking cocoa
1/3 cup milk
    1 teaspoon vanilla extract
1/4 cup vanilla *or* white chips

Prepare the brownie batter according to package directions. Spread into a greased 15-in. x 10-in. x 1-in. baking pan. Bake at 350° for 13-15 minutes or until a toothpick comes out clean. Cool on a wire rack. In a mixing bowl, cream butter, sugar, cocoa, milk and vanilla. Spread over cooled brownies. Loosely cover and chill for 1 hour or until frosting is set. Cut brownies into diamond shapes. In a microwave, melt chips at 50% power; stir until smooth. Place in a small heavy-duty resealable plastic bag; cut a small hole in a corner of bag. Pipe laces on brownies. **Yield:** about 3 dozen.

Sideline Snackers

Throw together this munchable mixture that has some zip.

    3 quarts popped popcorn
    2 cups pretzel sticks
    2 cups salted peanuts
1-1/4 teaspoons chili powder
3/4 teaspoon paprika
1/2 teaspoon garlic salt
1/4 teaspoon onion salt
1/4 teaspoon ground mustard
1/4 teaspoon ground cumin
    6 tablespoons butter *or* margarine, melted

In a large bowl, combine popcorn, pretzels and peanuts. Combine the seasonings. Drizzle butter over popcorn mixture and sprinkle with seasonings; toss to coat. Store in an airtight container. **Yield:** about 3-1/2 quarts.

Chapter 4

LIKE OTHER time-pressed cooks across the country, you probably steer clear of recipes with long lists of ingredients.

After all, fewer ingredients mean you can offer your family a wholesome hearty meal in a hurry and spend less time cleaning up.

With just five ingredients—or even fewer—these mouth-watering main courses, side dishes, soups, salads, desserts and more are a snap to prepare.

Although these delectable dishes are short on ingredients, you can be sure each and every one is long on flavor.

MAKING THE SHORT LIST.
Clockwise from upper left: Tortilla Beef Bake, Chocolate Ice Cream Syrup and Salsa Strips (all recipes on pp. 54 and 55).

Honey-Mustard Chicken

(Pictured below)

Ready in 15 minutes or less

I get bored with the same old chicken, so I came up with this simple recipe. The coating adds fast flavor to tender chicken cooked on the stovetop. —Laura Theofilis
Leonardtown, Maryland

 Uses less fat, sugar or salt. Includes Nutritional Analysis and Diabetic Exchanges.

> **4 boneless skinless chicken breast halves (1 pound)**
> **1 cup dry bread crumbs**
> **1 teaspoon plus 2 tablespoons Dijon mustard, divided**
> **3 tablespoons honey**
> **2 tablespoons butter or margarine**

Flatten chicken to 1/4-in. thickness. In a shallow bowl, combine bread crumbs and 1 teaspoon of mustard. In another shallow bowl, combine honey and remaining mustard. Dip chicken in honey-mustard mixture, then coat with crumbs. In a nonstick skillet over medium heat, cook chicken in butter on both sides until juices run clear, about 8 minutes. **Yield:** 4 servings. **Nutritional Analysis:** One serving (prepared with reduced-fat margarine) equals 338 calories, 583 mg sodium, 73 mg cholesterol, 34 gm carbohydrate, 31 gm protein, 9 gm fat, 1 gm fiber. **Diabetic Exchanges:** 4 very lean meat, 2 starch, 1 fat.

Basil Green Beans

(Pictured below)

Ready in 15 minutes or less

Basil and lemon-pepper really come through in this speedy way to dress up frozen green beans. My husband and I find that being retired does not mean we're idle. Some days we're very busy, so this side dish is a favorite.
—Marilou Candela, Licking, Missouri

 Uses less fat, sugar or salt. Includes Nutritional Analysis and Diabetic Exchanges.

> **2 cups frozen French-style green beans**
> **2 teaspoons butter or margarine**
> **1/2 teaspoon dried basil**
> **1/2 teaspoon lemon-pepper seasoning**
> **Salt to taste, optional**

Cherry Yogurt Parfaits
Basil Green Beans
Honey-Mustard Chicken

Combine all ingredients in a saucepan. Cover and bring to a boil. Reduce heat; simmer for 6-8 minutes or until beans are tender. **Yield:** 2-3 servings. **Nutritional Analysis:** One 1/2-cup serving (prepared with salt-free lemon-pepper and reduced-fat margarine and without salt) equals 42 calories, 32 mg sodium, 0 cholesterol, 7 gm carbohydrate, 2 gm protein, 2 gm fat, 3 gm fiber. **Diabetic Exchanges:** 1 vegetable, 1/2 fat.

Cherry Yogurt Parfaits

(Pictured below left)

Ready in 15 minutes or less

These attractive parfaits are a cool and light finish to a meal. Our two young children enjoy assembling them... and eating them, of course. —Pam Masters
Derby, Kansas

✓ Uses less fat, sugar or salt. Includes Nutritional Analysis and Diabetic Exchanges.

- 1 can (21 ounces) cherry pie filling, *divided*
- 2 cartons (8 ounces *each*) vanilla yogurt, *divided*
- 1 cup graham cracker crumbs (about 16 squares), *divided*

Combine 1 cup pie filling and one carton of yogurt; place about 2 tablespoons each in six parfait glasses. Top each with 1-2 tablespoons of the graham cracker crumbs, about 2 tablespoons pie filling and about 2 tablespoons yogurt. Divide remaining cracker crumbs and pie filling/yogurt mixture between parfait glasses. **Yield:** 6 servings. **Nutritional Analysis:** One serving (prepared with nonfat yogurt, reduced-sugar pie filling and reduced-fat graham crackers) equals 218 calories, 192 mg sodium, 4 mg cholesterol, 45 gm carbohydrate, 6 gm protein, 3 gm fat, 3 gm fiber. **Diabetic Exchanges:** 2 starch, 1 fruit, 1/2 fat.

Pizza Crescent Bake

Ready in 1 hour or less

When my husband and I were first married, I didn't have many recipes. When my cousin found out, she wrote out nearly 50 of them, including this family favorite. —Laurie Malyuk, River Falls, Wisconsin

- 2 tubes (8 ounces *each*) refrigerated crescent rolls
- 1-1/2 pounds ground beef
- 1 can (15 ounces) pizza sauce
- 1 cup (4 ounces) shredded cheddar cheese
- 1 cup (4 ounces) shredded mozzarella cheese

Unroll one tube of crescent dough; place in a lightly greased 13-in. x 9-in. x 2-in. baking dish. Press to seal perforations. In a skillet, cook beef over medium heat until no longer pink; drain. Sprinkle over dough. Top with pizza sauce and sprinkle with cheeses. Unroll remaining crescent dough and place over cheese; seal perforations. Bake, uncovered, at 350° for 30 minutes or until golden brown. **Yield:** 6-8 servings.

Mandarin Salad

Ready in 15 minutes or less

You can use the oranges and french-fried onions in your pantry to prepare this refreshingly different salad when unexpected company shows up at the door. It goes equally well with beef, pork, poultry or fish. —Elsie Mauriello
Atkinson, New Hampshire

- 1 can (15 ounces) mandarin oranges
- 1/2 cup mayonnaise
- 10 cups torn salad greens
- 1 can (2.8 ounces) french-fried onions

Drain oranges, reserving 2 tablespoons juice (discard remaining juice or refrigerate for another use). In a small bowl, combine mayonnaise and reserved juice until smooth. In a large bowl, toss the greens, oranges and onions. Drizzle with dressing and toss to coat. Serve immediately. **Yield:** 8-10 servings.

Chocolate-Covered Crispies

Plan ahead...needs to chill

Candy bars are the "secret" ingredient in these sweet chewy treats. They taste great and are so quick to make. My family requests them often. —Patricia Carmichael
Gibsons, British Columbia

- 4 Milky Way candy bars* (2.05 ounces *each*), cut up
- 3/4 cup butter *or* margarine, *divided*
- 3 cups crisp rice cereal
- 1 cup (6 ounces) semisweet chocolate chips

In a saucepan over low heat or in a microwave-safe bowl, melt candy bars and 1/2 cup butter; stir until blended. Stir in cereal. Pat into a greased 11-in. x 7-in. x 2-in. pan. In another saucepan or microwave-safe bowl, melt the chocolate chips and remaining butter; stir until smooth. Spread over cereal mixture. Refrigerate until firm. **Yield:** 2 to 2-1/2 dozen. *****Editor's Note:** In Canada, substitute Mars Bars for Milky Way bars.

Vegetable Noodle Soup

Ready in 30 minutes or less

This creamy soup is great on a cold winter day. I created it when I didn't have all the ingredients for broccoli soup. I like this combo even better. —Judie Peters
Camden, Indiana

- 3-1/2 cups milk
- 1 package (16 ounces) frozen California-blend vegetables
- 1/2 cup cubed process American cheese
- 1 envelope chicken noodle soup mix

In a large saucepan, bring milk to a boil. Stir in vegetables and return to a boil. Reduce heat; cover and simmer for 6 minutes. Stir in cheese and soup mix. Return to a boil. Reduce heat. Simmer, uncovered, for 5-7 minutes or until the noodles are tender and the cheese is melted, stirring occasionally. **Yield:** 5-6 servings.

Creamy Cauliflower Soup

Ready in 15 minutes or less

My aunt always made this smooth, rich-tasting soup for me when I came to visit. I could smell it simmering as soon as I arrived. I think of her whenever I have a bowlful.
—Heather Kasprick, Keewatin, Ontario

> 1 medium head cauliflower, broken into florets
> 2 cans (10-3/4 ounces *each*) condensed cream of chicken soup, undiluted
> 1 can (10-3/4 ounces) condensed cheddar cheese soup, undiluted
> 1 can (14-1/2 ounces) chicken broth
> 2 cups milk

Place cauliflower in a saucepan with 1 in. of water; bring to a boil. Reduce heat; cover and simmer for 5-10 minutes or until crisp-tender. Meanwhile, in another saucepan, combine soups, broth and milk; heat through. Drain the cauliflower; stir into soup. **Yield:** 9 servings.

Cocoa Mocha Pie

Plan ahead…needs to freeze

I combined coffee and Milky Way candy bars to create this cool and creamy dessert. I usually prepare the pie the night before, then garnish each slice with extra candy bar chunks before serving. —Carolyn Crump, Center, Texas

> 6 Milky Way candy bars* (2.05 ounces *each*), *divided*
> 1/4 cup milk
> 2 to 3 teaspoons instant coffee granules
> 1 quart vanilla ice cream, softened
> 1 graham cracker *or* chocolate crumb crust (8 *or* 9 inches)

Finely chop four candy bars; place in a microwave-safe bowl or double boiler. Add milk and coffee granules; heat and stir until melted and smooth. Place ice cream in a bowl; fold in mocha mixture. Spoon into crust; freeze. Remove from the freezer 15 minutes before serving. Cut remaining candy bars into 1/2-in. pieces for garnish. **Yield:** 6-8 servings. ***Editor's Note:** In Canada, substitute Mars Bars for Milky Way bars.

Tangy Beef Turnovers

Ready in 30 minutes or less

My mom's recipe for these flavorful pockets called for dough made from scratch, but I streamlined it by using crescent rolls. My children love them plain or dipped in ketchup. —Claudia Bodeker, Ash Flat, Arkansas

> 1 pound ground beef
> 1 medium onion, chopped
> 1 jar (16 ounces) sauerkraut, rinsed, drained and chopped
> 1 cup (4 ounces) shredded Swiss cheese
> 3 tubes (8 ounces *each*) refrigerated crescent rolls

In a skillet, cook beef and onion over medium heat un-til meat is no longer pink; drain. Add sauerkraut and cheese; mix well. Unroll crescent roll dough and separate into rectangles. Place on greased baking sheets; pinch seams to seal. Place 1/2 cup beef mixture in the center of each rectangle. Bring corners to the center and pinch to seal. Bake at 375° for 15-18 minutes or until golden brown. **Yield:** 1 dozen.

Soft Lemon Frosting

Ready in 15 minutes or less

This fresh-tasting citrus icing makes a pretty topping for white cake or cupcakes, especially when garnished with grated lemon peel. Plus, it's a snap to stir up in a jiffy.
—Madge Robertson, Murfreesboro, Arkansas

> 1 can (14 ounces) sweetened condensed milk
> 3/4 cup lemonade concentrate
> 1 carton (8 ounces) frozen whipped topping, thawed

In a bowl, combine milk and lemonade concentrate. Fold in whipped topping. Store in the refrigerator. **Yield:** about 4 cups (enough to frost 24 cupcakes or a two-layer, tube or 13- x 9-inch cake).

Parmesan Broccoli Bake

Ready in 1 hour or less

This cheesy casserole is a terrific way to dress up every-day broccoli. It's quick, easy and has great flavor.
—Robin Blakeley, East Syracuse, New York

> 1 can (10-3/4 ounces) condensed cream of mushroom soup, undiluted
> 1 can (5 ounces) evaporated milk
> 1/2 cup grated Parmesan cheese
> 1/2 teaspoon salt
> 2 packages (10 ounces *each*) frozen chopped broccoli, thawed and drained

In a bowl, combine all ingredients. Transfer to a greased 11-in. x 7-in. x 2-in. baking dish. Bake, uncovered, at 350° for 30-35 minutes or until broccoli is tender. **Yield:** 6 servings.

Double Cheddar Hash Browns

(Pictured above right)

This comforting side dish starts with convenient frozen hash browns and canned soups. Shredded cheese and crunchy cornflake crumbs are the fast finishing touch to this potato bake. —Renee Hatfield, Marshallville, Ohio

> 1 can (10-3/4 ounces) condensed cream of onion soup, undiluted
> 1 can (10-3/4 ounces) condensed cheddar cheese soup, undiluted
> 1 package (30 ounces) frozen shredded hash browns
> 2 cups (8 ounces) shredded cheddar cheese
> 1 cup crushed cornflakes

Double Cheddar Hash Browns
Mom's Coleslaw
Chili Chops

In a large bowl, combine the soups. Stir in hash browns. Pour into a greased 2-1/2-qt. baking dish. Sprinkle with cheese and cornflake crumbs. Cover and bake at 350° for 50 minutes. Uncover; bake 10 minutes longer or until golden. **Yield:** 8 servings.

Chili Chops

(Pictured above)

Ready in 1 hour or less

I often accompany this dish with mashed potatoes and serve the chili sauce as gravy. It's easy to make after a long day. In summer, I cook it in the microwave to keep the kitchen cool. —Nicole Svacina, St. Nazianz, Wisconsin

- 4 pork loin chops, 1/2 inch thick
- 4 onion slices, 1/4 inch thick
- 4 green pepper slices, 1/4 inch thick
- 1 bottle (12 ounces) chili sauce

Place the pork chops in a greased 9-in. square baking dish. Top with the onion, green pepper and chili sauce.

Cover and bake at 350° for 20-30 minutes or until the meat juices run clear. **Yield:** 4 servings.

Mom's Coleslaw

(Pictured above)

Ready in 15 minutes or less

You won't have to fuss with a lot of seasonings to fix this tangy coleslaw. This speedy salad is an old family favorite that we've shared with many friends over the years.
—Denise Augostine, Saxonburg, Pennsylvania

- 1 small head cabbage, shredded
- 3 medium carrots, shredded
- 1 cup mayonnaise
- 1/3 cup sugar
- 1/4 cup cider vinegar

In a large bowl, combine cabbage and carrots. In a small bowl, combine the mayonnaise, sugar and vinegar. Pour over cabbage mixture and toss to coat. Serve with a slotted spoon. **Yield:** 10-12 servings.

Crisp Peanut Candies

Ready in 1 hour or less

My sister gave me this quick-and-easy recipe one year when I was tired of making the same old holiday cookies. My husband absolutely loves these sweet treats, and I love their no-bake convenience. —Christine Kehler
Nebo, North Carolina

      2-2/3 cups vanilla *or* white chocolate chips
        1/4 cup peanut butter
          3 cups crisp rice cereal
          1 cup peanuts

In a heavy saucepan, heat vanilla chips and peanut butter over low until melted; stir until smooth. Add cereal and peanuts; stir to coat. Drop by tablespoonfuls onto waxed paper; let stand until set. Store in an airtight container at room temperature. **Yield:** about 4-1/2 dozen.

Spinach Potato Soup

Ready in 30 minutes or less

I first made this fresh-tasting soup for a school potluck on St. Patrick's Day. It was a hit, and now I make it throughout the year. —Lois McAtee, Oceanside, California

      3 cups milk
      1 can (15 ounces) sliced potatoes, drained
      1 package (10 ounces) frozen creamed
        spinach, thawed
    1/2 teaspoon dried basil
    1/2 to 3/4 teaspoon garlic salt

Combine all ingredients in a saucepan. Bring to a boil. Reduce heat; cover and simmer for 15 minutes. Cool slightly. Transfer mixture to a blender; cover and process until small pieces of potato remain. Return to the pan and heat through. **Yield:** 4-6 servings.

Dilly Crab Salad

Ready in 30 minutes or less

This summery seafood salad is one of my husband's favorites. For a tasty variation, add peas, pimientos or green onions to the colorful mixture. —Christy Herbert
Muskegon, Michigan

      1 package (1 pound) medium shell pasta
      2 packages (8 ounces *each*) imitation crabmeat,
        flaked
  1-1/2 cups (12 ounces) sour cream
  1-1/2 cups mayonnaise
      1 to 2 tablespoons dill weed

Speedy Side Dish

To quickly round out a meal, I defrost a package of frozen strawberries and add it to a jar of applesauce. This fruity combination makes an excellent side dish.
—Betty Pedigo, Green River, Wyoming

Cook pasta according to package directions; rinse in cold water and drain. Place in a large bowl. Add crab. Combine sour cream, mayonnaise and dill; add to pasta mixture and mix well. Chill until serving. **Yield:** 8-10 servings.

Crumb-Coated Cod

Ready in 30 minutes or less

Fish fillets pick up flavor from Italian salad dressing mix and a breading made with seasoned stuffing mix. I serve this baked fish with a tossed salad or relishes. —Julia Bruce, Tuscola, Illinois

      2 tablespoons vegetable oil
      2 tablespoons water
      1 envelope Italian salad dressing mix
      2 cups crushed stuffing mix
      4 cod fillets (about 6 ounces *each*)

In a shallow bowl, combine the oil, water and salad dressing mix. Place the stuffing mix in another bowl. Dip fillets in salad dressing mixture, then in stuffing. Place on a greased baking sheet. Bake at 425° for 15-20 minutes or until fish flakes easily with a fork. **Yield:** 4 servings.

Golden Potato Rounds

My mom used to fix these crisp coated potatoes when she served baked chicken or pork chops. Now I enjoy making the thick, tender slices for my family of four. —Lisa Shafer, Oregon, Missouri

      1 cup crushed cornflakes
  1-1/2 teaspoons seasoned salt
      4 medium potatoes, peeled and sliced
        1/2-inch thick
    1/4 cup butter *or* margarine, melted

In a bowl, combine the cornflakes and seasoned salt. Dip potatoes in butter, then coat with cornflake mixture. Place on greased foil-lined baking sheets. Bake at 350° for 55-60 minutes or until tender. **Yield:** 6 servings.

Tortilla Beef Bake

(Pictured at right and on page 48)

Ready in 1 hour or less

My family loves Mexican food, so I came up with this simple satisfying casserole that gets its spark from salsa. We rarely have leftovers. —Kim Osburn, Ligonier, Indiana

  1-1/2 pounds ground beef
      1 can (10-3/4 ounces) condensed cream of
        chicken soup, undiluted
  2-1/2 cups crushed tortilla chips, *divided*
      1 jar (16 ounces) salsa
  1-1/2 cups (6 ounces) shredded cheddar cheese

In a skillet, cook beef over medium heat until no longer pink; drain. Stir in soup. Sprinkle 1-1/2 cups tortilla chips in a greased shallow 2-1/2-qt. baking dish. Top with beef mixture, salsa and cheese. Bake, uncovered, at 350° for 25-30 minutes or until bubbly. Sprinkle with the remaining chips. Bake 3 minutes longer or until chips are lightly toasted. **Yield:** 6 servings.

Chocolate Ice Cream Syrup

(Pictured below and on page 49)

Ready in 30 minutes or less

When our four children were growing up, we served this sweet chocolate sauce over hand-cranked ice cream. Now when we have friends over for cards, we finish the evening with sundaes made with this syrup.
—*Dorothy Mekemson, Humboldt, Iowa*

6 squares (1 ounce *each*) unsweetened
   chocolate
3 tablespoons butter (no substitutes), cubed
2 cups sugar
1 can (12 ounces) evaporated milk
Ice cream

In a heavy saucepan over low heat or double boiler over simmering water, melt the chocolate. Add butter; cook and stir until melted. Add sugar alternately with milk, stirring constantly. Cook for 15 minutes, stirring often. Serve warm over ice cream. Refrigerate leftovers. **Yield:** 2-

1/2 cups. **Editor's Note:** If desired, add 1 teaspoon vanilla extract or 1/2 teaspoon orange or peppermint extract. Stir into syrup after removing from the heat.

Salsa Strips

(Pictured below and on page 48)

Ready in 1 hour or less

I rely on refrigerated crescent rolls to make these crisp Southwestern appetizers. Choose mild, medium or hot salsa to suit your taste.
—*Joann Woloszyn*
Fredonia, New York

1 tube (8 ounces) refrigerated crescent rolls
2 tablespoons Dijon mustard
3/4 cup salsa
1 cup (4 ounces) shredded mozzarella cheese
Minced fresh cilantro *or* parsley

Unroll crescent roll dough and separate into four rectangles. Place on greased baking sheets. Spread mustard and salsa on each rectangle. Bake at 350° for 10 minutes. Sprinkle with cheese; bake 8-10 minutes longer or until golden brown. Cool for 10 minutes. Cut each into four strips; sprinkle with cilantro. **Yield:** 16 appetizers.

Chocolate Ice Cream Syrup
Tortilla Beef Bake
Salsa Strips

Zippy French Bread
Tomato Tossed Salad
Glazed Chicken Wings

Zippy French Bread

(Pictured above)

Ready in 30 minutes or less

Instead of serving plain French bread with butter, I prepare a loaf of this tasty bread while our steaks are cooking on the grill. It's quick, easy to make and oh-so-good with its creamy filling. I usually add a salad to complete the menu.
—Sue Mackey, Galesburg, Illinois

2 packages (3 ounces *each*) cream cheese, softened
1/4 cup butter *or* margarine, softened
2 tablespoons minced chives
2 to 4 teaspoons prepared horseradish
1 loaf (1 pound) French bread

In a small mixing bowl, beat the cream cheese, butter, chives and horseradish until combined. Cut the bread into 1-in. slices to within 1/2 in. of bottom. Spread cream cheese mixture between slices. Wrap the loaf in a large piece of heavy-duty foil (about 28 in. x 18 in.). Bake at 400° for 14-17 minutes or until heated through. **Yield:** 10 servings.

Fresh Fruit Dip

Ready in 15 minutes or less

This rich, sweet dip is a must at family gatherings. We serve it with a platter of strawberries, sliced kiwi and other fresh fruit in season.
—Jean Gribskov
Carmichael, California

1 cup marshmallow creme
2/3 cup sour cream
1/3 cup mayonnaise
Assorted fresh fruit

In a small bowl, combine the first three ingredients; whisk until smooth. Refrigerate until serving. Serve with fruit. **Yield:** 2 cups.

Tomato Tossed Salad

(Pictured above)

Ready in 15 minutes or less

I stir in chives and thyme to add interest to a simple oil and vinegar dressing, then drizzle it over this refreshing salad. It's es-

pecially good with sun-ripened tomatoes right out of the garden. —Edna Hoffman, Hebron, Indiana

6 cups shredded lettuce
2 medium tomatoes, cut into wedges
1/4 cup oil and vinegar salad dressing
1 teaspoon snipped chives
1/4 teaspoon dried thyme

Place lettuce and tomatoes in a salad bowl. Combine salad dressing, chives and thyme; drizzle over salad and toss gently. **Yield:** 4 servings.

Glazed Chicken Wings

(Pictured at left)

I received the recipe for these yummy wings from a cousin on Vancouver Island during a visit there a few years ago. They're an appealing appetizer, but also a favorite for Sunday lunch with rice and a salad. —Joan Airey
Rivers, Manitoba

12 whole chicken wings* (about 2-1/2 pounds)
1/2 cup barbecue sauce
1/2 cup honey
1/2 cup soy sauce

Cut chicken wings into three sections; discard wing tip section. Place in a greased 13-in. x 9-in. x 2-in. baking dish. Combine barbecue sauce, honey and soy sauce; pour over wings. Bake, uncovered, at 350° for 50-60 minutes or until chicken juices run clear. **Yield:** 4 servings. *Editor's Note: 2-1/2 pounds of uncooked chicken wing sections may be substituted for the whole chicken wings. Omit the first step of the recipe.

Tangy Potato Slices

Ready in 1 hour or less

A snappy sauce gives spuds a German potato salad-like taste that is sure to tingle your taste buds. This is a perfect way to use up leftover cooked potatoes. —Ilene Soroko
Norfolk, Virginia

4 medium potatoes
1/4 cup mayonnaise
4 teaspoons vinegar
1-1/2 teaspoons sugar
1/4 teaspoon salt

Place potatoes in a saucepan; cover with water. Bring to a boil; reduce heat. Cover and cook for 20-25 minutes or until tender; drain and cool slightly. Meanwhile, in a skillet, combine the mayonnaise, vinegar, sugar and salt. Cook and stir over low heat just until heated through. Peel potatoes and cut into 1/4-in. slices. Gently stir into mayonnaise mixture; heat through. **Yield:** 4 servings.

Cucumber Sandwiches

Ready in 15 minutes or less

I was introduced to a similar sandwich by a friend many years ago. I sometimes add thinly sliced onions for a change of pace. Along with fruit salad, it makes a light summer lunch. —Karen Schriefer, Stevensville, Maryland

1 carton (8 ounces) cream cheese spread
2 teaspoons ranch salad dressing mix
12 slices pumpernickel rye bread
2 to 3 medium cucumbers

In a bowl, combine cream cheese and dressing mix. Spread on one side of each slice of bread. Peel cucumbers if desired; thinly slice and place on six slices of bread. Top with remaining bread. Serve immediately. **Yield:** 6 servings.

Barbecue Beef Patties

Ready in 1 hour or less

My family loves these patties, which taste like individual meat loaves. Barbecue sauce brushed on top gives them great flavor. —Marlene Harguth, Maynard, Minnesota

1 egg
1/2 cup barbecue sauce, *divided*
3/4 cup crushed cornflakes
1/2 to 1 teaspoon salt
1 pound ground beef

In a bowl, combine egg, 1/4 cup barbecue sauce, cornflake crumbs and salt. Add beef and mix well. Shape into four oval patties, about 3/4 in. thick. Place in a greased 11-in. x 7-in. x 2-in. baking pan. Spread with remaining barbecue sauce. Bake, uncovered, at 375° for 25-30 minutes or until meat is no longer pink and a meat thermometer reads 160°; drain. **Yield:** 4 servings.

Lemon Grape Cooler

Plan ahead...needs to chill

While on vacation, we sampled this refreshing grape beverage that has hints of lemon and tea. We enjoyed it so much, I had to ask for the recipe. —Delores George
St. Louis, Missouri

1-1/2 cups sugar
1 cup lemon juice
1 cup white grape juice
2 tablespoons unsweetened instant tea
Water

In a gallon container, combine the sugar, juices and tea. Add water to measure 1 gallon. Cover and refrigerate until chilled. **Yield:** 16 servings (1 gallon).

Buying Chives

Fresh chives are easy to spot in your local supermarket. Just look for an even green color with no signs of wilting or browning. Keep chives fresh up to 1 week by wrapping in a paper towel and placing them in a plastic bag in the refrigerator. To freeze, wash chives and pat dry. Place in an airtight plastic bag and keep for up to 6 months. There is no need to defrost the chives before using.

Raisin Finger Sandwiches

Ready in 15 minutes or less

As a registered nurse and mother of four, I'm very busy. That's why I like these sweet sandwiches for an any time snack...they're simple to assemble but look and taste like you put a lot of effort into them. —Jeannie Dobbs
Bartlesville, Oklahoma

    1 package (8 ounces) cream cheese, softened
    1/4 cup mayonnaise
    1/2 cup chopped pecans
    10 slices raisin bread

In a mixing bowl, beat cream cheese and mayonnaise until smooth. Stir in pecans. Spread over five slices of bread; top with remaining bread. Cut each sandwich into three strips. Serve immediately. **Yield:** 5 servings.

Potato Beef Casserole

I sometimes add chopped onion when browning the ground beef for this fast-to-fix main dish. I often serve this comforting casserole for dinner or double the recipe to take to potlucks. —Shirley Goering, New Ulm, Minnesota

    4 medium potatoes, peeled and sliced
    1 pound ground beef, cooked and drained
    1 can (10-3/4 ounces) condensed cream of
      chicken soup, undiluted
    1 can (10-1/2 ounces) condensed vegetable
      beef soup, undiluted
    1/2 teaspoon salt

In a large bowl, combine all ingredients. Transfer to a greased 2-qt. baking dish. Cover and bake at 350° for 1-1/2 hours or until potatoes are tender. **Yield:** 4-6 servings.

Chocolate Cookie Mousse

Plan ahead...needs to freeze

I have family members who beg for this yummy dessert whenever I visit. It calls for just four ingredients, and it's handy to keep in the freezer for a special occasion.
—Carol Mullaney, Pittsburgh, Pennsylvania

    1 package (16 ounces) cream-filled chocolate
      sandwich cookies, *divided*
    2 tablespoons milk
    2 cups whipping cream, *divided*
    2 cups (12 ounces) semisweet chocolate chips

Crush 16 cookies; sprinkle into an 8-in. square dish. Drizzle with milk. In a microwave-safe bowl, combine 2/3 cup cream and chocolate chips. Microwave, uncovered, on high for 1 minute. Stir; microwave 30-60 seconds longer or until chips are melted. Stir until smooth; cool to room temperature. Meanwhile, in a mixing bowl, beat remaining cream until soft peaks form. Fold into chocolate mixture. Spread a third of the chocolate mixture over crushed cookies. Separate eight cookies; place over chocolate mixture. Repeat. Top with remaining chocolate mixture. Garnish with remaining whole

cookies. Cover and freeze for up to 2 months. Thaw in the refrigerator for at least 3 hours before serving. **Yield:** 16 servings. **Editor's Note:** This recipe was tested in an 850-watt microwave.

Creamy Broccoli Cabbage

Ready in 15 minutes or less

My kids hated cabbage, but when times were hard, I wanted to make the most of this economical vegetable, so I invented this creamy combination. They gobbled it up. Now it's a must at our holiday dinners. —Lee Silvey
Snohomish, Washington

    4 cups shredded cabbage
    1/2 pound fresh broccoli florets
    2 tablespoons butter *or* margarine
    4 ounces cream cheese, cubed
Salt to taste

Place cabbage and broccoli in a saucepan; add 1 in. of water. Bring to a boil. Reduce heat; cover and simmer for 5-8 minutes or until crisp-tender. Meanwhile, in another saucepan, melt butter. Stir in cream cheese until melted. Drain vegetables; top with cream sauce. Add salt and toss to coat. **Yield:** 4-6 servings.

Pasta with Basil

(Pictured at right)

Ready in 15 minutes or less

If you like basil, you'll enjoy the Italian flavor of this speedy side dish. This is one of my husband's favorites. It's super easy to make and tastes wonderful.
—Jaime Hampton, Birmingham, Alabama

☑ Uses less fat, sugar or salt. Includes Nutritional Analysis and Diabetic Exchanges.

    2-1/2 cups uncooked small tube pasta
        1 small onion, chopped
        1 to 3 tablespoons olive *or* vegetable oil
        2 to 3 tablespoons dried basil
        1 cup (4 ounces) shredded mozzarella cheese

Cook pasta according to package directions. Meanwhile, in a skillet, saute onion in oil until tender. Stir in basil; cook and stir for 1 minute. Drain pasta; add to basil mixture. Remove from the heat; stir in cheese just until it begins to melt. Serve immediately. **Yield:** 4 servings. **Nutritional Analysis:** One serving (prepared with 1 tablespoon oil and part-skim mozzarella cheese) equals 332 calories, 135 mg sodium, 16 mg cholesterol, 48 gm carbohydrate, 15 gm protein, 9 gm fat, 2 gm fiber. **Diabetic Exchanges:** 3 starch, 1 meat, 1 fat.

Cherry Gelatin Squares

(Pictured above right)

Plan ahead...needs to chill

I like to take advantage of gelatin mixes and pie fillings

**Cherry Gelatin Squares
Pasta with Basil
Bacon-Wrapped Chicken**

to make colorful salads that can be prepared the day before you need them. These fruity squares are great for everyday suppers yet special enough for company.
—Chris Rentmeister, Ripon, Wisconsin

 Uses less fat, sugar or salt. Includes Nutritional Analysis and Diabetic Exchanges.

>   1 package (6 ounces) cherry gelatin
> 1-1/2 cups boiling water
>   1 can (21 ounces) cherry pie filling
> 1-1/4 cups lemon-lime soda, chilled
> Whipped topping, optional

In a bowl, dissolve gelatin in water. Stir in pie filling; mix well. Slowly stir in soda (mixture will foam). Pour into an 8-in. square dish. Cover and refrigerate until firm. Cut into squares. Garnish with whipped topping if desired. **Yield:** 9 servings. **Nutritional Analysis:** One serving (prepared with sugar-free gelatin, reduced-sugar pie filling and diet soda and without whipped topping) equals 59 calories, 52 mg sodium, 0 cholesterol, 13 gm carbohydrate, 1 gm protein, 1 gm fat, trace fiber. **Diabetic Exchange:** 1 fruit.

Bacon-Wrapped Chicken

(Pictured above)

Ready in 1 hour or less

Tender chicken takes on a wonderful new flavor when spread with a creamy filling and wrapped with bacon.
—MarlaKaye Skinner, Tucson, Arizona

>   6 boneless skinless chicken breast halves
>   1 carton (8 ounces) whipped cream cheese with onion and chives
>   1 tablespoon butter or margarine, cubed
> Salt to taste
>   6 bacon strips

Flatten the chicken to 1/2-in. thickness. Spread 3 tablespoons cream cheese over each. Dot with the butter and sprinkle with salt; roll up. Wrap each with a bacon strip. Place, seam side down, in a greased 13-in. x 9-in. x 2-in. baking pan. Bake, uncovered, at 400° for 35-40 minutes or until juices run clear. Broil 6 in. from the heat for 5 minutes or until bacon is crisp. **Yield:** 6 servings.

Cherry Cinnamon Cobbler

(Pictured below)

Ready in 30 minutes or less

Two convenience items come together in this cobbler. It's a snap to whip up for a brunch treat or a warming dessert.
—*Terri Robinson, Muncie, Indiana*

1 can (21 ounces) cherry pie filling
1 tube (12.4 ounces) refrigerated cinnamon rolls

Spread pie filling into a greased 8-in. square baking dish. Set aside icing from cinnamon rolls. Arrange rolls around edge of baking dish. Bake at 400° for 15 minutes. Cover and bake 10 minutes longer or until golden. Spread icing over rolls. Serve warm. **Yield:** 8 servings.

Savory Sprouts

(Pictured below)

Ready in 30 minutes or less

Cream of chicken soup creates the easy sauce that coats these tender sprouts. Seasoned with thyme and sprinkled with sliced almonds, this vegetable side dish is special.
—*Daphne Blandford, Gander, Newfoundland*

1 package (16 ounces) frozen brussels sprouts
1 can (10-3/4 ounces) condensed cream of chicken soup, undiluted
3 tablespoons milk
1/4 teaspoon dried thyme
1/4 cup sliced almonds, toasted

In a saucepan, cook brussels sprouts according to package directions; drain. Remove sprouts and set aside. To the saucepan, add soup, milk and thyme; heat through. Return sprouts to pan; stir to coat. Transfer to a serving dish; sprinkle with almonds. **Yield:** 4-6 servings.

Shrimp Newburg

(Pictured below)

Ready in 15 minutes or less

A friend gave me the recipe for this tasty time-saving dish that takes advantage of cooked shrimp. It's a quick company meal when served over rice with a tossed salad and dessert. —*Donna Souders, Hagerstown, Maryland*

Savory Sprouts
Cherry Cinnamon Cobbler
Shrimp Newburg

1 can (10-3/4 ounces) condensed cream of
 shrimp *or* mushroom soup, undiluted
1/4 cup water
1 teaspoon seafood seasoning
1 package (1 pound) frozen cooked medium
 salad shrimp, thawed
Hot cooked rice

In a saucepan, combine soup, water and seafood seasoning. Bring to a boil. Reduce heat; stir in shrimp. Heat through. Serve over rice. **Yield:** 4 servings.

Corny Clam Chowder

Ready in 15 minutes or less

Cream gives richness to the canned items that make up this satisfying chowder. I sometimes make it in the slow cooker, so it can simmer while I work around the house.
—Karen Johnston, Syracuse, Nebraska

1 can (14-3/4 ounces) cream-style corn
1 can (10-3/4 ounces) condensed cream of
 potato soup, undiluted
1-1/2 cups half-and-half cream
1 can (6-1/2 ounces) minced clams, drained
6 bacon strips, cooked and crumbled

In a saucepan, combine corn, soup and cream; heat through. Stir in clams; heat through. Garnish with bacon. **Yield:** 4 servings.

Mocha Punch

Plan ahead...needs to chill

Coffee lovers will delight in this yummy beverage that tastes like a chilled cappuccino. I add chocolate ice cream to make it rich and creamy.
—Shirley Glaab
Hattiesburg, Mississippi

4 cups brewed coffee
1/4 cup sugar
4 cups milk
4 cups chocolate ice cream, softened

In a container, combine coffee and sugar; stir until sugar is dissolved. Refrigerate for 2 hours. Just before serving, pour into a punch bowl. Add milk; mix well. Top with scoops of ice cream and stir well. **Yield:** about 3 quarts.

Apple Sausage Appetizers

Ready in 1 hour or less

I bake sausage slices in a sweet glaze. This no-fuss appetizer makes plenty, so it's great for a football party or holiday gathering...just serve with toothpicks.
—Dolores Barnas, Blasdell, New York

✓ Uses less fat, sugar or salt. Includes Nutritional Analysis and Diabetic Exchanges.

2 jars (23 ounces *each*) unsweetened
 chunky applesauce

1/2 cup packed brown sugar
2 pounds fully cooked kielbasa *or* Polish
 sausage, cut into 1/2-inch slices
1 medium onion, chopped

In a bowl, combine applesauce and brown sugar. Stir in sausage and onion. Transfer to a greased 13-in. x 9-in. x 2-in. baking dish. Bake, uncovered, at 350° for 40-45 minutes or until bubbly. **Yield:** 20 servings. **Nutritional Analysis:** One 1/2-cup serving (prepared with reduced-fat turkey Polish sausage) equals 117 calories, 404 mg sodium, 30 mg cholesterol, 14 gm carbohydrate, 7 gm protein, 4 gm fat, 1 gm fiber. **Diabetic Exchanges:** 1 fruit, 1 lean meat.

Turkey and Stuffing Pie

Ready in 1 hour or less

For a fast and flavorful way to use up Thanksgiving leftovers, try this main-dish pie. This is such a handy recipe during the holidays. *—Debbi Baker, Green Springs, Ohio*

✓ Uses less fat, sugar or salt. Includes Nutritional Analysis and Diabetic Exchanges

3 cups prepared stuffing
2 cups cubed cooked turkey
1 cup (4 ounces) shredded Swiss cheese
3 eggs
1/2 cup milk

Press stuffing onto the bottom and up the sides of a well-greased 9-in. pie plate. Top with turkey and cheese. Beat eggs and milk; pour over cheese. Bake at 350° for 35-40 minutes or until a knife inserted near the center comes out clean. Let stand 5-10 minutes before serving. **Yield:** 8 servings. **Nutritional Analysis:** One serving (prepared with reduced-fat Swiss cheese, skim milk and egg substitute equivalent to 3 eggs) equals 327 calories, 1,065 mg sodium, 46 mg cholesterol, 39 gm carbohydrate, 28 gm protein, 6 gm fat, 2 gm fiber. **Diabetic Exchanges:** 3 lean meat, 2 starch.

Orange Cream Dessert

Plan ahead...needs to chill

For a light and refreshing ending to a meal, I fill a cookie crumb crust with a combination of orange gelatin and ice cream. I top slices with a dollop of whipped cream.
—Peggy Detjen, Lakeville, Minnesota

2 cups crushed cream-filled chocolate
 sandwich cookies (about 20 cookies)
1/3 cup butter *or* margarine, melted
1 package (6 ounces) orange *or* lime gelatin
2 cups boiling water
1 quart vanilla ice cream, softened

In a bowl, combine cookie crumbs and butter; set aside 1/4 cup for topping. Press remaining crumb mixture into a greased 13-in. x 9-in. x 2-in. dish. In a bowl, dissolve gelatin in water; cover and refrigerate for 10 minutes. Stir in ice cream until smooth. Pour over the crust. Sprinkle with reserved crumb mixture. Chill until firm. **Yield:** 12-15 servings.

Chapter 5

THE NEXT TIME you're feeling harried in the kitchen, take a deep breath, turn to this handy chapter and count to 10.

Before long, you'll be heading to the table with a delectable dish...and your family will be following closely behind!

That's because every long-on-flavor recipe featured here can be ready in a mere 10 minutes. So you can count on them on those days when you truly are "down to the wire".

From snacks, soups and breads to main dishes, salads and desserts, you'll find a table-ready recipe to please every palate in your family.

READY IN A FLASH. Top to bottom: Fancy Ham 'n' Cheese and Crunchy Coleslaw (both recipes on page 68).

Hot Pizza Dip

(Pictured below)

I can assemble this effortless appetizer in a jiffy. The pizza-flavored dip goes fast, so you may want to make two.
—Stacie Morse, South Otselic, New York

1 package (8 ounces) cream cheese, softened
1 teaspoon Italian seasoning
1 cup (4 ounces) shredded mozzarella cheese
3/4 cup grated Parmesan cheese
1 can (8 ounces) pizza sauce
2 tablespoons chopped green pepper
2 tablespoons thinly sliced green onion
Breadsticks *or* tortilla chips

In a mixing bowl, beat cream cheese and Italian seasoning. Spread in an ungreased 9-in. microwave-safe pie plate. Combine mozzarella and Parmesan cheeses; sprinkle half over the cream cheese. Top with the pizza sauce, remaining cheese mixture, green pepper and onion. Microwave, uncovered, on high for 3-4 minutes or until cheese is almost melted, rotating a half turn several times. Let stand for 1-2 minutes. Serve with breadsticks or tortilla chips. **Yield:** about 3 cups. **Editor's Note:** This recipe was tested in an 850-watt microwave.

Tasty Turkey Soup

You'll love this quick-and-easy way to jazz up a can of soup. Enjoy the comforting results in a hurry by using leftover turkey and convenient ramen noodles.
—Laurie Todd, Columbus, Mississippi

✓ Uses less fat, sugar or salt. Includes Nutritional Analysis and Diabetic Exchanges.

2 tablespoons chopped celery
2 tablespoons chopped onion
1 tablespoon butter *or* margarine
1 package (3 ounces) chicken-flavored ramen noodles
1-1/2 cups water
1 can (10-3/4 ounces) condensed turkey noodle soup, undiluted
1 cup chicken broth
1/2 cup cubed cooked turkey
Pepper to taste

In a saucepan, saute celery and onion in butter until tender. Discard seasoning packet from ramen noodles or save for another use. Stir noodles, water, soup, broth, turkey and pepper into celery mixture. Cook for 3 minutes or until noodles are tender and heated through. **Yield:** 4 servings. **Nutritional Analysis:** One serving (prepared with reduced-fat margarine and low-sodium broth) equals 166 calories, 1,042 mg sodium, 18 mg cholesterol, 22 gm carbohydrate, 10 gm protein, 4 gm fat, 1 gm fiber. **Diabetic Exchanges:** 1-1/2 starch, 1 lean meat.

School Day Biscuits

A sweet buttery coating disguises refrigerator biscuits in this recipe. With a houseful of children and now grandchildren, I've found these cinnamony treats are a classic for breakfast or a snack. —Dixie Terry, Marion, Illinois

1/2 cup packed brown sugar
1 teaspoon ground cinnamon
1 tube (12 ounces) refrigerated buttermilk biscuits
1/4 cup butter *or* margarine, melted

In a small bowl, combine brown sugar and cinnamon. Separate biscuits; dip the top of each in butter, then in cinnamon-sugar. Place sugared side up on an ungreased baking sheet. Bake at 400° for 6-8 minutes or until golden brown. Serve warm. **Yield:** 10 biscuits.

Hot Pizza Dip

Fast Fiesta Soup

(Pictured at right)

This spicy soup was served at a very elegant lunch, and the hostess was deluged with requests for the recipe. The colorful combination is a snap to throw together...just open the cans and heat. —Patricia White
Monrovia, California

 Uses less fat, sugar or salt. Includes Nutritional Analysis and Diabetic Exchanges.

2 cans (10 ounces *each*) diced tomatoes and green chilies
1 can (15-1/4 ounces) whole kernel corn, drained
1 can (15 ounces) black beans, rinsed and drained
Shredded cheddar cheese and sour cream, optional

In a saucepan, combine tomatoes, corn and beans; heat through. Garnish servings with cheese and sour cream if desired. **Yield:** 4 servings. **Nutritional Analysis:** One serving (prepared with no-salt-added diced tomatoes and without cheese and sour cream) equals 210 calories, 576 mg sodium, 0 cholesterol, 42 gm carbohydrate, 10 gm protein, 2 gm fat, 10 gm fiber. **Diabetic Exchanges:** 2-1/2 starch, 1 vegetable.

Fast Fiesta Soup

Creamy Chicken 'n' Rice

This was my favorite dish when I was growing up. Now I appreciate it even more because it's fast, easy and nutritious. Served with biscuits and a fresh salad, it makes a hearty meal. —Renee Leetch, Canton, Ohio

1 cup instant rice
1 cup water
1 can (15 ounces) mixed vegetables, drained
1 can (10-3/4 ounces) condensed cream of chicken soup, undiluted
1 can (5 ounces) white chicken, drained
1/4 to 1/2 teaspoon dried basil
Pinch pepper

In a saucepan, cook rice in water according to package directions. Add the remaining ingredients; heat through. **Yield:** 4 servings.

Broccoli with Mustard Sauce

Broccoli is among the vegetables that we are able to grow well, so we eat a lot of it. Tossing it with this tangy sauce is one of the fun ways I serve it. —Elizabeth Schuk
Tatlayoko, British Columbia

 Uses less fat, sugar or salt. Includes Nutritional Analysis and Diabetic Exchanges.

4 tablespoons water, *divided*
1 tablespoon butter *or* margarine, melted
1 tablespoon brown sugar
1 tablespoon Dijon mustard
1 pound broccoli, cut into florets (4 cups)
1 tablespoon vegetable oil

In a small bowl, combine 1 tablespoon water, butter, brown sugar and mustard; set aside. In a skillet or wok, stir-fry broccoli in oil for 1 minute; add remaining water. Reduce heat; cover and cook for 3-4 minutes or until crisp-tender. Add mustard sauce and toss to coat. **Yield:** 4 servings. **Nutritional Analysis:** One serving (prepared with reduced-fat margarine) equals 83 calories, 148 mg sodium, 0 cholesterol, 7 gm carbohydrate, 2 gm protein, 6 gm fat, 2 gm fiber. **Diabetic Exchanges:** 1-1/2 vegetable, 1 fat.

Peachy Fruit Salad

Peach pie filling is the unexpected ingredient in this yummy medley of canned and fresh fruits. This is the kind of recipe I really appreciate when time is short. —Deanna Richter, Elmore, Minnesota

1 can (21 ounces) peach pie filling
1 can (20 ounces) pineapple chunks, drained
1 can (11 ounces) mandarin oranges, drained
2 medium firm bananas, sliced
1 cup green grapes
1 cup miniature marshmallows

In a bowl, combine all ingredients; stir gently. Refrigerate until serving. **Yield:** 6-8 servings.

Cilantro Chicken Salad

2 tablespoons chopped onion
3 tablespoons butter *or* margarine
1 can (15-1/4 ounces) whole kernel corn, drained
1 package (3 ounces) cream cheese, cubed
1/3 cup milk
1/2 teaspoon curry powder
Salt and pepper to taste

In a saucepan, saute green pepper and onion in butter until tender. Stir in the remaining ingredients. Cook until cheese is melted and corn is heated through. **Yield:** about 3 servings. **Nutritional Analysis:** One 1/2-cup serving (prepared with reduced-fat margarine, light cream cheese and skim milk and without salt) equals 224 calories, 651 mg sodium, 16 mg cholesterol, 25 gm carbohydrate, 7 gm protein, 13 gm fat, 4 gm fiber. **Diabetic Exchanges:** 2-1/2 fat, 1-1/2 starch.

Chipped Beef on Toast

This fast-to-fix dish makes a hearty breakfast or light lunch. A creamy sauce prepared in the microwave coats convenient packaged dried beef. I serve it over toast.
—Jane Fry, Lancaster, Pennsylvania

1/4 cup butter *or* margarine
1/4 cup all-purpose flour
2 cups milk
2 packages (2-1/2 ounces *each*) dried beef, cut into strips
4 slices bread, toasted and halved

In a microwave-safe bowl, heat butter on high for 45 seconds or until melted. Stir in flour until smooth. Gradually stir in milk. Microwave, uncovered, on high for 3-4 minutes or until thickened, stirring every minute. Stir in beef; cook on high for 1 minute or until heated through. Serve on toast. **Yield:** 4 servings. **Editor's Note:** This recipe was tested in an 850-watt microwave.

Banana Split Salad

This pretty pink mixture, chock-full of yummy fruit and nuts, is sure to disappear in a hurry. It's a sweet and speedy treat that can be served as a dessert or salad.
—Anne Powers, Munford, Alabama

1 can (14 ounces) sweetened condensed milk
1 carton (12 ounces) frozen whipped topping, thawed
1 can (21 ounces) cherry pie filling
3 medium firm bananas, cut into chunks
1 can (8 ounces) crushed pineapple, drained
1/2 cup chopped nuts

In a large bowl, combine the milk and whipped topping until well blended. Fold in pie filling, bananas, pineapple and nuts. **Yield:** 10 servings.

Cilantro Chicken Salad

(Pictured above)

This lively recipe has a distinctive dressing of cilantro, cumin and lime that is refreshing over crisp lettuce and tender chicken. Toss in cherry tomatoes, if you'd like, for color. —Linda Schwab-Edmundson, Shokan, New York

2/3 cup olive *or* vegetable oil
1/4 cup lime juice
1/4 cup minced fresh cilantro *or* parsley
1/2 teaspoon ground cumin
1/2 teaspoon salt
1/4 teaspoon crushed red pepper flakes
4 cups torn leaf lettuce
2 cups cubed cooked chicken
1 pint cherry tomatoes, optional

In a jar with a tight-fitting lid, combine the oil, lime juice, cilantro, cumin, salt and red pepper flakes; shake well. In a bowl, combine the lettuce, chicken and tomatoes if desired. Drizzle with dressing; toss to coat. **Yield:** 4 servings.

Curried Cream Corn

I like to find creative ways to serve vegetables to my husband and daughters. Curry gives a different twist to this side dish that has become my family's favorite treatment for corn. —Kelly Malloy, Baltimore, Maryland

✔ Uses less fat, sugar or salt. Includes Nutritional Analysis and Diabetic Exchanges.

2 tablespoons chopped green pepper

Cannoli Pudding

This subtly sweet blend lets you enjoy the taste of a traditional Italian dessert in only minutes. It makes any meal special. —Kat Thompson, Prineville, Oregon

   1 carton (15 ounces) ricotta cheese
  1/4 cup miniature semisweet chocolate chips
  1/4 cup chopped pecans
  1/4 cup chopped maraschino cherries
   3 tablespoons sugar
   3 tablespoons whipping cream
Whole maraschino cherries, optional

In a mixing bowl, beat the ricotta cheese until smooth. Stir in the chocolate chips, pecans, cherries, sugar and cream. Spoon into dessert dishes. Refrigerate until serving. Garnish with whole cherries if desired. **Yield:** 4 servings.

Creamy Garlic Dressing

Garlic lovers will savor this delicious, creamy dressing. Just blend ingredients until smooth and serve over salad. It's a little different than other dressings I've tried.
—Myra Innes, Auburn, Kansas

1-1/2 cups mayonnaise
  3/4 cup vegetable oil
  1/4 cup vinegar
   3 tablespoons chopped onion
1-1/2 teaspoons sugar
  3/4 teaspoon salt
   1 garlic clove, minced

In a blender, combine all ingredients. Cover and process until smooth. Serve over a tossed salad. **Yield:** 3 cups.

Crunchy Shrimp Salad

I received the recipe for this fresh-tasting shrimp and veggie salad from a co-worker several years ago. Dollop the dressing over the top or stir into the medley for a lunch treat that brings a bit of summer to any season. —Suzanne Strocsher
Bothell, Washington

 Uses less fat, sugar or salt. Includes Nutritional Analysis and Diabetic Exchanges.

   1 cup frozen cooked shrimp,
    thawed
  1/2 cup frozen peas, thawed
  1/2 cup sliced water chestnuts
   2 tablespoons diced pimientos,
    drained
   1 green onion, thinly sliced
  1/3 cup mayonnaise
   2 tablespoons seafood sauce
   1 teaspoon lemon juice

In a bowl, combine the first five ingredients. In another bowl, combine the mayonnaise, seafood sauce and lemon juice; serve with the shrimp salad. **Yield:**

2 servings. **Nutritional Analysis:** One serving (prepared with fat-free mayonnaise) equals 150 calories, 692 mg sodium, 111 mg cholesterol, 19 gm carbohydrate, 15 gm protein, 1 gm fat, 3 gm fiber. **Diabetic Exchanges:** 1 starch, 1 very lean meat, 1 vegetable.

Corny Chicken Wraps

(Pictured below)

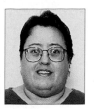

My girls like these tortilla roll-ups very much—they'll ask for them practically every week! Tender chicken is mixed with canned corn and salsa for a fast-to-fix main dish.
—Sue Seymour, Valatie, New York

✓ Uses less fat, sugar or salt. Includes Nutritional Analysis and Diabetic Exchanges.

   2 cups cubed cooked chicken breast
   1 can (11 ounces) whole kernel corn, drained
   1 cup salsa
   1 cup (4 ounces) shredded cheddar cheese
   8 flour tortillas (6 inches), warmed

In a saucepan or microwave-safe bowl, combine the chicken, corn and salsa. Cook until heated through. Sprinkle cheese over the tortillas. Place about 1/2 cup of the chicken mixture down the center of each tortilla; roll up. Secure with toothpicks. **Yield:** 4 servings. **Nutritional Analysis:** One serving (prepared with reduced-fat cheese and tortillas) equals 374 calories, 1,088 mg sodium, 61 mg cholesterol, 50 gm carbohydrate, 26 gm protein, 8 gm fat, 3 gm fiber. **Diabetic Exchanges:** 3 starch, 2 lean meat, 1 vegetable.

Corny Chicken Wraps

Fancy Ham 'n' Cheese

(Pictured below and on page 62)

Garden-fresh ingredients including spinach, cucumber and onion add appeal to this zippy sandwich. It has a touch of class that turns the ordinary into something special.
—*James Gauthier, Oak Creek, Wisconsin*

- 1/4 cup butter *or* margarine, softened
- 8 slices rye bread
- 12 fresh spinach leaves
- 16 slices cucumber
- 4 thin slices red onion
- 12 slices fully cooked ham
- 2 tablespoons Dijon mustard
- 8 slices cheddar cheese

Spread butter on one side of each slice of bread. On half of the slices, layer spinach, cucumber, onion, ham, mustard and cheese. Top with remaining bread. **Yield:** 4 servings.

Crunchy Coleslaw

(Pictured below and on page 62)

This crunchy cabbage salad is so easy to put together that we often have it for spur-of-the-moment picnics or when unexpected company stops by. It gets its nutty flavor from almonds. —*Julie Vavroch, Montezuma, Iowa*

- 1/3 cup vegetable oil
- 1 package (3 ounces) beef-flavored ramen noodles
- 1/2 teaspoon garlic salt
- 1 package (16 ounces) shredded coleslaw mix
- 1 package (5 ounces) sliced almonds

In a small saucepan, heat oil. Stir in contents of noodle seasoning packet and garlic salt; cook for 3-4 minutes or until blended. Meanwhile, crush the noodles and place in a bowl. Add coleslaw mix and almonds. Drizzle with oil mixture and toss to coat. Serve immediately. **Yield:** 6-8 servings.

No-Fuss Meatballs

When I had some girlfriends over, one of them fixed these sweet and spicy appetizers. We were amazed that something so good took so little time to prepare.
—*Valerie Solar*
San Francisco, California

- 1 package (14 ounces) frozen cooked meatballs, thawed
- 1 tablespoon soy sauce
- 1/2 cup chili sauce
- 1/2 cup grape jelly
- 1/4 cup Dijon mustard

In a skillet, cook meatballs in soy sauce until heated through. Combine the chili sauce, jelly and mustard; pour over the meatballs. Cook and stir until jelly is dissolved and mixture comes to a boil. Reduce heat; cover and simmer for 1-2 minutes. **Yield:** about 2 dozen.

Cucumber Fruit Salad

Cool cucumber and juicy grapes give this summer salad its light and refreshing difference. It's a tasty twist on a traditional Waldorf salad. —*Trudie Hagen, Roggen, Colorado*

 Uses less fat, sugar or salt. Includes Nutritional Analysis and Diabetic Exchanges.

- 1 medium cucumber, peeled, seeded and diced
- 1 medium tart apple, chopped
- 1 cup halved seedless green grapes
- 1 cup halved seedless red grapes
- 1/2 cup sour cream
- 1 tablespoon sugar
- 1 tablespoon minced fresh parsley
- 1/3 cup chopped walnuts, optional

In a bowl, combine the cucumber, apple and grapes. In a small bowl, combine the sour cream, sugar and parsley. Pour over cucumber mixture and toss to coat. Stir in walnuts if desired. Serve immediately. **Yield:** 6 servings. **Nutritional Analysis:** One serving (prepared with nonfat sour cream and without walnuts) equals 87 calories, 19 mg sodium, 2 mg cholesterol, 20 gm carbohydrate, 2 gm protein, trace fat, 2 gm fiber. **Diabetic Exchange:** 1-1/2 fruit.

Fancy Ham 'n' Cheese
Crunchy Coleslaw

Mexicali Pork Chops

Corned Beef Bagel Dip

Guests enjoy dipping bite-size bagel chunks into this creamy dip that's made with sour cream, chopped corned beef and a little horseradish. I've taken this appetizer to many potlucks over the years, and it's always a hit.
—Shari Stensrud, Cambridge, Minnesota

　3/4 cup mayonnaise
　3/4 cup sour cream
　　2 packages (2-1/2 ounces *each*) thinly sliced
　　　deli corned beef, chopped
　1/4 cup chopped onion
　　1 tablespoon minced fresh parsley
　1/2 teaspoon seasoned salt
　　1 to 2 teaspoons prepared horseradish,
　　　optional
　　3 to 4 bagels, cut into bite-size pieces

In a bowl, combine mayonnaise and sour cream. Stir in the corned beef, onion, parsley, seasoned salt and horseradish if desired. Serve with bagel pieces. **Yield:** about 2 cups.

Dressed-Up Applesauce

I jazz up applesauce with lemon juice and a sprinkling of spices to create this speedy side dish. It's wonderful warm or cold with a savory helping of pork or chicken.
—Therian Mendelsohn, Cincinnati, Ohio

✓ Uses less fat, sugar or salt. Includes Nutritional Analysis and Diabetic Exchanges.

　　2 cups unsweetened applesauce
　1/4 cup sugar
1-1/2 teaspoons lemon juice
　1/2 teaspoon rum extract
　1/4 teaspoon ground cinnamon
　1/4 teaspoon ground allspice
　1/8 to 1/4 teaspoon ground cloves
　1/8 teaspoon ground ginger

In a saucepan, combine all ingredients. Bring to a boil. Cook, uncovered, for 1 minute. Serve warm or refriger-

ate. **Yield:** about 2 cups. **Nutritional Analysis:** One 1-cup serving equals 205 calories, 6 mg sodium, 0 cholesterol, 53 gm carbohydrate, trace protein, trace fat, 3 gm fiber. **Diabetic Exchange:** 3-1/2 fruit.

Mexicali Pork Chops

(Pictured above)

You'll need just four ingredients to fix these tender pork chops. They get their zesty flavor from a packet of taco seasoning and salsa.
—Laura Cohen
Eau Claire, Wisconsin

　　1 envelope taco seasoning
　　4 boneless pork loin chops (1/2 inch thick)
　　1 tablespoon vegetable oil
Salsa

Rub taco seasoning over pork chops. In a skillet, cook chops in oil over medium-high heat until meat is no longer pink and juices run clear, about 9 minutes. Serve with salsa. **Yield:** 4 servings.

Tangy Salad Dressing

This was my family's all-time favorite dressing when I was growing up. Both tangy and sweet, it's delicious drizzled over any variety of crisp greens or fresh veggies.
—Kathryn Anderson, Wallkill, New York

　1/2 cup olive *or* vegetable oil
　1/4 cup cider vinegar
　　3 tablespoons sugar
　1/2 teaspoon salt
　1/2 teaspoon seasoned salt
　1/4 teaspoon pepper
　1/4 teaspoon ground mustard
Mixed salad greens

In a jar with a tight-fitting lid, combine the first seven ingredients; shake well. Toss with salad greens just before serving. **Yield:** 3/4 cup.

Chapter 6

GOOD EATING doesn't require a lot of effort. Sometimes just by peeking in your pantry or freezer, you can put together a meal pronto!

When the clock is ticking closer to dinnertime, rely on canned goods, boxed mixes, prepared sauces and other convenience foods for fast fixes to your dining dilemmas.

Or, when you have a little extra time, assemble your own economical assortment of tasty homemade mix recipes. Then keep them on hand as a head start on a last-minute meal.

With these handy mix tricks, you'll save money and shopping time without sacrificing flavor!

PANTRY FAVORITES. Top to bottom: Sausage Cheese Muffins and Peanut Butter Pancakes (both recipes on p. 84).

Fast Fixes With Mixes

WITH the wide range of packaged convenience foods available on grocery store shelves today, you can have a tasty home-prepared meal ready in minutes. Creating a memorable meal can be as simple as jazzing up a box mix or combining canned goods.

Banana Nut Cake

(Pictured below)

Boxed pudding and cake mixes speed up the preparation of this moist banana cake. It doesn't last long at our house. In fact, my family and the hired men have it finished almost before it has time to cool. —Karen Ann Bland Gove, Kansas

    1 package (18-1/4 ounces) yellow cake mix
    1 package (3.4 ounces) instant banana cream
      pudding mix
  1/4 cup vegetable oil
    4 eggs
    1 cup water
1-1/2 cups mashed ripe bananas (about 2 medium)
  3/4 cup chopped walnuts
Confectioners' sugar, optional

In a mixing bowl, combine the first five ingredients. Beat on medium speed for 2 minutes. Add bananas; mix well. Stir in nuts. Pour into a greased 13-in. x 9-in. x 2-in. baking pan. Bake at 350° for 50-55 minutes or until a toothpick inserted near the center comes out clean. Cool on a wire rack. Dust with confectioners' sugar if desired. **Yield:** 12 servings.

Chocolate Chip Cake Bars

(Pictured below)

Ready in 1 hour or less

Whenever I need a quick dessert for a bake sale or get-together, I rely on this recipe. I keep cake mixes on hand, so these chocolate chip-studded treats are a snap to stir up. —Tammy Haugen, Mayville, Wisconsin

    1 package (18-1/4 ounces) yellow cake mix
    2 eggs
  1/4 cup packed brown sugar
  1/4 cup butter *or* margarine, melted
  1/4 cup water
    2 cups (12 ounces) semisweet chocolate chips,
      divided
  1/2 cup chopped pecans *or* walnuts
    1 tablespoon shortening

In a mixing bowl, combine the first five ingredients. Beat on medium speed for 2 minutes. Stir in 1-1/2 cups of chocolate chips and nuts. Spread in a greased 13-in. x 9-in. x 2-in. baking pan. Bake at 375° for 20-25 minutes or until lightly browned and a toothpick inserted near the center comes out clean. Cool on a wire rack. Melt shortening with the remaining chocolate chips; drizzle over the top. Cut into bars. **Yield:** about 3-1/2 dozen.

Banana Nut Cake
Chocolate Chip Cake Bars

Ham Potato Scallop

Ham Potato Scallop

(Pictured above)

Ready in 1 hour or less

It's simple to jazz up a box of scalloped potatoes and pop them in the oven while the kids are doing their homework. This casserole disappears in a hurry whenever I serve it. I round out the meal with a tossed salad.
—Jennifer Skipper, Great Lakes, Illinois

  1 package (5 ounces) scalloped potatoes
  2 cups boiling water
  2 tablespoons butter *or* margarine
3/4 cup milk
  2 cups cubed fully cooked ham
  1 package (10 ounces) frozen cut green beans
  1 cup (4 ounces) shredded cheddar cheese

In an ungreased 1-1/2-qt. baking dish, combine potatoes with sauce mix, boiling water and butter. Stir in milk, ham and beans. Bake, uncovered, at 400° for 35 minutes or until the potatoes are tender, stirring occasionally. Sprinkle with cheese. Bake 5 minutes longer or until cheese is melted. Let stand 5 minutes before serving. **Yield:** 4 servings.

Smoked Sausage Soup

Ready in 1 hour or less

Whenever I serve this thick stew-like soup to new friends, they never fail to ask for the recipe. Each satisfying bowl is chock-full of tasty smoked sausage, hash browns, green beans, carrots and more.
—Marge Wheeler
San Benito, Texas

4-1/2 cups water
  1 can (28 ounces) diced tomatoes, undrained

  1 envelope onion soup mix
  1 package (9 ounces) frozen cut green beans
  3 small carrots, halved and thinly sliced
  2 celery ribs, thinly sliced
  1 tablespoon sugar
1/2 teaspoon salt
1/2 teaspoon dried oregano
1/8 teaspoon hot pepper sauce
  1 pound fully cooked smoked sausage, halved and thinly sliced
2-1/2 cups frozen shredded hash brown potatoes

In a soup kettle or Dutch oven, combine the first 10 ingredients. Bring to a boil. Reduce heat; cover and simmer for 20-25 minutes or until the vegetables are tender. Stir in the sausage and hash browns. Bring to a boil. Reduce heat; cover and cook for 5 minutes or until heated through. **Yield:** 12 servings.

Spiced-Up Sauces

- I have a quick way to make a bottle of barbecue sauce taste like homemade. I add 3/4 cup of orange juice concentrate, two tablespoons of brown sugar and a dash of hot pepper sauce. Everyone thinks it's the best barbecue sauce ever. —Joyce Oosterwal
Ada, Michigan

- I couldn't cook without instant cream of chicken soup mix. I use it as a base for white sauces. I also add a teaspoon or two to any other sauce for an extra flavor boost. —Esther Cochrane
Los Angeles, California

- I can make a cheese sauce in just minutes by emptying a package of chicken gravy mix into a sauce pan, tossing in some shredded cheese, then adding the liquid called for on the package.
—Mona Russell, Tulsa, Oklahoma

Santa Fe Enchiladas

Onion Beef Stroganoff

Ready in 1 hour or less

Onion soup mix gives great flavor to this tender beef and creamy sauce. I threw this together one night using ingredients I had on hand. The cream of potato soup makes it a real meat-and-potatoes meal.

—Priscilla Callis, Nashville, Tennessee

1-1/2 pounds eye of round steak, cut into strips
    1 to 2 tablespoons vegetable oil
    1 envelope onion soup mix
    1 can (10-3/4 ounces) condensed cream of potato soup, undiluted
1-1/4 cups milk
    1 jar (4-1/2 ounces) sliced mushrooms, drained
Hot cooked rice or noodles

In a large skillet over medium heat, cook beef in oil until no longer pink. Stir in soup mix, potato soup, milk and mushrooms. Cover and simmer for 35-40 minutes or until meat is tender. Serve over rice or noodles. **Yield:** 4-6 servings.

Santa Fe Enchiladas

(Pictured above)

Ready in 30 minutes or less

These flavorful enchiladas are my sister's favorite—she requests them whenever we get together. This meaty main dish is cooked in the microwave, so it's done in a jiffy.

—Lisa Zamora, Beloit, Wisconsin

1-1/2 pounds lean ground beef
    1 medium onion, chopped
    1 can (12 ounces) tomato paste
    1 cup water
    1 envelope taco seasoning
  10 flour tortillas (6 inches), warmed

    1 jar (8 ounces) process cheese sauce
    1 can (4 ounces) chopped green chilies, drained

Crumble beef into a large microwave-safe bowl; stir in onion. Cover and microwave on high for 6 to 7-1/2 minutes or until meat is no longer pink, stirring every 1-1/2 minutes; drain. Stir in tomato paste, water and taco seasoning. Cover and cook on high for 3-4 minutes or until heated through, stirring once. Spoon about 1/3 cup meat mixture down the center of each tortilla; roll up tightly. Set remaining meat mixture aside. Place tortillas, seam side down, in a greased shallow 2-1/2-qt. dish. In a microwave-safe bowl, combine cheese sauce and chilies. Cover and cook on high for 1 minute; stir. Pour over tortillas. Spoon remaining meat mixture down the center of tortillas. Cover and cook on high for 5-6 minutes or until heated through. Let stand 5 minutes before serving. **Yield:** 5 servings. **Editor's Note:** This recipe was tested in an 850-watt microwave.

Special Side Dishes

- I mix a small amount of bottled barbecue sauce with a can of green beans. Sprinkle with crumbled bacon to make this side dish even more enticing.
  —Nancy Cruz, Baltimore, Maryland

- For candied carrots, follow this simple recipe: Cook 1 package of baby carrots until tender. Fold in 1 jar orange marmalade. Continue cooking carrots until glazed and heated through. —Donna Gonda North Canton, Ohio

- Prepare canned peas with a dash of ketchup and a sprinkle of sugar, then add salt and pepper to taste. I created this recipe for my family, and now it's the only way they'll eat canned peas.
  —Shirley Creamer, Milnesand, New Mexico

Poppy Seed Biscuits

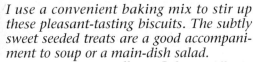

(Pictured below)

Ready in 30 minutes or less

I use a convenient baking mix to stir up these pleasant-tasting biscuits. The subtly sweet seeded treats are a good accompaniment to soup or a main-dish salad.
—Diane Molberg, Calgary, Alberta

✓ Uses less fat, sugar or salt. Includes Nutritional Analysis and Diabetic Exchanges.

> 1/4 cup milk
> 2 tablespoons honey
> 1/2 cup cream-style cottage cheese
> 2-1/4 cups biscuit/baking mix
> 1 tablespoon poppy seeds

In a blender, combine milk, honey and cottage cheese. Cover and process until smooth. In a bowl, combine biscuit mix and poppy seeds. Stir in cottage cheese mixture just until blended. Turn onto a floured surface; pat or knead to 1/2-in. thickness. Cut with a 2-1/2-in. biscuit cutter. Place on an ungreased baking sheet. Bake at 425° for 8-10 minutes or until golden brown. **Yield:** about 1 dozen. **Nutritional Analysis:** One biscuit (prepared with skim milk, low-fat cottage cheese and reduced-fat biscuit/ baking mix) equals 119 calories, 323 mg sodium, 1 mg cholesterol, 21 gm carbohydrate, 3 gm protein, 2 gm fat, trace fiber. **Diabetic Exchange:** 1-1/2 starch.

Sweet Tropical Loaves

(Pictured below)

These pineapple coconut loaves are so good and moist that sometimes I don't even bother to glaze them. But the glaze makes them extra special for company. The golden bread gets its tender cake-like texture from a handy boxed cake mix.
—Sybil Brown, Highland, California

> 1 package (18-1/4 ounces) yellow cake mix
> 1 can (8 ounces) crushed pineapple, undrained
> 1 cup evaporated milk
> 2 eggs
> 1/2 teaspoon ground nutmeg
> 1/2 cup flaked coconut
> GLAZE:
> 1-1/2 cups confectioners' sugar
> 2 tablespoons milk
> 1 to 2 drops coconut extract, optional
> 2 tablespoons flaked coconut, toasted

In a mixing bowl, combine the first five ingredients. Beat on low speed just until moistened. Beat on high for 2 minutes. Stir in the coconut. Pour into two greased 8-in. x 4-in. x 2-in. loaf pans. Bake at 325° for 45-50 minutes or until a toothpick inserted near the center comes out clean. Cool for 10 minutes before removing from pans to wire racks to cool completely. For the glaze, in a mixing bowl, combine the sugar and milk until smooth. Add the extract if desired. Drizzle over loaves; sprinkle with coconut. **Yield:** 2 loaves.

Poppy Seed Biscuits
Sweet Tropical Loaves

Chocolate Pudding Pizza

1/4 cup olive *or* vegetable oil
2 cups cubed cooked chicken *or* turkey
Shredded Parmesan cheese

Cook the pasta according to package directions. Meanwhile, in a large saucepan, whisk together pesto mix, milk and oil. Bring to a boil. Reduce heat; simmer, uncovered, for 5 minutes. Add chicken; heat through. Drain pasta. Add to the sauce and toss to coat. Sprinkle with cheese. **Yield:** 4-6 servings.

Artichoke Tuna Toss

Ready in 30 minutes or less

I do volunteer work one evening a week and leave a meal behind for my family. On one occasion, I left this made-in-minutes medley. When I came home, my husband said it was the best pasta dish I'd ever fixed! —Emily Perez
Alexandria, Virginia

3-1/2 cups water
1/4 cup butter *or* margarine
2 packages (4.6 ounces *each*) garlic and olive oil vermicelli mix
1 can (16 ounces) artichoke hearts, undrained and quartered
2 cans (6 ounces *each*) tuna, drained and flaked
1 package (10 ounces) frozen peas
1 tablespoon olive *or* vegetable oil
1 tablespoon cider *or* red wine vinegar
4 to 6 garlic cloves, minced

In a saucepan, bring water and butter to a boil. Stir in vermicelli with contents of seasoning packets, artichokes, tuna, peas, oil, vinegar and garlic. Return to a boil; cook, uncovered, for 8-10 minutes or until vermicelli is tender. Let stand 5 minutes before serving. **Yield:** 6 servings.

Chocolate Pudding Pizza

(Pictured above)

Plan ahead...needs to chill

My sister Brenda and I made up this recipe while talking on the phone. My family loves the classic pairing of chocolate and peanut butter presented in a whole new way.
—LaDonna Reed, Ponca City, Oklahoma

1 package (17-1/2 ounces) peanut butter cookie mix
1 carton (12 ounces) whipped cream cheese
1-3/4 cups cold milk
1 package (3.9 ounces) instant chocolate pudding mix
1 carton (8 ounces) frozen whipped topping, thawed
1/4 cup miniature semisweet chocolate chips

Prepare cookie mix dough according to package directions. Press into a greased 12-in. pizza pan. Bake at 375° for 15 minutes or until set; cool. In a mixing bowl, beat cream cheese until smooth. Spread over crust. In another mixing bowl, beat milk and pudding mix on medium speed for 2 minutes. Spread over the cream cheese layer. Refrigerate for 20 minutes or until set. Spread with whipped topping. Sprinkle with chips. Chill for 1-2 hours. **Yield:** 12 servings.

Pesto Chicken Penne

Ready in 15 minutes or less

A convenient pesto sauce mix provides the pleasant basil flavor in this simple chicken and pasta combination. This entree requires little effort, yet seems elegant.
— Beth Martin Sine, Faulkner, Maryland

8 ounces penne *or* any medium pasta
1 envelope pesto sauce mix
3/4 cup milk

Turkey Stuffing Roll-Ups

Ready in 1 hour or less

When I worked at a local deli, a customer gave me this family-pleasing recipe. After a busy day, I tried it with quicker boxed stuffing mix in place of homemade dressing. It's wonderful with salad and green beans.
—Darlene Ward, Hot Springs, Arkansas

1 package (6 ounces) stuffing mix*
1 can (10-3/4 ounces) condensed cream of chicken soup, undiluted

No More Cooked-On Messes

When I cook any type of pasta or rice, I spritz the pan with nonstick cooking spray, let it sit for a moment, then add the water. Once the water boils, I add the pasta and stir as needed. When it's done, there's no sticky mess on the bottom of the pan.
—*Judith Wenzel, Hemlock, Michigan*

3/4 cup milk
1 pound sliced deli smoked turkey
1 can (2.8 ounces) french-fried onions, crushed

Prepare stuffing mix according to package directions. Meanwhile, in a bowl, combine soup and milk; set aside. Spoon about 1/4 cup stuffing onto each turkey slice. Roll up and place in a greased 13-in. x 9-in. x 2-in. baking dish. Pour soup mixture over roll-ups. Bake, uncovered, at 350° for 20 minutes. Sprinkle with onions. Bake 5 minutes longer or until heated through. **Yield:** 6 servings. ***Editor's Note:** 3 cups of any prepared stuffing can be substituted for the stuffing mix.

Curly Noodle Pork Supper

(Pictured below)

Ready in 30 minutes or less

This hearty meal-in-one is loaded with tender pork and ramen noodles. Broccoli and red pepper add a bounty of fresh-from-the-garden flavor that will bring 'em back for seconds. —*Carmen Carlson, Kent, Washington*

1 pound pork tenderloin, cut into 1/4-inch strips
1 medium sweet red pepper, cut into 1-inch pieces
1 cup broccoli florets
4 green onions, cut into 1-inch pieces
1 tablespoon vegetable oil
1-1/2 cups water
2 packages (3 ounces *each*) pork ramen noodles
1 tablespoon minced fresh parsley
1 tablespoon soy sauce

In a large skillet, cook pork, red pepper, broccoli and onions in oil until meat is no longer pink. Add the water, noodles with contents of seasoning packets, parsley

and soy sauce. Bring to a boil. Reduce heat; cook for 3-4 minutes or until noodles are tender. **Yield:** 3-4 servings.

Pizza Potatoes

For a simple side dish that's sure to appeal to kids, try this twist on traditional pizza. Packaged scalloped potatoes, canned tomatoes and pepperoni slices are combined for fast Italian fare that's delightfully different.
—*Kathy White, Chicopee, Massachusetts*

1 package (5 ounces) scalloped potatoes
1 can (14-1/2 ounces) Italian stewed tomatoes
1-1/2 cups water
1/4 teaspoon dried oregano
1 package (3-1/2 ounces) sliced pepperoni
1 cup (4 ounces) shredded mozzarella cheese

Combine the potatoes and contents of sauce mix in a greased 1-1/2-qt. baking dish. In a saucepan, bring tomatoes, water and oregano to a boil. Pour over potatoes. Top with pepperoni. Bake, uncovered, at 375° for 50-60 minutes or until the potatoes are tender. Sprinkle with cheese. Bake 5-10 minutes longer or until cheese is melted. **Yield:** 4 servings.

Effortless Entree

I always have jars of Alfredo sauce, frozen ravioli and cooked crumbled bacon on hand so I can whip up a meal in minutes. While the ravioli is cooking, I zap the sauce and some bacon in the microwave. Tossed together, this tasty combination makes a special main dish for drop-in guests. I serve it with a salad, vegetable and frozen garlic bread for a delicious meal that doesn't require a lot of time in the kitchen.
—*Cheryl Norwood, Canton, Georgia*

Curly Noodle Pork Supper

Franks and Corn Bread
Chili-Stuffed Peppers

Franks and Corn Bread

(Pictured above)

Ready in 1 hour or less

We ate this corn bread-topped casserole often when our children were growing up, and it was always well received. It's so easy to throw together after work that I still make it for my husband and me.
—Marilyn Hoiten
Rockford, Illinois

- 2 cans (16 ounces each) pork and beans
- 1 package (12 ounces) hot dogs, halved lengthwise and sliced
- 2 tablespoons brown sugar
- 2 tablespoons Worcestershire sauce
- 2 tablespoons prepared mustard
- 1 package (8-1/2 ounces) corn bread/muffin mix

1 cup (4 ounces) shredded cheddar cheese

In a bowl, combine the first five ingredients; mix well. Transfer to a greased 9-in. square baking dish. Prepare corn bread batter according to package directions; stir in cheese. Drop by spoonfuls onto bean mixture. Bake, uncovered, at 350° for 40-45 minutes or until heated through. **Yield:** 6 servings.

Chili-Stuffed Peppers

(Pictured above)

Ready in 1 hour or less

My family loves chili, so I decided to try stuffing green peppers with it. Everyone agreed the peppers tasted great; they're really good made with leftover chili, too.
—Verna Redman, Dade City, Florida

6 medium green peppers
1 pound ground beef
1/2 cup chopped onion
1 can (15 ounces) chili beans, undrained
1 can (10 ounces) diced tomatoes and green chilies, undrained
1 teaspoon chili powder
1/2 teaspoon salt, optional
1/4 teaspoon pepper
1/4 teaspoon cayenne pepper
3/4 cup shredded cheddar cheese

Cut tops off peppers and remove seeds. Place peppers in a large kettle and cover with water. Bring to a boil; cook until crisp-tender, about 3 minutes. Drain and rinse in cold water; set aside. In a large skillet, cook beef and onion over medium heat until meat is no longer pink; drain. Add beans, tomatoes, chili powder, salt if desired, pepper and cayenne. Bring to a boil. Reduce heat; cover and simmer for 5 minutes. Spoon meat mixture into peppers; place in an ungreased 3-qt. baking dish. Cover and bake at 350° for 20-25 minutes or until heated through. Sprinkle with cheese. **Yield:** 6 servings. **Nutritional Analysis:** One serving (prepared with lean ground beef and reduced-fat cheese and without salt) equals 259 calories, 656 mg sodium, 31 mg cholesterol, 24 gm carbohydrate, 24 gm protein, 9 gm fat, 6 gm fiber. **Diabetic Exchanges:** 3 lean meat, 1 starch, 1 vegetable.

Golden Chicken Casserole

Ready in 1 hour or less

Apricot preserves give a different twist to this saucy sweet-and-sour chicken. With just five ingredients, it's a snap to stir up and serve over rice. This is a frequent request for dinner at my house. —Melanie May
Fishers, Indiana

2 cups cubed cooked chicken
1 can (20 ounces) unsweetened pineapple chunks, drained
1 jar (12 ounces) apricot preserves *or* spreadable fruit
1 can (10-3/4 ounces) condensed cream of chicken soup, undiluted
1 can (8 ounces) water chestnuts, drained
Hot cooked rice

In a bowl, combine the first five ingredients. Transfer to a greased 2-qt. baking dish. Bake, uncovered, at 350° for 30 minutes or until heated through. Serve over rice. **Yield:** 6 servings. **Nutritional Analysis:** One serving (prepared with low-fat soup and spreadable fruit; calculated without rice) equals 259 calories, 413 mg sodium, 44 mg cholesterol, 41 gm carbohydrate, 16 gm protein, 3 gm fat, 3 gm fiber. **Diabetic Exchanges:** 2 lean meat, 2 fruit, 1/2 vegetable.

Pork Chops with Orange Rice

Ready in 1 hour or less

My husband is delighted every time we have this pork and rice bake for dinner. I've also made it for new moms who need meals brought in, and I'm frequently asked to share the recipe. —Karen Hossink, Lansing, Michigan

4 loin *or* pork chops (1/2 inch thick)
1 tablespoon vegetable oil
1-1/3 cups uncooked instant rice
1 cup orange juice
Salt and pepper to taste
1 can (10-1/2 ounces) condensed chicken with rice soup, undiluted

In a skillet, brown pork chops on both sides in oil. Sprinkle rice into a greased 9-in. square baking dish. Add juice; arrange chops over rice. Sprinkle with salt and pepper. Pour soup over chops. Cover and bake at 350° for 20 minutes. Uncover; bake 10-15 minutes longer or until meat juices run clear and rice is tender. **Yield:** 4 servings.

Lively Salads

- Mayonnaise mixed with salsa makes a great salad dressing if you're tired of the usual ranch dressing.
  —Marianne Segall, Cody, Wyoming
- When I make tuna salad, I add 1/4 to 1/3 cup of peanut butter and a small peeled chopped apple. It's nutritious, makes the mixture go further and has a unique taste. Everyone who tries it compliments me on this different tuna salad.
  —Rose Adamson, Fairfax, Missouri
- Bagel chips that I keep on hand for snacking are great on salads, too. The various flavors spark the taste of any salad. —Emilio Esquibel
  Denver, Colorado
- I jazz up gelatin salads by replacing 1 cup cold water with 1 cup vanilla ice cream. I also include sliced bananas, but almost any combination of fresh or canned fruit is tasty. My kids gobble this up and hold out their bowls for seconds! —Lisa Shoemaker
  Middletown, Pennsylvania
- When I was sick a few years ago, a friend brought us a meal that included a green salad with raisins in it. We liked it so much that now I always sprinkle raisins on my tossed salads. —Carol Koekkoek
  Sioux Center, Iowa
- Once when I was making potato salad, I ran out of regular salad dressing, so I added ranch dressing instead. It was the best potato salad I ever made. I still make it this way. —Laurie Hobart
  Wisconsin Rapids, Wisconsin
- To make tuna salad a bit more special, I add chopped water chestnuts to the mixture. —Vera Hamilton
  Loveland, Colorado
- I make bread salad quite often and find that packaged croutons are a great time-saving substitute. I use them instead of cutting and toasting bread cubes. Our favorite varieties are the cheese and garlic croutons found in the produce section of our supermarket. —Judith Miller, Walnut, California

Crunchy Celery Casserole

Ready in 1 hour or less

I first sampled this tempting treatment for celery when a friend brought it to a 4-H covered-dish dinner. We could not believe how good it tastes or how easy it is to prepare in the microwave. —Michelle Garretson
Newcomerstown, Ohio

10 celery ribs, thinly sliced
 2 cans (10-3/4 ounces *each*) condensed cream of celery soup, undiluted
 1 can (8 ounces) sliced water chestnuts, drained
 1 can (2.8 ounces) french-fried onions

In a bowl, combine the celery, soup and water chestnuts. Pour into a greased microwave-safe 8-in. square dish. Cover and microwave on high for 27 minutes or until the celery is tender, stirring every 5 minutes. Sprinkle with onions. Microwave, uncovered, 5 minutes longer. **Yield:** 8 servings. **Editor's Note:** This recipe was tested in an 850-watt microwave.

Broccoli Wild Rice Soup

(Pictured below)

Ready in 30 minutes or less

My daughter relies on a boxed rice mix to get a head start on this rich and colorful soup. She likes to serve it to friends after football games in autumn, but it's a favorite with our family any time of year. —Janet Sawyer, Dysart, Iowa

✓ Uses less fat, sugar or salt. Includes Nutritional Analysis and Diabetic Exchanges.

1 package (6 ounces) chicken and wild rice mix
5 cups water
1 package (10 ounces) frozen chopped broccoli, thawed
1 medium carrot, shredded
2 teaspoons dried minced onion
1 can (10-3/4 ounces) condensed cream of chicken soup, undiluted
1 package (8 ounces) cream cheese, cubed
1/4 cup slivered almonds, optional

In a large saucepan, combine rice, contents of seasoning packet and water; bring to a boil. Reduce heat; cover and simmer for 10 minutes, stirring once. Stir in the broccoli, carrot and onion. Cover and simmer for 5 minutes. Stir in soup and cream cheese. Cook and stir until cheese is melted. Stir in almonds if desired. **Yield:** 8 servings (about 2 quarts). **Nutritional Analysis:** One 1-cup serving (prepared with reduced-fat, reduced-sodium soup and light cream cheese and without almonds) equals 178 calories, 582 mg sodium, 19 mg cholesterol, 25 gm carbohydrate, 7 gm protein, 6 gm fat, 2 gm fiber. **Diabetic Exchanges:** 1-1/2 starch, 1 vegetable, 1 fat.

Creamy Turkey and Biscuits

Ready in 1 hour or less

Leftover holiday turkey goes into a quick, comforting casserole that gets plenty of appeal when topped with refrigerator biscuits. Even my finicky youngster likes this one! —Annette Gorton, Miles City, Montana

1/3 cup chopped green pepper
1/3 cup chopped onion
 3 tablespoons butter *or* margarine

Broccoli Wild Rice Soup

Quick Fruitcake
Cherry Almond Tart

1/4 cup biscuit/baking mix
1-1/2 cups milk
1 can (10-3/4 ounces) condensed cream of mushroom soup, undiluted
2 cups cubed cooked turkey
1 cup frozen peas
2 tubes (7-1/2 ounces *each*) refrigerated buttermilk biscuits
3/4 cup shredded cheddar cheese

In a large saucepan, saute green pepper and onion in butter until tender. Stir in biscuit mix until blended. Gradually add milk and soup; stir until blended. Bring to a boil; cook and stir for 2 minutes. Stir in turkey and peas. Transfer to a greased 13-in. x 9-in. x 2-in. baking dish. Separate biscuits and arrange over the top. Sprinkle with cheese. Bake, uncovered, at 425° for 17-20 minutes or until golden brown. **Yield:** 4-6 servings.

Quick Fruitcake

(Pictured above)

This moist loaf is the perfect choice for people who don't like the candied fruits that go into traditional fruitcake. Each slice is chock-full of goodies. —Diane Hixon
Niceville, Florida

1 package (15.6 ounces) cranberry *or* blueberry quick bread mix
1/2 cup chopped pecans
1/2 cup raisins *or* chopped dates
1/4 cup chopped maraschino cherries
1/4 cup crushed pineapple, drained

Prepare quick bread batter according to package directions. Stir in the remaining ingredients. Pour into a greased 9-in. x 5-in. x 3-in. loaf pan. Bake at 350° for 55-60 minutes or until a toothpick inserted near the center comes out clean. Cool for 10 minutes before removing from pan to a wire rack. **Yield:** 1 loaf.

Cherry Almond Tart

(Pictured above)

Ready in 1 hour or less

I used on-hand ingredients, including canned pie filling and a cake mix, to create this pretty dessert. It's fast to fix, looks elegant and tastes delicious. The red cherries make it perfect for Christmas and Valentine's Day.
—Connie Raterink, Caledonia, Michigan

1 package (18-1/4 ounces) yellow cake mix
2/3 cup graham cracker crumbs (about 11 squares)
1/2 cup butter *or* margarine, softened
1 egg
1/2 cup chopped almonds
1 package (8 ounces) cream cheese, softened
1/4 cup confectioners' sugar
1 can (21 ounces) cherry pie filling
1/2 cup sliced almonds, toasted

In a mixing bowl, combine the dry cake mix, cracker crumbs and butter until crumbly. Add the egg; mix well. Stir in the chopped almonds. Press onto the bottom and up the sides of a greased 14-in. pizza pan. Bake at 350° for 11-13 minutes or until lightly browned. Cool completely. In a mixing bowl, beat the cream cheese and sugar. Spread over the crust. Top with the pie filling. Sprinkle with the sliced almonds. Store leftovers in the refrigerator. **Yield:** 14-16 servings.

Caramel Apple Pizza

(Pictured above)

Ready in 1 hour or less

Sweet wedges of this fun fall dessert are sure to impress guests. It has an appealing appearance and a tempting combination of flavors. —Tami Lucas, Wooster, Ohio

      1 tube (18 ounces) refrigerated sugar cookie dough
      1 package (8 ounces) cream cheese, softened
  1/2 cup peanut butter
  1/2 cup packed brown sugar
      2 tablespoons milk
      4 cups sliced peeled tart apples (about 3 large)
      1 can (12 ounces) lemon-lime soda
      1 teaspoon ground cinnamon
  1/2 cup caramel ice cream topping*
  1/3 cup chopped pecans

Press cookie dough into a greased 14-in. pizza pan. Bake at 350° for 20 minutes or until golden brown. Cool on a wire rack. Run a large flat spatula under crust to loosen from pan. In a mixing bowl, beat the cream cheese, peanut butter, brown sugar and milk until smooth. Spread over the cooled crust. In a bowl, combine the apples and soda; drain well. Toss apples with cinnamon; arrange over cream cheese. Drizzle with the caramel topping and sprinkle with pecans. Cut into wedges. **Yield:** 8-10 servings. ***Editor's Note:** Fat-free caramel ice cream topping is not recommended for this recipe.

Super Soups and Chili

● I mix about 1/4 to 1/2 teaspoon of poultry seasoning into turkey vegetable soup to give it special flavor. You can also add it to vegetable beef soup.
—*Pam West, Centralia, Missouri*

● For the best chili you've ever tasted, add a can of sloppy joe sauce to your favorite recipe. My family won't eat chili without this easy addition!
—*John Kroll, Escanaba, Michigan*

● Here's a simple way to dress up a can of cream of mushroom soup. Chop various salad fixings, such as green pepper, onion and broccoli, then microwave them until crisp-tender. Stir them into the soup to make a quick meal. —*Chris Tucker Portland, Oregon*

● To brighten up a bowl of chicken soup, I add 1/2 teaspoon of lemon juice and a pinch of grated lemon peel just before serving. This works with any clear chicken soup—canned or homemade.
—*Kathryn Alkire, Oak Harbor, Washington*

● Especially in the winter, I like to spice up tomato soup with a teaspoon of chili powder, a couple shakes of garlic powder and crushed red pepper flakes. Then I top bowls of it with seasoned croutons. The extra heat from the spices really warms us up.
—*Alyce Leythan, Liberty, Missouri*

● To give homemade flavor to a can of cream of mushroom soup, stir in a 1/4 teaspoon of garlic powder.
—*Stephen Dowe, Brooklyn, New York*

Tex-Mex Pitas

(Pictured below)

Ready in 1 hour or less

I sometimes treat my friends at work to these peppy pitas. I prepare them in advance, then heat in the microwave. —Helen Overman, Pottsboro, Texas

2 pounds ground beef
1 envelope taco seasoning
1/3 cup water
1 can (16 ounces) refried beans
1 can (10 ounces) diced tomatoes and green chilies, undrained
Pinch ground cumin
7 pita breads (6 inches), halved
3 cups (12 ounces) shredded cheddar cheese
Sliced jalapenos

In a skillet, cook beef over medium heat until no longer pink; drain. Stir in taco seasoning, water, beans, tomatoes and cumin. Simmer, uncovered, for 20 minutes, stirring occasionally. Spoon about 1/3 cup into each pita half; top with about 2 tablespoons cheese and a few jalapeno slices. Place in an ungreased 13-in. x 9-in. x 2-in. baking pan. Bake at 350° for 10 minutes or until cheese is melted. **Yield:** 7 servings.

Taco Mac

(Pictured below)

Ready in 30 minutes or less

Pork sausage, taco seasoning and taco sauce add plenty of zip to easy macaroni and cheese. This zesty dish is just as yummy the next day. Just warm it up and garnish with shredded lettuce, diced tomatoes and cheese. — JoLynn Fribley, Winchester, Indiana

1 package (24 ounces) shells and cheese mix*
1/2 pound bulk pork sausage, cooked and drained
1/3 cup taco sauce
1 tablespoon taco seasoning
4 cups shredded lettuce
2 medium tomatoes, chopped
1 cup (4 ounces) shredded cheddar cheese, optional

Prepare shells and cheese mix according to package directions. Stir in sausage, taco sauce and seasoning. Garnish with lettuce, tomatoes and cheddar cheese if desired. Serve immediately. **Yield:** 6 servings. ***Editor's Note:** This recipe was tested with Kraft Velveeta Family-Size Shells & Cheese.

Taco Mac
Tex-Mex Pitas

Sausage Cheese Muffins

(Pictured below and on page 71)

Ready in 1 hour or less

These small savory muffins are fun to serve as appetizers or at a brunch. With just five ingredients, the tasty bites are easy to whip up to take to a party, the office or a sick friend. —Willa Paget, Nashville, Tennessee

- 1 pound bulk hot pork sausage
- 1 can (10-3/4 ounces) condensed cheddar cheese soup, undiluted
- 1/2 cup milk
- 2 to 3 teaspoons rubbed sage
- 3 cups biscuit/baking mix

In a skillet over medium heat, cook sausage until no longer pink; drain. In a bowl, combine soup, milk, sage and sausage. Stir in the biscuit mix just until moistened. Fill greased miniature or regular muffin cups two-thirds full. Bake at 400° for 15-20 minutes or until muffins test done. **Yield:** 4 dozen mini-muffins or 2 dozen regular muffins.

Peanut Butter Pancakes

(Pictured below and on page 70)

Ready in 15 minutes or less

Pancakes are one of my husband's specialties. So it's not unusual for him to wake me with these hot-from-the-griddle cakes that get their delicious difference from creamy peanut butter. —Dorothy Pritchett, Wills Point, Texas

- 1 cup pancake mix
- 2 tablespoons sugar
- 1 egg
- 1/3 cup peanut butter*
- 1 can (5 ounces) evaporated milk
- 1/3 cup water

HONEY BUTTER:
- 1/4 cup butter (no substitutes), softened
- 2 tablespoons honey

In a bowl, combine pancake mix and sugar. In a small bowl, beat egg and peanut butter; add milk and water. Stir into dry ingredients just until moistened. Pour batter by 1/4 cupfuls onto a lightly greased medium-hot griddle. Turn when bubbles form on top of pancakes; cook until second side is golden brown. Combine butter and honey in a small bowl. Serve with the pancakes. **Yield:** 10 pancakes. ***Editor's Note:** This recipe was tested with Jif brand peanut butter.

Raspberry Cake

Plan ahead...needs to chill

I jazz up a plain cake with raspberry gelatin and frozen berries. Spread with a light, fruity whipped topping, the festive results make a cool and refreshing dessert. —Marion Anderson, Dalton, Minnesota

- 1 package (18-1/4 ounces) white cake mix
- 1 package (3 ounces) raspberry gelatin
- 1 package (10 ounces) frozen sweetened raspberries, thawed, undrained

Sausage Cheese Muffins
Peanut Butter Pancakes

        4 eggs
    1/2 cup vegetable oil
    1/4 cup hot water
FROSTING:
        1 carton (12 ounces) frozen whipped topping,
          thawed
        1 package (10 ounces) frozen sweetened
          raspberries, thawed, undrained

In a large bowl, combine dry cake mix and gelatin powder. Add raspberries with juice, eggs, oil and water. Beat until well blended. Pour into a greased 13-in. x 9-in. x 2-in. baking pan. Bake at 350° for 35-40 minutes or until a toothpick inserted near the center comes out clean. Cool. For frosting, fold whipped topping into raspberries. Spread over cake. Refrigerate for 2 hours before serving. Store in the refrigerator. **Yield:** 12-16 servings.

Artichoke Rice Salad

Plan ahead...needs to chill

A close friend shared this make-ahead recipe that starts with a packaged rice mix. Curry and artichoke hearts give it a flavorful change of pace that's welcome at a picnic or potluck. —Sonja Blow
Groveland, California

    1 package (6.9 ounces) chicken-flavored
      rice mix
    2 jars (6-1/2 ounces *each*) marinated
      artichoke hearts
    3 cups cooked long grain rice
    3 cups chopped green onions
    3/4 cup mayonnaise
    1/2 teaspoon curry powder

Prepare rice mix according to package directions; cool. Drain artichokes, reserving marinade. Chop artichokes; place in a large bowl. Add prepared rice, long grain rice and onions. In a small bowl, combine mayonnaise, curry powder and reserved marinade. Pour over rice mixture and toss to coat. Cover and refrigerate until serving. **Yield:** 10-12 servings.

Cinnamon Peach Cobbler

Ready in 1 hour or less

Biscuit mix makes this comforting cobbler a quick favorite. My husband loves the warm peaches, cinnamony sauce and golden crumb topping. —Victoria Lowe
Lititz, Pennsylvania

    4 cups sliced peeled fresh *or* frozen
      unsweetened peaches, thawed
    1/2 cup sugar
    1 tablespoon plus 2/3 cup biscuit/baking
      mix, *divided*
    1/2 teaspoon ground cinnamon
    2 to 3 tablespoons brown sugar
    1/4 cup cold butter *or* margarine
    3 tablespoons milk

In a bowl, combine peaches, sugar, 1 tablespoon of biscuit mix and cinnamon. Transfer to a greased shallow 1-1/2-qt. baking dish. In a bowl, combine the brown sugar and remaining biscuit mix. Cut in butter until crumbly. Stir in milk just until blended. Drop by rounded tablespoonfuls onto peach mixture. Bake at 400° for 20-25 minutes or until top is golden brown and filling is bubbly. **Yield:** 6-8 servings.

Lemon Berry Cake

Ready in 1 hour or less

This recipe starts out with simple ingredients but it tastes special when it's done. Lemon gelatin and blackberries add tangy taste to a plain yellow cake mix. I like to serve it warm with a dollop of sweet whipped cream or a big scoop of vanilla ice cream. —Karen Ehatt, Chester, Maryland

    1 package (18-1/4 ounces) yellow cake mix
    1 tablespoon grated lemon peel
    2 cups fresh *or* frozen blueberries
    1 package (6 ounces) lemon gelatin
1-1/2 cups boiling water
Confectioners' sugar
Whipped cream *or* topping, optional

Prepare the cake batter according to package directions. Stir in the lemon peel. Pour into a lightly greased 13-in. x 9-in. x 2-in. baking dish. Sprinkle with the blueberries. In a bowl, whisk together the gelatin and water until gelatin is dissolved. Slowly pour over the batter. Bake at 350° for 33-38 minutes or until a toothpick inserted near the center of cake layer comes out with moist crumbs (cake will set upon cooling). Cool slightly on a wire rack. Dust with confectioners' sugar. Serve warm with whipped cream if desired. Store in the refrigerator. **Yield:** 12 servings.

Better Beverages

- To give my homemade hot chocolate mix richer taste and texture, I add a small package of instant pudding mix to the batch. It's wonderful! I use one package of pudding to the 3 cups of instant nonfat dry milk powder called for in the recipe. —Rena Hall, Grandview, Missouri

- When I make fruit punch of any kind, I sprinkle in an envelope or two of unsweetened lemonade soft drink mix. It perks up the flavor and I always get lots of compliments on it. —Marybell Seeber
Delavan, Wisconsin

- While preparing a cup of instant coffee, I mixed in vanilla extract and vanilla flavored non-dairy creamer. I was amazed that simple pantry ingredients could make it taste like store-bought specialty coffee. —Anna Reich, Albuquerque, New Mexico

- The next time you're looking for a way to sweeten tea and add a little refreshing lemon flavor, try this simple trick. For every glass, stir in a teaspoon or two of lemonade drink mix. I've found this works well with both iced and hot tea. —J.F. Lizakowski
Wilomar, California

Homemade Mixes

HOMEMADE mixes deliver all the great taste of the popular specialty products offered today but for far less cost. They're convenient to have on hand, too.

Buttermilk Biscuit Mix

I stir up a big batch of this versatile biscuit mix to use in dozens of recipes. This mix is easy to make and handy to use, plus it saves money! —Katie Koziolek
Hartland, Minnesota

   8 cups all-purpose flour
1-1/2 cups buttermilk blend powder
   4 tablespoons baking powder
   3 tablespoons sugar
   2 teaspoons salt
   2 teaspoons cream of tartar
   1 teaspoon baking soda
2-1/3 cups shortening

In a bowl, combine the first seven ingredients; cut in the shortening until crumbly. Store in an airtight container in a cool dry place for up to 6 months. **Yield:** about 13-1/2 cups.

Quick Chicken Pie

(Pictured at right)

I use my homemade biscuit mix to create a golden crust over this comforting combination of chicken chunks and vegetables in a creamy sauce. —Katie Koziolek

1-2/3 cups frozen mixed vegetables, thawed
   1 can (10-3/4 ounces) condensed cream of chicken soup, undiluted
   1 cup cubed cooked chicken
   1 egg, beaten
1/2 cup milk
   1 cup Buttermilk Biscuit Mix (recipe on this page)

In a bowl, combine vegetables, soup and chicken. Transfer to an ungreased 9-in. pie plate. In another bowl, combine egg, milk and biscuit mix just until moistened. Pour over chicken mixture. Bake at 400° for 30-35 minutes or until golden brown. **Yield:** 6 servings.

Bacon 'n' Egg Biscuits

(Pictured at right)

On busy mornings, you can fix these tasty sandwiches in about 15 minutes. While the flaky biscuits bake, cook the eggs and warm up precooked bacon. —Katie Koziolek

   2 cups Buttermilk Biscuit Mix (recipe on this page)
   7 tablespoons water
   8 eggs
   8 slices process American cheese
   8 bacon strips, halved and cooked

In a bowl, combine biscuit mix and water just until blended. Turn onto a lightly floured surface and knead 5 times. Roll out to 1/2-in. thickness; cut with a 3-in. biscuit cutter. Place on an ungreased baking sheet. Bake at 425° for 9-10 minutes or until golden brown. Meanwhile, scramble the eggs. Split the biscuits; fill each with a slice of cheese, scrambled egg and two bacon pieces. **Yield:** 8 servings.

Cheesecake Squares

(Pictured at right)

This is my favorite cheesecake made easy. It bakes in a jiffy and is rich, creamy and irresistible, especially when served with fresh fruit. —Katie Koziolek

   2 packages (8 ounces *each*) cream cheese, softened
   1 cup sugar
   2 eggs
1/2 cup plain yogurt
   2 teaspoons vanilla extract
   1 teaspoon lemon juice
1/2 cup Buttermilk Biscuit Mix (recipe on this page)
TOPPING:
   1 cup (8 ounces) sour cream
   2 tablespoons sugar
   2 teaspoons vanilla extract
Fresh fruit, optional

In a mixing bowl, beat cream cheese and sugar. Add eggs, yogurt, vanilla, lemon juice and biscuit mix; mix just until smooth. Pour into a greased 9-in. square baking dish. Bake at 350° for 25-30 minutes or until center is nearly set. Place on a wire rack while preparing topping. In a bowl, combine sour cream, sugar and vanilla until smooth. Carefully spread over cheesecake. Bake for 4 minutes (topping will not brown or set). Cool on a wire rack for 1 hour. Refrigerate until completely cooled. Garnish with fruit if desired. **Yield:** 9 servings.

Cheese Pizza

You can use this dough to make one 12-inch pizza or a half dozen individual pizzas. Just roll it out and add your favorite toppings. —Katie Koziolek

1-1/2 cups Buttermilk Biscuit Mix (recipe on this page)
  1/3 cup hot water
    1 can (8 ounces) pizza sauce
1-1/2 cups (6 ounces) shredded mozzarella cheese

In a bowl, combine biscuit mix and water; mix well. Press into a greased 12-in. pizza pan. Spread with pizza sauce; sprinkle with cheese. Bake at 450° for 12-15 minutes or until golden brown. **Yield:** 4 servings.

Quick Chicken Pie
Cheesecake Squares
Bacon 'n' Egg Biscuits

Beef Pinwheels with Gravy

Basil in the biscuit dough provides the pleasant seasoning in these beef-filled swirls. The attractive slices are especially good with additional gravy. —Katie Koziolek, Hartland, Minnesota

> 2 cups Buttermilk Biscuit Mix (recipe on page 86)
> 1 teaspoon dried basil
> 7 tablespoons water
> 1/2 pound ground beef, cooked and drained
> 1/4 cup beef gravy
> Additional gravy, warmed

In a bowl, combine biscuit mix, basil and water just until moistened. Turn onto a lightly floured surface; knead 5 times. Roll out into a 12-in. x 9-in. rectangle. Combine beef and gravy; spoon over dough. Roll up, jelly-roll style, starting with a long side. Cut into 1/2-in. slices; place in a lightly greased 13-in. x 9-in. x 2-in. baking pan. Bake at 450° for 14-16 minutes or until golden brown. Serve with gravy. **Yield:** 4-6 servings.

Pigs in Biscuits

Cornmeal gives a nice twist to these spiral-wrapped hot dogs. Kids love dipping them in ketchup and mustard. —Katie Koziolek, Hartland, Minnesota

> 2 cups Buttermilk Biscuit Mix (recipe on page 86)
> 2 tablespoons cornmeal
> 7 tablespoons water
> 10 hot dogs

In a bowl, combine biscuit mix, cornmeal and water just until moistened. Turn onto a lightly floured surface; knead 5 times. Roll out into a 10-in. square; cut into 10 strips. Starting at one end, wrap each strip in a spiral around a hot dog; pinch ends. Place on an ungreased baking sheet. Bake at 425° for 10-12 minutes or until golden brown. **Yield:** 10 servings.

Cornmeal-Coated Chicken

The pepper really comes through in this quick and convenient coating mix for chicken. Not only is it tasty, it's certainly more economical than the store-bought kind. —Aljene Wendling, Seattle, Washington

 Uses less fat, sugar or salt. Includes Nutritional Analysis and Diabetic Exchanges.

> 1 cup all-purpose flour
> 1 cup cornmeal
> 4 teaspoons ground cumin
> 2 teaspoons onion powder
> 2 teaspoons garlic powder
> 2 teaspoons dried oregano
> 1 teaspoon salt, optional
> 1 teaspoon pepper
> 1/2 teaspoon cayenne pepper
> ADDITIONAL INGREDIENTS:
> 1 broiler/fryer chicken (3 pounds), cut up and skin removed
> 3 tablespoons butter *or* margarine, melted

In a large resealable plastic bag, combine the first nine ingredients. Store in a cool dry place for up to 6 months. **Yield:** 3 batches (2-1/4 cups total). **To prepare chicken:** Place 3/4 cup coating mix in a resealable plastic bag. Dip chicken in butter; add chicken to bag, a few pieces at a time, and shake to coat. Place in a greased 15-in. x 10-in. x 1-in. baking pan. Bake, uncovered, at 375° for 45-50 minutes or until juices run clear. **Yield:** 4 servings per batch. **Nutritional Analysis:** One serving (prepared with reduced-fat margarine and without salt) equals 314 calories, 218 mg sodium, 106 mg cholesterol, 18 gm carbohydrate, 35 gm protein, 10 gm fat, 1 gm fiber. **Diabetic Exchanges:** 4 lean meat, 1 starch.

Gingerbread Cake Mix

(Pictured at left)

With this mix you can bake moist, nicely spiced gingerbread in no time. It's especially handy during the hectic holiday season. —Ruth Seitz, Columbus Junction, Iowa

> 6-2/3 cups all-purpose flour
> 1-1/2 cups sugar
> 3/4 cup plus 1 tablespoon nonfat dry milk powder
> 1/4 cup baking powder
> 1 tablespoon salt
> 2-1/2 teaspoons ground cinnamon
> 2 teaspoons cream of tartar
> 1-1/4 teaspoons ground cloves
> 1-1/4 teaspoons ground ginger
> 1-1/2 cups shortening

Gingerbread Cake Mix

Graham Pie Crust Mix

ADDITIONAL INGREDIENTS (for each batch):
- 1 egg
- 1/2 cup water
- 1/2 cup molasses

In a large bowl, combine the first nine ingredients; mix well. Cut in shortening until the mixture resembles coarse crumbs. Store in an airtight container in a cool dry place for up to 6 months. **Yield:** 5 batches (10 cups total). **To prepare cake:** In a mixing bowl, lightly beat egg, water and molasses. Add 2 cups cake mix; beat until well blended. Spread into a greased 8-in. square baking pan. Bake at 350° for 35-40 minutes or until a toothpick inserted near the center comes out clean. Cool on a wire rack. **Yield:** 9 servings per batch. **Editor's Note:** Contents of cake mix may settle during storage. When preparing recipe, spoon mix into measuring cup.

Raisin Oatmeal Mix

We like the sweet cinnamony flavor of this instant oatmeal at our house. The mix makes it convenient to zap a bowl in the microwave for a speedy breakfast.
—Robert Caummisar, Grayson, Kentucky

- 6 cups quick-cooking oats
- 1/2 cup raisins
- 1/2 cup chopped dried apples *or* bananas
- 1/4 cup sugar
- 1/4 cup packed brown sugar
- 1 tablespoon ground cinnamon
- 1 teaspoon salt

ADDITIONAL INGREDIENT FOR OATMEAL:
- 3/4 cup water

In a bowl, combine the first seven ingredients. Store in an airtight container for up to 1 month. **Yield:** 14 batches (about 7 cups total). **To prepare oatmeal:** In a deep microwave-safe bowl, combine 1/2 cup oatmeal mix and 3/4 cup water. Microwave, uncovered, on high for 1 minute; stir. Cook 30-60 seconds longer or until bubbly. Let stand 1-2 minutes. **Yield:** 1 serving per batch. **Editor's Note:** This recipe was tested in an 850-watt microwave.

Graham Pie Crust Mix

(Pictured above)

To save time when I needs a dessert in a jiffy, I keep this versatile crust mix on hand. The crumb mixture makes enough for four pies. I've found it complements the taste of most any filling. —Sue Ross
Casa Grande, Arizona

- 5 cups graham cracker crumbs (about 40 squares)
- 1 cup sugar
- 1 teaspoon ground cinnamon
- 1 cup cold butter (no substitutes)

In a food processor or bowl, combine crumbs, sugar and cinnamon; pulse or cut in butter until mixture begins to clump together. Store in an airtight container in the refrigerator for up to 3 months. **Yield:** about 7-1/2 cups mix (about 4 pie crusts). **To prepare one crust:** Press about 1-3/4 cups crust mix onto the bottom and up the sides of a 9-in. pie plate. Bake at 375° for 8-10 minutes or until lightly browned. Chill 30 minutes before filling.

Quick Bread Mix

Quick Bread Mix
(Pictured above)

Looking for a speedy breakfast or some take-along treats for the office? This mix is so convenient to have on hand to bake a batch of moist tropical muffins or a loaf of nutty banana bread. —Doris Barb, El Dorado, Kansas

10 cups all-purpose flour
1/3 cup baking powder
1/4 cup sugar
1 tablespoon salt
2 cups shortening
ADDITIONAL INGREDIENTS FOR MUFFINS:
1/4 cup sugar
1-1/2 teaspoons grated orange peel
1 egg
1 can (8 ounces) crushed pineapple, undrained
1/4 cup milk
ADDITIONAL INGREDIENTS FOR BREAD:
1 package (8 ounces) cream cheese, softened
1 cup sugar
2 eggs
3/4 cup mashed ripe banana (about 1 banana)
1/2 cup chopped pecans

In a large bowl, combine the dry ingredients. Cut in shortening until crumbly. Store in an airtight container in a cool dry place or in the freezer for up to 6 months. **Yield:** about 7 batches of muffins and about 5 batches of bread (13 cups total). **To prepare muffins:** In a bowl, combine 1-3/4 cups quick bread mix, sugar and orange peel. In a small bowl, combine the egg, pineap-

ple and milk; stir into dry ingredients just until moistened. Fill greased or paper-lined muffin cups two-thirds full. Bake at 400° for 25 minutes or until a toothpick comes out clean. Cool for 5 minutes before removing from pan to a wire rack. **Yield:** 8 muffins. **To prepare bread:** In a mixing bowl, beat cream cheese and sugar. Add eggs, one at a time. Beat in banana. Stir in 2-1/4 cups quick bread mix and pecans just until moistened. Pour into a greased 9-in. x 5-in. x 3-in. loaf pan. Bake at 350° for 65-70 minutes or until a toothpick comes out clean. Cool for 10 minutes before removing from pan to a wire rack to cool completely. **Yield:** 1 loaf.

Friendship Tea Mix

I combine seven simple ingredients to make a big batch of this hot spiced drink mix. Placed in a jar and tied with pretty ribbon, this is one of my favorite gifts for neighbors. —Arma White, Golconda, Illinois

1 jar (21.1 ounces) orange breakfast drink mix
1 cup sugar
1/2 cup sweetened lemonade soft drink mix
1/2 cup unsweetened instant tea
1 package (3 ounces) apricot gelatin
2-1/2 teaspoons ground cinnamon
1 teaspoon ground cloves
ADDITIONAL INGREDIENTS:
1 cup boiling water

In a bowl, combine the first seven ingredients; mix well. Store in an airtight container in a cool dry place for up to 6 months. **Yield:** 50 batches (about 5 cups total). **To prepare 1 cup of tea:** Dissolve 4-1/2 teaspoons tea mix in boiling water; stir well. **Yield:** 1 serving.

Italian Meatball Mix

I keep this blend for moist meatballs in the fridge for a quick Italian meal. Sometimes my daughter stops by on her way home from work, so a cupful will be missing and I'll find a little note on the refrigerator door. —Lois Crissman, Mansfield, Ohio

2-1/2 cups dry bread crumbs
2/3 cup dried minced onion
2/3 cup grated Parmesan cheese
1/3 cup dried parsley flakes
1 tablespoon garlic powder
1 tablespoon garlic salt
ADDITIONAL INGREDIENTS (for each batch):
1 egg, lightly beaten
1 pound ground beef

In a bowl, combine the first six ingredients; mix well. Store in the refrigerator for up to 2 months. **Yield:** 4 batches (about 4 cups total). **To prepare meatballs:** In a bowl, combine egg and 1 cup meatball mix. Add the beef and mix well. Shape into 1-1/2-in. balls. In a skillet, brown the meatballs; drain. Transfer to a 13-in. x 9-in. x 2-in. baking dish. Bake at 400° for 20-25 minutes or until meat is no longer pink. **Yield:** 16 meatballs per batch.

Ranch Dressing and Dip Mix

(Pictured below)

This versatile recipe converts easily into a creamy dip or smooth dressing. It's delicious served with fresh veggies or drizzled over greens.
—Carolyn Zimmerman
Fairbury, Illinois

- 2 tablespoons plus 2 teaspoons dried minced onion
- 1 tablespoon dried parsley flakes
- 2-1/2 teaspoons paprika
- 2 teaspoons sugar
- 2 teaspoons salt
- 2 teaspoons pepper
- 1-1/2 teaspoons garlic powder

ADDITIONAL INGREDIENTS FOR DRESSING:
- 1 cup mayonnaise
- 1 cup buttermilk

ADDITIONAL INGREDIENTS FOR DIP:
- 1 cup (8 ounces) sour cream

In a small bowl, combine the first seven ingredients. Store in an airtight container in a cool dry place for up to 1 year. **Yield:** about 6 tablespoons mix (enough to make 6 batches). **To prepare dressing:** In a bowl, combine 1 tablespoon mix with mayonnaise and buttermilk; refrigerate. **Yield:** 2 cups. **To prepare dip:** In a bowl, combine 1 tablespoon mix and sour cream; refrigerate for at least 1 hour before serving. **Yield:** 1 cup.

Whole Wheat Brownie Mix

Here's one way to get your kids to eat whole wheat—use it to make brownies! My mom baked these often when I was younger. They're so good, they don't need frosting.
—Roni Goodell, Spanish Fork, Utah

- 4 cups sugar
- 3 cups whole wheat flour
- 1 cup baking cocoa
- 2 teaspoons baking powder
- 2 teaspoons salt
- 1 cup shortening

ADDITIONAL INGREDIENTS (for each batch):
- 2 eggs
- 1 teaspoon vanilla extract
- 1/2 cup chopped walnuts, optional

In a large bowl, combine the dry ingredients. Cut in shortening until the mixture resembles coarse crumbs. Store in an airtight container in the refrigerator or freezer for up to 3 months. **Yield:** about 4 batches (about 11 cups total). **To prepare brownies:** In a bowl, combine eggs, vanilla and 2-1/2 cups brownie mix until blended (batter will be stiff). Stir in nuts if desired. Spread into a greased 8-in. square baking pan. Bake at 350° for 20-25 minutes or until a toothpick inserted near the center comes out clean. Cool on a wire rack. Cut into bars. **Yield:** 16 brownies per batch. **Editor's Note:** Contents of brownie mix may settle during storage. When preparing recipe, spoon mix into measuring cup.

Ranch Dressing and Dip Mix

Chicken-Flavored Rice Mix

Preparing a flavorful rice side dish is a snap with this mixture. With just five ingredients, it's simple to make and can be stored in an airtight container for up to 6 months. I frequently turn to it when I'm in a hurry. —Florence Arbes, Courtland, Minnesota

- 3 tablespoons chicken bouillon granules
- 3 tablespoons dried parsley flakes
- 1 tablespoon dried celery flakes
- 1 tablespoon dried minced onion
- 1 tablespoon sugar

ADDITIONAL INGREDIENTS:
- 1 cup uncooked long grain rice
- 2 tablespoons butter *or* margarine
- 2 cups water

In a bowl, combine the first five ingredients. Store in an airtight container for up to 6 months. **Yield:** 3 batches (about 3/4 cup total). **To prepare rice:** In a saucepan, saute rice in butter until lightly browned. Add water and about 1/4 cup of seasoning mix. Bring to a boil; reduce heat. Cover and simmer for 20 minutes or until the rice is tender. **Yield:** 4-6 servings.

Vegetable Seasoning Mix

My husband wouldn't eat green beans until I seasoned them with this simple blend. Now he asks for seconds. Try this mix with most any vegetable for a zippy side dish that's sure to please. —Susan Johnson, Arlington, Texas

- 2 tablespoons garlic salt
- 2 tablespoons garlic powder
- 2 tablespoons dried minced onion
- 2 tablespoons onion powder
- 2 tablespoons salt

ADDITIONAL INGREDIENTS:
- 2 cups fresh *or* frozen cut green beans *or* vegetable of your choice
- 1 tablespoon butter *or* margarine
- 1 tablespoon slivered almonds, toasted

In a bowl, combine the first five ingredients. Store in an airtight container in a cool dry place for up to 1 year. **Yield:** 24-30 batches (1/2 cup total). **To use seasoning mix:** Cook and drain vegetables. Add butter and 1/2 to 1 teaspoon seasoning mix; toss until butter is melted. Sprinkle with almonds. **Yield:** 3-4 servings per batch.

Seasoned Noodle Mix

You can get a head start on a side dish with this pleasant seasoning mixture that works with most any type of noodles you have in your pantry. Add water and pop the dish in the oven alongside your entree. —Dawn Fagerstrom, Warren, Minnesota

- 2 tablespoons chicken bouillon granules
- 2 tablespoons dried parsley flakes
- 1 tablespoon dried minced onion
- 1/4 teaspoon pepper

ADDITIONAL INGREDIENTS:
- 2 cups uncooked medium egg noodles
- 1 teaspoon butter *or* margarine
- 1-1/4 cups boiling water

In a bowl, combine bouillon, parsley, onion and pepper. Store in an airtight container in a cool dry place for up to 6 months. **Yield:** 3 batches (about 1/3 cup total). **To prepare noodles:** Place noodles in a greased 1-qt. baking dish. Dot with butter. Add water and 5 teaspoons seasoning mix. Cover and bake at 350° for 15 minutes; stir. Cover and bake 5 minutes longer or until noodles are tender. Let stand 5 minutes before serving. **Yield:** 4 servings per batch.

Snack Cake Mix

Your family can enjoy two distinctly different snack cakes with this simple mix. The moist and sweet banana version is chock-full of crunchy nuts while the applesauce cake has plenty of spicy goodness. Both are popular at my house. —Kathy Nieratko, Fair Haven, Vermont

- 8 cups all-purpose flour
- 4 cups sugar
- 1 tablespoon baking soda
- 1 tablespoon salt

ADDITIONAL INGREDIENTS FOR BANANA SNACK CAKE:
- 1 egg
- 1/3 cup milk
- 1/3 cup vegetable oil
- 1/2 cup mashed ripe banana
- 1 cup chopped walnuts

ADDITIONAL INGREDIENTS FOR APPLESAUCE SNACK CAKE:
- 1 egg
- 3/4 cup applesauce
- 1/4 cup vegetable oil
- 1-1/2 teaspoons ground cinnamon
- 1 teaspoon ground allspice
- 1/8 teaspoon ground cloves
- 1 cup raisins
- 1/2 cup chopped walnuts

In a large bowl, combine flour, sugar, baking soda and salt. Store in an airtight container for up to 6 months. **Yield:** about 11-1/2 cups (about 5 batches). **To prepare banana cake:** In a mixing bowl, beat egg, milk and oil. Stir in 2-1/4 cups cake mix and banana; mix well. Fold in walnuts. Pour into a greased 8-in. square baking pan. Bake at 350° for 30-35 minutes or until a toothpick inserted near the center comes out clean. Cool on a wire rack. **Yield:** 6-8 servings. **To prepare applesauce cake:** In a mixing bowl, beat egg, applesauce and oil. Add cinnamon, allspice, cloves and 2-1/4 cups cake mix; mix well. Fold in the raisins and walnuts. Pour into a greased 8-in. square baking pan. Bake at 350° for 30-35 minutes or until a toothpick inserted near the center comes out clean. Cool on a wire rack. **Yield:** 6-8 servings. **Editor's Note:** Contents of mix may settle during storage. When preparing recipe, spoon the mix into a measuring cup.

Versatile Oat Mix
Peach Crisp

Versatile Oat Mix

(Pictured above)

For breakfast, savor a stack of pleasant pancakes, or spread warm muffins with butter, honey or jam. For dessert, a golden fruit crisp offers old-fashioned flavor with the ease of canned pie filling. —Dorothy Smith
El Dorado, Arkansas

    3 cups all-purpose flour
    1 cup packed brown sugar
    1/2 cup sugar
    3-1/2 teaspoons baking powder
    1-1/2 teaspoons salt
    1-1/2 cups shortening
    3 cups quick-cooking oats
ADDITIONAL INGREDIENTS FOR OAT PANCAKES:
    1 egg, beaten
    1 cup water
ADDITIONAL INGREDIENTS FOR OATMEAL MUFFINS:
    1 egg, beaten
    2/3 cup milk
ADDITIONAL INGREDIENTS FOR PEACH CRISP:
    1/4 cup packed brown sugar

    1 can (21 ounces) peach pie filling
    Ice cream *or* whipped topping, optional

In a large bowl, combine the flour, sugars, baking powder and salt; mix well. Cut in shortening until mixture resembles fine crumbs. Stir in oats. Store in airtight containers in a cool dry place for up to 6 months. **Yield:** 9 cups (number of batches varies depending on recipe used). **To prepare pancakes:** Combine 1-1/2 cups oat mix, egg and water in a bowl; mix well. Let stand for 5 minutes. Pour by 1/4 cupfuls onto a lightly greased hot griddle. Turn when bubbles form on top; cook until second side is golden brown. **Yield:** 10 pancakes. **To prepare muffins:** Combine 3 cups oat mix, egg and milk in a bowl; mix well. Fill paper-lined muffin cups two-thirds full. Bake at 400° for 15-20 minutes or until toothpick comes out clean. Cool for 5 minutes before removing from pan to a wire rack. Serve warm. **Yield:** 1 dozen. **To prepare peach crisp:** Combine 2 cups oat mix and brown sugar in a bowl and mix well. Pat 1-1/4 cups into a greased 8-in. baking pan. Spread with the pie filling. Sprinkle with the remaining oat mixture. Bake at 375° for 30 minutes or until lightly browned. Serve warm with ice cream or whipped topping if desired. **Yield:** 6-8 servings.

Chapter 7

IF FAMILY MEMBERS typically turn up their noses when you reheat the same dish over and over again, maybe all you need to do is dress up the food in a different disguise!

The secret is to first cook up a hearty dish on the weekend and then use the "planned leftovers" in an entirely different recipe or two during the week.

For example, start by treating your family to Yeast Pancakes pictured at left and featured on page 100. (Like all the weekend dishes that supply the main ingredient for the weekday recipes, its title is highlighted in a colored box.) Later, surprise them with such lively leftovers as Spinach Pancake Quesadillas and Fruit Pancake Roll-Ups.

Your family will never again look at leftovers the same way!

TWICE AS TASTY. Top to bottom: Yeast Pancakes, Spinach Pancake Quesadillas and Fruit Pancake Roll-Ups (all recipes on p. 100).

Baked Potatoes

The next time you make baked potatoes as a side dish, pop a few extra in the oven.

4 medium baking potatoes (about 1-1/3 pounds)

Oven: Scrub and pierce potatoes. Bake at 400° for 40-60 minutes or until tender. **Microwave:** Scrub and pierce potatoes; place on a microwave-safe plate. Microwave, uncovered, on high for 12-14 minutes or until tender, turning once. **Yield:** 4 servings.

Baked Potato Soup

Ready in 30 minutes or less

This creamy potato soup recipe is a winter favorite in our home.   —Kristi Teague, Southside, Tennessee

    3 bacon strips, diced
    1 small onion, chopped
    1 garlic clove, minced
    3 tablespoons all-purpose flour
    1 teaspoon salt
    1 teaspoon dried basil
1/2 teaspoon pepper
    3 cups chicken broth
    2 large potatoes, baked, peeled and cubed
        (about 2 cups)
    1 cup half-and-half cream
1/2 teaspoon hot pepper sauce
Shredded cheddar cheese
Minced fresh parsley

In a large saucepan, cook bacon until crisp. Drain, reserving 1 tablespoon drippings. Set bacon aside. Saute onion and garlic in the drippings until tender. Stir in flour, salt, basil and pepper; mix well. Gradually add broth. Bring to a boil; boil and stir for 2 minutes. Add the potatoes, cream and hot pepper sauce; heat through but do not boil. Garnish with bacon, cheese and parsley. **Yield:** 4-5 servings.

Fiesta Potatoes

Ready in 30 minutes or less

I originally served this zippy ham filling on open-faced French rolls. One day I added some to a baked potato.
          —Socorro Kimble, Bakersfield, California

    4 medium potatoes, baked
1/2 cup sour cream
1/2 cup diced fully cooked ham
    3 tablespoons grated Parmesan cheese
    2 tablespoons mayonnaise
    1 to 2 tablespoons chopped green chilies
Salt and pepper to taste
    1 cup (4 ounces) shredded cheddar cheese

Place potatoes in a 13-in. x 9-in. x 2-in. baking dish. With a sharp knife, cut an X in the top of each potato. Bake, uncovered, at 350° for 10 minutes or until warm.

Meanwhile, combine the sour cream, ham, Parmesan, mayonnaise, chilies, salt and pepper; mix well. Fluff potato pulp with a fork. Top with ham mixture; sprinkle with cheese. Bake, uncovered, 10-15 minutes longer or until cheese is melted. **Yield:** 4 servings. **Editor's Note:** If using hot baked potatoes, omit the baking time before adding the topping.

Tasty Potato Bake

Ready in 1 hour or less

This cheesy dish is a time-saver because there's no need to peel the potatoes.   —Jane Carlovsky, Sebring, Florida

    5 medium potatoes, baked and cubed
    8 ounces process American cheese, cubed
1/4 cup chopped onion
    2 tablespoons chopped sweet red pepper or
        pimientos
    2 slices bread, cubed
1/8 teaspoon onion salt or onion powder
1/8 teaspoon garlic salt or garlic powder
1/3 cup butter or margarine, melted

Place potato cubes in a greased 11-in. x 7-in. x 2-in. baking dish. Top with cheese. In a bowl, combine the onion, red pepper, bread cubes, onion salt and garlic salt. Sprinkle over potatoes and cheese. Drizzle with butter. Bake, uncovered, at 350° for 25-30 minutes or until heated through. **Yield:** 8 servings.

Green Pepper Meat Loaf

(Pictured above right)

We like spicy meat loaf, so we use hot pork sausage rather than mild.   —Edna Lauderdale, Milwaukee, Wisconsin

☑ Uses less fat, sugar or salt. Includes Nutritional Analysis and Diabetic Exchanges.

    2 eggs, lightly beaten
    2 medium green peppers, chopped
    1 large onion, finely chopped
1/4 cup chopped celery leaves
1/4 cup minced fresh parsley
    1 envelope onion soup mix
    2 pounds ground beef
    1 pound bulk pork sausage
    4 bacon strips, optional

In a large bowl, combine eggs, green peppers, onion, celery leaves, parsley and soup mix. Crumble beef and sausage over the mixture and mix well. Shape into a 12-in. x 4-in. loaf. Place on a rack in a shallow baking pan. Bake, uncovered, at 350° for 1 hour. Place bacon strips over top if desired. Bake 45-60 minutes longer or until no pink remains and a meat thermometer reads 160°. **Yield:** 14 slices. **Nutritional Analysis:** One slice (prepared with egg substitute equivalent to 2 eggs, reduced-sodium soup mix, lean ground beef and bulk turkey sausage) equals 193 calories, 398 mg sodium, 51 mg cholesterol, 5 gm carbohydrate, 20 gm protein,

Green Pepper Meat Loaf
Meat Loaf Shepherd's Pie
Meat Loaf Burritos

10 gm fat, 1 gm fiber. **Diabetic Exchanges:** 3 lean meat, 1 vegetable.

Meat Loaf Burritos

(Pictured above)

Ready in 15 minutes or less

I deliciously disguise leftover meat loaf in these hearty burritos. They get plenty of flavor from tasty toppings.
—Lori Thompson, New London, Texas

 Uses less fat, sugar or salt. Includes Nutritional Analysis and Diabetic Exchanges.

    1 tablespoon butter *or* margarine
    1 can (15 ounces) pinto beans, rinsed and
      drained
    2 cups crumbled cooked meat loaf (3 slices)
    6 flour tortillas (7 inches), warmed
Shredded cheddar cheese, shredded lettuce,
    chopped tomatoes and salsa, optional

Melt butter in a skillet; add half of the beans and mash with a fork. Stir in meat loaf and remaining beans; heat through. Spoon about 1/2 cup meat loaf mixture onto each tortilla. Top with cheese if desired. Fold up bottom and sides over filling. Serve with lettuce, tomatoes and salsa if desired. **Yield:** 6 burritos. **Nutritional Analysis:** One burrito (prepared with fat-free flour tortillas and reduced-fat margarine; calculated without toppings)

equals 251 calories, 691 mg sodium, 31 mg cholesterol, 37 gm carbohydrate, 13 gm protein, 5 gm fat, 4 gm fiber. **Diabetic Exchanges:** 2-1/2 starch, 1 meat.

Meat Loaf Shepherd's Pie

(Pictured above)

Ready in 1 hour or less

This meal-in-one is quick and easy to make, plus it tastes so much better than plain warmed-up meat loaf.
—Jennifer Haines, Redford, Michigan

    5 slices cooked meat loaf
    1 jar (12 ounces) beef gravy
    1 can (15-1/4 ounces) whole kernel corn,
      drained
    4 cups warm mashed potatoes (prepared with
      milk and butter)
  3/4 cup shredded cheddar cheese, *divided*
  1/2 cup sour cream
  1/4 cup sliced green onions

Place meat loaf slices in a greased 2-1/2-qt. baking dish. Cover with gravy; top with corn. Combine potatoes, 1/2 cup cheese, sour cream and onions; spread over corn. Bake, uncovered, at 375° for 25-30 minutes or until heated through. Sprinkle with remaining cheese. Bake 2 minutes longer or until the cheese is melted. **Yield:** 4-6 servings.

Potato Egg Supper
Scotch Eggs
Spinach Deviled Eggs

Hard-Cooked Eggs

Unpeeled hard-cooked eggs will stay fresh in the refrigerator for up to one week.

12 eggs
Water

Place eggs in a single layer in a large saucepan; add enough cold water to cover by 1 in. Cover and quickly bring to a boil. Remove from the heat. Let stand for 15 minutes for large eggs (18 minutes for extra-large eggs and about 12 minutes for medium eggs). Rinse in cold water and place eggs in ice water until completely cooled. **Yield:** 12 servings.

Spinach Deviled Eggs

(Pictured above)

Ready in 15 minutes or less

Spinach adds unexpected color and flavor to this tasty variation on deviled eggs. They're easy to make with leftover hard cooked eggs. —Dorothy Sander, Evansville, Indiana

  12 hard-cooked eggs
1/4 cup mayonnaise
  2 tablespoons vinegar
  2 tablespoons butter *or* margarine, softened
  1 tablespoon sugar

1/2 teaspoon pepper
1/4 teaspoon salt
1/2 cup frozen chopped spinach, thawed and squeezed dry
  4 bacon strips, cooked and crumbled

Slice eggs in half lengthwise; remove yolks and set whites aside. In a small bowl, mash yolks with a fork. Stir in the mayonnaise, vinegar, butter, sugar, pepper and salt. Add spinach and mix well. Stir in the bacon; spoon into egg whites. Serve immediately. **Yield:** 2 dozen.

Scotch Eggs

(Pictured above)

Ready in 1 hour or less

A crispy pork-sausage coating livens up these hard-cooked eggs.   —Dorothy Smith El Dorado, Arkansas

  1 pound bulk pork sausage
Salt and pepper to taste
  6 hard-cooked eggs
  1 egg, lightly beaten
3/4 cup crushed cornflakes

Divide the sausage into six portions; flatten and sprinkle with salt and pepper. Shape each portion around a peeled hard-cooked egg. Roll in beaten egg, then in cornflake crumbs. Place on a rack in a baking pan. Bake, uncovered, at 400° for 30 minutes or until meat is no longer pink, turning every 10 minutes. **Yield:** 6 servings.

Potato Egg Supper

(Pictured at left)

Ready in 1 hour or less

I serve this convenient all-in-one casserole with a green salad or pickled beets. I've taken it to church suppers many times. —Rosemary Flexman, Waukesha, Wisconsin

    4 cups diced cooked peeled potatoes
    8 bacon strips, cooked and crumbled
    4 hard-cooked eggs, sliced
    1 can (10-3/4 ounces) condensed cream of
        mushroom soup, undiluted
  1/2 cup milk
    1 small onion, chopped
    1 tablespoon chopped green pepper
    1 tablespoon chopped sweet red pepper
    1 cup (4 ounces) shredded cheddar cheese

Place half of the potatoes in a greased 2-qt. baking dish. Top with bacon, eggs and remaining potatoes. In a saucepan, combine the soup, milk, onion and peppers. Cook over medium heat until heated through. Pour over the potatoes. Cover and bake at 350° for 20 minutes. Uncover; sprinkle with cheese. Bake 10-15 minutes longer or until heated through. **Yield:** 4 servings.

South Shore Pork Roast

I surround this moist pork roast with a pretty combination of carrots and onion. It feeds a family of four with plenty left over for dishes later in the week. And since the creamy gravy is served on the side, the leftover pork is easy to use. —Pat Botine, Storm Lake, Iowa

    1 boneless pork loin roast (3 to 3-1/2 pounds)
  1/4 cup butter *or* margarine
    1 cup chopped onion
    1 cup diced carrots
    1 teaspoon paprika
  3/4 cup chicken broth
    2 tablespoons all-purpose flour
  1/2 cup sour cream
    1 tablespoon minced fresh parsley
  1/2 teaspoon salt

In a large skillet over medium heat, brown roast in butter for 5 minutes on each side. Transfer to a roasting pan. In the same skillet, saute onion and carrots until crisp-tender. Place around roast. Sprinkle with paprika. Add broth to pan. Cover and bake at 350° for 1-1/2 hours. Uncover; bake 50 minutes longer or until a meat thermometer reads 160°-170°. Remove roast and vegetables to a serving platter; keep warm. Pour pan drippings into a measuring cup; skim fat. Add water to measure 2-2/3 cups. In a saucepan, combine flour and sour cream until smooth. Add drippings, parsley and salt. Bring to a boil; cook and stir for 2 minutes or until thickened. Serve with the roast. **Yield:** 10-12 servings (3-1/3 cups gravy).

Pork Chow Mein

Ready in 30 minutes or less

This crunchy combination is quick to fix and a great way to use up leftover pork roast. I've substituted leftover turkey for the pork with equally pleasing results. —Deborah Stark Cavalier, North Dakota

  2/3 cup uncooked instant rice
    2 tablespoons butter *or* margarine
  1/2 teaspoon salt
    1 large onion, chopped
    2 celery ribs, sliced
    1 medium green pepper, chopped
    1 teaspoon chicken bouillon granules
1-1/2 cups boiling water
    1 cup cubed cooked pork roast
    1 tablespoon cornstarch
    1 tablespoon cold water
    1 tablespoon soy sauce
Chow mein noodles

In a skillet, saute rice in butter and salt until golden. Add the onion, celery and green pepper; cook until crisp-tender. Dissolve bouillon in boiling water; add to the rice mixture. Add pork; bring to a boil. Reduce heat; cover and cook for 5 minutes or until the rice is tender. Combine cornstarch, cold water and soy sauce until smooth; add to the skillet. Bring to a boil; cook and stir for 2 minutes or until thickened. Serve over chow mein noodles. **Yield:** 3 servings.

Roast Pork Soup

Ready in 15 minutes or less

This satisfying soup has a rich full-bodied broth brimming with tender chunks of pork, potatoes and navy beans. —Sue Gulledge, Springville, Alabama

 Uses less fat, sugar or salt. Includes Nutritional Analysis and Diabetic Exchanges.

    3 cups cubed cooked pork roast
    2 medium potatoes, peeled and chopped
    1 large onion, chopped
    1 can (15 ounces) navy beans, rinsed and
        drained
    1 can (14-1/2 ounces) Italian diced tomatoes,
        undrained
    4 cups water
  1/2 cup unsweetened apple juice
  1/2 teaspoon salt, optional
  1/2 teaspoon pepper
Minced fresh basil

In a soup kettle or Dutch oven, combine the first nine ingredients. Bring to a boil. Reduce heat; cover and simmer for 45 minutes or until vegetables are crisp-tender. Sprinkle with basil. **Yield:** 9 servings. **Nutritional Analysis:** One 1-cup serving (prepared with no-salt-added tomatoes and without salt) equals 192 calories, 236 mg sodium, 29 mg cholesterol, 22 gm carbohydrate, 16 gm protein, 5 gm fat, 4 gm fiber. **Diabetic Exchanges:** 1 starch, 1 meat, 1 vegetable.

Yeast Pancakes

(Pictured below and on page 94)

Ready in 1 hour or less

These tender, golden pancakes are a little thicker than traditional versions, so they make a substantial breakfast. The leftovers can be used in the unique recipes that follow.
—Dorothy Smith, El Dorado, Arkansas

    4 cups all-purpose flour
    2 packages (1/4 ounce *each*) quick-rise yeast
    2 teaspoons sugar
    2 teaspoons salt
    3 cups warm milk (120° to 130°)
    2 eggs, beaten
    1/4 cup butter *or* margarine, melted

In a mixing bowl, combine the flour, yeast, sugar and salt. Add milk, eggs and butter; beat for 2 minutes. Cover and let rise in a warm place until doubled, about 30 minutes. Pour batter by 1/2 cupfuls onto a lightly greased hot griddle; turn when bubbles form and start to burst on top of pancakes. Cook until second side is golden brown. **Yield:** about 1 dozen.

Spinach Pancake Quesadillas

(Pictured below and on page 95)

Ready in 15 minutes or less

I give a savory twist to pancakes with this fancy treatment. Leftover pancakes, folded over a delicious spinach filling, become a special lunch or side dish for dinner when garnished with sour cream and tomatoes. *—Anna Free*
Loudonville, Ohio

    1 package (10 ounces) fresh spinach
    3 tablespoons water
    1 package (3 ounces) cream cheese, softened
    1/8 teaspoon ground nutmeg
    4 large pancakes
    1/4 cup shredded Swiss cheese
    1/4 cup shredded mozzarella cheese
Sour cream and chopped tomato, optional

In a saucepan, bring spinach and water to a boil. Reduce heat; cover and cook for 3-4 minutes or until spinach is wilted. Drain well and chop. In a mixing bowl, beat cream cheese and nutmeg. Stir in the spinach. Spread over pancakes; sprinkle with cheeses. Place each on a microwave-safe plate. Microwave, uncovered, on high for 1 to 1-1/2 minutes or until cheese is melted. Fold in half; top with sour cream and tomato if desired. **Yield:** 4 servings. **Editor's Note:** This recipe was tested in an 850-watt microwave.

Fruit Pancake Roll-Ups

(Pictured below and on page 94)

Ready in 15 minutes or less

Sweetened sour cream and fruit pie filling add flavor and richness to these pretty rolled pancakes. They're tasty for brunch...or dessert.
—Wendy Moylan
Crystal Lake, Illinois

    1/4 cup sour cream

Yeast Pancakes
Spinach Pancake Quesadillas
Fruit Pancake Roll-Ups

1/2 teaspoon confectioners' sugar
4 large pancakes, warmed
1/2 cup strawberry *or* raspberry pie filling
Fresh fruit and additional pie filling, optional

In a bowl, combine the sour cream and sugar. Spread over warm pancakes; top with pie filling. Roll up jelly-roll style. Garnish with fruit and additional pie filling if desired. **Yield:** 4 servings.

Pointers for Perfect Pancakes

To make pancakes that are nicely shaped and properly cooked, follow these suggestions:

1 For perfectly shaped pancakes, use a 1/4- or 1/2- cup measure and slowly pour batter onto the preheated griddle. Be sure to leave several inches between pancakes to allow for spreading.

2 Allow pancakes to cook until bubbles form on top and some have burst. Turn and cook until the bottom of the pancake is browned, about 1 minute.

Brats with Onions

Ready in 1 hour or less

After years of eating plain old brats, I came up with this great-tasting version slathered in onions. Your family can enjoy juicy bratwurst for dinner with plenty left over for meals later in the week. —*Gunnard Stark*
Englewood, Florida

3 cans (12 ounces *each*) beer *or* 4-1/2 cups water
3 large onions, thinly sliced and separated into rings
6 garlic cloves, minced
1 tablespoon hot pepper sauce
2 to 3 teaspoons celery salt
2 to 3 teaspoons pepper
1 teaspoon chili powder
15 fresh bratwurst links (3-1/2 to 4 pounds)
5 hot dog buns *or* brat buns, split

In a large saucepan or Dutch oven, combine the first seven ingredients. Bring to a boil. Add bratwurst. Reduce heat; simmer, uncovered, for 20-25 minutes or until bratwurst is firm and cooked. Drain, reserving onions. Refrigerate or freeze 10 bratwurst. Broil or grill remaining bratwurst for 4-5 minutes or until browned, turning once. Serve on buns with reserved onions. **Yield:** 5 servings.

Bratwurst Stew

Ready in 1 hour or less

Using leftover brats hurries along the preparation of this satisfying stew. When time is short, this flavorful combination is so good and so easy. I usually have all the ingredients handy. —*Deborah Elliott*
Ridge Spring, South Carolina

2 cans (14-1/2 ounces *each*) chicken broth
4 medium carrots, cut into 3/4-inch chunks
2 celery ribs, cut into 3/4-inch chunks
1 medium onion, chopped
1/2 to 1 teaspoon dried thyme
1/2 teaspoon dried basil
1/2 teaspoon salt
1/4 to 1/2 teaspoon garlic powder
3 cups chopped cabbage
2 cans (15-1/2 ounces *each*) great northern beans, rinsed and drained
5 fully cooked bratwurst links, cut into 3/4-inch slices

In a large saucepan, combine the first eight ingredients. Bring to a boil. Reduce heat; cover and simmer for 15 minutes. Add the cabbage; cover and cook for 10 minutes. Stir in beans and bratwurst; heat through. **Yield:** 8-10 servings.

Brat 'n' Kraut Supper

Ready in 1 hour or less

Brown sugar and sauerkraut provide the sweet and sour flavor in this super skillet meal. The family-pleasing fare is chock-full of hearty bratwurst slices and potato chunks. —*Emily Chaney, Penobscot, Maine*

2 large onions, cut into 1/4-inch slices
3 tablespoons butter *or* margarine
3 medium potatoes, peeled and cubed
1 can (14 ounces) sauerkraut, rinsed and drained
2 cups white wine *or* chicken broth
2 tablespoons brown sugar
2 tablespoons cider *or* red wine vinegar
3 tablespoons Dijon mustard
2 teaspoons caraway seeds
1 bay leaf
Pepper to taste
5 fully cooked bratwurst links, cut into 1/2-inch slices

In a large skillet, saute onions in butter until tender. Add the potatoes, sauerkraut, wine or broth, brown sugar, vinegar, mustard, caraway seeds, bay leaf and pepper. Cover and simmer for 35-40 minutes or until potatoes are tender. Stir in the bratwurst; heat through. Discard bay leaf. **Yield:** 4-6 servings.

Baked Barbecued Broilers

You'll need just six ingredients for the simple sauce that coats these tender chickens. The recipe makes enough for a hearty supper yet leaves plenty for other meals.
—Mary Ellen Wix, Harrington, Delaware

   2 broiler/fryer chickens (3-1/2 to 4 pounds
      each)
   1 can (15 ounces) tomato sauce
1/2 cup finely chopped green pepper
1/4 cup cider *or* red wine vinegar
   1 tablespoon molasses
   1 tablespoon Worcestershire sauce
1/2 teaspoon salt

Place chickens, breast side up, in a large shallow roasting pan. Combine the remaining ingredients; pour over chickens. Bake, uncovered, at 350° for 1 hour. Cover and bake 20-30 minutes longer or until a meat thermometer reads 180° and juices run clear. Let stand for 10 minutes before cutting. **Yield:** 6-8 servings.

Chicken Tortellini Soup

Ready in 30 minutes or less

Whenever I make this soup for my husband, he enjoys it so much he never leaves room for anything else! When you're pressed for time, it's a breeze to make with leftover chicken, refrigerated tortellini and canned tomatoes.
—Laurie Vincent, Erie, Pennsylvania

7-3/4 cups chicken broth
   1 can (14-1/2 ounces) stewed tomatoes, cut up
   1 package (10 ounces) frozen chopped
      spinach, thawed
1/4 cup grated Parmesan cheese
1/2 teaspoon salt
1/4 teaspoon pepper
   1 package (9 ounces) refrigerated cheese
      tortellini
2-1/2 cups cubed cooked chicken

In a Dutch oven or soup kettle, combine the broth, tomatoes, spinach, Parmesan cheese, salt and pepper. Cook for 10 minutes; add the tortellini and chicken. Cook for 5 minutes or until tortellini is heated through. **Yield:** 12 servings (3 quarts).

Crispy Chicken Wontons

Ready in 1 hour or less

Served with a choice of sauces, these crunchy appetizers are a big hit at parties. They're so popular that my family has even requested them as a main dish for dinner.
—Connie Blesse, Auberry, California

   3 cups finely chopped cooked chicken
1/2 cup shredded carrot
1/4 cup finely chopped water chestnuts
   2 teaspoons cornstarch
   1 tablespoon water
   1 tablespoon soy sauce

1/2 to 1 teaspoon ground ginger
   1 package (16 ounces) wonton wrappers*
   2 tablespoons butter *or* margarine, melted
   1 tablespoon vegetable oil
Plum *or* sweet-sour sauce

In a bowl, combine chicken, carrot and water chestnuts. In another bowl, combine cornstarch, water, soy sauce and ginger until smooth. Add to chicken mixture; toss to coat. Spoon 1 teaspoon of filling in the center of each wonton wrapper. Moisten edges with water. Bring opposite points together; pinch to seal. Place on greased baking sheets. Combine butter and oil; brush over wontons. Bake at 375° for 10-12 minutes or until golden brown. Serve with plum or sweet-sour sauce. **Yield:** about 4 dozen. ***Editor's Note:** Fill wonton wrappers a few at a time, keeping the others covered until ready to use.

Grilled Corn and Peppers

(Pictured at right)

Plan ahead…needs to marinate

Every Fourth of July, we invite friends to our houseboat for a cookout. We always have corn on the cob prepared this way, and everyone loves it. The onions and peppers add fantastic flavor to the sweet ears of corn.
—Cindy Williams, Fort Myers, Florida

✓ Uses less fat, sugar or salt. Includes Nutritional Analysis and Diabetic Exchanges.

   3 cups Italian salad dressing
   8 large ears fresh corn, husked and cleaned
   4 medium green peppers, julienned
   4 medium sweet red peppers, julienned
   2 medium red onions, sliced and separated
      into rings

Place salad dressing in a large resealable plastic bag or shallow glass container. Add corn, peppers and onions; turn to coat. Seal or cover and refrigerate for 30 minutes. Drain and discard marinade. Place vegetables in a grill pan or disposable foil pan with holes punched in the bottom. Grill, covered, over medium heat for 25 minutes or until corn is tender, turning frequently. **Yield:** 8 servings. **Nutritional Analysis:** One serving (prepared with fat-free Italian dressing) equals 145 calories, 452 mg sodium, 0 cholesterol, 33 gm carbohydrate, 4 gm protein, 1 gm fat, 5 gm fiber. **Diabetic Exchanges:** 1-1/2 starch, 1 vegetable.

Cactus Corn Muffins

(Pictured at right)

Ready in 1 hour or less

I adapted a recipe from a Texas cafe to come up with these moist, spicy corn bread muffins. They're wonderful alone or with butter. —*Marion Lowery, Medford, Oregon*

1/2 cup butter *or* margarine, softened
1/2 cup sugar

5 eggs
1 cup buttermilk
1 can (4 ounces) chopped green chilies, drained
1-1/4 cups cornmeal
1 cup all-purpose flour
2 teaspoons baking powder
1/2 teaspoon salt
1 cup whole kernel corn*
1 cup (4 ounces) shredded cheddar cheese
1 cup (4 ounces) shredded Monterey Jack cheese

In a mixing bowl, cream butter and sugar. Add eggs, one at a time, beating well after each addition. Beat in buttermilk and chilies; mix well. Combine the dry ingredients; gradually add to creamed mixture. Fold in corn and cheeses. Fill well-greased cactus-shaped or regular muffin cups with about 1/3 cup batter. Bake at 375° for 20-25 minutes or until a toothpick comes out clean. Cool for 5 minutes before removing from pans to wire racks. **Yield:** about 1-1/2 dozen. ***Editor's Note:** Leftover corn from Grilled Corn and Peppers (on previous page) may be used in this recipe. One ear of corn equals about 1/2 cup kernels.

Corn with a Kick

(Pictured below)

Ready in 30 minutes or less

This zesty summer side dish is great with canned, frozen or leftover corn. Tomato and green pepper add bright color and taste. —Nancy McDonald, Burns, Wyoming

1/4 cup chopped onion
1/4 cup chopped green pepper
1 tablespoon butter *or* margarine
2 cups whole kernel corn*
1/2 medium tomato, diced
1 teaspoon salt
1/8 teaspoon pepper
Cayenne pepper to taste

In a large saucepan, saute onion and green pepper in butter until tender. Stir in corn, tomato, salt, pepper and cayenne. Reduce heat; cover and cook for 5-10 minutes or until heated through, stirring occasionally. **Yield:** 4 servings. ***Editor's Note:** Leftover corn from Grilled Corn and Peppers (on previous page) may be used in this recipe. One ear of corn equals about 1/2 cup kernels.

Grilled Corn and Peppers
Corn with a Kick
Cactus Corn Muffins

Garden-Fresh Spaghetti
Sausage Broccoli Manicotti
Parmesan Chicken

Garden-Fresh Spaghetti

(Pictured above)

This thick pasta sauce with fresh-from-the-garden flavor is chock-full of peppers, mushrooms, carrots and onion. It makes a big batch, so you'll have plenty to serve over spaghetti with leftovers for other meals. —Sue Yaeger
Boone, Iowa

4 cups sliced fresh mushrooms
3 medium carrots, coarsely chopped
1 cup chopped celery
1 cup chopped onion
1/2 cup chopped green pepper
1/2 cup chopped sweet red pepper
4 garlic cloves, minced
1/4 cup vegetable oil
2 cans (28 ounces *each*) crushed tomatoes
2 cans (15 ounces *each*) tomato sauce
1 can (12 ounces) tomato paste
1 cup beef broth
2 teaspoons dried basil
2 teaspoons dried oregano
1-1/2 teaspoons brown sugar
1 teaspoon salt
1/2 teaspoon pepper
1 cup grated Parmesan cheese
Hot cooked spaghetti

In a Dutch oven, saute the mushrooms, carrots, celery, onion, peppers and garlic in oil until tender. Add the next 10 ingredients. Bring to a boil. Reduce heat; cover and simmer for 1 hour. Serve over spaghetti. **Yield:** 15 cups sauce.

Sausage Broccoli Manicotti

(Pictured above)

Even kids will eat their broccoli when it's served this way. I dress up spaghetti sauce with Italian sausage and garlic, then drizzle it over shells stuffed with broccoli and cheese. —Jason Jost, Manitowoc, Wisconsin

1 package (8 ounces) manicotti shells
2 cups (16 ounces) small-curd cottage cheese
1 package (10 ounces) frozen chopped broccoli, thawed and well drained
1-1/2 cups (6 ounces) shredded mozzarella cheese, *divided*
3/4 cup shredded Parmesan cheese, *divided*
1 egg
2 teaspoons minced fresh parsley
1/2 teaspoon onion powder
1/2 teaspoon pepper
1/8 teaspoon garlic powder
1 pound bulk Italian sausage
4 cups meatless spaghetti sauce
2 garlic cloves, minced

Cook manicotti shells according to package directions. Meanwhile, in a large bowl, combine the cottage cheese, broccoli, 1 cup mozzarella cheese, 1/4 cup Parmesan cheese, egg, parsley, onion powder, pepper and garlic powder. Set aside. In a skillet, cook the sausage over medium heat until no longer pink; drain. Add spaghetti sauce and garlic. Spread 1 cup meat sauce in a greased 13-in. x 9-in. x 2-in. baking dish. Rinse and drain shells; stuff with broccoli mixture. Arrange over sauce. Top with remaining sauce. Sprinkle with remaining mozzarella and Parmesan. Bake, uncovered, at 350° for 40-50 minutes or until heated through. **Yield:** 6-8 servings.

Parmesan Chicken

(Pictured at left)

Ready in 30 minutes or less

I like to make this yummy recipe when I have extra spaghetti sauce on hand. The herbed coating on the tender chicken gets nice and golden. —Margie Eddy
Ann Arbor, Michigan

```
  1/2 cup seasoned bread crumbs
  1/2 cup grated Parmesan cheese, divided
1-1/2 teaspoons dried oregano, divided
  1/2 teaspoon dried basil
  1/2 teaspoon salt
  1/4 teaspoon pepper
    1 egg
    1 tablespoon water
    4 boneless skinless chicken breast halves
    2 tablespoons butter or margarine
    2 cups meatless spaghetti sauce
  1/2 teaspoon garlic salt
    1 cup (4 ounces) shredded mozzarella cheese
Hot cooked fettuccine or pasta of your choice
```

In a bowl, combine the bread crumbs, 1/4 cup Parmesan cheese, 1 teaspoon oregano, basil, salt and pepper. In a bowl, combine the egg and water. Dip chicken in egg mixture, then coat with crumb mixture. In a skillet, cook chicken in butter on both sides until juices run clear. Meanwhile, combine the spaghetti sauce, garlic salt and remaining oregano in a saucepan; heat through. Spoon over chicken; sprinkle with mozzarella and remaining Parmesan. Serve with pasta. **Yield:** 4 servings.

Spiced Applesauce

Ready in 1 hour or less

We have an apple-picking party every year. It's a bushel of fun, and I look forward to cooking a batch of this easy applesauce seasoned with cinnamon, cloves and allspice. —Marian Platt, Sequim, Washington

✓ Uses less fat, sugar or salt. Includes Nutritional Analysis and Diabetic Exchanges.

```
16 medium tart apples, peeled and sliced
 1 cup apple juice
 1 teaspoon ground cinnamon
```

1/2 teaspoon ground cloves
1/2 teaspoon ground allspice

Place all ingredients in a Dutch oven. Cover and cook over medium-low heat for 30-40 minutes or until apples are tender. Remove from the heat; mash apples to desired consistency. Serve warm or cold. Store in the refrigerator. **Yield:** 8 cups. **Nutritional Analysis:** One serving (1 cup) equals 162 calories, 1 mg sodium, 0 cholesterol, 42 gm carbohydrate, trace protein, trace fat, 5 gm fiber. **Diabetic Exchange:** 3 fruit.

Applesauce Bread

I make this applesauce loaf with plump raisins and crunchy nuts. My kids love a slice of this moist bread in their lunch box or as a snack after school. —Tracey Jo Schley, Sherburn, Minnesota

```
  1/2 cup butter or margarine, softened
    1 cup sugar
    1 egg
1-1/4 cups applesauce
1-1/2 cups all-purpose flour
1-1/2 teaspoons baking soda
    1 teaspoon ground cinnamon
  3/4 teaspoon ground nutmeg
  1/2 teaspoon salt
  1/4 teaspoon ground cloves
  1/2 cup raisins
  1/2 cup chopped walnuts
```

In a mixing bowl, cream butter and sugar. Add the egg and applesauce; mix well. Combine flour, baking soda, cinnamon, nutmeg, salt and cloves; gradually add to the creamed mixture just until combined. Fold in raisins and nuts. Pour into a greased 8-in. x 4-in. x 2-in. loaf pan. Bake at 350° for 50-55 minutes or until a toothpick inserted near the center comes out clean. Cool for 10 minutes before removing from pan to a wire rack. **Yield:** 1 loaf.

Saucy Apple Pork Chops

Ready in 1 hour or less

My mother gave me the recipe for these juicy pork chops oven-baked in a slightly sweet sauce. This effortless entree is a snap to prepare using leftover applesauce. —Amy Church, Camby, Indiana

```
  2 cups applesauce
1/3 cup sugar
  2 tablespoons soy sauce
  1 garlic clove, minced
1/4 teaspoon ground ginger
  6 boneless pork loin chops (1/2 inch thick)
  2 tablespoons butter or margarine
```

In a bowl, combine the applesauce, sugar, soy sauce, garlic and ginger; mix well. Pour into a greased 13-in. x 9-in. x 2-in. baking dish. In a skillet, brown pork chops in butter; place over applesauce mixture. Bake, uncovered, at 325° for 30 minutes or until meat is tender. **Yield:** 6 servings.

Sweet Potato Wedges

Quartered sweet potatoes bake in a mildly spiced butter sauce in this recipe. Leftovers can be made into either of the following second-day dishes with excellent results.
—Donna Howard, Stoughton, Wisconsin

3 pounds sweet potatoes, peeled and
   quartered lengthwise (about 10 cups)
6 tablespoons butter *or* margarine, melted
6 tablespoons orange juice
3/4 teaspoon salt
3/4 teaspoon ground cinnamon

Arrange sweet potatoes in a greased 13-in. x 9-in. x 2-in. baking dish. Combine the butter, orange juice, salt and cinnamon; drizzle over sweet potatoes. Cover and bake at 350° for 55-60 minutes or until tender. **Yield:** 10 servings (8 cups).

Sweet Potato Apple Bake

Ready in 1 hour or less

A caramel-like sauce made with apricot nectar sets this casserole apart from ordinary sweet potato dishes. It's great for the holidays or anytime.
—Gail Glende Woodland, California

4 cups cooked sweet potato wedges
1 medium tart apple, peeled and thinly sliced
1/2 cup packed brown sugar
2-1/4 teaspoons cornstarch
1/8 teaspoon salt
1/2 cup apricot nectar
1/4 cup water
1 teaspoon grated orange peel
1 tablespoon butter *or* margarine
1/4 cup chopped pecans, optional

Arrange sweet potatoes and apple slices in a greased 11-in. x 7-in. x 2-in. baking pan. In a saucepan, combine brown sugar, cornstarch and salt. Stir in the apricot nectar, water and orange peel until blended; add butter. Bring to a boil; cook and stir for 2 minutes or until thickened. Stir in pecans if desired. Pour over sweet potato mixture. Cover and bake at 375° for 35 minutes or until apples are tender. **Yield:** 6 servings.

Sweet Potato Pie

I've been preparing this glazed pecan-topped pie for so long that I can't recall when I came across the combination of ingredients my family likes best.
—Anita Ammerman Albemarle, North Carolina

1-1/2 cups sugar
2 tablespoons all-purpose flour
1 can (5 ounces) evaporated milk
1 egg, lightly beaten
1 teaspoon vanilla extract
2 cups mashed cooked sweet potatoes (about
   3 potatoes)

1 unbaked pastry shell (9 inches)
GLAZE:
1/2 cup sugar
2-1/4 teaspoons all-purpose flour
2 tablespoons butter *or* margarine, melted
2 tablespoons evaporated milk
1/4 cup pecan halves

In a bowl, combine sugar, flour, milk, egg and vanilla. Stir in the sweet potatoes. Pour into pastry shell. For glaze, combine the sugar, flour, butter and milk; drizzle over sweet potato mixture. Garnish with pecans. Cover edges of pastry loosely with foil. Bake at 375° for 45 minutes. Remove foil; bake 15 minutes longer or until crust is golden brown and a knife inserted near the center comes out clean. **Yield:** 6-8 servings.

Apricot-Glazed Ham

(Pictured at right)

Glaze a bone-in ham with apricot jam to give it an attractive look and delicious flavor. It's the star of a special Sunday supper and yields lots of extra ham for made-in-minutes meals later in the week.
—Galelah Dowell Fairland, Oklahoma

1/2 fully cooked bone-in ham (6 to 8 pounds)
1/2 cup packed brown sugar
2 to 3 tablespoons ground mustard
Whole cloves
1/2 cup apricot preserves

Score the surface of the ham, making shallow diagonal diamond shapes 1/2 in. deep. Combine brown sugar and mustard; rub over surface of ham. Insert a clove in the center of each diamond. Place ham on a rack in a shallow roasting pan. Bake, uncovered, at 325° for 1 hour. Spoon preserves over ham. Bake 15-30 minutes longer or until a meat thermometer reads 140° and ham is heated through. **Yield:** 20-24 servings.

Scalloped Potatoes with Ham

(Pictured above right)

Ready in 30 minutes or less

This saucy skillet dish takes so little time to prepare. The recipe won first prize in our local paper some years back.
—Emma Magielda, Amsterdam, New York

4 medium potatoes, peeled *and* thinly sliced
2 tablespoons butter *or* margarine
1/3 cup water
1/2 cup milk
2 to 3 tablespoons dry onion soup mix
3 tablespoons minced fresh parsley
1 cup cubed process American cheese
1 cup cubed fully cooked ham

In a large skillet, cook potatoes in butter until potatoes are evenly coated. Add water; bring to a boil. Reduce heat; cover and simmer for 14 minutes or until potatoes are tender. In a bowl, combine the milk, soup mix

Apricot-Glazed Ham
Scalloped Potatoes with Ham
Ham and Bean Chili

and parsley; stir in cheese. Pour over potatoes. Add ham; cook and stir gently until cheese is melted and sauce is smooth. Serve immediately. **Yield:** 4 servings.

Ham and Bean Chili

(Pictured above)

Ready in 1 hour or less

Leftover ham gets an unusual treatment in this creative chili blend that features three kinds of convenient canned beans. Serve it in bowls over rice or corn bread and garnish it with cheese. —Carol Forcum, Marion, Illinois

- 2 cups cubed fully cooked ham
- 1 medium onion, chopped
- 1 medium green pepper, chopped
- 1 garlic clove, minced
- 1 tablespoon olive *or* vegetable oil
- 1 can (28 ounces) diced tomatoes, undrained
- 1 can (16 ounces) kidney beans, rinsed and drained
- 1 can (15 ounces) black beans, rinsed and drained
- 1 can (15 ounces) pinto beans, rinsed and drained
- 1 jar (8 ounces) picante sauce
- 1 can (8 ounces) tomato sauce
- 1/2 cup water, optional
- 1 can (2-1/4 ounces) sliced ripe olives, drained
- 1 teaspoon beef bouillon granules
- 1 teaspoon dried thyme
- 1 teaspoon salt
- 1/4 teaspoon pepper
- Shredded cheddar cheese

In a large saucepan, cook the ham, onion, green pepper and garlic in oil until tender. Stir in tomatoes, beans, picante sauce, tomato sauce and water if desired. Bring to a boil. Stir in olives, bouillon, thyme, salt and pepper. Reduce heat; simmer, uncovered, for 15-20 minutes. Garnish with cheese. **Yield:** 10 servings (about 2-1/2 quarts).

Sweet Selections

When choosing sweet potatoes, pick small- to medium-size ones that have smooth skins and no soft spots. (Larger ones may be fibrous.) If you're not going to cook them right away, keep them in a cool dry place instead of the fridge. They'll be fine for up to a week.

Chapter 8

IT'S EASY to keep your cool in the kitchen—and offer your family a home-cooked meal—even on the most hurried and hectic days. To give hunger the cold shoulder, all it takes is a little advance planning.

By setting aside a bit of time on your more leisurely days, you can prepare mouthwatering main courses, side dishes, desserts and more, then simply pop them into the freezer.

So at the end of those days when you don't have the energy to do more than switch on the stove, just turn to your well-stocked freezer for a fast-to-fix meal in a snap!

COOL RECIPES. Top to bottom: Mint Chocolate Chip Pie and Ice Cream Sandwich Dessert (both recipes on p. 118).

No-Crust Tropical Pie

As a mother of two, a part-time student and a full-time employee, I appreciate freezer dishes that don't take away from family time in the evening. These creamy coconut wedges are a frequent request in my home.
—Kim Ridgeway, Okeechobee, Florida

1 package (8 ounces) cream cheese, softened
1/3 cup sugar
1/2 teaspoon rum extract
1 can (8 ounces) crushed pineapple, undrained
2-1/3 cups flaked coconut, *divided*
1 carton (8 ounces) frozen whipped topping, thawed, *divided*

In a mixing bowl, beat cream cheese, sugar and extract. Fold in pineapple, 2 cups coconut and 2 cups whipped topping. Pour into an ungreased 9-in. pie plate. Top with remaining whipped topping. Toast remaining coconut and sprinkle over the top. Cover and freeze for at least 3 hours before cutting. May be frozen up to 3 months. **Yield:** 6-8 servings.

Make-Ahead Squash Soup

I make a big batch of this soup when I have an abundance of zucchini from the garden. In winter, I just heat and serve it to be reminded of summer's goodness. It's also a nice treat to take to a shut-in or sick friend.
—Suzanne McKinley, Lyons, Georgia

SOUP BASE:
3 pounds zucchini, sliced
2 cups water
1 can (14-1/2 ounces) beef broth
1 cup chopped onion
1-1/2 teaspoons salt
1/8 teaspoon garlic powder
ADDITIONAL INGREDIENTS (for each batch):
1 cup half-and-half cream
Grated Parmesan cheese and crumbled cooked bacon, optional

Combine soup base ingredients in a large kettle or Dutch oven; bring to a boil. Reduce heat; simmer for 20 min-

Freezing Single Portions

To freeze individual servings of uncooked meat or chicken, place the food on waxed paper-lined baking sheets, making sure pieces are not touching one another. Freeze the items, uncovered, until firm.

Wrap frozen pieces in freezer paper or heavy-duty foil or transfer to freezer bags, removing as much air as possible. Label each package and include the date. Properly packaged, most meats can be stored in the freezer for up to 3 months.

utes or until the zucchini is tender. Cool slightly. Puree in batches in a blender or food processor; cool. Place 2 cups each into freezer containers. May be frozen for up to 3 months. **Yield:** 4 batches (8 cups total). **To prepare soup:** Thaw soup base in the refrigerator. Transfer to a saucepan. Add cream; cook and stir over medium heat until heated through. Garnish with Parmesan cheese and bacon if desired. **Yield:** 3 servings per batch.

Triple-Batch Beef

Because I work full-time, I like to cook ahead and freeze meals so things aren't so hectic when I get home. I keep portions of this economical meat mixture in heavy-duty resealable plastic bags in the freezer. After a busy day, it's easy to fix one of the three variations I've included here.
—Heidee Manrose, Burns, Wyoming

1 boneless chuck roast (4 to 5 pounds), cut into 3/4-inch cubes
2 medium onions, chopped
4 garlic cloves, minced
2 tablespoons vegetable oil
1-1/2 cups water
1 teaspoon salt
1/2 teaspoon pepper

In a Dutch oven, cook beef, onions and garlic in oil until beef is brown; drain. Stir in water, salt and pepper. Bring to a boil. Reduce heat; cover and simmer for 1-3/4 to 2 hours or until meat is tender. Cool. Divide beef and cooking liquid between three freezer containers; cover and freeze. May be frozen for up to 3 months. **Yield:** 3 batches.

Chunky Chili
(Pictured at right)

My meat mixture is the starting point for a hearty chili that cooks up in a jiffy. Choose different salsa if you like your chili milder or hotter. This is a nice alternative to chili made with ground beef.
—Heidee Manrose

1 portion Triple-Batch Beef,* thawed
1 jar (11 ounces) salsa
1/4 cup water
1 to 2 teaspoons chili powder
1 can (16 ounces) kidney beans, rinsed and drained

In a saucepan, combine beef, salsa, water and chili powder. Bring to a boil. Reduce heat; cover and simmer for 10 minutes. Stir in kidney beans; heat through. **Yield:** 3-4 servings. ***Editor's Note:** 2 cups of cubed cooked beef and 1/2 cup beef broth may be substituted.

Herbed Beef Barley Soup
(Pictured above right)

Thyme comes through in this colorful soup that's chock-full of tender beef. You can use any combination of vegetables you have on hand. Leftovers work especially well.
—Heidee Manrose

Herbed Beef Barley Soup
Thick Beef Stew
Chunky Chili

1 portion Triple-Batch Beef,* thawed
3 cups water
1 cup frozen cut green beans
1 cup frozen sliced carrots
1/4 cup quick-cooking barley
1 tablespoon beef bouillon granules
1 teaspoon dried thyme
1/2 teaspoon salt

In a large saucepan, combine all ingredients. Bring to a boil. Reduce heat; cover and simmer for 10-14 minutes or until vegetables and barley are tender. Let stand for 5 minutes before serving. **Yield:** 4 servings. ***Editor's Note:** 2 cups of cubed cooked beef and 1/2 cup beef broth may be substituted.

Thick Beef Stew

(Pictured above)

For a real meat-and-potatoes meal, this comforting stew is sure to satisfy the heartiest of appetites. Unlike other stew recipes, this one simmers for just a few minutes because it calls for a batch of my cooked beef mixture.
—*Heidee Manrose*

1 portion Triple-Batch Beef,* thawed
3 medium red potatoes, quartered and cut into 1/4-inch slices
1-1/4 cups water
1 to 1-1/2 teaspoons dried oregano
1 teaspoon salt
1 cup frozen peas
1 tablespoon cornstarch
2 tablespoons lemon juice

In a saucepan, combine the beef, potatoes, water, oregano and salt. Bring to a boil. Reduce heat; cover and simmer for 10-15 minutes or until potatoes are tender. Add peas; heat through. Combine cornstarch and lemon juice until smooth; gradually add to beef mixture. Bring to a boil; cook and stir for 2 minutes or until thickened and bubbly. **Yield:** 3 servings. ***Editor's Note:** 2 cups of cubed cooked beef and 1/2 cup beef broth may be substituted.

Giant Ice Cream Sandwich
Peppery Pizza Loaves

Peppery Pizza Loaves

(Pictured above)

I often take these French bread pizzas to church picnics or potluck suppers and there is never any left. When I fix them for the two of us for lunch, a snack or dinner, I freeze two halves in foil to enjoy later.
—Lou Stasny
Poplarville, Mississippi

1-1/2 pounds ground beef
1/2 teaspoon garlic powder
1/2 teaspoon salt
2 loaves (8 ounces *each*) French bread, halved lengthwise
1 jar (8 ounces) process cheese sauce
1 can (4 ounces) mushroom stems and pieces, drained
1 cup chopped green onions
1 can (4 ounces) sliced jalapenos, drained
1 can (8 ounces) tomato sauce
1/2 cup grated Parmesan cheese
4 cups (16 ounces) shredded mozzarella cheese

In a skillet, cook beef over medium heat until no longer pink; drain. Stir in garlic powder and salt. Place each bread half on a large piece of heavy-duty foil. Spread with cheese sauce. Top with beef mixture, mushrooms, onions and jalapenos. Drizzle with tomato sauce. Top with Parmesan and mozzarella cheeses. Wrap and freeze. May be frozen for up to 3 months. **To bake:** Unwrap loaves and thaw on baking sheets in the refrigerator. Bake at 350° for 18 minutes or until cheese is melted. **Yield:** 4 loaves (2-3 servings each).

Giant Ice Cream Sandwich

(Pictured at left)

I was an inexperienced cook when I married. A good friend, who was a cooking inspiration to me, shared many of her recipes, including this scrumptious dessert. It's handy to pull out of the freezer for unexpected guests.
—Charlene Turnbull, Wainwright, Alberta

2 packages brownie mix (8-inch-square pan size)
1 cup (6 ounces) semisweet chocolate chips
4 cups vanilla ice cream, softened
1/2 cup English toffee bits *or* almond brickle chips
CHOCOLATE SAUCE:
1/3 cup evaporated milk
1/4 cup butter (no substitutes)
1/3 cup semisweet chocolate chips
2 cups confectioners' sugar
1/2 teaspoon vanilla extract

Prepare the brownie mixes according to package directions, adding chocolate chips to batter. Pour into two greased 9-in. springform pans or two 9-in. round cake pans. Bake at 350° for 25-30 minutes or until a toothpick inserted near the center comes out clean. Cool for 10 minutes before removing from pans to wire racks to cool completely. Freeze for 2 hours or until easy to handle. Spoon ice cream on top of one brownie layer; top with toffee bits and second brownie layer. Wrap in plastic wrap; freeze until set. May be frozen for up to 2 months. Remove from freezer 10-15 minutes before serving. For chocolate sauce, combine milk, butter and chocolate chips in a saucepan. Heat until chips are melted; stir until smooth. Stir in confectioners' sugar and vanilla. Cut the ice cream sandwich into wedges; serve with chocolate sauce. **Yield:** 10-12 servings.

Ice Cream Dessert

Three easy ingredients you likely have on hand form the rich crumb coating on these fun frozen squares. My sister-in-law gave me this recipe, and it's one of my family's favorite desserts. —Rosemary White
Oneida, New York

1 cup packed brown sugar
1/2 cup butter *or* margarine
1-3/4 cups graham cracker crumbs (about 22 squares)
1/2 gallon vanilla ice cream *or* flavor of your choice, softened

In a saucepan, combine brown sugar and butter; cook and stir until sugar is melted. Remove from the heat; stir in cracker crumbs. Place half of crumb mixture in a greased 11-in. x 7-in. x 2-in. dish. Carefully spread ice cream over crumbs (pan will be full). Sprinkle with remaining crumbs; gently press down. Cover and freeze until firm. Remove from the freezer 10 minutes before cutting. May be frozen for up to 2 months. **Yield:** 8-10 servings.

Fuss-Free Future Meals

- To simplify preparation of stir-fries, I cook two or three meals worth of diced chicken, pork or beef in store-bought stir-fry sauce. I freeze the cooked meat and sauce in meal-sized portions. Then when I want to serve a stir-fry, it's a snap to remove the meat from the freezer, toss it in a skillet with fresh vegetables and reheat it. —*Amanda Smith Cincinnati, Ohio*

- During grilling weather, I always make extra of whatever we're having, whether it be chicken, burgers or sausage. I freeze the extras in dinner-size portions to be reheated in the microwave. Then when I'm rushed at dinnertime, our family can still enjoy that "just off the grill" flavor, even in winter. —*Diana Duda, Glenwood, Illinois*

- When I have time, I do the prep work for this speedy yet special side dish. I cut 6-8 baked potatoes in half, scoop out the insides and mash them with butter, milk, cheese and a bit of green onion. Then I stuff the mixture back into the potato skins and freeze them on baking sheets. The individually frozen potatoes transfer easily to freezer bags until I'm ready to use them. They're a snap to serve. A dash of paprika or parsley on top is all that's needed after heating them in the oven or microwave. —*Dee Kirk Toledo, Ohio*

Corn Bread Turkey Casserole

Folks who love turkey and stuffing will appreciate the flavor and convenience of this casserole. The recipe makes three pans, so you can enjoy one for dinner and freeze the other two for future meals. —Michelle Flynn
Philadelphia, Pennsylvania

3 packages (6 ounces *each*) crushed corn bread stuffing mix
10 to 11 cups cubed cooked turkey *or* chicken
2 cups (8 ounces) shredded cheddar cheese
2 cans (10-3/4 ounces *each*) condensed cream of celery soup, undiluted
2 cans (10-3/4 ounces *each*) condensed cream of chicken soup, undiluted
1 can (10-3/4 ounces) condensed cream of mushroom soup, undiluted
1 can (12 ounces) evaporated milk
1-1/2 cups (6 ounces) shredded Swiss cheese

Prepare stuffing mix according to package directions. Add turkey and cheddar cheese. Combine the soups and milk. Pour 1 cup each into three greased 13-in. x 9-in. x 2-in. baking dishes. Top each with turkey mixture and remaining soup mixture. Sprinkle with Swiss cheese. Cover and freeze two casseroles for up to 3 months. Cover and bake the remaining casserole at 350° for 30-35 minutes or until bubbly. Let stand for 5-10 minutes before serving. **To use frozen casseroles:** Thaw in the refrigerator. Bake, uncovered, at 350° for 35-40 minutes or until bubbly. Let stand for 5-10 minutes before serving. **Yield:** 3 casseroles (8-10 servings each).

Big-Batch Beef Sauce

I prepare this beef mixture on weekends when I have a little more time. Having it in the freezer is a real time-saver during the week and a great way to serve unexpected guests. I use the versatile sauce to get a head start on casseroles, stews and the swift suppers I share here.
—Debbie Hodge, Kitscoty, Alberta

4 pounds ground beef
4 medium onions, chopped
5 celery ribs, thinly sliced
4 garlic cloves, minced
3 cans (28 ounces *each*) diced tomatoes, undrained
2 cans (6 ounces *each*) tomato paste
2 jars (4-1/2 ounces *each*) sliced mushrooms, drained, optional
1/4 cup minced fresh parsley
1 tablespoon salt
2 teaspoons dried oregano
2 teaspoons dried basil
1 teaspoon pepper
1/2 teaspoon crushed red pepper flakes

In a Dutch oven over medium heat, cook beef, onions, celery and garlic until meat is no longer pink and vegetables are tender; drain. Stir in the remaining ingredients. Bring to a boil; reduce heat. Simmer, uncovered, for 1 to 1-1/2 hours, stirring occasionally. Cool. Transfer to freezer bags or containers, about 2 cups in each. May be frozen for up to 3 months. **Yield:** about 15 cups total.

Weekday Chili

It's so convenient to pull a batch of the meat mixture out of the freezer to make this hearty soup. Chili powder and red pepper flakes are the easy seasonings that give it zesty flavor. *—Debbie Hodge*

2 cups Big-Batch Beef Sauce
1 can (16 ounces) kidney beans, rinsed and drained
1 can (8 ounces) tomato sauce
1 to 2 tablespoons chili powder
1/4 teaspoon crushed red pepper flakes
Shredded cheddar cheese

In a saucepan, combine the beef sauce, beans, tomato sauce, chili powder and red pepper flakes. Bring to a boil; reduce heat. Cover and simmer until heated through. Garnish servings with cheese. **Yield:** 2-3 servings.

Speedy Spaghetti

(Pictured at far right)

On a busy weekday, you can rely on my premade meat sauce to put an Italian spaghetti dinner on the table in mere minutes. It's nicely seasoned and has plenty of meat and mushrooms. Just add a tossed salad and fresh bread to round out the meal. *—Debbie Hodge*

2 cups Big-Batch Beef Sauce
1 can (8 ounces) tomato sauce
1 jar (4-1/2 ounces) sliced mushrooms, drained
2 teaspoons Italian seasoning
Hot cooked spaghetti

In a saucepan, combine the beef sauce, tomato sauce, mushrooms and Italian seasoning. Bring to a boil; reduce heat. Simmer, uncovered, for 5 minutes. Serve over spaghetti. **Yield:** 2-3 servings.

Organizing Your Freezer

- Here's an easy way to seal bags of frozen food. Starting about 1 inch from the top of the bag, create a strip partway across the top, cutting through both layers of plastic and stopping in the middle. Pour out the amount of food you need. To close the bag, tie together the 1-inch strip and the cut corner. One tight knot will hold the food in and the air out, and it's much easier than hunting for a twist tie.
—Barbara Jones, Moweaqua, Illinois
- One of the handiest tools in my kitchen is a roll of masking tape. When putting leftovers into the refrigerator or freezer, I tear off some tape, write the name of the food and the date, then place the tape on the lid of the storage container. This makes it easy see at a glance what's in the fridge or freezer and how fresh it is. We waste less food this way.
—Barb Leaman, Hornell, New York
- To organize my freezer, I sort chicken, beef, pork and vegetables into separate labeled boxes. That way I know at a glance if I have the ingredients I need for a recipe on hand. After grocery shopping, it's simple to put the fresh items on the bottom of the box and move the older ones to the top.
—Darlene White, Hobson, Montana
- Buy inexpensive multicolored plastic baskets and use different colors to store a variety of meats and vegetables. The baskets stack nicely and you can see at a glance what you have on hand. *—Kathie Morris Redmond, Oregon*

Time-Saving Tacos

(Pictured at right)

An envelope of taco seasoning gives Mexican flair to the meat mixture in this tasty taco dinner. It has such a different flavor from the other variations that your family will never realize it's made from the same sauce.
—Debbie Hodge

2 cups Big-Batch Beef Sauce
1 envelope taco seasoning
1/4 cup water
6 to 8 taco shells *or* flour tortillas
Toppings: shredded lettuce, chopped tomatoes, sliced ripe olives, shredded cheddar cheese, chopped onions, sour cream, salsa

In a saucepan, combine beef sauce, taco seasoning and water. Bring to a boil; reduce heat. Simmer, uncovered, until heated through. Spoon about 1/4 cup meat mixture into each taco shell or tortilla. Serve with toppings of your choice. **Yield:** 3-4 servings.

Oven-Ready Lasagna

(Pictured below)

When company drops in, I use the sauce to assemble this cheesy lasagna. No-cook noodles further speed preparation of this easy entree. —Debbie Hodge

- 2 cups Big-Batch Beef Sauce
- 1 can (6 ounces) tomato paste
- 2 teaspoons dried basil
- 2 cups (16 ounces) small-curd cottage cheese
- 1 egg
- 6 no-cook lasagna noodles
- 4 cups (16 ounces) shredded mozzarella cheese
- 1/3 cup shredded Parmesan cheese

In a saucepan, combine beef sauce, tomato paste and basil. Bring to a boil; reduce heat. Cover and simmer for 5 minutes. Combine cottage cheese and egg; mix well. Spoon a third of the meat sauce into a greased 13-in. x 9-in. x 2-in. baking dish. Layer with three noodles, half of the cottage cheese mixture and a third of the mozzarella cheese. Repeat layers. Top with remaining meat sauce and mozzarella. Cover and bake at 350° for 30 minutes. Uncover; sprinkle with Parmesan cheese. Bake 5-10 minutes longer or until bubbly and the cheese is melted. Let stand 10 minutes before serving. **Yield:** 9-12 servings. **Editor's Note:** Cooked lasagna noodles may be substituted for no-cook lasagna noodles.

**Oven-Ready Lasagna
Speedy Spaghetti
Time-Saving Tacos**

Crescent Chicken Bundles

When I was expecting our third child, this was one of the meals I put in the freezer ahead of time. We now have four kids and they all like these rich chicken pockets. I've also made them with ham or smoked turkey. —Jo Groth, Plainfield, Iowa

- 2 packages (3 ounces *each*) cream cheese, softened
- 4 tablespoons butter *or* margarine, melted, *divided*
- 2 tablespoons minced chives
- 2 tablespoons milk
- 1/2 teaspoon salt
- 1/4 teaspoon pepper
- 4 cups cubed cooked chicken
- 2 tubes (8 ounces *each*) refrigerated crescent rolls
- 1 cup crushed seasoned stuffing croutons

In a mixing bowl, beat cream cheese, 2 tablespoons butter, chives, milk, salt and pepper until smooth. Stir in the chicken. Unroll crescent roll dough and separate into eight rectangles; press perforations together. Spoon about 1/2 cup chicken mixture onto the center of each rectangle. Bring edges up to the center and pinch to seal. Brush with remaining butter. Sprinkle with crushed croutons, lightly pressing down. Transfer to two ungreased baking sheets. Cover one baking sheet and freeze until firm; transfer squares to a covered container. May be frozen for up to 2 months. Bake remaining squares at 350° for 20-25 minutes or until golden brown. **To use frozen squares:** Thaw in the refrigerator and bake as directed. **Yield:** 8 servings.

Freezer Frosting

(Pictured at right)

It's handy to have this sweet creamy frosting in the freezer when you need to decorate a cake or cupcakes. Just thaw in the fridge and spread. It's easy to tint with food coloring for a special look. —Evelyn Comeau Virden, Manitoba

- 1/3 cup shortening
- 4-1/2 cups confectioners' sugar, *divided*
- 1-1/2 teaspoons vanilla extract
- 1/4 teaspoon salt
- 3/4 to 1 cup whipping cream

In a mixing bowl, cream shortening, 1 cup of sugar, vanilla and salt. Add the remaining sugar alternately with cream. Beat until the frosting reaches desired consistency. Cover and freeze for up to 2 months. Thaw before using. **Yield:** about 3 cups (enough to frost 24 cupcakes or a two-layer, tube, 13- x 9-inch or 15- x 10-inch cake).

Strawberry-Topped Yogurt Pie

(Pictured at right)

This tangy make-ahead pie has been one of our family's favorite desserts for more than 15 years. You can top it with most any fruit. —Nancy Gordon Kansas City, Missouri

☑ Uses less fat, sugar or salt. Includes Nutritional Analysis and Diabetic Exchanges.

- 1 package (8 ounces) cream cheese, softened
- 2/3 cup plain yogurt
- 1/3 cup nonfat dry milk powder
- 1/3 cup honey
- 1 graham cracker crust (8 inches)
- 2 cups diced fresh strawberries

Orange peel strips, optional

In a mixing bowl, beat cream cheese, yogurt, milk powder and honey. Spoon into crust. Cover and freeze for up to 1 month. Remove from the freezer 30 minutes before serving. Top with strawberries. Garnish with orange peel if desired. **Yield:** 8 servings. **Nutritional Analysis:** One serving (prepared with fat-free cream cheese, nonfat yogurt and a reduced-fat graham cracker crust) equals 194 calories, 272 mg sodium, 3 mg cholesterol, 33 gm carbohydrate, 8 gm protein, 4 gm fat, 1 gm fiber. **Diabetic Exchanges:** 2 starch, 1 fat.

Miscellaneous Freezer Hints

- I like having shredded cheese on hand to add to casseroles or sprinkle on various dishes. So I buy a block of cheese, shred it, spread it in a pan and put it in the freezer. Once frozen, the shredded cheese doesn't stick together and can be stored in heavy-duty plastic bags or freezer containers to use in recipes at any time. —*Cheryl Miller Fort Collins, Colorado*

- Do you often need fresh, crunchy bacon bits for salads and other recipes but hate the mess? I have a method that works great. I store the bacon in the freezer. Before frying it, I cut the frozen slices crosswise into little strips. Then I fry them on medium until crisp, separating the strips during cooking. I drain the bits on paper towels and they're ready for use. No greasy fingers! —*Claire Menges Leonardtown, Maryland*

- If you rely on a lot of recipes that call for fresh parsley, try this trick: Chop extra fresh parsley, put it in ice cube trays and cover with a little water. Once the cubes are frozen, transfer them to a heavy-duty resealable bag. Then you can toss one or two (or the amount of parsley you need) into soups, stews, casseroles, etc. It's so handy and tastes just like fresh. You'll never buy dried parsley flakes again! —*O.O. Kepler, Prospect, Ohio*

- I live in Florida and often have extra limes during the growing season. To make sure they don't go to waste, I squeeze the juice into ice cube trays and place them in the freezer. The frozen cubes can be left in the trays or transferred into a plastic bag. When you need a few tablespoons of lime juice for a recipe, just pull out a few cubes and thaw. —*Nancy Dunn, Naples, Florida*

**Freezer Frosting
Strawberry-Topped Yogurt Pie**

Mint Chocolate Chip Pie
Ice Cream Sandwich Dessert

Ice Cream Sandwich Dessert

(Pictured above and on page 108)

No one will believe this awesome dessert is just dressed-up ice cream sandwiches. For my son's birthday party, I decorated it with race cars and checkered flags because he's a big racing fan. —Jody Koerber, Caledonia, Wisconsin

19 ice cream sandwiches
1 carton (12 ounces) frozen whipped topping, thawed
1 jar (11-3/4 ounces) hot fudge ice cream topping
1 cup salted peanuts

Cut one ice cream sandwich in half. Place one whole and one half sandwich along a short side of an ungreased 13-in. x 9-in. x 2-in. pan. Arrange eight sandwiches in opposite direction in the pan. Spread with half of the whipped topping. Spoon fudge topping by teaspoonfuls onto whipped topping. Sprinkle with 1/2 cup peanuts. Repeat layers with remaining ice cream sandwiches, whipped topping and peanuts (pan will be full). Cover and freeze for up to 2 months. Remove from the freezer 20 minutes before serving. Cut into squares. **Yield:** 12-15 servings.

Mint Chocolate Chip Pie

(Pictured above and on page 109)

You'll need only three ingredients to fix this refreshing make-ahead dessert featuring a cool combination of mint and chocolate. When time is short, it's so handy to pull this no-fuss pie out of the freezer for company. —Dolores Scofield, West Shokan, New York

6 to 8 cups mint chocolate chip ice cream, softened
1 chocolate crumb crust (9 inches)
2 squares (1 ounce *each*) semisweet chocolate

Spoon ice cream into crust. In a microwave-safe bowl, melt chocolate; stir until smooth. Drizzle over ice cream. Freeze for 6-8 hours or overnight. Remove from the freezer 15 minutes before serving. Pie may be frozen for up to 2 months. **Yield:** 6-8 servings.

Miniature Meat Pies

These cute little bites of flaky dough are stuffed with an easy-to-season ground beef mixture. They're filling and oh-so-good served with ketchup.
—Gayle Lewis
Yucaipa, California

    1 pound ground beef
  1/2 cup chili sauce
    1 envelope onion soup mix
  1/4 teaspoon salt
DOUGH:
    3 cups all-purpose flour
    1 to 2 tablespoons sesame seeds, optional
1-1/4 teaspoons salt
    1 cup shortening
  3/4 cup shredded cheddar cheese
  3/4 cup evaporated milk
    1 tablespoon cider vinegar

In a skillet over medium heat, cook beef until no longer pink; drain. Stir in chili sauce, soup mix and salt; set aside. In a bowl, combine flour, sesame seeds if desired and salt. Cut in shortening and cheese until crumbly. Combine milk and vinegar; gradually add to flour mixture, tossing with a fork until dough forms a ball. Divide dough in half; roll out to 1/8-in. thickness. Cut with a 2-1/2-in. round cutter. Place half of the circles 2 in. apart on ungreased baking sheets. Top each with about 1-1/2 tablespoons of beef mixture; cover with remaining circles. Moisten edges with water and press with a fork to seal. Cut a slit in the top of each. Bake at 425° for 12-16 minutes or until golden brown. Serve immediately; or cool, wrap and freeze for up to 3 months. **To use frozen meat pies:** Place on an ungreased baking sheet. Bake at 425° for 14-16 minutes or until heated through. **Yield:** about 1-1/2 dozen.

Pearl Onion Mushroom Bake

Assemble this saucy side dish days before you need it. Take one out of the freezer in the morning, and it's ready to be baked for dinner. It's great with turkey or ham.
—Diane Caragio, Livermore, California

   24 pearl onions
    1 cup water
    3 teaspoons salt
    3 cups sliced fresh mushrooms
   10 tablespoons butter *or* margarine, *divided*
    2 teaspoons lemon juice
  1/4 cup all-purpose flour
    2 cups milk
    1 cup (4 ounces) shredded cheddar cheese
  1/2 cup soft bread crumbs

In a small saucepan, combine the onions, water and salt. Cover and cook for 20 minutes or until crisp-tender; drain. Transfer to two greased 1-qt. baking pans; set aside. In a skillet, saute mushrooms in 4 tablespoons butter and lemon juice. In a small saucepan, melt 4 tablespoons butter; stir in flour until smooth. Gradually add milk. Bring to a boil; cook and stir for 2 minutes or until thickened. Stir into mushroom mixture. Pour over onions. Melt the remaining butter. Add cheese and bread crumbs; toss to coat. Sprinkle over each casserole. Cover and freeze one casserole for up to 3 months. Cover and bake the second casserole at 375° for 15 minutes. Uncover; bake 10 minutes longer or until golden brown. **To use frozen casserole:** Thaw in the refrigerator for 8 hours. Bake as directed. **Yield:** 2 casseroles (4 servings each).

Beef Mushroom Spaghetti

This hearty spaghetti casserole calls for just six simple ingredients, so it's made in a flash. I like to garnish it with Parmesan cheese and serve it with a tossed salad and garlic bread.
—Norene Wright
Manilla, Indiana

    1 pound ground beef
    1 medium onion, chopped
    1 can (15 ounces) tomato sauce
    1 can (10-3/4 ounces) condensed cream of mushroom soup, undiluted
  1/4 cup water
    1 package (7 ounces) thin spaghetti, cooked and drained

In a skillet, cook beef and onion over medium heat until the meat is no longer pink; drain. Stir in tomato sauce, soup and water. Add spaghetti; mix well. Place in a greased 8-in. square baking dish. Cover and freeze for up to 3 months. **To bake:** Thaw in the refrigerator. Cover and bake at 350° for 35-40 minutes or until heated through. **Yield:** 4 servings.

Fresh Baked from the Freezer

- I buy big loaves of French bread from the supermarket bakery and keep them in my freezer. When I need a few slices to make garlic bread for supper, I take out the loaf and slice off what I need and put the rest back in the freezer. Because the bread is frozen, it slices cleanly without mashing the rest of the loaf, and the frozen slices take just minutes to thaw. Best of all, I don't have to worry about using up the remaining loaf before it gets stale.
  —Janet Taylor, Osceola, Missouri

- On Saturday mornings, I mix up a big batch of pancakes or waffles. What our family doesn't eat, I freeze in a single layer on a cookie sheet, transfer to a heavy-duty resealable plastic bag and return to the freezer. On weekday mornings, it's a snap to heat up individual servings in the toaster.
  —Jennifer Plummer, Haveloc, North Carolina

- Often I make an extra batch of cookie dough and spoon dollops onto waxed paper. After freezing them solid, I put a dozen in a freezer bag labeled with the cookies' name, baking time and temperature. They stay in the freezer (for up to 4 months) until we're hungry for their fresh-baked flavor. (You'll likely need to bake this frozen cookie dough a little longer.)
  —Maribeth Edwards, Follansbee, West Virginia

Stew Turned into Chili

A big pot of this versatile blend can be enjoyed two ways. As is, it's a satisfying stew brimming with tender chunks of beef, tomato and two kinds of beans. Or add picante sauce and chili powder to create a zippy chili.
—Don Trumbly, Paola, Kansas

> 5 pounds beef stew meat, cut into 3/4-inch cubes
> 5 garlic cloves, minced
> 3 tablespoons vegetable oil
> 4 cans (14-1/2 ounces *each*) diced tomatoes with green pepper and onion, undrained
> 2 teaspoons salt
> 1 teaspoon pepper
> 2 cans (16 ounces *each*) kidney beans, rinsed and drained
> 2 cans (15-1/2 ounces *each*) great northern beans, rinsed and drained
> **ADDITIONAL INGREDIENTS (for each batch of chili):**
> 1 jar (16 ounces) picante sauce
> 1 to 2 teaspoons chili powder
> **Sour cream and chopped green onions, optional**

In a Dutch oven, brown beef and garlic in oil; drain. Add tomatoes, salt and pepper. Bring to a boil. Reduce heat; cover and simmer for 1-1/4 hours. Stir in the beans. Cover and simmer 30-45 minutes longer or until meat is tender. Serve immediately, or cool slightly and freeze in 4-cup portions. May be frozen for up to 3 months. **Yield:** 4 batches of stew (16 cups total). **To prepare chili:** Thaw one batch of stew in the refrigerator. Place in a saucepan; add picante sauce and chili powder. Cook over medium heat until hot and bubbly. Garnish servings with sour cream and green onions if desired. **Yield:** 4 servings per batch.

Frozen Cranberry Salad

This frosty fruit salad is a marvelous make-ahead addition to any menu, especially during the Christmas season. It gets its appealing appearance from cranberries and its fun crunch from chopped walnuts. —Freda Triano
Milwaukie, Oregon

> 1 package (12 ounces) fresh *or* frozen cranberries, thawed
> 1-1/2 cups sugar
> 1 can (20 ounces) crushed pineapple
> 1 package (16 ounces) miniature marshmallows
> 2 cups whipping cream
> 2 tablespoons confectioners' sugar
> 1 teaspoon vanilla extract
> 1 cup chopped walnuts

In a blender or food processor, process cranberries until coarsely ground. Pour into a bowl; add sugar. Cover and chill for 1 hour. Drain pineapple, reserving 1/4 cup of juice (discard remaining juice or save for another use). In a large bowl, combine pineapple, juice and marshmallows. Cover and chill for 1 hour. Add cranberry mixture. In a mixing bowl, beat cream until soft peaks form; beat in sugar and vanilla. Fold into the cranberry-pineapple mixture. Stir in walnuts. Transfer to two greased 8-in. square dishes. Cover and freeze for up to 2 months. Remove from the freezer about 45 minutes before serving. Cut into squares. **Yield:** 2 salads (6-8 servings each).

Cranberry Cream Pie

Busy cooks appreciate the make-ahead convenience of this fast-to-fix frozen pie. If you like cranberries, you'll enjoy the fruity flavor and creamy texture of this no-bake dessert. It's great to get a jump on your holiday cooking!
—Pauline Zunk, Oak Harbor, Ohio

> 1 package (8 ounces) cream cheese, softened
> 1 cup whipping cream
> 1/4 cup sugar
> 1/2 teaspoon vanilla extract
> 1 can (16 ounces) whole-berry cranberry sauce
> 1 graham cracker crust (8 *or* 9 inches)

In a mixing bowl, beat cream cheese until smooth. In another mixing bowl, combine cream, sugar and vanilla; beat until soft peaks form. Beat into the cream cheese until blended. Fold in cranberry sauce. Spoon into crust. Cover and freeze for up to 2 months. Remove from the freezer 15 minutes before slicing. **Yield:** 6-8 servings.

Ham 'n' Cheese Crepes

(Pictured at right)

The beauty of these crepes is that they can be cooked ahead and stored in the freezer until you need them. I thaw a few at a time, roll them with ham and cheese and serve them for breakfast, lunch or a quick snack.
—Marion Lowery, Medford, Oregon

> 2/3 cup cold water
> 2/3 cup plus 4 to 6 tablespoons cold milk, *divided*
> 1 cup all-purpose flour
> 2 eggs
> 1/4 cup butter *or* margarine, melted
> 1/4 teaspoon salt
> **ADDITIONAL INGREDIENTS (for 8 crepes):**
> 1 to 2 tablespoons Dijon mustard
> 8 thin slices deli ham
> 1 cup (4 ounces) shredded cheddar cheese

In a blender, combine the water, 2/3 cup of milk, flour, eggs, butter and salt. Cover and process until smooth. Refrigerate for at least 30 minutes; stir. Add remaining milk if batter is too thick. Heat a lightly greased 8-in. skillet; add about 3 tablespoons batter. Lift and tilt pan to evenly coat bottom. Cook until the top appears dry; turn and cook 15-20 seconds longer. Repeat with remaining batter, greasing skillet as needed. Stack crepes with waxed paper between layers. Cover and freeze for up to 3 months. **Yield:** 16 crepes. **To use frozen crepes:** Thaw 8 crepes in the refrigerator for about 2 hours. Spread each with mustard; top with a slice of ham and sprinkle with cheese. Roll up tightly. Place in a greased 11-in. x 7-in. x 2-in. baking dish. Bake, uncovered, at 375° for 10-14 minutes or until heated through. **Yield:** 4 servings.

Apple Coffee Cake

(Pictured below)

Tart apples and sour cream flavor this moist coffee cake covered with brown sugar and crunchy nuts. The recipe makes two pans. You can serve one and freeze the other.
—Dawn Fagerstrom, Warren, Minnesota

1/2 cup butter-flavored shortening
1 cup sugar
2 eggs
1 teaspoon vanilla extract
2 cups all-purpose flour
1 teaspoon baking powder
1 teaspoon baking soda
1/2 teaspoon salt
1 cup (8 ounces) sour cream
1-3/4 to 2 cups chopped peeled tart apples
TOPPING:
3/4 cup packed brown sugar
1 teaspoon ground cinnamon
2 tablespoons cold butter *or* margarine
1/2 cup chopped walnuts

In a mixing bowl, cream shortening and sugar. Add eggs and vanilla; mix well. Combine flour, baking powder, baking soda and salt; add to the creamed mixture alternately with sour cream. Stir in apples. Transfer to two greased 8-in. square baking dishes. For topping, combine brown sugar and cinnamon. Cut in butter until crumbly. Stir in nuts; sprinkle over batter. Bake at 350° for 30-35 minutes or until a toothpick inserted near the center comes out clean. Cool completely. Cover and freeze for up to 6 months. Thaw overnight in the refrigerator. **Yield:** 2 coffee cakes (6-9 servings each).

Apple Coffee Cake
Ham 'n' Cheese Crepes

Chapter 9

DOES YOUR FAMILY often rush off to work, school or other activities and either go without breakfast altogether or head to the nearest drive-thru?

Steer clear of fasting...and fast food! With this chapter's bounty of ready-in-minutes morning meals, even folks who usually aren't in a hurry to rise and shine will eagerly clamor to the kitchen table—instead of the front door—for a wholesome hearty breakfast.

From fast-to-fix egg dishes, beverages and fruit to easy French toast, pancakes and waffles, you can offer your family a delicious, nutritious start to the day in a matter of minutes.

RISE-'N'-SHINE RECIPES. Top to bottom: Oven Denver Omelet, Sweet Ham Steak and Strawberry French Toast (all recipes on p. 128).

French Toast Casserole

(Pictured at right)

Plan ahead...start the night before

Cinnamon and sugar top this fuss-free fare that tastes like French toast. —Sharyn Adams, Crawfordsville, Indiana

 Uses less fat, sugar or salt. Includes Nutritional Analysis and Diabetic Exchanges.

- 1 loaf (10 ounces) French bread, cut into 1-inch cubes (10 cups)
- 8 eggs
- 3 cups milk
- 4 teaspoons sugar
- 1 teaspoon vanilla extract
- 3/4 teaspoon salt, optional

TOPPING:
- 2 tablespoons butter *or* margarine, cubed
- 3 tablespoons sugar
- 2 teaspoons ground cinnamon

Maple syrup, optional

Place bread cubes in a greased 13-in. x 9-in. x 2-in. baking dish. In a mixing bowl, beat eggs, milk, sugar, vanilla and salt if desired. Pour over bread. Cover and refrigerate for 8 hours or overnight. Remove from the refrigerator 30 minutes before baking. Dot with butter. Combine sugar and cinnamon; sprinkle over the top. Cover and bake at 350° for 45-50 minutes or until a knife inserted near the center comes out clean. Let stand for 5 minutes. Serve with syrup if desired. **Yield:** 12 servings. **Nutritional Analysis:** One serving (prepared with egg substitute equivalent to 8 eggs, skim milk and reduced-fat margarine and without salt and syrup) equals 147 calories, 271 mg sodium, 2 mg cholesterol, 19 gm carbohydrate, 9 gm protein, 3 gm fat, 1 gm fiber. **Diabetic Exchanges:** 1 starch, 1 lean meat.

Tart Grapefruit Cooler

(Pictured at right)

Ready in 15 minutes or less

I pour this pretty pink beverage over ice to make a refreshing breakfast drink. —Connie Cooper
Charleston, Illinois

 Uses less fat, sugar or salt. Includes Nutritional Analysis and Diabetic Exchanges.

- 1-1/2 cups cranberry juice
- 1 cup grapefruit juice
- 1/2 cup sugar
- 1/4 cup lemon juice
- 1 cup club soda, chilled

In a bowl or pitcher, combine cranberry juice, grapefruit juice, sugar and lemon juice. Cover and refrigerate. Just before serving, stir in soda. **Yield:** 4 servings. **Nutritional Analysis:** One serving (prepared with unsweetened cranberry and grapefruit juices and artificial sweetener equivalent to 1/2 cup sugar) equals 57 calories, 16 mg sodium, 0 cholesterol, 14 gm carbohydrate, trace protein, trace fat, trace fiber. **Diabetic Exchange:** 1 fruit.

Cheesy Ham Cups

(Pictured at right)

Ready in 1 hour or less

These individual ham and cheese casseroles are a unique way to serve brunch, and they're easy to make, too. —Barbara Nowakowski, North Tonawanda, New York

- 6 slices deli ham
- 1/2 cup finely chopped green onions
- 2 cups (8 ounces) shredded cheddar cheese, *divided*
- 6 eggs
- 1 carton (8 ounces) plain yogurt
- 2 tablespoons minced fresh parsley

Place each ham slice in a greased 10-oz. ramekin or custard cup. Sprinkle with onions and 1 cup cheese. In a bowl, beat eggs and yogurt until blended; pour into cups. Sprinkle with parsley and the remaining cheese. Bake, uncovered, at 350° for 25-30 minutes or until a knife inserted near the center comes out clean. Serve immediately. **Yield:** 6 servings.

Apple-Banana Oatmeal

Ready in 15 minutes or less

This special oatmeal gets me going in the morning and makes me feel great all day. My husband and son race mountain bikes, so they need foods like this that provide energy. —Linda Hocking, Mackay, Idaho

 Uses less fat, sugar or salt. Includes Nutritional Analysis and Diabetic Exchanges.

- 1 cup water
- 1 tablespoon orange juice concentrate
- 1/2 cup chopped unpeeled tart apple
- 1/4 cup sliced firm banana
- 1/4 cup raisins
- 1/4 teaspoon salt, optional
- 1/8 teaspoon ground cinnamon
- 2/3 cup quick-cooking oats
- 1/4 to 1/3 cup oat bran

Brown sugar, optional

In a saucepan, combine water, orange juice concentrate, apple, banana, raisins, salt if desired and cinnamon; bring to a boil. Stir in oats and oat bran. Cook for 1-2 minutes, stirring occasionally. Sprinkle with brown sugar if desired. **Yield:** 2 servings. **Nutritional Analysis:** One serving (prepared without salt and brown sugar) equals 235 calories, 4 mg sodium, 0 cholesterol, 52 gm carbohydrate, 7 gm protein, 3 gm fat, 7 gm fiber. **Diabetic Exchanges:** 2-1/2 starch, 1 fruit.

Super Spread

I spread peanut butter on waffles and pancakes. Then I top it with maple syrup for a butterscotchy treat. Kids love it, and even I won't eat frozen waffles any other way. —*Monica Hunter, Kansas City, Missouri*

French Toast Casserole
Tart Grapefruit Cooler
Cheesy Ham Cups

Fruit Salad Dressing
Crab Quiche Bake
Sausage Brunch Braid

Fruit Salad Dressing

(Pictured at left)

Plan ahead...needs to chill

I like to top seasonal fruit with this smooth, citrusy dressing. It makes a cool, colorful salad for breakfast, lunch or picnics in the summer. —Frances Poste, Wall, South Dakota

    3 tablespoons all-purpose flour
    2 cans (6 ounces *each*) pineapple juice
    1 can (6 ounces) frozen orange juice
       concentrate, thawed
  1/2 to 1 cup sugar
  1/4 cup honey
  1/4 cup lemon juice
Assorted fresh fruit

In a saucepan, combine the flour, pineapple juice, orange juice concentrate, sugar, honey and lemon juice. Bring to a boil; cook and stir for 2 minutes or until thickened and bubbly. Cool. Serve over fruit. Leftover dressing may be refrigerated for up to 1 week. **Yield: 2 cups.**

Crab Quiche Bake

(Pictured at left)

Ready in 1 hour or less

On a farm, a hearty breakfast is a given. Loaded with cheese, this satisfying crab casserole is an easy-to-assemble addition to a brunch buffet. —Nancy Robaidek Krakow, Wisconsin

    8 eggs, beaten
    2 cups half-and-half cream
    1 large sweet red pepper, chopped
    1 package (8 ounces) imitation crabmeat,
       chopped
    1 cup soft bread crumbs
    1 cup (4 ounces) shredded Swiss cheese
    1 cup (4 ounces) shredded cheddar cheese
  1/2 cup chopped green onions
    1 teaspoon salt
  1/2 teaspoon pepper

In a bowl, combine all ingredients. Transfer to a greased 13-in. x 9-in. x 2-in. baking dish. Bake, uncovered, at 350° for 30-35 minutes or until a knife inserted near the center comes out clean. Let stand 10 minutes before cutting. **Yield: 6-8 servings.**

Sausage Brunch Braid

(Pictured at left)

Ready in 1 hour or less

I created this sausage-stuffed bread when I needed something special to bring to a party. The versatile braid can be served at breakfast or as an appetizer or entree. —Amelia Meaux, Crowley, Louisiana

  12 ounces bulk pork sausage
  1/2 cup chopped onion
  1/4 cup chopped celery

  1/4 cup chopped green pepper
    1 garlic clove, minced
    1 package (3 ounces) cream cheese, cubed
    2 tablespoons chopped green onion tops
    2 tablespoons minced fresh parsley
    1 tube (8 ounces) refrigerated crescent rolls
    1 egg, lightly beaten

In a skillet, cook sausage, onion, celery, green pepper and garlic until meat is no longer pink and vegetables are tender; drain. Add cream cheese, green onion and parsley. Cook and stir over low heat until cheese is melted; set aside. Unroll crescent dough on a greased baking sheet; press perforations together. Roll into a 12-in. x 10-in. rectangle. Spoon sausage mixture to within 3 in. of long sides and 1 in. of ends. On each long side, cut 3/4-in.-wide strips 3 in. into center. Starting at one end, fold alternating strips at an angle, forming a braid. (See how-to photo on page 327.) Brush dough with egg. Bake at 350° for 20-25 minutes or until golden brown. Refrigerate leftovers. **Yield: 8-10 servings.**

Eggs Ahoy

Ready in 15 minutes or less

This dish is not quite eggs Benedict, but it's really good. A can of cream of celery soup substitutes for traditional hollandaise sauce in this quick-and-easy version. —Martha Creech, Kinston, North Carolina

    2 tablespoons chopped green pepper
    2 tablespoons butter *or* margarine, *divided*
    1 can (10-3/4 ounces) condensed cream of
       celery soup, undiluted
  1/4 cup milk
    3 English muffins, split and toasted
  12 bacon strips, cooked
    6 poached eggs

In a saucepan, saute green pepper in 1 tablespoon butter until tender. Add the soup and milk; cook and stir until heated through. Spread remaining butter over muffin halves. Place two bacon strips on each half; top each with a poached egg and the soup mixture. **Yield: 3 servings.**

Perfect Poached Eggs

For best results, follow this method for poaching eggs:

    Fill a saucepan or skillet with 1 to 3 inches of water. Bring liquid to a boil, then reduce heat to a gentle simmer. Crack a cold egg into a custard cup or measuring cup. Holding the cup close to the water, let the egg gently slide into it. Repeat with remaining eggs, one at a time.

    Cook, uncovered, until the egg whites are completely set and the yolks begin to thicken, about 3-5 minutes. Remove eggs with a slotted spoon.

Asparagus Crab Omelets

Ready in 30 minutes or less

These eggs are elegant with crab, asparagus and lemon-colored hollandaise sauce prepared from a convenient mix.
—Dave Eddy, Miles City, Montana

      1 envelope (1-1/4 ounces) hollandaise sauce
      8 eggs
      2 tablespoons milk
Salt, pepper and garlic powder to taste
1-1/2 teaspoons vegetable oil
      2 cups (8 ounces) shredded cheddar cheese, *divided*
      2 cups cut fresh asparagus, cooked, *divided*
      2 cups flaked imitation crabmeat, coarsely chopped, *divided*
Minced chives

Prepare hollandaise sauce according to package directions; set aside and keep warm. In a bowl, beat eggs, milk, salt, pepper and garlic powder. Heat oil in a 10-in. skillet over medium-low; add half of the egg mixture. As the eggs set, lift edges, letting uncooked portion flow underneath. Sprinkle with 1/2 cup cheese, 1 cup asparagus, 1 cup crab and another 1/2 cup cheese. Fold omelet in half. Cover for 1-2 minutes or until the cheese is melted. Repeat for second omelet. Serve with hollandaise sauce. Garnish with chives. **Yield: 2-4 servings.**

Oven Denver Omelet

(Pictured at right and on page 123)

Ready in 1 hour or less

Hearty with hash browns and ham chunks, squares of this flavorful dish are wonderful for a Sunday brunch.
—Pat Clark, Richmond, Indiana

      8 eggs
      1 cup milk
  1/2 teaspoon seasoned salt
      2 cups frozen shredded hash brown potatoes
      1 cup diced fully cooked ham
      1 cup (4 ounces) shredded cheddar cheese
      1 tablespoon dried minced onion

In a large bowl, beat the eggs, milk and seasoned salt. Stir in the remaining ingredients. Pour into a greased 8-in. square baking dish. Bake, uncovered, at 350° for 45-50 minutes or until a knife inserted near the center comes out clean. **Yield: 6-8 servings.**

Sweet Ham Steak

(Pictured at right and on page 122)

Ready in 15 minutes or less

I need just three ingredients to fix this sweetly seasoned ham slice. —Nancy Smits, Markesan, Wisconsin

      1 fully cooked ham steak (2 pounds)
      5 tablespoons butter *or* margarine
      5 tablespoons brown sugar

In a large skillet over medium heat, brown ham steak on both sides; drain. Remove ham. In the same skillet, melt the butter; stir in brown sugar. Return ham to skillet; cook until heated through, turning often. **Yield: 6-8 servings.**

Strawberry French Toast

(Pictured at right and on page 123)

Plan ahead...start the night before

Berries and cream cheese create the creamy middle in these French toast sandwiches. Because you prepare this breakfast bake the night before, it's perfect for overnight guests.
—Karen Sharp, Harvard, Illinois

      2 packages (3 ounces *each*) cream cheese, softened
  3/4 cup sliced fresh strawberries
  1/3 cup confectioners' sugar
      1 loaf (1 pound) French bread, cut into 1-inch slices
    10 eggs
  2/3 cup half-and-half *or* whipping cream
      1 teaspoon vanilla extract
STRAWBERRY SAUCE:
      4 cups sliced fresh strawberries
  1/2 cup sugar
      2 tablespoons water
Maple syrup, optional

In a mixing bowl, beat cream cheese, strawberries and confectioners' sugar until combined. Spread about 2 tablespoons on one side of half the bread slices; top with remaining bread. Place sandwiches in an ungreased 13-in. x 9-in. x 2-in. baking dish. In a bowl, beat the eggs, cream and vanilla. Pour over the bread. Turn each sandwich. Cover and refrigerate for 8 hours or overnight. With a slotted spatula, transfer sandwiches to a greased 15-in. x 10-in. x 1-in. baking pan. Discard any remaining egg mixture. Bake at 375° for 15 minutes; turn and bake 10 minutes longer or until golden brown. Meanwhile, for the sauce, combine the strawberries, sugar and water in a saucepan. Cook over medium heat for 5 minutes, stirring occasionally. Serve French toast with strawberry sauce and maple syrup if desired. **Yield:** 10 servings.

Corny Scrambled Eggs

Ready in 15 minutes or less

Vary the flavor of these eggs by adding 1/4 cup of chopped onion and 3 tablespoons of chopped green pepper.
—Mrs. John Perschke, Michigan City, Indiana

      6 eggs
      1 can (14-3/4 ounces) cream-style corn
  1/2 pound sliced bacon, cooked and crumbled
      2 tablespoons butter *or* margarine

In a bowl, beat eggs. Add corn and bacon. Melt butter in a skillet over medium heat; add egg mixture. Cook and stir until the eggs are completely set. **Yield:** 3 servings.

Oven Denver Omelet
Sweet Ham Steak
Strawberry French Toast

Melon Fruit Bowl
Brunch Scramble
Cornmeal Waffle Sandwiches

Brunch Scramble

(Pictured at left)

Ready in 30 minutes or less

When I have overnight guests, I serve this speedy skillet dish for breakfast. Onion, green pepper and mushrooms add a bounty of flavor they love. —Valerie Putsey
Winamac, Indiana

    1 medium red onion, chopped
    1 medium green pepper, chopped
    1 jar (4-1/2 ounces) sliced mushrooms, drained
    3 tablespoons butter *or* margarine
  12 eggs
  3/4 cup half-and-half cream
1-1/2 teaspoons salt
  1/4 teaspoon pepper
1-1/2 cups (6 ounces) shredded cheddar cheese
    1 tablespoon minced chives

In a skillet, saute the onion, green pepper and mushrooms in butter until crisp-tender. In a mixing bowl, beat the eggs, cream, salt and pepper; add to skillet. Cook over medium heat until eggs are almost set, stirring occasionally. Sprinkle with cheese and chives. Cover and cook until eggs are completely set and cheese is melted. **Yield:** 6 servings.

Cornmeal Waffle Sandwiches

(Pictured at left)

Ready in 30 minutes or less

Craving a BLT for breakfast? Try this deliciously different version that features crisp bacon and fresh tomatoes between two golden cornmeal waffles. Prepare the waffles ahead of time and reheat in the toaster for quick assembly. —Stacy Joura, Stoneboro, Pennsylvania

  3/4 cup all-purpose flour
  3/4 cup cornmeal
    1 tablespoon baking powder
    1 tablespoon sugar
    1 teaspoon salt
    2 eggs, *separated*
    1 cup milk
    3 tablespoons butter *or* margarine, melted
  1/2 cup shredded cheddar cheese
Mayonnaise
  12 bacon strips, cooked and drained
    2 small tomatoes, sliced
Salt and pepper to taste

In a mixing bowl, combine the first five ingredients. In another bowl, beat egg yolks. Add milk and butter; stir into dry ingredients just until moistened. Stir in cheese.

Breakfast Berries

I always keep bulk dried cranberries on hand and sprinkle them over cereal and toss them into the batter when baking muffins and breads. —Beverly Deen
Newcastle, California

In a small mixing bowl, beat egg whites until stiff peaks form; fold into the batter. Bake 12 waffles in a preheated waffle iron according to manufacturer's directions until golden brown. Spread mayonnaise on six waffles; top each with bacon, tomato, salt, pepper and remaining waffles. Serve immediately. **Yield:** 6 servings.

Melon Fruit Bowl

(Pictured at left)

Ready in 15 minutes or less

This medley of strawberries, melon and pineapple gets its rich sweet taste from a creamy banana dressing. Drizzle it over any fresh fruit for an eye-appealing salad that's perfect for breakfast or brunch. —Edie DeSpain, Logan, Utah

✓ Uses less fat, sugar or salt. Includes Nutritional Analysis and Diabetic Exchanges.

    1 medium cantaloupe, cut into chunks
    1 medium honeydew, cut into chunks
    3 cups fresh pineapple chunks
    1 cup halved strawberries
BANANA DRESSING:
    1 medium ripe banana, cut into chunks
  1/2 cup sour cream
    2 tablespoons brown sugar
1-1/2 teaspoons lemon juice

In a large bowl, combine the melon, pineapple and strawberries; set aside. Place the dressing ingredients in a blender; cover and process until smooth. Serve with fruit salad. **Yield:** 12 servings. **Nutritional Analysis:** One serving (prepared with nonfat sour cream) equals 100 calories, 48 mg sodium, trace cholesterol, 24 gm carbohydrate, 2 gm protein, trace fat, 2 gm fiber. **Diabetic Exchange:** 1-1/2 fruit.

Simple Sausage Strata

Ready in 1 hour or less

I start this convenient casserole with a simple bread base. Then I add cheese, eggs and pork sausage to create a satisfying sunrise meal. —Bonnie Coffman
Clarksville, Tennessee

    6 slices bread, crusts removed
    1 pound bulk pork sausage
    1 teaspoon prepared mustard
  3/4 cup shredded Swiss cheese
    3 eggs
1-1/4 cups milk
  2/3 cup half-and-half cream
Pinch pepper

Place bread in a greased 13-in. x 9-in. x 2-in. baking dish; set aside. In a skillet, cook sausage over medium heat until no longer pink; drain. Stir in mustard. Sprinkle sausage and cheese evenly over bread. In a bowl, beat eggs, milk, cream and pepper. Pour over cheese. Bake, uncovered, at 350° for 25-30 minutes or until a knife inserted near the center comes out clean. Cut into squares; serve immediately. **Yield:** 6-8 servings.

Hearty Hotcakes

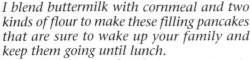

(Pictured at right)

Ready in 30 minutes or less

I blend buttermilk with cornmeal and two kinds of flour to make these filling pancakes that are sure to wake up your family and keep them going until lunch.
—Nancy Horsburgh, Everett, Ontario

✓ Uses less fat, sugar or salt. Includes Nutritional Analysis and Diabetic Exchanges.

1 cup all-purpose flour
1/2 cup whole wheat flour
1/2 cup cornmeal
1/2 cup quick-cooking oats
2 tablespoons sugar
1/2 teaspoon baking powder
1/2 teaspoon baking soda
1/2 teaspoon salt
1 egg
2-1/2 cups buttermilk
3 tablespoons butter *or* margarine, melted
Maple syrup *or* topping of your choice

In a bowl, combine the dry ingredients. In a small bowl, beat egg, buttermilk and butter; stir into dry ingredients just until moistened. Pour batter by 1/4 cupfuls onto a lightly greased hot griddle; turn when bubbles form on top. Cook until second side is golden brown. Serve with syrup or topping of your choice. **Yield:** 16 hotcakes. **Nutritional Analysis:** One hotcake (prepared with 1% buttermilk; calculated without toppings) equals 111 calories, 189 mg sodium, 15 mg cholesterol, 17 gm carbohydrate, 4 gm protein, 3 gm fat, 1 gm fiber. **Diabetic Exchanges:** 1 starch, 1 fat.

Orange Coffee Cake

Ready in 1 hour or less

I like to make this quick breakfast treat because I don't have to lug out my big mixer. The cake's mild orange flavor is complemented by a tasty streusel topping.
—Cheryl Palla, Cannon Falls, Minnesota

2 cups all-purpose flour
1/2 cup sugar
2 teaspoons baking powder
1 teaspoon salt
1 egg
3/4 cup orange juice
1/3 cup vegetable oil
1/4 cup milk
1 tablespoon grated orange peel
STREUSEL TOPPING:
1/4 cup sugar
1/4 cup all-purpose flour
2 tablespoons cold butter *or* margarine

In a bowl, combine the dry ingredients. Combine egg, orange juice, oil, milk and orange peel; add to the dry ingredients just until combined. Pour into a greased 10-in. pie plate. For topping, combine sugar and flour in a bowl; cut in butter until crumbly. Sprinkle over batter. Bake at 350° for 30-35 minutes or until a toothpick inserted near the center comes out clean. **Yield:** 8 servings.

Nutty Fruit Medley

(Pictured at right)

Ready in 15 minutes or less

I coat apples, green grapes, banana and walnuts with a creamy dressing to make this Waldorf-like salad. I experimented with many different versions of this recipe until I got it just right. *—Ruth Glick, Apple Creek, Ohio*

2 large red apples, chopped
1 cup green grapes
1 medium firm banana, sliced
1/2 cup chopped walnuts
1/4 cup mayonnaise
2 tablespoons sour cream
1/2 teaspoon sugar
1/2 teaspoon lemon juice
Pinch salt

In a large bowl, combine the apples, grapes, banana and walnuts. Combine mayonnaise, sour cream, sugar, lemon juice and salt; pour over fruit mixture and toss gently to coat. **Yield:** 6-8 servings.

Hot 'n' Spicy Omelet

(Pictured at right)

Ready in 15 minutes or less

Red pepper flakes add fiery zip to this omelet. It's a favorite at our house—for breakfast, brunch or supper—with sausage or bacon, home fries and hot biscuits.
—Dixie Terry, Marion, Illinois

8 eggs
2 tablespoons water
4 garlic cloves, minced
1/2 teaspoon salt
1/4 teaspoon pepper
1 tablespoon vegetable oil
1 tablespoon butter *or* margarine
1/4 teaspoon crushed red pepper flakes

In a bowl, beat eggs. Add water, garlic, salt and pepper. In a large nonstick skillet over medium heat, heat oil and butter. Add egg mixture; as eggs set, lift edges, letting the uncooked portion flow underneath. When eggs are completely set, remove from the heat. Fold omelet in half and transfer to a warm platter. Sprinkle with red pepper flakes. **Yield:** 4 servings.

Spice Up Your Day

I shake some ground cinnamon on my fresh coffee grounds before I start brewing a pot. The cinnamon gives a hint of flavor and aroma that's so warm and welcome on chilly winter mornings. *—Laura Edick Pulaski, New York*

**Hot 'n' Spicy Omelet
Nutty Fruit Medley
Hearty Hotcakes**

**Frosty Orange Drink
Picante Potato Pie
Bacon 'n' Egg Wraps**

Frosty Orange Drink

(Pictured at left)

Ready in 15 minutes or less

If you're looking for a refreshing drink, I can guarantee that you'll find it in an orange frosty. This wonderful drink tastes delicious and is so easy to make in the blender.
—Karen Radford, Seattle, Washington

✓ Uses less fat, sugar or salt. Includes Nutritional Analysis and Diabetic Exchanges.

   1 cup water
   1 cup milk
  1/2 cup orange breakfast drink mix
  1/2 cup sugar
   1 teaspoon vanilla extract
 10 to 12 ice cubes

Combine all ingredients in a blender; cover and process until smooth. Serve immediately. **Yield:** 4 servings. **Nutritional Analysis:** One serving (prepared with skim milk, sugar-free orange breakfast drink mix and artificial sweetener equivalent to 1/2 cup sugar) equals 77 calories, 46 mg sodium, 1 mg cholesterol, 16 gm carbohydrate, 8 gm protein, trace fat, 1 gm fiber. **Diabetic Exchanges:** 1/2 fruit, 1/2 skim milk.

Picante Potato Pie

(Pictured at left)

Plan ahead...start the night before

This bacon-topped pie is a tasty and convenient addition to a brunch menu. It's great to serve overnight guests because you prepare it the night before and bake it in the morning. —Janet Hill, Sacramento, California

    5 eggs
2-1/2 cups frozen shredded hash brown potatoes
    1 cup (4 ounces) shredded Monterey Jack cheese
  1/2 cup shredded sharp cheddar cheese
  2/3 cup picante sauce
    2 green onions, sliced
  1/4 teaspoon salt
    6 bacon strips, cooked and crumbled
Additional picante sauce, optional

In a bowl, beat eggs. Stir in the hash browns, cheeses, picante sauce, onions and salt. Pour into a greased 9-in. pie plate. Cover and refrigerate overnight. Remove from the refrigerator 30 minutes before baking. Bake at

---

Skillet Savvy

When making pancakes in my electric skillet, I place a plate underneath the skillet to hold the cooked pancakes. The plate is far enough away from the bottom of the skillet to avoid a safety hazard, yet close enough to keep the pancakes warm until I finish using all of the batter. —Amanda Smith, Cincinnati, Ohio

---

350° for 25 minutes. Sprinkle with bacon; bake 5-10 minutes longer or until a knife inserted near the center comes out clean. Serve with additional picante sauce if desired. **Yield:** 6 servings.

Bacon 'n' Egg Wraps

(Pictured at left)

Ready in 30 minutes or less

The zip from salsa will wake up your taste buds when you bite into this hearty handheld meal on-the-go. It makes a quick and very filling breakfast.
—Sharonda Baker, Joliet, Illinois

   1 medium onion, chopped
 3/4 cup chopped green pepper
   1 tablespoon butter *or* margarine
   5 eggs
   1 tablespoon milk
 1/2 teaspoon salt
 1/4 teaspoon pepper
   2 cups (8 ounces) shredded cheddar cheese
 1/2 pound sliced bacon, cooked and crumbled
   4 flour tortillas (10 inches), warmed
Salsa, optional

In a nonstick skillet, saute onion and green pepper in butter until tender. In a bowl, beat the eggs, milk, salt and pepper. Pour over vegetables in the skillet. Sprinkle with cheese and bacon. Cook and stir gently over medium heat until the eggs are completely set. Spoon 1/2 cup down the center of each tortilla; fold sides over filling. Serve with salsa if desired. **Yield:** 4 servings.

Mini Ham Quiches

Ready in 1 hour or less

These cute quiches are easy to fix for an after-church brunch when you don't want to fuss. They're versatile, too. Replace the ham with bacon, sausage, chicken or shrimp...or substitute chopped onion, red pepper or zucchini for the olives.
—Marilou Robinson
Portland, Oregon

 3/4 cup diced fully cooked ham
 1/2 cup shredded sharp cheddar cheese
 1/2 cup chopped ripe olives
   3 eggs, beaten
   1 cup half-and-half cream
 1/4 cup butter *or* margarine, melted
   3 drops hot pepper sauce
 1/2 cup biscuit/baking mix
   2 tablespoons grated Parmesan cheese
 1/2 teaspoon ground mustard

In a bowl, combine the ham, cheddar cheese and olives; divide among 12 greased muffin cups. In a mixing bowl, combine the remaining ingredients just until blended. Pour over ham mixture. Bake at 375° for 20-25 minutes or until a knife inserted near the center comes out clean. Let stand for 5 minutes before serving. **Yield:** 1 dozen.

Chapter 10

THESE DAYS, convenience is the key ingredient for folks who don't have a lot of extra time to spend cooking.

That's what makes all-in-one casseroles so appealing. Just toss the ingredients together and turn on the oven. In no time (often in less than an hour), you'll be dishing out hearty helpings of an enjoyable main course or side dish that will surely please the family.

And for even less fuss, you can rely on this chapter's slew of skillet suppers. Each one requires only minutes to make and calls for a single pan. So cleanup's quick, too!

QUICK COMFORT. Biscuit Pizza Bake (recipe on p. 141).

Catchall Casseroles

WITH a blend of meat, vegetables, pasta, rice and sauces, it's no wonder hot and hearty casseroles top the list of comfort foods.

Chicken Noodle Casserole

(Pictured below)

Ready in 1 hour or less

Friends and family who try this comforting cheesy combination always ask for the recipe. It's so simple to make.
—Kay Pederson, Yellville, Arkansas

- 1 can (10-3/4 ounces) condensed cream of chicken soup, undiluted
- 1/2 cup mayonnaise
- 2 tablespoons lemon juice
- 2 cups cubed cooked chicken
- 1 small onion, chopped
- 1/4 cup chopped green pepper
- 1/4 cup chopped sweet red pepper
- 1 cup (4 ounces) shredded Monterey Jack cheese, *divided*
- 1 cup (4 ounces) shredded sharp cheddar cheese, *divided*
- 12 ounces medium egg noodles, cooked and drained

In a large bowl, combine soup, mayonnaise and lemon juice. Add the chicken, onion, peppers, 1/2 cup of Monterey Jack cheese and 1/2 cup of cheddar cheese; mix well. Add noodles and toss to coat. Transfer to a greased 2-qt. baking dish. Bake, uncovered, at 350° for 30-35 minutes. Sprinkle with remaining cheeses. Bake 10 minutes longer or until vegetables are tender and cheese is melted. **Yield:** 6 servings.

Chicken Noodle Casserole

Beef Potato Casserole

This comforting casserole is a snap to prepare. To give this meat-and-potatoes meal a flavorful change of pace, I sometimes use cream of chicken soup.   —Sandra Jongs
Abbotsford, British Columbia

✓ Uses less fat, sugar or salt. Includes Nutritional Analysis and Diabetic Exchanges.

- 1 pound ground beef
- 1/2 cup chopped onion
- 1/2 cup chopped celery
- 2 tablespoons chopped celery leaves
- 1 can (10-3/4 ounces) condensed cream of mushroom soup, undiluted
- 1/2 cup milk
- 1 teaspoon Worcestershire sauce
- 1/2 teaspoon pepper
- 4 medium potatoes, peeled and thinly sliced
- 1 teaspoon salt, optional

In a skillet, cook beef, onion, celery and celery leaves over medium heat until meat is no longer pink and vegetables are tender; drain. Remove from the heat; stir in soup, milk, Worcestershire sauce and pepper. Place half of the potatoes in a greased 2-qt. baking dish; sprinkle with 1/2 teaspoon salt if desired. Top with half of the beef mixture. Repeat layers. Cover and bake at 400° for 1 hour and 10 minutes or until the potatoes are tender. **Yield:** 4 servings. **Nutritional Analysis:** One serving (prepared with lean ground beef and low-fat soup and without salt) equals 353 calories, 428 mg sodium, 48 mg cholesterol, 32 gm carbohydrate, 28 gm protein, 12 gm fat, 3 gm fiber. **Diabetic Exchanges:** 3 meat, 2 starch.

Beef Stuffing Bake

Ready in 1 hour or less

This quick and easy dish includes two of my children's favorite foods—ground beef and stuffing. It also goes over great at potluck suppers.
—Denise Goedeken
Platte Center, Nebraska

- 1 pound ground beef
- 1 small onion, chopped
- 1 package (10 ounces) beef- *or* pork-flavored stuffing mix
- 1 can (10-3/4 ounces) condensed cream of celery soup, undiluted
- 1 can (10-3/4 ounces) condensed cream of mushroom soup, undiluted
- 1 jar (4-1/2 ounces) sliced mushrooms, drained
- 1 cup water
- 1 cup frozen mixed vegetables

In a skillet, cook beef and onion over medium heat until meat is no longer pink; drain. Transfer to an ungreased 13-in. x 9-in. x 2-in. baking dish. In a bowl, combine contents of stuffing seasoning packet, soups, mushrooms, water and vegetables. Sprinkle stuffing over beef mixture; top with soup mixture. Bake, uncovered, at 350° for 30 minutes or until heated through. **Yield:** 6-8 servings.

Mexican Manicotti

Spinach Surprise

Ready in 1 hour or less

If you're looking for a good way to get kids to eat spinach, try this zippy side dish spiced with picante sauce. My daughter likes it so much she makes it herself. —Sandra Weaver
Fort Gordon, Georgia

    1 medium onion,
      chopped
    2 tablespoons butter *or*
      margarine
    2 tablespoons all-purpose flour
  1/2 teaspoon salt
  3/4 to 1 cup milk
    2 packages (10 ounces *each*)
      frozen chopped spinach,
      thawed
  1/2 cup picante sauce *or*
      salsa
    1 cup (4 ounces) shredded
      cheddar cheese, *divided*

In a saucepan, saute onion in butter until tender. Stir in flour and salt until blended. Slowly stir in milk. Bring to a boil; cook and stir 2 minutes or until thickened and bubbly. Stir in spinach and picante sauce. Stir in 3/4 cup cheese. Transfer to a greased 8-in. square baking dish. Sprinkle with rest of cheese. Bake, uncovered, at 350° for 20-25 minutes or until heated through. **Yield:** 4-6 servings.

Mexican Manicotti

(Pictured above)

Plan ahead...start the night before

My family enjoys this hearty dish with spanish rice, salsa and chips. —Lucy Shifton, Wichita, Kansas

✓ Uses less fat, sugar or salt. Includes Nutritional Analysis and Diabetic Exchanges.

    1 pound lean ground beef
    1 can (16 ounces) refried beans
2-1/2 teaspoons chili powder
1-1/2 teaspoons dried oregano
    1 package (8 ounces) manicotti shells
2-1/2 cups water
    1 jar (16 ounces) picante sauce
    2 cups (16 ounces) sour cream
  1/4 cup sliced green onions
    1 can (2-1/4 ounces) sliced ripe olives, drained,
      optional
    1 cup (4 ounces) shredded Monterey Jack *or*
      Mexican-style cheese

In a bowl, combine the uncooked beef, beans, chili powder and oregano. Spoon into uncooked manicotti shells; arrange in a greased 13-in. x 9-in. x 2-in. baking dish. Combine water and picante sauce; pour over shells. Cover and refrigerate overnight. Remove from the refrigerator 30 minutes before baking. Cover and bake at 350° for 1 hour. Uncover; spoon sour cream over top. Sprinkle with onions, olives if desired and cheese. Bake 5-10 minutes longer or until cheese is melted. **Yield:** 8 servings. **Nutritional Analysis:** One serving (prepared with fat-free refried beans, light sour cream and reduced-fat Monterey Jack cheese and without olives) equals 383 calories, 785 mg sodium, 47 mg cholesterol, 40 gm carbohydrate, 26 gm protein, 13 gm fat, 4 gm fiber. **Diabetic Exchanges:** 3 meat, 2-1/2 starch.

Salmon Macaroni Bake

Ready in 1 hour or less

A neighbor brought our family this creamy casserole the night after our newborn daughter came home from the hospital. It was so good, we couldn't resist heating up the leftovers for breakfast the next morning. It's since become a favorite of the entire family—especially because it's so quick to make. —Carrie Mitchell
Raleigh, North Carolina

    1 package (14 ounces) deluxe macaroni and
      cheese dinner mix
    1 can (10-3/4 ounces) condensed cream of
      mushroom soup, undiluted
  1/2 cup milk
    1 can (6 ounces) skinless boneless salmon,
      drained
    1 tablespoon grated onion *or* 1/2 teaspoon
      onion powder
  1/2 cup shredded cheddar cheese
  1/2 cup dry bread crumbs
    2 tablespoons butter *or* margarine, cubed

Prepare macaroni and cheese according to package directions. Stir in the soup, milk, salmon, onion and cheddar cheese. Transfer to a greased 1-1/2-qt. baking dish. Sprinkle with bread crumbs; dot with butter. Bake, uncovered, at 375° for 30 minutes or until heated through. **Yield:** 4 servings.

Cashew Chicken Casserole

crumbs; sprinkle over casserole. Top with cashews. Bake, uncovered, at 350° for 35-40 minutes or until macaroni is tender. **Yield:** 6 servings.

Chicken Macaroni

Ready in 1 hour or less

I often put together this yummy chicken and pasta combination for my daughter and her family. All she has to do is heat and serve it with a salad.
—*Donna V'Dovec, Veradale, Washington*

 Uses less fat, sugar or salt. Includes Nutritional Analysis and Diabetic Exchanges.

   1 can (10-3/4 ounces) condensed cream
     of mushroom soup, undiluted
   1 can (4 ounces) chopped green chilies
1/2 cup chicken broth
1/2 cup finely chopped onion
1/2 teaspoon pepper
   2 cups cooked elbow macaroni
   1 cup cubed cooked chicken
   1 cup (4 ounces) shredded cheddar
     cheese

In a bowl, combine the first five ingredients. Fold in the macaroni and chicken. Transfer to a greased 1-1/2-qt. baking dish; sprinkle with cheese. Bake, uncovered, at 350° for 30 minutes or until bubbly. **Yield:** 4 servings. **Nutritional Analysis:** One serving (prepared with low-fat mushroom soup, low-sodium broth and reduced-fat cheese) equals 268 calories, 420 mg sodium, 40 mg cholesterol, 31 gm carbohydrate, 19 gm protein, 8 gm fat, 4 gm fiber. **Diabetic Exchanges:** 2 starch, 2 lean meat.

Country-Style Casserole

Even my little sister, who is a picky eater, asks for seconds of this dish. —*Katie Shea, Brigham, Utah*

 Uses less fat, sugar or salt. Includes Nutritional Analysis and Diabetic Exchanges.

   2 cans (10-3/4 ounces *each*) condensed cream
     of chicken soup, undiluted
3/4 cup mayonnaise *or* salad dressing
1/2 cup milk
   3 tablespoons honey
   2 tablespoons Dijon mustard
   4 cups cubed cooked chicken *or* fully cooked
     ham
   1 package (26 ounces) frozen shredded hash
     brown potatoes
   3 cups sliced frozen carrots, optional

In a large bowl, combine the first five ingredients. Stir in chicken, hash browns and carrots if desired. Transfer to a greased 13-in. x 9-in. x 2-in. baking dish. Cover and bake at 350° for 45-50 minutes. Uncover; bake 15-20 minutes longer or until bubbly. **Yield:** 8 servings. **Nutritional Analysis:** One serving (prepared with low-fat cream of chicken soup, light mayonnaise, skim milk

Cashew Chicken Casserole

(Pictured above)

Plan ahead...start the night before

I especially like this dish because I can get it ready the day before I need it. It's easy to whip up with common pantry items. —*Julie Ridlon, Solway, Minnesota*

   2 cups uncooked elbow macaroni
   3 cups cubed cooked chicken
1/2 cup cubed process American cheese
   1 small onion, chopped
1/2 cup chopped celery
1/2 cup chopped green pepper
   1 can (8 ounces) sliced water chestnuts,
     drained
   1 can (10-3/4 ounces) condensed cream of
     mushroom soup, undiluted
   1 can (10-3/4 ounces) condensed cream of
     chicken soup, undiluted
1-1/3 cups milk
   1 can (14-1/2 ounces) chicken broth
1/4 cup butter *or* margarine, melted
2/3 cup crushed saltines (about 20 crackers)
3/4 cup cashew halves

In a greased 13-in. x 9-in. x 2-in. baking dish, layer the first seven ingredients in the order listed. In a bowl, combine the soups, milk and broth. Pour over water chestnuts. Cover and refrigerate overnight. Toss butter and cracker

and chicken and without carrots) equals 252 calories, 390 mg sodium, 51 mg cholesterol, 31 gm carbohydrate, 14 gm protein, 8 gm fat, 1 gm fiber. **Diabetic Exchanges:** 2 starch, 1 meat, 1/2 fat.

Chicken Meal-in-One

As the parents of a young son, my husband and I don't have much time to prepare meals. While our boy is napping, I can assemble this dinner-in-a-dish in just 10 minutes and then pop it in the oven. —Jina Nickel
Lawton, Oklahoma

✓ Uses less fat, sugar or salt. Includes Nutritional Analysis and Diabetic Exchanges.

4-1/2 cups frozen shredded hash brown potatoes
    2 cups frozen cut green beans
    1 cup frozen sliced carrots
    4 bone-in chicken breasts (6 ounces *each*)
    1 can (10-3/4 ounces) condensed cream of chicken *or* mushroom soup, undiluted
    3/4 cup water
    2 tablespoons dry onion soup mix
Salt and pepper to taste

In an ungreased 13-in. x 9-in. x 2-in. baking dish, combine hash browns, beans and carrots. Top with chicken. Combine remaining ingredients; pour over chicken and vegetables. Cover and bake at 375° for 50 minutes. Uncover; bake 25-30 minutes longer or until chicken juices run clear. **Yield:** 4 servings. **Nutritional Analysis:** One serving (prepared with skinless chicken breasts, low-fat reduced-sodium mushroom soup and reduced-sodium onion soup mix and without salt) equals 428 calories, 685 mg sodium, 73 mg cholesterol, 62 gm carbohydrate, 34 gm protein, 5 gm fat, 8 gm fiber. **Diabetic Exchanges:** 3-1/2 starch, 3 very lean meat, 1 vegetable, 1/2 fat.

Salmon Stroganoff

Ready in 1 hour or less

A golden bread crumb topping is the finishing touch on this rich noodle casserole that takes advantage of canned salmon. It's so good that I'm always asked for the recipe. —Joan Sherlock, Belle Plaine, Minnesota

    4 cups cooked wide egg noodles
    1 can (14-3/4 ounces) salmon, drained, bones and skin removed
    1 jar (4-1/2 ounces) sliced mushrooms, drained
    1 jar (2 ounces) diced pimientos, drained
1-1/2 cups small-curd cottage cheese
1-1/2 cups (12 ounces) sour cream
    1/2 cup mayonnaise *or* salad dressing
    3 tablespoons grated onion
    1 garlic clove, minced
1-1/2 teaspoons Worcestershire sauce
    1 teaspoon salt
    1 cup (4 ounces) shredded cheddar cheese
    1/3 cup dry bread crumbs
    2 tablespoons butter *or* margarine, melted

In a bowl, combine the noodles, salmon, mushrooms and pimientos. Combine cottage cheese, sour cream, mayonnaise, onion, garlic, Worcestershire sauce and salt; add to noodle mixture and mix well. Stir in cheddar cheese. Transfer to a greased 2-qt. baking dish. Toss bread crumbs and butter; sprinkle over the casserole. Bake, uncovered, at 350° for 30-35 minutes or until bubbly. **Yield:** 4-6 servings.

Biscuit Pizza Bake

(Pictured below and on page 136)

Ready in 1 hour or less

This recipe provides all the flavor of traditional pizza in a convenient casserole. It's chock-full of ground beef, pepperoni and veggies, so it's perfect for a potluck or to feed the men in the fields. —Emma Hageman, Waucoma, Iowa

    1 pound ground beef
    2 tubes (12 ounces *each*) refrigerated buttermilk biscuits
    1 can (15 ounces) pizza sauce
    1 cup chopped green pepper
    1/2 cup chopped onion
    1 can (4 ounces) mushroom stems and pieces, drained
    1 package (3-1/2 ounces) sliced pepperoni
    1 cup (4 ounces) shredded mozzarella cheese
    1 cup (4 ounces) shredded cheddar cheese

In a skillet, cook beef over medium heat until no longer pink. Meanwhile, quarter the biscuits; place in a greased shallow 3-qt. baking dish. Top with pizza sauce. Drain beef; sprinkle over biscuits and sauce. Layer with green pepper, onion, mushrooms, pepperoni and cheeses. Bake, uncovered, at 350° for 25-30 minutes or until cheese is melted. Let stand for 5-10 minutes before serving. **Yield:** 6-8 servings.

Biscuit Pizza Bake

Rice 'n' Black Bean Bake

Ready in 30 minutes or less

When I come home from work, I start cooking the rice for this meatless casserole right away. The rest is a breeze, because it's just opening cans and mixing. That's my kind of cooking. —Kathy Prado, Fort Worth, Texas

    1 can (15 ounces) black beans, rinsed and drained
    1 can (10 ounces) diced tomatoes and green chilies, undrained
    1 can (8 ounces) tomato sauce
    1 jar (8 ounces) picante sauce
    2 cups cooked rice
    1 cup (8 ounces) sour cream
    2 cups (8 ounces) shredded cheddar cheese, *divided*
Corn *or* tortilla chips

In a bowl, combine the first four ingredients. Stir in the rice, sour cream and 1 cup of cheese. Transfer to a greased 13-in. x 9-in. x 2-in. baking dish. Sprinkle with the remaining cheese. Bake, uncovered, at 350° for 20 minutes or until the cheese is melted. Serve with corn or tortilla chips. **Yield:** 6 main-dish or 8-10 side-dish servings.

Chicken Biscuit Bake

(Pictured below)

Ready in 1 hour or less

Golden biscuits cover this homespun dish filled with chicken, broccoli and cheese. It's then topped with a celery seed mixture. My family requests this all-in-one dinner once a month. —Karen Weirick, Bourbon, Indiana

    1 can (10-3/4 ounces) condensed cream of chicken soup, undiluted
  2/3 cup mayonnaise*
    2 to 3 teaspoons Worcestershire sauce
    4 cups cubed cooked chicken
    3 cups chopped broccoli, cooked
    1 medium onion, chopped
    1 cup (4 ounces) shredded cheddar cheese

Chicken Biscuit Bake

    2 tubes (12 ounces *each*) refrigerated buttermilk biscuits
    2 eggs
  1/2 cup sour cream
    2 teaspoons celery seed
    1 teaspoon salt

In a bowl, combine the soup, mayonnaise and Worcestershire sauce. Stir in chicken, broccoli and onion. Transfer to a greased 13-in. x 9-in. x 2-in. baking dish. Sprinkle with cheese. Cover and bake at 375° for 20 minutes. Separate biscuits; cut each in half. Arrange, cut side down, over hot chicken mixture. In a bowl, combine remaining ingredients; pour over biscuits. Bake, uncovered, 20 minutes longer or until golden brown. **Yield:** 6-8 servings. ***Editor's Note:** Light or fat-free mayonnaise may not be substituted for regular mayonnaise.

Chops with Sauerkraut

Ready in 1 hour or less

Tender pork chops are topped with crumbled bacon, sauerkraut and applesauce in this tasty down-home dish. My family wouldn't eat sauerkraut until they sampled this flavorful bake. —Phyllis Hastie, Salem, Oregon

    6 bone-in pork loin chops (1/2 inch thick, about 2-1/4 pounds)
    1 tablespoon vegetable oil
    1 cup applesauce
    1 jar (16 ounces) sauerkraut, rinsed and drained
  1/4 cup white wine *or* apple juice
    4 bacon strips, cooked and crumbled
  1/2 teaspoon brown sugar
  1/4 teaspoon ground mustard
Pepper to taste

In a skillet, brown the pork chops on both sides in oil. Transfer to a greased 13-in. x 9-in. x 2-in. baking pan. Combine the remaining ingredients; spoon over chops. Bake, uncovered, at 350° for 20-25 minutes or until meat juices run clear. **Yield:** 6 servings.

Beef Veggie Casserole

Ready in 30 minutes or less

This satisfying stew is a breeze to fix because it uses leftover roast beef and refrigerated biscuits. With hearty chunks of potato and plenty of mixed vegetables, it makes a wonderful meal with a loaf of garlic bread. —Patti Keith, Ebensburg, Pennsylvania

    1 envelope mushroom gravy mix
  3/4 cup water
    2 cups cubed cooked beef
    2 cups frozen mixed vegetables, thawed
    2 medium potatoes, peeled, cooked and cubed
    1 tube (12 ounces) refrigerated buttermilk biscuits, separated into 10 biscuits

In a saucepan, combine gravy mix and water until smooth. Bring to a boil; cook and stir for 1 minute or un-

Broccoli Bean Bake

til thickened. Stir in beef, mixed vegetables and potatoes; heat through. Transfer to a greased 8-in. square baking dish. Top with biscuits. Bake at 400° for 12-16 minutes or until biscuits are golden and meat mixture is bubbly. **Yield:** 5 servings.

Broccoli Bean Bake

(Pictured above)

Ready in 1 hour or less

This may sound like an unusual combination, but it's really delicious. It's a great way to get my husband and son to eat broccoli. —*Valerie McInroy, Waterloo, Iowa*

- 6 cups broccoli florets (about 1 large bunch)
- 1 small onion, chopped
- 2 garlic cloves, minced
- 3 tablespoons butter *or* margarine, *divided*
- 1 can (15-1/2 ounces) great northern beans, rinsed and drained
- 1 jar (4 ounces) diced pimientos, drained
- 1 teaspoon dried oregano
- 1/2 teaspoon salt
- 1/8 teaspoon pepper
- 2 cups (8 ounces) shredded cheddar cheese
- 3 tablespoons dry bread crumbs

Place broccoli in a saucepan; add 1 in. of water. Bring to a boil. Reduce heat; cover and simmer for 5-8 minutes or until crisp-tender. Meanwhile, in a skillet, saute onion and garlic in 1 tablespoon butter. Spread in a greased 11-in. x 7-in. x 2-in. baking dish. Drain broccoli; place over onion mixture. Top with beans and pimientos. Sprinkle with oregano, salt, pepper, cheese and bread crumbs. Melt remaining butter; pour over the top. Bake, uncovered, at 375° for 20 minutes or until heated through. **Yield:** 8 servings.

Cheesy Beef 'n' Rice

This herb-seasoned casserole is one dish that all six of our kids love. I usually serve it with garlic bread. —*Gwen Bradshaw, Kennewick, Washington*

- 1 cup uncooked long grain rice
- 1 garlic clove, minced
- 2 tablespoons butter *or* margarine
- 3 cups water
- 2 medium carrots, shredded
- 2 teaspoons beef bouillon granules
- 1 teaspoon dried parsley flakes
- 1/2 teaspoon salt
- 1/2 teaspoon dried basil
- 1/2 teaspoon dried minced onion
- 1 pound ground beef, cooked and drained
- 1/2 cup shredded cheddar cheese

In a large saucepan, saute rice and garlic in butter until golden brown. Stir in water, carrots, bouillon, parsley, salt, basil and onion. Bring to a boil. Reduce heat; cover and simmer for 5 minutes. Stir in beef. Transfer to a greased 9-in. square baking dish. Cover and bake at 325° for 45 minutes, stirring twice. Uncover; sprinkle with cheese. Bake 5 minutes longer or until cheese is melted. **Yield:** 6 servings.

Dash in the Pan

ENJOYED by themselves or served over hot cooked rice, stovetop specialties fit any active lifestyle. You'll be filing these skillet suppers under "F" files for filling, flavorful...and flat-out fast!

Crunchy Cashew Pork

Ready in 30 minutes or less

I enjoy the crunchiness of the cashews and fresh veggies in this colorful medley. —Myra Innes, Auburn, Kansas

- 2 teaspoons cornstarch
- 1/2 cup chicken broth
- 1/4 cup cider *or* red wine vinegar
- 2 tablespoons soy sauce
- 2 teaspoons plus 2 tablespoons vegetable oil, *divided*
- 3/4 pound boneless pork, cut into thin strips
- 1 cup thinly sliced carrots
- 1 cup broccoli florets
- 3 green onions, thinly sliced
- 1/2 cup cashews
- Hot cooked rice

In a bowl, combine cornstarch, broth, vinegar, soy sauce and 2 teaspoons oil until smooth; set aside. In a large skillet or wok over medium-high heat, stir-fry pork in 1 tablespoon oil until no longer pink; remove and keep warm. Heat remaining oil; stir-fry carrots and broccoli until crisp-tender. Stir in broth mixture and green onions. Bring to a boil; cook and stir for 2 minutes or until thickened. Return meat to pan and heat through. Stir in cashews. Serve over rice. **Yield:** 4 servings.

Flavorful Beef Stir-Fry

(Pictured at right)

Ready in 30 minutes or less

I'm a working mom, so I appreciate meals like this one that I can whip up in no time using whatever vegetables I have on hand. —Tere Abel, Muskegon, Michigan

☑ Uses less fat, sugar or salt. Includes Nutritional Analysis and Diabetic Exchanges.

- 2 tablespoons cornstarch
- 2 teaspoons sugar
- 6 tablespoons soy sauce
- 1/4 cup white wine, apple juice *or* water
- 1 pound boneless round steak, cut into thin strips
- 3 cups broccoli florets
- 2 medium carrots, thinly sliced

- 1 package (6 ounces) frozen pea pods, thawed
- 2 tablespoons chopped onion
- 2 tablespoons vegetable oil, *divided*
- 1 can (8 ounces) sliced water chestnuts, undrained
- Hot cooked rice

In a bowl, combine cornstarch, sugar, soy sauce and wine, apple juice or water until smooth. Add beef and toss to coat; set aside. In a large skillet, stir-fry broccoli, carrots, pea pods and onion in 1 tablespoon oil for 1 minute. Stir in water chestnuts. Cover and simmer for 4 minutes; remove and keep warm. In the same skillet, stir-fry beef in remaining oil until meat reaches desired doneness. Return vegetables to pan; toss. Serve over rice. **Yield:** 4 servings. **Nutritional Analysis:** One serving (prepared with light soy sauce and water; calculated without rice) equals 313 calories, 466 mg sodium, 70 mg cholesterol, 21 gm carbohydrate, 31 gm protein, 12 gm fat, 7 gm fiber. **Diabetic Exchanges:** 4 lean meat, 1 starch, 1 vegetable.

Walnut Chicken Skillet

Ready in 1 hour or less

This is the best stir-fry I've ever found...and the only way my son will eat chicken. —Kay Hatfield, Elgin, Illinois

- 2 teaspoons cornstarch, *divided*
- 3 tablespoons soy sauce, *divided*
- 1 pound boneless skinless chicken breasts, cut into 1/4-inch strips
- 1 tablespoon water
- 1-1/2 teaspoons vinegar
- 1-1/2 teaspoons sugar
- Dash hot pepper sauce
- 1/2 cup walnut halves
- 3 tablespoons vegetable oil
- 1 medium green pepper, cut into 1-inch pieces
- 1/2 teaspoon ground ginger
- Hot cooked rice

Flavorful Beef Stir-Fry

In a bowl, combine 1 teaspoon of cornstarch and 1 tablespoon soy sauce until smooth; add chicken and toss to coat. Cover and refrigerate for 30 minutes. Meanwhile, in a bowl, combine water, vinegar, sugar, hot pepper sauce, and remaining cornstarch and soy sauce; set aside. In a skillet, saute walnuts in oil until toasted; remove with a slotted spoon and set aside. In the same skillet, stir-fry chicken until juices run clear. Remove and keep warm. Add green pepper and ginger to skillet; cook and stir for 3 minutes or until pepper is crisp-tender. Stir cornstarch mixture; add to skillet. Bring to a boil; cook and stir for 2 minutes or until thickened and bubbly. Return chicken and walnuts to pan. Serve over rice. **Yield:** 4 servings.

Chicken and Egg Hash

Chicken and Egg Hash

Ready in 30 minutes or less

This recipe is one of my daughter's favorites. To reduce cooking time and clean out the fridge, dice up leftover potatoes and use cooked chicken or ham instead.
—*Joyce Price, Whitefish, Ontario*

       4 bacon strips, diced
       1 medium onion, chopped
       2 garlic cloves, minced
       1 pound boneless skinless chicken breasts, cubed
       2 large potatoes, peeled and diced
       1 tablespoon vegetable oil
   1/2 cup frozen peas, thawed
   1/2 cup frozen corn, thawed
       2 tablespoons minced fresh parsley
   3/4 teaspoon salt
   1/8 teaspoon pepper
       4 eggs

In a skillet, cook bacon until crisp. Remove with a slotted spoon to paper towels to drain. In the drippings, saute onion and garlic until tender. Stir in the chicken, potatoes and oil. Cover and cook for 10 minutes or until the potatoes and chicken are tender, stirring once. Stir in peas, corn, parsley, salt and pepper. Make four wells in the hash; break an egg into each well. Cover and cook over low heat for 8-10 minutes or until eggs are completely set. Sprinkle with bacon. **Yield:** 4 servings.

Hawaiian Ham Skillet

Ready in 30 minutes or less

Pineapple tidbits give island appeal to this sweet-and-sour ham dish. —*Ona Nelson, Muskegon, Michigan*

 Uses less fat, sugar or salt. Includes Nutritional Analysis and Diabetic Exchanges.

       1 can (20 ounces) unsweetened pineapple
         tidbits
       1 pound fully cooked ham, julienned
   1/4 cup packed brown sugar
       3 tablespoons cornstarch
   1-1/2 cups cold water
       2 tablespoons vinegar

       4 teaspoons prepared mustard
       2 medium green peppers, julienned
   Hot cooked rice

Drain pineapple, reserving juice; set aside. In a skillet, stir-fry ham until golden. In a bowl, combine brown sugar and cornstarch. Stir in water, vinegar, mustard and pineapple juice until blended. Add to the ham; bring to a boil. Reduce heat; cook and stir for 2 minutes or until thickened and bubbly. Add green pepper and pineapple; simmer for 5-8 minutes. Serve over rice. **Yield:** 6 servings. **Nutritional Analysis:** One serving (prepared with reduced-sodium ham and artificial sweetener equivalent to 1/4 cup sugar; calculated without rice) equals 171 calories, 781 mg sodium, 40 mg cholesterol, 16 gm carbohydrate, 17 gm protein, 5 gm fat, 2 gm fiber. **Diabetic Exchanges:** 2 lean meat, 1 fruit.

Clock-Watcher Chicken

Ready in 1 hour or less

I appreciate not having to dirty extra pans when I make this one-skillet dish. —*Anne Drouin, Dunnville, Ontario*

       4 boneless skinless chicken breast halves
       1 medium onion, chopped
       2 tablespoons vegetable oil
       1 can (14-1/2 ounces) Italian diced tomatoes,
         undrained
       2 cups chicken broth
       1 teaspoon dried basil
   1/4 teaspoon pepper
       8 ounces uncooked spaghetti, broken into
         2-inch pieces
   1/4 cup grated Parmesan cheese

In a large skillet, cook chicken and onion in oil until onion is tender; remove and keep warm. Add tomatoes, broth, basil and pepper to the skillet. Bring to a boil; stir in spaghetti. Reduce heat; cover and simmer for 15-20 minutes. Return chicken to pan; cook until juices run clear and spaghetti is tender. Sprinkle with Parmesan cheese. **Yield:** 4 servings.

Pork Slaw Skillet

(Pictured at right)

Ready in 30 minutes or less

Tender, moist slices of pork tenderloin and crispy slaw combine in this deliciously different recipe.
—Jerry Harrison, St. Mary's, Georgia

Pork Slaw Skillet

2 pork tenderloins (about 3/4 pound *each*),
   cut into 1/4-inch slices
2 tablespoons vegetable oil
Salt and pepper to taste
SLAW:
   1 tablespoon all-purpose flour
1/2 cup water
   2 tablespoons vinegar
   1 tablespoon sugar
   1 tablespoon prepared mustard
   2 teaspoons Worcestershire sauce
   1 teaspoon salt
1/2 to 1 teaspoon celery seed
Dash pepper
   7 cups shredded cabbage
1-1/2 cups shredded carrots
   1 medium onion, chopped
   1 cup chopped green pepper, optional

In a large skillet, cook pork in oil over medium heat for 2-3 minutes on each side or until juices run clear. Season with salt and pepper. Remove and keep warm. In a bowl, combine the flour and water until smooth. Stir in the vinegar, sugar, mustard, Worcestershire sauce, salt, celery seed and pepper; pour into the skillet. Add vegetables. Cook and stir over medium heat until mixture comes to a boil. Cook and stir for 2 minutes or until thickened and vegetables are crisp-tender. Top with pork; cover and heat through. **Yield:** 4-6 servings.

Italian Beans and Pasta

Ready in 30 minutes or less

This hearty recipe calls for pantry items, so it's extremely easy to prepare. —Judy Henfey, Carlisle, Pennsylvania

 Uses less fat, sugar or salt. Includes Nutritional Analysis and Diabetic Exchanges.

2 cans (14-1/2 ounces *each*) stewed tomatoes,
   cut up
1 can (15-1/2 ounces) great northern beans,
   rinsed and drained
1 jar (14 ounces) spaghetti sauce
2 celery ribs, sliced
1 small onion, chopped
Pepper to taste
1/4 teaspoon garlic salt *or* garlic powder
1/4 teaspoon dried basil
1/4 teaspoon dried parsley flakes
Hot cooked pasta

In a large saucepan, combine the tomatoes, beans, spaghetti sauce, celery, onion and seasonings. Bring to a boil. Reduce heat; cover and simmer for 20 minutes or until vegetables are tender. Serve over pasta. **Yield:** 6 servings. **Nutritional Analysis:** One serving (prepared with garlic powder and no-salt-added diced tomatoes; calculated without pasta) equals 205 calories, 360 mg sodium, 0 cholesterol, 36 gm carbohydrate, 8 gm protein, 3 gm fat, 9 gm fiber. **Diabetic Exchanges:** 2-1/2 starch, 1/2 fat.

Jiffy Jambalaya

Ready in 30 minutes or less

My husband and I like this nicely spiced combination on days when we're pressed for time. —Carolyn Gubser Waukesha, Wisconsin

Uses less fat, sugar or salt. Includes Nutritional Analysis and Diabetic Exchanges.

1 medium onion, chopped
1/2 cup chopped green pepper
2 tablespoons vegetable oil
1 pound fully cooked kielbasa *or* Polish
   sausage, cut into 1/4-inch slices
1 can (28 ounces) diced tomatoes, undrained
1/2 cup water
1 tablespoon sugar
1 teaspoon paprika
1/2 teaspoon dried thyme
1/2 teaspoon dried oregano
1/4 teaspoon garlic powder
3 drops hot pepper sauce
1-1/2 cups uncooked instant rice

In a skillet, saute onion and green pepper in oil until tender. Stir in the sausage, tomatoes, water, sugar and seasonings. Bring to a boil; add the rice. Cover and cook for 5 minutes or until the rice is tender. **Yield:** 6 servings. **Nutritional Analysis:** One serving (prepared with reduced-fat smoked turkey sausage and no-salt-added diced tomatoes) equals 278 calories, 680 mg sodium, 49 mg cholesterol, 31 gm carbohydrate, 15 gm protein, 11 gm fat, 3 gm fiber. **Diabetic Exchanges:** 1-1/2 starch, 1-1/2 lean meat, 1 vegetable, 1 fat.

Golden Chicken and Autumn Vegetables

Ready in 30 minutes or less

This comforting dish from the Taste of Home Cooking School Recipe Collection will warm you up on a chilly day.

    4 bone-in chicken breast halves, skin removed
    2 large sweet potatoes, peeled and cut into
       large chunks
    2 cups fresh *or* frozen cut green beans
    1 cup chicken broth
    1 tablespoon minced fresh parsley
    1/2 teaspoon garlic powder
    1/2 teaspoon dried rosemary, crushed
    1/4 teaspoon dried thyme

In a nonstick skillet over medium-high heat, cook chicken until browned on both sides. Add sweet potatoes and beans. Combine the remaining ingredients; pour over chicken and vegetables. Bring to a boil. Reduce heat; cover and cook over low heat for 20 minutes or until chicken juices run clear. **Yield:** 4 servings.

Country Pork Chop Dinner

(Pictured below)

Ready in 1 hour or less

This satisfying supper, smothered in a golden sauce, is truly spirit-warming. —Jean Lawson, Dover, Delaware

☑ Uses less fat, sugar or salt. Includes Nutritional Analysis and Diabetic Exchanges.

    4 pork loin chops (1/2 inch thick)
    1 small onion, chopped
    1 tablespoon vegetable oil
    4 medium red potatoes, cubed
    1 cup thinly sliced carrots
    1 jar (4-1/2 ounces) sliced mushrooms, drained
       or 1 cup sliced fresh mushrooms

    1 can (10-3/4 ounces) condensed cream of
       celery soup, undiluted
    1/2 cup water
    1 teaspoon salt, optional
    1/2 to 1 teaspoon dried thyme

In a large skillet, cook pork and onion in oil until meat is browned; drain. Top with potatoes, carrots and mushrooms. Combine the soup, water, salt if desired and thyme; pour over vegetables. Bring to a boil; reduce heat. Cover and simmer for 25-30 minutes or until vegetables are tender. **Yield:** 4 servings. **Nutritional Analysis:** One serving (prepared with low-fat soup and fresh mushrooms and without salt) equals 282 calories, 362 mg sodium, 55 mg cholesterol, 25 gm carbohydrate, 23 gm protein, 10 gm fat, 5 gm fiber. **Diabetic Exchanges:** 3 lean meat, 1-1/2 starch, 1 vegetable.

Corned Beef Stir-Fry

Ready in 30 minutes or less

The celery seed really comes through in this colorful combination of carrots, cabbage and corned beef.
—Alesha Padgett, Franklin, Georgia

    7 tablespoons vegetable oil, *divided*
    3 tablespoons vinegar
    2 tablespoons sugar
    1 teaspoon celery seed
    1/4 teaspoon salt
    6 cups coarsely chopped cabbage
    1 cup shredded carrots
    1/4 cup chopped green onions
    1/2 pound thinly sliced fully cooked corned beef

In a bowl, whisk 4 tablespoons oil, vinegar, sugar, celery seed and salt until sugar is dissolved; set aside. In a large skillet, saute the vegetables in remaining oil until crisp-tender, about 15 minutes. Stir in vinegar-oil mixture and corned beef. Cover and simmer for 10 minutes or until heated through. **Yield:** 4-6 servings.

Country Pork Chop Dinner

Herbed Chicken Fettuccine

Herbed Chicken Fettuccine

(Pictured above)

Ready in 1 hour or less

Every time I fix this dish, the kids ask for more. It goes well with steamed broccoli and glazed carrots.
—Kathy Kirkland, Denham Springs, Louisiana

    1 to 2 teaspoons salt-free seasoning blend
    1 teaspoon poultry seasoning
    1 pound boneless skinless chicken breasts, cut into 1-inch strips
    2 tablespoons olive *or* vegetable oil
    4 tablespoons butter *or* margarine, *divided*
  2/3 cup water
    2 tablespoons teriyaki sauce
    2 tablespoons onion soup mix
    1 envelope savory herb and garlic soup mix, *divided*
    8 ounces uncooked fettuccine *or* pasta of your choice
    2 tablespoons grated Parmesan cheese
    1 tablespoon Worcestershire sauce

Combine seasoning blend and poultry seasoning; sprinkle over chicken. In a skillet, saute chicken in oil and 2 tablespoons butter for 5 minutes or until juices run clear. Add the water, teriyaki sauce, onion soup mix and 2 tablespoons herb and garlic soup mix. Bring to a boil. Reduce heat; cover and simmer for 15 minutes. Meanwhile, cook the fettuccine according to package directions. Drain; add to the chicken mixture. Add cheese, Worcestershire sauce, remaining butter, and remaining herb and garlic soup mix; toss to coat. **Yield:** 4 servings.

Sausage Spanish Rice

Ready in 1 hour or less

When I want to add a little more zip to this hearty entree, I use hot salsa. —Grace Riele, Addison, Illinois

    1 pound bulk pork sausage
    1 medium onion, chopped
    1 cup chopped celery
    1 can (28 ounces) diced tomatoes, undrained
2-1/2 cups water
1-1/4 cups uncooked long grain rice
  1/2 cup chili sauce *or* salsa
1-1/2 cups (6 ounces) shredded sharp cheddar cheese

In a skillet, cook sausage, onion and celery over medium heat until meat is no longer pink and vegetables are tender; drain. Add tomatoes, water, rice and chili sauce. Cover and cook over low heat for 30 minutes or until rice is tender. Remove from the heat. Sprinkle with cheese; cover and let stand for 5 minutes or until cheese is melted. **Yield:** 4 servings.

Harvest Ham Skillet

Ready in 30 minutes or less

An eye-catching sauce features diced apple, green onions and dried cranberries, so it tastes as special as it looks.
—Jann Van Massenhoven, Hensall, Ontario

    1 tablespoon brown sugar
1-1/2 teaspoons cornstarch
  2/3 cup apple juice
1-1/2 teaspoons Dijon mustard
    1 teaspoon lemon juice
    1 fully cooked ham slice (about 1-1/2 pounds and 1 inch thick), quartered
    1 tablespoon butter *or* margarine
    1 medium tart apple, peeled and diced
  1/4 cup dried cranberries
    2 green onions, chopped

In a small bowl, combine the brown sugar and cornstarch. Stir in the apple juice, mustard and lemon juice until smooth; set aside. In a large skillet, brown the ham slice on both sides in butter. Remove and set aside. Add the apple, cranberries and onions to the skillet; cook for 2-3 minutes or until the apple is tender. Stir in the apple juice mixture. Bring to a boil; cook and stir for 2 minutes or until thickened. Return the ham to the skillet; heat through. **Yield:** 4 servings.

Spinach Pepperoni Spaghetti

Ready in 15 minutes or less

I use fresh basil to flavor this medley of mushrooms, pepperoni, spinach and spaghetti. —Joanne Laing Soyk
Milwaukee, Wisconsin

   1 package (7 ounces) thin spaghetti
1/2 pound fresh mushrooms, sliced
   1 package (3-1/2 ounces) pepperoni, cut into thin strips
   2 tablespoons butter *or* margarine
   6 cups torn fresh spinach
   2 tablespoons minced fresh basil
   2 teaspoons lemon juice
   4 tablespoons grated Parmesan cheese, *divided*

Cook spaghetti according to package directions. Meanwhile, in a skillet, saute mushrooms and pepperoni in butter until mushrooms are tender. Stir in spinach, basil and lemon juice. Cook and stir for 2 minutes or until spinach is wilted. Drain spaghetti. Toss with pepperoni mixture and 3 tablespoons Parmesan cheese. Sprinkle with the remaining Parmesan cheese. **Yield:** 4 servings.

Ground Beef and Veggies

Ready in 1 hour or less

Fresh tomato and green pepper add color to this filling family dinner. —Pauletta Bushnell, Lebanon, Oregon

✓ Uses less fat, sugar or salt. Includes Nutritional Analysis and Diabetic Exchanges.

   1 pound ground beef
2-1/2 cups water
   1 cup uncooked long grain rice
   1 large onion, chopped
   1 tablespoon beef bouillon granules
1/2 teaspoon ground mustard
   8 slices cheddar *or* process American cheese, *divided*
   1 medium green pepper, chopped
   1 medium tomato, chopped

In a skillet, cook beef over medium heat until no longer pink; drain. Stir in water, rice, onion, bouillon and mustard. Bring to a boil; reduce heat. Cover and simmer for 20 minutes. Cut six cheese slices into small pieces; add to rice mixture with green pepper and tomato. Cut remaining cheese slices diagonally into four triangles; arrange over top. Cover and remove from the heat. Let stand until liquid is absorbed and cheese is melted. **Yield:** 6 servings. **Nutritional Analysis:** One serving (prepared with lean ground beef, low-sodium bouillon and reduced-fat process American cheese product) equals 327 calories, 465 mg sodium, 37 mg cholesterol, 33 gm carbohydrate, 26 gm protein, 9 gm fat, 2 gm fiber. **Diabetic Exchanges:** 3 lean meat, 2 starch.

Sesame Chicken

Ready in 30 minutes or less

My mother passed down the recipe for this tasty stir-fry, which is so simple to make. We like it with wild rice.
—Elizabeth Limestahl, Port Clinton, Ohio

✓ Uses less fat, sugar or salt. Includes Nutritional Analysis and Diabetic Exchanges.

1-1/4 pounds boneless skinless chicken breasts, cubed
   2 tablespoons vegetable oil
1/4 cup soy sauce
1/4 cup sesame seeds
   1 large onion, sliced
   2 jars (4-1/2 ounces *each*) sliced mushrooms, drained, *or* 2 cups sliced fresh mushrooms

In a large skillet, cook chicken in oil until no longer pink. Stir in the soy sauce and sesame seeds. Cook and stir over medium heat for 5 minutes. Remove chicken with a slotted spoon; set aside and keep warm. In the same skillet, saute onion and mushrooms until onion is tender. Return chicken to pan; heat through. **Yield:** 5 servings. **Nutritional Analysis:** One serving (prepared with light soy sauce and fresh mushrooms) equals 272 calories, 474 mg sodium, 73 mg cholesterol, 8 gm carbohydrate, 31 gm protein, 13 gm fat, 2 gm fiber. **Diabetic Exchanges:** 4 very lean meat, 2 fat, 1 vegetable.

Lamb Ratatouille

Ready in 1 hour or less

This quick recipe is a great way to use up leftover lamb or beef. Your family will never guess it's a second-day dish.
—Maxine Cenker, Weirton, West Virginia

   1 package (6.9 ounces) beef-flavored rice mix
   2 tablespoons butter *or* margarine
2-1/2 cups water
   3 medium tomatoes, peeled, seeded and chopped
   1 medium zucchini, sliced
1-1/2 cups sliced fresh mushrooms
   1 small onion, chopped
   6 green onions, sliced
   3 garlic cloves, minced
   2 tablespoons olive *or* vegetable oil
   1 pound cooked lamb *or* beef, cut into thin strips

Set rice seasoning packet aside. In a large skillet, saute the rice mix in butter until browned. Stir in water and contents of seasoning packet; bring to a boil. Reduce heat; cover and simmer for 15 minutes. Meanwhile, in another skillet, saute vegetables in oil until crisp-tender. Add lamb and vegetables to the rice. Cover and simmer for 5-10 minutes or until rice is tender. **Yield:** 4-6 servings.

Chapter 11

EVEN the best store-bought loaf can't compare with homemade breads. But who has time to bake them from scratch? You do!

The sweet and savory quick breads featured here promise true fresh-from-the-oven flavor without the work traditional yeast breads require. In fact, many get a head start from such convenience items as biscuit or cake mixes and frozen or refrigerated bread dough.

Nowadays, bread machines make it more convenient to bake bread at home than to pick it up at the supermarket. It takes only minutes to put ingredients in the pan, flick a few switches and make a simple check.

Soon the aroma of just-baked bread will fill your kitchen!

BREAD MACHINE MAGIC.
Clockwise from upper left: Multigrain Bread (p. 172), Golden Honey Pan Rolls (p. 167), Frosted Cinnamon Rolls (p. 173) and Sour Cream Lemon Bread (p. 171).

Oven-Fresh Quick Breads

ARE YOU looking for a quick accompaniment to a delicious breakfast, hearty lunch or speedy supper? You need not worry about kneading—or spending too much time in the kitchen—with these sweet and savory loaves, rolls, coffee cakes, muffins and more.

Chocolate Chip Muffins

(Pictured below)

Ready in 1 hour or less

Both of my daughters love these sweet muffins. I usually double the recipe so I have extras to keep in the freezer for a quick breakfast or snack.
—Lori Thompson
New London, Texas

  2 cups all-purpose flour
1/2 cup sugar
  1 tablespoon baking powder
1/2 teaspoon salt
  1 egg
3/4 cup milk
1/3 cup vegetable oil
3/4 cup miniature semisweet chocolate chips

In a large bowl, combine the first four ingredients. In a small bowl, beat egg, milk and oil. Stir into dry ingredients just until moistened. Fold in chocolate chips. Fill greased or paper-lined muffin cups three-fourths full. Bake at 400° for 18-20 minutes or until a toothpick comes out clean. Cool for 5 minutes before removing to a wire rack. **Yield:** 1 dozen.

Zucchini Chip Bread

(Pictured below)

These mild orange-flavored loaves are chock-full of chocolate chips, nuts and spices. The bread is easy to stir up, yet it tastes like you spent hours in the kitchen.
—Edie DeSpain, Logan, Utah

  3 cups all-purpose flour
  2 cups sugar
  1 teaspoon baking soda
  1 teaspoon salt
  1 teaspoon ground nutmeg
1/2 teaspoon ground cinnamon
1/4 teaspoon baking powder
  3 eggs
1/2 cup unsweetened applesauce
1/2 cup vegetable oil
  1 tablespoon grated orange peel
  2 teaspoons vanilla extract
  2 cups shredded zucchini
  1 cup chopped walnuts
  1 cup (6 ounces) semisweet chocolate chips

In a large bowl, combine the first seven ingredients. In another bowl, beat eggs, applesauce, oil, orange peel

Chocolate Chip Muffins
Zucchini Chip Bread

and vanilla. Stir into the dry ingredients just until moistened. Fold in zucchini, nuts and chocolate chips. Divide batter between two greased 9-in. x 5-in. x 3-in. loaf pans. Bake at 350° for 55-60 minutes or until a toothpick inserted near the center comes out clean. Cool for 10 minutes before removing from pans to wire racks to cool completely. **Yield:** 2 loaves.

French Breakfast Puffs

Ready in 1 hour or less

Rather than serve typical pastries, I like to make these light tender treats when I have guests at breakfast. Everyone enjoys their sweet cinnamon and sugar coating.
—Kimberly Flora, Peru, Indiana

      1/3 cup shortening
        1 cup sugar, *divided*
        1 egg
    1-1/2 cups all-purpose flour
    1-1/2 teaspoons baking powder
      1/2 teaspoon salt
      1/4 teaspoon ground nutmeg
      1/2 cup milk
        1 teaspoon ground cinnamon
        6 tablespoons butter *or* margarine, melted

In a mixing bowl, beat shortening, 1/2 cup sugar and egg until smooth. Combine flour, baking powder, salt and nutmeg; add to the sugar mixture alternately with milk. Fill greased muffin cups two-thirds full. Bake at 350° for 20 minutes or until a toothpick comes out clean. Meanwhile, combine cinnamon and remaining sugar in a shallow bowl. Roll the warm puffs in butter, then in cinnamon-sugar. Serve immediately. **Yield:** 1 dozen.

Parmesan Muffins

Ready in 1 hour or less

These aromatic muffins are a nice change from garlic bread. I serve them warm. —Irene Muller, Wray, Colorado

✓ Uses less fat, sugar or salt. Includes Nutritional Analysis and Diabetic Exchanges.

        2 cups all-purpose flour
      3/4 cup grated Parmesan cheese
        2 teaspoons sugar
        2 teaspoons baking powder
        2 teaspoons Italian seasoning
        2 teaspoons dried basil, parsley *or* cilantro flakes
      1/2 teaspoon baking soda
      1/2 teaspoon salt, optional
        1 egg
    1-1/4 cups buttermilk
      1/4 cup vegetable oil

In a large bowl, combine the first eight ingredients. In a small bowl, beat egg, buttermilk and oil. Stir into dry ingredients just until moistened. Fill greased or paper-lined muffin cups two-thirds full. Bake at 400° for 20-22 minutes or until a toothpick comes out clean.

Cool for 5 minutes before removing from pan to a wire rack. **Yield:** 1 dozen. **Nutritional Analysis:** One muffin (prepared with egg substitute equivalent to one egg and without salt) equals 164 calories, 287 mg sodium, 6 mg cholesterol, 19 gm carbohydrate, 6 gm protein, 7 gm fat, 1 gm fiber. **Diabetic Exchanges:** 1 starch, 1 fat, 1/2 meat.

Praline Biscuits

Ready in 30 minutes or less

These upside-down biscuits have an appealing nut topping that adds a special touch to a company brunch. Best of all, they bake in just minutes. —Merrill Powers
Spearville, Kansas

      1/2 cup butter *or* margarine, melted
      1/2 cup packed brown sugar
       36 pecan halves
   Ground cinnamon
        2 cups biscuit/baking mix
      1/3 cup unsweetened applesauce
      1/3 cup milk

Grease 12 muffin cups. In each cup, place 2 teaspoons butter, 2 teaspoons brown sugar, three pecan halves and a dash of cinnamon. In a bowl, combine biscuit mix, applesauce and milk just until moistened. Spoon into muffin cups. Bake at 450° for 10 minutes. Immediately invert onto a serving platter. Serve warm. **Yield:** 1 dozen.

Cinnamon-Raisin Coffee Cake

Ready in 1 hour or less

Raisins add sweetness and nuts add crunch to this moist coffee cake. Feel free to substitute chopped cranberries or finely chopped apple.
—Dorothy Bateman, Carver, Massachusetts

      2/3 cup sugar
      1/2 cup vegetable oil
        2 eggs
        1 teaspoon vanilla extract
    1-1/2 cups all-purpose flour
        1 teaspoon baking soda
      1/4 teaspoon salt
        1 cup (8 ounces) plain yogurt
      1/2 cup raisins
   TOPPING:
      1/2 cup walnuts, chopped
      1/3 cup packed brown sugar
        2 teaspoons ground cinnamon

In a mixing bowl, beat sugar, oil, eggs and vanilla until smooth. Combine flour, baking soda and salt; add to the sugar mixture alternately with yogurt. Stir in raisins. Pour half of the batter into a greased 9-in. square baking pan. Combine topping ingredients; sprinkle half over batter. Top with remaining batter and topping. Cut through batter with a knife to swirl the topping. Bake at 350° for 30-35 minutes or until a toothpick inserted near the center comes out clean. Cool on a wire rack. **Yield:** 9 servings.

Country Apple Coffee Cake

Ready in 1 hour or less

Refrigerated biscuits make this apple-pecan delight a breeze to prepare for brunch or dessert.
—Katie Strzyzewski, Midlothian, Illinois

> 2 medium tart apples, peeled and chopped, *divided*
> 1 tube (12 ounces) refrigerated buttermilk biscuits
> 1 egg
> 1/3 cup corn syrup
> 1/3 cup packed brown sugar
> 1 tablespoon butter *or* margarine, softened
> 1/2 teaspoon ground cinnamon
> 1/2 cup chopped pecans
> GLAZE:
> 1/3 cup confectioners' sugar
> 1/4 teaspoon vanilla extract
> 1 to 2 teaspoons milk

Place 1-1/2 cups apples in a greased 9-in. round baking pan. Separate biscuits into 10 pieces; cut each biscuit into quarters. Place over apples with point side up. Top with remaining apples. In a mixing bowl, combine egg, corn syrup, brown sugar, butter and cinnamon. Stir in pecans. Spoon over apples. Bake at 350° for 30-35 minutes or until biscuits are browned. For glaze, combine confectioners' sugar, vanilla and enough milk to achieve desired consistency. Drizzle over warm coffee cake. Serve immediately. **Yield:** 8-10 servings.

Simple Sticky Buns

Plan ahead...start the night before

I make these rolls Christmas Eve to enjoy on Christmas morning. —Tyan Cadwell, St. Johns, Michigan

> 2 loaves (1 pound *each*) frozen bread dough,* thawed, *divided*
> Ground cinnamon to taste
> 1/2 cup butter *or* margarine
> 1 cup packed brown sugar
> 1 package (4.6 ounces) cook-and-serve vanilla pudding mix
> 2 tablespoons milk
> 1 cup chopped pecans
> 1/2 cup raisins, optional

Cut each loaf of dough into 18 pieces. Arrange half in a greased 13-in. x 9-in. x 2-in. baking dish. Sprinkle with cinnamon. In a saucepan over low heat, melt butter. Remove from the heat; stir in brown sugar, pudding mix and milk until smooth. Pour over dough. Sprinkle with pecans and raisins if desired. Arrange remaining pieces of dough over top. Cover and refrigerate overnight or let stand at room temperature for 3 hours. Bake, uncovered, at 350° for 35 minutes or until center sounds hollow when tapped with fingers. Invert onto a serving platter or baking sheet. **Yield:** 12-15 servings. ***Editor's Note:** Frozen dinner roll dough (24 rolls) may be substituted for 2 loaves of bread dough.

Pineapple Bran Muffins

Ready in 1 hour or less

Tidbits of pineapple add a touch of sweetness to these mild bran muffins. —Ruth Bolduc Conway, New Hampshire

> 1-1/3 cups all-purpose flour
> 2 teaspoons baking soda
> 1-1/3 cups bran cereal
> 1/3 cup shortening
> 1/4 cup sugar
> 2 eggs
> 1 cup half-and-half cream
> 1/3 cup honey
> 1 can (8 ounces) crushed pineapple, drained

In a bowl, combine flour, baking soda and cereal. In a mixing bowl, cream shortening and sugar. Beat in eggs, cream and honey; stir into dry ingredients just until moistened. Fold in pineapple. Fill greased muffin cups two-thirds full. Bake at 350° for 20-25 minutes or until a toothpick comes out clean. Cool for 5 minutes; remove from pans to wire racks. **Yield:** 1-1/2 dozen.

BLT Muffins

(Pictured at right)

Ready in 1 hour or less

If you like the taste of a classic bacon, lettuce and tomato sandwich, you will enjoy these muffins. You can spread them with softened cream cheese or butter, but they're plenty moist and rich all by themselves.
—Katie Koziolek, Hartland, Minnesota

> 2 cups all-purpose flour
> 1 tablespoon baking powder
> 1 tablespoon sugar
> 1 cup milk
> 1/2 cup mayonnaise*
> 3/4 cup cooked crumbled bacon (about 12 strips)
> 1/2 cup chopped seeded plum tomatoes
> 2 tablespoons minced fresh parsley

In a large bowl, combine the flour, baking powder and sugar. In another bowl, beat the milk and mayonnaise until smooth. Stir into the dry ingredients just until moistened. Fold in the bacon, tomatoes and parsley. Fill greased or paper-lined muffin cups two-thirds full. Bake at 400° for 20-25 minutes or until a toothpick comes out clean. Cool for 5 minutes before removing from pan to a wire rack. Serve warm. **Yield:** 1 dozen. ***Editor's Note:** Light or fat-free mayonnaise may not be substituted for regular mayonnaise.

Nice Slices

An electric knife is a great way to slice quick breads. It makes it easy to cut regular slices and even thin slices for tea sandwiches. Refrigerating the loaf overnight also makes slicing easier—and improves the flavor of fruited loaves. —Doris McCollum, Corona, California

BLT Muffins
Round Cheese Bread

Round Cheese Bread

(Pictured above)

Ready in 1 hour or less

This savory loaf has an Italian flair. Warm buttered wedges are tasty with a pasta dinner or tossed salad.
—Deborah Bitz, Medicine Hat, Alberta

1-1/2 cups biscuit/baking mix
    1 cup (4 ounces) shredded mozzarella cheese
1/4 cup grated Parmesan cheese
1/2 teaspoon dried oregano
1/2 cup milk
    1 egg, beaten
    2 tablespoons butter *or* margarine, melted
Additional Parmesan cheese

In a bowl, combine the first six ingredients (batter will be thick). Spoon into a greased 8-in. round baking pan. Drizzle with butter; sprinkle with additional Parmesan cheese. Bake at 400° for 20-25 minutes or until a toothpick inserted near the center comes out clean. Cool for 10 minutes. Cut into wedges. Serve warm. **Yield:** 6-8 servings.

Pecan Poppy Seed Loaves

This bread is wonderful for brunch or with a cup of tea or coffee. I keep some on hand in case friends drop in. Wrapped in foil, the loaves stay moist for quite a while.
—Jean Switzer, Pauline, South Carolina

2 tablespoons poppy seeds
1 cup hot water
1 package (18-1/4 ounces) yellow cake mix
1 package (3.4 ounces) instant coconut cream *or* lemon pudding mix
4 eggs
1/2 cup vegetable oil
1/2 cup chopped pecans, toasted

In a mixing bowl, combine poppy seeds and water. Add cake and pudding mixes, eggs and oil. Beat on medium speed for 2 minutes. Stir in pecans. Pour into two greased 8-in. x 4-in. x 2-in. loaf pans. Bake at 350° for 45-50 minutes or until a toothpick inserted near the center comes out clean. Cool for 10 minutes; remove from pans to wire racks to cool completely. **Yield:** 2 loaves.

Orange Coconut Crescents
Cherry Danish

Orange Coconut Crescents

(Pictured above)

Ready in 30 minutes or less

These rich rolls are perfect for brunch when served with fresh fruit and just-perked coffee. They start with convenient crescent rolls and get their special flavor from coconut and grated orange peel. —Becky Bobier
South Sioux City, Nebraska

> 1 tube (8 ounces) refrigerated crescent rolls
> 2 tablespoons butter *or* margarine, softened
> 1/3 cup flaked coconut
> 1/3 cup sugar
> 1 tablespoon grated orange peel
> GLAZE:
>   1/4 cup sugar
>   1/4 cup sour cream
>   2 tablespoons orange juice
>   2 tablespoons butter *or* margarine

Separate crescent rolls; spread with butter. In a bowl, combine coconut, sugar and orange peel. Set aside 2 tablespoons for topping. Sprinkle remaining coconut mixture over butter. Roll up and place, point side down, on a greased baking sheet. Bake at 375° for 16-18 minutes or until golden brown. Meanwhile, combine glaze ingredients in a saucepan. Bring to a boil; boil for 3 minutes or until mixture is glossy. Cool slightly; pour over warm rolls. Sprinkle with reserved coconut mixture. **Yield:** 8 rolls.

Cherry Danish

(Pictured above)

Ready in 30 minutes or less

These delightful Danish are so quick to fix, you don't even have to uncoil the refrigerated breadsticks. We prefer them with cherry pie filling, but you can use peach or blueberry instead. —Margaret McNeil, Memphis, Tennessee

> 2 tubes (11 ounces *each*) refrigerated
>   breadsticks
> 1/3 cup butter *or* margarine, melted
> 1 tablespoon sugar
> 1 cup cherry pie filling
> 1 cup confectioners' sugar
> 1-1/2 teaspoons water

Separate breadsticks into 12 sections but leave coiled. Place in a greased 15-in. x 10-in. x 1-in. baking pan. Brush generously with butter and sprinkle with sugar.

Make an indentation in the top of each; fill with about 1 tablespoon of pie filling. Bake at 400° for 15-20 minutes or until golden brown. Combine confectioners' sugar and water; drizzle over warm rolls. **Yield:** 1 dozen.

Lemony Corn Muffins

Ready in 1 hour or less

When my son's class went on a 3-day field trip, I tagged along as one of the cooks. We made these sweet corn muffins as a special treat. They went over so well, the children wanted them at every meal! —Sandra Vaux
Lantzville, British Columbia

  1-3/4 cups all-purpose flour
   3/4 cup shredded cheddar cheese
   1/4 cup cornmeal
   1/4 cup sugar
   1/4 cup chopped almonds
     2 teaspoons baking powder
   1/2 teaspoon ground nutmeg
   1/2 teaspoon grated lemon peel
   1/4 teaspoon salt
     1 egg
     1 can (14-3/4 ounces) cream-style corn
   1/4 cup vegetable oil

In a large bowl, combine the first nine ingredients. In another bowl, beat egg, corn and oil; stir into dry ingredients just until blended. Fill greased muffin cups two-thirds full. Bake at 375° for 25-30 minutes or until golden brown. Cool for 10 minutes before removing from pan to a wire rack. **Yield:** 1 dozen.

Orange Toast

Ready in 30 minutes or less

A friend gave me the recipe for this sweet snack. I make it with thinly sliced bread from Pepperidge Farm. It's lovely with tea. —Helen Applequist, Minneapolis, Minnesota

   1/2 cup butter *or* margarine, softened
   1/2 cup confectioners' sugar
     2 teaspoons grated orange peel
     1 loaf white bread, thinly sliced (about 18
       slices)

In a small bowl, combine butter, sugar and orange peel; mix well. Spread on both sides of bread; cut in half diagonally. Place on ungreased baking sheets. Bake at 350° for 8-10 minutes. Turn slices over; bake 7 minutes longer (watch carefully). **Yield:** about 3 dozen.

Honey Fruit Loaves

I'm always looking for quick-and-easy recipes. These mini loaves are simple to make, and breakfast guests love them. —Norma Pederson, Colman, South Dakota

  1-3/4 cups all-purpose flour
     1 cup graham cracker crumbs (about 16
       squares)
  1-1/2 teaspoons baking powder
     2 eggs

   1/2 cup honey
   1/4 cup vegetable oil
   1/4 cup orange juice
     2 teaspoons grated orange peel
     1 cup chopped peeled apple
   1/2 cup chopped dates
   1/2 cup chopped dried apricots

In a large bowl, combine flour, crumbs and baking powder. In another bowl, beat eggs, honey, oil, orange juice and peel. Stir into dry ingredients just until moistened. Fold in apple, dates and apricots. Spoon into three greased 5-3/4-in. x 3-in. x 2-in. loaf pans. Bake at 350° for 45-50 minutes or until a toothpick inserted near the center comes out clean. Cool for 10 minutes before removing from pans to wire racks to cool completely. **Yield:** 3 mini loaves.

Bacon-Onion Pan Rolls

These buttery bacon-filled rolls are a favorite item at family get-togethers. We have to hide them from our two sons-in-law or there wouldn't be any left for dinner!
—Liz Vaughn, Mt. Prospect, Illinois

     1 loaf (1 pound) frozen bread dough, thawed
   1/4 cup butter *or* margarine, melted, *divided*
   1/2 pound sliced bacon, cooked and crumbled
   1/2 cup chopped onion

On a lightly floured surface, roll out dough to 1/4-in. thickness. Cut with a 2-1/2-in. biscuit cutter; brush with 3 tablespoons butter. Place 1 teaspoon of bacon and onion on half of each roll. Fold over and pinch to seal. Place, pinched edge up, in a greased 9-in. square baking pan, forming three rows of six. Brush tops with remaining butter. Let rise until doubled, about 30 minutes. Bake at 350° for 25-30 minutes or until golden brown. **Yield:** 1-1/2 dozen.

Peppy Cheese Bread

Ready in 1 hour or less

I enjoy entertaining and find this zippy cheese bread complements most meals. It's easy to assemble before guests arrive. —Leslie Sheldon-Kloss
Quakertown, Pennsylvania

     1 loaf (1 pound) unsliced French bread
   1/4 cup butter *or* margarine
   1/4 cup finely chopped onion
  1-1/2 teaspoons chili powder
     2 cups (8 ounces) shredded pepper Jack cheese
     1 cup (4 ounces) shredded mozzarella cheese

Cut bread in half lengthwise. In a microwave-safe bowl, combine the butter, onion and chili powder. Cover and microwave on high for 2-3 minutes or until the onion is tender, stirring once. Spread over cut side of bottom of bread. Sprinkle with cheeses. Replace bread top; wrap in heavy-duty foil. Bake at 350° for 35 minutes or until the cheese is melted. Slice and serve warm. **Yield:** 10-12 servings. **Editor's Note:** This recipe was tested in an 850-watt microwave.

Rosemary Lemon Muffins

Ready in 1 hour or less

These mouth-watering muffins are nicely spiced with rosemary and a hint of lemon. My husband and I especially enjoy them with a home-cooked meal.   —Felicia Fiocchi Vineland, New Jersey

      1 cup milk
      2 tablespoons minced fresh rosemary
      2 teaspoons grated lemon peel
      2 cups all-purpose flour
  1-1/2 teaspoons baking powder
      1/4 teaspoon salt
      2 eggs
      1/2 cup butter *or* margarine, melted
      2 tablespoons sugar

In a saucepan, combine the milk, rosemary and lemon peel. Bring to a simmer; cook and stir over low heat for 2 minutes. Remove from the heat; cool slightly. In a bowl, combine the flour, baking powder and salt; set aside. In another bowl, whisk the eggs until foamy. Stir in butter, sugar and milk mixture until combined. Stir into the dry ingredients just until moistened. Fill greased or paper-lined muffin cups two-thirds full. Bake at 375° for 20-22 minutes or until a toothpick comes out clean. Cool for 5 minutes before removing from pan to a wire rack. **Yield:** about 1 dozen.

Banana-Berry Nut Bread

I first made this pretty loaf after picking strawberries one year. The berries complement its banana and nut flavors. —Gina Todd, Louisville, Kentucky

✓ Uses less fat, sugar or salt. Includes Nutritional Analysis and Diabetic Exchanges.

  1-1/2 cups all-purpose flour
      1 teaspoon ground cinnamon
      1/2 teaspoon baking soda
      1/2 teaspoon salt
      1/4 teaspoon ground nutmeg
      2 eggs
      1 cup sugar
      1/4 cup vegetable oil
      3/4 cup mashed fresh strawberries
      1/2 cup mashed ripe banana (about 1 large)
      1/2 to 1 cup chopped walnuts

Speedy Solution

My children love garlic bread with pasta meals. One evening, while preparing a spaghetti dinner, I realized I didn't have garlic bread. To avoid disappointing the kids, I melted margarine, mixed it with garlic powder and brushed it on English muffin halves—the only bread in the house. I broiled the muffins for 2 minutes to make instant garlic bread. Now this is the only way my youngsters like their garlic bread.   —Jim Benson Glen Burnie, Maryland

In a bowl, combine the first five ingredients. In another bowl, beat eggs, sugar and oil until smooth; add the strawberries and banana. Stir into the dry ingredients just until moistened. Fold in walnuts. Pour into a greased 9-in. x 5-in. x 3-in. loaf pan. Bake at 350° for 60-65 minutes or until a toothpick inserted near the center comes out clean. Cool for 10 minutes before removing from pan to a wire rack. **Yield:** 1 loaf (16 slices). **Nutritional Analysis:** One slice (recipe prepared with 1/2 cup walnuts) equals 166 calories, 121 mg sodium, 27 mg cholesterol, 25 gm carbohydrate, 3 gm protein, 6 gm fat, trace fiber. **Diabetic Exchanges:** 1 starch, 1 fat, 1/2 fruit.

Tennessee Fry Bread

Ready in 30 minutes or less

You'll need only four ingredients to fix this time-easing bread. We like it with scrambled eggs and fried potatoes for breakfast.   —Theresa Sanchez, Franklin, Tennessee

      3 tablespoons butter *or* margarine
      1 cup self-rising flour*
      1/2 cup buttermilk
  All-purpose flour

Place butter in a 12-in. ovenproof skillet; place in a 450° oven for 2-3 minutes or until melted. In a bowl, combine flour and buttermilk just until moistened. Turn onto a surface dusted with all-purpose flour; knead 4-5 times. Pat dough to 1/4-in. thickness. Cut with a 2-1/2-in. biscuit cutter. Place in a single layer in prepared pan; carefully turn to coat. Bake at 450° for 12-13 minutes or until golden brown. **Yield:** 8 servings. ***Editor's Note:** As a substitute for self-rising flour, place 1-1/2 teaspoons baking powder and 1/2 teaspoon salt in a measuring cup. Add all-purpose flour to measure 1 cup.

Blueberry Coffee Cake

Ready in 1 hour or less

I assemble this cake the night before I need it, then just pop it in the oven the next morning. We enjoy its light texture and fruity taste. —Marian Platt, Sequim, Washington

      1 egg
      1/2 cup plus 2 tablespoons sugar, *divided*
  1-1/4 cups all-purpose flour
      2 teaspoons baking powder
      3/4 teaspoon salt
      1/3 cup milk
      3 tablespoons butter *or* margarine, melted
      1 cup fresh blueberries

In a mixing bowl, beat egg. Gradually add 1/2 cup sugar; mix well. Combine the flour, baking powder and salt; add to sugar mixture alternately with milk. Stir in the butter. Gently fold in blueberries. Pour into a greased 8-in. square baking pan. Sprinkle with remaining sugar. Bake at 350° for 35 minutes or until a toothpick inserted near the center comes out clean. **Yield:** 9 servings. **Editor's Note:** Coffee cake can be prepared the night before and refrigerated; sprinkle with sugar just before baking.

Pecan Coffee Cake

(Pictured below)

Ready in 1 hour or less

Mom serves this nutty coffee cake for Christmas breakfast each year. The simple recipe is a big time-saver on such an event-filled morning. Everyone loves the crunchy topping. —Becky Wax, Tuscola, Illinois

- 1 package (18-1/4 ounces) yellow cake mix
- 1 package (3.4 ounces) instant vanilla pudding mix
- 4 eggs
- 1 cup (8 ounces) sour cream
- 1/3 cup vegetable oil
- 2 teaspoons vanilla extract
- 2/3 cup chopped pecans
- 1/3 cup sugar
- 2 teaspoons ground cinnamon
- 1/2 cup confectioners' sugar
- 2 tablespoons orange juice

In a mixing bowl, combine the first six ingredients. Beat on medium speed for 2 minutes. Pour into a greased 13-in. x 9-in. x 2-in. baking pan. Combine pecans, sugar and cinnamon; sprinkle over batter. Cut through with a knife to swirl. Bake at 350° for 30-35 minutes or until a toothpick inserted near the center comes out clean. In a small bowl, combine confectioners' sugar and orange juice until smooth; drizzle over warm coffee cake. **Yield:** 12-15 servings.

Cinnamon Coffee Cake Loaf

(Pictured below)

This cinnamony bread tastes just like a coffee cake. When I worked as an elementary school secretary, I used to take a slice of this cake with me in the morning for a snack. —Lynda Atteberry Hoskins, Mathis, Texas

- 2 cups all-purpose flour
- 1-1/4 cups sugar, *divided*
- 3 teaspoons baking powder
- 3-1/2 teaspoons ground cinnamon, *divided*
- 1-1/4 teaspoons salt
- 2 eggs
- 1 cup buttermilk
- 1/3 cup vegetable oil
- 2 teaspoons vanilla extract
- 3 tablespoons butter *or* margarine, melted

In a bowl, combine the flour, 1 cup sugar, baking powder, 1-1/2 teaspoons cinnamon and salt. In another bowl, combine the eggs, buttermilk, oil and vanilla; stir into dry ingredients just until smooth. Pour half of the batter into a greased 9-in. x 5-in. x 3-in. loaf pan. In a small bowl, combine the remaining sugar and cinnamon; stir in butter. Drizzle half over batter; cut through with a knife to swirl. Top with remaining batter. Drizzle with remaining cinnamon-sugar mixture; swirl with a knife. Bake at 350° for 55-60 minutes or until a toothpick inserted near the center comes out clean. Cool for 10 minutes before removing from pan to a wire rack. **Yield:** 1 loaf.

Cinnamon Coffee Cake Loaf
Pecan Coffee Cake

Swiss Mushroom Loaf

(Pictured below)

Ready in 1 hour or less

I get oodles of recipe requests when I serve this outstanding loaf stuffed with Swiss cheese and mushrooms. It's excellent as an appetizer or served with pasta or chili.
—Heidi Mellon, Waukesha, Wisconsin

    1 unsliced loaf (1 pound) Italian bread
    1 block (8 ounces) Swiss cheese, cut into cubes
    1 cup sliced fresh mushrooms
 1/4 cup butter *or* margarine
    1 small onion, finely chopped
1-1/2 teaspoons poppy seeds
    2 garlic cloves, minced
 1/2 teaspoon seasoned salt
 1/2 teaspoon ground mustard
 1/2 teaspoon lemon juice

Cut bread diagonally into 1-in. slices to within 1 in. of bottom of loaf. Repeat cuts in opposite direction. Place cheese cubes and mushrooms in each slit. In a microwave-safe bowl, combine the remaining ingredients; cover and microwave on high for 2 minutes or until butter is melted. Spoon over bread. Wrap loaf in foil. Bake at 350° for 40 minutes or until cheese is melted. **Yield:** 10-12 servings.

Cheddar Zucchini Wedges

(Pictured below)

Ready in 1 hour or less

I stir together convenient biscuit mix, tender zucchini, cheddar cheese and toasted almonds to create this flavorful round bread. The golden wedges look as appealing as they taste. —Vevie Clarke, Camano Island, Washington

    1 medium onion, chopped
 1/4 cup butter *or* margarine
2-1/2 cups biscuit/baking mix
    1 tablespoon minced fresh parsley
 1/2 teaspoon dried basil
 1/2 teaspoon dried thyme
    3 eggs, beaten
 1/4 cup milk
1-1/2 cups shredded zucchini
    1 cup (4 ounces) shredded cheddar cheese
 3/4 cup chopped almonds, toasted

In a skillet, saute onion in butter until tender. In a bowl, combine the biscuit mix, parsley, basil, thyme and onion mixture. Stir in eggs and milk just until combined. Fold in the zucchini, cheese and almonds. Transfer to a greased 9-in. round baking pan. Bake at 400° for 25-30 minutes or until a toothpick inserted near the center comes out clean. Cut into wedges. **Yield:** 6-8 servings.

Crisp Onion Squares

Ready in 30 minutes or less

Three easy ingredients season this fun flat bread. It's simple to make with refrigerated crescent roll dough and easy to slice into savory squares with a pizza cutter.
—Myra Innes, Auburn, Kansas

1 tube (8 ounces) refrigerated crescent rolls
1 tablespoon butter *or* margarine, softened
2 tablespoons dried minced onion
1/4 to 1/2 teaspoon garlic salt

Unroll crescent dough and place on an ungreased baking sheet; seal perforations and press into an 8-in. x 6-in. rectangle. Spread with butter; sprinkle with onion and garlic salt. Bake at 400° for 10 minutes or until golden brown. Cut into squares. **Yield:** 1 dozen.

Cheddar Zucchini Wedges
Swiss Mushroom Loaf

Orange Poppy Muffins

Ready in 1 hour or less

The creamy spread makes these mild orange muffins such a treat. They won a blue ribbon at our county fair. Even the judge asked for the recipe! —Pam Severance
Herman, Minnesota

```
1-1/3 cups all-purpose flour
    1 cup sugar
    1 tablespoon poppy seeds
  1/2 teaspoon baking soda
  1/4 teaspoon salt
    1 egg
  1/2 cup sour cream
  1/3 cup butter or margarine, melted
    2 tablespoons orange juice
    1 tablespoon grated orange peel
ORANGE SPREAD:
  1/2 cup butter or margarine, softened
    1 package (3 ounces) cream cheese, softened
  1/4 cup confectioners' sugar
    1 tablespoon grated orange peel
```

In a bowl, combine the first five ingredients. In another bowl, beat egg, sour cream, butter, orange juice and peel. Stir in dry ingredients just until moistened. Fill paper-lined muffin cups two-thirds full. Bake at 400° for 18-20 minutes or until a toothpick comes out clean. Cool for 5 minutes before removing from pan to a wire rack. Combine spread ingredients in a small mixing bowl; beat until smooth. Serve with muffins. **Yield:** 10 muffins.

Jelly-Filled Muffins

Ready in 1 hour or less

As a child, I always loved the gooey surprise in the center of jelly-filled doughnuts. These yummy muffins offer that same sweet filling, but they're baked instead of fried. You can substitute raspberry jelly—or any other flavor you like.
—Darlene Markel, Mt. Hood, Oregon

```
1-1/2 cups all-purpose flour
  1/2 cup sugar
    2 teaspoons baking powder
  1/4 teaspoon salt
  1/4 teaspoon ground nutmeg
    1 egg
  1/2 cup milk
  1/3 cup butter or margarine, melted
  1/2 teaspoon vanilla extract
  1/4 cup strawberry or plum jelly
TOPPING:
    3 tablespoons butter or margarine, melted
  1/3 cup sugar
  1/2 teaspoon ground cinnamon
```

In a bowl, combine the first five ingredients. In another bowl, whisk the egg, milk, butter and vanilla. Stir into dry ingredients just until moistened. Spoon half of the batter into 12 greased or paper-lined muffin cups. Spoon 1 teaspoon jelly in center of each. Fill muffin cups two-thirds full with remaining batter. Bake at 400° for 20 min-

utes or until a toothpick inserted 1 in. from the edge comes out clean. Cool for 5 minutes before removing from pan to a wire rack. Brush tops with butter. Combine sugar and cinnamon; dip tops of muffins in mixture. Serve warm. **Yield:** 1 dozen.

Banana-Nut Chip Bread

Leftover bananas inspired me to make this homespun bread. The loaves are nicely spiced with nutmeg and include lots of crunchy nuts, sweet chocolate chips and hearty oats. —Raymond Lux, Arlington, Texas

```
1-1/2 cups mashed ripe bananas (about 3 medium)
1-1/4 cups sugar
    3 eggs
  1/3 cup vegetable oil
    1 tablespoon vanilla extract
2-1/4 cups all-purpose flour
  3/4 cup quick-cooking oats
    2 teaspoons ground cinnamon
    1 teaspoon baking powder
    1 teaspoon baking soda
    1 teaspoon salt
  1/4 teaspoon ground nutmeg
    1 cup (6 ounces) semisweet chocolate chips
  3/4 cup chopped walnuts
```

In a mixing bowl, beat bananas, sugar, eggs, oil and vanilla. Combine the dry ingredients; stir into banana mixture. Fold in chocolate chips and nuts. Pour into two greased 8-in. x 4-in. x 2-in. loaf pans. Bake at 350° for 55 minutes or until a toothpick inserted near the center comes out clean. Cool for 10 minutes before removing from pans to wire racks. **Yield:** 2 loaves.

Honey-Raisin Quick Bread

This fiber-rich bread, packed with plump raisins and bran cereal, is a tasty way to start the day. My husband likes to eat a slice spread with a little vanilla frosting for breakfast. —Judy Kern, Clovis, New Mexico

```
1-1/2 cups all-purpose flour
  2/3 cup packed brown sugar
2-1/2 teaspoons baking powder
  1/2 teaspoon salt
    1 cup bran cereal flakes
    1 cup milk
    1 egg, lightly beaten
  1/4 cup honey
    2 tablespoons butter or margarine, melted
    1 cup raisins
```

In a bowl, combine the flour, brown sugar, baking powder and salt. In another bowl, combine the cereal and milk; let stand for 5 minutes. Add the egg, honey and butter to cereal mixture; mix well. Stir into dry ingredients just until moistened. Fold in raisins. Pour into a greased 8-in. x 4-in. x 2-in. loaf pan. Bake at 350° for 1 hour or until a toothpick inserted near the center comes out clean. Cool for 10 minutes before removing from pan to a wire rack. **Yield:** 1 loaf.

Fruit Bread Twists
Cranberry Zucchini Bread

Cranberry Zucchini Bread

(Pictured above)

Nutmeg and cinnamon add spice to these flavorful loaves. The flecks of green zucchini and red cranberries give each slice a festive look that's just right for the holidays.
—*Alice Manzo, South Easton, Massachusetts*

    3 cups all-purpose flour
    2 cups sugar
2-1/2 teaspoons ground cinnamon
1-1/4 teaspoons salt
    1 teaspoon baking soda
1/2 teaspoon baking powder
1/4 teaspoon ground nutmeg
    3 eggs
1-1/2 cups shredded zucchini
    1 cup vegetable oil
    1 tablespoon vanilla extract
    1 cup chopped fresh *or* frozen cranberries
1/2 cup chopped walnuts

In a large bowl, combine the first seven ingredients. In another bowl, beat eggs; add zucchini, oil and vanilla. Stir into dry ingredients just until blended. Fold in the cranberries and walnuts. Pour into two greased and floured 9-in. x 5-in. x 3-in. loaf pans. Bake at 350° for 50-60 minutes or until a toothpick inserted near the center

comes out clean. Cool for 10 minutes before removing from pans to wire racks. **Yield:** 2 loaves.

Fruit Bread Twists

(Pictured above)

My husband loves this fruit-filled bread, so I fix it for him often. It's easy to prepare with frozen white and wheat bread dough, yet it's lovely enough for a special occasion.
—*Sandra Hessler, Caro, Michigan*

    1 loaf (1 pound) frozen white bread dough, thawed
    1 loaf (1 pound) frozen wheat bread dough, thawed
1/2 cup sugar
    1 teaspoon ground cinnamon
    1 package (8 ounces) mixed dried fruit, chopped
GLAZE:
    1 cup confectioners' sugar
    1 tablespoon water
    1 teaspoon vanilla extract

Cut each loaf of bread dough in half lengthwise. Roll each portion into an 18-in. x 5-in. rectangle. Brush lightly with water. Combine sugar and cinnamon; sprinkle over dough. Sprinkle with fruit. Roll up each rectangle, jelly-roll style, starting with a long side. For each loaf, twist one white and one wheat rope together, pinching ends to seal. Place on greased baking sheets. Cover with plastic wrap coated with nonstick cooking spray; let rise in a warm place until doubled, about 30 minutes. Remove plastic wrap. Bake at 350° for 25-30 minutes or until golden brown. Remove from pans to cool on wire racks. Combine glaze ingredients; drizzle over loaves. **Yield:** 2 loaves.

Broccoli-Cheese Corn Bread

Ready in 1 hour or less

This moist corn bread, which relies on convenient muffin mix and frozen broccoli, is a breeze to whip up anytime. It's especially good in the winter with a steaming bowl of soup. —Charlotte McDaniel
Anniston, Alabama

4 eggs
1/2 cup butter *or* margarine, melted
3/4 teaspoon salt
1 package (8-1/2 ounces) corn bread/muffin mix
1 package (10 ounces) frozen chopped broccoli, thawed and drained
1 cup (4 ounces) shredded cheddar cheese
1 medium onion, chopped

In a bowl, combine eggs, butter and salt. Stir in corn bread mix just until blended. Stir in the remaining ingredients. Pour into a greased 11-in. x 7-in. x 2-in. baking pan. Bake at 350° for 30-35 minutes or until a toothpick inserted near the center comes out clean. Slice and serve warm. **Yield:** 12 servings.

Apricot Oatmeal Muffins

Ready in 1 hour or less

Our family enjoys all types of muffins, including this tempting apricot variety. I like that they can be stirred together in a jiffy for a breakfast treat or anytime snack.
—Nelly Smees, Hopewell, Nova Scotia

2-1/2 cups all-purpose flour
1/2 cup packed brown sugar
3 teaspoons baking powder
1/2 teaspoon salt
1 cup quick-cooking oats
1 cup chopped dried apricots
1/2 cup butter *or* margarine
3/4 cup boiling water
2 eggs, lightly beaten
1 cup milk
2 teaspoons grated orange peel, optional

In a bowl, combine the first four ingredients. In another bowl, combine the oats, apricots, butter and boiling water; stir until butter is melted. Cool for 5 minutes.

Stir in eggs, milk and orange peel if desired. Stir into dry ingredients just until moistened. Fill greased or paper-lined muffin cups two-thirds full. Bake at 400° for 20-22 minutes or until a toothpick comes out clean. Cool for 5 minutes before removing from pans to wire racks. **Yield:** 1-1/2 dozen.

Banana Coffee Cake

Ready in 1 hour or less

You're sure to go bananas over this yummy coffee cake topped with cinnamon, sugar and pecans. This recipe is so delicious that a local pecan grower asked permission to use it in one of his brochures. —Georgia Courtney
Las Cruces, New Mexico

1 package (8 ounces) cream cheese, softened
1/2 cup butter *or* margarine, softened
1-1/4 cups sugar
2 eggs
1 cup mashed ripe bananas (about 3 medium)
1 teaspoon vanilla extract
2-1/4 cups all-purpose flour
1-1/2 teaspoons baking powder
1/2 teaspoon baking soda
TOPPING:
1 cup chopped pecans
2 tablespoons sugar
1 teaspoon ground cinnamon

In a mixing bowl, beat the cream cheese, butter and sugar. Add eggs, one at a time, beating well after each addition. Add the bananas and vanilla. Combine flour, baking powder and baking soda; gradually add to the creamed mixture. Combine topping ingredients; add half to batter. Transfer to a greased 13-in. x 9-in. x 2-in. baking pan. Sprinkle with the remaining topping. Bake at 350° for 25-30 minutes or until a toothpick inserted near the center comes out clean. Cool on a wire rack. **Yield:** 12-15 servings.

Parmesan Walnut Bread

Parmesan cheese and crunchy walnuts flavor this tender golden loaf. It's one of my all-time favorite breads.
—Cindy Hudson, Crawfordsville, Indiana

3 cups all-purpose flour
2/3 cup sugar
2/3 cup grated Parmesan cheese
4 teaspoons baking powder
1/2 teaspoon salt
1 egg
1-3/4 cups milk
1/3 cup vegetable oil
1 cup finely chopped walnuts

In a large bowl, combine the first five ingredients. In another bowl, beat the egg, milk and oil until smooth. Stir into dry ingredients just until moistened. Fold in the nuts. Pour into a greased 9-in. x 5-in. x 3-in. loaf pan. Bake at 350° for 50-60 minutes or until a toothpick inserted near the center comes out clean. Cool for 10 minutes before removing from pan to a wire rack. **Yield:** 1 loaf.

Paprika Onion Bread

Bread at The Touch Of a Button

WHEN IT COMES to offering family and friends warm, fresh-from-the-oven bread, convenient bread machine recipes really rise to the occasion. With these handy appliances, it's easy to enjoy the from-scratch flavor of home-baked breads and rolls with a lot less work than traditional methods.

Paprika Onion Bread

(Pictured above)

Paprika adds both color and flavor to this aromatic onion bread that's delicious spread with cream cheese. My family likes it served with goulash. —Jackie Robbins
Flint, Michigan

    1 cup water (70° to 80°)
    2 tablespoons butter *or* margarine, softened
1/3 cup finely chopped onion
    1 teaspoon sugar
1-1/2 teaspoons salt
    1 teaspoon paprika
    3 cups bread flour
    1 package (1/4 ounce) active dry yeast

In bread machine pan, place all ingredients in order suggested by manufacturer. Select basic bread setting. Choose crust color and loaf size if available. Bake according to bread machine directions (check dough af-ter 5 minutes of mixing; add 1 to 2 tablespoons water or flour if needed). **Yield:** 1 loaf (1-1/2 pounds).

Soft Sandwich Buns

I bake these soft and golden sandwich buns a few times a week because my whole family loves them. I made 300 for a wedding reception and received compliments for weeks afterward. —Lesa Young, Turpin, Oklahoma

1-1/4 cups milk (70° to 80°)
    1 egg, beaten
    2 tablespoons butter *or* margarine, softened
1/4 cup sugar
3/4 teaspoon salt
3-3/4 cups bread flour
1-1/4 teaspoons active dry yeast
    1 tablespoon butter *or* margarine, melted

In bread machine pan, place the first seven ingredients in order suggested by manufacturer. Select dough set-ting (check dough after 5 minutes of mixing; add 1 to 2 tablespoons of water or flour if needed). When cycle is completed, turn dough onto a lightly floured surface and punch down. Divide dough in half. Roll each por-tion to 3/4-in. thickness; cut with a 2-1/2-in. biscuit cutter. Place on lightly greased baking sheets. Brush tops with melted butter. Cover and let rise in a warm place until doubled, about 1 hour. Bake at 350° for 10-15 min-utes or until lightly browned. **Yield:** 1-1/2 dozen.

No-Fry Potato Doughnuts

(Pictured at far right)

I adapted a recipe from my Czechoslovakian in-laws to make the dough for these sweet treats in my bread machine.

They are the best baked doughnuts you'll ever eat. They're tender and terrific. —Jill Shramek, Smith, Nevada

      3 medium potatoes, peeled and quartered
      1 cup milk (70° to 80°)
      2 eggs, well beaten
    3/4 cup shortening
    1/2 cup sugar
      1 teaspoon salt
  4-1/2 cups bread flour
  2-1/4 teaspoons active dry yeast
TOPPING:
    3/4 cup sugar
  1-1/4 teaspoons ground cinnamon
    1/4 cup butter *or* margarine, melted

Place potatoes in a saucepan and cover with water. Bring to a boil; cook until tender. Drain, reserving 1/4 cup cooking liquid; set liquid aside to cool to 70°-80°. Mash potatoes; set aside 1 cup to cool to room temperature. (Refrigerate any remaining mashed potatoes for another use.) In bread machine pan, place dough ingredients in order suggested by manufacturer, adding reserved cooking liquid and potatoes. Select dough setting (check dough after 5 minutes of mixing; some flour may remain on top; add 1 to 2 tablespoons water or flour if needed). When cycle is completed, turn dough onto a lightly floured surface. Knead in an additional 1/4 to 1/2 cup flour if necessary. Roll out to 1/2-in. thickness. Cut with a 2-1/2-in. doughnut cutter. Place on greased baking sheets; cover and let rise until almost doubled, about 25 minutes. Bake at 350° for 15-20 minutes or until lightly browned. Combine sugar and cinnamon. Brush warm doughnuts with butter; dip in cinnamon-sugar. **Yield:** about 2-1/2 dozen. **Editor's Note:** Use of the timer feature is not recommended.

Apricot Nutmeg Bread

(Pictured at right)

Slices of this fruity bread are good for breakfast when toasted and spread with strawberry jam. Nutmeg complements the apricot flavor in this golden soft-textured loaf. —Anna Kinney, Farmington, New Mexico

      1 cup water (70° to 80°)
      3 tablespoons vegetable oil
      1 teaspoon lemon juice
      2 tablespoons plus 1-1/2 teaspoons
        brown sugar
      1 teaspoon salt
  2-1/4 teaspoons active dry yeast
      3 cups bread flour
      1 tablespoon plus 1-1/2 teaspoons instant
        nonfat dry milk powder
      1 cup chopped dried apricots
    3/4 teaspoon ground nutmeg

In bread machine pan, place the first eight ingredients in order suggested by manufacturer. Select sweet bread cycle. Choose medium crust color and loaf size if available. Bake according to bread machine directions (check dough after 5 minutes of mixing; add 1 to 2 tablespoons water or flour if needed). Just before final kneading (your machine may audibly signal this), add apricots and nutmeg. **Yield:** 1 loaf (1-1/2 pounds).

Bread Machine Basics

- Bread machines vary somewhat, depending on the manufacturer. It will be easier for you to use your machine if you first become very familiar with it. Before trying new recipes, make a variety of those provided in your manual—they were developed specifically for your machine.

- When trying any new recipe, be sure to stay within the limits of the maximum flour amounts listed in the recipes in your machine's manual.

- Canadian cooks should use 3 to 4 tablespoons less flour than called for in the bread recipes published in this chapter.

- Add the ingredients only in the order recommended by the manufacturer (which isn't always how they may appear in a recipe here).

- Your bread machine does the mixing and kneading for you. Because of that, you must learn to judge the bread with your eyes and ears to decide whether a recipe is right for your machine or needs adjusting.

  Listen to your bread machine as it's kneading the dough. If the machine sounds labored, the dough might be too dry. After 5 minutes of mixing, take a look at it. It should be forming a smooth satiny ball. If the dough looks dry or cracked, add 1 to 2 tablespoons of water. If the dough is flat and wet-looking, add 1 to 2 tablespoons of flour.

- The crispness of bread machine crusts varies depending on the manufacturer. If you don't care for a crisp crust, use your machine's lightest crust setting and remove the loaf from the machine as soon as the baking cycle is complete. If the loaf is still too crusty for your liking, brush the loaf with melted butter while it's warm for a softer texture.

No-Fry Potato Doughnuts
Apricot Nutmeg Bread

Poppy Seed Egg Bread

I prepare this light eggy loaf with poppy seeds throughout. It's simple to make in the bread machine...or use the dough setting, shape it into a traditional braided challah loaf and bake it in the oven.
—Lorraine Darocha
Berkshire, Massachusetts

    3/4 cup water (70° to 80°)
    1/4 cup butter *or* margarine, softened
      2 eggs
      1 egg yolk
      2 tablespoons sugar
  1-1/2 teaspoons salt
      1 tablespoon poppy seeds
      3 cups bread flour
  1-3/4 teaspoons active dry yeast

In bread machine pan, place all ingredients in order suggested by manufacturer. Select basic bread setting. Choose crust color and loaf size if available. Bake according to bread machine directions (check dough after 5 minutes of mixing; add 1 to 2 tablespoons of water or flour if needed). **Yield:** 1 loaf (2 pounds). **Editor's Note:** Use of the timer feature is not recommended.

Pizza with Wheat Crust

If you're looking for a change from traditional pizza crust, try this whole wheat version. Covered with your choice of pizza toppings, the homemade crust is thick, tender and tasty.
—Kathryn Maxson
Mountlake Terrace, Washington

      1 cup water (70° to 80°)
      2 tablespoons olive *or* vegetable oil
      1 tablespoon sugar
  1-1/2 teaspoons salt
    1/2 teaspoon dried oregano
    1/2 teaspoon dried basil
    1/4 teaspoon garlic powder
      2 cups all-purpose flour
      1 cup whole wheat flour
  2-1/4 teaspoons active dry yeast
      1 can (15 ounces) pizza sauce
      3 cups (12 ounces) shredded
        mozzarella cheese
Pizza toppings of your choice

In bread machine pan, place the first 10 ingredients in order suggested by manufacturer. Select dough setting (check dough after 5 minutes of mixing; add 1 to 2 tablespoons of water or flour if needed). When the cycle is completed, turn dough onto a lightly floured surface. Punch down; cover and let stand for 10 minutes. Divide dough in half; press each portion into a greased 12-in. pizza pan. Spread sauce over crusts; sprinkle with cheese and toppings. Bake at 400° for 18-20 minutes or until the crust and cheese are lightly browned. **Yield:** 2 pizzas (8 slices each).

Pepperoni Bread

(Pictured below)

This chewy bread, flecked with spicy pepperoni, is a favorite no matter where I take it. I often use slices of it to make garlic bread when I serve Italian meals.
—Annette Self, Junction City, Ohio

      1 cup plus 2 tablespoons water (70° to 80°)
    1/3 cup shredded mozzarella cheese
      2 tablespoons sugar
  1-1/2 teaspoons garlic salt
  1-1/2 teaspoons dried oregano
  3-1/4 cups bread flour
  1-1/2 teaspoons active dry yeast
    2/3 cup sliced pepperoni

In bread machine pan, place the first seven ingredients in order suggested by manufacturer. Select basic bread setting. Choose medium crust color and loaf size if available. Bake according to bread machine directions (check dough after 5 minutes of mixing; add 1 to 2 tablespoons of water or flour if needed). Just before the final kneading (your machine may audibly signal this), add the pepperoni. **Yield:** 1 loaf (about 1-1/2 pounds). **Editor's Note:** Use of the timer feature is not recommended for this recipe.

Pepperoni Bread

Golden Honey Pan Rolls

(Pictured on page 151)

A cousin in North Carolina gave me the recipe for these delicious honey-glazed rolls. Using my bread machine to make the dough saves me about 2 hours compared to the traditional method. The rich, buttery taste of these rolls is so popular with family and friends that I usually make two batches so I have enough! —*Sara Wing*
Philadelphia, Pennsylvania

    1 cup milk (70° to 80°)
    1 egg
    1 egg yolk
  1/2 cup vegetable oil
    2 tablespoons honey
1-1/2 teaspoons salt
3-1/2 cups bread flour
2-1/4 teaspoons active dry yeast
GLAZE:
  1/3 cup sugar
    2 tablespoons butter *or* margarine, melted
    1 tablespoon honey
    1 egg white
Additional honey, optional

In bread machine pan, place the first eight ingredients in order suggested by manufacturer. Select dough setting (check dough after 5 minutes of mixing; add 1 to 2 tablespoons of water or flour if needed.) When cycle is completed, turn dough onto a lightly floured surface. Punch down; cover and let rest for 10 minutes. Divide into 24 pieces; shape each into a ball. Place 12 balls each in two greased 8-in. baking pans. Cover and let rise in a warm place until doubled, about 30 minutes. For glaze, combine sugar, butter, honey and egg white; drizzle over dough. Bake at 350° for 20-25 minutes or until golden brown. Brush with additional honey if desired. **Yield:** 2 dozen. **Editor's Note:** Use of the timer feature is not recommended for this recipe.

Granola Raisin Bread

(Pictured above right)

Made with granola, oats, raisins and honey, this bread has a subtle sweetness. It's so delightful that friends often request the recipe. Slices of the crusty loaf are especially good toasted. If you prefer a softer crust, rub margarine or butter on the loaf while it's still warm. —*Patricia Nelson*
Kenosha, Wisconsin

1-2/3 cups water (70° to 80°)
  1/3 cup honey
    2 tablespoons butter *or* margarine
1-1/2 teaspoons salt
3-1/2 cups bread flour
    1 cup quick-cooking oats
    1 tablespoon active dry yeast
    1 cup granola cereal
  3/4 cup golden raisins

In bread machine pan, place the first seven ingredients in order suggested by manufacturer. Select basic bread

Granola Raisin Bread

setting. Choose crust color and loaf size if available. Bake according to bread machine directions (check dough after 5 minutes of mixing; add 1 to 2 tablespoons of water or flour if needed). Just before the final kneading (your machine may audibly signal this), add the granola and raisins. **Yield:** 1 loaf (2 pounds).

Cinnamon Flat Bread

Wedges of this chewy cinnamon bread are a big hit with our eight children. The bread machine does most of the work, so I can move on to other things.
    —*Patricia Spurrill, Pritchard, British Columbia*

    1 cup water (70° to 80°)
    2 tablespoons butter *or* margarine
    2 tablespoons nonfat dry milk powder
    1 tablespoon sugar
1-1/2 teaspoons salt
    1 tablespoon wheat germ
    2 teaspoons molasses
    3 cups all-purpose flour
2-1/4 teaspoons active dry yeast
TOPPING:
    3 tablespoons butter *or* margarine, softened
  1/2 cup packed brown sugar
    1 teaspoon ground cinnamon

In bread machine pan, place the first nine ingredients in order suggested by manufacturer. Select dough setting (check dough after 5 minutes of mixing; add 1 to 2 tablespoons water or flour if needed). When the cycle is completed, turn dough onto a lightly floured surface. Roll into a 14-in. circle; transfer to a lightly greased 14-in. pizza pan. Make indentations in top of dough with fingers. Spread with butter; sprinkle with brown sugar and cinnamon. Cover and let rise in a warm place until doubled, about 25 minutes. Bake at 375° for 30 minutes or until golden brown. Cool for 5 minutes; cut into wedges and serve warm. **Yield:** 16 wedges.

Garlic Herb Bubble Loaf

Soft Italian Breadsticks

I use the "dough only" cycle on my bread machine to prepare these melt-in-your-mouth breadsticks that my family of five gobbles up! The soft, chewy breadsticks are irresistible when brushed with butter and sprinkled with Parmesan cheese. They're the perfect accompaniment to soups or Italian entrees. —Christy Eichelberger
Jesup, Iowa

      1 cup water (70° to 80°)
      3 tablespoons butter *or* margarine, softened
  1-1/2 teaspoons salt
      3 cups bread flour
      2 tablespoons sugar
      1 teaspoon Italian seasoning
      1 teaspoon garlic powder
  2-1/4 teaspoons active dry yeast
TOPPING:
      1 tablespoon butter *or* margarine, melted
      1 tablespoon grated Parmesan cheese

In bread machine pan, place the first eight ingredients in order suggested by manufacturer. Select dough setting (check dough after 5 minutes of mixing; add 1 to 2 tablespoons of water or flour if needed). When cycle is completed, turn dough onto a lightly floured surface; divide in half. Cut each portion into 12 pieces; roll each into a 4-in. to 6-in. rope. Place 2 in. apart on greased baking sheets. Cover and let rise in a warm place until doubled, about 20 minutes. Bake at 350° for 15-18 minutes or until golden brown. Immediately brush with butter; sprinkle with Parmesan cheese. Serve warm. **Yield:** 2 dozen.

Garlic Herb Bubble Loaf

(Pictured above)

I adapted an old sour cream bread recipe to make the dough for this deliciously different pull-apart loaf. It smells heavenly while baking, has a light crust and tender interior and is packed with herb and butter flavor. It's wonderful with a bowl of potato soup. —Katie Crill
Priest River, Idaho

  1/2 cup water (70° to 80°)
  1/2 cup sour cream
      2 tablespoons butter *or* margarine, softened
      3 tablespoons sugar
  1-1/2 teaspoons salt
      3 cups bread flour
  2-1/4 teaspoons active dry yeast
GARLIC HERB BUTTER:
  1/4 cup butter *or* margarine, melted
      4 garlic cloves, minced
  1/4 teaspoon *each* dried oregano, thyme and
      rosemary, crushed

In bread machine pan, place the first seven ingredients in order suggested by manufacturer. Select dough setting (check dough after 5 minutes of mixing; add 1 to 2 tablespoons of water or flour if needed). When cycle is completed, divide dough into 36 pieces. Shape each into a ball. In a bowl, combine butter, garlic and herbs. Dip each ball in mixture; place in an ungreased 9-in. x 5-in. x 3-in. loaf pan. Cover and let rise in a warm place until doubled, about 45 minutes. Bake at 375° for 35-40 minutes or until golden brown. Serve warm. **Yield:** 1 loaf.

Herbed Tomato Bread

I added my favorite herbs to another recipe to create this savory tomato loaf. For extra flavor, I serve it with a garlic chive spread my family loves. In fact, my sister confiscated all the leftovers at our last gathering! Slices of this moist bread also make great grilled cheese sandwiches. —Sherry Letson, Trinity, Alabama

  1/2 cup plus 2 tablespoons milk (70° to 80°)
      1 can (6 ounces) tomato paste
      1 egg
      2 tablespoons olive *or* vegetable oil
  1/2 teaspoon salt
      2 tablespoons minced fresh parsley
      1 tablespoon sugar
      2 teaspoons dried minced onion
  1/2 teaspoon garlic powder
  1/2 teaspoon dried tarragon
      3 cups bread flour
  2-1/4 teaspoons active dry yeast
GARLIC CHIVE SPREAD:
  1/2 cup butter *or* margarine, softened
      1 tablespoon minced chives
      1 garlic clove, minced

In bread machine pan, place the first 12 ingredients in order suggested by manufacturer. Select basic bread setting. Choose crust color and loaf size if available. Bake according to bread machine directions (check dough after 5 minutes of mixing; add 1 to 2 tablespoons of water or flour if needed). In a bowl, combine spread ingredients. Serve with bread. **Yield:** 1 loaf (1-1/2 pounds) and 1/2 cup spread. **Editor's Note:** Use of the timer feature is not recommended for this recipe.

Focaccia Bread Squares

(Pictured below)

Looking for an alternative to garlic bread? Try this golden focaccia bread that's a big hit at our house. The dough is easy to whip up in the bread machine, then season with rosemary, garlic salt and Parmesan cheese. I serve it warm whenever we're having spaghetti or another Italian dish. —Kay King, Dyersville, Iowa

   3/4 cup plus 3 tablespoons water (70° to 80°)
   3 tablespoons butter *or* margarine, softened
   2 tablespoons nonfat dry milk powder
   3 tablespoons sugar
1-1/2 teaspoons salt
   3 cups bread flour
2-1/4 teaspoons active dry yeast
TOPPING:
   2 tablespoons olive *or* vegetable oil
   3 tablespoons grated Parmesan cheese
   2 teaspoons minced fresh rosemary *or* 3/4
     teaspoon dried rosemary, crushed
   1/2 teaspoon garlic salt

In bread machine pan, place the first seven ingredients in order suggested by manufacturer. Select dough setting (check dough after 5 minutes of mixing; add 1 to 2 tablespoons of water or flour if needed). When cycle is completed, turn dough onto a lightly floured surface. Cover and let rest for 15 minutes. Knead for 1 minute. Roll into a 15-in. x 10-in. rectangle. Transfer to a greased 15-in. x 10-in. x 1-in. baking pan. Press dough 1/4 in. up the sides of pan. Cover and let rise in a warm place for

20-30 minutes or until slightly risen. With a wooden spoon handle, make indentations at 1-in. intervals. Brush dough with oil; sprinkle with Parmesan cheese, rosemary and garlic salt. Bake at 400° for 13-15 minutes or until lightly browned. Cool slightly. Cut into squares; serve warm. **Yield:** 2 dozen.

Zucchini Raisin Bread

I make this moist bread with shredded zucchini, plump raisins and cinnamon. Try slices of it toasted.
—Billie Hersh, Ritzville, Washington

✓ Uses less fat, sugar or salt. Includes Nutritional Analysis and Diabetic Exchanges.

   3/4 cup plus 2 tablespoons water (70° to 80°)
   2 tablespoons butter *or* margarine, softened
   1 cup shredded zucchini
   2 tablespoons sugar
4-1/2 teaspoons nonfat dry milk powder
   1 teaspoon salt
   1/2 teaspoon ground cinnamon
3-1/2 cups bread flour
2-1/2 teaspoons active dry yeast
   1/2 cup raisins

In bread machine pan, place the first nine ingredients in order suggested by manufacturer. Select basic bread setting. Choose crust color and loaf size if available. Bake according to bread machine directions (check dough after 5 minutes of mixing; add 1 to 2 tablespoons of water or flour if needed). Just before the final kneading (your machine may audibly signal this), add the raisins. **Yield:** 1 loaf (16 slices, about 1-1/2 pounds). **Nutritional Analysis:** One slice (prepared with margarine) equals 126 calories, 166 mg sodium, trace cholesterol, 26 gm carbohydrate, 4 gm protein, 2 gm fat, 1 gm fiber. **Diabetic Exchanges:** 1-1/2 starch, 1/2 fat. **Editor's Note:** Use of the timer feature is not recommended.

Caraway Dill Bread

The caraway really comes through in this herb bread. The nicely textured loaf is an especially good accompaniment to pork. —Margaret Runhardt, Aledo, Illinois

   2/3 cup water (70° to 80°)
   1 tablespoon butter *or* margarine, softened
   1 tablespoon nonfat dry milk powder
   2 tablespoons sugar
   1 teaspoon salt
   2 tablespoons dried parsley flakes
   1 tablespoon caraway seeds
   1 tablespoon dill weed
   2 cups bread flour
1-1/2 teaspoons active dry yeast

In a bread machine pan, place all ingredients in order suggested by manufacturer. Select basic bread setting. Choose crust color and loaf size if available. Bake according to bread machine directions (check dough after 5 minutes of mixing; add 1 to 2 tablespoons of water or flour if needed). **Yield:** 1 loaf (1 pound).

Focaccia Bread Squares

Fruited Pull-Apart Bread

(Pictured below)

My mother made this wreath-shaped coffee cake each Christmas. The dough is kneaded in the bread machine, so it turns out perfectly every time. —Bonnie Wilde
Springville, Utah

    3/4 cup water (70° to 80°)
      1 tablespoon butter *or* margarine, softened
      3 tablespoons sugar
      1 teaspoon salt
      1 tablespoon nonfat dry milk powder
2-1/4 cups bread flour
1-1/2 teaspoons active dry yeast
TOPPING:
      1 cup sugar
1-1/4 teaspoons ground cinnamon
    1/2 cup pecan halves
    1/3 cup halved maraschino cherries
      2 tablespoons raisins
      2 tablespoons dried cranberries
    1/3 cup butter *or* margarine, melted

In bread machine pan, place the first seven ingredients in order suggested by manufacturer. Select the dough setting (check dough after 5 minutes of mixing; add 1 to 2 tablespoons of water or flour if needed). When cycle is completed, turn dough onto a floured surface and punch down. Divide into 40 portions. In a bowl, combine the sugar and cinnamon; sprinkle 2 teaspoons in a greased 10-in. fluted tube pan. Arrange about a third of the pecans, cherries, raisins and cranberries in bottom of pan. Dip half of the dough pieces in butter, then roll in sugar mixture. Arrange evenly in pan. Repeat. Arrange remaining pecans and fruit over top. Cover and let rise in a warm place until doubled, about 1 hour. Bake at 350° for 30 minutes or until golden brown. Cool in pan for 5 minutes before inverting onto a serving platter. **Yield:** 1 loaf.

Italian Holiday Bread

A subtle anise flavor highlights this traditional bread dotted with chunks of citron. Before bread machines, I made a similar recipe by hand. —Betty Alexander
Kelowna, British Columbia

    2/3 cup milk (70° to 80°)
      1 egg
      4 teaspoons butter *or* margarine, softened
      1 teaspoon salt
    1/2 teaspoon ground aniseed
      2 cups all-purpose flour
1-1/2 teaspoons active dry yeast
    1/4 cup chopped candied citron
    1/4 cup chopped candied pineapple

In a bread machine pan, place all ingredients in order suggested by manufacturer. Select basic bread setting. Choose crust color and loaf size if available. Bake according to bread machine directions (check dough after 5 minutes of mixing; add 1 to 2 tablespoons of water or flour if needed). **Yield:** 1 loaf (1 pound). **Editor's Note:** Use of the timer feature is not recommended for this recipe.

Fruited Pull-Apart Bread

Pumpernickel Caraway Bread

(Pictured at right)

This rich, dark bread has an old-fashioned homemade taste that's oh-so-satisfying. Made with molasses and caraway seeds, it's moist and flavorful. My family prefers slices of it slathered with apple butter or cream cheese.
—Lorraine Darocha, Berkshire, Massachusetts

3/4 cup water (70° to 80°)
2 tablespoons molasses
4-1/2 teaspoons butter *or* margarine
1 teaspoon salt
1 cup bread flour
2/3 cup rye flour
1/3 cup whole wheat flour
2 tablespoons cornmeal
5 teaspoons baking cocoa
4-1/2 teaspoons sugar
3 teaspoons nonfat dry milk powder
1 teaspoon caraway seeds
1/4 teaspoon instant coffee granules
1-1/2 teaspoons active dry yeast

In bread machine pan, place all ingredients in order suggested by manufacturer. Select basic bread setting. Choose crust color and loaf size if available. Bake according to bread machine directions (check dough after 5 minutes of mixing; add 1 to 2 tablespoons of water or flour if needed). **Yield:** 1 loaf (1 pound).

Pumpernickel Caraway Bread

ter 5 minutes of mixing; add 1 to 2 tablespoons of water or flour if needed). In a mixing bowl, beat spread ingredients until smooth; serve with the bread. **Yield:** 1 loaf (1 pound) and about 1/2 cup spread. **Editor's Note:** Use of the timer feature is not recommended for this recipe. If your bread machine does not have a sweet bread setting, follow the manufacturer's directions using the basic setting.

Sour Cream Lemon Bread

(Pictured on page 150)

My family always requests this light, tender bread with a hint of lemon. This loaf is so scrumptious that it complements almost any meal. I serve slices with a creamy lemon spread for an early-morning treat or late-night snack that's simply dreamy. —Barbara Strickler, Syracuse, Indiana

1/4 cup sour cream
2 tablespoons lemon juice
2 to 3 tablespoons milk (70° to 80°)
2 tablespoons butter *or* margarine, softened
1 egg
2 teaspoons grated lemon peel
2 tablespoons sugar
1 teaspoon salt
1/4 teaspoon baking soda
2 cups bread flour
1-1/2 teaspoons active dry yeast
LEMON SPREAD:
1 package (3 ounces) cream cheese, softened
1/4 cup confectioners' sugar
1 tablespoon lemon juice
1 teaspoon lemon peel

In a measuring cup, combine sour cream and lemon juice. Add enough milk to measure 1/2 cup. In bread machine pan, place the sour cream mixture, butter, egg, lemon peel, sugar, salt, baking soda, flour and yeast in order suggested by manufacturer. Select sweet bread setting. Choose crust color and loaf size if available. Bake according to bread machine directions (check dough af-

Honey Oatmeal Bread

My mother served this honey-flavored loaf at a family gathering, and I had to have the recipe.
—Megan Schwartz, Burbank, Ohio

✓ Uses less fat, sugar or salt. Includes Nutritional Analysis and Diabetic Exchanges.

1-1/4 cups water (70° to 80°)
1/2 cup honey
2 tablespoons vegetable oil
1 cup quick-cooking oats
1-1/2 teaspoons salt
3 cups plus 2 tablespoons bread flour
2-1/4 teaspoons active dry yeast

In bread machine pan, place all ingredients in order suggested by manufacturer. Select basic bread setting. Choose crust color and loaf size if available. Bake according to bread machine directions (check dough after 5 minutes of mixing; add 1 to 2 tablespoons of water or flour if needed). **Yield:** 1 loaf (16 slices, 1-1/2 pounds). **Nutritional Analysis:** One slice equals 165 calories, 219 mg sodium, 0 cholesterol, 32 gm carbohydrate, 4 gm protein, 2 gm fat, 1 gm fiber. **Diabetic Exchanges:** 2 starch, 1/2 fat.

Multigrain Bread

(Pictured on page 150)

It's hard to get a good whole-grain bread where I live, so my bread machine comes in very handy when making this hearty loaf. I adapted it from an old recipe, and I've been enjoying it ever since. Cornmeal and wheat germ give it a wonderful texture and nutty flavor I love.
—Michele MacKinlay, Madoc, Ontario

    1 cup water (70° to 80°)
    2 tablespoons vegetable oil
    2 egg yolks
    1/4 cup molasses
    1 teaspoon salt
    1-1/2 cups bread flour
    1 cup whole wheat flour
    1/2 cup rye flour
    1/2 cup nonfat dry milk powder
    1/4 cup quick-cooking oats
    1/4 cup wheat germ
    1/4 cup cornmeal
    2-1/4 teaspoons active dry yeast

In bread machine pan, place all ingredients in order suggested by manufacturer. Select basic bread setting. Choose crust color and loaf size if available. Bake according to bread machine directions (check dough after 5 minutes of mixing; add 1 to 2 tablespoons water or flour if needed). **Yield:** 1 loaf (2 pounds). **Editor's Note:** Use of the timer feature is not recommended for this recipe.

Sweet Potato Bread

This pleasant bread is a welcome addition to fall meals. No one at our Thanksgiving table can get enough hearty slices slathered with creamy butter.
—Christi Ross
Mill Creek, Oklahoma

    1/2 cup plus 2 tablespoons milk (70° to 80°)
    1 egg, lightly beaten
    1-1/2 teaspoons salt
    4-1/2 teaspoons butter *or* margarine
    2 tablespoons brown sugar
    1/2 cup chopped canned sweet potatoes, drained
    1/3 cup miniature marshmallows
    3 cups bread flour
    2-1/4 teaspoons active dry yeast

In bread machine pan, place all ingredients in order suggested by manufacturer. Select basic bread setting. Choose crust color and loaf size if available. Bake according to bread machine directions (check dough after 5 minutes of mixing; add 1 to 2 tablespoons of water or flour if needed). **Yield:** 1 loaf (about 1-1/2 pounds). **Editor's Note:** Use of the timer feature is not recommended for this recipe.

Cranberry Biscuits

(Pictured below left)

I like the texture and nutrition of potato rolls and the taste of orange-cranberry bread, so I combined them in these yummy breakfast biscuits. Dotted with dried cranberries and drizzled with a sweet glaze, these tender treats are a family favorite.
—Debra Fulenwider
Colfax, California

    1-2/3 cups milk (70° to 80°)
    2 eggs
    3 tablespoons butter *or* margarine, softened
    3/4 cup mashed potato flakes
    1/4 cup sugar
    2 teaspoons salt
    1-1/4 teaspoons ground cinnamon
    1 teaspoon grated orange peel
    4 cups bread flour
    1 tablespoon active dry yeast
    1 cup dried cranberries
ORANGE GLAZE:
    1 cup confectioners' sugar
    2 to 3 tablespoons orange juice
    3 tablespoons chopped dried cranberries, optional

In bread machine pan, place the first 10 ingredients in order suggested by manufacturer. Select dough setting (check dough after

Cranberry Biscuits

5 minutes of mixing; add 1 to 2 tablespoons of water or flour if needed). Just before final kneading (your machine may audibly signal this), add cranberries. When cycle is completed, turn dough onto a lightly floured surface. Cover and let rest for 15 minutes. Roll or pat to 1/2-in. thickness. Cut with a 2-1/2-in. biscuit cutter. Place in a greased 15-in. x 10-in. x 1-in. baking pan. Cover and let rise in a warm place until almost doubled, about 40 minutes. Bake at 375° for 10-15 minutes or until golden brown. Combine confectioners' sugar and enough orange juice to achieve a glaze consistency. Drizzle over warm biscuits. Sprinkle with chopped cranberries if desired. **Yield:** about 1-1/2 dozen. **Editor's Note:** Use of the timer feature is not recommended.

Turkey Stuffing Bread

(Pictured at right)

My father-in-law had a ball experimenting with his bread machine to come up with this unique bread that tastes just like real turkey stuffing. It's fabulous with a chicken or turkey dinner ...and works well with all those Thanksgiving leftovers, too.
—Gayl Koster
Nunica, Michigan

   1 cup plus 1 tablespoon milk (70° to 80°)
   1 egg
   1 tablespoon butter *or* margarine, softened
   2 tablespoons brown sugar
1-1/2 teaspoons salt
   1/3 cup cornmeal
   3 cups bread flour
4-1/2 teaspoons dried minced onion
1-1/2 teaspoons celery seed
   3/4 teaspoon poultry seasoning
   1/2 teaspoon rubbed sage
   1/2 teaspoon pepper
2-1/4 teaspoons active dry yeast

In bread machine pan, place all ingredients in order suggested by manufacturer. Select basic bread setting. Choose crust color and loaf size if available. Bake according to bread machine directions (check dough after 5 minutes of mixing; add 1 to 2 tablespoons of water or flour if needed). **Yield:** 1 loaf (1-1/2 pounds). **Editor's Note:** Use of the timer feature is not recommended for this recipe.

Frosted Cinnamon Rolls

(Pictured on page 151)

These pretty cinnamon rolls are absolutely marvelous and taste just like the ones sold at the mall. Topped with a cream cheese frosting, they're best served warm with coffee.
—Velma Horton, LaGrange, California

   1 cup milk (70° to 80°)
   1/4 cup water (70° to 80°)
   1/4 cup butter *or* margarine, softened
   1 egg
   1 teaspoon salt
   4 cups bread flour
   1/4 cup instant vanilla pudding mix

Turkey Stuffing Bread

   1 tablespoon sugar
   1 tablespoon active dry yeast
FILLING:
   1/4 cup butter *or* margarine, softened
   1 cup packed brown sugar
   2 teaspoons ground cinnamon
FROSTING:
   4 ounces cream cheese, softened
   1/4 cup butter *or* margarine, softened
1-1/2 cups confectioners' sugar
1-1/2 teaspoons milk
   1/2 teaspoon vanilla extract

In bread machine pan, place first nine ingredients in order suggested by manufacturer. Select dough setting (check dough after 5 minutes of mixing; add 1 to 2 tablespoons water or flour if needed). When cycle is completed, turn dough onto lightly floured surface. Roll into a 17-in. x 10-in. rectangle. Spread with butter; sprinkle with brown sugar and cinnamon. Roll up, jelly-roll style, starting from a long side; pinch seam to seal. Cut into 21 slices. Place 12 slices, cut side down, in a greased 13-in. x 9-in. x 2-in. baking pan and nine rolls in a 9-in. square baking pan. Cover; let rise in a warm place until doubled, about 45 minutes. Bake at 350° for 20-25 minutes or until golden brown. Cool on wire racks for 5 minutes. In a mixing bowl, beat frosting ingredients. Frost warm rolls. Store in refrigerator. **Yield:** 21 rolls. **Editor's Note:** Use of timer feature is not recommended.

Chapter 12

IF YOU have only a few minutes to prepare a satisfying lunch or dinner for your family, turn to some souped-up suppers!

This chapter is brimming with easy-to-prepare chowder, soup and chili. Each recipe swiftly simmers on the stovetop, so your family won't have to wait long to hear you say, "Soup's on!"

You'll appreciate the amazing versatility of garden-fresh salads. While some offer make-ahead convenience, others can be tossed together on a moment's notice.

And for a hearty meal in hand, easy-to-assemble sandwiches are fast, filling fare for busy folks.

HAND-HELD MEALS. Clockwise from upper left: The Ultimate Grilled Cheese (p. 178), Fresh Veggie Pockets (p. 183), Bacon 'n' Egg Sandwiches (p. 182) and Mushroom Steak Hoagies (p. 199).

Marinated Broccoli Salad

(Pictured at right)

Plan ahead...needs to chill

I rely on bottled salad dressing to flavor this crunchy veggie combination. A bowlful makes a nice presentation at the table. You're the only person who has to know how simple it is to make this tasty salad! —Martha Smith
Rockledge, Georgia

✓ Uses less fat, sugar or salt. Includes Nutritional Analysis and Diabetic Exchanges.

> 4 cups broccoli florets
> 4 medium carrots, thinly sliced
> 2 small onions, sliced and separated into rings
> 1 can (2-1/4 ounces) sliced ripe olives, drained
> 1 jar (2 ounces) diced pimientos, drained
> 1 bottle (8 ounces) Italian salad dressing
> 1 teaspoon sugar
> 3/4 cup chopped walnuts, optional

In a bowl, combine the broccoli, carrots, onions, olives and pimientos. Add dressing and sugar; toss to coat. Cover and refrigerate for at least 4 hours, stirring occasionally. Just before serving, stir in walnuts if desired. **Yield:** 8 servings. **Nutritional Analysis:** One serving (prepared with fat-free Italian dressing and without walnuts) equals 59 calories, 378 mg sodium, 0 cholesterol, 11 gm carbohydrate, 2 gm protein, 1 gm fat, 3 gm fiber. **Diabetic Exchange:** 2 vegetable.

Sweet Club Sandwich

(Pictured at right)

Ready in 1 hour or less

I first tasted this delicious layered loaf at a potluck at work. This stacked sandwich seems fancy with its raspberry jam surprise, yet it's convenient because it can be assembled ahead of time and then warmed just before serving.
—Joanne Klopfenstein, North Liberty, Indiana

> 2 tubes (8 ounces *each*) refrigerated crescent rolls
> 2 tablespoons butter *or* margarine, melted
> 4 tablespoons honey, *divided*
> 6 ounces thinly sliced deli turkey
> 6 ounces sliced Muenster *or* Monterey Jack cheese
> 6 ounces thinly sliced deli ham
> 1/3 cup raspberry preserves
> 1 tablespoon sesame seeds

Unroll each tube of crescent roll dough into two rectangles. Place 2 in. apart on ungreased baking sheets; press perforations to seal. In a small bowl, combine butter and 2 tablespoons honey. Brush over dough. Bake at 375° for 10-12 minutes or until lightly browned. Cool on pans for 15 minutes. Carefully transfer one crust to a greased 15-in. x 10-in. x 1-in. baking pan. Layer with turkey, second crust, cheese and ham. Add third crust; spread with preserves. Top with remaining crust; spread with remaining honey. Sprinkle with sesame seeds. Bake,

uncovered, at 375° for 10-15 minutes or until crust is golden brown and loaf is heated through. Carefully cut into slices. **Yield:** 8 servings.

Cheesy Wild Rice Soup

(Pictured at right)

Ready in 30 minutes or less

We often eat easy-to-make soups when there's not a lot of time to cook. I replaced the wild rice requested in the original recipe with a boxed rice mix. This creamy concoction is now a family favorite. —Lisa Hofer
Hitchcock, South Dakota

> 1 package (6 ounces) quick-cooking long grain and wild rice mix
> 4 cups milk
> 1 can (10-3/4 ounces) condensed cream of potato soup, undiluted
> 8 ounces process American cheese, cubed
> 1/2 pound sliced bacon, cooked and crumbled

In a large saucepan, prepare rice according to package directions. Stir in milk, soup and cheese; mix well. Cook and stir until cheese is melted. Garnish with bacon. **Yield:** 6-8 servings.

Tangy Hot Dogs

Ready in 30 minutes or less

The young at heart will enjoy the zippy flavor of these hot dog sandwiches with all the toppings mixed right in. Our grown sons still ask me to prepare these for them.
—Janet Garski, Wisconsin Rapids, Wisconsin

> 1 package (1 pound) hot dogs, chopped
> 1 medium onion, chopped
> 1 teaspoon vegetable oil
> 1/4 cup all-purpose flour
> 1/2 teaspoon ground mustard
> 1/4 teaspoon pepper
> 1 cup finely chopped celery
> 1/2 cup water
> 1/2 cup ketchup
> 1/2 cup shredded process American cheese
> 8 hot dog buns, split

In a large saucepan, saute hot dogs and onion in oil until onion is tender. Sprinkle with flour, mustard and pepper. Stir in celery, water and ketchup until blended. Cook and stir over medium heat for 10 minutes; remove from the heat. Stir in cheese. Spoon about 1/2 cup hot dog mixture into each bun. **Yield:** 8 servings.

Ready Relish

When I have my food processor out, I chop pickles and olives and store them in covered plastic containers in the refrigerator. It's a snap to add the amounts I need to macaroni salad, potato salad, stuffed celery, etc.
—*Kathy Richardson, Falkner, Mississippi*

Marinated Broccoli Salad
Sweet Club Sandwich
Cheesy Wild Rice Soup

Crabby Bagels

Crabby Bagels

(Pictured above)

Ready in 15 minutes or less

Because I have a preschooler and new baby at home, sandwiches are a lunchtime staple. When my husband and I get tired of the peanut butter and jelly our daughter favors, we make this "grown-up" fare shared by a dear lady at church. The onion flavor from the bagels complements the crabmeat nicely. —Connie Faulkner, Moxee, Washington

> 1 can (6 ounces) crabmeat, drained, flaked and cartilage removed
> 1/2 cup shredded cheddar cheese
> 1/4 cup finely chopped celery
> 1/4 cup sour cream
> 3/4 teaspoon Worcestershire sauce
> 1/4 teaspoon salt
> 4 onion bagels, split
> 1 package (3 ounces) cream cheese, softened
> 4 lettuce leaves

In a bowl, combine the first six ingredients. Toast bagels; spread with cream cheese. On the bottom of each bagel, place a lettuce leaf and 1/4 cup of crab mixture. Replace tops. **Yield:** 4 servings.

The Ultimate Grilled Cheese

(Pictured on page 174)

Ready in 15 minutes or less

These gooey grilled cheese sandwiches, subtly seasoned with garlic, taste great for lunch with sliced apples. And they're really fast to whip up, too. To save seconds, I soften the cream cheese in the microwave, then blend it with the rest of the ingredients in the same bowl. That makes cleanup a breeze. —Kathy Norris, Streator, Illinois

> 1 package (3 ounces) cream cheese, softened
> 3/4 cup mayonnaise
> 1 cup (4 ounces) shredded cheddar cheese
> 1 cup (4 ounces) shredded mozzarella cheese
> 1/2 teaspoon garlic powder
> 1/8 teaspoon seasoned salt
> 10 slices Italian bread (1/2 inch thick)
> 2 tablespoons butter *or* margarine, softened

In a mixing bowl, beat cream cheese and mayonnaise until smooth. Stir in cheeses, garlic powder and seasoned salt. Spread five slices of bread with the cheese mixture, about 1/3 cup on each. Top with remaining bread. Butter the outsides of sandwiches; cook in a large skillet over medium heat until golden brown on both sides. **Yield:** 5 servings.

Colorful Chicken Croissants

(Pictured below)

Ready in 15 minutes or less

A friend of mine invented this fruity chicken salad. I've made it many times, and guests are always surprised at the pleasant blend of tastes and textures. It's handy to take in a cooler to a picnic, where you can assemble the croissants on site. —Sheila Lammers, Englewood, Colorado

 Uses less fat, sugar or salt. Includes Nutritional Analysis and Diabetic Exchanges.

> 2 cups cubed cooked chicken breast
> 1/4 cup diced celery
> 1/4 cup golden raisins
> 1/4 cup dried cranberries
> 1/4 cup sliced almonds
> 3/4 cup mayonnaise *or* salad dressing
> 2 tablespoons chopped red onion
> 1/4 teaspoon salt, optional

Colorful Chicken Croissants

1/4 teaspoon pepper
4 croissants, split

In a bowl, combine the first nine ingredients. Spoon about 1/2 cup into each croissant. **Yield:** 4 servings. **Nutritional Analysis:** One serving (prepared with fat-free mayonnaise and without salt; calculated without croissant) equals 184 calories, 331 mg sodium, 43 mg cholesterol, 20 gm carbohydrate, 13 gm protein, 5 gm fat, 2 gm fiber. **Diabetic Exchanges:** 2 lean meat, 1 fruit, 1 vegetable.

Hearty Eight-Layer Salad

(Pictured at right)

Plan ahead...needs to chill

I'm a great-grandmother and have been making this satisfying salad for years. It's my most requested recipe for family gatherings. It's simple to make ahead of time and looks lovely with all of its tasty layers. Dijon mustard gives a nice kick to the dressing.
—Noreen Meyer
Madison, Wisconsin

1-1/2 cups uncooked small shell macaroni
1 tablespoon vegetable oil
3 cups shredded lettuce
3 hard-cooked eggs, sliced
1/4 teaspoon salt
1/8 teaspoon pepper
1 cup julienned fully cooked ham
1 cup julienned hard salami
1 package (10 ounces) frozen peas, thawed
1 cup mayonnaise
1/4 cup sour cream
1/4 cup chopped green onions
2 teaspoons Dijon mustard
1 cup (4 ounces) shredded Colby *or* Monterey Jack cheese
2 tablespoons minced fresh parsley

Cook macaroni according to package directions; drain and rinse with cold water. Drizzle with oil; toss to coat. Place the lettuce in a 2-1/2-qt. glass serving bowl; top with macaroni and eggs. Sprinkle with salt and pepper. Layer with ham, salami and peas. Combine mayonnaise, sour cream, green onions and mustard. Spread over the top. Cover and refrigerate for several hours or overnight. Just before serving, sprinkle with cheese and parsley. **Yield:** 10 servings.

Fajita Pitas

Ready in 1 hour or less

I was late coming home one evening and forgot to pick up tortillas for the fajitas we planned for dinner. So we used pita bread that I had in the freezer instead. The warm chicken-filled pockets, garnished with a homemade sauce and other tasty toppings, are often requested when we're hungry for something in a hurry.
—Diana Jones
Springtown, Texas

✓ Uses less fat, sugar or salt. Includes Nutritional Analysis and Diabetic Exchanges.

Hearty Eight-Layer Salad

6 boneless skinless chicken breast halves
1 large onion, sliced
1 large green pepper, thinly sliced
1 tablespoon vegetable oil
2 cups (8 ounces) shredded Mexican cheese blend *or* cheddar cheese
8 pita breads, halved, warmed
SAUCE:
1 medium onion, finely chopped
1 medium tomato, finely chopped
1/2 jalapeno pepper, finely chopped*
1 tablespoon minced fresh cilantro *or* parsley
1 tablespoon vegetable oil
Guacamole and sour cream, optional

Grill chicken, covered, over medium heat for 16-20 minutes or until juices run clear, turning occasionally. Cut into strips. In a skillet, saute onion and green pepper in oil. Add chicken and cheese. Stuff into pita halves; place on an ungreased baking sheet. Bake at 325° for 10 minutes or until cheese is melted. Meanwhile, for sauce, combine the onion, tomato, jalapeno, cilantro and oil in a bowl; mix well. Serve sauce, guacamole and sour cream if desired with pitas. **Yield:** 8 servings. **Nutritional Analysis:** One serving (prepared with reduced-fat cheddar cheese and without guacamole and sour cream) equals 341 calories, 530 mg sodium, 42 mg cholesterol, 40 gm carbohydrate, 27 gm protein, 8 gm fat, 3 gm fiber. **Diabetic Exchanges:** 2 starch, 2 very lean meat, 1 fat, 1 vegetable. ***Editor's Note:** When cutting or seeding hot peppers, use rubber or plastic gloves to protect your hands. Avoid touching your face.

Herbed Vinaigrette
Broccoli Ham Turnovers
Creamy Tomato Soup

Creamy Tomato Soup

(Pictured at left)

Ready in 30 minutes or less

My husband, who doesn't like tomato soup, really likes this rich and creamy version. It's easy, but it tastes like you put a lot of work into it. When I share it with co-workers, everyone loves it. —Marie Keyes, Cheney, Washington

✓ Uses less fat, sugar or salt. Includes Nutritional Analysis and Diabetic Exchanges.

    1 medium onion, chopped
    2 tablespoons butter *or* margarine
    2 cans (14-1/2 ounces *each*) diced tomatoes, undrained
    2 cans (10-3/4 ounces *each*) condensed tomato soup, undiluted
1-1/2 cups milk
    1 teaspoon sugar
  1/2 to 1 teaspoon dried basil
  1/2 to 1 teaspoon paprika
  1/8 to 1/4 teaspoon garlic powder
    1 package (8 ounces) cream cheese, cubed

In a saucepan, saute onion in butter until tender. Stir in tomatoes, soup, milk, sugar, basil, paprika and garlic powder. Bring to a boil. Reduce heat; cover and simmer for 10 minutes. Stir in cream cheese until melted. Serve immediately. **Yield:** 8 servings (2 quarts). **Nutritional Analysis:** One 1-cup serving (prepared with reduced-fat margarine, no-salt-added diced tomatoes, low-fat condensed tomato soup, skim milk and light cream cheese) equals 157 calories, 457 mg sodium, 11 mg cholesterol, 21 gm carbohydrate, 6 gm protein, 5 gm fat, 2 gm fiber. **Diabetic Exchanges:** 1-1/2 starch, 1 fat.

Broccoli Ham Turnovers

(Pictured at left)

Ready in 1 hour or less

I enjoy creating special dishes for my family and friends. Although I don't make sandwiches often, these attractive turnovers with their fresh-tasting filling are an exception. —Lupie Molinar, Tucson, Arizona

    2 cups broccoli florets
1-1/2 cups (6 ounces) shredded sharp cheddar cheese
  1/2 cup cubed fully cooked ham
  1/2 cup sliced green onions
    1 tablespoon minced fresh parsley
  1/4 teaspoon ground nutmeg
Salt and pepper to taste
Pastry for a double-crust pie
    1 egg
    1 tablespoon whipping cream

Place broccoli in a steamer basket over 1 in. of boiling water in a saucepan. Cover and steam for 5-8 minutes or until crisp-tender. Rinse in cold water; drain well. In a bowl, combine the broccoli, cheese, ham, onions, pars-ley, nutmeg, salt and pepper. On a floured surface, roll out the pastry; cut each in half. Place 1-1/2 cups of the filling on one side of each half; flatten filling with a spoon. Combine the egg and cream; brush some over pastry edges. Fold pastry over filling. Seal edges and prick tops with a fork. Place on a baking sheet; brush with remaining egg mixture. Bake at 400° for 18-22 minutes or until golden brown. Let stand 5 minutes before serving. **Yield:** 4 servings.

Herbed Vinaigrette

(Pictured at left)

Ready in 15 minutes or less

This simple vinegar and oil dressing is seasoned with three herbs for robust flavor. We like balsamic vinegar, so we often use it in place of wine vinegar as a nice change of pace. —Mildred Sherrer, Bay City, Texas

✓ Uses less fat, sugar or salt. Includes Nutritional Analysis and Diabetic Exchanges.

  1/4 cup olive *or* vegetable oil
  1/4 cup cider *or* red wine vinegar
    1 to 2 tablespoons sugar
    1 teaspoon minced fresh basil *or* 1/4 teaspoon dried basil
    1 teaspoon minced fresh thyme *or* 1/4 teaspoon dried thyme
  1/2 teaspoon minced fresh marjoram *or* 1/8 teaspoon dried marjoram

In a jar with a tight-fitting lid, combine all ingredients; shake well. Serve over greens. **Yield:** 1/2 cup. **Nutritional Analysis:** 1 tablespoon (prepared with artificial sweetener equivalent to 1 tablespoon sugar) equals 62 calories, trace sodium, 0 cholesterol, trace carbohydrate, trace protein, 7 gm fat, 0 fiber. **Diabetic Exchange:** 1-1/2 fat.

Success with Salads

- For a really delicious coleslaw, substitute your favorite bottled French dressing for the traditional dressing. Even folks who don't like coleslaw like this salad. —*Sue Leone, Eagan, Minnesota*

- To make potato salad in a hurry, I quickly bake the potatoes in the microwave oven until tender and then mash them with a potato masher. I add chopped onions, eggs and celery, then finish with my family's favorite dressing and seasonings. —*Joyce Wilson Somerset, Kentucky*

- To make the most of day-old bread, I prepare my own croutons. I drizzle bread cubes with garlic butter and sprinkle with parsley, salt, white pepper and a dried vegetable blend used for seasoning soups and stews. Then I bake them until they're crunchy. When my croutons are down to mostly crumbs, I grind them and use them as a flavorful coating for baked chicken. —*Zola Brown, Waianae, Hawaii*

eggs and crunchy green onions make these special sandwiches look impressive when company drops by for lunch. Best of all, they're a snap to assemble.
—Ann Fuemmeler, Glasgow, Missouri

1/2 cup sour cream
8 slices bread
4 green onions, chopped
4 slices process American cheese
2 hard-cooked eggs, cut into 1/4-inch slices
8 bacon strips, cooked and drained
1/4 cup butter *or* margarine, softened

Spread sour cream on one side of four slices of bread. Top with onions, cheese, eggs and bacon. Top with the remaining bread. Butter outsides of sandwiches; cook in a large skillet over medium heat until golden brown on both sides. **Yield:** 4 servings.

Sour Cream Macaroni Salad

Plan ahead...needs to chill

This make-ahead macaroni salad never fails to stay moist. I double the recipe for potluck dinners. It's a reliable standby that always satisfies. —Rita Morris
Gastonia, North Carolina

 Uses less fat, sugar or salt. Includes Nutritional Analysis and Diabetic Exchanges.

1 package (8 ounces) elbow macaroni
3/4 cup diced green pepper
1/3 cup sweet pickle relish
1 jar (2 ounces) diced pimientos, drained
1 tablespoon grated onion
1/2 cup mayonnaise
1/2 cup sour cream
1/4 cup milk
1-1/2 teaspoons salt *or* salt-free seasoning blend
Pepper to taste

Cook macaroni according to package directions; rinse in cold water and drain. Place in a large bowl; add green pepper, pickle relish, pimientos and onion. In a small bowl, combine the remaining ingredients; mix well. Pour over macaroni mixture and toss to coat. Cover and refrigerate until serving. **Yield:** 6 servings. **Nutritional Analysis:** One 1/2-cup serving (prepared with fat-free mayonnaise, light sour cream, skim milk and salt-free seasoning blend) equals 138 calories, 198 mg sodium, 5 mg cholesterol, 26 gm carbohydrate, 4 gm protein, 2 gm fat, 1 gm fiber. **Diabetic Exchanges:** 1-1/2 starch, 1/2 fat.

Apple-Walnut Turkey Sandwiches

Apple-Walnut Turkey Sandwiches

(Pictured above)

Ready in 15 minutes or less

When you live where temperatures easily climb to 100° or more in the summer, you look for recipes that get you in and out of the kitchen in minutes. This luscious sandwich, with its cool Waldorf salad filling, is a breeze to prepare.
—Cathy Dobbins, Rio Rancho, New Mexico

3/4 cup mayonnaise
1/4 cup chopped celery
1/4 cup raisins
1/4 cup chopped walnuts, toasted
1 medium tart apple, chopped
3/4 pound sliced deli turkey
8 slices sourdough bread
Lettuce leaves

In a bowl, combine mayonnaise, celery, raisins and walnuts. Stir in apple; set aside. Place turkey on four slices of bread. Top with apple mixture, lettuce and remaining bread. **Yield:** 4 servings.

Bacon 'n' Egg Sandwiches

(Pictured on page 175)

Ready in 15 minutes or less

I came across this unique grilled combo when I was digging in my mom's recipe box. The crisp bacon, hard-cooked

Bacon Bits in Brief

Do you often need fresh, crunchy bacon bits for soups, salads and other recipes? I have a method that works great. I store bacon in the freezer. Before frying it, I cut the frozen slices crosswise into little strips. Then I fry them on medium until crisp, separating the strips during cooking. I drain the bits on paper towel and they're ready for use.
—Claire Menges
Leonardtown, Maryland

Fresh Veggie Pockets

(Pictured on page 175)

Ready in 15 minutes or less

One summer I worked at a health food store that sold sandwiches. We were close to a college campus, so I made lots of these fresh filled pitas for the students. Crunchy with crisp vegetables and nutty sunflower kernels, they're a fast-to-fix lunch when you're on the go.
—Linda Reeves, Cloverdale, Indiana

✓ Uses less fat, sugar or salt. Includes Nutritional Analysis and Diabetic Exchanges.

  1 carton (8 ounces) cream cheese spread
1/4 cup sunflower kernels
  1 teaspoon seasoned salt *or* salt-free seasoning blend
  4 wheat pita breads, halved
  1 medium tomato, thinly sliced
  1 medium cucumber, thinly sliced
  1 cup sliced fresh mushrooms
  1 ripe avocado, peeled and sliced

In a bowl, combine the cream cheese, sunflower kernels and seasoned salt; spread about 2 tablespoons on the inside of each pita half. Layer with tomato, cucumber, mushrooms and avocado. **Yield:** 4 servings. **Nutritional Analysis:** One serving (prepared with fat-free cream cheese, unsalted sunflower kernels and salt-free seasoning blend) equals 378 calories, 660 mg sodium, 5 mg cholesterol, 48 gm carbohydrate, 18 gm protein, 15 gm fat, 9 gm fiber. **Diabetic Exchanges:** 3 starch, 2 fat, 1 vegetable, 1 meat.

BLT Chicken Salad

(Pictured at right)

Ready in 30 minutes or less

I like this salad because I can prepare all the ingredients ahead of time and just throw it together at the last minute. Barbecue sauce in the dressing gives a different taste to this salad, which features the fun fixings for a BLT chicken sandwich. Even picky eaters love it. —Cindy Moore
Mooresville, North Carolina

1/2 cup mayonnaise
  3 to 4 tablespoons barbecue sauce
  2 tablespoons finely chopped onion
  1 tablespoon lemon juice
1/4 teaspoon pepper
  8 cups torn salad greens
  2 large tomatoes, chopped
1-1/2 pounds boneless skinless chicken breasts, cooked and cubed
 10 bacon strips, cooked and crumbled
  2 hard-cooked eggs, sliced

In a small bowl, combine the first five ingredients; mix well. Cover and refrigerate until serving. Place salad greens on a large serving platter. Sprinkle with tomatoes, chicken and bacon; garnish with eggs. Drizzle with dressing. **Yield:** 8 servings.

Pea 'n' Cheese Salad

Plan ahead...needs to chill

Radish slices add color and crunch to this fresh-tasting potluck favorite. I usually serve it in a bowl lined with romaine leaves, then garnish it with radish roses.
—Inez Orsburn, Demotte, Indiana

  1 package (20 ounces) frozen peas, thawed
  1 cup chopped celery
  2 hard-cooked eggs, chopped
1/4 cup chopped green onions
  1 cup cubed cheddar cheese
1/2 cup thinly sliced radishes *or* 1 jar (2 ounces) pimientos, drained
  1 cup mayonnaise
  3 tablespoons sweet pickle relish
  1 teaspoon sugar
  1 teaspoon seasoned salt
  1 teaspoon ground mustard

In a bowl, combine the first six ingredients. In a small bowl, combine the mayonnaise, relish and seasonings. Stir into pea mixture. Cover and refrigerate until serving. **Yield:** 8-10 servings.

BLT Chicken Salad

Almond-Raspberry Tossed Salad

Ready in 15 minutes or less

My husband and I helped prepare this summery salad for a weekend retreat. The recipe served 60 to 80 people, so I modified it to use at home. The sweet-tart dressing is wonderful over romaine with toasted almonds and fresh raspberries. —Jennifer Long, St. Peters, Missouri

    8 cups torn romaine
    1 cup fresh raspberries
  1/2 cup sliced almonds, toasted
  1/2 cup seedless raspberry jam
  1/4 cup cider *or* white wine vinegar
  1/4 cup honey
    2 tablespoons plus 2 teaspoons vegetable oil

In a salad bowl, combine the romaine, raspberries and almonds. In a blender, combine the remaining ingredients; cover and process until smooth. Serve with salad. **Yield:** 10 servings.

Dilly Chicken Sandwiches

(Pictured at right)

Ready in 30 minutes or less

A creamy lemon-dill spread adds fresh flavor to tender chicken served between slices of grilled French bread. People who have tried this sandwich say it's "to die for". —Orien Major, Hinton, Alberta

    4 boneless skinless chicken breast halves
    6 tablespoons butter *or* margarine, softened, *divided*
    1 garlic clove, minced
  3/4 teaspoon dill weed, *divided*
    8 slices French bread (1/2 inch thick)
    4 tablespoons cream cheese, softened
    2 teaspoons lemon juice
    4 lettuce leaves
    8 slices tomato

Pound chicken to flatten evenly; set aside. In a skillet, melt 3 tablespoons of butter; add garlic and 1/2 teaspoon dill. Add chicken; cook until juices run clear. Remove and keep warm. Spread both sides of bread with remaining butter. In a skillet or griddle, grill bread on both sides until golden brown. In a small bowl, combine cream cheese, lemon juice and remaining dill; spread on one side of grilled bread. Place lettuce, chicken and tomato on four slices of bread; top with remaining bread. **Yield:** 4 servings.

Berry-Mandarin Tossed Salad

(Pictured at right)

Ready in 30 minutes or less

The recipe for this beautiful blend came from a local berry farm some years ago. We like to take the sweet and savory salad on picnics to accompany cold chicken and a loaf of crusty bread. Every bite tastes like summer. —Linda Jo Wahlgren, Mt. Horeb, Wisconsin

  1/4 cup sugar
    2 tablespoons cider vinegar
    2 tablespoons honey
1-1/4 teaspoons lemon juice
  1/2 teaspoon paprika
  1/2 teaspoon ground mustard
  1/2 teaspoon grated onion
  1/4 teaspoon celery seed
Dash salt
  1/3 cup vegetable oil
    8 cups torn mixed salad greens
    2 cups sliced fresh strawberries
    1 can (11 ounces) mandarin oranges, drained
    1 medium sweet onion, sliced into rings
  1/3 cup slivered almonds, toasted
    4 bacon strips, cooked and crumbled

In a 2-cup microwave-safe bowl, combine the first nine ingredients. Microwave, uncovered, on high for 1-1/2 to 2 minutes; stir until sugar is dissolved. Whisk in oil. Cover and refrigerate until serving. In a salad bowl, combine the greens, strawberries, oranges, onion, almonds and bacon. Drizzle with dressing and gently toss to coat. **Yield:** 12-14 servings. **Editor's Note:** This recipe was tested in an 850-watt microwave.

Zippy Corn Chowder

(Pictured at right)

Ready in 1 hour or less

This thick colorful chowder was so well received the first time I made it that some of us had to go without seconds. Now I make this hearty soup often. —Kera Bredin, Vancouver, British Columbia

    1 medium onion, chopped
    1 medium green pepper, chopped
    2 tablespoons butter *or* margarine
    1 can (14-1/2 ounces) chicken broth
    2 large red potatoes, cubed
    1 jalapeno pepper, chopped*
    2 teaspoons Dijon mustard
    1 teaspoon salt
  1/2 teaspoon paprika
  1/4 to 1/2 teaspoon crushed red pepper flakes
    3 cups frozen corn
    4 green onions, chopped
    3 cups milk, *divided*
  1/4 cup all-purpose flour

In a large saucepan, saute the onion and green pepper in butter until tender. Add the broth and potatoes. Bring to a boil. Reduce heat; cover and simmer for 15 minutes or until potatoes are almost tender. Stir in the jalapeno, mustard, salt, paprika and red pepper flakes. Add the corn, green onions and 2-1/2 cups milk. Bring to a boil. Combine flour and remaining milk until smooth; gradually add to the soup. Bring to a boil. Cook and stir for 2 minutes or until thickened and bubbly. **Yield:** 8 servings (2 quarts). ***Editor's Note:** When cutting or seeding hot peppers, use rubber or plastic gloves to protect your hands. Avoid touching your face. Leave the seeds in for spicier flavor.

Berry-Mandarin Tossed Salad
Zippy Corn Chowder
Dilly Chicken Sandwiches

Fruit-Filled Raspberry Ring
Summer Spinach Salad
Shrimp Taco Salad
Nutty Broccoli Slaw

Nutty Broccoli Slaw

(Pictured above)

Ready in 15 minutes or less

My daughter gave me the recipe for this delightful salad. The sweet dressing nicely coats a crisp blend of broccoli slaw mix, carrots, onions, almonds and sunflower kernels. Crushed ramen noodles provide even more crunch. It's a smash hit wherever I take it. —Dora Clapsaddle
Kensington, Ohio

　1 package (3 ounces) chicken ramen noodles
　1 package (16 ounces) broccoli slaw mix
　2 cups sliced green onions (about 2 bunches)
1-1/2 cups broccoli florets
　1 can (6 ounces) ripe olives, drained and
　　　halved
　1 cup sunflower kernels, toasted
1/2 cup slivered almonds, toasted

1/2 cup sugar
1/2 cup cider vinegar
1/2 cup olive *or* vegetable oil

Set aside the noodle seasoning packet; crush the noodles and place in a large bowl. Add the slaw mix, onions, broccoli, olives, sunflower kernels and almonds. In a jar with a tight-fitting lid, combine the sugar, vinegar, oil and contents of seasoning packet; shake well. Drizzle over salad and toss to coat. Serve immediately. **Yield:** 16 servings.

Summer Spinach Salad

(Pictured above)

Ready in 30 minutes or less

Guests always request the recipe for this fabulous spinach salad. Tossed with ripe banana chunks, fresh strawberries and toasted almonds, it looks and tastes special enough

for company. The tangy poppy seed dressing is a snap to combine in the blender. —Callie Berger
Diamond Springs, California

1/2 cup vegetable oil
1/4 cup chopped onion
2 tablespoons plus 2 teaspoons cider *or* red wine vinegar
2 tablespoons plus 2 teaspoons sugar
1-1/2 teaspoons ground mustard
1/2 teaspoon salt
1-1/2 teaspoons poppy seeds
8 cups torn fresh spinach
3 green onions, sliced
2 pints fresh strawberries, sliced
3 large ripe bananas, cut into 1/2-inch slices
1/2 cup slivered almonds, toasted

Place the first six ingredients in a blender or food processor; cover and process until the sugar is dissolved. Add the poppy seeds; process just until blended. In a salad bowl, combine the remaining ingredients. Drizzle with dressing; toss to coat. Serve immediately. **Yield:** 14 servings.

Shrimp Taco Salad

(Pictured at left)

Ready in 30 minutes or less

I created this main-dish salad to satisfy our family's love of shrimp. It has lots of contrasting textures, including firm taco-seasoned shrimp, crispy tortilla strips and hearty black beans. A convenient bag of salad greens cuts down on prep time, so I can have this meal ready in half an hour.
—Ellen Morrell, Hazleton, Pennsylvania

1 pound uncooked large shrimp, peeled and deveined
1 envelope taco seasoning, *divided*
1/2 cup plus 3 tablespoons olive *or* vegetable oil, *divided*
1 small onion, finely chopped
3 tablespoons cider *or* red wine vinegar
2 tablespoons diced green *or* sweet red pepper
6 garlic cloves, minced
1/2 teaspoon ground coriander
1/4 teaspoon sugar
3 corn tortillas (6 inches), cut into 1/4-inch strips
1 package (8 ounces) ready-to-serve salad greens
1 medium tomato, chopped
1 can (8 ounces) black beans, rinsed and drained
2 cups (8 ounces) finely shredded Colby/ Monterey Jack cheese

Remove shrimp tails if desired. Place shrimp in a bowl; sprinkle with half of the taco seasoning. Set aside. In another bowl, combine 1/2 cup oil, onion, vinegar, green pepper, garlic, coriander and sugar; set aside. In a skillet, stir-fry tortilla strips in remaining oil; drain on paper towels. Sprinkle with remaining taco seasoning. In the same skillet, saute shrimp for 8-10 minutes or until

pink. In a large bowl, combine the greens, tomato, beans, shrimp and tortilla strips. Drizzle with dressing. Sprinkle with cheese; toss. **Yield:** 6-8 servings.

Fruit-Filled Raspberry Ring

(Pictured at left)

Plan ahead...start the night before

People love this fruity gelatin ring that gets extra flavor from an ambrosia-like mixture in the center. I've been bringing it to potlucks, buffets and showers for 20 years. While it looks like you fussed, it's easy to make the night before a special occasion. —Janice Steinmetz
Somers, Connecticut

2 packages (6 ounces *each*) raspberry gelatin
4 cups boiling water
1 quart raspberry sherbet
1 can (14 ounces) pineapple tidbits, drained
1 can (11 ounces) mandarin oranges, drained
1 cup flaked coconut
1 cup miniature marshmallows
1 cup (8 ounces) sour cream

In a bowl, dissolve gelatin in boiling water. Stir in sherbet until melted. Pour into an 8-cup ring mold coated with nonstick cooking spray. Chill overnight or until firm. In a bowl, combine the pineapple, oranges, coconut, marshmallows and sour cream. Cover and chill. To serve, unmold gelatin onto a serving plate. Spoon fruit mixture into center of ring. **Yield:** 12-16 servings.

Sandwich Secrets

- Tuna salad sandwiches are a must at our picnics. To avoid soggy slices of bread, I pack the tuna salad mixture in a plastic container with a tight-fitting lid and keep it in the cooler with ice. I bring along bread or rolls and assemble the sandwiches at the site. They taste fresh and terrific. —*Charlotte Baillargeon Hinsdale, Massachusetts*

- When making sloppy joes, do you have trouble keeping the mixture on the bun? Next time, stir in a few mashed potato flakes. The thicker mixture is less likely to crumble and fall out. For easier serving, use an ice cream scoop to place the right amount on each bun. —*Carolyn Street Fort Collins, Colorado*

- To make hamburger patties of the same size and shape, I save the lid from a carton of cottage cheese, cover it with a plastic sandwich bag and pat ground beef on top of it. The edge on the lid stops the hamburger from spilling over, and once the patty is formed, it's easy to flip the lid upside down onto a tray. The patty comes out nicely and the bag can be removed for quick cleanup. —*Doris Rector Comanche, Oklahoma*

- Here's a hurry-up way to make grilled cheese sandwiches for a crowd: Prepare the sandwiches as you would for the griddle, but place them all on a cookie sheet instead. Bake in a 350° oven for 5-8 minutes on each side until they're golden brown. —*Sharon Sullivan, Lake Villa, Illinois*

**Grilled Chicken Salad
Herbed Gazpacho
Italian Deli Rollers**

Grilled Chicken Salad

(Pictured at left)

Ready in 1 hour or less

This tasty salad is fast to assemble, and cleanup's a breeze because the chicken is cooked on the grill. Serve with the warmed dressing and crusty bread or rolls, and you have a complete meal that the whole family is sure to love.
—Dawn Davidson, Thornton, Ontario

- 1/4 cup olive *or* vegetable oil
- 1/4 cup chicken broth
- 3 tablespoons lemon juice
- 1 teaspoon dried basil
- 1 teaspoon dried oregano
- 1 teaspoon Dijon mustard
- 1/4 teaspoon salt
- 1/4 teaspoon lemon-pepper seasoning
- 4 boneless skinless chicken breast halves
- 1 large red onion, sliced and separated into rings
- 10 cups torn romaine
- 1 medium sweet red pepper, chopped
- 3/4 cup crumbled feta *or* blue cheese

In a bowl, combine the first eight ingredients; mix well. Place half in a saucepan and set aside. Brush remaining vinaigrette over chicken and onion rings. Grill chicken and onion, covered, over medium heat for 12 minutes or until meat juices run clear, turning once. Cut chicken into 1/2-in. slices. In a large bowl or on salad plates, layer romaine, onion, chicken, red pepper and cheese. Heat the reserved vinaigrette; drizzle over salad. Serve immediately. **Yield:** 8 servings.

Herbed Gazpacho

(Pictured at left)

Plan ahead…needs to chill

For a unique first course, serve this colorful soup. Chilled V-8 juice is the base for this soup that's chock-full of generous chunks of chopped tomatoes, green pepper and cucumber. For a fancier finish, I sometimes garnish individual bowls with cooked shrimp.
—Carole Benson, Cabazon, California

- 1 can (46 ounces) V-8 juice, chilled
- 1 can (14-1/2 ounces) Italian stewed tomatoes
- 3 medium tomatoes, chopped
- 1 medium green pepper, chopped
- 1 medium cucumber, chopped
- 1/2 cup Italian salad dressing
- 1/4 cup minced fresh parsley
- 4 to 6 garlic cloves, minced
- 1 teaspoon Italian seasoning
- 1 teaspoon salt
- 1/4 teaspoon pepper
- Cooked shrimp, optional

In a large bowl, combine the first 11 ingredients; mix well. Cover and refrigerate for at least 1 hour. Garnish with shrimp if desired. **Yield:** 10-12 servings (about 3 quarts).

Italian Deli Rollers

(Pictured at left)

Ready in 15 minutes or less

I make these handy roll-ups on summer days when it's too hot for stovetop cooking. They're a fun change of pace from traditional sandwiches.
—Carol Bassett, Kentwood, Michigan

- 2 tablespoons butter *or* margarine, softened
- 3 flour tortillas (10 inches)
- 6 slices provolone cheese
- 6 thin slices deli ham
- 6 thin slices bologna
- 30 thin slices pepperoni
- 18 banana pepper rings
- 9 thin slices tomato
- 6 lettuce leaves
- 2 tablespoons mayonnaise

Spread butter on one side of tortillas. Layer each with cheese, ham, bologna, pepperoni, peppers, tomato and lettuce to within 2 in. of edge. Spread mayonnaise over lettuce. Roll up tightly. Serve immediately or wrap in plastic wrap and chill up to 2 hours. **Yield:** 3 servings.

Tortellini Caesar Salad

Ready in 30 minutes or less

This salad was served at a dear friend's baby shower by a health-conscious friend who suggested the dressing be prepared with low-fat or fat-free ingredients. Either way, the creamy dressing has plenty of garlic flavor and coats the pasta, romaine and croutons nicely.
—Tammy Steenbock, Sembach Air Base, Germany

✓ Uses less fat, sugar or salt. Includes Nutritional Analysis and Diabetic Exchanges.

- 1 package (9 ounces) frozen cheese tortellini
- 1/2 cup mayonnaise
- 1/4 cup milk
- 1/4 cup plus 1/3 cup shredded Parmesan cheese, *divided*
- 2 tablespoons lemon juice
- 2 garlic cloves, minced
- 8 cups torn romaine
- 1 cup seasoned croutons
- Halved cherry tomatoes, optional

Cook tortellini according to package directions. Meanwhile, in a small bowl, combine the mayonnaise, milk, 1/4 cup Parmesan cheese, lemon juice and garlic; mix well. Drain tortellini and rinse in cold water; place in a large bowl. Add the romaine and remaining Parmesan. Just before serving, drizzle with dressing and toss to coat. Top with croutons and tomatoes if desired. **Yield:** 10 servings. **Nutritional Analysis:** One serving (prepared with fat-free mayonnaise and skim milk and without tomatoes) equals 144 calories, 318 mg sodium, 14 mg cholesterol, 18 gm carbohydrate, 8 gm protein, 4 gm fat, 1 gm fiber. **Diabetic Exchanges:** 1 starch, 1 vegetable, 1 fat.

Ground Beef Gyros

(Pictured at right)

Ready in 30 minutes or less

If your family likes gyros as much as mine, they'll love this easy version that's made with ground beef instead of lamb. I found the recipe in a newspaper and adapted it to fit our tastes. They're very much like the ones served at a local restaurant. A cucumber yogurt sauce adds an authentic finishing touch. —Ruth Stahl, Shepherd, Montana

 Uses less fat, sugar or salt. Includes Nutritional Analysis and Diabetic Exchanges.

> 1 carton (8 ounces) plain yogurt
> 1/3 cup chopped seeded cucumber
> 2 tablespoons finely chopped onion
> 1 garlic clove, minced
> 1 teaspoon sugar
> FILLING:
> 1 pound ground beef
> 1-1/2 teaspoons dried oregano
> 1 teaspoon garlic powder
> 1 teaspoon onion powder
> 1 teaspoon salt, optional
> 3/4 teaspoon pepper
> 4 pita breads, halved, warmed
> 3 cups shredded lettuce
> 1 large tomato, chopped
> 1 small onion, sliced

In a bowl, combine the first five ingredients. Cover and refrigerate. In a bowl, combine beef and seasonings; mix well. Shape into four patties. Grill, covered, over medium-hot heat for 10-12 minutes or until no longer pink, turning once. Cut patties into thin slices; stuff into pita halves. Add lettuce, tomato and onion. Serve with the yogurt sauce. **Yield:** 4 servings. **Nutritional Analysis:**

Ground Beef Gyros

One serving (prepared with fat-free yogurt and lean ground beef and without salt) equals 422 calories, 453 mg sodium, 42 mg cholesterol, 45 gm carbohydrate, 33 gm protein, 11 gm fat, 3 gm fiber. **Diabetic Exchanges:** 3-1/2 meat, 3 starch.

Grandma's Potato Salad

(Pictured at left)

Plan ahead...needs to chill

I've never found a better potato salad recipe than this one handed down from my grandma. Like many grandmothers, mine cooked with a dash of this and a dash of that, so I estimated the measurements on this recipe. Feel free to change them according to taste, just like Grandma did! —Susan Plocher, Oklahoma City, Oklahoma

> 6 to 7 medium red potatoes (about 2 pounds)
> 3/4 cup mayonnaise
> 1/2 cup sour cream
> 1/2 cup plain yogurt
> 1/3 cup thinly sliced green onions
> 2 to 3 dill pickle spears, chopped
> 4-1/2 teaspoons Dijon mustard
> 1 teaspoon prepared horseradish
> 2 garlic cloves, minced
> 1/2 teaspoon celery seed
> 1/2 teaspoon salt

Grandma's Potato Salad

1/4 teaspoon pepper
Dash onion salt
Dash garlic powder
   4 hard-cooked eggs, coarsely chopped

Place potatoes in a saucepan and cover with water; bring to a boil. Cook for 20-30 minutes or until tender; drain and cool slightly. Slice potatoes into a large bowl. In a small bowl, combine the mayonnaise, sour cream, yogurt, onions, pickles, mustard, horseradish, garlic and seasonings. Pour over potatoes and toss to coat. Gently stir in eggs. Cover and refrigerate for 2-3 hours. **Yield:** 8 servings.

Chicken Chopped Salad

(Pictured at right)

Ready in 30 minutes or less

Lime dressing gives lively flavor to this crunchy salad tossed with peaches, peppers and peanuts. The unusual combination is a great way to use up leftover chicken or turkey and packs well for lunches or picnics. It's also terrific with grapefruit sections or pineapple tidbits.
—*Diane Halferty, Corpus Christi, Texas*

   2 cups chopped *or* torn mixed salad greens
   2 cups chopped cooked chicken
   1 cup chopped celery
   1 can (15-1/4 ounces) peaches, drained and chopped
   1 cup chopped sweet red *or* yellow pepper
1/3 cup limeade concentrate
1/4 cup vegetable oil
   2 tablespoons vinegar
   2 to 3 tablespoons minced fresh cilantro *or* parsley
1/4 teaspoon ground ginger *or* 1-1/2 teaspoons minced fresh gingerroot
1/4 teaspoon salt
1/2 cup dry roasted peanuts

In a large salad bowl, combine the first five ingredients. In a jar with a tight-fitting lid, combine the limeade concentrate, oil, vinegar, cilantro, ginger and salt; shake well. Pour over salad and toss to coat. Sprinkle with peanuts. Serve immediately. **Yield:** 6 servings.

Sausage Corn Chili

Ready in 30 minutes or less

Nicely spiced Italian sausage and crunchy corn distinguish this thick chili from usual offerings. My daughter won a national contest with this zesty recipe.
—*Rhea Lease, Colman, South Dakota*

   1 pound bulk Italian sausage
   1 tablespoon dried minced onion
   1 can (16 ounces) kidney beans, rinsed and drained
   1 can (15-1/4 ounces) whole kernel corn, drained
   1 can (15 ounces) tomato sauce

2/3 cup picante sauce
1/3 to 1/2 cup water
   1 teaspoon chili powder

In a large saucepan, cook sausage and onion over medium heat until meat is no longer pink; drain. Stir in the remaining ingredients. Simmer, uncovered, for 5-10 minutes or until heated through. **Yield:** 6 servings.

Chicken Chopped Salad

"Souper" Hints

- When making a pot of soup with chicken or turkey that has lots of bones, I cook it in my pasta pot. After the meat is cooked, I just lift the colander part out and let the liquid drain. This makes it easy to strain the broth. While I wait for the meat to cool so I can remove it from the bones, I add noodles and vegetables to the broth so my soup can be completed in a snap.   —*Marilyn Weaver, Sparks, Maryland*

- When you're short on time and making homemade soup, add frozen hash browns instead of peeling and cubing potatoes. It saves time, and there's no difference in taste. When I'm in a hurry, I sometimes use frozen mixed vegetables, too.   —*Irene Anderson Kamloops, British Columbia*

- I add a small can of V-8 juice to a pot of chili to give it extra flavor. It's delicious and couldn't be easier.
                —*Betty Brye, Milwaukee, Wisconsin*

Sweet Potato Chowder

(Pictured at right)

Ready in 30 minutes or less

My husband came up with this spicy soup that's a snap to make yet tastes wonderful. Creamy bowls of it are warm and winning on a cool night. —Kathy Whitford
Oscoda, Michigan

> 1 celery rib, chopped
> 2 tablespoons butter *or* margarine
> 2 cans (14-1/2 ounces *each*) chicken broth
> 2 cups water
> 2 teaspoons chicken bouillon granules
> 4 medium potatoes, peeled and cubed
> 1 large sweet potato, peeled and cubed
> 2 cups cubed fully cooked turkey ham
> 2 tablespoons dried minced onion
> 1/2 teaspoon *each* garlic powder, seasoned salt, dried oregano and parsley flakes
> 1/4 teaspoon *each* pepper and crushed red pepper flakes
> 1/4 cup all-purpose flour
> 2 cups milk

In a large saucepan, saute celery in butter until tender. Stir in broth, water and bouillon. Add potatoes, sweet potato, turkey ham and seasonings. Bring to a boil. Reduce heat; cover and simmer for 12 minutes or until potatoes are tender. Combine flour and milk until smooth; gradually stir into soup. Bring to a boil; cook and stir for 2 minutes or until thickened and bubbly. **Yield:** 11 servings.

Dijon Spinach Salad

(Pictured at right)

Ready in 30 minutes or less

For an unusual mix of tastes and textures, try this medley. This salad goes nicely with roasted chicken or London broil. —Kara de la Vega, Suisun City, California

 Uses less fat, sugar or salt. Includes Nutritional Analysis and Diabetic Exchanges.

> 8 cups torn fresh spinach
> 1 cup shredded red cabbage
> 1 cup thinly sliced cauliflowerets
> 1 cup thinly sliced red onion
> 1/2 cup sliced radishes
> 1/4 to 1/2 cup vegetable oil
> 1/4 cup cider *or* tarragon vinegar
> 2 tablespoons Dijon mustard
> 2 teaspoons sugar
> 1/4 teaspoon salt
> 2 tablespoons sesame seeds, toasted

In a bowl, combine the first five ingredients. In a jar with a tight-fitting lid, combine the oil, vinegar, mustard, sugar and salt; shake well. Pour over the salad and toss to coat. Sprinkle with sesame seeds. Serve immediately. **Yield:** 10 servings. **Nutritional Analysis:** One 3/4-cup serving (prepared with 1/4 cup oil) equals 80 calories, 156 mg sodium, 0 cholesterol, 5 gm carbohydrate, 2 gm protein, 7 gm fat, 2 gm fiber. **Diabetic Exchanges:** 1 vegetable, 1 fat.

Turkey Divan Croissants

(Pictured at right)

Ready in 30 minutes or less

I always served these tasty sandwiches at ladies' luncheons. One time I had leftovers and discovered my fussy family enjoyed them, too. —Ann Pirrung
Cleveland, Wisconsin

✓ Uses less fat, sugar or salt. Includes Nutritional Analysis and Diabetic Exchanges.

> 1/3 cup mayonnaise
> 1/4 cup Dijon mustard
> 1-1/2 teaspoons lemon juice
> 1/2 teaspoon dill weed
> 1 pound broccoli, finely chopped
> 1/2 cup chopped onion
> 2 tablespoons butter *or* margarine
> 1 cup sliced fresh mushrooms
> 6 croissants *or* hamburger buns, split
> 6 ounces thinly sliced cooked turkey
> 6 slices Swiss cheese

In a bowl, combine mayonnaise, mustard, lemon juice and dill; set aside. In a skillet, saute broccoli and onion in butter for 10 minutes. Add mushrooms; cook and stir until tender. Spread mustard mixture over bottom halves of croissants. Top with turkey, broccoli mixture and cheese; replace tops. Place on a baking sheet. Bake at 350° for 5 minutes or until heated through and cheese is melted. **Yield:** 6 servings. **Nutritional Analysis:** One sandwich (prepared with fat-free mayonnaise, reduced-fat margarine and fat-free Swiss cheese; served on a hamburger bun) equals 239 calories, 846 mg sodium, 3 mg cholesterol, 37 gm carbohydrate, 11 gm protein, 6 gm fat, 3 gm fiber. **Diabetic Exchanges:** 2 starch, 1 lean meat, 1 vegetable.

Berry Gelatin Ring

Plan ahead...needs to chill

Cranberries give extra holiday appeal to this gelatin salad. A co-worker always shares this festive fruit ring with us at staff potlucks. —Elise Spring, Bellevue, Ohio

> 1 package (6 ounces) raspberry gelatin
> 2 cups boiling water
> 1 can (16 ounces) whole-berry cranberry sauce
> 1 can (8 ounces) crushed pineapple, undrained
> 1/2 cup red wine *or* grape juice
> 1/3 cup chopped walnuts
> 1 package (8 ounces) cream cheese, softened
> 1/4 cup mayonnaise
> 1 teaspoon grated orange peel

In a bowl, dissolve gelatin in water. Add cranberry sauce, pineapple, wine or juice and walnuts; mix well. To evenly distribute fruit and nuts, chill until partially set, about 2 hours. Then pour into a 6-cup ring mold coated with nonstick cooking spray. Refrigerate until set. Unmold onto a serving plate. In a small mixing bowl, combine cream cheese, mayonnaise and orange peel. Serve with the salad. **Yield:** 8 servings.

Sweet Potato Chowder
Dijon Spinach Salad
Turkey Divan Croissants

Fruity Green Salad

8 cups torn mixed salad greens
1 medium red apple, chopped
1 medium pear, chopped
1 cup chopped pecans, toasted
1 cup (4 ounces) shredded Swiss cheese
1/4 cup dried cranberries

In a jar with a tight-fitting lid, combine the oil, lemon juice, sugar, onions, salt and poppy seeds; shake well. In a large bowl, combine the remaining ingredients. Drizzle with dressing and toss to coat. Serve immediately. **Yield:** 16 servings.

Layered Deli Loaf

(Pictured below)

Plan ahead...needs to chill

This recipe is special to me because it was handed down from my grandma. A tangy sauce, flavored with horseradish and Dijon mustard, sparks a hearty assortment of meats and cheeses. It's perfect for a party or potluck. My husband says it's the best sub sandwich he's ever had.
—Sarah Kraemer, Rockford, Illinois

1/4 cup mayonnaise
2 tablespoons prepared horseradish, drained
1 tablespoon Dijon mustard
1 loaf (1 pound) unsliced round bread
2 tablespoons butter *or* margarine, softened
1/3 pound thinly sliced deli ham
1/3 pound sliced Monterey Jack *or* Muenster cheese
1/3 pound thinly sliced deli turkey
1/3 pound sliced cheddar *or* Colby cheese
1/3 pound thinly sliced deli roast beef
1 medium tomato, sliced
1 large dill pickle, sliced lengthwise
1 small red onion, thinly sliced
Lettuce leaves

In a small bowl, combine the mayonnaise, horseradish and mustard. Cut bread in half. Carefully hollow out bottom and top of loaf, leaving a 3/4-in. shell (discard removed bread or save for another use). Spread butter

Fruity Green Salad

(Pictured above)

Ready in 15 minutes or less

My family enjoys this fast and refreshing salad. It's jazzed up with a beautiful blend of red apple, pear, dried cranberries, toasted pecans and Swiss cheese. No matter when I serve it, the light dressing and fruity flavor remind me of springtime.
—Helen Petisi
Palm Coast, Florida

2/3 cup vegetable oil
1/3 cup lemon juice
1/4 cup sugar
2 teaspoons chopped green onions
3/4 teaspoon salt
1 teaspoon poppy seeds

Easy Deviled Eggs

● Here's a fuss-free way to fill deviled eggs. Put the cooked yolks in a resealable plastic bag along with the mayonnaise and seasonings. Knead the mixture through the plastic. Cut one small hole in the corner of the bag and pipe the filling into the cooked whites. Presto—you're finished with no mess. Just throw the bag away.
—Virginia Ingrum
Tuscumbia, Alabama

● When making deviled eggs, I use a plastic-coated baby spoon to scoop out the egg yolks. It fits perfectly under the yolks and is gentle on the tender whites.
—Katie Foshee, Lawrenceville, Georgia

Layered Deli Loaf

on cut sides of bread. In the shell, layer ham, a third of the mayonnaise mixture, Monterey Jack cheese, turkey, a third of the mayonnaise mixture, cheddar cheese, roast beef, remaining mayonnaise mixture, tomato, pickle, onion and lettuce. Replace top. Wrap tightly in plastic wrap; cover and refrigerate for at least 1 hour. **Yield:** 8 servings.

Open-Faced Turkey Sandwiches

Ready in 30 minutes or less

I use a flavorful garlic spread to give Italian flair to my warm turkey sandwiches. Mozzarella cheese melted on top adds a fast final touch to the open-faced rolls.
—Tiffany Mouren, Oakdale, California

  1/3 cup chopped onion
    2 garlic cloves, minced
    1 teaspoon Italian seasoning
    1 tablespoon olive *or* vegetable oil
  1/4 cup minced fresh parsley
    1 tablespoon lemon juice
    1 tablespoon Worcestershire sauce
Dash pepper
    4 sandwich rolls, split
    1 pound thinly sliced deli turkey
    1 cup (4 ounces) shredded mozzarella cheese

In a skillet, saute the onion, garlic and Italian seasoning in oil. Add parsley, lemon juice, Worcestershire sauce and pepper; spread on cut sides of rolls. Top with turkey; sprinkle with cheese. Bake at 350° for 8-10 minutes or until heated through. **Yield:** 4 servings.

Cheesy Chicken Subs

(Pictured at right)

Ready in 30 minutes or less

I've been part of the Food Services staff at Appalachian State University for 33 years. One summer we created this flavorful sandwich that combines seasoned grilled chicken, Swiss cheese and sauteed mushrooms and onions. Thousands of students have enjoyed this wonderful sub since then. —Jane Hollar, Vilas, North Carolina

  12 ounces boneless skinless chicken breasts, cut into strips
    1 envelope Parmesan Italian *or* Caesar salad dressing mix
    1 cup sliced fresh mushrooms
  1/2 cup sliced red onion
  1/4 cup olive *or* vegetable oil
    4 submarine sandwich rolls, split and toasted
    4 slices Swiss cheese

Place chicken in a bowl; sprinkle with the salad dressing mix. In a skillet, saute the mushrooms and onion in oil for 3 minutes. Add the chicken; saute for 6 minutes or until chicken juices run clear. Spoon mixture onto roll bottoms; top with cheese. Broil 4 in. from the heat for 4 minutes or until cheese is melted. Replace tops. **Yield:** 4 servings.

Cheesy Chicken Subs

Toasted Ham Salad Sandwiches

I'm always looking for easy recipes that are good and different. This delightful grilled sandwich definitely meets those requirements. —Margaret DeLong Gainesville, Florida

1-1/3 cups diced fully cooked ham
1-1/3 cups diced cooked chicken
  1/2 cup diced celery
    1 can (8 ounces) crushed pineapple, drained
  1/3 cup mayonnaise
    3 tablespoons chopped pecans
4-1/2 teaspoons chopped green pepper
    1 teaspoon sliced green onion
  1/4 teaspoon salt
Dash pepper
  16 slices bread
    8 slices mozzarella cheese
    6 tablespoons butter *or* margarine, softened

In a bowl, combine the first 10 ingredients. Spread eight slices of bread with ham mixture (about 1/2 cup each). Top with cheese and the remaining bread. Spread butter on outsides of sandwiches. Cook on a griddle or in a large skillet over medium heat until golden brown on both sides. **Yield:** 8 servings.

Zucchini Beef Soup
Super Pizza Subs
Tomato Bread Salad

Zucchini Beef Soup

(Pictured at left)

Ready in 1 hour or less

I make this wonderful garden-fresh soup as soon as my homegrown zucchini is plentiful. I often double the recipe and freeze some to enjoy later. —Betty Claycomb
Alverton, Pennsylvania

✓ Uses less fat, sugar or salt. Includes Nutritional Analysis and Diabetic Exchanges.

    1/2 pound ground beef
      2 celery ribs, thinly sliced
    1/3 cup chopped onion
    1/2 cup chopped green pepper
      1 can (28 ounces) diced tomatoes, undrained
      3 medium zucchini, cubed
      2 cups water
  1-1/2 teaspoons Italian seasoning
      1 teaspoon salt, optional
      1 teaspoon beef bouillon granules
    1/2 teaspoon sugar
Pepper to taste
Shredded Parmesan cheese, optional

In a large saucepan, cook beef, celery, onion and green pepper over medium heat until meat is no longer pink and vegetables are tender; drain. Stir in the tomatoes, zucchini, water, Italian seasoning, salt if desired, bouillon, sugar and pepper. Bring to a boil. Reduce heat; cover and simmer for 20-25 minutes or until zucchini is tender. Garnish with Parmesan cheese if desired. **Yield:** 6 servings. **Nutritional Analysis:** One serving (prepared with lean ground beef and without salt and Parmesan cheese) equals 106 calories, 628 mg sodium, 14 mg cholesterol, 10 gm carbohydrate, 10 gm protein, 4 gm fat, 2 gm fiber. **Diabetic Exchanges:** 2 vegetable, 1 lean meat.

Super Pizza Subs

(Pictured at left)

Ready in 30 minutes or less

My husband loves this zippy sub sandwich. Italian sausage, pepperoni and salami provide the robust flavors in this family-pleasing fare. —Kathy Bennett
Hattiesburg, Mississippi

      6 submarine sandwich buns (about 9 inches), split
    1/2 pound bulk Italian sausage, cooked and drained
      1 pound shaved deli ham
      1 can (8 ounces) pizza sauce
      1 pound sliced mozzarella cheese
      1 medium onion, halved and thinly sliced
     36 mild banana pepper rings
      2 packages (3-1/2 ounces *each*) sliced pepperoni
    1/4 pound thinly sliced hard salami

On bottom half of sandwich buns, layer sausage, ham, pizza sauce, cheese, onion, banana peppers, pepperoni

and salami. Replace tops. Wrap each sandwich in heavy-duty foil; place on baking sheets. Bake at 425° for 12-15 minutes or until cheese is melted. Serve immediately. **Yield:** 6 servings.

Tomato Bread Salad

(Pictured at left)

Ready in 1 hour or less

While "bread salad" may sound unusual, you'll find that this blend is unusually good. A simple dressing jazzes up a medley of bread cubes, tomatoes, basil and red onion. —Joan Gwynn, Watsonville, California

      8 cups cubed Italian *or* French bread
      3 cups chopped tomatoes
      1 cup minced fresh basil
    1/2 cup thinly sliced red onion
    1/2 cup olive *or* vegetable oil
      2 tablespoons cider *or* red wine vinegar
    1/2 teaspoon salt
    1/2 teaspoon pepper
      1 garlic clove, minced

In a large bowl, combine the bread, tomatoes, basil and onion. In a small bowl, whisk together the remaining ingredients; drizzle over bread mixture. Cover and let stand for 30 minutes before serving. **Yield:** 8 servings.

Hot Italian Patties

Ready in 30 minutes or less

I've been making these spicy sandwiches for more than a dozen years. On occasion, I substitute country sausage for the Italian sausage and they taste just as good. Served with a zesty sauce for dipping, they're my family's favorite. —Brenda Jackson, Garden City, Kansas

      1 can (8 ounces) tomato sauce
    1/4 teaspoon dried basil
    1/4 teaspoon crushed red pepper flakes
    1/8 teaspoon garlic powder
      1 pound bulk Italian sausage
      1 medium onion, thinly sliced and separated into rings
      8 slices mozzarella cheese (about 6 ounces)
      8 slices French bread (3/4 inch thick)
    1/4 to 1/2 cup butter *or* margarine, softened

In a saucepan, combine tomato sauce, basil, pepper flakes and garlic powder. Bring to a boil over medium heat. Reduce heat; simmer for 15 minutes. Meanwhile, shape sausage into four thin oval patties. In a skillet over medium heat, cook patties until no longer pink; remove and keep warm. In the drippings, saute onion until tender. Place a slice of cheese on four slices of bread; top each with a sausage patty, onion and remaining cheese. Top with remaining bread. Butter the outsides of sandwiches. Cook on a griddle or in a large skillet over medium heat until both sides are golden brown and cheese is melted. Serve with herbed tomato sauce for dipping. **Yield:** 4 servings.

White Chili with Chicken

(Pictured below)

Ready in 30 minutes or less

Folks who enjoy a change from traditional tomato-based chilies will enjoy this version. The flavorful blend has tender chunks of chicken, white beans and just enough zip. Serve it with warm, crusty bread or rolls.
—*Christy Campos, Richmond, Virginia*

1 medium onion, chopped
1 jalapeno pepper, seeded and chopped,* optional
2 garlic cloves, minced
1 tablespoon vegetable oil
2 cans (15-1/2 ounces *each*) great northern beans, rinsed and drained
4 cups chicken broth
2 tablespoons minced fresh parsley
1 tablespoon lime juice
1 to 1-1/4 teaspoons ground cumin
2 tablespoons cornstarch
1/4 cup cold water
2 cups cubed cooked chicken

In a large saucepan, cook onion, jalapeno if desired and garlic in oil until tender. Stir in beans, broth, parsley, lime juice and cumin; bring to a boil. Reduce heat; cover and simmer for 10 minutes, stirring occasionally. Combine cornstarch and water until smooth; stir into chili. Add chicken. Bring to a boil; cook and stir for 2 minutes or until thickened. **Yield:** 6 servings. ***Editor's Note:** When cutting and seeding hot peppers, use rubber or plastic gloves to protect your hands. Avoid touching your face. Leave the seeds in for spicier flavor.

White Chili with Chicken
Salsa Chili

Salsa Chili

(Pictured below left)

Ready in 15 minutes or less

You'll need just five ingredients to stir up this quick-and-easy chili. We like to use medium salsa for zippy flavor, but sometimes I use half mild and half medium.
—Jane Bone, Cape Coral, Florida

　1 pound ground beef
　1 medium onion, chopped
　1 jar (16 ounces) salsa
　1 can (15 ounces) pinto beans, rinsed and
　　　drained
　1 can (5-1/2 ounces) tomato juice
Shredded cheddar cheese, diced peppers, sour
　cream and sliced green onions, optional

In a saucepan, cook beef and onion over medium heat until meat is no longer pink; drain. Stir in salsa, beans and tomato juice; heat through. If desired, garnish with cheese and peppers and serve with sour cream and onions. **Yield:** 5 servings.

Mushroom Steak Hoagies

(Pictured on page 174)

Plan ahead...needs to marinate

My Aunt Diane perfected the recipe for these hearty hoagies. We often double or triple it for family gatherings since they're such a hit.　—Jennifer Walker, Logan, Utah

　1 cup water
　1/3 cup soy sauce
　1-1/2 teaspoons garlic powder
　1-1/2 teaspoons pepper
　1 pound round steak, cut into 1/4-inch strips
　1 medium onion, chopped
　1 medium green pepper, julienned
　1 can (4 ounces) mushroom stems and pieces,
　　　drained
　2 cups (8 ounces) shredded mozzarella cheese
　6 hoagie buns, split and toasted
Sliced tomatoes

In a large resealable plastic bag or shallow glass container, combine first four ingredients. Add steak and turn to coat. Seal or cover and refrigerate for 6-8 hours or overnight. Drain and discard marinade. In a large skillet, brown steak over medium heat. Add onion, green pepper and mushrooms; stir-fry until tender. Reduce heat. Sprinkle with cheese. Remove from heat; stir until cheese is melted and meat is coated. Spoon onto buns; top with tomatoes. **Yield:** 6 servings.

Cut Cleanup

Whenever I need to chop something juicy, like a tomato or melon, I use a plastic tray with a lip or small edge for a cutting board. All the juice is caught on the tray, so there's less mess.　—Jane Lamkin, Brownwood, Texas

Crunchy Corn Medley

Crunchy Corn Medley

Plan ahead...needs to chill

This recipe came from my husband's aunt, who's an excellent cook, friend and mentor. It's crunchy, colorful and combined with a light tasty dressing. I've shared it with friends and relatives, who think it's a great addition to their recipe collection.　—Meredith Cecil, Plattsburg, Missouri

　2 cups frozen peas, thawed
　1 can (15-1/4 ounces) whole kernel corn,
　　　drained
　1 can (15-1/4 ounces) white *or* shoepeg corn,
　　　drained
　1 can (8 ounces) water chestnuts, drained and
　　　chopped
　1 jar (4 ounces) diced pimientos, drained
　8 green onions, thinly sliced
　2 celery ribs, chopped
　1 medium green pepper, chopped
　1/2 cup vinegar
　1/2 cup sugar
　1/4 cup vegetable oil
　1 teaspoon salt
　1/4 teaspoon pepper

In a large bowl, combine the first eight ingredients. In a small bowl, combine vinegar, sugar, oil, salt and pepper; whisk until sugar is dissolved. Pour over corn mixture; mix well. Cover and refrigerate for at least 3 hours. Stir just before serving; serve with a slotted spoon. **Yield:** 10 servings.

Chapter 13

⏱ *Delectable Desserts*

FOLKS will think you fussed all day in the kitchen when you serve a savory selection of these sweet desserts for a special occasion, or when you present them at a bake sale or potluck.

But all of these cakes, cookies, pies, candies and more are so easy to prepare, you'll likely whip them up for family, co-workers, unexpected company and dinner guests even when you *do* have time to spare.

The memorable results of these impressive after-dinner delights are sure to have everyone asking for more...and for the recipe!

SWEET INSPIRATION. Clockwise from upper left: Chocolate and Fruit Trifle (p. 222), Chocolate Mint Cookies (p. 213), Cream Puff Dessert (p. 217) and German Chocolate Ice Cream (p. 220).

Coconut Pineapple Pie

(Pictured at right)

Plan ahead...needs to chill

I found this tropical custard pie in an old church cookbook in my collection. When I sent one to the office with my husband, one of his co-workers said, "It doesn't get any better than this."
—Judi Oudekerk
Buffalo, Minnesota

1 cup sugar
3 tablespoons all-purpose flour
1 cup light corn syrup
1 cup flaked coconut
1 can (8 ounces) crushed pineapple, undrained
3 eggs, beaten
1 teaspoon vanilla extract
1 unbaked pastry shell (9 inches)
1/4 cup butter *or* margarine, melted

In a bowl, combine sugar and flour. Add the corn syrup, coconut, pineapple, eggs and vanilla; mix well. Pour into pastry shell. Drizzle with butter. Bake at 350° for 50-55 minutes or until a knife inserted near the center comes out clean. (Cover loosely with foil if the top browns too quickly.) Cool on a wire rack. Chill before cutting. Store in the refrigerator. **Yield:** 6-8 servings.

Mom's Buttermilk Cookies

(Pictured at right)

This was my mother's recipe for comforting "cookie pillows", which may explain why they're such a wonderful bedtime snack. The tender treats are jazzed up with thick frosting and a sprinkling of chopped walnuts.
—Jane Darling, Simi Valley, California

1/2 cup butter (no substitutes), softened
1 cup sugar
1 egg
1 teaspoon vanilla extract
2-1/2 cups all-purpose flour
1/2 teaspoon baking soda
1/2 teaspoon salt
1/2 cup buttermilk
FROSTING:
3 tablespoons butter (no substitutes), softened
3-1/2 cups confectioners' sugar
1/4 cup milk
1 teaspoon vanilla extract
1/2 cup finely chopped walnuts, optional

In a mixing bowl, cream butter and sugar until light and fluffy. Beat in egg and vanilla. Combine flour, baking soda and salt; add to the creamed mixture alternately with buttermilk and mix well. Drop by rounded tablespoonfuls 2 in. apart onto greased baking sheets. Bake at 375° for 10-12 minutes or until edges are lightly browned. Remove to wire racks to cool. For frosting, combine butter, sugar, milk and vanilla in a mixing bowl; beat until smooth. Frost cookies; sprinkle with walnuts if desired. **Yield:** 3 dozen.

Ladyfinger Cheesecake

(Pictured at right and on cover)

Plan ahead...needs to chill

Raspberry, strawberry or cherry pie filling gives a festive appearance to this rich no-bake cheesecake. It's perfect for Valentine's Day, Christmas or other special occasions. This elegant-looking dessert makes a dramatic presentation. Get ready to share the recipe.
—Irene Pitzer
Madison, Tennessee

2 packages (11.1 ounces *each*) no-bake cheesecake mix
2/3 cup butter *or* margarine, melted
1/4 cup sugar
1 package (3 ounces) ladyfingers (25 cookies)
1 package (8 ounces) cream cheese, softened
3 cups cold milk, *divided*
1 carton (12 ounces) frozen whipped topping, thawed
1 can (21 ounces) raspberry pie filling *or* flavor of your choice

In a bowl, combine contents of crust mix packages, butter and sugar. Press onto the bottom of an ungreased 10-in. springform pan. Arrange ladyfingers around edge of pan. In a mixing bowl, beat cream cheese and 1/2 cup milk until smooth. Gradually beat in remaining milk. Add contents of filling mix packages; beat until smooth. Beat on medium for 3 minutes. Fold in whipped topping. Pour over crust. Cover and refrigerate for at least 1 hour. Top with pie filling. Remove sides of pan before serving. **Yield:** 12 servings.

Pecan Lemon Bars

I use quick-and-easy refrigerated cookie dough to make these luscious lemon squares. All 27 of my grandchildren love the bars' sweet and tangy flavor.
—June Trom
Blooming Prairie, Minnesota

1 tube (18 ounces) refrigerated sugar cookie dough
1 cup chopped pecans, *divided*
1/3 cup corn syrup
1/4 cup lemon juice
1 egg, beaten
1 tablespoon butter *or* margarine, melted
1 tablespoon grated lemon peel
1/2 cup sugar
5 teaspoons all-purpose flour
Confectioners' sugar

Cut dough into 1/2-in. slices; press into an ungreased 13-in. x 9-in. x 2-in. baking pan. Sprinkle with 1/2 cup pecans; press firmly into crust. Bake at 375° for 10-12 minutes or until light golden brown. Reduce heat to 350°. In a bowl, combine the corn syrup, lemon juice, egg, butter and lemon peel. Combine sugar, flour and remaining pecans; stir into lemon mixture until blended. Pour over crust. Bake for 18-20 minutes or until golden brown. Cool on a wire rack. Dust with confectioners' sugar. Cut into bars. **Yield:** 2 to 2-1/2 dozen.

Ladyfinger Cheesecake
Coconut Pineapple Pie
Mom's Buttermilk Cookies

Poppin' Cereal Bars

(Pictured below)

Ready in 15 minutes or less

A melted marshmallow coating holds together all sorts of goodies in these yummy bars. The addition of colorful M&M's makes them especially appealing to kids of all ages.
—Edna Hoffman, Hebron, Indiana

- 2 cups popped popcorn
- 2 cups Life cereal
- 1 cup miniature pretzels
- 1 cup M&M's, *divided*
- 1 package (10-1/2 ounces) miniature marshmallows
- 1/4 cup butter *or* margarine

In a bowl, combine the popcorn, cereal, pretzels and 1/2 cup M&M's. In a microwave-safe bowl, melt marshmallows and butter; stir until smooth. Fold into cereal mixture. Spread into a greased 11-in. x 7-in. x 2-in. dish. Sprinkle with remaining M&M's; press lightly. Cut into bars. **Yield:** 1-1/2 dozen.

Peanut Butter Cookie Cups

(Pictured below)

Ready in 1 hour or less

I'm a busy schoolteacher and pastor's wife who always looks for shortcuts. I wouldn't dare show my face at a church dinner or bake sale without these tempting peanut butter treats. They're quick and easy to make and always a hit.
—Kristi Tackett, Banner, Kentucky

- 1 package (17-1/2 ounces) peanut butter cookie mix*
- 36 miniature peanut butter cups, unwrapped

Prepare cookie mix according to package directions. Roll the dough into 1-in. balls. Place in greased miniature muffin cups. Press dough evenly onto bottom and up sides of each cup. Bake at 350° for 11-13 minutes or until set. Immediately place a peanut butter cup in each cup; press down gently. Cool for 10 minutes; carefully remove from pans. **Yield:** 3 dozen. ***Editor's Note:** 2-1/4 cups peanut butter cookie dough of your choice can be substituted for the mix.

Caramel Fudge Cheesecake

Plan ahead...needs to chill

It's hard to resist this chocolaty cheesecake with its fudgy crust, crunchy pecans and gooey layer of caramel. I combined several recipes to create this version, which always satisfies both the chocolate lovers and the cheesecake lovers in my family. —Brenda Ruse, Truro, Nova Scotia

- 1 package fudge brownie mix (8-inch square pan size)

Poppin' Cereal Bars
Peanut Butter Cookie Cups

1 package (14 ounces) caramels*
1/4 cup evaporated milk
1-1/4 cups coarsely chopped pecans
2 packages (8 ounces *each*) cream cheese, softened
1/2 cup sugar
2 eggs
2 squares (1 ounce *each*) semisweet chocolate, melted
2 squares (1 ounce *each*) unsweetened chocolate, melted

Prepare brownie batter according to the package directions. Spread into a greased 9-in. springform pan. Bake at 350° for 20 minutes. Cool for 10 minutes on a wire rack. Meanwhile, in a microwave-safe bowl, melt caramels with milk. Pour over brownie crust; sprinkle with pecans. In a mixing bowl, combine the cream cheese and sugar; mix well. Add eggs, beating on low speed just until combined. Stir in melted chocolate. Pour over pecans. Bake at 350° for 35-40 minutes or until the center is almost set. Cool on a wire rack for 10 minutes. Run a knife around edge of pan to loosen; cool completely. Chill overnight. Remove sides of pan before serving. Store leftovers in the refrigerator. **Yield:** 12 servings. ***Editor's Note:** This recipe was tested using Hershey-brand caramels.

Fudgy Raspberry Torte

Fudgy Raspberry Torte

(Pictured above right)

Guests will think you fussed when you serve this three-layer torte made with convenient cake and pudding mixes, a bit of raspberry jam and fresh berries. It looks elegant for most any special occasion and always brings lots of compliments. —Dolores Hurtt, Florence, Montana

1 package (18-1/4 ounces) chocolate fudge cake mix
1-1/3 cups water
3 eggs
1/3 cup vegetable oil
3/4 cup ground pecans
1-1/2 cups cold milk
1 package (3.9 ounces) instant chocolate fudge *or* chocolate pudding mix
1/2 cup seedless raspberry jam
1-1/2 cups whipped topping
1/4 cup finely chopped pecans
Fresh raspberries

In a mixing bowl, combine dry cake mix, water, eggs and oil; mix well. Add ground pecans; mix just until combined. Pour into three greased and floured 9-in. round baking pans. Bake at 350° for 15-20 minutes or until a toothpick inserted near the center comes out clean. Cool for 10 minutes before removing from pans to wire racks to cool completely. In a mixing bowl, beat milk and pudding mix on low speed for 2 minutes or until thickened. In a saucepan, melt jam. Brush over the top of each cake. Place one cake on a serving plate; spread with half of the pudding. Repeat layers. Top with third cake layer; spread top with whipped topping. Sprinkle with chopped pecans. Garnish with raspberries. Store in the refrigerator. **Yield:** 12 servings.

Crunchy Drop Cookies

I stir up a batch of these rich, buttery cookies when I want to satisfy a crowd. They get their crunch from coconut, walnuts and crisp rice cereal. —Ellie Kocar, Avon Lake, Ohio

1 cup butter *or* margarine, softened
1 cup sugar
1 cup packed brown sugar
1 egg
1 cup vegetable oil
1 teaspoon vanilla extract
3-1/2 cups all-purpose flour
1 teaspoon salt
1 teaspoon cream of tartar
1 teaspoon baking soda
1 cup quick-cooking oats
1 cup crisp rice cereal
1 cup flaked coconut
1/2 cup chopped walnuts

In a mixing bowl, cream butter and sugars. Beat in egg, oil and vanilla. Combine flour, salt, cream of tartar and baking soda; gradually add to the creamed mixture. Stir in remaining ingredients. Drop by tablespoonfuls 2 in. apart onto ungreased baking sheets. Press tops lightly with a fork. Bake at 350° for 8-10 minutes or until lightly browned. Remove to wire racks to cool. **Yield:** 10-1/2 dozen.

Coconut Chocolate Trifle
Peanut Butter Brownies
White Chocolate Fudge Cake

Coconut Chocolate Trifle

(Pictured at left)

Plan ahead...needs to chill

This luscious dessert will wow everyone who sees it, let alone tries it. Apricot preserves add a fruity touch to the pleasing pairing of chocolate and toasted coconut in this easy-to-assemble trifle.
—Donna Cline
Pensacola, Florida

> 1 loaf (10-3/4 ounces) frozen pound cake, thawed
> 1/3 cup apricot preserves
> 1/3 cup plus 2 tablespoons orange juice, *divided*
> 1 package (4 ounces) German sweet chocolate
> 1-1/4 cups flaked coconut, toasted, *divided*
> 1-3/4 cups cold milk
> 1 cup half-and-half cream
> 1 package (5.9 ounces) instant chocolate pudding mix

Trim crust from top, sides and bottom of cake. Cut cake into 16 slices. Spread preserves over eight slices; top with remaining cake. Cut into 1-in. cubes. Place in a 2-qt. serving bowl; drizzle with 1/3 cup orange juice. Chop chocolate; set aside 2 tablespoons for garnish. Sprinkle remaining chocolate and 1 cup coconut over cake. In a mixing bowl, combine milk, cream, pudding mix and remaining orange juice; beat on low for 2 minutes. Spoon over cake. Sprinkle with remaining coconut and reserved chocolate. Refrigerate for at least 4 hours before serving. **Yield:** 10-14 servings.

Peanut Butter Brownies

(Pictured at left)

The combination of chocolate and peanut butter makes these brownies a real crowd-pleaser. They're so good, they won a ribbon at the fair.
—Margaret McNeil
Memphis, Tennessee

> 3 eggs
> 1 cup butter *or* margarine, melted
> 2 teaspoons vanilla extract
> 2 cups sugar
> 1-1/4 cups all-purpose flour
> 3/4 cup baking cocoa
> 1/2 teaspoon baking powder
> 1/4 teaspoon salt
> 1 cup milk chocolate chips

FILLING:
> 2 packages (8 ounces *each*) cream cheese, softened
> 1/2 cup creamy peanut butter
> 1/4 cup sugar
> 1 egg
> 2 tablespoons milk

In a large mixing bowl, combine eggs, butter and vanilla. Combine dry ingredients; add to egg mixture and mix well. Stir in chocolate chips. Set aside 1 cup for topping. Spread remaining batter into a greased 13-in. x 9-in. x 2-in. baking pan. In a small mixing bowl, beat cream cheese, peanut butter and sugar until smooth. Add egg and milk, beating on low just until combined. Carefully spread over batter. Drop reserved batter by tablespoonfuls over filling. Cut through batter with a knife to swirl. Bake at 350° for 35-40 minutes or until a toothpick inserted in the center comes out clean. Cool on a wire rack before cutting. Refrigerate until serving. **Yield:** 3 dozen.

White Chocolate Fudge Cake

(Pictured at left)

This sweet cake, with its thick frosting and rich chocolate layer, is a big hit at office potlucks. I have one co-worker who tells everyone it's awful so he can have it all to himself!
—Denise VonStein, Shelby, Ohio

> 1 package (18-1/4 ounces) white cake mix
> 1-1/4 cups water
> 3 egg whites
> 1/3 cup vegetable oil
> 1 teaspoon vanilla extract
> 3 squares (1 ounce *each*) white baking chocolate, melted

FILLING:
> 3/4 cup semisweet chocolate chips
> 2 tablespoons butter (no substitutes)

FROSTING:
> 1 can (16 ounces) vanilla frosting
> 3 squares (1 ounce *each*) white baking chocolate, melted
> 1 teaspoon vanilla extract
> 1 carton (8 ounces) frozen whipped topping, thawed

In a mixing bowl, combine the dry cake mix, water, egg whites, oil and vanilla. Beat on low for 2 minutes. Stir in white chocolate. Pour into a greased 13-in. x 9-in. x 2-in. baking pan. Bake at 350° for 25-30 minutes or until a toothpick inserted near the center comes out clean. Cool for 5 minutes. Meanwhile, in a microwave or heavy saucepan over low heat, melt chocolate chips and butter; stir until smooth. Carefully spread over warm cake. Cool completely. In a mixing bowl, beat frosting; stir in white chocolate and vanilla. Fold in whipped topping; frost cake. Store in the refrigerator. **Yield:** 16 servings.

Tasty Cake Toppings

- I use this quick fix when I don't have prepared frosting on hand for a 13-in. x 9-in. chocolate cake. When I take the cake out of the oven, I immediately sprinkle it with 4 cups of miniature marshmallows and a 1/4 cup of flaked coconut. —Jennifer McKinney Washington, Illinois

- No time to ice a cake? Just sprinkle semisweet chocolate chips on it as it comes out of the oven. They'll melt and can be spread into a rich topping. —Janet Champion, North Vancouver, British Columbia

- Is your frosting too thin and you're out of confectioner's sugar? Try adding instant pudding, a spoonful at a time. The frosting will thicken right up. —Nita Benefield, Ola, Arkansas

Cookie Pizza

(Pictured below)

Ready in 30 minutes or less

I contribute this quick-and-easy treat to every bake sale our two daughters are involved in. Everyone seems to love the great-tasting combination of yummy chocolate and marshmallows on a homemade peanut butter cookie crust. It sells fast. In fact, it goes quickly at home, too.
—Debbie Johnson, New Bloomfield, Missouri

1/2 cup butter *or* margarine, softened
1/2 cup peanut butter
1/2 cup sugar
1/2 cup packed brown sugar
  1 egg
1/2 teaspoon vanilla extract
1-1/2 cups all-purpose flour
  2 cups miniature marshmallows
  1 cup (6 ounces) semisweet chocolate chips

In a mixing bowl, cream butter, peanut butter and sugars. Beat in egg and vanilla. Stir in flour until blended. Spread dough onto a greased 12-in. pizza pan. Bake at 375° for 12 minutes. Sprinkle with marshmallows and chocolate chips. Bake 5-6 minutes longer or until lightly browned. **Yield:** 10-12 servings. **Editor's Note:** This recipe is best eaten the same day it's prepared.

Favorite Chocolate Cookies

(Pictured below)

Ready in 1 hour or less

These crispy cookies, studded with white chocolate, are my husband's absolute favorite. I often double the recipe and freeze half of the dough, so I can bake a warm batch in a jiffy.
—Selena Redel, Consort, Alberta

  1 cup butter *or* margarine, softened
1-1/2 cups sugar
  2 eggs
  2 teaspoons vanilla extract
  2 cups all-purpose flour
2/3 cup baking cocoa
3/4 teaspoon baking soda
1/4 teaspoon salt
  1 package (12 ounces) vanilla *or* white chips
1/2 cup chopped pecans, optional

In a mixing bowl, cream butter and sugar. Add the eggs, one at a time, beating well after each addition. Beat in vanilla. Combine the flour, cocoa, baking soda and salt; gradually add to creamed mixture. Stir in chips and pecans if desired. Drop by tablespoonfuls 2 in. apart onto ungreased baking sheets. Bake at 350° for 10-12 minutes or until set. Remove to wire racks to cool. **Yield:** 4-1/2 dozen.

Favorite Chocolate Cookies
Cookie Pizza

Jumbo Molasses Cookies
Popcorn Snack Mix

Popcorn Snack Mix

(Pictured above)

For a big crunch that kids will love, try this munchable snack mix. A sweet coating makes this combination of popcorn, crispy cereal and salty peanuts hard to resist, even for grownups. —Shirley Engstrom, Genoa, Nebraska

- 3 quarts popped popcorn
- 4 cups Cheerios
- 4 cups Corn *or* Rice Chex
- 2 cups salted peanuts
- 1 cup packed brown sugar
- 3/4 cup corn syrup
- 1/4 cup butter *or* margarine
- 2 teaspoons vanilla extract
- 1/2 teaspoon baking soda

In a large greased roasting pan, combine popcorn, cereal and peanuts. In a large saucepan, combine brown sugar, corn syrup and butter; bring to a rolling boil. Boil for 6 minutes, stirring occasionally. Remove from the heat; quickly stir in vanilla and baking soda until mixture is light and foamy. Immediately pour over popcorn mixture; mix well. Bake, uncovered, at 250° for 1 hour, stirring every 15 minutes. Cool completely. **Yield:** about 5-1/2 quarts.

Jumbo Molasses Cookies

(Pictured above)

Plan ahead...needs to chill

These gigantic molasses cookies remind me of the wonderful ones my grandmother used to make years ago. At nearly 4 inches across, they're nicely spiced, delightfully chewy and bound to be noticed. It's like getting a taste of the good old days! —Joan Stull, Titusville, Florida

- 3 cups butter-flavored shortening
- 4 cups sugar
- 1 cup molasses
- 4 eggs
- 8 cups all-purpose flour
- 2 tablespoons plus 2 teaspoons baking soda
- 2 teaspoons ground cinnamon
- 1 teaspoon salt
- 1 teaspoon ground cloves
- 1 teaspoon ground ginger
Additional sugar

In a large mixing bowl, cream shortening and sugar. Add molasses and eggs; mix well. Combine the flour, baking soda, cinnamon, salt, cloves and ginger; gradually add to creamed mixture. Cover and refrigerate for 1-2 hours. Shape 1/4 cupfuls of dough into balls; roll in sugar. Place four cookies on a greased baking sheet at a time. Bake at 350° for 18-20 minutes or until edges are set. Remove to wire racks to cool. **Yield:** 3-1/2 dozen. **Editor's Note:** In order to fit the ingredients in a large mixing bowl, prepare half of the recipe at a time.

Dynamic Duo

If you need a delicious dessert in a hurry, try this easy ice cream topping. Simply add enough chunky peanut butter to chocolate syrup to get the consistency you'd like. It's wonderful over vanilla ice cream.
—Betty Pedigo, Green River, Wyoming

Pineapple Layer Cake

(Pictured at right)

I often prepare this moist golden cake at Easter, but it's wonderful just about any time of year. Pineapple frosting provides the fast finishing touch. —Linda Sakal
Biloxi, Mississippi

 Uses less fat, sugar or salt. Includes Nutritional Analysis and Diabetic Exchanges.

   1 package (18-1/4 ounces) yellow cake mix
   1 can (11 ounces) mandarin oranges, drained
   1 can (20 ounces) unsweetened crushed pineapple, drained
   1 package (3.4 ounces) instant vanilla pudding mix
   1 carton (12 ounces) frozen whipped topping, thawed

Prepare cake batter according to package directions. Beat in oranges until blended. Pour into two greased and floured 9-in. round baking pans. Bake at 350° for 25-30 minutes or until a toothpick inserted near the center comes out clean. Cool for 10 minutes before removing from pans to wire racks to cool completely. Combine pineapple and dry pudding mix; fold in whipped topping. Spread between layers and over top and sides of cake. Store in the refrigerator. **Yield:** 12 servings. **Nutritional Analysis:** One serving (prepared with light cake mix, sugar-free pudding mix and nonfat whipped topping) equals 216 calories, 523 mg sodium, 0 cholesterol, 46 gm carbohydrate, 2 gm protein, 2 gm fat, 1 gm fiber. **Diabetic Exchanges:** 2 fruit, 1 starch, 1/2 fat.

Strawberry Cheesecake Pie

(Pictured at right)

Plan ahead...needs to chill

This creamy concoction is so refreshing on a hot day. With its appealing look, company will never know how simple it is.
—Janis Plourde, Smooth Rock Falls, Ontario

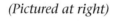

 Uses less fat, sugar or salt. Includes Nutritional Analysis and Diabetic Exchanges.

   2 cups sliced fresh strawberries
 1/4 cup chopped almonds, toasted
   1 tablespoon sugar
   1 graham cracker crust (9 inches)
   1 package (8 ounces) cream cheese, softened
   2 cups cold milk, *divided*
   1 package (3.4 ounces) instant vanilla pudding mix

In a bowl, combine the strawberries, almonds and sugar. Pour into crust. In a mixing bowl, beat cream cheese until smooth; gradually add 1/2 cup of milk. Add pudding mix and remaining milk. Beat for 1 minute or until blended; pour over strawberries. Cover and refrigerate for 2 hours or until set. **Yield:** 8 servings. **Nutritional**

Analysis: One serving (prepared with a reduced-fat graham cracker crust, fat-free cream cheese, skim milk and sugar-free pudding mix) equals 189 calories, 311 mg sodium, 3 mg cholesterol, 25 gm carbohydrate, 9 gm protein, 6 gm fat, 1 gm fiber. **Diabetic Exchanges:** 1 starch, 1 fruit, 1 fat.

Lime Chiffon Dessert

(Pictured at right)

Plan ahead...needs to chill

This make-ahead recipe was given to me by an aunt many years ago. Her recipe called for lemon gelatin, but we like this dessert with more of a bite to it, so we use lime instead. My whole family thinks the light fluffy squares are great, especially in summer. —Joyce Key
Snellville, Georgia

1-1/2 cups crushed graham crackers (about 24 squares)
 1/3 cup sugar
 1/2 cup butter *or* margarine, melted
FILLING:
   1 package (3 ounces) lime gelatin
   1 cup boiling water
   2 packages (one 8 ounces, one 3 ounces) cream cheese, softened
   1 cup sugar
   1 teaspoon vanilla extract
   1 carton (16 ounces) frozen whipped topping, thawed

Combine the first three ingredients; set aside 2 tablespoons for topping. Press remaining crumbs onto the bottom of an ungreased 13-in. x 9-in. x 2-in. baking dish; set aside. In a bowl, dissolve gelatin in boiling water; cool. In a mixing bowl, beat cream cheese and sugar. Add vanilla; mix well. Slowly add gelatin until combined. Fold in whipped topping. Spoon over crust; sprinkle with reserved crumbs. Cover and refrigerate for 3 hours or until set. **Yield:** 12-15 servings.

Chocolate Yummies

Ready in 1 hour or less

Loaded with coconut and oats, these chewy chocolate treats are my daughter's absolute favorite cookie. When she fixed these no-bake bites for a party, one guest couldn't keep his hands out of the cookie jar. —Brenda Meurer
Snyder, Texas

   1 cup (6 ounces) semisweet chocolate chips
 1/3 cup butter *or* margarine
  16 large marshmallows
   2 cups quick-cooking oats
   1 cup flaked coconut
 1/2 teaspoon vanilla extract

In a saucepan over low heat, melt the chocolate chips, butter and marshmallows; stir until smooth. Stir in oats, coconut and vanilla; mix well. Drop by rounded teaspoonfuls onto waxed paper-lined baking sheets. Chill until set, about 30 minutes. **Yield:** 4 dozen.

Pineapple Layer Cake
Strawberry Cheesecake Pie
Lime Chiffon Dessert

Toffee Crunch Grahams

(Pictured below)

Ready in 1 hour or less

Only four ingredients make up these toffee bars loaded with crunchy almonds. My sister gave me the recipe years ago, and it's still a family favorite. Not only are they good, they're quick and easy. —Carol Horne, Perth, Ontario

  12 whole graham crackers (about 5 inches x
      2-1/2 inches)
1-1/2 cups butter (no substitutes)
   1 cup packed brown sugar
   2 cups sliced almonds

Line a 15-in. x 10-in. x 1-in. baking pan with heavy-duty foil. Place graham crackers in pan. In a saucepan, combine butter and brown sugar; bring to a boil, stirring constantly. Carefully pour over graham crackers. Sprinkle with almonds. Bake at 400° for 6-8 minutes or until bubbly. Cool in pan for 4 minutes. Cut each cracker into four sections; transfer to wire racks to cool completely. **Yield:** 4 dozen.

Coffee Chip Cookies

(Pictured below)

My daughter loves the subtle coffee flavor in these soft cookies. Now that she's away at college, I send her goody boxes with these freshly baked treats inside. The recipe makes plenty for her to share with her friends. They all seeem to enjoy a change from traditional chocolate chip cookies. —Maurane Ramsey, Fort Wayne, Indiana

Coffee Chip Cookies
Toffee Crunch Grahams

1 cup shortening
2 cups packed brown sugar
2 eggs
1 cup boiling water
2 tablespoons instant coffee granules
4 cups all-purpose flour
2 teaspoons baking powder
1 teaspoon baking soda
4 cups (24 ounces) semisweet chocolate chips

In a mixing bowl, cream shortening and brown sugar. Add eggs, one at a time, beating well after each addition. Combine water and coffee; set aside. Combine the flour, baking powder and baking soda; add to creamed mixture alternately with coffee. Stir in the chocolate chips. Refrigerate for 1 hour. Drop dough by rounded tablespoonfuls 2 in. apart onto greased baking sheets. Bake at 350° for 10-12 minutes or until golden around the edges. Remove to wire racks to cool. **Yield:** 3-1/2 dozen.

Spiced Apple Bars

I bake chopped walnuts and hearty oats into these moist apple and cinnamon squares. —Evelyn Winchester
Hilton, New York

1/2 cup butter *or* margarine, softened
1 cup sugar
2 eggs
1 cup all-purpose flour
1 cup quick-cooking oats
1 tablespoon baking cocoa
1 teaspoon baking powder
1 teaspoon ground cinnamon
1/2 teaspoon baking soda
1/2 teaspoon salt
1/2 teaspoon ground nutmeg
1/4 teaspoon ground cloves
1-1/2 cups diced peeled tart apple
1/2 cup chopped walnuts
Confectioners' sugar

In a mixing bowl, cream butter and sugar. Add the eggs, one at a time, beating well after each. Combine dry ingredients; add to creamed mixture and mix well. Stir in apple and nuts. Spread into a greased 13-in. x 9-in. x 2-in. baking pan. Bake at 375° for 20-25 minutes or until a toothpick comes out clean. Cool. Dust with confectioners' sugar. Cut into bars. **Yield:** about 2-1/2 dozen.

Brownie Crackles

Ready in 1 hour or less

Chocolate chips and a convenient brownie mix provide the rich chocolate flavor in these sweet cookies. Rolling the dough in powdered sugar gives them an inviting crackled appearance. —Ellen Govertsen, Wheaton, Illinois

1 package fudge brownie mix (13-inch x 9-inch pan size)
1 cup all-purpose flour
1 egg

1/2 cup water
1/4 cup vegetable oil
1 cup (6 ounces) semisweet chocolate chips
Confectioners' sugar

In a mixing bowl, combine the brownie mix, flour, egg, water and oil; mix well. Stir in the chocolate chips. Place confectioners' sugar in a shallow dish. Drop dough by tablespoonfuls into sugar; roll to coat. Place 2 in. apart on greased baking sheets. Bake at 350° for 8-10 minutes or until set. Remove to wire racks to cool. **Yield:** 4-1/2 dozen.

Chocolate Mint Cookies

(Pictured on page 201)

Ready in 1 hour or less

My dad sandwiches mint patties between two tender chocolate cookies to create these chewy treats. The blend of chocolate and mint is a big hit at our house. Best of all, these cookies are easy and fun to make.
—Christina Burbage, Spartanburg, South Carolina

1-1/4 cups butter (no substitutes), softened
2 cups sugar
2 eggs
2 teaspoons vanilla extract
2 cups all-purpose flour
3/4 cup baking cocoa
1 teaspoon baking soda
1/2 teaspoon salt
32 round thin chocolate-covered mint patties

In a mixing bowl, cream butter and sugar. Add eggs, one at a time, beating well after each addition. Beat in vanilla. Combine the flour, cocoa, baking soda and salt; gradually add to the creamed mixture, beating until well combined. Drop by tablespoonfuls 2 in. apart onto ungreased baking sheets. Bake at 350° for 8-9 minutes or until puffy and tops are cracked. Invert half of the cookies onto wire racks. Immediately place a mint patty on each, then top with remaining cookies. Press lightly to seal. Cool completely. **Yield:** 32 sandwich cookies.

Dressed-Up Desserts

- Looking for a fun way to decorate a cake in a hurry? After covering a cake with frosting, experiment with whatever goodies you have on hand. I use coconut, licorice, LifeSavers, Teddy Grahams and more.
  —Nancy Decker, Lemoore Naval Air Station, California
- To make any cake mix more delicious, stir an envelope of whipped topping mix into the cake batter.
  —Michelle Yach, Independence, Missouri
- I blend peanut butter with a can of prepared butter frosting. It adds an extra luscious layer to chocolate cake. —Lori Michelli, Sheboygan, Wisconsin
- Try substituting eggnog for milk in your next homemade pumpkin pie. We tried it, and everyone thought it was the best pumpkin pie they ever ate.
  —Clifford Koss, Chandler, Arizona

**Make-Ahead Shortcake
Blueberry Lemon Trifle
Almond Mocha Pie**

Make-Ahead Shortcake

(Pictured at left)

Plan ahead...needs to chill

Here's a lovely layered dessert that showcases strawberries. This family favorite has all the satisfaction of traditional strawberry shortcake with just a dash of distinction.
—Karen Bland, Gove, Kansas

      1 loaf (14 ounces) angel food cake, cut into
        1-inch slices
  1/2 cup cold milk
      1 package (5.1 ounces) instant vanilla pudding
        mix
      1 pint vanilla ice cream, softened
      1 package (6 ounces) strawberry gelatin
      1 cup boiling water
      2 packages (10 ounces *each*) frozen sweetened
        sliced strawberries
Sliced fresh strawberries, optional

Arrange cake slices in a single layer in an ungreased 13-in. x 9-in. x 2-in. dish. In a mixing bowl, beat milk and pudding mix for 2 minutes or until thickened; beat in ice cream. Pour over cake. Chill. In a bowl, dissolve gelatin in boiling water; stir in frozen strawberries. Chill until partially set. Spoon over pudding mixture. Chill until firm. Garnish with fresh strawberries if desired. **Yield:** 12 servings.

Almond Mocha Pie

(Pictured at left)

Plan ahead...needs to freeze

I received this recipe from an aunt years ago. The creamy chocolate pie—with a hint of coffee—is nice to have in the freezer for a quick reward on a hectic day.
—Edna Johnson, St. Croix Falls, Wisconsin

      1 teaspoon instant coffee granules
      2 tablespoons boiling water
      1 milk chocolate candy bar with almonds
        (7 ounces)
      1 carton (8 ounces) frozen whipped topping,
        thawed
      1 pastry shell (9 inches), baked
Chocolate curls and additional whipped topping,
  optional

In a small bowl, dissolve coffee in boiling water; set aside. In a microwave or saucepan, melt the candy bar; cool slightly. Fold in half of the whipped topping. Fold in coffee and remaining whipped topping. Pour into pas-

Handy Hint

To keep my mixing bowl from sliding around on the countertop, I place it on a wet dishcloth. The cloth holds the bowl steady, which makes it easier to whip ingredients with my hand mixer.
—Leah Ragsdale
Conrad, Montana

try shell; freeze. Remove from the freezer 15 minutes before serving. Garnish with chocolate curls and additional whipped topping if desired. **Yield:** 6-8 servings.

Blueberry Lemon Trifle

(Pictured at left)

Plan ahead...needs to chill

A refreshing lemon filling and fresh blueberries give this sunny dessert sensation plenty of color. It doesn't require baking, so you don't have to heat up the oven.
—Ellen Peden, Houston, Texas

      3 cups fresh blueberries, *divided*
      2 cans (15-3/4 ounces *each*) lemon pie filling
      2 cartons (8 ounces *each*) lemon yogurt
      1 prepared angel food cake (8 inches),
        cut into 1-inch cubes
      1 carton (8 ounces) frozen whipped topping,
        thawed
Lemon slices and fresh mint, optional

Set aside 1/4 cup blueberries for garnish. In a bowl, combine pie filling and yogurt. In a 3-1/2-qt. serving or trifle bowl, layer a third of the cake cubes, lemon mixture and blueberries. Repeat layers twice. Top with whipped topping. Cover and refrigerate for at least 2 hours. Garnish with reserved blueberries, and lemon and mint if desired. **Yield:** 12-14 servings.

Jumbo Raisin Cookies

When I was growing up, my mother would make these soft and spicy raisin cookies once a month. Since the recipe makes a huge batch, she would freeze some to snack on later. —Becky Melander, Clinton, Michigan

      2 cups water
      4 cups raisins
      1 cup butter *or* margarine, softened
      1 cup shortening
      4 cups sugar
      6 eggs
      2 teaspoons vanilla extract
      8 cups all-purpose flour
      4 teaspoons baking soda
      4 teaspoons baking powder
      4 teaspoons salt
      1 tablespoon ground cinnamon
      1 teaspoon ground nutmeg
  1/2 teaspoon ground allspice
      2 cups (12 ounces) semisweet chocolate chips

In a saucepan, combine the water and raisins. Bring to a boil. Remove from the heat; cool to room temperature (do not drain). In a large mixing bowl, cream butter, shortening and sugar. Add eggs, one at a time, beating well after each addition. Beat in vanilla. Combine the dry ingredients; gradually add to the creamed mixture. Stir in chocolate chips and raisins with any liquid. Drop by heaping tablespoonfuls 2 in. apart onto greased baking sheets. Bake at 350° for 12-15 minutes or until golden brown. Remove to wire racks to cool. **Yield:** 13 dozen.

Cinnamon Rock Candy
Spritz Cookies

Cinnamon Rock Candy

(Pictured above)

My mother made this hard cinnamon candy many times for us as kids. Now I fix it for my own family and I give it as gifts at Christmas. —Marganne Winter Oxley
Klamath Falls, Oregon

> 1 cup water
> 3-3/4 cups sugar
> 1-1/4 cups light corn syrup
> 1 teaspoon red liquid food coloring
> 1 teaspoon cinnamon oil*
> 1/3 cup confectioners' sugar

Line a 15-in. x 10-in. x 1-in. baking pan with foil; butter the foil and set aside. In a large heavy saucepan, combine water, sugar, corn syrup and food coloring. Bring to a boil over medium heat, stirring occasionally. Cover and cook for 3 minutes to dissolve sugar crystals. Uncover; cook on medium-high heat, without stirring, until a candy thermometer reads 300° (hard-crack stage), about 25 minutes. Remove from the heat; stir in cinnamon oil (keep face away from mixture as odor is very strong). Immediately pour onto prepared pan. Cool completely, about 45 minutes. Break into pieces using the edge of a metal mallet. Sprinkle both sides of candy with confectioners' sugar. Store in airtight containers. **Yield:** about 2 pounds.
*Editor's Note: Cinnamon oil can be found in some pharmacies or at kitchen and cake decorating supply stores.

Spritz Cookies

(Pictured above)

These almond-flavored cookies are great for holiday bake sales. They can be left plain or decorated with colored sugar and frosting. In our house, it just wouldn't be Christmas without them. —Tanya Hart, Muncie, Indiana

> 1 cup butter (no substitutes), softened
> 1/2 cup sugar
> 1/2 cup packed brown sugar
> 1 egg
> 1/2 teaspoon almond extract
> 1/2 teaspoon vanilla extract
> 2-1/2 cups all-purpose flour
> 1/4 teaspoon baking soda
> 1/4 teaspoon salt
> Green and red colored sugar, chopped candied cherries and red frosting, optional

In a mixing bowl, cream the butter and sugars. Beat in the egg and extracts. Combine the flour, baking soda and salt; gradually add to the creamed mixture. Using a cookie press fitted with the disk of your choice, press dough 2 in. apart onto ungreased baking sheets. Sprinkle with colored sugar if desired. Bake at 375° for 7-9 minutes or until the edges just begin to brown. Immediately add cherries if desired, lightly pressing onto cookies. Cool on wire racks. Decorate with frosting if desired. **Yield:** about 7 dozen.

Homemade Chocolate Cake

A creamy chocolate frosting is the flavorful finishing touch to this moist from-scratch cake that's mixed in one bowl. It always turns out and is quickly gobbled up by friends and family. I'm asked to fix this favorite so often that the recipe card is an absolute mess!
—Cindy Miller
Riverside, Iowa

      3 cups all-purpose flour
      2 cups sugar
  1/3 cup baking cocoa
      2 teaspoons baking soda
      1 teaspoon salt
      2 cups water
  3/4 cup vegetable oil
      2 teaspoons vanilla extract
      2 teaspoons vinegar
CHOCOLATE CREAM CHEESE FROSTING:
      1 package (3 ounces) cream cheese, softened
  1/4 cup butter *or* margarine, softened
      2 cups confectioners' sugar
  1/3 cup baking cocoa
Dash salt
      3 tablespoons milk
  1/2 teaspoon vanilla extract

In a mixing bowl, combine the first five ingredients. Add the water, oil, vanilla and vinegar; mix well (batter will be thin). Pour into a greased 13-in. x 9-in. x 2-in. baking pan. Bake at 350° for 25-30 minutes or until a toothpick inserted near the center comes out clean. Cool completely. For frosting, in a mixing bowl, beat the cream cheese and butter. Add the confectioners' sugar, cocoa, salt, milk and vanilla; mix well. Spread over the cake. **Yield:** 12-15 servings. **Editor's Note:** This recipe contains no egg.

Cream Puff Dessert

(Pictured on page 201)

I recently took this rich dessert to a fellowship meeting at our church. Everyone loved it! In fact, so many people asked for the recipe that the church secretary printed it in our monthly newsletter. —Lisa Nash, Blaine, Minnesota

      1 cup water
  1/2 cup butter (no substitutes)
      1 cup all-purpose flour
      4 eggs
FILLING:
      1 package (8 ounces) cream cheese, softened
  3-1/2 cups cold milk
      2 packages (3.9 ounces *each*) instant chocolate
          pudding mix
TOPPING:
      1 carton (8 ounces) frozen whipped topping,
          thawed
  1/4 cup milk chocolate ice cream topping
  1/4 cup caramel ice cream topping
  1/3 cup chopped almonds

In a saucepan over medium heat, bring the water and butter to a boil. Add the flour all at once; stir until a smooth ball forms. Remove from the heat; let stand for

5 minutes. Add the eggs, one at a time, beating well after each addition. Beat until smooth. Spread into a greased 13-in. x 9-in. x 2-in. baking dish. Bake at 400° for 30-35 minutes or until puffed and golden brown. Cool completely on a wire rack. Meanwhile, in a mixing bowl, beat the cream cheese, milk and pudding mix until smooth. Spread over puff; refrigerate for 20 minutes. Spread with whipped topping; refrigerate until serving. Drizzle with the chocolate and caramel toppings; sprinkle with almonds. Store leftovers in the refrigerator. **Yield:** 12 servings.

Chocolate Chip Cheese Ball

(Pictured below)

Plan ahead...needs to chill

Your guests are in for a sweet surprise when they try this unusual cheese ball...it tastes just like cookie dough! Rolled in chopped pecans, the chip-studded spread is wonderful on regular or chocolate graham crackers. I especially like it because it can be assembled in a wink.
—Kelly Glascock, Syracuse, Missouri

      1 package (8 ounces) cream cheese, softened
  1/2 cup butter (no substitutes), softened
  1/4 teaspoon vanilla extract
  3/4 cup confectioners' sugar
      2 tablespoons brown sugar
  3/4 cup miniature semisweet chocolate chips
  3/4 cup finely chopped pecans
Graham crackers

In a mixing bowl, beat the cream cheese, butter and vanilla until fluffy. Gradually add sugars; beat just until combined. Stir in chocolate chips. Cover and refrigerate for 2 hours. Place cream cheese mixture on a large piece of plastic wrap; shape into a ball. Refrigerate for at least 1 hour. Just before serving, roll cheese ball in pecans. Serve with graham crackers. **Yield:** 1 cheese ball (about 2 cups).

Chocolate Chip Cheese Ball

Apple Spice Drops

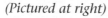

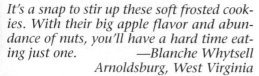

(Pictured at right)

Ready in 1 hour or less

It's a snap to stir up these soft frosted cookies. With their big apple flavor and abundance of nuts, you'll have a hard time eating just one. —Blanche Whytsell
Arnoldsburg, West Virginia

1/2 cup butter *or* margarine, softened
2/3 cup sugar
2/3 cup packed brown sugar
1 egg
1/4 cup apple juice
2 cups all-purpose flour
1 teaspoon ground cinnamon
1/2 teaspoon baking soda
1/2 teaspoon ground nutmeg
1 cup finely chopped peeled tart apple
1 cup chopped walnuts
FROSTING:
1/4 cup butter *or* margarine, softened
3 cups confectioners' sugar
1 teaspoon vanilla extract
3 to 4 tablespoons apple juice

In a mixing bowl, cream butter and sugars. Beat in egg and apple juice. Combine the dry ingredients; gradually add to the creamed mixture. Fold in apple and walnuts. Drop by teaspoonfuls 2 in. apart onto greased baking sheets. Bake at 375° for 12-14 minutes or until golden brown. Remove to wire racks to cool. For frosting, cream butter, sugar, vanilla and enough apple juice to achieve spreading consistency. Frost cooled cookies. **Yield:** about 3-1/2 dozen.

Peanut Butter Apple Dessert

(Pictured at right)

Plan ahead...needs to chill

My mom, who's well-known in our community for her cooking, shared the recipe for this yummy layered dessert. It's very popular with my husband. He made it in a 9 x 13 pan for his men's Bible study group and ended up giving out the recipe! —Kim Spencer, Hickman, Nebraska

1-1/2 cups graham cracker crumbs (about 24 squares)
1/2 cup packed brown sugar
1/2 cup plus 1/3 cup peanut butter, *divided*
1/4 cup butter *or* margarine, melted
1 package (8 ounces) cream cheese, softened
3/4 cup sugar
1 carton (16 ounces) frozen whipped topping, thawed
2 cans (21 ounces *each*) apple pie filling
3/4 cup confectioners' sugar
1 teaspoon ground cinnamon

In a bowl, combine the cracker crumbs, brown sugar, 1/2 cup peanut butter and butter; spoon half into a 3-

qt. bowl. In a mixing bowl, beat cream cheese and sugar until smooth; fold in whipped topping. Spread half over crumb mixture in the bowl. Top with one can of pie filling. Combine confectioners' sugar, cinnamon and remaining peanut butter until crumbly; sprinkle half over pie filling. Repeat layers. Refrigerate until serving. **Yield:** about 20 servings.

All-Star Apple Pie

(Pictured at right)

My two boys, Ben and Andy, made this scrumptious apple pie with a sweet, crunchy topping. It's simple to assemble with a store-bought crust and canned pie filling, yet it tastes like it's made from scratch. —Cindy Glick
Bradford, New York

1 can (21 ounces) apple pie filling
1 tablespoon lemon juice
1/4 teaspoon ground cinnamon
1 pastry shell (9 inches), baked
1/4 cup all-purpose flour
1/4 cup packed brown sugar
2 tablespoons cold butter *or* margarine
1/4 cup chopped pecans *or* walnuts
1/4 cup quick-cooking oats
2 tablespoons flaked coconut

In a bowl, combine pie filling, lemon juice and cinnamon; spoon into pastry shell. In another bowl, combine the flour and brown sugar; cut in butter until the mixture resembles coarse crumbs. Stir in nuts, oats and coconut; sprinkle over pie filling. Bake at 400° for 12-15 minutes or until topping is golden brown, covering edge of pastry with foil to prevent overbrowning if needed. Cool on a wire rack before cutting. **Yield:** 6-8 servings.

Minty Cocoa Mousse

Ready in 1 hour or less

Junior Mints give the refreshing mint taste to this scrumptious smooth-as-silk mousse. It's one of my best desserts because it's a snap to prepare, yet the flavor is beyond compare. —Melissa Tarbox, Allen, Texas

2 tablespoons baking cocoa
2 tablespoons milk
1 cup Junior Mints
2 tablespoons butter *or* margarine
1 carton (8 ounces) frozen whipped topping, thawed, *divided*
1/2 teaspoon vanilla extract
Fresh mint and additional whipped topping, optional

In a saucepan, combine cocoa and milk until smooth. Add mints and butter; cook and stir over low heat until smooth. Cool for 15 minutes. Stir in 1 cup whipped topping and vanilla. Fold in the remaining whipped topping. Spoon into dessert dishes. Refrigerate until serving. Garnish with mint and whipped topping if desired. **Yield:** 4 servings.

Peanut Butter Apple Dessert
All-Star Apple Pie
Apple Spice Drops

Layered Brownies

I have always enjoyed cooking and baking. Now I have grandchildren that like to help me in the kitchen. These chocolaty bars are one of our favorites. —Sharon Miller
Elkhart, Indiana

  1 package (18-1/4 ounces) chocolate cake mix
  1 cup chopped nuts
1/3 cup vegetable oil
  1 egg
  1 can (14 ounces) sweetened condensed milk
  1 cup (6 ounces) semisweet chocolate chips
1/8 teaspoon salt
  1 teaspoon vanilla extract

In a mixing bowl, combine dry cake mix, nuts, oil and egg; mix until crumbly. Set aside 1-1/2 cups for topping. Press the remaining crumb mixture into a greased 13-in. x 9-in. x 2-in. baking pan. In a saucepan, combine milk, chocolate chips and salt. Cook and stir over low heat until chips are melted. Stir in vanilla. Spread evenly in pan. Sprinkle with reserved crumb mixture. Bake at 350° for 25-30 minutes or until a toothpick inserted near the center comes out clean. Cool before cutting. **Yield:** 4 dozen.

Chocolate Peanut Delight

(Pictured below)

Plan ahead...needs to chill

Peanut lovers will appreciate this yummy dessert I dreamed up. A brownie-like crust is packed with nuts, topped with a fluffy peanut butter layer and covered with whipped topping and more nuts. It was so well received that I made it for a local restaurant where I used to work.
—Karen Kutruff, New Berlin, Pennsylvania

Chocolate Peanut Delight

  1 package (18-1/4 ounces) chocolate cake mix
1/2 cup butter *or* margarine, melted
1/4 cup milk
  1 egg
  1 cup chopped peanuts, *divided*
  1 package (8 ounces) cream cheese, softened
  1 cup peanut butter
  1 cup confectioners' sugar
  1 can (14 ounces) sweetened condensed milk
1-1/2 teaspoons vanilla extract
  1 carton (16 ounces) frozen whipped topping, thawed, *divided*
1/2 cup semisweet chocolate chips
4-1/2 teaspoons butter *or* margarine
1/2 teaspoon vanilla extract

In a mixing bowl, combine dry cake mix, butter, milk and egg. Add 3/4 cup of peanuts. Spread into a greased 13-in. x 9-in. x 2-in. baking pan. Bake at 350° for 30 minutes or until a toothpick inserted near the center comes out clean. Cool on a wire rack. In a mixing bowl, beat the cream cheese, peanut butter, sugar, condensed milk and vanilla until smooth. Fold in 3 cups whipped topping. Spread over the crust; top with the remaining whipped topping and peanuts. In a microwave-safe bowl, heat chocolate chips and butter on high for 1 minute or until melted. Stir in vanilla until smooth; drizzle over cake. Refrigerate for 2-3 hours before cutting. **Yield:** 12-15 servings.

German Chocolate Ice Cream

(Pictured on page 200)

Plan ahead...needs to freeze

I found this recipe years ago and have been taking it to ice cream socials ever since. But you won't want to wait for a get-together to enjoy it. The cool combination of chocolate, coconut and pecans is delicious anytime. My family requests it regularly, regardless of the season.
—Peggy Key, Grant, Alabama

1-1/2 cups sugar
1/4 cup all-purpose flour
1/4 teaspoon ground cinnamon
1/4 teaspoon salt
  4 cups milk
  3 eggs, beaten
  1 quart half-and-half cream
  2 packages (4 ounces *each*) German sweet chocolate, melted
  1 cup flaked coconut
  1 cup chopped pecans

In a large heavy saucepan, combine the sugar, flour, cinnamon and salt. Gradually add milk and eggs; stir until smooth. Cook and stir over medium-low heat until mixture is thick enough to coat a metal spoon and reaches 160°, about 15 minutes. Stir in the remaining ingredients. Refrigerate for several hours or overnight. Fill ice cream freezer cylinder two-thirds full; freeze according to manufacturer's instructions. Refrigerate remaining mixture until ready to freeze. Remove ice cream from the freezer 10 minutes before serving. **Yield:** 1 gallon.

St. Patrick's Day Cupcakes
Peppermint Patty Brownies

St. Patrick's Day Cupcakes

(Pictured above)

Ready in 1 hour or less

These stir-and-bake cupcakes go together super-quick. Pistachio pudding mix gives them a mild flavor and pretty pastel color that makes them perfect for St. Patrick's Day.
—Kathy Meyer, Almond, Wisconsin

1-3/4 cups all-purpose flour
2/3 cup sugar
   1 package (3.4 ounces) instant pistachio
      pudding mix
   2 teaspoons baking powder
1/2 teaspoon salt
   2 eggs
1-1/4 cups milk
1/2 cup vegetable oil
   1 teaspoon vanilla extract
Green food coloring, optional
Cream cheese frosting

In a bowl, combine the dry ingredients. In another bowl, beat eggs, milk, oil and vanilla; add to dry ingredients and mix until blended. Fill paper-lined muffin cups three-fourths full. Bake at 375° for 18-22 minutes or until a toothpick inserted in the center comes out clean. Cool on a wire rack. If desired, add food coloring to frosting. Frost cupcakes. **Yield:** 1 dozen.

Peppermint Patty Brownies

(Pictured above)

I add a special ingredient to these fudgy brownies. A layer of chocolate-covered mint patties provides the rich, refreshing surprise. —Clara Bakke, Coon Rapids, Minnesota

1-1/2 cups butter *or* margarine, softened
   3 cups sugar
   5 eggs
   1 tablespoon vanilla extract
   2 cups all-purpose flour
   1 cup baking cocoa
   1 teaspoon baking powder
   1 teaspoon salt
   1 package (13 ounces) chocolate-covered
      peppermint patties

In a mixing bowl, cream butter and sugar. Add eggs, one at a time, beating well after each addition. Beat in vanilla. Combine the dry ingredients; add to creamed mixture and mix well. Spread about two-thirds of the batter in a greased 13-in. x 9-in. x 2-in. baking pan. Arrange peppermint patties over top. Carefully spread remaining batter over patties. Bake at 350° for 35-40 minutes or until edges begin to pull away from sides of pan and a toothpick inserted near the center comes out clean (top will appear uneven). Cool completely before cutting. **Yield:** 2 to 2-1/2 dozen.

Chocolate and Fruit Trifle

semble, spread 2-1/2 cups pudding mixture in a 4-qt. glass bowl. Top with half of the crumbled cake; sprinkle with 1 tablespoon orange juice. Arrange half of the berries and kiwi over cake. Repeat pudding and cake layers; sprinkle with remaining orange juice. Top with remaining pudding mixture. Spoon remaining fruit around edge of bowl. Cover and refrigerate until serving. **Yield:** 12-16 servings.

Fudgy Brownies

I can stir up these moist and chocolaty brownies in a snap. They're oh-so-easy to make and oh-so-scrumptious to eat.
—*Evie Gloistein, Susanville, California*

      1/2 cup butter (no substitutes)
        4 squares (1 ounce *each*)
            unsweetened chocolate
        2 cups sugar
        4 eggs, beaten
        1 teaspoon vanilla extract
      1/2 cup all-purpose flour
      1/2 teaspoon salt
        2 cups chopped pecans, optional
Confectioners' sugar, optional

In a heavy saucepan, melt the butter and chocolate; stir until smooth. Remove from the heat. Stir in sugar. Add eggs and vanilla; mix well. Stir in flour and salt. Add pecans if desired. Spread into two greased 8-in. square baking pans. Bake at 325° for 35-40 minutes or until a toothpick inserted near the center comes out clean. Cool on a wire rack. Dust with confectioners' sugar if desired. Cut into bars. **Yield:** 32 brownies.

Card Club Dessert

Plan ahead...needs to chill

My bridge club loves squares of this rich and creamy peanut butter filling over a cookie-crumb crust. Everyone always asks for seconds!
—*Margaret Wochos*
Mt. Home, Arkansas

     30 cream-filled chocolate sandwich cookies,
            finely crushed (about 2-1/4 cups)
      1/3 cup butter *or* margarine, melted
  1-3/4 cups cold milk
        1 package (3.4 ounces) instant vanilla pudding
            mix
        1 cup peanut butter
        1 package (4 ounces) German sweet chocolate,
            chopped
        1 carton (12 ounces) frozen whipped topping,
            thawed

In a bowl, combine cookie crumbs and butter; set aside 1/4 cup for topping. Press remaining crumb mixture into an ungreased 13-in. x 9-in. x 2-in. baking pan. Bake at 375° for 5 minutes; cool completely. In a mixing bowl,

Chocolate and Fruit Trifle

(Pictured above and on page 200)

This refreshing dessert layered with devil's food cake, a creamy pudding mixture, red berries and green kiwi is perfect for the holidays. I like making it in a clear glass trifle bowl to show off its festive colors. —*Angie Dierikx*
State Center, Iowa

        1 package (18-1/4 ounces) devil's food cake
            mix
        1 can (14 ounces) sweetened condensed milk
        1 cup cold water
        1 package (3.4 ounces) instant vanilla pudding
            mix
        2 cups whipping cream, whipped
        2 tablespoons orange juice
        2 cups fresh strawberries, chopped
        2 cups fresh raspberries
        2 kiwifruit, peeled and chopped

Prepare cake batter according to package directions; pour into a greased 15-in. x 10-in. x 1-in. baking pan. Bake at 350° for 20 minutes or until a toothpick inserted near the center comes out clean. Cool completely on a wire rack. Crumble enough cake to measure 8 cups; set aside. (Save remaining cake for another use.) In a mixing bowl, combine milk and water until smooth. Add pudding mix; beat on low speed for 2 minutes or until slightly thickened. Fold in the whipped cream. To as-

beat milk and pudding mix for 2 minutes or until thickened. Immediately stir in peanut butter and chocolate. Fold in whipped topping. Spread over cooled crust. Sprinkle with reserved crumb mixture. Cover and refrigerate for 4 hours or overnight. **Yield:** 12-15 servings.

Frozen Mocha Marbled Loaf

(Pictured below right)

Plan ahead...needs to freeze

This showstopping marbled dessert seems fancy, but it's really simple to prepare ahead of time and pop in the freezer. Frosty slices have a creamy blend of chocolate and coffee that's delightful any time of year.
—*Cheryl Martinetto, Grand Rapids, Minnesota*

  2 cups finely crushed chocolate cream-filled sandwich cookies (about 22 cookies)
  3 tablespoons butter *or* margarine, melted
  1 package (8 ounces) cream cheese, softened
  1 can (14 ounces) sweetened condensed milk
  1 teaspoon vanilla extract
  2 cups whipping cream, whipped
  2 tablespoons instant coffee granules
  1 tablespoon hot water
1/2 cup chocolate syrup

Line a 9-in. x 5-in. x 3-in. loaf pan with foil. In a bowl, combine the cookie crumbs and butter. Press firmly onto the bottom and 1-1/2 in. up the sides of prepared pan. In a mixing bowl, beat cream cheese until light. Add milk and vanilla; mix well. Fold in whipped cream. Spoon half of the mixture into another bowl and set aside. Dissolve coffee in hot water; fold into remaining cream cheese mixture. Fold in chocolate syrup. Spoon half of chocolate mixture over crust. Top with half of the reserved cream cheese mixture. Repeat layers. Cut through layers with a knife to swirl the chocolate (pan will be full). Cover and freeze for 6 hours or overnight. To serve, lift out of the pan; remove foil. Cut into slices. **Yield:** 12 servings.

Chocolate Cherry Bars

Plan ahead...needs to chill

These tempting bars are simple to make with cherry pie filling, crunchy almonds and chocolate chips. I took them to a church supper and everyone wanted the recipe. People said the sweet treats reminded them of chocolate-covered cherries.
—*Tina Dierking, Canaan, Maine*

1-3/4 cups all-purpose flour
  1 cup sugar
1/4 cup baking cocoa
  1 cup cold butter *or* margarine

  1 egg, lightly beaten
  1 teaspoon almond extract
  1 can (21 ounces) cherry pie filling
  2 cups (12 ounces) semisweet chocolate chips
  1 cup chopped almonds

In a bowl, combine the flour, sugar and cocoa. Cut in butter until crumbly. Add the egg and almond extract until blended; set aside 1 cup for topping. Press remaining crumb mixture into a greased 13-in. x 9-in. x 2-in. baking pan. Carefully top with pie filling. Combine chocolate chips, almonds and reserved crumb mixture; sprinkle over pie filling. Bake at 350° for 35-40 minutes or until a toothpick inserted near the center comes out clean. Cool; refrigerate for at least 2 hours before cutting. **Yield:** 3 dozen.

Homemade Taste

When I need a fussy cake for a special occasion and don't have much time, I add 1/2 teaspoon ground nutmeg to a basic yellow cake mix batter. The result is a nicely spiced cake that tastes like it was made with lots of loving care!
—*Carol Ann Lowes*
Clifton Park, New York

Frozen Mocha Marbled Loaf

Chapter 14

Fast, Delicious...and Nutritious

OF COURSE you're looking for tempting recipes that don't keep you in the kitchen for hours. But you're likely also looking for delicious dishes that fit today's healthy lifestyle.

The lighter versions featured in this chapter fit right in if you're watching your diet *and* if you're watching the kitchen clock.

Each and every delicious dish is lower in fat, sugar or salt and includes Nutritional Analysis and Diabetic Exchanges.

Even those who aren't on a special diet will enjoy this fast-to-fix, lighter fare.

(All the quick good-for-you foods in this book are flagged with a red checkmark in the indexes beginning on page 336.)

LIGHT 'N' LUSCIOUS. Clockwise from upper left: Turkey Taco Dip (p. 232), Honey-Dijon Potato Salad (p. 231), Chicken with Spicy Fruit (p. 240) and Light Lemon Mousse (p. 231).

No-Oil Salad Dressing
Vegetarian Lasagna Loaf

 All recipes in this chapter use less fat, sugar or salt and include Nutritional Analysis and Diabetic Exchanges.

Vegetarian Lasagna Loaf

(Pictured above)

Ready in 1 hour or less

I enjoy preparing this meatless casserole for my family. They love its creamy texture and think they're eating an extremely rich dish when in fact it's good for them.
—Francine Scott, DeLand, Florida

    5 no-cook lasagna noodles
    2 envelopes (1-1/4 ounces *each*) white sauce
      mix
    1 tablespoon Italian seasoning
    1 teaspoon garlic powder
    3 cups skim milk
    1 cup (8 ounces) fat-free ricotta cheese
    1 cup frozen California-blend vegetables,
      thawed
1/2 cup nonfat Parmesan cheese topping
    2 tablespoons light sour cream
1/2 cup seeded chopped fresh tomato

Break the noodles in half widthwise; set aside. In a saucepan, combine sauce mix, Italian seasoning and garlic powder. Gradually stir in milk. Bring to a boil; cook and stir for 2 minutes or until thickened and bubbly. In an 8-in. x 4-in. x 2-in. loaf pan coated with nonstick cooking spray, layer 1/2 cup sauce, two noodle pieces, 1/4 cup ricotta cheese, 1/4 cup vegetables and about 1-1/2 tablespoons Parmesan cheese topping. Repeat layers three times. Top with remaining noodles, sour cream, 1/2 cup sauce, tomato and remaining Parmesan cheese topping. Bake, uncovered, at 350° for 30-35 minutes or until bubbly and noodles are tender. Let stand 10 minutes before serving. Reheat remaining sauce; serve with lasagna. **Yield:** 4 servings. **Nutritional Analysis:** One serving equals 378 calories, 1211 mg sodium, 18 mg cholesterol, 52 gm carbohydrate, 24 gm protein, 8 gm fat, 3 gm fiber. **Diabetic Exchanges:** 3 starch, 2 meat, 1 vegetable.

No-Oil Salad Dressing

(Pictured above)

Plan ahead...needs to chill

A little horseradish gives a lot of zip to this tart cooked dressing. Cornstarch thickens this tangy blend without oil.
—Naomi Giddis, Two Buttes, Colorado

    1 tablespoon cornstarch
1/2 teaspoon ground mustard
    1 cup cold water
1/4 cup vinegar
1/4 cup ketchup
    1 garlic clove, minced
1/2 teaspoon paprika

1/2 teaspoon prepared horseradish
1/2 teaspoon Worcestershire sauce
Artificial sweetener equivalent to 2 teaspoons
  sugar, optional

In a saucepan, combine the cornstarch, mustard and water until smooth. Bring to a boil; cook and stir for 2 minutes or until thickened and bubbly. Cool completely. In a bowl, combine remaining ingredients. Whisk in cornstarch mixture. Store in refrigerator. Stir before serving. **Yield:** about 1 cup. **Nutritional Analysis:** 2 tablespoons equals 16 calories, 96 mg sodium, 4 mg cholesterol, 4 gm carbohydrate, trace protein, trace fat, trace fiber. **Diabetic Exchange:** Free food.

Low-Fat Corn Bread

Ready in 30 minutes or less

I love corn bread, and I think this version is much better than traditional ones. Served warm, it's moist and tasty yet low in fat. —Heather Andersen, Norfolk, Nebraska

1 cup all-purpose flour
1 cup cornmeal
2 tablespoons sugar
2 teaspoons baking powder
1/2 teaspoon salt
2 egg whites
1 cup skim milk
1/4 cup unsweetened applesauce

In a bowl, combine the flour, cornmeal, sugar, baking powder and salt. In another bowl, combine egg whites, milk and applesauce. Stir into dry ingredients just until moistened. Pour into a 9-in. square baking pan coated with nonstick cooking spray. Bake at 400° for 15-20 minutes or until a toothpick inserted near the center comes out clean. Serve warm. **Yield:** 12 servings. **Nutritional Analysis:** One serving equals 101 calories, 198 mg sodium, trace cholesterol, 21 gm carbohydrate, 3 gm protein, trace fat, 1 gm fiber. **Diabetic Exchange:** 1-1/2 starch.

Fruit Cocktail Salad

Ready in 15 minutes or less

Convenient canned fruit and instant pudding mix streamline preparation of this refreshing medley. This shortcut salad can also be served as a sweet dessert for diabetics. —Karen Buhr, Gasport, New York

2 cans (16 ounces *each*) fruit cocktail in juice,
  undrained
1 can (20 ounces) unsweetened pineapple
  tidbits, drained
1 can (11 ounces) mandarin oranges, drained
1 tablespoon lemon juice
1 package (1 ounce) instant sugar-free vanilla
  pudding mix
2 medium firm bananas, sliced

In a bowl, combine the fruit and lemon juice. Sprinkle with pudding mix. Stir gently for 1 minute or until mix-

ture is thickened. Fold in bananas. Refrigerate until serving. **Yield:** 12 servings. **Nutritional Analysis:** One serving equals 88 calories, 101 mg sodium, 0 cholesterol, 22 gm carbohydrate, 1 gm protein, trace fat, 2 gm fiber. **Diabetic Exchange:** 1-1/2 fruit.

Light Lemon Cake

(Pictured below)

I revised a recipe that appeared in the newspaper to come up with this lemony cake topped with a light and creamy frosting. Not only is it fast to fix, but it serves a crowd. —Edna Thomas, Warsaw, Indiana

1 package (18-1/4 ounces) light yellow
  cake mix
1 package (3.4 ounces) instant lemon
  pudding mix*
1-3/4 cups water
3 egg whites
3/4 cup cold skim milk
1/2 teaspoon lemon extract
1 package (1 ounce) instant sugar-free vanilla
  pudding mix
1 carton (8 ounces) frozen light whipped
  topping, thawed

In a mixing bowl, combine dry cake mix, lemon pudding mix, water and egg whites. Beat on low speed for 1 minute. Pour into a 13-in. x 9-in. x 2-in. baking pan coated with nonstick cooking spray. Bake at 350° for 23-28 minutes or until a toothpick inserted near the center comes out clean. Cool. In a mixing bowl, combine milk, extract and vanilla pudding mix. Beat on low for 2 minutes. Fold in whipped topping. Spread over cake. Store in the refrigerator. **Yield:** 20 servings. **Nutritional Analysis:** One serving equals 163 calories, 294 mg sodium, trace cholesterol, 31 gm carbohydrate, 2 gm protein, 3 gm fat, trace fiber. **Diabetic Exchanges:** 2 starch, 1/2 fat. ***Editor's Note:** Sugar-free lemon pudding mix is not available.

Light Lemon Cake

Lime Garlic Shrimp

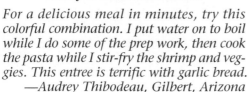

(Pictured below right)

Ready in 30 minutes or less

For a delicious meal in minutes, try this colorful combination. I put water on to boil while I do some of the prep work, then cook the pasta while I stir-fry the shrimp and veggies. This entree is terrific with garlic bread.
—Audrey Thibodeau, Gilbert, Arizona

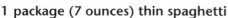

    1 package (7 ounces) thin spaghetti
    4 garlic cloves, minced
    2 tablespoons reduced-fat margarine
    1 pound uncooked medium shrimp, peeled
      and deveined
    1 package (6 ounces) frozen snow peas,
      thawed
    1 medium sweet red pepper, julienned
    3 tablespoons minced fresh basil *or*
      1 tablespoon dried basil
    2 tablespoons minced fresh parsley
Pepper to taste
    1/4 cup white wine *or* low-sodium chicken broth
      1 tablespoon lime juice
    1/2 cup grated nonfat Parmesan cheese topping
      (no substitutes)
    1/4 cup skim milk
    1/2 teaspoon grated lime peel

Cook spaghetti according to package directions. Meanwhile, in a skillet, saute garlic in margarine for 1 minute. Add the shrimp, peas, red pepper, basil, parsley and pepper. Stir-fry for 4 minutes or until shrimp turn pink and vegetables are crisp-tender. Add wine or broth and lime juice. Cook and stir for 1 minute. Drain spaghetti; stir in cheese topping, milk and lime peel. Serve shrimp mixture over spaghetti. **Yield:** 4 servings. **Nutritional Analysis:** One serving (prepared with low-sodium broth) equals 407 calories, 447 mg sodium, 176 mg cholesterol, 49 gm carbohydrate, 37 gm protein, 7 gm fat, 4 gm fiber. **Diabetic Exchanges:** 3 starch, 3 lean meat, 1 vegetable.

Peanutty Chocolate Pudding

(Pictured at right)

Ready in 15 minutes or less

I jazz up instant chocolate pudding by stirring in a small amount of peanut butter. The smooth results are sure to satisfy the dessert lovers in your family.
—Naomi Giddis
Two Buttes, Colorado

    2 cups cold skim milk
    1 package (1.4 ounces) instant
      sugar-free chocolate pudding mix
    1/3 cup reduced-fat peanut butter
Nonfat whipped topping, optional

In a mixing bowl, combine milk and pudding mix. Beat on low speed for 2 minutes. Beat in peanut butter until smooth. Spoon into dessert dishes. Top with whipped topping if desired. **Yield:** 4 servings. **Nutritional Analysis:** One serving (prepared without whipped topping) equals 157 calories, 235 mg sodium, 2 mg cholesterol, 14 gm carbohydrate, 10 gm protein, 7 gm fat, 1 gm fiber. **Diabetic Exchanges:** 1 starch, 1 meat.

Chicken-Fried Steak

Ready in 30 minutes or less

We raise cattle, so beef is a mainstay at our house. I adapted this traditional dish to leave a lot of the fat behind. This lighter version is now a family favorite.　—Carol Dale
Greenville, Texas

    3/4 cup all-purpose flour
    1/4 teaspoon pepper
      1 pound boneless round steak, cut into
        serving-size pieces
    1/2 cup skim milk
      2 tablespoons vegetable oil
GRAVY:
      2 tablespoons water
  4-1/2 teaspoons all-purpose flour
    3/4 cup skim milk
    1/8 teaspoon pepper

In a shallow bowl, combine flour and pepper. Add beef; turn to coat. Remove meat and pound with a mallet to tenderize. Pour milk into another shallow bowl. Heat oil in a skillet. Dip meat in milk, then coat again in flour mixture; add to skillet. Cover and cook over low heat

Peanutty Chocolate Pudding
Lime Garlic Shrimp

for 10 minutes. Turn; cook 10 minutes longer. Remove and keep warm. For gravy, add water to skillet; stir to loosen browned bits from pan. In a small bowl, combine flour, milk and pepper until smooth. Stir into skillet. Bring to a boil; cook and stir for 1-2 minutes or until thickened. Serve with steak. **Yield:** 4 servings. **Nutritional Analysis:** One serving (calculated without gravy) equals 307 calories, 67 mg sodium, 71 mg cholesterol, 19 gm carbohydrate, 30 gm protein, 11 gm fat, 1 gm fiber. **Diabetic Exchanges:** 4 meat, 1-1/2 starch.

Crustless Spinach Quiche

(Pictured at right)

Ready in 1 hour or less

My daughter is a vegetarian, so I eliminated the ham called for in the original recipe. Wedges of this healthy quiche make a fast and flavorful brunch, lunch or supper. —Vicki Schrupp
Little Falls, Minnesota

Crustless Spinach Quiche

3 ounces light cream cheese, softened
1 cup skim milk
Egg substitute equivalent to 4 eggs
1/4 teaspoon pepper
3 cups (12 ounces) shredded reduced-fat cheddar cheese
1 package (10 ounces) frozen chopped spinach, thawed and squeezed dry
1 cup frozen chopped broccoli, thawed and well drained
1 small onion, finely chopped
5 fresh mushrooms, sliced

In a small mixing bowl, beat cream cheese. Add milk, egg substitute and pepper; beat until smooth. Stir in remaining ingredients. Transfer to a 10-in. quiche pan coated with nonstick cooking spray. Bake at 350° for 45-50 minutes or until a knife inserted near the center comes out clean. **Yield:** 8 servings. **Nutritional Analysis:** One serving equals 151 calories, 404 mg sodium, 14 mg cholesterol, 8 gm carbohydrate, 18 gm protein, 5 gm fat, 2 gm fiber. **Diabetic Exchanges:** 1 starch, 1 meat.

Six-Veggie Bake

Plan ahead...needs to chill

I altered the original recipe for this strata-like dish and replaced the sausage with fresh vegetables. I can easily assemble it the night before a busy day. Then all I have to do for dinner is bake it and make a salad. —Kate Hilts
Fairbanks, Alaska

1 loaf (1 pound) Italian bread, cut into 1/2-inch cubes
1 can (14-1/2 ounces) diced tomatoes, undrained
1 package (10 ounces) frozen chopped spinach, thawed and well drained

1 cup chopped fresh mushrooms
1 cup (4 ounces) shredded part-skim mozzarella cheese
1/2 cup chopped green pepper
1/2 cup chopped zucchini
2 green onions, chopped
1 teaspoon dried basil
1/2 teaspoon dried oregano
1 cup skim milk
Egg substitute equivalent to 4 eggs
1 teaspoon salt-free seasoning blend
1/4 teaspoon pepper

In a large bowl, combine the first 10 ingredients; mix well. Place in a 13-in. x 9-in. x 2-in. baking dish coated with nonstick cooking spray. In a small bowl, combine milk, egg substitute, seasoning blend and pepper; pour over the vegetable mixture. Cover and refrigerate for 2 hours or overnight. Remove from the refrigerator 30 minutes before baking. Cover and bake at 425° for 15 minutes. Uncover; bake 15 minutes longer or until a knife inserted near the center comes out clean. **Yield:** 16 servings. **Nutritional Analysis:** One serving equals 128 calories, 292 mg sodium, 5 mg cholesterol, 18 gm carbohydrate, 8 gm protein, 3 gm fat, 2 gm fiber. **Diabetic Exchanges:** 1 starch, 1 vegetable, 1/2 meat.

Creamy Chicken Salad

Apple Carrot Salad

Ready in 15 minutes or less

I toss together sweet raisins, bright carrots and crunchy apple chunks to create this fresh-tasting side dish. This creamy salad is a breeze to prepare and a nice accompaniment to any meal. —Diane Molberg, Calgary, Alberta

    4 large carrots, shredded
    1 medium tart apple, chopped
    1/3 cup raisins
    1/4 cup plain nonfat yogurt
    1/4 cup fat-free mayonnaise
    2 teaspoons Dijon mustard
    2 teaspoons lemon juice
    1/8 teaspoon pepper
Artificial sweetener equivalent to 2 teaspoons sugar
    1/3 cup shredded reduced-fat cheddar cheese

In a bowl, combine the carrots, apple and raisins. In a small bowl, combine yogurt, mayonnaise, mustard, lemon juice, pepper and sweetener. Pour over carrot mixture and toss to coat. Stir in cheese. **Yield:** 8 servings. **Nutritional Analysis:** One serving equals 66 calories, 133 mg sodium, 1 mg cholesterol, 14 gm carbohydrate, 2 gm protein, 1 gm fat, 2 gm fiber. **Diabetic Exchanges:** 1/2 starch, 1/2 fruit.

Creamy Chicken Salad

(Pictured above)

Ready in 15 minutes or less

I modified the original recipe for this chicken salad to make it healthier. The ingredients are so flavorful that my changes didn't take away from the taste. This refreshing salad never lasts long at our house. Even if I double the recipe, my husband asks, "Why didn't you make more?"
—Kristi Abernathy, Kalispell, Montana

    2 cups cubed cooked chicken breast
    1 cup cooked small ring pasta
    1 cup halved seedless red grapes
    1 can (11 ounces) mandarin oranges, drained
    3 celery ribs, chopped
    1/2 cup sliced almonds
    1 tablespoon grated onion
    1 cup reduced-fat mayonnaise
    1 cup light whipped topping
    1/4 teaspoon salt
Lettuce leaves, optional

In a bowl, combine the chicken, pasta, grapes, oranges, celery, almonds and onion. In another bowl, combine the mayonnaise, whipped topping and salt. Add to the chicken mixture; stir to coat. Serve in a lettuce-lined bowl if desired. **Yield:** 6 servings. **Nutritional Analysis:** One 1-cup serving equals 261 calories, 307 mg sodium, 38 mg cholesterol, 25 gm carbohydrate, 11 gm protein, 13 gm fat, 2 gm fiber. **Diabetic Exchanges:** 1-1/2 fat, 1 starch, 1 meat, 1/2 fruit.

Open-Faced Omelet

Ready in 30 minutes or less

This tasty breakfast dish is a snap to make with convenient frozen hash browns. It gets its colorful look and fresh flavor from broccoli, red pepper and green onions. I take this egg dish to all of our church brunches and bring home an empty skillet every time. It's also a snappy morning dish when company spends the weekend.
—Cynthia Hinkle, Front Royal, Virginia

    1 cup broccoli florets
    1/2 cup chopped sweet red pepper
    1/4 cup thinly sliced green onions
1-1/2 cups cubed reduced-sodium fully cooked
        ham
    1 cup frozen shredded hash brown potatoes,
        thawed
Egg substitute equivalent to 10 eggs
    1/4 teaspoon pepper
    1/2 cup shredded reduced-fat cheddar cheese

In a 9-in. or 10-in. skillet coated with nonstick cooking spray, saute broccoli, red pepper and onions until crisp-tender. Add ham and hash browns. Cook for 2 minutes, stirring frequently. In a bowl, whisk together the egg substitute and pepper. Pour over vegetable mixture. Reduce heat; cover and cook for 10-12 minutes or until set. Remove from the heat. Sprinkle with cheese; cover and let stand for 5 minutes or until cheese is melted. Cut into wedges. **Yield:** 6 servings. **Nutritional Analysis:** One serving equals 172 calories, 490 mg sodium, 15 mg cholesterol, 10 gm carbohydrate, 21 gm protein, 5 gm fat, 1 gm fiber. **Diabetic Exchanges:** 2-1/2 lean meat, 1/2 starch.

Sweet 'n' Sour Meatballs

(Pictured below)

Ready in 1 hour or less

Convenience items, including bottled barbecue sauce and canned pineapple and cranberry sauce, speed preparation of this sweet and tangy main dish. It's a cinch to throw together, yet tastes like it took a lot of work. My family loves its Hawaiian flavor. —Nancy Decker
Lemoore Naval Air Station, California

Egg substitute equivalent to 1 egg
   2 tablespoons skim milk
   1 cup seasoned bread crumbs
   2 tablespoons chopped onion
1/8 teaspoon pepper
   1 pound lean ground beef
   1 tablespoon cornstarch
3/4 cup unsweetened pineapple juice
1/2 cup barbecue sauce
1/4 cup water
   1 cup whole-berry cranberry sauce
   6 unsweetened pineapple slices
   6 green pepper rings
Hot cooked rice

In a bowl, combine egg substitute and milk. Stir in crumbs, onion and pepper. Add beef; mix well. Shape into 36 balls, about 1 in. each. In a skillet coated with nonstick cooking spray, brown meatballs; drain if necessary. Combine cornstarch, pineapple juice, barbecue sauce and water until smooth; stir in cranberry sauce. Pour over meatballs. Bring to a boil; cook and stir for 2 minutes or until thickened. Reduce heat; top with pineapple and green pepper. Cover and simmer 10 minutes or until meatballs are no longer pink. Serve over rice. **Yield:** 6 servings. **Nutritional Analysis:** One serving (calculated without rice) equals 351 calories, 790 mg sodium, 28 mg cholesterol, 49 gm carbohydrate, 21 gm protein, 8 gm fat, 2 gm fiber. **Diabetic Exchanges:** 2 meat, 2 fruit, 1 starch.

Sweet 'n' Sour Meatballs

Honey-Dijon Potato Salad

(Pictured on page 225)

Plan ahead...needs to chill

No matter which recipe I tried, my potato salad always turned out bland. So I came up with this creamy version that has plenty of pizzazz. It's so tangy and flavorful and is a favorite at family picnics. —Kristie Kline Jones
Douglas, Wyoming

2-1/4 pounds red potatoes (about 14 small)
   3 tablespoons vinegar
3/4 cup chopped green pepper
1/2 cup chopped onion
   5 tablespoons chopped dill pickles
   1 teaspoon salt-free seasoning blend
1/4 teaspoon pepper
   1 cup fat-free mayonnaise
1/3 cup fat-free honey-Dijon salad dressing
   2 tablespoons Dijon mustard
   2 hard-cooked egg whites, chopped

Place potatoes in a saucepan; cover with water. Bring to a boil; cook until tender, 15-30 minutes. Drain and cool. Cube the potatoes and place in a large bowl. Sprinkle with vinegar. Add green pepper, onion, pickles, seasoning blend and pepper. Fold in mayonnaise, salad dressing, mustard and egg whites. Cover and refrigerate for at least 1 hour. **Yield:** 8 servings. **Nutritional Analysis:** One 3/4-cup serving equals 165 calories, 513 mg sodium, 0 cholesterol, 36 gm carbohydrate, 4 gm protein, 1 gm fat, 3 gm fiber. **Diabetic Exchanges:** 2 starch, 1 vegetable.

Light Lemon Mousse

(Pictured on page 224)

Plan ahead...needs to chill

This smooth and refreshing dessert is popular at summer cookouts, but it makes a delicious light finish to hearty winter meals, too. —Joan Jay, Frisco, Texas

3/4 cup sugar
1/2 cup cornstarch
   3 cups skim milk
2/3 cup lemon juice
1-1/2 teaspoons grated lemon peel
1/4 teaspoon vanilla extract
   2 cups light whipped topping
   3 drops yellow food coloring, optional

In a saucepan, combine the sugar and cornstarch; gradually stir in milk until smooth. Bring to a boil over medium heat, stirring constantly. Cook and stir for 2 minutes or until thickened and bubbly. Remove from the heat. Stir in lemon juice, peel and vanilla. Set saucepan in ice; stir until mixture reaches room temperature, about 5 minutes. Fold in whipped topping and food coloring if desired. Spoon into dessert dishes. Refrigerate for at least 1 hour before serving. **Yield:** 10 servings. **Nutritional Analysis:** One 1/2-cup serving equals 145 calories, 39 mg sodium, 1 mg cholesterol, 29 gm carbohydrate, 3 gm protein, 2 gm fat, trace fiber. **Diabetic Exchanges:** 1 starch, 1 fruit.

Zucchini Ricotta Bake

(Pictured below)

I have made this lasagna-like zucchini casserole frequently over the years and shared the recipe with many people. Recently, my daughter had heart trouble, so I adapted the recipe to cut fat and calories. We think this version is just as delicious.
—Eleanor Hauserman
Huntsville, Alabama

      2 pounds zucchini
      1 carton (15 ounces) light ricotta cheese
Egg substitute equivalent to 2 eggs
   1/2 cup dry bread crumbs, *divided*
      5 tablespoons grated Parmesan cheese, *divided*
      1 tablespoon minced parsley
   1/4 teaspoon dried oregano
   1/4 teaspoon dried basil
   1/8 teaspoon pepper
      1 jar (26 ounces) low-sodium spaghetti sauce
1-1/2 cups (6 ounces) shredded part-skim
      reduced-fat mozzarella cheese

Cut zucchini lengthwise into 1/4-in. slices. Place in a basket over 1 in. of boiling water. Cover and steam for 5-6 minutes or until just tender. Drain; pat dry. In a bowl, combine ricotta, egg substitute, 3 tablespoons bread crumbs, 3 tablespoons Parmesan, parsley, oregano, basil and pepper; set aside. Spread a third of the spaghetti sauce in a 13-in. x 9-in. x 2-in. baking dish coated with nonstick cooking spray. Sprinkle with 2 tablespoons bread crumbs. Cover with half of the zucchini, ricotta mixture and mozzarella. Repeat layers of sauce, zucchini, ricotta mixture and mozzarella. Cover with remaining sauce. Combine remaining crumbs and Parmesan; sprinkle over top. Cover and bake at 350° for 45 minutes. Uncover; bake 15 minutes longer. Let stand 15 minutes before cutting. **Yield:** 12 servings. **Nutritional Analysis:** One serving equals 201 calories, 237 mg sodium, 21 mg cholesterol, 18 gm carbohydrate, 12 gm protein, 9 gm fat, 3 gm fiber. **Diabetic Exchanges:** 1 starch, 1 meat, 1 fat, 1/2 vegetable.

Turkey Taco Dip

(Pictured on page 224)

Ready in 30 minutes or less

I created this zippy snack when I had a craving for tacos, but didn't want all the fat and calories that go along with them. It's quick to fix and uses ingredients I usually have on hand. I served this appetizer at a bridal shower, and the bride liked it so much she asked me to make it for her wedding reception!
—Liz Adcock
Rayville, Louisiana

   1 pound ground turkey breast
   1 envelope reduced-sodium taco seasoning
   1 cup water
   1 package (8 ounces) fat-free cream cheese,
      softened
   1 cup (8 ounces) nonfat sour cream
3/4 cup picante sauce
1/2 cup shredded lettuce
   1 cup chopped fresh tomato
   1 cup (4 ounces) shredded fat-free cheddar
      cheese
Baked tortilla chips

In a skillet, cook turkey over medium heat until no longer pink; drain. Add taco seasoning and water; cover and simmer for 10 minutes. Spoon turkey onto a 12-in. serving plate or pizza pan. In a mixing bowl, beat the cream cheese until smooth. Add sour cream; spread over the meat mixture. Spread with picante sauce. Top with lettuce, tomato and cheese. Serve with tortilla chips. **Yield:** 10 servings. **Nutritional Analysis:** One serving (calculated without chips) equals 135 calories, 569 mg sodium, 18 mg cholesterol, 11 gm carbohydrate, 19 gm protein, 1 gm fat, trace fiber. **Diabetic Exchanges:** 2 very lean meat, 1 vegetable, 1/2 starch.

Apple Tuna Sandwiches

(Pictured above right)

Ready in 15 minutes or less

My husband and his buddies love to pack these tasty sandwiches when they go on fishing trips. The tangy tuna salad gets fun flavor from sweet pickle relish and lots of crunch from apples, celery and walnuts. The satisfying sandwiches are a complete meal in themselves.
—Ivy Eresmas, Dade City, Florida

Zucchini Ricotta Bake

Apple Tuna Sandwiches

1 can (6 ounces) tuna in water, drained
1/2 cup chopped red apple
1/3 cup fat-free mayonnaise
1/4 cup finely chopped celery
1/4 cup finely chopped walnuts
2 tablespoons finely chopped onion
1 tablespoon sweet pickle relish
1 teaspoon sugar
1/4 teaspoon salt
6 slices reduced-calorie bread, toasted
6 lettuce leaves

In a bowl, combine the first nine ingredients. Spread 1/2 cup on three slices of bread. Top with lettuce and remaining bread. **Yield:** 3 servings. **Nutritional Analysis:** One serving (calculated without bread) equals 262 calories, 817 mg sodium, 17 mg cholesterol, 31 gm carbohydrate, 22 gm protein, 7 gm fat, 5 gm fiber. **Diabetic Exchanges:** 2 starch, 2 lean meat.

Low-Fat Devil's Food Cake

I adjusted the original recipe for this cake so my father, who's on a low-fat diet, can enjoy it. This moist bundt cake is a breeze to make because it starts with convenient reduced-fat cake mix. It's terrific for parties...no one can believe it's low in fat. —Nancy Lamber
Jacksonville, Florida

1 package (18-1/4 ounces) reduced-fat devil's food cake mix
1 carton (8 ounces) nonfat plain yogurt
1/2 cup orange juice
1/2 cup water
Egg substitute equivalent to 2 eggs
2 tablespoons unsweetened applesauce

2 tablespoons grated orange peel
1 teaspoon ground cinnamon
GLAZE:
1 cup confectioners' sugar
2 tablespoons baking cocoa
2 tablespoons orange juice
1/2 teaspoon vanilla extract

In a mixing bowl, combine the first eight ingredients; beat on low speed for 1 minute, scraping the bowl constantly. Coat a 10-in. fluted tube pan with nonstick cooking spray and dust with flour. Pour batter into pan. Bake at 350° for 50-55 minutes or until a toothpick comes out clean. Cool for 10 minutes before removing to a wire rack to cool completely. Combine the glaze ingredients; drizzle over cake. **Yield:** 12 servings. **Nutritional Analysis:** One serving equals 243 calories, 368 mg sodium, trace cholesterol, 48 gm carbohydrate, 5 gm protein, 4 gm fat, 2 gm fiber. **Diabetic Exchanges:** 2 starch, 1 fruit, 1 fat.

Vegetable Lentil Stew

This delicious stew is nothing but good for you! The chunky mixture, seasoned with chili powder and cumin, is chock-full of hearty beans, lentils and other veggies. Steaming bowls of it make a warm and satisfying supper.
—Vi Toews, Bluffton, Alberta

4 cups reduced-sodium V-8 *or* tomato juice
2 cans (14-1/2 ounces *each*) Italian stewed tomatoes
1 can (16 ounces) kidney beans, rinsed and drained
1 can (15 ounces) garbanzo beans, rinsed and drained
2 medium carrots, thinly sliced
2 medium potatoes, cubed
1 large onion, chopped
1 green pepper, chopped
1 sweet red pepper, chopped
1 cup lentils
2 tablespoons minced parsley
2 tablespoons chili powder
2 teaspoons dried basil
1 teaspoon garlic powder
1 teaspoon ground cumin
1 package (10 ounces) frozen chopped spinach, thawed
TOPPING:
1/2 cup light sour cream
1/2 cup low-fat plain yogurt
2 tablespoons snipped chives

In a Dutch oven, combine the first 15 ingredients. Bring to a boil. Reduce heat; cover and simmer for 35-40 minutes or until lentils and vegetables are tender. Stir in spinach; heat through. Combine topping ingredients; dollop about 1 tablespoon on each serving. **Yield:** 13 servings. **Nutritional Analysis:** One 1-cup serving equals 216 calories, 392 mg sodium, 4 mg cholesterol, 38 gm carbohydrate, 12 gm protein, 2 gm fat, 12 gm fiber. **Diabetic Exchanges:** 2 starch, 1 vegetable, 1/2 meat.

Blueberry Oat Muffins

Blueberry Oat Muffins

(Pictured above)

Ready in 1 hour or less

For a tasty option to cold cereal or toast for breakfast, try these tender muffins. They're so full of blueberry and oat flavor that no one ever believes they are low in fat.
—Mildred Mummau, Mt. Joy, Pennsylvania

  1-1/4 cups all-purpose flour
      1 cup quick-cooking oats
    1/2 cup sugar
      1 teaspoon baking powder
    1/2 teaspoon baking soda
    1/4 teaspoon salt
      2 egg whites
    1/2 cup water
    1/3 cup vegetable oil
      1 cup fresh *or* frozen blueberries*
TOPPING:
      2 tablespoons sugar
    1/4 teaspoon ground cinnamon

In a bowl, combine the first six ingredients. In another bowl, beat egg whites, water and oil. Stir into dry ingredients just until moistened. Fold in blueberries. Fill paper-lined muffin cups or muffin cups coated with nonstick cooking spray three-fourths full. Combine sugar and cinnamon; sprinkle over muffins. Bake at 400° for 18-22 minutes or until a toothpick comes out clean. Cool for 5 minutes before removing from pan to a wire rack. **Yield:** 1 dozen. **Nutritional Analysis:** One muffin equals 177 calories, 131 mg sodium, 0 cholesterol, 27 gm carbohydrate, 3 gm protein, 7 gm fat, 1 gm fiber. **Diabetic Exchanges:** 1-1/2 starch, 1-1/2 fat. ***Editor's Note:** If using frozen blueberries, do not thaw before adding to the batter.

Light Tiramisu

Plan ahead...needs to chill

I call this my "skinny" dessert. It tastes just as rich as the traditional Italian dessert, but uses low-fat and sugar-free ingredients. If you don't tell people, they won't even know they're eating light.
—Jackie Newell
Roanoke, Virginia

      1 prepared angel food cake (8 inches), cut into 1-inch cubes
    1/2 cup instant sugar-free cappuccino mix, *divided*
      2 cups cold skim milk, *divided*
      1 package (8 ounces) nonfat cream cheese, softened
      1 package (1 ounce) sugar-free instant vanilla pudding mix
      2 cups light whipped topping
    1/2 teaspoon baking cocoa

Place cake cubes in an ungreased 13-in. x 9-in. x 2-in. dish. In a small bowl, combine 1/4 cup cappuccino mix and 1/2 cup milk until dissolved. Pour over cake. In a mixing bowl, beat cream cheese. In another bowl, combine pudding mix and remaining cappuccino mix and milk; whisk until smooth and thickened. Add to the cream cheese; mix well. Fold in whipped topping; spoon over cake mixture. Refrigerate for 3 hours or overnight. Sprinkle with cocoa just before serving. **Yield:** 8 servings. **Nutritional Analysis:** One serving equals 351 calories, 797 mg sodium, 3 mg cholesterol, 62 gm carbohydrate, 11 gm protein, 6 gm fat, trace fiber. **Diabetic Exchanges:** 4 starch, 1 fat.

Veggie Burgers

(Pictured at right)

Ready in 15 minutes or less

We created these quick vegetable patties to use up some of our garden bounty. To suit your family's tastes, include more of the vegetables you like and leave out the ones you don't for a specialty sandwich that's all your own.
—Mary James, Port Orchard, Washington

      1 small zucchini, grated
      1 medium uncooked potato, peeled and grated
      1 medium carrot, grated
    1/4 cup grated onion
Egg substitute equivalent to 3 eggs
Pepper to taste
    12 slices whole wheat bread, toasted
Sliced red onion and lettuce leaves, optional

In a bowl, combine the first six ingredients; mix well. Pour about 1/2 cup batter onto a hot griddle lightly coated with nonstick cooking spray. Fry for 2-3 minutes on each side or until golden brown. Serve on toasted bread with onion and lettuce if desired. **Yield:** 6 burgers. **Nutritional Analysis:** One burger (calculated without bread) equals 57 calories, 63 mg sodium, trace cholesterol, 8 gm carbohydrate, 5 gm protein, 1 gm fat, 1 gm fiber. **Diabetic Exchanges:** 1 vegetable, 1/2 lean meat.

Strawberry Slush

(Pictured below)

Plan ahead...needs to freeze

This make-ahead slush is really refreshing on hot summer days. Pour lemon-lime soda over scoops of the strawberry blend for a fast fruity treat that's so thick you'll have to eat it with a spoon.
—Patricia Schroedl
Jefferson, Wisconsin

 1 quart fresh strawberries
 2 cups nonfat vanilla ice cream, softened
 1 package (.3 ounce) sugar-free strawberry gelatin
 1/2 cup boiling water
 2 teaspoons lemon juice
 2 liters diet lemon-lime soda, chilled
Additional fresh strawberries, optional

In a large bowl, mash strawberries; add ice cream. In a small bowl, dissolve gelatin in water; stir in lemon juice. Add to the strawberry mixture; mix well. Pour into a 1-1/2-qt. freezer container; cover and freeze overnight. Remove from the freezer 15 minutes before serving. Spoon into glasses; add soda. Garnish with strawberries if desired. **Yield:** 10 servings. **Nutritional Analysis:** One 1/2-cup serving (calculated without garnish) equals 63 calories, 40 mg sodium, 0 cholesterol, 12 gm carbohydrate, 2 gm protein, 1 gm fat, 2 gm fiber. **Diabetic Exchanges:** 1/2 starch, 1/2 fruit.

Baked Basil Fries

(Pictured below)

Ready in 1 hour or less

A Parmesan cheese and basil coating gives these fries a pleasant taste. Seasoned with garlic powder and baked in the oven, they're a zippy alternative to deep-fat fried potatoes.
—Tammy Neubauer, Ida Grove, Iowa

 1/4 cup grated Parmesan cheese
 1 tablespoon olive *or* vegetable oil
 1 tablespoon dried basil
 1/4 teaspoon garlic powder
 4 medium red potatoes

In a bowl, combine Parmesan cheese, oil, basil and garlic powder. Cut potatoes into 1/4-in. sticks. Add to cheese mixture; toss to coat. Place in a 15-in. x 10-in. x 1-in. baking pan coated with nonstick cooking spray. Bake at 425° for 15 minutes; turn potatoes. Bake 15-20 minutes longer or until crisp and tender. **Yield:** 4 servings. **Nutritional Analysis:** One serving equals 162 calories, 117 mg sodium, 5 mg cholesterol, 27 gm carbohydrate, 7 gm protein, 5 gm fat, 3 gm fiber. **Diabetic Exchanges:** 1-1/2 starch, 1 fat.

Strawberry Slush
Veggie Burgers
Baked Basil Fries

Parmesan Zucchini Strips

Ready in 1 hour or less

My friends say these crispy zucchini sticks remind them of a restaurant appetizer. Little do they know how simple they are to make. With only four ingredients, they couldn't be easier. —Marilyn Hutter, Costa Mesa, California

- 1/3 cup seasoned bread crumbs
- 1/4 cup nonfat Parmesan cheese topping
- 4 small zucchini, quartered lengthwise
- Egg substitute equivalent to 1 egg

In a bowl, combine the bread crumbs and cheese topping. Dip zucchini in egg substitute, then in crumb mixture. Place on a baking sheet coated with nonstick cooking spray. Bake at 450° for 20-25 minutes or until golden brown and tender. **Yield:** 4 servings. **Nutritional Analysis:** One serving equals 91 calories, 390 mg sodium, 2 mg cholesterol, 14 gm carbohydrate, 7 gm protein, 1 gm fat, 3 gm fiber. **Diabetic Exchanges:** 1 vegetable, 1/2 starch, 1/2 lean meat.

Do-Ahead Brunch Bake

Plan ahead...start the night before

I wake up my clan with this convenient breakfast casserole that I assemble the night before. Loaded with hearty ham and hash browns, it starts their day in a tasty way. —Joy Maynard, St. Ignatius, Montana

- 8 frozen hash brown potato patties
- 1 package (8 ounces) thinly sliced fully cooked ham, chopped
- 1-1/4 cups shredded reduced-fat cheddar cheese, *divided*
- 2 cups skim milk
- 1 can (10-3/4 ounces) low-fat condensed cream of mushroom soup, undiluted
- Egg substitute equivalent to 4 eggs
- 1 teaspoon ground mustard
- 1/4 teaspoon pepper

Place potato patties in a 13-in. x 9-in. x 2-in. baking dish coated with nonstick cooking spray. Top with ham and 1 cup cheese. Combine milk, soup, egg substitute, mustard and pepper; pour over cheese. Cover and refrigerate overnight. Remove from the refrigerator 30 minutes before baking. Bake at 350° for 1 hour. Uncover and sprinkle with remaining cheese. Bake 20-25 minutes longer or until a knife inserted near the center comes out clean. Let stand 10 minutes before serving. **Yield:** 12 servings. **Nutritional Analysis:** One serving equals 122 calories, 463 mg sodium, 13 mg cholesterol, 9 gm carbohydrate, 11 gm protein, 5 gm fat, trace fiber. **Diabetic Exchanges:** 1 meat, 1/2 starch.

Pepper Steak with Squash

(Pictured at right)

Ready in 30 minutes or less

I fix this colorful stir-fry with savory strips of flank steak and plenty of veggies. Serve it over rice for a satisfying supper that's on the table in less than half an hour. —Gayle Lewis, Yucaipa, California

- 1 pound flank steak, cut into strips
- 2 tablespoons vegetable oil, *divided*
- 1 medium green pepper, julienned
- 1 medium sweet red pepper, julienned
- 2 medium zucchini, julienned
- 1 small onion, cut into 1/4-inch strips
- 3 garlic cloves, minced
- 1 cup fresh *or* frozen snow peas
- 1 cup sliced fresh mushrooms
- 1 can (8 ounces) sliced water chestnuts, drained
- 3 tablespoons cornstarch
- 1 can (14-1/2 ounces) low-sodium beef broth
- 2 tablespoons light soy sauce
- Hot cooked rice

In a large skillet, cook steak in 1 tablespoon oil over medium-high heat until no longer pink; drain. Remove and keep warm. In the same skillet, heat remaining oil; saute peppers for 2 minutes. Stir in zucchini, onion and garlic; cook and stir 2 minutes longer. Add peas, mushrooms and water chestnuts. Saute until the vegetables are tender, about 2 minutes. Return beef to the skillet. Combine cornstarch, broth and soy sauce until smooth; add to skillet. Bring to a boil; cook and stir for 2 minutes or until thickened. Serve over rice. **Yield:** 6 servings. **Nutritional Analysis:** One serving (calculated without rice) equals 245 calories, 547 mg sodium, 39 mg cholesterol, 17 gm carbohydrate, 19 gm protein, 11 gm fat, 3 gm fiber. **Diabetic Exchanges:** 2 meat, 2 vegetable, 1/2 starch.

Ginger Biscuits

(Pictured above right)

Ready in 30 minutes or less

These mildly spiced biscuits taste best served warm. They rely on convenient baking mix and orange yogurt, so they're virtually fuss-free. —Elaine Green Mechanicsville, Maryland

- 3 cups reduced-fat biscuit/baking mix
- 3 tablespoons sugar
- 1/2 teaspoon ground ginger
- 2 tablespoons cold margarine
- 1 carton (6 ounces) low-fat orange yogurt
- 1/4 cup plus 1 tablespoon egg substitute, *divided*

Ginger Biscuits
Pepper Steak with Squash

In a bowl, combine the biscuit mix, sugar and ginger. Cut in margarine until the mixture resembles coarse crumbs. With a fork, stir in yogurt and 1/4 cup egg substitute until mixture forms a ball. Turn onto a floured surface; knead 5-6 times. Roll out to 1/2-in. thickness; cut with a 2-1/2-in. biscuit cutter. Place on an ungreased baking sheet. Brush tops with remaining egg substitute. Bake at 425° for 14-16 minutes or until golden brown. **Yield:** 16 biscuits. **Nutritional Analysis:** One biscuit equals 123 calories, 289 mg sodium, 1 mg cholesterol, 21 gm carbohydrate, 3 gm protein, 3 gm fat, trace fiber. **Diabetic Exchanges:** 1 starch, 1/2 fat.

Pork Stroganoff

Ready in 30 minutes or less

Pork tenderloin is deliciously showcased in a smooth sauce with fresh lemon and herb flavor. Served over noodles, this entree has become one of our family's favorites.
—Darlene Sheridan, Phoenix, Arizona

  1 **pound pork tenderloin, thinly sliced**
  1 **tablespoon olive** *or* **vegetable oil**
1/2 **pound fresh mushrooms, quartered**

1-1/2 **cups coarsely chopped onions**
  2 **garlic cloves, minced**
1/2 **cup low-sodium beef broth**
  1 **tablespoon no-salt-added tomato paste**
  1 **teaspoon lemon juice**
  1 **teaspoon dried tarragon**
1/4 **teaspoon pepper**
  1 **tablespoon all-purpose flour**
1/2 **cup light sour cream**
1/3 **cup minced fresh parsley**
Hot cooked noodles

In a skillet, stir-fry pork in oil for 3-4 minutes or until no longer pink. Remove and keep warm. In the same skillet, saute mushrooms, onions and garlic for 3 minutes. Add the broth, tomato paste, lemon juice, tarragon and pepper. Simmer, uncovered, for 5 minutes. Return pork to the pan. Combine flour and sour cream; stir into pork mixture. Bring to a gentle boil; cook and stir for 2 minutes. Sprinkle with parsley. Serve over noodles. **Yield:** 4 servings. **Nutritional Analysis:** One serving (calculated without noodles) equals 266 calories, 92 mg sodium, 78 mg cholesterol, 13 gm carbohydrate, 29 gm protein, 11 gm fat, 2 gm fiber. **Diabetic Exchanges:** 3-1/2 lean meat, 2 vegetable.

Chicken Cutlets

(Pictured below)

Ready in 1 hour or less

I keep baked chicken moist and juicy with a golden coating of bread crumbs, wheat germ and Parmesan cheese. If you like a crunchier coating, substitute cornflake crumbs. —Cathy Kierstead, Easton, Maine

    6 boneless skinless chicken breast halves
        (1-1/2 pounds)
1-1/4 cups dry bread crumbs
  1/2 cup nonfat Parmesan cheese topping
    2 tablespoons wheat germ
    1 teaspoon dried basil
  1/2 teaspoon garlic powder
    1 cup plain yogurt
Refrigerated butter-flavored spray

Flatten chicken to 1/2-in. thickness. In a shallow dish, combine the bread crumbs, Parmesan topping, wheat germ, basil and garlic powder. Place the yogurt in another shallow dish. Dip chicken in yogurt, then coat with the crumb mixture. Place in a 15-in. x 10-in. x 1-in. baking pan coated with nonstick cooking spray. Spritz chicken with butter-flavored spray. Bake, uncovered, at 350° for 20-25 minutes or until the juices run clear. **Yield:** 6 servings. **Nutritional Analysis:** One serving equals 264 calories, 347 mg sodium, 78 mg cholesterol, 22 gm carbohydrate, 33 gm protein, 4 gm fat, 1 gm fiber. **Diabetic Exchanges:** 3 lean meat, 1 starch.

Tarragon Green Beans

(Pictured below)

Ready in 30 minutes or less

A mixture of celery, onion and green pepper adds spark to this simple green bean side dish. It's pleasantly seasoned with dried tarragon and lemon-pepper, so its flavor complements most main-dish meats. —Ruby Williams
Bogalusa, Louisiana

    4 cups fresh *or* frozen cut green beans
  1/2 cup water
  1/2 teaspoon salt
    1 large onion, chopped
    1 celery rib, chopped
  1/2 cup finely chopped green pepper
    2 tablespoons margarine
  3/4 teaspoon dried tarragon
  1/2 teaspoon salt-free lemon-pepper seasoning
Pepper to taste

In a large saucepan, combine the beans, water and salt; bring to a boil. Reduce heat; cover and simmer for 15 minutes or until tender. Meanwhile, in a small saucepan, saute the onion, celery and green pepper in margarine until tender. Stir in the tarragon, lemon-pepper and pepper. Drain beans; add vegetable mixture and toss to coat. **Yield:** 6 servings. **Nutritional Analysis:** One serving equals 74 calories, 274 mg sodium, 0 cholesterol, 9 gm carbohydrate, 2 gm protein, 4 gm fat, 2 gm fiber. **Diabetic Exchanges:** 1-1/2 vegetable, 1 fat.

Tarragon Green Beans
Chicken Cutlets

Blueberry Crisp

Ready in 1 hour or less

I take advantage of frozen blueberries to make this fruity crisp with a sweet golden topping. A dollop of vanilla yogurt adds to its homemade taste. —Betty Geiger
Marion, Michigan

   2 packages (12 ounces *each*) frozen
      unsweetened blueberries, thawed
   2 tablespoons plus 1/2 cup all-purpose flour,
      divided
   2 tablespoons brown sugar
   1/4 teaspoon ground cinnamon
   3 tablespoons cold margarine
TOPPING:
   1 cup (8 ounces) plain nonfat yogurt
   1/2 teaspoon vanilla extract
Artificial sweetener equivalent to 2 teaspoons sugar

Place the blueberries in an 8-in. baking dish coated with nonstick cooking spray. Sprinkle with 2 tablespoons flour. In a bowl, combine brown sugar, cinnamon and remaining flour; cut in margarine until crumbly. Sprinkle over berries. Bake at 350° for 25-30 minutes or until bubbly and golden brown. For topping, combine yogurt, vanilla and sweetener; serve with the crisp. **Yield:** 6 servings. **Nutritional Analysis:** One serving equals 198 calories, 99 mg sodium, 1 mg cholesterol, 31 gm carbohydrate, 5 gm protein, 7 gm fat, 3 gm fiber. **Diabetic Exchanges:** 1-1/2 fat, 1 starch, 1 fruit.

Chocolate Raspberry Dessert

(Pictured above right)

Plan ahead...needs to freeze

Guests are sure to find wedges of this fruity frozen pie irresistible. The crustless concoction has a creamy mousse-like consistency that's melt-in-your-mouth good. Plus, with drizzled chocolate and fresh raspberries, it has true eye appeal.
—Judy Schut, Grand Rapids, Michigan

   1 cup low-fat cottage cheese
   3/4 cup skim milk
   1/3 cup raspberry spreadable fruit
   1 package (1.4 ounces) instant sugar-free
      chocolate pudding mix
   1 carton (8 ounces) light frozen whipped
      topping, thawed
   1 square (1 ounce) semisweet chocolate, melted
   1/2 cup unsweetened raspberries

In a blender, combine cottage cheese, milk and spreadable fruit; cover and process until smooth. Add pudding mix and mix well. Pour into a bowl; fold in whipped topping. Spoon into a 9-in. pie plate. Drizzle with chocolate. Cover and freeze for 8 hours or overnight. Let stand at room temperature for 20 minutes before serving. Garnish with raspberries. **Yield:** 8 servings. **Nutritional Analysis:** One serving equals 161 calories, 250 mg sodium, 4 mg cholesterol, 22 gm carbohydrate, 5 gm protein, 5 gm fat, 1 gm fiber. **Diabetic Exchanges:** 1-1/2 fruit, 1 starch.

Chocolate Raspberry Dessert

Colorful Chicken Stew

Plan ahead...uses slow cooker

I rely on chili powder to spice up this hearty stew brimming with chicken and fresh-tasting veggies. Since it simmers in a slow cooker all day, it's ready when you walk in the door. —Ila Alderman, Galax, Virginia

   1 pound boneless skinless chicken breasts,
      cubed
   1 can (14-1/2 ounces) Italian diced tomatoes,
      undrained
   2 medium potatoes, peeled and cut into
      1/2-inch cubes
   5 medium carrots, chopped
   3 celery ribs, chopped
   1 large onion, chopped
   1 medium green pepper, chopped
   2 cans (4 ounces *each*) mushroom stems and
      pieces, drained
   2 low-sodium chicken bouillon cubes
Artificial sweetener equivalent to 2 teaspoons sugar
   1 teaspoon chili powder
   1/4 teaspoon pepper
   1 tablespoon cornstarch
   2 cups cold water

In a 5-qt. slow cooker, combine the first 12 ingredients. In a small bowl, combine cornstarch and water until smooth. Stir into chicken mixture. Cover and cook on low for 8-10 hours or until vegetables are tender. **Yield:** 10 servings. **Nutritional Analysis:** One 1-cup serving equals 123 calories, 209 mg sodium, 25 mg cholesterol, 16 gm carbohydrate, 11 gm protein, 1 gm fat, 3 gm fiber. **Diabetic Exchanges:** 2 vegetable, 1 very lean meat, 1/2 starch.

Pumpkin Streusel Muffins

(Pictured at right)

Ready in 1 hour or less

These nicely spiced muffins are a great accompaniment to any meal—or try them for breakfast, dessert or a snack. The pumpkin flavor is complemented by a sweet brown sugar topping. You'll never know they're made with egg substitute. —Connie Pietila, Atlantic Mine, Michigan

1/4 cup margarine, softened
1/2 cup sugar
1/4 cup packed brown sugar
2/3 cup cooked *or* canned pumpkin
1/2 cup buttermilk
Egg substitute equivalent to 2 eggs
2 tablespoons molasses
1 teaspoon grated orange peel
2 cups all-purpose flour
2 teaspoons baking powder
1 teaspoon baking soda
1 teaspoon pumpkin pie spice
1/4 teaspoon salt
STREUSEL TOPPING:
1/3 cup all-purpose flour
3 tablespoons brown sugar
2 tablespoons cold margarine

In a mixing bowl, cream margarine and sugars. Add pumpkin, buttermilk, egg substitute, molasses and orange peel; mix well. Combine dry ingredients; gradually add to pumpkin mixture just until blended. Use paper liners or coat muffin cups with nonstick cooking spray; fill two-thirds full. For topping, combine flour and brown sugar; cut in margarine until crumbly. Sprinkle over batter. Bake at 375° for 20-25 minutes or until a toothpick comes out clean. Cool in pan for 5 minutes before removing to a wire rack. **Yield:** 1 dozen. **Nutritional Analysis:** One muffin equals 229 calories, 336 mg sodium, trace cholesterol, 39 gm carbohydrate, 4 gm protein, 6 gm fat, 1 gm fiber. **Diabetic Exchanges:** 2 starch, 1 fat, 1/2 fruit.

Spinach Artichoke Spread

Ready in 1 hour or less

This baked spinach and artichoke blend makes a great appetizer for any occasion. I always serve it warm with reduced-fat crackers. —Nancy Farmer, Jordan, Arkansas

1 package (8 ounces) light cream cheese, softened
1 cup (8 ounces) light sour cream
1 package (10 ounces) frozen chopped spinach, thawed and well drained
1 package (9 ounces) frozen artichoke hearts, thawed, drained and chopped
2 teaspoons lemon juice
1/2 teaspoon salt-free seasoning blend
1/2 teaspoon pepper
Reduced-fat crackers

In a mixing bowl, beat cream cheese and sour cream until smooth. Stir in spinach and artichokes; mix well. Add

Pumpkin Streusel Muffins

lemon juice, seasoning blend and pepper. Transfer to a 9-in. pie plate coated with nonstick cooking spray. Bake at 350° for 20-30 minutes or until mixture bubbles around the edges. Serve warm with crackers. **Yield:** 4 cups. **Nutritional Analysis:** One 1/4-cup serving (calculated without crackers) equals 49 calories, 82 mg sodium, 10 mg cholesterol, 3 gm carbohydrate, 3 gm protein, 3 gm fat, 2 gm fiber. **Diabetic Exchanges:** 1 vegetable, 1/2 fat.

Chicken with Spicy Fruit

(Pictured on page 225)

Ready in 30 minutes or less

This speedy stovetop entree is special enough to serve company, yet easy enough for everyday. The moist chicken gets wonderful flavor from a sweet sauce made with strawberry jam, dried cranberries and pineapple juice. I like to serve it with rice pilaf, peas, a garden salad and warm cloverleaf rolls. —Kathy Rairigh, Milford, Indiana

1-1/4 cups unsweetened pineapple juice
1/4 cup dried cranberries
2 garlic cloves, minced
1/8 to 1/4 teaspoon crushed red pepper flakes
4 boneless skinless chicken breast halves (1 pound)
1/4 cup reduced-sugar strawberry fruit spread
1 teaspoon cornstarch
2 green onions, thinly sliced

In a large skillet, combine pineapple juice, cranberries, garlic and red pepper flakes; bring to a boil. Add chicken. Reduce heat; cover and simmer for 10 minutes or until chicken juices run clear. Remove chicken to a platter and keep warm. Bring cooking liquid to a boil; cook for 5-7 minutes or until liquid is reduced to 3/4 cup. Combine fruit spread and cornstarch until blended; add to the skillet. Boil and stir for 1 minute or until thickened. Spoon over chicken. Sprinkle with onions. **Yield:** 4 servings. **Nutritional Analysis:** One serving equals 248 calories, 66 mg sodium, 73 mg cholesterol, 26 gm carbohydrate, 27 gm protein, 3 gm fat, 1 gm fiber. **Diabetic Exchanges:** 4 very lean meat, 1-1/2 fruit.

Zippy White Chili

Ready in 1 hour or less

This chunky chicken chili doesn't require any fancy preparation or exotic ingredients. I usually serve the zesty mixture over crunchy tortilla chips. —Jenny Schmidtbauer
Sioux Falls, South Dakota

1 pound boneless skinless chicken breasts, cut into cubes
1 small onion, chopped
1-3/4 cups low-sodium chicken broth
1 can (4 ounces) chopped green chilies
1/2 teaspoon garlic powder
1/2 teaspoon dried oregano
1/2 teaspoon minced fresh cilantro *or* parsley
1/8 to 1/4 teaspoon cayenne pepper
1 can (15 ounces) white kidney *or* cannelini beans, rinsed and drained
Reduced-fat tortilla chips, optional

In a saucepan coated with nonstick cooking spray, saute chicken and onion until juices run clear; drain if desired. Stir in broth, chilies, garlic powder, oregano, cilantro and cayenne. Bring to a boil. Reduce heat; simmer, uncovered, for 30 minutes. Stir in beans; cook 10 minutes longer. Serve over tortilla chips if desired. **Yield:** 4 servings. **Nutritional Analysis:** One serving (calculated without tortilla chips) equals 235 calories, 428 mg sodium, 64 mg cholesterol, 19 gm carbohydrate, 29 gm protein, 4 gm fat, 6 gm fiber. **Diabetic Exchanges:** 3-1/2 very lean meat, 1 starch, 1 vegetable.

Creamed Crab

Ready in 15 minutes or less

This snappy crab sauce is so delicious over steamed rice that your guests will never guess it's good for them. Complete the meal with green beans, a tossed salad and fruit for dessert. —Emily Chaney, Penobscot, Maine

1/4 cup all-purpose flour
1 packet (1/2 ounce) butter-flavored granules*
2-1/2 cups skim milk
3 tablespoons reduced-fat mayonnaise
1-1/2 teaspoons ground mustard
1 teaspoon hot pepper sauce
1/4 teaspoon pepper

2 cans (6 ounces *each*) crabmeat, drained, flaked and cartilage removed *or* 2 cups imitation crabmeat
2 hard-cooked egg whites, chopped
Hot cooked rice

In a saucepan, combine flour and butter-flavored granules. Gradually stir in milk. Bring to a boil; cook and stir for 2 minutes or until thick and bubbly. Stir in mayonnaise, mustard, hot pepper sauce and pepper until smooth. Stir in the crab and cooked egg whites; heat through. Serve over rice. **Yield:** 4 servings. **Nutritional Analysis:** One serving (prepared with canned crab; calculated without rice) equals 185 calories, 446 mg sodium, 61 mg cholesterol, 16 gm carbohydrate, 21 gm protein, 4 gm fat, trace fiber. **Diabetic Exchanges:** 2-1/2 very lean meat, 1 starch. *Editor's Note:* This recipe was tested with Butter Buds Butter Flavor Mix.

Tomato-Topped Cod

Ready in 1 hour or less

Fresh tomato slices and a tasty topping jazz up plain fish fillets in this easy oven entree. The tempting treatment helps keep the cod moist and flavorful. —Kathleen Taugher
East Troy, Wisconsin

1-1/2 cups water
2 tablespoons lemon juice
1-1/2 pounds cod fillets
Pepper to taste
1 small onion, finely chopped
2 large tomatoes, sliced
1/2 cup chopped green pepper
1/2 cup seasoned bread crumbs
1/4 cup grated Parmesan cheese
1/2 teaspoon dried basil
1 tablespoon vegetable oil

In a bowl, combine the water and lemon juice. Add fish; soak for 5 minutes. Drain and place fish in an 11-in. x 7-in. x 2-in. baking dish coated with nonstick cooking spray. Sprinkle with pepper. Layer with onion, tomatoes and green pepper. Combine the remaining ingredients; sprinkle over top. Bake, uncovered, at 375° for 20-30 minutes or until fish flakes easily with a fork. **Yield:** 6 servings. **Nutritional Analysis:** One serving equals 158 calories, 391 mg sodium, 33 mg cholesterol, 13 gm carbohydrate, 16 gm protein, 4 gm fat, trace fiber. **Diabetic Exchanges:** 2 lean meat, 1 starch.

Sweet Substitute

Applesauce works well as a substitute for fat in baked goods. It can be used in muffins, quick breads, brownies and cakes—in both homemade and boxed-mix recipes.

Substitute the same amount of unsweetened applesauce for up to 1 cup of the butter, margarine or vegetable oil in the recipe. If you are unsure of the results in a particular recipe, first experiment by replacing only half of the fat with applesauce.

Chapter 15

⏱ Centsible Foods—Fast and Frugal

WHILE they may save time, store-bought packaged entrees and carryout meals aren't always money-savers. As a matter of fact, if you rely on them too much, they could quickly break the family budget.

So when you're in a pinch and counting pennies as well as minutes, look to these "centsible" quick dishes that are not only easy and economical but appetizing as well.

Our test kitchen staff has figured out the cost per serving for each of these express-eating alternatives. So these fast and frugal recipes are guaranteed to please your pocketbook as well as your palate.

THE PRICE IS RIGHT. Tangy Chicken Legs (p. 249).

Pasta Primavera

Pasta Primavera

(Pictured above)

Ready in 30 minutes or less

This colorful pasta and vegetable toss is a great quick meal. It has such a special taste, it's hard to believe it's inexpensive. —Charlotte McDaniel, Anniston, Alabama

 Uses less fat, sugar or salt. Includes Nutritional Analysis and Diabetic Exchanges.

  2 cups broccoli florets
  1 can (10-3/4 ounces) condensed cream of chicken *or* mushroom soup, undiluted
  1 large carrot, julienned
  1/2 cup milk
  1/4 cup grated Parmesan cheese
  1 garlic clove, minced
  1/8 teaspoon pepper
  3 cups cooked spaghetti

In a large saucepan, combine the first seven ingredients. Cook, uncovered, over medium heat until vegetables are tender, about 12 minutes. Stir in spaghetti; heat through. **Yield:** 4 servings (50¢ per serving). **Nutritional Analysis:** One serving (prepared with low-fat cream of chicken soup, skim milk and nonfat Parmesan cheese topping) equals 238 calories, 425 mg sodium, 8 mg cholesterol, 43 gm carbohydrate, 11 gm protein, 2 gm fat, 3 gm fiber. **Diabetic Exchanges:** 2 starch, 2 vegetable, 1/2 fat.

Chicken Dumpling Soup

Ready in 30 minutes or less

Although we were on a tight budget when I was a youngster, we always had good food. This comforting soup with soft dumplings was one of Mom's mainstays.
—Brenda Risser, Willard, Ohio

 Uses less fat, sugar or salt. Includes Nutritional Analysis and Diabetic Exchanges.

  2 cans (10-3/4 ounces *each*) condensed cream of chicken soup, undiluted
3-1/3 cups milk, *divided*
1-2/3 cups biscuit/baking mix

In a 3-qt. saucepan, combine soup and 2-2/3 cups of milk. Bring to a boil over medium heat; reduce heat. In a bowl, combine biscuit mix with remaining milk just until blended. Drop by rounded tablespoons onto simmering soup. Cook, uncovered, for 10 minutes. Cover and simmer 10-12 minutes longer or until dumplings test done (do not lift lid while simmering). Serve immediately. **Yield:** 4 servings (82¢ per serving). **Nutritional Analysis:** One serving (prepared with low-fat cream of chicken soup, skim milk and reduced-fat biscuit mix) equals 359 calories, 1276 mg sodium, 16 mg cholesterol, 60 gm carbohydrate, 13 gm protein, 6 gm fat, 1 gm fiber. **Diabetic Exchanges:** 3 starch, 1 skim milk, 1 fat.

Salmonettes

Ready in 30 minutes or less

Canned salmon makes these delicious salmon patties so fast to fix. And they always get rave reviews.
—Juanita Gross, Clearwater, Kansas

1 can (14-3/4 ounces) salmon
1 egg, lightly beaten
1/2 cup all-purpose flour
1/4 teaspoon dill weed
1-1/2 teaspoons baking powder
2 tablespoons vegetable oil

Drain salmon, reserving 1/4 cup juice. Discard salmon bones and skin. In a bowl, combine the salmon, egg, flour and dill; mix well. Stir baking powder into the reserved juice; add to the salmon mixture. Heat oil in a skillet over medium-high heat. Drop batter by 1/4 cupfuls into skillet. Cook the patties for 2-3 minutes on each side or until golden brown. Drain on paper towels. Serve warm. **Yield:** 6 patties (39¢ per patty).

Zucchini Corn Medley

Ready in 15 minutes or less

I concocted this fresh-tasting side dish when I needed to use up zucchini and a little leftover spaghetti sauce. The colorful combination is on the table in minutes.
—Mary Ann Pals, Chesterton, Indiana

2 small zucchini, cubed
1 cup frozen corn
1/4 cup chopped onion
2 tablespoons butter *or* margarine
1/4 cup spaghetti sauce
1/2 teaspoon salt
1/4 teaspoon dried basil
1/4 teaspoon dried oregano
1/8 teaspoon pepper
1/4 cup shredded cheddar cheese

In a saucepan, saute the zucchini, corn and onion in butter until tender. Stir in spaghetti sauce and seasonings; heat through. Stir in the cheese until melted. **Yield:** 4 servings (31¢ per serving).

Drop Biscuits and Gravy

Ready in 30 minutes or less

We enjoy these flaky biscuits covered with gravy not only for breakfast, but also for dinner. It's hard to find a more stick-to-the-ribs meal at such a low cost.
—Darlene Markel, Mt. Hood, Oregon

1 cup all-purpose flour
1-1/2 teaspoons baking powder
1/8 teaspoon salt
1/2 cup milk
1 teaspoon butter *or* margarine, melted
GRAVY:
1/2 pound bulk pork sausage
1 tablespoon butter *or* margarine
3 tablespoons all-purpose flour
1-3/4 cups milk
1/8 teaspoon salt
1/2 teaspoon pepper

In a bowl, combine the flour, baking powder and salt. Combine milk and butter; stir into dry ingredients just

until blended. Drop by rounded tablespoonfuls onto a greased baking sheet. Bake at 450° for 10-12 minutes or until golden brown. Meanwhile, in a saucepan, cook the sausage over medium heat until no longer pink. Stir in butter until melted. Sprinkle with flour. Gradually stir in milk, salt and pepper. Bring to a boil; cook and stir for 2 minutes. Serve over biscuits. **Yield:** 4 servings (27¢ per serving).

Beef and Tomato Pie

(Pictured below)

Ready in 1 hour or less

I bake this hot and hearty ground beef pie when my grandchildren come to visit. They like its down-home flavor. I like that it's a family-pleasing meal.
—June Mullins, Livonia, Missouri

1 pound ground beef
1 large onion, chopped
2 tablespoons ketchup
1/2 teaspoon salt
2 cups biscuit/baking mix
2/3 cup milk
1 cup diced fresh tomato
1/2 cup shredded cheddar cheese

In a skillet over medium heat, cook beef and onion until meat is no longer pink; drain. Remove from the heat. Stir in ketchup and salt; set aside. Combine biscuit mix and milk just until moistened. Turn onto a lightly floured surface and knead 6-8 times. Roll into a 10-in. circle; transfer to a greased 9-in. pie plate. Flute edges. Spoon meat mixture into crust. Sprinkle with tomatoes. Bake at 425° for 20-25 minutes. Sprinkle with cheese; bake 2 minutes longer or until cheese is melted. **Yield:** 6 servings (57¢ per serving).

Beef and Tomato Pie

Lazy Day Cake

Lazy Day Cake

(Pictured above)

Ready in 1 hour or less

The rich frosting really makes this delicious cake. I frequently rely on this recipe when I want something good in a hurry. —Lillian Marcotte, Woodstock, Vermont

- 1/4 cup butter *or* margarine, softened
- 2/3 cup sugar
- 1 egg
- 1 teaspoon vanilla extract
- 1-1/2 cups all-purpose flour
- 2 teaspoons baking powder
- 1/4 teaspoon salt
- 3/4 cup milk

TOPPING:
- 1-1/2 cups flaked coconut
- 1/2 cup packed brown sugar
- 5 tablespoons whipping cream
- 1-1/2 teaspoons vanilla extract

In a mixing bowl, cream butter and sugar. Beat in egg and vanilla. Combine the flour, baking powder and salt; add to creamed mixture alternately with milk. Pour into a greased 8-in. square baking pan. Bake at 350° for 30 minutes or until a toothpick inserted near the center comes out clean. Meanwhile, combine topping ingredients. Spread over warm cake. Broil 3-5 in. from the heat for 3-5 minutes or until golden brown. **Yield:** 9 servings (20¢ per serving).

Tuna Melt Sandwiches

Ready in 30 minutes or less

When our children were young, I often fixed these warm crunchy sandwiches. They're great for a quick lunch. —Carole Anhalt, Manitowoc, Wisconsin

- 3/4 cup chopped celery
- 3/4 cup diced cheddar cheese
- 1 can (6 ounces) tuna, drained and flaked
- 1 small onion, chopped
- 1/4 cup mayonnaise
- 1/8 teaspoon salt
- 1/4 cup butter *or* margarine, softened
- 6 hamburger buns, split

In a bowl, combine the first six ingredients; set aside. Spread butter over cut sides of buns. Spread tuna mixture on bun bottoms; replace tops. Wrap in foil. Bake at 350° for 15 minutes or until the cheese is melted. **Yield:** 6 servings.

Meat Loaf Patties

Ready in 30 minutes or less

I copied this recipe from my mom before my husband and I were married. These moist burgers are still a favorite. —Nancy Carpenter, Sidney, Montana

- 1 egg, beaten
- 1/4 cup milk
- 2 tablespoons finely chopped onion
- 1 teaspoon chili powder
- 1/4 teaspoon salt
- 1/4 teaspoon Worcestershire sauce
- 1 cup coarsely crushed saltines (about 20), *divided*
- 1 pound lean ground beef
- 1 tablespoon vegetable oil
- 1/3 cup ketchup

In a bowl, combine egg, milk, onion, chili powder, salt and Worcestershire sauce. Mix in 1/2 cup cracker crumbs. Add beef; mix well. Shape into six patties, about 1/2 in. thick. Coat with remaining crumbs. In a large skillet over medium heat, cook patties in oil for 5 minutes on each side or until meat is no longer pink. Serve with ketchup. **Yield:** 6 servings (39¢ per serving).

Souper Joes

Ready in 30 minutes or less

It's a snap to prepare these beefed-up sandwiches that get their flavor from onion soup mix and cheddar cheese. —Erlene Cornelius, Spring City, Tennessee

✓ Uses less fat, sugar or salt. Includes Nutritional Analysis and Diabetic Exchanges.

- 1 pound ground beef
- 1 can (10-3/4 ounces) condensed cream of mushroom soup, undiluted
- 1 tablespoon onion soup mix
- 1 cup (4 ounces) shredded cheddar cheese
- 8 hamburger buns, split

In a saucepan, cook beef over medium heat until no longer pink; drain. Stir in soup and soup mix; heat through. Stir in cheese until melted. Place about 1/3 cupful on each bun. **Yield:** 8 servings (47¢ per serving). **Nutritional Analysis:** One serving (prepared with lean ground beef, low-fat mushroom soup, reduced-sodium onion soup mix and reduced-fat cheese; calculated without the bun) equals 162 calories, 256 mg sodium, 30 mg cholesterol, 5 gm carbohydrate, 17 gm protein, 8 gm fat, 1 gm fiber. **Diabetic Exchanges:** 2 lean meat, 1/2 starch.

Oregano Chicken

Salad dressing mix and a generous sprinkling of oregano add the rich herb flavor to this tender baked chicken.
—*Nancy Moore, Candler, North Carolina*

    1/4 cup butter *or* margarine, melted
      1 envelope Italian salad dressing mix
      2 tablespoons lemon juice
      1 broiler/fryer chicken (3-1/2 to 4 pounds),
        cut up
      1 to 2 tablespoons dried oregano

Combine the butter, salad dressing mix and lemon juice. Place chicken in an ungreased 13-in. x 9-in. x 2-in. baking dish. Spoon butter mixture over chicken. Cover and bake at 350° for 45 minutes. Uncover. Baste with pan drippings; sprinkle with oregano. Bake 15-20 minutes longer or until the chicken juices run clear. **Yield:** 6 servings (83¢ per serving).

Tomato Spiral Toss

(Pictured below)

Ready in 30 minutes or less

When my husband and I don't have a lot of time to spare, we fix this pleasing pasta dish. It's easy to prepare and the price per serving comes down even more if you use homegrown tomatoes. —*Nicole Lync*
Powell River, British Columbia

Tomato Spiral Toss

      8 ounces uncooked spiral pasta
  2-1/2 cups diced fresh tomatoes
      1 tablespoon dried basil
    1/4 to 1/2 cup vegetable oil
      2 tablespoons cider vinegar
      2 garlic cloves, minced
    1/4 teaspoon salt
    1/8 teaspoon pepper
      3 tablespoons grated Parmesan cheese

Cook pasta according to package directions. Meanwhile, combine tomatoes and basil in a serving bowl; set aside. In a small bowl, combine the oil, vinegar, garlic, salt and pepper. Drain pasta; add to tomato mixture. Drizzle with oil mixture and toss to coat. Sprinkle with Parmesan cheese. Serve immediately. **Yield:** 6 servings (42¢ per serving). **Nutritional Analysis:** One serving (prepared with 1/4 cup oil) equals 237 calories, 163 mg sodium, 2 mg cholesterol, 29 gm carbohydrate, 6 gm protein, 11 gm fat, 2 gm fiber. **Diabetic Exchanges:** 2 fat, 1-1/2 starch, 1 vegetable.

Beef Cabbage Hash

Ready in 30 minutes or less

As a busy working mother, I often rely on this comforting all-in-one skillet recipe when we need a quick meal.
—*Penny Wolverton, Parsons, Kansas*

      1 pound ground beef
      4 medium baking potatoes, peeled and
        julienned
      4 cups shredded cabbage
      1 large onion, sliced and quartered
    3/4 cup water
      1 teaspoon salt
    1/2 teaspoon pepper

In a large skillet, cook beef over medium heat until no longer pink; drain. Add remaining ingredients. Cover and cook over medium-high heat for 10 minutes or until potatoes are tender. **Yield:** 4 servings (55¢ per serving).

Easy Chicken and Noodles

Ready in 15 minutes or less

Prepare this comforting stovetop supper in mere minutes. Canned soup makes the sauce a snap to throw together while the noodles boil. —*Shirley Heston, Lancaster, Ohio*

      1 can (10-3/4 ounces) condensed cream of
        chicken soup, undiluted
    3/4 cup milk
    1/3 cup grated Parmesan cheese
    1/8 teaspoon pepper
      3 cups cooked wide egg noodles
      2 cups cubed cooked chicken

In a saucepan, combine the soup, milk, Parmesan cheese and pepper. Stir in the noodles and chicken; heat through. **Yield:** 4 servings ($1.22 per serving).

Taco Meat Loaf

Taco Meat Loaf

(Pictured above)

Even your kids will enjoy this tasty meat loaf. I like to serve it with shredded cheese, salsa and sour cream.
—Cathy Streeter, De Kalb Junction, New York

1 cup crushed saltines (about 30 crackers)
1 envelope taco seasoning mix
1/2 cup ketchup
1 can (4 ounces) mushroom stems and pieces, drained
1 can (2-1/4 ounces) sliced ripe olives, drained
1 small onion, chopped
2 eggs, beaten
2 tablespoons Worcestershire sauce
2 pounds lean ground beef
Salsa, sour cream, shredded cheddar cheese and additional olives, optional

In a bowl, combine the first eight ingredients. Add beef; mix well. Press into a greased 9-in. x 5-in. x 3-in. loaf pan. Bake, uncovered, at 350° for 1 to 1-1/2 hours or until a meat thermometer reads 160°. Serve with salsa, sour cream, cheese and olives if desired. **Yield:** 8 servings (77¢ per serving).

Chocolate Snack Cake

Ready in 1 hour or less

This rich cocoa cake is so tasty, there's no need to frost it. But it's wonderful served warm with ice cream or whipped cream. It's just the right size for a small family.
—LeeAnn McCue, West Springfield, Massachusetts

1-1/2 cups all-purpose flour
1 cup sugar
1/3 cup baking cocoa
1 teaspoon baking soda
1/2 teaspoon salt
1 cup water
1/2 cup vegetable oil
2 tablespoons vinegar
2 teaspoons vanilla extract

In a mixing bowl, combine the first five ingredients. In another bowl, combine water, oil, vinegar and vanilla; add to dry ingredients and mix just until blended. Pour into a greased 8-in. square baking pan. Bake at 375° for 20-25 minutes or until a toothpick inserted near the center comes out clean. Cool slightly before cutting. **Yield:** 9 servings (8¢ per serving).

Crustless Zucchini Pie

Ready in 1 hour or less

I make the most of my zucchini harvest by baking this crowd-pleasing entree. The golden-brown pies slice so beautifully you can serve them to company!
—Peggy Gandy, South Amboy, New Jersey

1 large onion, finely chopped
1/2 cup vegetable oil
1/2 cup grated Parmesan cheese
4 eggs, beaten
1 tablespoon minced fresh parsley
3 cups grated zucchini
1 cup biscuit/baking mix
1 cup (4 ounces) shredded cheddar cheese

In a bowl, combine the first five ingredients. Stir in the zucchini, biscuit mix and cheese. Pour into two greased 9-in. pie plates. Bake at 350° for 35 minutes or until golden brown. **Yield:** 2 pies (6 servings each) (31¢ per serving).

Black Bean Nacho Bake

Ready in 1 hour or less

Pasta, black beans and nacho cheese soup combine in this zippy six-ingredient supper. —Melodie Gay
Salt Lake City, Utah

   1 package (7 ounces) shell *or* elbow macaroni, cooked and drained
   1 can (15 ounces) black beans, rinsed and drained
   1 can (11 ounces) nacho cheese soup
1/3 cup milk
1/2 cup crushed tortilla chips
1/2 cup shredded cheddar cheese

In a bowl, combine macaroni and beans. Combine soup and milk; stir into macaroni mixture. Transfer to a greased 8-in. square baking dish. Cover and bake at 350° for 25 minutes. Uncover; sprinkle with tortilla chips and cheese. Bake 5-10 minutes longer or until cheese is melted. **Yield:** 4 servings (87¢ per serving).

Beefy Tomato Soup

Ready in 30 minutes or less

Ground beef and macaroni add heartiness to this soup. It's nicely seasoned. —Patricia Staudt, Marble Rock, Iowa

 Uses less fat, sugar or salt. Includes Nutritional Analysis and Diabetic Exchanges.

   1 pound ground beef
   1 quart tomato juice
   3 cups water
3/4 cup uncooked elbow macaroni
   1 envelope onion soup mix
1/4 teaspoon chili powder

In a large saucepan, cook beef over medium heat until no longer pink; drain. Add the remaining ingredients. Bring to a boil. Reduce heat; simmer, uncovered, for 15-20 minutes or until macaroni is tender. **Yield:** 8 servings (37¢ per serving). **Nutritional Analysis:** One 1-cup serving (prepared with lean ground beef, reduced-sodium tomato juice and reduced-sodium onion soup mix) equals 176 calories, 307 mg sodium, 21 mg cholesterol, 16 gm carbohydrate, 15 gm protein, 5 gm fat, 1 gm fiber. **Diabetic Exchanges:** 1-1/2 meat, 1 starch.

Vegetable Wild Rice

(Pictured on cover)

Ready in 1 hour or less

A convenient packaged rice mix gives a jump start to this simple side dish. A bright blend of veggies adds color. —Helen Jacobs, Canton, Michigan

   1 package (6 ounces) long grain and wild rice mix
   2 medium carrots, cut into 1/4-inch slices
   1 cup diced yellow summer squash
2/3 cup chopped sweet red pepper
2/3 cup chopped green pepper
1/4 cup chopped onion
   2 tablespoons vegetable oil

In a saucepan, place rice mix, contents of seasoning packet and water as directed on package. Bring to a boil. Add carrots. Reduce heat; cover and simmer for 30 minutes or until rice is tender and water is absorbed. Meanwhile, in a skillet, saute squash, peppers and onion in oil until crisp-tender. Stir into rice mixture. **Yield:** 6 servings (52¢ per serving).

Tangy Chicken Legs

(Pictured below and on page 242)

Ready in 1 hour or less

This sweet and tangy sauce is easily assembled with basic pantry ingredients. Brushed on chicken leg quarters, it's bargain-priced. Try it over beef or pork, too. —Joey McGuire, Winchester, Indiana

   1 cup brewed coffee
   1 cup ketchup
1/2 cup sugar
1/2 cup Worcestershire sauce
1/4 cup vinegar
1/8 teaspoon pepper
   8 grilled *or* broiled chicken leg quarters

In a saucepan, combine the first six ingredients. Bring to a boil; reduce heat. Simmer, uncovered, for 30-35 minutes or until thickened, stirring occasionally. Brush over cooked chicken. **Yield:** 8 servings (1-1/2 cups barbecue sauce) (39¢ per serving).

Tangy Chicken Legs

Chapter 16

A SUREFIRE way to spark a child's interest in eating is to encourage a love of cooking!

Kids of all ages will jump at the chance to lend a hand in the kitchen when they see the fast, flavorful foods in this chapter.

From snappy snacks and hearty main dishes to delectable desserts and homemade breads, younger children can mix and measure ingredients, while older ones help you get a head start on dinner. (Toddlers can even help with "cleanup" by licking the bowl!)

With such rapid, kid-approved recipes, cooking can be a family activity that's as fun as it is delicious.

FAMILY-PLEASING FARE: Top to bottom: Tropical Island Dessert (p. 261) and Berry-Stuffed French Toast (p. 260).

Three-Cheese Spaghetti Bake
Taco Pizza

Three-Cheese Spaghetti Bake

(Pictured above)

Ready in 1 hour or less

My son Holden and I created this mild casserole that is such a hit there are never any leftovers. We serve it with a green salad and garlic bread. —Laura Linder
Provo, Utah

    1 package (16 ounces) spaghetti
    2 cups (8 ounces) shredded mozzarella cheese, *divided*
 3/4 cup grated Parmesan cheese
 1/2 cup grated Romano cheese
    3 eggs, beaten
    1 tablespoon olive *or* vegetable oil
    2 teaspoons garlic powder
Salt and pepper to taste
    1 jar (28 ounces) spaghetti sauce

Cook spaghetti according to package directions; drain. Add 1 cup mozzarella cheese, Parmesan, Romano, eggs, oil, garlic powder, salt and pepper. Press into a greased 13-in. x 9-in. x 2-in. baking dish. Top with spaghetti sauce. Cover and bake at 350° for 20 minutes. Uncover; sprinkle with the remaining mozzarella. Bake 10 minutes longer or until heated through and cheese is melted. **Yield:** 6-8 servings.

Taco Pizza

(Pictured above)

Ready in 1 hour or less

Convenient prebaked crust makes this tasty taco pizza as easy as can be. This is a great recipe, especially if you have teenagers. I keep the ingredients on hand so that we can make it anytime. —Mary Cass, Balto, Maryland

    1 pound ground beef
    1 envelope taco seasoning
    1 cup water
    2 prebaked Italian bread shell crusts (12 inches)
    1 can (16 ounces) refried beans

3/4 cup salsa
2 cups coarsely crushed tortilla chips
2 cups (8 ounces) shredded cheddar cheese
2 medium tomatoes, chopped, optional
1 cup shredded lettuce, optional

In a saucepan, cook beef over medium heat until no longer pink; drain. Stir in taco seasoning and water. Bring to a boil; reduce heat. Simmer, uncovered, for 10 minutes; set aside. Place crusts on ungreased pizza pans or baking sheets. Combine beans and salsa; spread over crusts. Top with beef mixture, chips and cheese. Bake at 350° for 13-16 minutes or until cheese is melted. Sprinkle with tomatoes and lettuce if desired. **Yield:** 2 pizzas (6-8 servings each).

Snowman Cookies Melt Hearts

ACCORDING to Leah Gallington of Corona, California, there's no mistaking the popularity of her Frosted Snowmen. But a mistake while following the recipe didn't harm the flavor of these winter treats.

"I was making the cookies for my son's classroom party," she recalls. "In my haste, I used regular sugar instead of the confectioners' sugar called for in the original recipe.

"I didn't realize the error until the first batch was baked. I sampled one and noticed that it was not as crunchy as usual," Leah explains. "But I thought it tasted even better, so I kept baking.

"When I took the frosty fellows to my son's class, everyone loved them. I got so many compliments on their delightful shape and taste that I've decided to always make them this way."

Frosted Snowmen
(Pictured at right)

1-1/2 cups butter (no substitutes), softened
2-1/4 cups sugar
1 egg
3 teaspoons vanilla extract
3-3/4 cups all-purpose flour
1/2 teaspoon baking powder
1 can (16 ounces) vanilla frosting
72 pretzel sticks
Red and blue decorating icing

In a mixing bowl, cream butter and sugar. Gradually beat in egg and vanilla. Combine flour and baking powder; add to creamed mixture. Shape dough into 1-in., 5/8-in. and 1/4-in. balls. For each snowman, place one of each size ball 1/4 in. apart on ungreased baking sheets; place snowmen 2 in. apart. Break pretzel sticks in half; press into sides of middle ball. Bake at 375° for 10-12 minutes or until bottoms are lightly browned. Cool 1 minute before removing to wire racks. Frost cooled cookies. Decorate with blue icing for eyes, mouth and buttons, and red for nose and scarf. **Yield:** 6 dozen.

Frosted Snowmen

Frosted Butter Cutouts
Rocky Road Fudge Pops

Frosted Butter Cutouts

(Pictured above)

Plan ahead...needs to chill

With their soft, tender insides, these cookies quickly disappear from the cookie jar. Vanilla pudding mix gives the frosting a velvety texture and fabulous flavor.
—Stephanie McKinnon, West Valley City, Utah

　1/2 cup butter (no substitutes), softened
　　1 cup sugar
　　1 egg
　1/2 cup sour cream
　　1 teaspoon vanilla extract
3-1/2 cups all-purpose flour
　　1 teaspoon baking soda
　1/2 teaspoon salt
FROSTING:
　1/4 cup cold milk
　　3 tablespoons instant vanilla pudding mix
　1/4 cup butter (no substitutes), softened
2-1/2 cups confectioners' sugar
　　1 teaspoon vanilla extract
Food coloring, optional

In a mixing bowl, cream butter and sugar. Beat in the egg, sour cream and vanilla. Combine flour, baking soda and salt; gradually add to creamed mixture. Cover and chill for 1 hour or until easy to handle. On a work surface that has been sprinkled heavily with confectioners' sugar, roll out dough to 1/8-in. thickness. Cut with 2-1/2-in. cookie cutters. Place 1 in. apart on greased baking sheets. Bake at 375° for 8-10 minutes or until lightly browned. Immediately remove to wire racks to cool. For frosting, combine milk and pudding mix until smooth; set aside. In a mixing bowl, cream butter. Beat in pudding mixture. Gradually add confectioners' sugar, vanilla and food coloring if desired; beat on high speed until light and fluffy. Frost cookies. **Yield:** 5-1/2 dozen.

Rocky Road Fudge Pops

(Pictured above)

Plan ahead...needs to freeze

These sweet frozen treats are simple to prepare and guaranteed to bring out the kid in anyone. The creamy pops feature a special chocolate and peanut topping.
—Karen Grant, Tulare, California

    1 package (3.4 ounces) cook-and-serve
        chocolate pudding mix
2-1/2 cups milk
    1/2 cup chopped peanuts
    1/2 cup miniature semisweet chocolate chips
    12 plastic cups (3 ounces *each*)
    1/2 cup marshmallow creme
    12 Popsicle sticks

In a large microwave-safe bowl, combine the pudding mix and milk. Microwave, uncovered, on high for 6 to 7-1/2 minutes or until bubbly and slightly thickened, stirring every 2 minutes. Cool for 20 minutes, stirring several times. Meanwhile, combine the peanuts and chocolate chips; place about 2 tablespoons in each plastic cup. Stir the marshmallow creme into pudding; spoon into cups. Insert Popsicle sticks; freeze. **Yield:** 12 servings. **Editor's Note:** This recipe was tested in an 850-watt microwave.

Golden Burger Spirals

Ready in 1 hour or less

This recipe was given to me by a fellow dental hygienist nearly 20 years ago. After a busy day, it's a convenient meal the whole family enjoys. It's also an excellent dish to take to potlucks and church socials. —Lisa Sinyard
Lexington, Alabama

    1 pound ground beef
    1 medium onion, chopped
    1 medium green pepper, chopped
    1 can (10-3/4 ounces) condensed golden
        mushroom soup, undiluted
    1 can (8 ounces) tomato sauce
1-1/2 cups (6 ounces) shredded cheddar cheese,
        divided
    1/2 teaspoon salt
    1 package (8 ounces) spiral pasta, cooked and
        drained

In a large skillet or saucepan over medium heat, cook beef, onion and green pepper until the meat is no longer pink; drain. Add the soup, tomato sauce, 1 cup cheese and salt. Stir in pasta. Transfer to a greased 2-1/2-qt. baking dish. Sprinkle with remaining cheese. Bake, uncovered, at 350° for 30 minutes or until bubbly. **Yield:** 4-6 servings.

Cooking with Kids

When you have four children like I do, it's sometimes difficult to find quality "alone" time with each child. Since my kids know I love to cook and I know they certainly love to eat, we designed a program that's perfect for our family.

Each child has a designated night during the week when they are the cook and I am the supervisor. On each child's special night, no one but the two of us is allowed in the kitchen. It's a fun way to share my love of cooking and spend one-on-one time with my children.   —Laura Linder, Provo, Utah

Cook Up Cute Candies

BREAKFAST will never be the same once you introduce your kids to Fried Egg Candy. These adorable confections look like miniature fried eggs served over two strips of bacon.

But bite into one and you're in for a sweet surprise. The yolks are actually yellow M&M's and the bacon strips are pretzel sticks.

"This is the only way I can get my daughter Haley to eat her bacon and eggs," jokes Melanie Hayes of Libby, Montana. "We have a great time together making these treats and munching on them, too," she adds.

Kids of all ages will have fun assembling these simple snacks.

"We give them as gifts at Easter and Christmas," Melanie shares.

The irresistible candies also would make a tasty treat for April Fool's Day...just tell your friends that "the yolk" is on them!

Fried Egg Candy

(Pictured below)

Ready in 30 minutes or less

    1 package (15 ounces) pretzel sticks
    1 package (12 ounces) vanilla *or* white chips
    48 yellow M&M's

Place pretzel sticks on waxed paper in groups of two, leaving a small space between each. In a microwave-safe bowl, heat vanilla chips at 70% power until melted; stir until smooth. Drop by tablespoonfuls over each pair of pretzel sticks. For "yolks", place one or two M&M's in the center of each "egg". **Yield:** about 3-1/2 dozen.

Banana-Pear Caterpillar
Apple-Raisin Ladybug

Apple-Raisin Ladybug

(Pictured above)

Ready in 15 minutes or less

Children seem to be fascinated by bugs. So during a spring visit, my great-nieces and I had fun making fresh fruit salads that looked like garden insects. Mandy Paige-Wrischnik assembled this lovely ladybug while her sister made the cute caterpillar, whose recipe is at right.

—Sherry Masters, Cincinnati, Ohio

2 lettuce *or* kale leaves
1 medium Red Delicious apple, quartered
   and cored
2 teaspoons creamy peanut butter
2 tablespoons raisins
5 red grapes

Place lettuce leaves on two salad plates. Arrange two apple quarters, peel side up, on the lettuce. Use dabs of peanut butter to place raisins in the space between apple quarters. Place one grape at the stem end of apple

for head. For legs, cut the remaining grapes lengthwise into four pieces; place three on each side of ladybugs. Place small dabs of peanut butter on remaining raisins; gently press onto apples for spots. **Yield:** 2 servings.

Banana-Pear Caterpillar

(Pictured above)

Ready in 15 minutes or less

My great-niece, Kendra Paige-Wrischnik, transformed banana and pear slices into this creepy crawler. The girls' brother, Joey, was too young to help prepare the salads, but he enjoyed eating them. —Sherry Masters

1 lettuce leaf
1 medium banana, peeled
1/2 medium red pear, cored and cut into
   1/4-inch slices
2 raisins

Place lettuce on a salad plate; top with the banana. Cut 1/4-in. V-shaped slices halfway through the banana, spacing cuts 1 in. apart. Place a pear slice, peel side up, in each cut. For eyes, gently press raisins into one end of banana. Serve immediately. **Yield:** 1 serving.

Bacon Bean Sandwiches

Ready in 30 minutes or less

My mother-in-law first shared this scrumptious open-faced sandwich with us, and it's now a favorite around our house. The flavors of the bacon, beans, onion and cheese complement each other wonderfully!
—Dorothy Klass, Tabor City, North Carolina

    5 slices bread, lightly toasted
    1 can (16 ounces) pork and beans
   10 bacon strips, cooked and drained
    4 slices onion, separated into rings
    5 slices process American cheese

Place toast on an ungreased baking sheet. Spread each slice with 3 tablespoons beans. Top each with two bacon strips, a few onion rings and a cheese slice. Bake at 350° for 15-20 minutes or until cheese is melted and lightly browned. **Yield:** 5 servings.

Kool-Aid Pie

Plan ahead...needs to freeze

A fun crust of vanilla wafers is easy for kids to make and holds an eye-catching fluffy filling that's refreshing in summer. Use different flavors of Kool-Aid to vary the pie's taste. — Ledia Black, Pineland, Texas

    1 can (12 ounces) evaporated milk
   36 vanilla wafers
    1 cup sugar
    1 envelope (.14 ounce) unsweetened lemon-
      lime Kool-Aid
Whipped topping, optional

Pour milk into a small metal or glass mixing bowl. Add mixer beaters to the bowl. Cover and chill for at least 2 hours. Coat a 9-in. pie plate with nonstick cooking spray. Line bottom and sides of plate with wafers. Beat milk until soft peaks form. Add sugar and drink mix; beat until thoroughly mixed. Spoon over wafers; freeze for at least 4 hours. Garnish with whipped topping if desired. **Yield:** 6-8 servings.

Ham and Cheese Puffs

Ready in 30 minutes or less

These tasty little bites go over great with kids. They have fun making and eating them. These puffs are delicious with soups or as party appetizers.
—Mrs. Marvin Buffington, Burlington, Iowa

    1 package (2-1/2 ounces) sliced fully cooked
      ham, chopped
    1 small onion, chopped
  1/2 cup shredded Swiss cheese
    1 egg
1-1/2 teaspoons Dijon mustard

Pizza Roll-Ups

  1/8 teaspoon pepper
    1 tube (8 ounces) refrigerated crescent rolls

In a bowl, combine the first six ingredients; set aside. Divide crescent dough into 24 portions. Press into greased miniature muffin cups. Spoon 1 tablespoon ham mixture into each cup. Bake at 350° for 13-15 minutes or until golden brown. **Yield:** 2 dozen.

Pizza Roll-Ups

(Pictured above)

Ready in 1 hour or less

Since receiving this recipe through 4-H, it's been a regular after-school snack. These bite-size pizza treats, made with refrigerated crescent rolls, are especially good served with spaghetti sauce for dipping.
—Donna Klettke
Wheatland, Missouri

  1/2 pound ground beef
    1 can (8 ounces) tomato sauce
  1/2 cup shredded mozzarella cheese
  1/2 teaspoon dried oregano
    2 tubes (8 ounces *each*) refrigerated crescent
      rolls

In a skillet, cook beef over medium heat until no longer pink; drain. Remove from the heat. Add tomato sauce, mozzarella cheese and oregano; mix well. Separate crescent dough into eight rectangles, pinching seams together. Place about 3 tablespoons of meat mixture along one long side of each rectangle. Roll up, jelly-roll style, starting with a long side. Cut each roll into three pieces. Place, seam side down, 2 in. apart on greased baking sheets. Bake at 375° for 15 minutes or until golden brown. **Yield:** 2 dozen.

Chicken Nugget Casserole
Root Beer Float Cake

Chicken Nugget Casserole

(Pictured above)

Ready in 1 hour or less

Youngsters will need just five ingredients to help prepare this easy entree. Our kids love to eat chicken nuggets this way. It's a satisfying supper with spaghetti and a salad.
—Tylene Loar, Mesa, Arizona

  1 package (13-1/2 ounces) frozen chicken
     nuggets
1/3 cup grated Parmesan cheese
  1 can (26-1/2 ounces) spaghetti sauce
  1 cup (4 ounces) shredded mozzarella cheese
  1 teaspoon Italian seasoning

Place chicken nuggets in a greased 11-in. x 7-in. x 2-in. baking dish. Sprinkle with Parmesan cheese. Top with spaghetti sauce, mozzarella cheese and Italian seasoning. Cover and bake at 350° for 30-35 minutes or until chicken is heated through and cheese is melted. **Yield:** 4-6 servings.

Root Beer Float Cake

(Pictured above)

I add root beer to both the cake batter and fluffy frosting of this sweet dessert to get that great root beer float taste. Serve this moist cake to a bunch of hungry kids and watch it disappear.
—Kat Thompson
LaPine, Oregon

    1 package (18-1/4 ounces) white cake mix
1-3/4 cups cold root beer, *divided*
  1/4 cup vegetable oil

  2 eggs
  1 envelope whipped topping mix

In a mixing bowl, combine dry cake mix, 1-1/4 cups root beer, oil and eggs. Beat on low speed for 2 minutes or stir by hand for 3 minutes. Pour into a greased 13-in. x 9-in. x 2-in. baking pan. Bake at 350° for 30-35 minutes or until a toothpick inserted near the center comes out clean. Cool completely on a wire rack. In a mixing bowl, combine the whipped topping mix and remaining root beer. Beat until soft peaks form. Frost cake. Store in the refrigerator. **Yield:** 12-16 servings.

Beef 'n' Cheese Macaroni

Ready in 30 minutes or less

I love to make this delicious main dish for my brother and me when our parents are at work at dinnertime. The mild-tasting combination of ground beef and noodles is sure to be a hit with even the pickiest eaters.
—Jamie Brown, Wichita, Kansas

1/2 pound ground beef
  1 package (7 ounces) elbow macaroni
  2 tablespoons butter *or* margarine
  1 cup cubed process American cheese
1/4 cup milk
1/4 teaspoon salt

In a skillet, cook beef over medium heat until no longer pink. Meanwhile, in a saucepan, cook macaroni according to package directions; drain and set aside. In the same pan, melt butter. Add the cheese, milk and salt; cook and stir until the cheese is melted. Drain beef. Stir beef and macaroni into cheese sauce; heat through. **Yield:** 4-6 servings.

Special Hamburger Sauce

Ready in 30 minutes or less

This thick sauce is the secret to making children happy. It turns an ordinary burger into their favorite fast-food version.
—Cairol Ostrander, Bainbridge, Georgia

 Uses less fat, sugar or salt. Includes Nutritional Analysis and Diabetic Exchanges.

    1 cup mayonnaise
  1/3 cup creamy French dressing
  1/4 cup sweet pickle relish
    1 tablespoon sugar
    1 teaspoon dried minced onion
Salt and pepper to taste

In a bowl, combine all ingredients. Store in the refrigerator. **Yield:** 1-1/2 cups. **Nutritional Analysis:** 2 tablespoons (prepared with light mayonnaise and fat-free French dressing and without salt) equals 87 calories, 255 mg sodium, 0 cholesterol, 7 gm carbohydrate, trace protein, 7 gm fat, trace fiber. **Diabetic Exchanges:** 1 fat, 1/2 starch.

Pennsylvania Milk Punch

Ready in 15 minutes or less

Children of all ages will savor the nostalgic flavor of this refreshing punch. It reminds me of the orange Creamsicles we enjoyed when we were young.
—Shirley Womer
Middleburg, Pennsylvania

 Uses less fat, sugar or salt. Includes Nutritional Analysis and Diabetic Exchanges

  4 cups milk
  1 quart orange sherbet, softened
  1 pint vanilla ice cream, softened
  1 liter lemon-lime soda

In a mixing bowl, beat milk, sherbet and ice cream until frothy. Pour into a punch bowl. Stir in soda. Serve immediately. **Yield:** 20 servings. **Nutritional Analysis:** One 3/4-cup serving (prepared with skim milk, fat-free ice cream and diet soda) equals 91 calories, 61 mg sodium, 3 mg cholesterol, 18 gm carbohydrate, 3 gm protein, 1 gm fat, 0 fiber. **Diabetic Exchange:** 1 starch.

Set Sail with Peachy Salad

YOU CAN STEER clear of a long list of ingredients when your family fixes these sensational Sailboat Salads shared by Lee Nelson of Waco, Texas.

"My grandson, Sean McGowan, likes to help his mom work in the kitchen," Lee says. "He always offers to make these delightful salads."

A calm lake of blue gelatin sets the scene for a boat made from a peach half. A slice of American cheese creates the sail, which gets support from a mast made with a frilled toothpick.

"These salads are fun to assemble and a terrific way to get kids to eat fruit," Lee adds.

These boats are so cute, kids will sail them right to the dinner table, where their siblings are sure to reward them with happy waves of applause.

Sailboat Salads

(Pictured at right)

Plan ahead...needs to chill

  1 package (3 ounces) berry blue gelatin
  1 cup boiling water
  1 cup cold water
  1 can (29 ounces) peach halves, drained
  4 toothpicks
  2 thick slices process American cheese
  2 cups torn lettuce

Place gelatin in a bowl; add boiling water and stir until gelatin is dissolved. Stir in cold water. Pour gelatin onto four salad plates; refrigerate until firm. For boat, place a peach half, cut side up, in the center of each plate (refrigerate any remaining peaches for another use). Cut cheese slices in half diagonally. For sail, carefully insert a toothpick into the top center of each cheese triangle. Bend cheese slightly; push toothpick through bottom center of cheese. Insert toothpick into edge of peach. Arrange lettuce around plate. **Yield:** 4 servings.

Pepperoni Hopple-Popple
Alfredo Potatoes

Pepperoni Hopple-Popple

(Pictured above)

Ready in 30 minutes or less

My grandma and I created this kids' version of a German breakfast dish. Serve it with toast or English muffins.
—Jaycee Gfeller, Russell, Kansas

2-1/2 cups frozen shredded hash brown potatoes
  1/3 cup chopped onion
    3 tablespoons butter *or* margarine
    5 eggs
  1/2 cup milk
    1 teaspoon Italian seasoning
  1/2 teaspoon salt
  1/2 teaspoon pepper
  25 slices pepperoni
    1 cup (4 ounces) shredded Mexican-cheese blend

In a large skillet, cook potatoes and onion in butter until tender and lightly browned. In a bowl, beat eggs, milk, Italian seasoning, salt and pepper. Pour over potato mixture. Sprinkle with pepperoni. Cover and cook on medium-low heat for 10-12 minutes or until eggs are set. Remove from the heat. Sprinkle with cheese; cover and let stand for 2 minutes. Cut into wedges. **Yield:** 6 servings.

Alfredo Potatoes

(Pictured above)

Ready in 30 minutes or less

I love baked potatoes, so I developed the recipe for these cheesy stuffed twice-baked potatoes myself. —Peter Barry Norrisville, Maryland

  2 large baking potatoes
  1 cup prepared Alfredo sauce

  1 teaspoon garlic powder
1/2 teaspoon pepper
1/8 teaspoon dried thyme
  1 cup (4 ounces) shredded cheddar cheese, *divided*
1/2 cup shredded mozzarella cheese

Pierce potatoes several times with a fork and place on a microwave-safe plate. Microwave on high for 6 minutes or until tender. Allow potatoes to cool slightly. Meanwhile, in a bowl, combine the Alfredo sauce, garlic powder, pepper and thyme. Stir in 1/2 cup cheddar cheese and mozzarella cheese. Cut potatoes in half lengthwise. Scoop out the pulp, leaving a thin shell. Mash the pulp and add to the sauce mixture; mix well. Spoon into potato shells. Sprinkle with remaining cheddar cheese. Microwave on high for 1 minute or until cheese is melted. **Yield:** 4 servings. **Editor's Note:** This recipe was tested in an 850-watt microwave.

Berry-Stuffed French Toast

(Pictured at right and on page 250)

Ready in 1 hour or less

Both kids and grown-ups will enjoy the creamy filling and sweet syrup that flavor these French toast sandwiches. I found a French toast recipe on the Internet, then made some changes to please my tastes. —Monica Hannahan Dayton, Ohio

RASPBERRY SYRUP:
  2 cups unsweetened raspberries
3/4 cup packed brown sugar
  3 tablespoons butter *or* margarine
  1 teaspoon ground cinnamon
1-1/2 teaspoons vanilla extract
FRENCH TOAST:
  1 package (8 ounces) cream cheese, softened
1/2 cup sour cream

18 slices sourdough bread
1/2 cup raspberry preserves
1 teaspoon vanilla extract
6 eggs
1/4 cup half-and-half cream
1-1/2 teaspoons ground cinnamon
Confectioners' sugar and additional raspberries, optional

For syrup, combine raspberries, brown sugar, butter and cinnamon in a saucepan. Bring to a boil. Reduce heat; simmer, uncovered, for 5-7 minutes or until syrup is desired consistency. Remove from the heat and stir in vanilla; set aside. In a mixing bowl, beat cream cheese and sour cream. Spread about 3 tablespoons on each slice of bread. Combine preserves and vanilla; spread over cream cheese mixture on nine slices. Top with remaining bread, cream cheese side down, to make a sandwich. In a shallow bowl, combine the eggs, cream and cinnamon. Dip both sides of bread into egg mixture. Cook on a hot greased griddle for 3-4 minutes on each side or until golden brown. Cut in half diagonally. If desired, sprinkle with confectioners' sugar and garnish with raspberries. Serve with raspberry syrup. **Yield:** 9 servings.

Tropical Island Dessert

(Pictured below and on page 250)

Plan ahead...needs to chill

Teens can easily assemble this pudding and gelatin treat.
—Ashley Walls, New Iberia, Louisiana

3 packages (3 ounces *each*) berry blue gelatin
2 cups boiling water
2-1/2 cups cold water

4 tablespoons fish-shaped gummy candies, *divided*
2 cups cold milk
1 package (3.4 ounces) instant vanilla pudding mix
1 medium lime
2 cinnamon sticks
1 round wooden toothpick
2 tablespoons graham cracker crumbs
6 whole allspice
1 disposable cup (2-ounce size)
Fresh blueberries and additional gummy candies, optional

In a bowl, dissolve gelatin in boiling water. Stir in cold water. Pour into a 6-cup ring mold coated with non-stick cooking spray. Add 2 tablespoons gummy candies. Chill for 1 hour. Stir in remaining candies. Chill for 1-2 hours or until set. In a bowl, whisk milk and pudding. Cover and chill until ready to use. To make palm tree leaves, cut lime in half; remove and discard pulp. Place lime halves, cut side down, on a cutting board. With a pencil, sketch five leaves from bottom to top on each half. Cut out leaves, leaving center intact; make little cuts to create a palm leaf appearance. To create a base for the trees, turn disposable cup upside down; cut two small slits in the bottom. Insert a cinnamon stick in each slit for tree trunks. Break toothpick in half. Insert pointed ends into center of lime halves; insert broken ends into cinnamon sticks. Unmold gelatin onto a 12-in. serving platter. Place cup in the center of gelatin ring. Spoon vanilla pudding over cup, filling center of ring. Sprinkle with graham cracker crumbs for sand. Place allspice at base of trees for coconuts (discard allspice before serving). Garnish with blueberries and additional gummy fish if desired. **Yield:** 12-16 servings.

Tropical Island Dessert
Berry-Stuffed French Toast

Wagon Wheel Chili
Corn Dog Muffins

Wagon Wheel Chili

(Pictured above)

Ready in 30 minutes or less

Youngsters are sure to love the fun shape of the wagon wheel pasta in this zippy chili. It's easy to whip up with canned chili and tomato sauce, so it's great for a hot lunch or quick dinner. —Lora Scroggins, El Dorado, Arkansas

   2 cups uncooked wagon wheel *or* spiral pasta
   1 can (15 ounces) chili
   1 can (8 ounces) tomato sauce
   3 tablespoons ketchup
 1/2 teaspoon chili powder
Shredded cheddar cheese, optional

Cook pasta according to package directions. Meanwhile, in a large saucepan, combine the chili, tomato sauce, ketchup and chili powder. Mix well; heat through. Drain and rinse pasta; stir into chili. Garnish with cheese if desired. **Yield:** 3-4 servings.

Corn Dog Muffins

(Pictured above)

Ready in 30 minutes or less

Our three boys were always asking for corn dogs, so I came up with this fast way to deliver the same flavor. These sweet corn bread muffins, chock-full of hot dog chunks and corn kernels, taste just like the real thing.
   —Lynita Arteberry, Plankinton, South Dakota

   2 packages (8-1/2 ounces *each*) corn bread/muffin mix
   2 tablespoons brown sugar
   2 eggs
   1 cup milk
   1 can (11 ounces) whole kernel corn, drained
   5 hot dogs, chopped

In a bowl, combine corn bread mix and brown sugar. Combine eggs and milk; stir into dry ingredients until moistened. Stir in corn and hot dogs (batter will be thin). Fill greased or paper-lined muffin cups three-fourths full. Bake at 400° for 14-18 minutes or until golden brown. Serve immediately or refrigerate. **Yield:** 1-1/2 dozen.

Cranberry Cinnamon Roll-Ups

Ready in 30 minutes or less

Children of all ages will have a ball assembling these yummy treats that start with plain white bread and other fuss-free ingredients. Cranberry sauce gives these appetizers holiday appeal. —Dorothy Pritchett, Wills Point, Texas

 12 slices bread, crusts removed
  7 tablespoons butter *or* margarine, softened, *divided*

2/3 cup whole-berry cranberry sauce
1/3 cup sugar
1-1/2 teaspoons ground cinnamon

Spread bread with 2 tablespoons butter. Spread each buttered slice with about 1 tablespoon cranberry sauce. Roll up jelly-roll style; secure with a toothpick if desired. In a shallow microwave-safe bowl, heat the remaining butter in the microwave until melted. Combine sugar and cinnamon in another shallow bowl. Dip roll-ups in butter, then roll in cinnamon-sugar. Place seam side down on an ungreased baking sheet. Bake at 400° for 6-8 minutes or until browned. Remove toothpicks before serving. **Yield:** 12 servings.

Cookbook Filled with Love

Over the years, I've encouraged my kids to join me when I'm cooking and baking. I've even compiled a cookbook of family favorite recipes to make the time they spend there even more enjoyable.

Every lunch break for 3 months, I busily typed up each recipe our family loves. I put two recipes to a page and covered each page with a plastic sleeve. Then I bound them into a 3-ring binder with tabs marking the different categories. This family cookbook is filled with good food and love for my kids! —*Deb Eilenfeld Ashland, Ohio*

Kringle Cupcakes Put on A Happy Holiday Face

LOOKING to make spirits bright during the holidays? Try these Santa Cupcakes shared by Sharon Skildum of Maple Grove, Minnesota.

"My daughter, Alison, and her cousin, Leah Voigt, decorate these cute cupcakes every year for Christmas," Sharon says. "Sometimes, my son Grant also gets involved."

The sweet treats are made with a packaged cake mix, so young children can easily stir together the ingredients. Older kids can spoon the batter into muffin cups, and, with an adult's supervision, pop the pans into the oven.

Once the cupcakes are baked and cooled, everyone will enjoy adding the festive finishing touches. Part of a can of prepared vanilla frosting creates an area for Kris Kringle's face, while the remaining frosting is tinted with red food coloring to form his hat. A mini marshmallow becomes the hat's tassel.

Then it's time to add some personality to the jolly old elf. "We use chocolate chips for Santa's eyes and a red-hot for his nose, but you can use any kind of candies you'd like," Sharon informs.

Santa Cupcakes
(Pictured at right)

1 package (18-1/4 ounces) white cake mix
1 can (16 ounces) *or* 2 cups vanilla frosting, *divided*
Red gel *or* paste food coloring
Miniature marshmallows, chocolate chips, red-hot candies and flaked coconut

Prepare cake batter according to package directions for cupcakes; fill paper-lined muffin cups two-thirds full. Bake according to package directions. Cool for 10 min-utes; remove from pans to wire racks. Place 2/3 cup frosting in a bowl; tint with red food coloring. Set aside 3 tablespoons white frosting for decorating. Cover two-thirds of the top of each cupcake with remaining white frosting. Frost the rest of cupcake top with red frosting for hat. Place reserved white frosting in a small heavy-duty resealable plastic bag; cut a 1/4-in. hole in one corner. On each cupcake, pipe a line of frosting to create fur band of hat. Press a marshmallow on one side of hat for pom-pom. Under hat, place two chocolate chips for eyes and one red-hot for nose. Gently press coconut onto face for beard. **Yield:** about 1-1/2 dozen.

Chapter 17

WHEN time isn't on their side, on-the-go cooks rely on the convenience of slow cookers, grills and microwave ovens.

Even though it simmers food ever-so-slowly, a slow cooker is indispensable for active families. So when a full schedule keeps you out of the kitchen, put your slow cooker to work making the meal.

Another way to spend less time in the kitchen is to step outdoors and fix a meal on the grill! It's easy to cook up an entire menu at once...plus there's less cleanup and mess.

With this chapter's made-in-minutes microwave recipes, you are sure to use your "zapper" for more than heating up coffee or warming leftovers.

SLOW-SIMMERED RECIPES.
Clockwise from top: Sweet 'n' Sour Ribs (p. 271), Rich French Onion Soup (p. 272), Slow Cooker Lasagna (p. 267) and Raisin Bread Pudding (p. 276).

Slow-Cooked Specialties

WITH just a little preparation, you can assemble all the ingredients for time-saving recipes in your slow cooker. Then just pop on the lid and switch on the pot as you head out the door.

Creamy Hash Browns

(Pictured below)

My mother often took this comforting side dish to social dinners because it was such a hit. Now I get the same compliments when I make it. Bacon and onion jazz up a creamy mixture that takes advantage of convenient frozen hash browns and canned soups. —Donna Downes
Las Vegas, Nevada

  1 package (2 pounds) frozen cubed hash
     brown potatoes
  2 cups (8 ounces) cubed *or* shredded process
     American cheese
  2 cups (16 ounces) sour cream
  1 can (10-3/4 ounces) condensed cream of
     celery soup, undiluted
  1 can (10-3/4 ounces) condensed cream of
     chicken soup, undiluted
  1 pound sliced bacon, cooked and crumbled
  1 large onion, chopped
1/4 cup butter *or* margarine, melted
1/4 teaspoon pepper

Creamy Hash Browns

Place potatoes in an ungreased 5-qt. slow cooker. In a bowl, combine the remaining ingredients. Pour over potatoes and mix well. Cover and cook on low for 4-5 hours or until potatoes are tender and heated through. **Yield:** 14 servings.

Steak Burritos

I like to spice up flank steak with taco seasoning packets. Slowly simmered all day, the beef is tender and a snap to shred. Just fill flour tortillas and add toppings for a tasty, time-easing meal. —Valerie Jones
Portland, Maine

✓ Uses less fat, sugar or salt. Includes Nutritional Analysis and Diabetic Exchanges.

  2 flank steaks (about 1 pound *each*)
  2 envelopes taco seasoning
  1 medium onion, chopped
  1 can (4 ounces) chopped green chilies
  1 tablespoon vinegar
10 flour tortillas (7 inches)
1-1/2 cups (6 ounces) shredded Monterey Jack
     cheese
1-1/2 cups chopped seeded plum tomatoes
3/4 cup sour cream

Cut steaks in half; rub with taco seasoning. Place in a slow cooker coated with nonstick cooking spray. Top with onion, chilies and vinegar. Cover and cook on low for 8-9 hours or until meat is tender. Remove steaks and cool slightly; shred meat with two forks. (Turn to page 277 for a tip on shredding meat.) Return to slow cooker; heat through. Spoon about 1/2 cup meat mixture down the center of each tortilla. Top with cheese, tomato and sour cream. Fold ends and sides over filling. **Yield:** 10 servings. **Nutritional Analysis:** One serving (prepared with reduced-sodium taco seasoning, fat-free tortillas, reduced-fat cheese and nonfat sour cream) equals 339 calories, 580 mg sodium, 57 mg cholesterol, 31 gm carbohydrate, 28 gm protein, 10 gm fat, 2 gm fiber. **Diabetic Exchanges:** 3 lean meat, 2 starch, 1 vegetable.

Savory Chicken Sandwiches

With eight children under the age of 12, I need to make family-pleasing meals. This tender chicken tastes like you fussed, but requires few ingredients. You can also thicken the juices and serve it over rice. —Joan Parker
Gastonia, North Carolina

  4 bone-in chicken breast halves
  4 chicken thighs
  1 envelope onion soup mix
1/4 teaspoon garlic salt
1/4 cup prepared Italian salad dressing
1/4 cup water
14 to 16 hamburger buns, split

Remove skin from chicken if desired. Place chicken in a 5-qt. slow cooker. Sprinkle with soup mix and garlic salt;

pour dressing and water over chicken. Cover and cook on low for 8-9 hours. Remove chicken; cool slightly. Skim fat from cooking juices. Remove chicken from bones; cut into bite-size pieces and return to slow cooker. Serve with a slotted spoon on buns. **Yield:** 14-16 servings.

Pennsylvania Pot Roast

This heartwarming one-dish meal is adapted from a Pennsylvania Dutch recipe. I start the pot roast cooking before I leave for church, add vegetables when I get home, and then just sit back and relax until it's done.
—Donna Wilkinson, Clarksburg, Maryland

2-1/2 to 3 pounds boneless pork shoulder roast
1-1/2 cups beef broth
1/2 cup sliced green onions
1 teaspoon dried basil
1 teaspoon dried marjoram
1/2 teaspoon salt
1/2 teaspoon pepper
1 bay leaf
6 medium red potatoes, cut into 2-inch chunks
4 medium carrots, cut into 2-inch chunks
7 to 8 fresh mushrooms, quartered
1/4 cup all-purpose flour
1/2 cup cold water
Browning sauce, optional

Place roast in a slow cooker; add broth, onions and seasonings. Cover and cook on high for 2 hours. Add potatoes, carrots and mushrooms. Cover and cook on low for 6 hours or until vegetables are tender. Remove the meat and vegetables; keep warm. Discard bay leaf. In a saucepan, combine flour and cold water until smooth; stir in 1-1/2 cups cooking juices. Bring to a boil. Cook and stir for 2 minutes or until thickened. Add browning sauce if desired. Serve with roast and vegetables. **Yield:** 6 servings.

Slow Cooker Lasagna

(Pictured on page 264)

Convenient no-cook lasagna noodles take the work out of this traditional favorite adapted for the slow cooker. It's great for workdays.
—Lisa Micheletti
Collierville, Tennessee

1 pound ground beef
1 large onion, chopped
2 garlic cloves, minced
1 can (29 ounces) tomato sauce
1 cup water
1 can (6 ounces) tomato paste
1 teaspoon salt
1 teaspoon dried oregano
1 package (8 ounces) no-cook lasagna noodles
4 cups (16 ounces) shredded mozzarella cheese
1-1/2 cups (12 ounces) small-curd cottage cheese
1/2 cup grated Parmesan cheese

In a skillet, cook beef, onion and garlic over medium heat until meat is no longer pink; drain. Add the tomato

Ham 'n' Swiss Chicken

sauce, water, tomato paste, salt and oregano; mix well. Spread a fourth of the meat sauce in an ungreased 5-qt. slow cooker. Arrange a third of the noodles over sauce (break the noodles if necessary). Combine the cheeses; spoon a third of the mixture over noodles. Repeat layers twice. Top with remaining meat sauce. Cover and cook on low for 4-5 hours or until noodles are tender. **Yield:** 6-8 servings.

Ham 'n' Swiss Chicken

(Pictured above)

This saucy casserole allows you to enjoy all the rich flavor of traditional chicken cordon bleu with less effort. It's a snap to layer the ingredients and let them cook all afternoon.
—Dorothy Witmer, Ephrata, Pennsylvania

2 eggs
2 cups milk, *divided*
1/2 cup butter *or* margarine, melted
1/2 cup chopped celery
1 teaspoon finely chopped onion
8 slices bread, cubed
12 thin slices deli ham, rolled up
2 cups (8 ounces) shredded Swiss cheese
2-1/2 cups cubed cooked chicken
1 can (10-3/4 ounces) condensed cream of chicken soup, undiluted

In a large bowl, beat the eggs and 1-1/2 cups milk. Add butter, celery and onion. Stir in bread cubes. Place half of the mixture in a greased slow cooker; top with half of the rolled-up ham, cheese and chicken. Combine soup and remaining milk; pour half over the chicken. Repeat layers once. Cover and cook on low for 4-5 hours or until a thermometer inserted into bread mixture reads 160°. **Yield:** 6 servings.

Teriyaki Pork Roast

pared with light soy sauce) equals 292 calories, 212 mg sodium, 101 mg cholesterol, 9 gm carbohydrate, 36 gm protein, 12 gm fat, trace fiber. **Diabetic Exchanges:** 4-1/2 lean meat, 1/2 starch.

Turkey in Cream Sauce

I've been relying on this recipe for tender turkey since I first moved out on my own years ago. I serve it whenever I invite new guests to the house. —Kathy-Jo Winterbottom
Pottstown, Pennsylvania

✓ Uses less fat, sugar or salt. Includes Nutritional Analysis and Diabetic Exchanges.

- 1-1/4 cups white wine *or* chicken broth
- 1 medium onion, chopped
- 2 garlic cloves, minced
- 2 bay leaves
- 2 teaspoons dried rosemary, crushed
- 1/2 teaspoon pepper
- 3 turkey breast tenderloins (3/4 pound *each*)
- 3 tablespoons cornstarch
- 1/2 cup half-and-half cream *or* milk
- 1/2 teaspoon salt

In a slow cooker, combine wine or broth, onion, garlic and bay leaves. Combine rosemary and pepper; rub over turkey. Place in slow cooker. Cover and cook on low for 7-8 hours or until meat is tender. Remove turkey and keep warm. Strain cooking juices; pour into a saucepan. Combine cornstarch, cream and salt until smooth; gradually add to juices. Bring to a boil; cook and stir for 2 minutes or until thickened and bubbly. Slice turkey; serve with cream sauce. **Yield:** 9 servings. **Nutritional Analysis:** One serving (prepared with wine and skim milk) equals 179 calories, 190 mg sodium, 82 mg cholesterol, 5 gm carbohydrate, 30 gm protein, 1 gm fat, 1 gm fiber. **Diabetic Exchanges:** 4 very lean meat, 1 vegetable.

Teriyaki Pork Roast

(Pictured above)

I'm always looking for no-fuss recipes, so I was thrilled to find this one. The moist teriyaki-seasoned pork roast has become a family favorite. —Roxanne Hulsey
Gainesville, Georgia

✓ Uses less fat, sugar or salt. Includes Nutritional Analysis and Diabetic Exchanges.

- 3/4 cup unsweetened apple juice
- 2 tablespoons sugar
- 2 tablespoons soy sauce
- 1 tablespoon vinegar
- 1 teaspoon ground ginger
- 1/4 teaspoon garlic powder
- 1/8 teaspoon pepper
- 1 boneless pork loin roast (about 3 pounds), halved
- 7-1/2 teaspoons cornstarch
- 3 tablespoons cold water

Combine the first seven ingredients in a greased slow cooker. Add roast and turn to coat. Cover and cook on low for 7-8 hours or until a thermometer inserted into the roast reads 160°. Remove roast and keep warm. In a saucepan, combine cornstarch and cold water until smooth; stir in cooking juices. Bring to a boil; cook and stir for 2 minutes or until thickened. Serve with the roast. **Yield:** 8 servings. **Nutritional Analysis:** One serving (pre-

San Francisco Chops

Simmered in a tangy sauce all day, these chops are so moist and delicious by dinnertime they practically melt in your mouth. —Tara Bonesteel, Dayton, New Jersey

- 4 bone-in pork loin chops (1 inch thick)
- 1 to 2 tablespoons vegetable oil
- 1 garlic clove, minced
- 1/4 cup soy sauce
- 1/4 cup red wine *or* chicken broth
- 2 tablespoons brown sugar
- 1/4 teaspoon crushed red pepper flakes
- 1 tablespoon cornstarch
- 1 tablespoon cold water

Hot cooked rice

In a skillet, brown pork chops on both sides in oil; transfer to a slow cooker. Add garlic to drippings; cook and stir for about 1 minute or until golden. Stir in soy sauce, wine or broth, brown sugar and red pepper flakes; cook and stir until sugar is dissolved. Pour over chops. Cover and cook on low for 7-8 hours or until meat is tender. Remove chops. Combine cornstarch and cold water until smooth; gradually stir into slow cooker. Return chops to slow cooker. Cover and cook for at least 30 minutes or until slightly thickened. Serve over rice. **Yield:** 4 servings.

Sweet-Sour Beef

Chock-full of tender beef, sliced carrots, green pepper and onion, this sweet-and-sour speciality is good over noodles or rice. —Beth Husband, Billings, Montana

        2 pounds boneless round *or* chuck steak, cut
            into 1-inch cubes
        2 tablespoons vegetable oil
        2 cans (8 ounces *each*) tomato sauce
        2 cups sliced carrots
        2 cups pearl onions
        1 large green pepper, cut into 1-inch pieces
    1/2 cup molasses
    1/3 cup vinegar
    1/4 cup sugar
        2 teaspoons chili powder
        2 teaspoons paprika
        1 teaspoon salt
Shell macaroni and snipped chives, optional

In a skillet, brown steak in oil; transfer to a slow cooker. Add the next 10 ingredients; stir well. Cover and cook on low for 7-8 hours or until meat is tender. Thicken if desired. Serve over macaroni and garnish with chives if desired. **Yield:** 10-12 servings.

Hot Dogs 'n' Beans

You'll please kids of all ages with this tasty combination that's good for casual get-togethers. —June Formanek
Belle Plaine, Iowa

        3 cans (two 28 ounces, one 16 ounces) pork
            and beans
        1 package (1 pound) hot dogs, halved
            lengthwise and cut into 1-inch pieces
        1 large onion, chopped
    1/2 cup packed brown sugar
        3 tablespoons prepared mustard
        4 bacon strips, cooked and crumbled

In a slow cooker, combine all ingredients; mix well. Cover and cook on low for 7-8 hours. **Yield:** 10 servings.

Tender Barbecued Chicken

I'm a teacher and work most of the day, so slow-cooked meals are a great help. One of my family's favorites is this moist, slow-simmered chicken. —Jacqueline Blanton
Gaffney, South Carolina

        1 broiler/fryer chicken (3 to 4 pounds), cut up
        1 medium onion, thinly sliced
        1 medium lemon, thinly sliced
        1 bottle (18 ounces) barbecue sauce*
    3/4 cup regular cola

Place chicken in a slow cooker. Top with onion and lemon slices. Combine barbecue sauce and cola; pour over all. Cover and cook on low for 8-10 hours or until chicken juices run clear. **Yield:** 4-6 servings. ***Editor's Note:** This recipe was tested with K.C. Masterpiece brand barbecue sauce.

Slow-Simmered Kidney Beans

(Pictured below)

My husband always puts us down for this popular side dish when we're invited to a potluck. —Sheila Vail
Long Beach, California

        6 bacon strips, diced
    1/2 pound fully cooked Polish sausage *or* kielbasa,
            chopped
        4 cans (16 ounces *each*) kidney beans, rinsed
            and drained
        1 can (28 ounces) diced tomatoes, drained
        2 medium sweet red peppers, chopped
        1 large onion, chopped
        1 cup ketchup
    1/2 cup packed brown sugar
    1/4 cup honey
    1/4 cup molasses
        1 tablespoon Worcestershire sauce
        1 teaspoon salt
        1 teaspoon ground mustard
        2 medium unpeeled red apples, cored and cut
            into 1/2-inch pieces

In a skillet, cook bacon until crisp. Remove with a slotted spoon to paper towels. Add sausage to drippings; cook and stir for 5 minutes. Drain and set aside. In an ungreased 5-qt. slow cooker, combine the beans, tomatoes, red peppers, onion, ketchup, brown sugar, honey, molasses, Worcestershire sauce, salt and mustard. Stir in the bacon and sausage. Cover and cook on low for 4-6 hours. Stir in apples. Cover and cook 2 hours longer or until bubbly. **Yield:** 16 servings.

Slow-Simmered Kidney Beans

Hot Cranberry Punch
Moist Poultry Dressing
Turkey with Mushroom Sauce

Moist Poultry Dressing

(Pictured above)

Tasty mushrooms and onions complement the big herb flavor in this stuffing. The dressing stays so moist when cooked this way.
—Ruth Ann Stelfox, Raymond, Alberta

> 2 jars (4-1/2 ounces *each*) sliced mushrooms, drained
> 4 celery ribs, chopped
> 2 medium onions, chopped
> 1/4 cup minced fresh parsley
> 3/4 cup butter *or* margarine
> 1-1/2 pounds day-old bread, crusts removed and cubed (about 13 cups)
> 1-1/2 teaspoons salt
> 1-1/2 teaspoons rubbed sage
> 1 teaspoon poultry seasoning
> 1 teaspoon dried thyme
> 1/2 teaspoon pepper
> 2 eggs
> 1 can (14-1/2 ounces) chicken broth

In a large skillet, saute the mushrooms, celery, onions and parsley in butter until the vegetables are tender. In a large bowl, toss the bread cubes with salt, sage, poultry seasoning, thyme and pepper. Add the mushroom mixture. Combine eggs and broth; add to the bread mixture and toss. Transfer to a slow cooker. Cover and cook on low for 4-5 hours or until a meat thermometer reads 160°. **Yield:** 12-16 servings.

Turkey with Mushroom Sauce

(Pictured above)

When we were first married, I didn't have an oven, so I made this tender turkey in the slow cooker. These days, I rely on this recipe because it frees up the oven to make other dishes for large get-togethers.
—Myra Innes
Auburn, Kansas

 Uses less fat, sugar or salt. Includes Nutritional Analysis and Diabetic Exchanges.

> 1 boneless turkey breast (3 pounds), halved
> 2 tablespoons butter *or* margarine, melted

2 tablespoons dried parsley flakes
1/2 teaspoon dried tarragon
1/2 teaspoon salt, optional
1/8 teaspoon pepper
1 jar (4-1/2 ounces) sliced mushrooms, drained
  or 1 cup sliced fresh mushrooms
1/2 cup white wine *or* chicken broth
2 tablespoons cornstarch
1/4 cup cold water

Place the turkey, skin side up, in a slow cooker. Brush with butter. Sprinkle with parsley, tarragon, salt if desired and pepper. Top with mushrooms. Pour wine or broth over all. Cover and cook on low for 7-8 hours. Remove turkey and keep warm. Skim fat from cooking juices. In a saucepan, combine cornstarch and water until smooth. Gradually add cooking juices. Bring to a boil; cook and stir for 2 minutes or until thickened. Serve with the turkey. **Yield:** 12 servings (2-1/2 cups sauce). **Nutritional Analysis:** One serving (prepared with reduced-fat margarine, fresh mushrooms and low-sodium broth and without salt) equals 181 calories, 76 mg sodium, 60 mg cholesterol, 2 gm carbohydrate, 24 gm protein, 8 gm fat, trace fiber. **Diabetic Exchanges:** 3 lean meat, 1/2 vegetable.

Hot Cranberry Punch

(Pictured at left)

I serve this rosy spiced beverage at parties and family gatherings during the winter. Friends like the tangy twist it gets from red-hots. It's a nice change from hot chocolate.
—Laura Burgess, Ballwin, Missouri

8 cups hot water
1-1/2 cups sugar
4 cups cranberry juice
3/4 cup orange juice
1/4 cup lemon juice
12 whole cloves, optional
1/2 cup red-hot candies

In a 5-qt. slow cooker, combine water, sugar and juices; stir until sugar is dissolved. If desired, place cloves in a double thickness of cheesecloth; bring up corners of cloth and tie with string to form a bag. Add spice bag and red-hots to slow cooker. Cover and cook on low for 2-3 hours or until heated though. Before serving, discard spice bag and stir punch. **Yield:** 3-1/2 quarts.

Sweet 'n' Sour Ribs

(Pictured on page 264)

If you're looking for a change from typical barbecue ribs, you'll enjoy this recipe my mom always prepared on birthdays and special occasions. The ribs have a slight sweet-and-sour taste. —Dorothy Voelz, Champaign, Illinois

3 to 4 pounds boneless country-style ribs
1 can (20 ounces) pineapple tidbits, undrained
2 cans (8 ounces *each*) tomato sauce
1/2 cup thinly sliced onion
1/2 cup thinly sliced green pepper

1/2 cup packed brown sugar
1/4 cup cider vinegar
1/4 cup tomato paste
2 tablespoons Worcestershire sauce
1 garlic clove, minced
Salt and pepper to taste

Place ribs in an ungreased slow cooker. In a bowl, combine the remaining ingredients; pour over the ribs. Cover and cook on low for 8-10 hours or until meat is tender. Thicken the sauce if desired. **Yield:** 8 servings.

Meal-in-One Casserole

Salsa adds zip to this hearty fix-and-forget-it meal. This recipe makes more than my husband and I can eat, so I freeze half.
—Dorothy Pritchett, Wills Point, Texas

1 pound ground beef
1 medium onion, chopped
1 medium green pepper, chopped
1 can (15-1/4 ounces) whole kernel corn, drained
1 can (4 ounces) mushroom stems and pieces, drained
1 teaspoon salt
1/4 teaspoon pepper
1 jar (11 ounces) salsa
5 cups uncooked medium egg noodles
1 can (28 ounces) diced tomatoes, undrained
1 cup water
1 cup (4 ounces) shredded cheddar cheese *or* blend of cheddar, Monterey Jack and American cheeses

In a skillet, cook beef and onion over medium heat until meat is no longer pink; drain. Transfer to a slow cooker. Top with the green pepper, corn and mushrooms. Sprinkle with salt and pepper. Pour salsa over mushrooms. Top with noodles. Pour tomatoes and water over all. Sprinkle with cheese. Cover and cook on low for 4 hours or until noodles are tender. **Yield:** 4-6 servings.

Mushroom Pork Tenderloin

This moist pork tenderloin in a savory gravy is the best you'll ever taste. Prepared with canned soups, it couldn't be easier to assemble.
—Donna Hughes
Rochester, New Hampshire

2 pork tenderloins (1 pound *each*)
1 can (10-3/4 ounces) condensed cream of mushroom soup, undiluted
1 can (10-3/4 ounces) condensed golden mushroom soup, undiluted
1 can (10-1/2 ounces) condensed French onion soup, undiluted
Hot mashed potatoes, optional

Place pork in a slow cooker. In a bowl, combine the soups; stir until smooth. Pour over pork. Cover and cook on low for 4-5 hours or until the meat is tender. Serve with mashed potatoes if desired. **Yield:** 6 servings.

Herbed Chicken and Shrimp

Herbed Chicken and Shrimp

(Pictured above)

This tasty dish is easy to prepare, yet elegant enough to serve at a dinner party. I serve it over cooked rice with crusty bread and a salad. —Diana Knight, Reno, Nevada

1 teaspoon salt
1 teaspoon pepper
1 broiler/fryer chicken (3 to 4 pounds), cut up and skin removed
1/4 cup butter *or* margarine
1 large onion, chopped
1 can (8 ounces) tomato sauce
1/2 cup white wine *or* chicken broth
1 garlic clove, minced
1 teaspoon dried basil
1 pound uncooked medium shrimp, peeled and deveined

Combine salt and pepper; rub over the chicken pieces. In a skillet, brown chicken on all sides in butter. Transfer to an ungreased slow cooker. In a bowl, combine the onion, tomato sauce, wine or broth, garlic and basil; pour over chicken. Cover and cook on low for 4-5 hours or until chicken juices run clear. Add the shrimp and mix well. Cover and cook on high for 20-30 minutes or until shrimp turn pink. **Yield:** 4 servings.

Pork Chops and Beans

A hearty combination of pork chops and two kinds of beans makes a satisfying supper in summer or winter.
—Dorothy Pritchett, Wills Point, Texas

✓ Uses less fat, sugar or salt. Includes Nutritional Analysis and Diabetic Exchanges.

4 pork loin chops (1/2 inch thick)
1/2 teaspoon salt, optional
1/4 teaspoon pepper
1 tablespoon vegetable oil
2 medium onions, chopped
2 garlic cloves, minced
1/4 cup chili sauce
1-1/2 teaspoons brown sugar
1 teaspoon prepared mustard
1 can (16 ounces) kidney beans, rinsed and drained
1 can (15-1/4 ounces) lima beans, rinsed and drained *or* 1-3/4 cups frozen lima beans

Sprinkle pork chops with salt if desired and pepper. In a skillet, brown chops in oil; transfer chops to a slow cooker. Reserve 1 tablespoon drippings in the skillet; saute onions and garlic until tender. Stir in chili sauce, brown sugar and mustard. Pour over chops. Cover and cook on low for 7-8 hours. Stir in beans. Cover and cook 1 to 1-1/2 hours longer or until meat juices run clear and beans are heated through. **Yield:** 4 servings. **Nutritional Analysis:** One serving (prepared with frozen lima beans and without salt) equals 427 calories, 564 mg sodium, 63 mg cholesterol, 48 gm carbohydrate, 36 gm protein, 10 gm fat, 14 gm fiber. **Diabetic Exchanges:** 3-1/2 lean meat, 3 starch, 1 vegetable.

Rich French Onion Soup

(Pictured on page 265)

When entertaining guests, I bring out this savory soup while we're waiting for the main course. It's easy to make—just saute the onions and let the soup simmer 'til dinnertime. —Linda Adolph, Edmonton, Alberta

6 large onions, chopped
1/2 cup butter *or* margarine
6 cans (10-1/2 ounces *each*) condensed beef broth, undiluted
1-1/2 teaspoons Worcestershire sauce
3 bay leaves
10 slices French bread, toasted
Shredded Parmesan and mozzarella cheeses

In a large skillet, saute onions in butter until crisp-tender. Transfer to an ungreased 5-qt. slow cooker. Add the broth, Worcestershire sauce and bay leaves. Cover and cook on low for 5-7 hours or until the onions are tender. Discard bay leaves. Top each serving with French bread and cheeses. **Yield:** 10 servings.

Simple Saucy Potatoes

These rich and creamy potatoes are simple to prepare for potlucks. This saucy side dish gets rave reviews wherever I take it. —Gloria Schroeder, Ottawa Lake, Michigan

4 cans (15 ounces *each*) sliced white potatoes, drained
2 cans (10-3/4 ounces *each*) condensed cream of celery soup, undiluted
2 cups (16 ounces) sour cream
10 bacon strips, cooked and crumbled
6 green onions, thinly sliced

Place potatoes in a slow cooker. Combine the remaining ingredients; pour over potatoes and mix well. Cover and cook on high for 4-5 hours. **Yield:** 12 servings.

Savory Cheese Soup

(Pictured below)

This creamy soup is great at parties. Let guests serve themselves and choose from fun garnishes such as popcorn, croutons, green onions and bacon bits. —Ann Huseby
Lakeville, Minnesota

 3 cans (14-1/2 ounces *each*) chicken broth
 1 small onion, chopped
 1 large carrot, chopped
 1 celery rib, chopped
 1/4 cup chopped sweet red pepper
 2 tablespoons butter *or* margarine
 1 teaspoon salt
 1/2 teaspoon pepper
 1/3 cup all-purpose flour
 1/3 cup cold water
 1 package (8 ounces) cream cheese, cubed and softened
 2 cups (8 ounces) shredded cheddar cheese
 1 can (12 ounces) beer, optional
Optional toppings: croutons, popcorn, cooked crumbled bacon, sliced green onions

In a slow cooker, combine the first eight ingredients. Cover and cook on low for 7-8 hours. Combine flour and water until smooth; stir into soup. Cover and cook on high 30 minutes longer or until soup is thickened. Stir in cream cheese and cheddar cheese until blended. Stir in beer if desired. Cover and cook on low until heated through. Serve with desired toppings. **Yield:** 6-8 servings.

Hot Ham Sandwiches

(Pictured below)

I came up with this crowd-pleasing recipe when trying to re-create a favorite sandwich from a restaurant near my hometown. Flavored with sweet relish, these ham sandwiches are oh-so-easy. My family likes them with coleslaw and French fries.—Susan Rehm, Grahamsville, New York

 3 pounds thinly sliced deli ham
 (about 40 slices)
 2 cups apple juice
 2/3 cup packed brown sugar
 1/2 cup sweet pickle relish
 2 teaspoons prepared mustard
 1 teaspoon paprika
 12 kaiser rolls, split
Additional sweet pickle relish, optional

Separate ham slices and place in a slow cooker. In a bowl, combine the apple juice, brown sugar, relish, mustard and paprika. Pour over ham. Cover and cook on low for 4-5 hours or until heated through. Place 3-4 slices of ham on each roll. Serve with additional relish if desired. **Yield:** 12 servings.

Savory Cheese Soup
Hot Ham Sandwiches

Sunday Chicken Supper

(Pictured below)

This hearty, homespun dish satisfies even the biggest appetites. The chicken, vegetables and seasonings meld into a supper that's special any day of the week.

—Ruthann Martin, Louisville, Ohio

4 medium carrots, cut into 2-inch pieces
1 medium onion, chopped
1 celery rib, cut into 2-inch pieces
2 cups cut fresh green beans (2-inch pieces)
5 small red potatoes, quartered
1 broiler/fryer chicken (3 to 3-1/2 pounds), cut up
4 bacon strips, cooked and crumbled
1-1/2 cups hot water
2 teaspoons chicken bouillon granules
1 teaspoon salt
1/2 teaspoon dried thyme
1/2 teaspoon dried basil
Pinch pepper

In a 5-qt. slow cooker, layer the first seven ingredients in order listed. In a bowl, combine the remaining ingredients; pour over the top. Do not stir. Cover and cook on low for 6-8 hours or until vegetables are tender and chicken juices run clear. Remove chicken and vegetables. Thicken juices for gravy if desired. **Yield:** 4 servings.

Mushroom Wild Rice

This is one of my favorite recipes from my mother. With only seven ingredients, it's quick to assemble in the morning before I leave for work. By the time I get home, mouth-watering aromas have filled the house.

—Bob Malchow, Monon, Indiana

2-1/4 cups water
1 can (10-1/2 ounces) condensed beef consomme, undiluted
1 can (10-1/2 ounces) condensed French onion soup, undiluted
3 cans (4 ounces *each*) mushroom stems and pieces, drained
1/2 cup butter *or* margarine, melted
1 cup uncooked brown rice
1 cup uncooked wild rice

In a slow cooker, combine all ingredients; stir well. Cover and cook on low for 7-8 hours or until rice is tender. **Yield:** 12-16 servings.

Garlic Beef Stroganoff

I'm a mom and work full-time, so I use my slow cooker whenever possible. This Stroganoff is perfect because I can get it ready in the morning before the kids get up.

—Erika Anderson, Wausau, Wisconsin

Sunday Chicken Supper

2 teaspoons beef bouillon granules
1 cup boiling water
1 can (10-3/4 ounces) condensed cream of
  mushroom soup, undiluted
2 jars (4-1/2 ounces *each*) sliced mushrooms,
  drained
1 large onion, chopped
3 garlic cloves, minced
1 tablespoon Worcestershire sauce
1-1/2 to 2 pounds boneless round steak, trimmed
  and cut into thin strips
2 tablespoons vegetable oil
1 package (8 ounces) cream cheese, cubed
Hot cooked noodles

In a slow cooker, dissolve bouillon in water. Add soup, mushrooms, onion, garlic and Worcestershire sauce. In a skillet, brown beef in oil. Transfer to the slow cooker. Cover and cook on low for 7-8 hours or until the meat is tender. Stir in cream cheese until smooth. Serve over noodles. **Yield:** 6-8 servings.

Creamy Ham and Potatoes

You can serve this stick-to-your-ribs dish with a green salad and dessert for a complete meal. The creamy mixture of hearty ham and tender potatoes is brimming with down-home flavor. —Peggy Key, Grant, Alabama

4 medium red potatoes, thinly sliced
2 medium onions, finely chopped
1-1/2 cups cubed fully cooked ham
2 tablespoons butter *or* margarine
2 tablespoons all-purpose flour
1 teaspoon ground mustard
1/2 teaspoon salt
1/2 teaspoon pepper
1 can (10-3/4 ounces) condensed cream of
  celery soup, undiluted
1-1/3 cups water
1 cup (4 ounces) shredded cheddar cheese,
  optional

In a slow cooker, layer potatoes, onions and ham. In a saucepan, melt butter. Stir in flour, mustard, salt and pepper until smooth. Combine soup and water; gradually stir into flour mixture. Bring to a boil; cook and stir for 2 minutes or until thickened and bubbly. Pour over ham. Cover and cook on low for 8-9 hours or until potatoes are tender. If desired, sprinkle with cheese before serving. **Yield:** 4 servings.

Beef Barbecue

(Pictured above right)

We like to keep our freezer stocked with plenty of beef roasts. When we're not in the mood for pot roast, I fix these satisfying sandwiches instead. The meat cooks in a tasty sauce while I'm at work. Then I just slice it thinly and serve it on rolls. —Karen Walker, Sterling, Virginia

✓ Uses less fat, sugar or salt. Includes Nutritional Analysis and Diabetic Exchanges.

Beef Barbecue

1 boneless chuck roast (3 pounds)
1 cup barbecue sauce
1/2 cup apricot preserves
1/3 cup chopped green *or* sweet red pepper
1 small onion, chopped
1 tablespoon Dijon mustard
2 teaspoons brown sugar
12 sandwich rolls, split

Cut the roast into quarters; place in a greased 5-qt. slow cooker. In a bowl, combine barbecue sauce, preserves, green pepper, onion, mustard and brown sugar; pour over roast. Cover and cook on low for 6-8 hours or until meat is tender. Remove roast and thinly slice; return meat to slow cooker and stir gently. Cover and cook 20-30 minutes longer. Skim fat from sauce. Serve beef and sauce on rolls. **Yield:** 12 servings. **Nutritional Analysis:** One serving (prepared with apricot spreadable fruit; calculated without roll) equals 218 calories, 253 mg sodium, 78 mg cholesterol, 11 gm carbohydrate, 26 gm protein, 7 gm fat, 1 gm fiber. **Diabetic Exchanges:** 3 lean meat, 1 fruit.

Easy Chocolate Clusters

You can use this simple recipe to make a big batch of chocolate candy without a lot of fuss. I've sent these clusters to my husband's office a number of times...and passed the recipe along as well. —Doris Reynolds Munds Park, Arizona

2 pounds white candy coating, broken into
  small pieces
2 cups (12 ounces) semisweet chocolate chips
1 package (4 ounces) German sweet chocolate
1 jar (24 ounces) dry roasted peanuts

In a slow cooker, combine candy coating, chocolate chips and German chocolate. Cover and cook on high for 1 hour. Reduce heat to low; cover and cook 1 hour longer or until melted, stirring every 15 minutes. Add peanuts; mix well. Drop by teaspoonfuls onto waxed paper. Let stand until set. Store at room temperature. **Yield:** 3-1/2 dozen.

Hot German Potato Salad

This zesty salad has potatoes, celery and onion. It's a terrific side dish when served warm with crumbled bacon and fresh parsley sprinkled on top.
—Marlene Muckenhirn, Delano, Minnesota

  8 medium potatoes, peeled and cut into 1/4-inch slices
  2 celery ribs, chopped
  1 large onion, chopped
  1 cup water
2/3 cup cider vinegar
1/3 cup sugar
  2 tablespoons quick-cooking tapioca
  1 teaspoon salt
3/4 teaspoon celery seed
1/4 teaspoon pepper
  6 bacon strips, cooked and crumbled
1/4 cup minced fresh parsley

In a slow cooker, combine potatoes, celery and onion. In a bowl, combine water, vinegar, sugar, tapioca, salt, celery seed and pepper. Pour over potatoes; stir gently to coat. Cover and cook on high for 4-5 hours or until potatoes are tender. Just before serving, sprinkle with bacon and parsley. **Yield:** 8-10 servings.

Easy and Elegant Ham

(Pictured below)

I fix this moist, tender ham to serve my large family. It can be readied quickly in the morning, frees up my oven, tastes outstanding and can feed a crowd. Covered with colorful pineapple slices, cherries and orange glaze, its showstopping appearance appeals to both children and adults.
—Denise DiPace, Medford, New Jersey

  2 cans (20 ounces *each*) sliced pineapple
  1 fully cooked boneless ham (about 6 pounds), halved

Easy and Elegant Ham

  1 jar (6 ounces) maraschino cherries, well drained
  1 jar (12 ounces) orange marmalade

Drain pineapple, reserving juice; set juice aside. Place half of the pineapple in an ungreased 5-qt. slow cooker. Top with the ham. Add cherries, remaining pineapple and reserved pineapple juice. Spoon marmalade over ham. Cover and cook on low for 6-7 hours or until heated through. Remove to a warm serving platter. Let stand for 10-15 minutes before slicing. Serve pineapple and cherries with sliced ham. **Yield:** 18-20 servings.

Raisin Bread Pudding

(Pictured on page 264)

My sister gave me the recipe for this delicious bread pudding that's dotted with raisins. It's a big hit with everyone who's tried it. A homemade vanilla sauce goes together quickly on the stovetop and is yummy drizzled over warm servings of this old-fashioned-tasting treat.
—Sherry Niese, McComb, Ohio

  8 slices bread, cubed
  4 eggs
  2 cups milk
1/4 cup sugar
1/4 cup butter *or* margarine, melted
1/4 cup raisins
1/2 teaspoon ground cinnamon
SAUCE:
  2 tablespoons butter *or* margarine
  2 tablespoons all-purpose flour
  1 cup water
3/4 cup sugar
  1 teaspoon vanilla extract

Place bread cubes in a greased slow cooker. In a bowl, beat eggs and milk; stir in sugar, butter, raisins and cinnamon. Pour over bread; stir. Cover and cook on high for 1 hour. Reduce heat to low; cook for 3-4 hours or until a thermometer reads 160°. Just before serving, melt butter in a saucepan. Stir in flour until smooth. Gradually add water, sugar and vanilla. Bring to a boil; cook and stir for 2 minutes or until thickened. Serve with warm bread pudding. **Yield:** 6 servings.

Chicken in Mushroom Sauce

My father thinks a restaurant could make a fortune with this flavorful main dish. Bacon and sour cream add richness to a simple sauce that really dresses up everyday chicken.
—Kathy Gallagher, La Crosse, Wisconsin

  4 boneless skinless chicken breast halves
  1 can (10-3/4 ounces) condensed cream of mushroom soup, undiluted
  1 cup (8 ounces) sour cream
  4 bacon strips, cooked and crumbled

Place chicken in a slow cooker. Combine soup and sour cream; pour over chicken. Cover and cook on low for 4-5 hours or until chicken is tender. Sprinkle with bacon. **Yield:** 4 servings.

Texas Black Bean Soup
Italian Beef Hoagies

Italian Beef Hoagies

(Pictured above)

You'll need just five ingredients to feed a crowd these tender, tangy sandwiches. On weekends, I start the roast the night before, so I can shred it in the morning.
—*Lori Piatt, Danville, Illinois*

> 1 boneless sirloin tip roast (about 4 pounds), halved
> 2 envelopes Italian salad dressing mix
> 2 cups water
> 1 jar (16 ounces) mild pepper rings, undrained
> 18 hoagie buns, split

Place roast in a 5-qt. slow cooker. Combine the salad dressing mix and water; pour over roast. Cover and cook on low for 8 hours or until meat is tender. Remove meat; shred with a fork and return to slow cooker. Add pepper rings; heat through. Spoon 1/2 cup meat mixture onto each bun. **Yield:** 18 servings.

Texas Black Bean Soup

(Pictured above)

This hearty stew made with convenient canned items is perfect for spicing up a family gathering on a cool day.
—*Pamela Scott, Garland, Texas*

Shredding Meat

To shred meat effectively, follow this method:

Remove cooked meat from pan with a slotted spoon if necessary. Reserve cooking liquid if called for. Place meat in a shallow pan. With two forks, pull meat into thin shreds. Return shredded meat to the pan to warm or use as recipe directs.

> 2 cans (15 ounces *each*) black beans, rinsed and drained
> 1 can (14-1/2 ounces) stewed tomatoes *or* Mexican stewed tomatoes, cut up
> 1 can (14-1/2 ounces) diced tomatoes *or* diced tomatoes with green chilies
> 1 can (14-1/2 ounces) chicken broth
> 1 can (11 ounces) Mexicorn, drained
> 2 cans (4 ounces *each*) chopped green chilies
> 4 green onions, thinly sliced
> 2 to 3 tablespoons chili powder
> 1 teaspoon ground cumin
> 1/2 teaspoon dried minced garlic

In a slow cooker, combine all ingredients. Cover and cook on high for 4-5 hours or until heated through. **Yield:** 8-10 servings (about 2-1/2 quarts).

Slow Cooker Mashed Potatoes
Cranberry Pork Chops

Slow Cooker Mashed Potatoes

(Pictured above)

These rich, creamy potatoes are wonderful for Thanksgiving or Christmas dinner since there's no last-minute mashing required.   —Trudy Vincent, Valles Mines, Missouri

> 1 package (3 ounces) cream cheese, softened
> 1/2 cup sour cream
> 1/4 cup butter *or* margarine, softened
> 1 envelope ranch salad dressing mix
> 1 teaspoon dried parsley flakes
> 6 cups warm mashed potatoes (prepared without milk or butter)

In a bowl, combine the cream cheese, sour cream, butter, salad dressing mix and parsley; stir in potatoes. Transfer to a slow cooker. Cover and cook on low for 2-4 hours. **Yield:** 8-10 servings. **Editor's Note:** This recipe was tested with fresh potatoes (not instant) in a slow cooker with heating elements surrounding the unit, not only in the base.

Cranberry Pork Chops

(Pictured above)

My husband and two kids rave over these moist chops. Use the mild sweet-and-sour sauce to make a gravy that can

be served over mashed potatoes or rice. Then add a salad and you have a very satisfying meal that didn't keep you in the kitchen for hours. —Robin Czachor
Appleton, Wisconsin

> 6 bone-in pork loin chops
> 1 can (16 ounces) jellied cranberry sauce
> 1/2 cup cranberry *or* apple juice
> 1/4 cup sugar
> 2 tablespoons spicy brown mustard
> 2 tablespoons cornstarch
> 1/4 cup cold water
> 1/2 teaspoon salt
> Dash pepper

Place pork chops in a slow cooker. Combine cranberry sauce, juice, sugar and mustard until smooth; pour over chops. Cover and cook on low for 7-8 hours or until meat is tender. Remove chops; keep warm. In a saucepan, combine cornstarch and cold water until smooth; gradually stir in cooking juices. Bring to a boil; cook and stir for 2 minutes or until thickened. Stir in salt and pepper. Serve over chops. **Yield:** 6 servings.

Seafood Chowder

Our family requests this creamy chowder for Christmas Eve supper. We enjoy it with a pot of chili, raw veggies, breadsticks and an array of baked goodies. It's an easy-

to-serve and easy-to-clean-up meal between our church service and gift exchange. —Marlene Muckenhirn
Delano, Minnesota

1 can (10-3/4 ounces) condensed cream of
potato soup, undiluted
1 can (10-3/4 ounces) condensed cream of
mushroom soup, undiluted
2-1/2 cups milk
4 medium carrots, finely chopped
2 medium potatoes, peeled and cut into
1/4-inch cubes
1 large onion, finely chopped
2 celery ribs, finely chopped
1 can (6-1/2 ounces) chopped clams, drained
1 can (6 ounces) medium shrimp, drained
4 ounces imitation crabmeat, flaked
5 bacon strips, cooked and crumbled

In a slow cooker, combine soups and milk. Stir in the vegetables. Cover and cook on low for 4-5 hours. Stir in clams, shrimp and crab; cover and heat through, about 20 minutes. Garnish each serving with bacon. **Yield:** 8 servings.

Spanish Hominy

I received this recipe from a friend who is a fabulous cook. It's a colorful side dish that gets its zesty flavor from spicy canned tomatoes with green chilies. —Donna Brockett
Kingfisher, Oklahoma

4 cans (15-1/2 ounces *each*) hominy, drained
1 can (14-1/2 ounces) diced tomatoes,
undrained
1 can (10 ounces) diced tomatoes and green
chilies, undrained
1 can (8 ounces) tomato sauce
3/4 pound sliced bacon, diced
1 large onion, chopped
1 medium green pepper, chopped

In a slow cooker, combine the hominy, tomatoes and tomato sauce. In a skillet, cook bacon until crisp; remove with a slotted spoon to paper towels. Drain, reserving 1 tablespoon drippings. Saute onion and green pepper in drippings until tender. Stir onion mixture and bacon into hominy mixture. Cover and cook on low for 6-8 hours or until heated through. **Yield:** 12 servings.

Stuffed Cabbage Casserole

I came up with this recipe because I love the taste of cabbage rolls, but don't always have the time to prepare them. My version uses the same ingredients in a simpler manner for hearty results everyone enjoys! —Joann Alexander
Center, Texas

1 pound ground beef
1 small onion, chopped
4 cups chopped cabbage
1 medium green pepper, chopped
1 cup uncooked instant rice

1 cup water
1 can (6 ounces) tomato paste
1 can (14-1/2 ounces) diced tomatoes,
undrained
1/2 cup ketchup
2 tablespoons vinegar
1 to 2 tablespoons sugar, optional
1 tablespoon Worcestershire sauce
1-1/2 teaspoons salt
1/2 teaspoon pepper
1/4 teaspoon garlic powder

In a skillet, cook beef and onion over medium heat until meat is no longer pink; drain. Transfer to a slow cooker; add cabbage, green pepper and rice. In a bowl, combine the water and tomato paste. Stir in the remaining ingredients. Pour over beef mixture; mix well. Cover and cook on low for 4-5 hours or until rice and vegetables are tender. **Yield:** 4-6 servings.

Polish Kraut and Apples

(Pictured below)

My family loves this hearty meal on cold winter nights. The tender apples, brown sugar and smoked sausage give this dish fantastic flavor. —Caren Markee, Cary, Illinois

1 can (14 ounces) sauerkraut, rinsed and well
drained
1 pound fully cooked Polish sausage *or* kielbasa,
cut into 2-inch pieces
3 medium tart apples, peeled and cut into
eighths
1/2 cup packed brown sugar
1/2 teaspoon caraway seeds, optional
1/8 teaspoon pepper
3/4 cup apple juice

Place half of the sauerkraut in an ungreased slow cooker. Top with sausage, apples, brown sugar, caraway seeds if desired and pepper. Top with remaining sauerkraut. Pour apple juice over all. Cover and cook on low for 4-5 hours or until apples are tender. **Yield:** 4 servings.

Polish Kraut and Apples

Great Grilling Recipes

GRILLING is hot no matter what the season. Fire up the grill throughout the year for a sizzling selection of fast, fuss-free fare and capture that great flavor of the outdoors.

Lemon Garlic Mushrooms

(Pictured below)

Ready in 30 minutes or less

To prepare this simple side dish, I baste whole mushrooms with a lemony sauce. Using skewers or a grill basket makes it easy to turn the mushrooms. —Diane Hixon
Niceville, Florida

     1/4 cup lemon juice
       3 tablespoons minced fresh parsley
       2 tablespoons olive *or* vegetable oil
       3 garlic cloves, minced
Pepper to taste
       1 pound large fresh mushrooms

In a small bowl, combine the first five ingredients; set aside. Grill mushrooms, covered, over medium-hot heat for 5 minutes. Brush generously with lemon mix-

ture. Turn mushrooms; grill 5-8 minutes longer or until tender. Brush with remaining lemon mixture before serving. **Yield:** 4 servings. **Nutritional Analysis:** One serving equals 96 calories, 7 mg sodium, 0 cholesterol, 8 gm carbohydrate, 3 gm protein, 7 gm fat, 2 gm fiber. **Diabetic Exchanges:** 1-1/2 fat, 1 vegetable.

Tender Flank Steak

(Pictured below)

Plan ahead...needs to marinate

This mildly marinated flank steak is my son's favorite. I usually slice it thinly and serve it with twice-baked potatoes and a green salad to round out the meal.
—Gayle Bucknam, Greenbank, Washington

✓ Uses less fat, sugar or salt. Includes Nutritional Analysis and Diabetic Exchanges.

     1/4 cup soy sauce
       2 tablespoons water
       3 garlic cloves, thinly sliced
       1 tablespoon brown sugar
       1 tablespoon vegetable oil
     1/2 teaspoon ground ginger
     1/2 teaspoon pepper
       1 flank steak (1 pound)

In a large resealable plastic bag or shallow glass container, combine the first seven ingredients; mix well. Add steak and turn to coat. Cover and refrigerate for 8 hours or overnight, turning occasionally. Drain and discard marinade. Grill, covered, over medium-hot heat for 6-8 minutes on each side or until meat reaches desired

Lemon Garlic Mushrooms
Tender Flank Steak

doneness (for rare, a meat thermometer should read 140°; medium, 160°; well-done, 170°). **Yield:** 4 servings. **Nutritional Analysis:** One serving (prepared with light soy sauce) equals 209 calories, 326 mg sodium, 59 mg cholesterol, 3 gm carbohydrate, 24 gm protein, 11 gm fat, trace fiber. **Diabetic Exchange:** 3-1/2 lean meat.

Paul Bunyan Burgers

Ready in 30 minutes or less

This is one of my favorite grilling recipes. To make these burgers even faster, I sometimes substitute canned mushrooms and bacon bits. —Jo Reed, Craig, Colorado

   6 bacon strips, diced
   1 cup sliced fresh mushrooms
   3 thin onion slices
   1 egg, beaten
   1 tablespoon Worcestershire sauce
1/2 teaspoon seasoned salt
1/2 teaspoon salt
1/2 teaspoon pepper
1/2 teaspoon prepared horseradish
   1 pound ground beef
   3 slices process American cheese
   3 hamburger buns, split

In a skillet, cook bacon until crisp. Remove with a slotted spoon to paper towels. In the drippings, saute mushrooms and onion until tender. Transfer to a bowl with a slotted spoon; add bacon. In another bowl, combine the egg, Worcestershire sauce, seasoned salt, salt, pepper and horseradish; add beef and mix well. Shape into six 1/4-in.-thick patties. Divide bacon mixture among three patties. Top with a cheese slice; fold in corners of cheese. Top with remaining patties; seal edges. Grill, uncovered, over medium-hot heat for 10-12 minutes or until meat juices run clear, turning once. Serve on buns. **Yield:** 3 servings.

Honey Barbecued Ribs

(Pictured above right)

My family celebrates four birthdays in July, and these tender ribs are a must at our joint get-together. Honey adds wonderful flavor to the homemade sauce. —Joyce Duff Mansfield, Ohio

   3 pounds country-style pork ribs
1/2 teaspoon garlic salt
1/2 teaspoon pepper
   1 cup ketchup
1/2 cup packed brown sugar
1/2 cup honey
1/4 cup spicy brown mustard
   2 tablespoons Worcestershire sauce
1-1/2 teaspoons liquid smoke, optional

Place ribs in a large kettle or Dutch oven; sprinkle with garlic salt and pepper. Add enough water to cover; bring to a boil. Reduce heat; cover and simmer for 1 hour or until juices run clear and ribs are tender; drain. Meanwhile, combine the remaining ingredients. Grill ribs, un-

Seafood Skewers
Honey Barbecued Ribs

covered, over medium heat for 10-12 minutes, basting with sauce and turning occasionally. **Yield:** 4 servings.

Seafood Skewers

(Pictured above)

Plan ahead…needs to marinate

My guests are always impressed when I make these shrimp and scallop kabobs. They taste great and look spectacular. —Carolyn Grier, Aurora, Illinois

✓ Uses less fat, sugar or salt. Includes Nutritional Analysis and Diabetic Exchanges.

1/4 cup olive *or* vegetable oil
1/4 cup chili sauce
   2 garlic cloves, minced
1/2 teaspoon hot pepper sauce
Pepper to taste
  16 uncooked large shrimp (about 1/2 pound),
     peeled and deveined
   8 sea scallops (about 1/2 pound)
Hot cooked rice

In a large resealable plastic bag or shallow glass container, combine the first five ingredients. Add shrimp and scallops. Seal or cover and turn to coat. Refrigerate for at least 1 hour. Discard marinade. Place shrimp and scallops on four metal or soaked bamboo skewers. Grill, covered, over medium heat for 5 minutes on each side or until shrimp turn pink. Serve over rice. **Yield:** 4 servings. **Nutritional Analysis:** One serving (calculated without rice) equals 231 calories, 440 mg sodium, 99 mg cholesterol, 4 gm carbohydrate, 18 gm protein, 16 gm fat, trace fiber. **Diabetic Exchanges:** 2-1/2 meat, 1 fat.

**Grilled Pineapple
Snappy Peas 'n' Mushrooms
Tangy Pork Tenderloin**

Grilled Pineapple

(Pictured above)

Ready in 30 minutes or less

Fresh pineapple adds an elegant touch to a barbecue when grilled, topped with butter and maple syrup and sprinkled with nuts. I suggest cutting each pineapple quarter into bite-size pieces before serving. —Polly Heer
Cabot, Arkansas

  1/4 cup maple syrup
    3 tablespoons butter (no substitutes), melted
    1 fresh pineapple
    2 tablespoons chopped macadamia nuts *or* hazelnuts, toasted

Combine syrup and butter; set aside. Quarter the pineapple lengthwise, leaving top attached. Grill, uncovered, over medium heat for 5 minutes. Turn; brush with maple butter. Grill 5-7 minutes longer or until heated through; brush with maple butter and sprinkle with nuts. Serve with remaining maple butter. **Yield:** 4 servings.

Snappy Peas 'n' Mushrooms

(Pictured above and on cover)

Ready in 30 minutes or less

You can make this dill-seasoned dish in minutes. Just wrap the vegetables in foil, seal tightly and grill until tender. —Laura Mahaffey, Annapolis, Maryland

    1 pound fresh sugar snap *or* snow peas
  1/2 cup sliced fresh mushrooms
    2 tablespoons sliced green onions
    1 tablespoon snipped fresh dill *or* 1 teaspoon dill weed

    2 tablespoons butter *or* margarine
Salt and pepper to taste

Place peas and mushrooms on a piece of double-layered heavy-duty foil (about 18 in. square). Sprinkle with onions and dill; dot with butter. Fold foil around the mixture and seal tightly. Grill, covered, over medium-hot heat for 5 minutes. Turn; grill 5-8 minutes longer or until the vegetables are tender. Season with salt and pepper. **Yield:** 8-10 servings.

Tangy Pork Tenderloin

(Pictured above and on cover)

Plan ahead...needs to marinate

A simple marinade adds sweet flavor and tangy zip to juicy pork. No one will know there are just four ingredients in this sauce. For a spicier version, add more chili powder. —Christopher Bingham, Lansing, Michigan

    2 pork tenderloins (1 pound *each*)
  2/3 cup honey
  1/2 cup Dijon mustard
  1/4 to 1/2 teaspoon chili powder
  1/4 teaspoon salt

Place pork tenderloins in a large resealable plastic bag or shallow glass container. In a bowl, combine the remaining ingredients; set aside 2/3 cup. Pour remaining marinade over pork; turn to coat. Seal or cover and refrigerate for at least 4 hours, turning occasionally. Drain and discard marinade. Grill pork, covered, over indirect medium heat for 8-9 minutes on each side or until meat juices run clear and a meat thermometer reads 160°-170°. In a saucepan, warm the reserved sauce; serve with the pork. **Yield:** 6 servings.

Marinated Turkey Slices

Plan ahead...start the night before

We love to entertain and have found this recipe makes plenty for a large get-together. The tender, flavorful turkey slices are always popular. —Shavon Hoopes
Vernal, Utah

1/2 cup soy sauce
1/2 cup vegetable oil
1/2 teaspoon prepared horseradish
1/4 teaspoon garlic powder
1 cup lemon-lime soda
3 pounds boneless skinless turkey breast slices

In a blender, combine soy sauce, oil, horseradish and garlic powder; cover and blend until smooth. Add soda and mix well. Pour into a 2-gal. resealable plastic bag or large shallow glass container. Add turkey slices and turn to coat. Cover and refrigerate overnight, turning once. Drain and discard marinade. Grill turkey, covered, over medium-hot heat for 5-6 minutes or until juices run clear, turning occasionally. **Yield:** 12 servings.

Glazed Salmon Fillet

Ready in 30 minutes or less

My husband caught a lot of salmon when we lived in Alaska, so I had to learn how to cook it. Basted with a sweet glaze, this tasty fillet is a staple in our house. Our six children absolutely love it. —Jerilyn Colvin
Foxboro, Massachusetts

1-1/2 cups packed brown sugar
6 tablespoons butter *or* margarine, melted
3 to 6 tablespoons lemon juice
2-1/4 teaspoons dill weed
3/4 teaspoon cayenne pepper
1 salmon fillet (about 2 pounds)
Lemon-pepper seasoning

In a small bowl, combine the first five ingredients; mix well. Remove 1/2 cup to a saucepan; simmer until heated through. Set aside remaining mixture for basting. Sprinkle salmon with lemon-pepper. Place on grill with skin side down. Grill, covered, over medium heat for 5 minutes. Brush with the reserved brown sugar mixture. Grill 10-15 minutes longer, basting occasionally. Serve with the warmed sauce. **Yield:** 6-8 servings.

Zucchini with Salsa

Ready in 30 minutes or less

I top zucchini slices with chunky homemade salsa to make this scrumptious side dish. We eat it often in the summer when I have the fresh vegetables on hand.
—Carole Hildebrand, Kelseyville, California

✓ Uses less fat, sugar or salt. Includes Nutritional Analysis and Diabetic Exchanges.

4 medium zucchini, sliced
3 medium tomatoes, diced
1 medium onion, diced

3 green onions, sliced
2 jalapeno peppers, seeded and minced*
2 garlic cloves, minced
1 tablespoon minced fresh cilantro *or* parsley
Salt and pepper to taste, optional

Divide zucchini between two pieces of heavy-duty foil (about 20 in. x 18 in.). In a bowl, combine the remaining ingredients; spoon over zucchini. Fold foil around vegetables and seal tightly. Grill, covered, over indirect heat for 15-20 minutes or until vegetables are tender. **Yield:** 10 servings. **Nutritional Analysis:** One 3/4-cup serving (prepared without salt) equals 26 calories, 7 mg sodium, 0 cholesterol, 6 gm carbohydrate, 1 gm protein, trace fat, 2 gm fiber. **Diabetic Exchange:** 1 vegetable. ***Editor's Note:** When cutting and seeding hot peppers, use rubber or plastic gloves to protect your hands. Avoid touching your face.

Grilled Peaches 'n' Berries

Ready in 30 minutes or less

This delightful dessert is so easy to prepare. Just halve peaches and sprinkle with fresh blueberries and a brown sugar mixture. Because they're grilled in foil, there are no messy dishes to wash. —Sharon Bickett
Chester, South Carolina

3 medium ripe peaches, halved and pitted
1 cup fresh blueberries
2 tablespoons brown sugar
2 tablespoons butter *or* margarine
1 tablespoon lemon juice

Place each peach half, cut side up, on a double thickness of heavy-duty foil (12 in. square). Sprinkle each with about 2 tablespoons blueberries, 1 teaspoon of brown sugar, 1 teaspoon butter and 1/2 teaspoon lemon juice. Fold foil around the peaches and seal tightly. Grill, covered, over medium-low heat for 18-20 minutes or until the peaches are tender. **Yield:** 3 servings.

Campfire Onions

Ready in 30 minutes or less

When cooking out, my family prefers these sweet tender onions instead of potatoes. They make an especially flavorful side dish alongside grilled steaks.
—Barbara Magruder, Odessa, Missouri

4 large sweet onions
1/4 cup butter *or* margarine
1/4 cup honey
1 teaspoon salt
1/8 teaspoon pepper
1/8 teaspoon garlic salt

Cut each onion into 12 wedges; divide between eight pieces of double-layered heavy-duty foil (about 12 in. square). Top onions with butter, honey and seasonings. Fold foil to seal packets tightly. Grill, covered, over medium-hot heat for 20 minutes or until onions are tender, turning once. **Yield:** 8 servings.

Veggie Skewers

(Pictured below)

Ready in 30 minutes or less

I discovered this recipe while trying to spruce up plain vegetables for dinner guests. —Monica Meek Flatford
Knoxville, Tennessee

        2 medium zucchini, cut into 1-inch slices
        2 medium yellow summer squash, cut into
          1-inch slices
      1/2 pound whole fresh mushrooms
      1/3 cup olive *or* vegetable oil
        2 tablespoons lemon juice
    1-1/2 teaspoons dried basil
    1-1/2 teaspoons dried parsley flakes
      3/4 teaspoon garlic powder
      3/4 teaspoon dried oregano
      1/2 teaspoon salt
      1/8 teaspoon pepper

On metal or soaked bamboo skewers, alternately thread zucchini, yellow squash and mushrooms. In a bowl, combine the remaining ingredients. Brush some of the mixture over vegetables. Grill, uncovered, over medium heat for 10-15 minutes or until vegetables are tender, turning and basting occasionally with herb mixture. **Yield:** 4 servings.

Favorite Pork Chops

(Pictured below)

Plan ahead...needs to marinate

As pork raisers, we've served pork many different ways, and this is our absolute favorite. —Alice Hermes
Glen Ullin, North Dakota

        1 cup soy sauce
      1/4 cup diced green pepper
      1/4 cup packed brown sugar
        4 teaspoons chopped onion

**Favorite Pork Chops
Veggie Skewers**

      1/2 teaspoon ground ginger
        2 garlic cloves, minced
        4 pork loin chops (1 inch thick)
        2 teaspoons sugar
        2 teaspoons cornstarch
      1/2 cup water

In a blender, combine first six ingredients; cover and process until smooth. Set aside 2 tablespoons for sauce. Pour remaining marinade into a large resealable plastic bag or shallow glass container. Add pork chops and turn to coat. Seal or cover and refrigerate for 8 hours or overnight; drain and discard marinade. Grill chops, covered, over medium-hot heat for 5-8 minutes on each side or until a meat thermometer reads 160°-170°. In a saucepan, combine sugar, cornstarch, water and reserved soy sauce mixture; stir until smooth. Bring to a boil; cook and stir for 2 minutes or until thickened. Serve over chops. **Yield:** 4 servings.

Campfire Chicken Stew

My family loves these chicken stew packets on camping trips, but they're equally good on our backyard grill.
—Florence Kreis, Beach Park, Illinois

        1 broiler/fryer chicken (3-1/2 to 4 pounds),
          cut up
        3 to 4 medium potatoes, peeled and sliced
        1 cup thinly sliced carrots
        1 medium green pepper, sliced
        1 can (10-3/4 ounces) condensed cream of
          mushroom soup, undiluted
      1/4 cup water
      1/2 teaspoon salt
      1/4 teaspoon pepper

Grill chicken, uncovered, over medium heat for 3 minutes on each side. Place two pieces of chicken each on four pieces of heavy-duty foil (about 18 in. x 12 in.). Divide the potatoes, carrots and green pepper between the four pieces of foil. Top each with 2 tablespoons soup, 1 tablespoon water, salt and pepper. Fold foil around mixture and seal tightly. Grill, covered, over medium heat for 20 minutes; turn and grill 20-25 minutes longer or until vegetables are tender and chicken juices run clear. **Yield:** 4 servings.

Cinnamon Flat Rolls

Ready in 15 minutes or less

I shared this recipe when 4-H leaders requested an activity for younger members. All the kids had a ball rolling out the dough. —Ethel Farnsworth, Yuma, Arizona

        1 package (16 ounces) frozen dinner rolls,
          thawed
        5 tablespoons olive *or* vegetable oil
      1/2 cup sugar
        1 tablespoon ground cinnamon

On a floured surface, roll each dinner roll into a 5-in. circle. Brush with oil. Grill, uncovered, over medium heat for 1 minute on each side or until golden brown (burst

Potato Floret Packets
Grilled Chicken Cordon Bleu

- 6 boneless skinless chicken breast halves
- 6 slices Swiss cheese
- 6 thin slices deli ham
- 3 tablespoons olive *or* vegetable oil
- 3/4 cup seasoned bread crumbs

Flatten the chicken to 1/4-in. thickness. Place a slice of cheese and ham on each to within 1/4 in. of edges. Fold in half; secure with thin metal skewers or toothpicks. Brush with oil and roll in bread crumbs. Grill, covered, over medium-hot heat for 15-18 minutes or until juices run clear. **Yield:** 6 servings.

Red-Hot Apples

Ready in 1 hour or less

I use red-hot candies to turn ordinary apples into something cinnamony and sensational. The treats bake on the grill during dinner.
—*Helen Shubert, Hays, Kansas*

- 4 medium tart apples, cored
- 4 teaspoons brown sugar
- 1/4 cup red-hot candies
Vanilla ice cream, optional

Place each apple in the center of a piece of heavy-duty foil (12 in. square). Spoon 1 teaspoon sugar and 1 tablespoon red-hots into the center of each apple. Fold foil around apple and seal tightly. Grill, covered, over medium-hot heat for 30 minutes or until apples are tender. Carefully transfer apples and syrup to bowls. Serve warm with ice cream if desired. **Yield:** 4 servings.

any large bubbles with a fork). Combine sugar and cinnamon; sprinkle over rolls. **Yield:** 1 dozen.

Potato Floret Packets

(Pictured above)

Ready in 1 hour or less

This dish was developed by my daughter, Betsey, who worked in a group home. This medley was a favorite of the residents there. —*Janet Hayes, Hermantown, Minnesota*

 Uses less fat, sugar or salt. Includes Nutritional Analysis and Diabetic Exchanges.

- 5 medium red potatoes, cubed
- 1 cup fresh broccoli florets
- 1 cup fresh cauliflowerets
- 1 small onion, chopped
- 1/4 teaspoon garlic salt *or* garlic powder
Pepper to taste
- 1/4 cup shredded cheddar cheese

In a bowl, combine the potatoes, broccoli, cauliflower, onion, garlic salt and pepper. Place on a double thickness of heavy-duty foil (about 17 in. x 12 in.). Fold foil around potato mixture and seal tightly. Grill, covered, over medium heat for 30 minutes or until the potatoes are tender. Sprinkle with cheese before serving. **Yield:** 6 servings. **Nutritional Analysis:** One 1-cup serving (prepared with garlic powder and reduced-fat cheese) equals 136 calories, 12 mg sodium, 1 mg cholesterol, 28 gm carbohydrate, 5 gm protein, 1 gm fat, 3 gm fiber. **Diabetic Exchanges:** 1-1/2 starch, 1 vegetable

Grilled Chicken Cordon Bleu

(Pictured above)

Ready in 1 hour or less

You can assemble these delicious chicken bundles up to 8 hours in advance and refrigerate. —*Shawna McCutcheon Homer City, Pennsylvania*

Rice on the Grill

Ready in 30 minutes or less

Since our kids love rice, we prepare this tangy side dish quite often. —*Shirley Hopkins, Olds, Alberta*

 Uses less fat, sugar or salt. Includes Nutritional Analysis and Diabetic Exchanges.

- 1-1/3 cups uncooked instant rice
- 1/3 cup sliced fresh mushrooms
- 1/4 cup chopped green pepper
- 1/4 cup chopped onion
- 1/2 cup chicken broth
- 1/2 cup water
- 1/3 cup ketchup
- 1 tablespoon butter *or* margarine

In a 9-in. round aluminum foil pie pan, combine the first seven ingredients. Dot with butter. Cover with heavy-duty foil; seal edges tightly. Grill, covered, for 14-15 minutes or until liquid is absorbed. Fluff with a fork and serve immediately. **Yield:** 6 servings. **Nutritional Analysis:** One serving (prepared with low-sodium broth and reduced-fat margarine) equals 104 calories, 195 mg sodium, trace cholesterol, 21 gm carbohydrate, 2 gm protein, 2 gm fat, 1 gm fiber. **Diabetic Exchanges:** 1 starch, 1 vegetable.

Microwave Magic

TIME-CONSCIOUS cooks use their microwave ovens for more than just defrosting foods and heating leftovers. They're also marvelous for preparing all kinds of delicious dishes.

Editor's Note: All of these recipes were tested in an 850-watt microwave.

Spinach Potatoes Au Gratin

(Pictured below)

Ready in 30 minutes or less

This creamy mixture of sliced potatoes and spinach makes a pretty side dish. It may sound like it's labor-intensive, but it's not.
—*Edna Shaffer, Beulah, Michigan*

> 5 cups thinly sliced red potatoes (about 7 large)
> 1/4 cup water
> 3 tablespoons butter *or* margarine
> 1/4 cup chopped onion
> 1/4 cup all-purpose flour
> 2 cups milk
> 1 cup (4 ounces) shredded cheddar cheese
> 1 teaspoon salt
> 1 cup chopped fresh spinach
> 1 tablespoon diced pimientos
> 4 bacon strips, cooked and crumbled

In a 2-qt. microwave-safe dish, combine potatoes and water. Cover and microwave on high for 8-9 minutes or until potatoes are tender, stirring twice. Drain; set potatoes aside. In a large microwave-safe bowl, heat butter on high until melted, about 30 seconds. Add onion. Microwave, uncovered, for 1-2 minutes or until tender, stirring once. Whisk in flour until blended. Gradually stir in the milk. Cook, uncovered, on high for 2-1/2 minutes; stir. Cook 3-4 minutes longer, stirring every minute, or until sauce is thickened and bubbly. Stir in cheese and salt. Pour over potatoes. Add spinach and pimientos; mix well. Microwave, uncovered, on high for 2-3 minutes or until heated through, stirring once. Sprinkle with bacon. **Yield:** 8 servings.

Microwave Apple Crisp

Ready in 30 minutes or less

When my siblings and I were young, we loved it when our mom made this old-fashioned-tasting treat. Now I frequently fix this comforting dessert for my family.
—*Sharon Missel, Penfield, New York*

> 6 to 8 medium tart apples, peeled and sliced (8 cups)
> 3/4 cup packed brown sugar, *divided*
> 1/2 cup all-purpose flour, *divided*
> 3/4 cup quick-cooking oats
> 1 teaspoon ground cinnamon
> 1/2 cup cold butter *or* margarine

Toss apples with 1/4 cup of brown sugar and 2 tablespoons of flour; place in a greased 8-in. microwave-safe deep-dish pie plate. In a bowl, combine oats, cinnamon, and remaining brown sugar and flour. Cut in butter until crumbly; sprinkle over apple mixture. Cover with waxed paper. Microwave on high for 10-12 minutes or until the apples are tender. **Yield:** 8 servings.

Mandarin Chicken

Ready in 30 minutes or less

I serve this tender chicken in a sweet sauce over hot rice. With fresh broccoli or asparagus, it makes a special meal for company. —*Maureen Readey, Farmingdale, New York*

 Uses less fat, sugar or salt. Includes Nutritional Analysis and Diabetic Exchanges.

> 4 boneless skinless chicken breast halves (1 pound)
> 2 tablespoons brown sugar
> 2 tablespoons cornstarch
> 1/2 cup teriyaki sauce
> 1/4 cup apple juice
> 1 tablespoon vegetable oil
> 1 garlic clove, minced
> 1 can (11 ounces) mandarin oranges
> Hot cooked rice
> 2 green onions, sliced

Flatten chicken to 1/4-in. thickness. Place in a greased 2-qt. microwave-safe dish. In a bowl, combine brown sugar and cornstarch; stir in the next four ingredients. Drain oranges, reserving juice; set oranges aside. Add juice to teriyaki mixture; pour over chicken. Cover and micro-

Spinach Potatoes Au Gratin

Casserole Chocolate Cake

wave on high for 8 minutes. Baste chicken with sauce. Cover and cook 3-5 minutes longer or until sauce is thickened. Serve over rice. Garnish with onions and oranges. **Yield:** 4 servings. **Nutritional Analysis:** One serving (calculated without rice) equals 245 calories, 425 mg sodium, 68 mg cholesterol, 20 gm carbohydrate, 28 gm protein, 5 gm fat, trace fiber. **Diabetic Exchanges:** 3-1/2 lean meat, 1 fruit, 1/2 starch.

Casserole Chocolate Cake

(Pictured above)

Ready in 1 hour or less

This cake "bakes" in minutes in the microwave, so it's the perfect snack to satisfy my chocolate cravings.
—Julie Finlayson, Greenville, North Carolina

  1/4 cup baking cocoa
  2/3 cup water, *divided*
    1 egg
  1/3 cup vegetable oil
    2 teaspoons vanilla extract
  3/4 cup plus 2 tablespoons all-purpose flour
    1 cup sugar
  1/2 teaspoon baking soda
  1/4 teaspoon baking powder
  1/4 teaspoon salt
FROSTING:
    3 tablespoons butter *or* margarine, softened
1-1/3 cups confectioners' sugar
  1/4 cup baking cocoa
  1/2 teaspoon vanilla extract
    3 to 4 tablespoons milk
    1 cup raspberries, optional
Additional confectioners' sugar

Line the bottom of a greased 8-in. round microwave-safe dish with waxed paper. In a microwave-safe bowl, com-

bine cocoa and 1/3 cup water. Microwave, uncovered, on high for 30-60 seconds or until thickened, stirring once. Add egg, oil, vanilla and remaining water. In a mixing bowl, combine dry ingredients. Add egg mixture; mix well. Pour into prepared dish. Cook, uncovered, on high for 3 minutes. Rotate a half turn. Cook 3-4 minutes longer or until a moist area about 1-1/2 in. in diameter remains in the center (when touched, cake will cling to finger while area underneath will be almost dry). Cool on a wire rack for 10-12 minutes. Invert onto serving plate; discard waxed paper. Cool completely. For frosting, in a mixing bowl, combine butter, sugar, cocoa, vanilla and enough milk to achieve spreading consistency. Frost cake. Top with raspberries and dust with confectioners' sugar. **Yield:** 6-8 servings. **Editor's Note:** This recipe was tested in a 2-qt. round Corning casserole dish.

Microwave Pickles

Plan ahead...needs to chill

You can enjoy a batch of these sweet crunchy pickles anytime without the work of traditional canning methods.
—Marie Wladyka, Land O'Lakes, Florida

    1 medium cucumber, thinly sliced
    2 small onions, thinly sliced
  3/4 cup sugar
  1/2 cup vinegar
    1 teaspoon salt
  1/2 teaspoon celery seed
  1/2 teaspoon mustard seed

In a large microwave-safe bowl, combine all of the ingredients. Microwave, uncovered, on high for 4 minutes; stir. Cook 3-4 minutes longer or until mixture is bubbly and cucumbers and onions are crisp-tender. Cover and refrigerate for at least 4 hours. Serve with a slotted spoon. **Yield:** 4-6 servings.

Horseradish Potatoes

Ready in 15 minutes or less

Looking for a speedy way to dress up potatoes? Try this zippy treatment. When our potatoes are fresh out of the garden, we eat them often, so I try to serve them in different ways. —Myra Innes, Auburn, Kansas

1/4 cup butter *or* margarine
1 tablespoon prepared horseradish
2 teaspoons lemon juice
1/2 teaspoon salt
1/8 teaspoon pepper
12 small new potatoes (about 1-1/4 pounds)

Place butter in an ungreased microwave-safe 1-qt. dish. Microwave, uncovered, on high for 40 seconds or until melted. Stir in horseradish, lemon juice, salt, pepper and potatoes. Cover and microwave on high for 10 minutes, stirring once. Let stand for 2 minutes. Stir before serving. **Yield:** 4 servings.

Swedish Meatballs

(Pictured below)

Ready in 30 minutes or less

This recipe relies on ingredients we always have on hand and doesn't dirty many dishes. While the tender meatballs cook in the microwave, boil the noodles on the stovetop to get this saucy entree on the table in minutes. I'm sure your family will like this as much as mine does.
—Sheryl Ludeman, Kenosha, Wisconsin

1 small onion, chopped
1 egg
1/4 cup seasoned bread crumbs
2 tablespoons milk
1/2 teaspoon salt
1/8 teaspoon pepper
1 pound ground beef

Swedish Meatballs

SAUCE:
1 can (10-3/4 ounces) condensed cream of mushroom soup, undiluted
1/2 cup sour cream
1/4 cup milk
1 tablespoon dried parsley flakes
1/4 teaspoon ground nutmeg, optional
Hot cooked noodles

In a bowl, combine the onion, egg, bread crumbs, milk, salt and pepper. Add beef; mix well. Shape into 1-in. meatballs, about 24. Place in a shallow 1-1/2-qt. microwave-safe dish. Cover and microwave on high for 10 minutes or until meat is no longer pink; drain. Combine the soup, sour cream, milk, parsley and nutmeg if desired; pour over meatballs. Cover and cook on high for 7-8 minutes or until heated through. Serve over noodles. **Yield:** 4 servings.

Raspberry Crumble

Ready in 30 minutes or less

I make the lunch box goodies I send with my son and husband. They love this snack, especially served warm.
—Linda Lundmark, Martinton, Illinois

3/4 cup butter *or* margarine
1 cup packed brown sugar
1-3/4 cups all-purpose flour
1-1/2 cups quick-cooking oats
1 teaspoon vanilla extract
1/2 teaspoon salt
1/2 teaspoon baking soda
1 cup raspberry jam

Place butter in a 2-qt. microwave-safe bowl. Heat, uncovered, at 50% power for 30-45 seconds or until softened. Add brown sugar; stir until creamy. Add flour, oats, vanilla, salt and baking soda; mix well. Pat half of the mixture into a greased 8-in. square microwave-safe dish. Microwave, uncovered, at 70% power for 5-6 minutes or until mixture sets, rotating a half turn after 3 minutes. (Crust will be uneven.) Spread with jam. Sprinkle with remaining dough; press down lightly. Cook, uncovered, at 70% power for 4-5 minutes or until set, rotating a half turn after 2 minutes. Serve warm. **Yield:** 9-12 servings.

Microwave Swiss Steak

Ready in 1 hour or less

I let my microwave do the work with this hassle-free Swiss steak dinner. Because this dish is so simple to assemble, it's perfect after a long day when I don't feel like cooking.
—Grace Ling, Winona, Minnesota

✓ Uses less fat, sugar or salt. Includes Nutritional Analysis and Diabetic Exchanges.

1-1/2 pounds boneless round steak (1/4 inch thick)
3 tablespoons onion soup mix
1 can (4 ounces) mushroom stems and pieces, drained
1 can (14-1/2 ounces) diced tomatoes

2 tablespoons cornstarch
1/4 to 1/2 teaspoon pepper
Dash cayenne pepper, optional

Cut steak into serving-size pieces; pound with a mallet to tenderize. Place the steak in an ungreased shallow microwave-safe dish. Sprinkle with soup mix and mushrooms. Drain tomatoes, reserving liquid; set tomatoes aside. In a bowl, combine the cornstarch and tomato liquid until smooth. Add pepper, cayenne if desired and tomatoes. Pour over meat. Cover and microwave on high for 6-7 minutes or until mixture begins to boil. Microwave, covered, at 50% power for 20 minutes. Turn meat and rotate dish. Cover and cook at 50% power 20-25 minutes longer or until meat is tender. **Yield:** 6 servings. **Nutritional Analysis:** One serving (prepared with reduced-sodium onion soup mix and no-salt-added whole tomatoes) equals 201 calories, 308 mg sodium, 70 mg cholesterol, 10 gm carbohydrate, 28 gm protein, 4 gm fat, 2 gm fiber. **Diabetic Exchanges:** 3 lean meat, 2 vegetable.

Italian Meat Loaf

(Pictured at right)

Ready in 1 hour or less

I received the recipe for this moist meat loaf in my high school home economics class. At the time, I made it for my mom and dad. Now I fix it for my husband and daughter. We all love it. —Lisa Malone, Cordell, Oklahoma

  1 egg, beaten
  1 can (8 ounces) tomato sauce, *divided*
1/2 cup dry bread crumbs
1/2 cup finely chopped onion, optional
1/2 cup finely chopped green pepper, optional
  1 teaspoon dried oregano, *divided*
  1 teaspoon salt
1/8 teaspoon pepper
1-1/2 pounds ground beef
1/2 cup shredded mozzarella cheese
  2 tablespoons grated Parmesan cheese

In a bowl, combine the egg, half of the tomato sauce, bread crumbs, onion and green pepper if desired, 1/2 teaspoon of oregano, salt and pepper. Add beef; mix well. On a large piece of heavy-duty foil, pat meat mixture into a 14-in. x 8-in. rectangle. Sprinkle cheeses to within 1/2 in. of edges. Roll up, jelly-roll style, starting with a short side and peeling foil away while rolling. Seal seam and ends. Transfer to a microwave-safe 9-in. x 5-in. x 3-in. loaf pan. Microwave, uncovered, at 50% power for 12 minutes, rotating a half turn once; drain. Continue cooking on 50% power for 20 minutes or until

Salad with Egg Dressing
Italian Meat Loaf

meat is no longer pink, rotating a half turn once. In a bowl, combine remaining tomato sauce and oregano. Pour over meat loaf. Microwave, uncovered, on high for 2 minutes. Cover loosely with foil; let stand 5 minutes before serving. **Yield:** 6 servings.

Salad with Egg Dressing

(Pictured above)

Ready in 15 minutes or less

Egg sparks the flavor of this pleasantly sweet cooked dressing. I serve it warm over greens tossed with bacon bits, tomato and more. Besides lettuce, it's also good over fresh spinach or cabbage. —Mary Bloom
Titusville, Pennsylvania

  2 eggs, beaten
1/2 cup sugar
1/4 cup water
1/4 cup vinegar
  8 cups mixed salad greens
  1 small onion, chopped
  4 bacon slices, cooked and crumbled
  1 medium tomato, cut into wedges
1/2 cup sliced cucumber

In a microwave-safe bowl, combine the eggs, sugar and water. Microwave, uncovered, on high for 1 minute. Stir in vinegar; cook for 1 to 1-1/2 minutes or until a thermometer reads 160°. Meanwhile, in a salad bowl, combine greens, onion, bacon, tomato and cucumber. Drizzle with warm dressing; toss to coat. **Yield:** 6-8 servings.

Meat Loaf in Minutes

Does your family love meat loaf? To shorten the cooking time, bake individual servings in a muffin pan. The smaller portions of the meat mixture cook more rapidly than a single loaf.

To save even more time, use a microwave-safe muffin pan and cook your entree in the microwave.
—Nora Beck, Crossville, Tennessee

Herbed Green Beans
Speedy Sweet Potatoes

2 tablespoons water
1/2 cup chopped onion
1/4 cup finely chopped celery
1 to 3 tablespoons butter *or* margarine
1 garlic clove, minced
1/2 teaspoon dried rosemary, crushed
1/2 teaspoon dried basil

Place the beans and water in a 2-qt. microwave-safe dish. Cover and microwave on high for 4-6 minutes or until tender; set aside. In another dish, combine the remaining ingredients. Cover and cook on high for 2 minutes or until onion is tender. Drain beans. Drizzle with onion mixture; toss to coat. **Yield:** 6 servings.

Flip-Over Pizza

Ready in 30 minutes or less

Your family is sure to enjoy this easy pizza that you flip over before serving. We like it in summer when we don't want to heat up the house.
—Karen Duncan, Franklin, Nebraska

1 pound ground beef
1 celery rib, chopped
1 medium onion, chopped
1/4 cup chopped green pepper
1 can (10-1/2 ounces) pizza sauce
Salt to taste
3/4 cup biscuit/baking mix
3 to 4 tablespoons milk
3/4 cup shredded mozzarella cheese
2 tablespoons grated Parmesan cheese

Crumble beef into a microwave-safe 9-in. pie plate. Sprinkle with celery, onion and green pepper. Cover and microwave on high for 7 minutes or until meat is no longer pink and vegetables are tender, stirring once; drain. Stir in the pizza sauce and salt. Combine biscuit mix and milk just until combined. Roll out on a lightly floured surface into a 9-in. circle; place over meat mixture. Cook, uncovered, on high for 8 minutes or until a toothpick inserted into crust comes out clean. Invert onto a serving plate. Sprinkle with cheeses. **Yield:** 4 servings.

Speedy Sweet Potatoes

(Pictured above)

Ready in 15 minutes or less

I discovered this yummy sweet potato recipe years ago. There's no need for lots of butter and sugar, because the pineapple and marshmallows provide plenty of sweetness. It's a holiday favorite at our house. —Beth Buhler
Lawrence, Kansas

2 cans (16 ounces *each*) sweet potatoes, drained
1/2 teaspoon salt
1 can (8 ounces) crushed pineapple, drained
1/4 cup coarsely chopped pecans
1 tablespoon brown sugar
1 cup miniature marshmallows, *divided*
Ground nutmeg

In a 1-1/2-qt. microwave-safe dish, layer sweet potatoes, salt, pineapple, pecans, brown sugar and 1/2 cup marshmallows. Cover and microwave on high for 5-7 minutes or until bubbly around the edges. Top with the remaining marshmallows. Heat, uncovered, on high for 1-2 minutes or until marshmallows puff. Sprinkle with nutmeg. **Yield:** 6 servings.

Herbed Green Beans

(Pictured above)

Ready in 30 minutes or less

Rosemary and basil complement green beans, celery and onion in this savory side dish. My mother always cooked with fresh herbs from her garden. Now I find myself doing the same. —Ruth Andrewson, Peck, Idaho

1 pound fresh green beans, cut into 2-inch pieces

Barbecued Pork Chops

Ready in 30 minutes or less

Homemade barbecue sauce tops these moist, tender chops. We like to use the microwave and love this recipe because it's so quick and easy to prepare. —David Bray
Hoover, Alabama

6 boneless pork chops (1/2 inch thick)
1 medium onion, chopped
1 cup ketchup
1/2 cup water
1/2 cup chopped celery
2 tablespoons lemon juice
1 tablespoon brown sugar
1 tablespoon Worcestershire sauce
1/2 teaspoon salt

1/2 teaspoon ground mustard
1 teaspoon cornstarch
1 tablespoon cold water

Place porks chops in an ungreased 11-in. x 7-in. x 2-in. microwave-safe dish. In a bowl, combine the next nine ingredients. Pour over the chops. Cover with plastic wrap; peel back one corner to vent. Microwave on high for 18-20 minutes or until juices run clear. Remove chops; set aside and keep warm. In a small bowl, combine cornstarch and cold water until smooth. Stir into barbecue sauce. Microwave for 1 minute or until thickened. Serve sauce over chops. **Yield:** 6 servings.

Crumb-Topped Scallops

Ready in 15 minutes or less

A pretty crumb topping blankets this tasty seafood entree. I won't make scallops any other way. —*Kathy Brodin*
Wauwatosa, Wisconsin

✓ Uses less fat, sugar or salt. Includes Nutritional Analysis and Diabetic Exchanges.

1/4 cup dry bread crumbs
1 tablespoon butter *or* margarine, melted
1 to 2 teaspoons dried parsley flakes
1 pound sea scallops
6 fresh mushrooms, quartered
1 tablespoon white wine *or* chicken broth
1-1/2 teaspoons lemon juice
1/4 teaspoon dried thyme
1/8 teaspoon garlic powder
1/8 teaspoon seasoned salt
1/8 teaspoon pepper
Lemon wedges, optional

In a small bowl, combine bread crumbs, butter and parsley; set aside. Place scallops and mushrooms in a 9-in. microwave-safe pie plate. Combine wine or broth, lemon juice and seasonings; pour over scallop mixture. Cover and microwave at 50% power for 2 minutes; drain. Sprinkle with crumb mixture. Cover and microwave at 50% power 4-1/2 minutes longer or until scallops are opaque, stirring once. Serve with lemon if desired. **Yield:** 4 servings. **Nutritional Analysis:** One serving (prepared with margarine and low-sodium broth) equals 162 calories, 321 mg sodium, 38 mg cholesterol, 10 gm carbohydrate, 21 gm protein, 4 gm fat, 1 gm fiber. **Diabetic Exchanges:** 3 very lean meat, 1/2 starch.

Cashew Brittle

(Pictured at right)

Ready in 30 minutes or less

I like this quick-and-easy recipe because it doesn't require a candy thermometer. It also makes a great gift.
—*Rhonda Glenn, Prince Frederick, Maryland*

1 cup sugar
1/2 cup light corn syrup
1 to 1-1/2 cups salted cashew halves

1 teaspoon butter (no substitutes)
1 teaspoon baking soda
1 teaspoon vanilla extract

In a microwave-safe bowl, combine the sugar and corn syrup. Microwave, uncovered, on high for 4 minutes; stir. Heat 3 minutes longer. Stir in cashews and butter. Microwave on high for 30-60 seconds or until mixture turns a light amber (mixture will be very hot). Quickly stir in baking soda and vanilla until light and foamy. Immediately pour onto a greased baking sheet and spread with a metal spatula. Chill for 20 minutes or until set; break into small pieces. Store in an airtight container. **Yield:** 3/4 pound.

Sweet Pretzel Nuggets

(Pictured below)

Ready in 30 minutes or less

This crowd-pleasing snack has been a tremendous hit both at home and at work. The fun crunchy bites have a sweet cinnamon-toast taste and just a hint of saltiness that make them very munchable. —*Billie Sue Ebinger*
Holton, Indiana

1 package (15 to 18 ounces) sourdough pretzel nuggets
2/3 cup vegetable oil
1/3 cup sugar
1 to 2 teaspoons ground cinnamon

Place pretzels in a microwave-safe bowl. In a small bowl, combine oil, sugar and cinnamon; pour over pretzels; toss to coat. Microwave, uncovered, on high for 2 minutes; stir. Microwave 3-4 minutes longer, stirring after each minute or until oil is absorbed. Cool to room temperature. **Yield:** 12-16 servings.

Cashew Brittle
Sweet Pretzel Nuggets

HERE'S a collection of reliable theme-related recipes that are tops for taste and time-saving.

When you want to prepare old-fashioned fare but don't have a second to spare, reach for streamlined "makeover" recipes that cut preparation time but not taste.

Kick-start fast, flavorful meals with zippy garlic or with two versatile ingredients—rice and chicken breasts.

Looking to capture the flavors of summer or slice a bit of time from holiday baking? This chapter offers recipes for campfire cuisine and easy icebox cookies.

And if you have a smaller household, you'll appreciate the perfectly portioned dishes that are great for the two of you.

OUTDOOR DINING. Top to bottom: S'mores Bars, Orange Vegetable Kabobs and Honey-Lime Grilled Chicken (all recipes on p. 297).

Makeovers Make Favorites Faster

THESE RECIPE "rehabs" from the home economists in our test kitchen trim ingredients and preparation time—not taste—for delicious old-fashioned dishes. The home-style flavors are so appealing you might even fool Grandma!

WHEN IT COMES to serving an extra-special dessert to company, Mary Ann Kosmas of Minneapolis, Minnesota relies on Traditional Caramel Flan.

The delectable dessert is baked over a layer of caramelized sugar, so when it's inverted, a delicious golden sauce runs down the edges of the flan and forms a pool on the serving platter.

"This smooth egg custard looks so elegant and tastes so rich," Mary Ann relates. "But I only make it for special occasions, because it's time-consuming. It needs to bake for about an hour, cool at room temperature, then be thoroughly chilled."

To get the palate-pleasing flavor and texture in less time, our test kitchen staff came up with Quicker Caramel Flan.

This shortcut version is made with convenient caramel ice cream topping to reduce prep time. Since it's prepared in individual custard cups, the baking time is nearly cut in half.

Traditional Caramel Flan

Plan ahead…needs to chill

1-1/4 cups sugar, *divided*
2-3/4 cups milk
5 eggs
1/8 teaspoon salt
1 teaspoon vanilla extract

In a heavy saucepan or skillet over medium-low, heat 3/4 cup sugar. As sugar begins to melt, slowly stir until all granules are melted into a smooth golden syrup. Quickly pour into an ungreased souffle dish or 2-qt. round baking dish, tilting to coat the bottom of the dish. Let stand for 10 minutes. Meanwhile, in a saucepan, heat milk until steaming. In a bowl, whisk eggs, salt and remaining sugar. Stir 1 cup of warm milk into egg mixture; return all to pan and mix well. Add vanilla. Pour into prepared pan. Place dish in a large baking pan. Pour boiling water into pan to a depth of 1 in. Bake at 325° for 55-60 minutes or until center is just set (mixture will jiggle). Remove flan dish to a wire rack; cool for 1 hour. Refrigerate for 3-4 hours or until thoroughly chilled. Run a knife around edge and invert onto a rimmed serving platter. **Yield:** 6 servings.

Quicker Caramel Flan

(Pictured below)

Plan ahead…needs to chill

5 eggs
1/2 cup sugar
1 teaspoon vanilla extract
1/8 teaspoon salt
2-1/2 cups milk
2 tablespoons caramel ice cream topping

In a bowl, lightly beat eggs. Add sugar, vanilla and salt; mix well. Gradually stir in milk. Divide caramel topping among six ungreased 6-oz. custard cups, 1 teaspoon in each. Place cups in a 13-in. x 9-in. x 2-in. baking dish. Pour egg mixture into each cup (cups will be full). Fill baking dish with hot water to a depth of 1 in. Bake, uncovered, at 350° for 30-35 minutes or until center of each is almost set (mixture will jiggle). Remove custard cups from water to a wire rack; cool for 30 minutes. Refrigerate for 3 hours or until thoroughly chilled. Invert and unmold onto rimmed dessert dishes. **Yield:** 6 servings.

Quicker Caramel Flan

MAKING homemade yeast bread has been a frustrating endeavor for Kelly Jo Yaksich. For quite a long time, the St. Cloud, Minnesota cook has been trying to produce a fresh-baked loaf of bread using a recipe she received from a special neighbor.

"About 14 years ago, my husband and I were newly married and had just moved to Seattle, Washington, 2,000 miles from our families," she relates.

"A wonderful lady in our neighborhood, Gloria Rose, took me under her wing and shared many fabulous recipes with me. Her recipe for whole wheat bread became one of our favorites," Kelly Jo notes.

"Gloria and I were determined that I'd learn to make this homemade bread, but to no avail. Every batch I made would flop terribly," she recalls.

"For years I tried to make Gloria's Traditional Wheat Bread by hand until I received a bread machine as a gift from my brother-in-law. I attempted to adapt her recipe to use in my machine, but was unsuccessful. Can you try?"

To help Kelly Jo enjoy this bread whenever she wants, our test kitchen staff came up with Bread Machine Wheat Bread.

To fit her bread machine, our home economists adjusted the amounts of ingredients to produce one loaf rather than three. While this version retains the same sweet taste and tender texture as the original loaf, there's no need to knead the dough by hand.

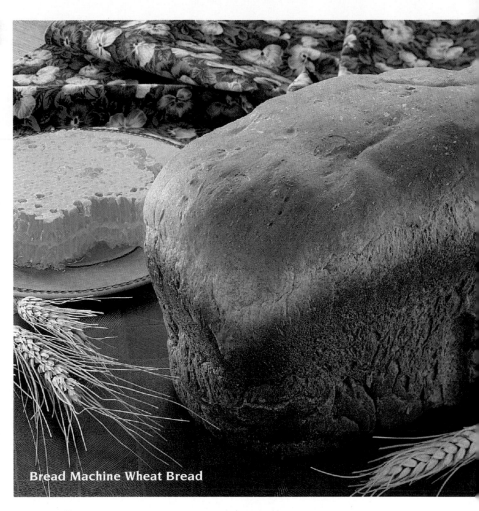

Bread Machine Wheat Bread

Traditional Wheat Bread

3-1/2 to 4 cups bread flour, *divided*
2-1/2 cups whole wheat flour, *divided*
    2 tablespoons active dry yeast
    1 tablespoon salt
    1 cup milk
    1 cup water
1/2 cup honey
    3 tablespoons butter *or* margarine
    1 egg
All-purpose flour

In a mixing bowl, combine 2 cups bread flour, 1 cup whole wheat flour, yeast and salt. In a saucepan, heat the milk, water, honey and butter to 120°-130°. Stir into dry ingredients just until moistened. Beat in egg until smooth. Stir in the remaining whole wheat flour and enough remaining bread flour to form a stiff dough. Turn onto a surface lightly dusted with all-purpose flour; knead until smooth and elastic, 8-10 minutes. Place in a greased bowl, turning once to grease top. Cover and let rise in a warm place until doubled, about 1 hour.

Punch dough down; let rest 10 minutes. Divide into thirds; shape into loaves. Place in three greased 9-in. x 5-in. x 3-in. loaf pans. Cover and let rise until doubled, about 45 minutes. Bake at 350° for 35-40 minutes or until golden. Cover loosely with foil if tops brown too fast. Remove from pans to wire racks to cool. **Yield:** 3 loaves.

Bread Machine Wheat Bread

(Pictured above)

1/2 cup milk (70° to 80°)
1/2 cup water (70° to 80°)
    1 egg
    3 tablespoons honey
    2 tablespoons butter *or* margarine, softened
1-1/2 teaspoons salt
    2 cups bread flour
    1 cup whole wheat flour
2-1/4 teaspoons active dry yeast

In bread machine pan, place all ingredients in order suggested by manufacturer. Select basic bread setting. Choose crust color and loaf size if available. Bake according to bread machine directions (check dough after 5 minutes of mixing; add 1 to 2 tablespoons of water or flour if needed). **Yield:** 1 loaf (1-1/2 pounds). **Editor's Note:** Use of the timer feature is not recommended for this recipe.

It Takes Two!

ARE YOU STUCK in a rut, serving the same old ingredients in the same old ways? These recipes transform versatile rice and popular boneless chicken breasts into three deliciously different dishes.

Chicken Carrot Pilaf

(Pictured below right)

Ready in 1 hour or less

While this colorful stovetop supper is perfect for everyday family meals, it makes a lovely company dinner, too.
—Frances Musser, Newmanstown, Pennsylvania

 Uses less fat, sugar or salt. Includes Nutritional Analysis and Diabetic Exchanges.

> 1 pound boneless skinless chicken breasts, cut into thin strips
> 1/4 cup butter *or* margarine
> 1-1/2 cups uncooked long grain rice
> 5 medium carrots, sliced
> 1 medium onion, chopped
> 1/2 cup sliced fresh mushrooms
> 1/4 cup chopped sweet red pepper
> 4 cups chicken broth
> 2 tablespoons minced fresh parsley

In a large skillet, brown chicken in butter. Remove and keep warm. Add rice, carrots, onion, mushrooms and red pepper to the skillet. Cook and stir until rice is browned and onion is tender. Stir in broth. Place chicken over rice mixture. Bring to a boil. Reduce heat; cover and simmer for 20-25 minutes or until rice is tender. Stir in parsley. Let stand 5 minutes before serving. **Yield:** 6 servings. **Nutritional Analysis:** One serving (prepared with reduced-fat margarine and low-sodium broth) equals 355 calories, 245 mg sodium, 46 mg cholesterol, 48 gm carbohydrate, 24 gm protein, 7 gm fat, 3 gm fiber. **Diabetic Exchanges:** 2-1/2 meat, 2 starch, 1-1/2 vegetable.

Creamy Chicken Hot Dish

(Pictured at right)

Ready in 1 hour or less

A potato chip topping adds some crunch to this creamy mixture. —Frances Walker, Jonesboro, Arkansas

> 2 celery ribs, chopped
> 1 small onion, chopped
> 1 tablespoon butter *or* margarine
> 1-1/2 cups mayonnaise*
> 1 can (10-3/4 ounces) condensed cream of chicken soup, undiluted
> 1 cup frozen peas, thawed
> 1 tablespoon lemon juice
> 1 teaspoon salt
> 3 cups cubed cooked chicken

> 2 cups cooked rice
> 1 cup crushed potato chips

In a small skillet, saute celery and onion in butter until crisp-tender. Place in a bowl; add the mayonnaise, soup, peas, lemon juice and salt. Stir in chicken and rice. Transfer to a greased 11-in. x 7-in. x 2-in. baking dish. Sprinkle with potato chips. Bake, uncovered, at 350° for 25-30 minutes or until heated through. **Yield:** 6 servings. ***Editor's Note:** Light or fat-free mayonnaise may not be substituted for regular mayonnaise.

Spicy Chicken Rice Soup

Ready in 1 hour or less

This zesty chicken and rice soup is brimming with flavor and color. —Elaine Grover, Santa Maria, California

 Uses less fat, sugar or salt. Includes Nutritional Analysis and Diabetic Exchanges.

> 4 cups chicken broth
> 2 cups cubed cooked chicken
> 2 celery ribs, chopped
> 2 medium carrots, chopped
> 1 medium green pepper, chopped
> 1 medium onion, chopped
> 1/3 cup uncooked long grain rice
> 1/4 cup minced fresh cilantro *or* parsley
> 1/2 teaspoon dried oregano
> 1/2 teaspoon salt, optional
> 1/2 teaspoon pepper
> 1/4 teaspoon ground cumin
> 1/8 to 1/4 teaspoon crushed red pepper flakes

In a large saucepan, combine all ingredients. Bring to a boil. Reduce heat; cover and simmer for 20-25 minutes or until rice and vegetables are tender. **Yield:** 6 servings. **Nutritional Analysis:** One serving (prepared with low-sodium broth and without salt) equals 135 calories, 100 mg sodium, 31 mg cholesterol, 17 gm carbohydrate, 11 gm protein, 3 gm fat, 2 gm fiber. Diabetic **Exchanges:** 1-1/2 very lean meat, 1 starch.

Creamy Chicken Hot Dish
Chicken Carrot Pilaf

Campfire Cuisine

S'mores Bars
Orange Vegetable Kabobs
Honey-Lime Grilled Chicken

WHETHER you prefer to pitch a tent in the wilderness or make camp closer to home, your family will enjoy this fun outdoor menu.

Honey-Lime Grilled Chicken

(Also pictured on page 292)

Plan ahead...needs to marinate

This easy marinade requires only three ingredients and gives fabulous lime flavor to tender chicken breasts. —Dorothy Smith, El Dorado, Arkansas

    1/2 cup honey
    1/3 cup soy sauce
    1/4 cup lime juice
      4 boneless skinless chicken breast halves

In a resealable plastic bag or shallow glass container, combine the honey, soy sauce and lime juice; mix well. Add chicken and turn to coat. Seal or cover and refrigerate for 30-45 minutes. Drain and discard marinade. Grill chicken, uncovered, over medium heat for 6-7 minutes on each side or until juices run clear. **Yield:** 4 servings.

Orange Vegetable Kabobs

(Also pictured on page 292)

Ready in 1 hour or less

I created this recipe to add some zip to grilled vegetables. Their color, crispness and taste are tempting to all ages. — Laurie Whitney, Bradford, Massachusetts

 Uses less fat, sugar or salt. Includes Nutritional Analysis and Diabetic Exchanges.

      1 large sweet onion
      1 large unpeeled navel orange
      1 medium sweet red pepper, cut into
        1-inch pieces
      1 medium sweet yellow pepper, cut into
        1-inch pieces
      8 medium fresh mushrooms
      8 cherry tomatoes
      2 small yellow summer squash, cut into
        1-inch slices
    MARINADE:
    1/2 cup olive *or* vegetable oil
    1/3 cup lemon juice
    1-1/2 teaspoons sugar
      1 teaspoon salt, optional
    1/4 teaspoon garlic powder
    1/4 teaspoon pepper
      2 tablespoons orange juice

Cut the onion and orange into eight wedges; halve each wedge. Alternately thread vegetables and orange pieces onto eight metal or soaked wooden skewers. Place in a shallow oblong dish. In a bowl, whisk together the oil, lemon juice, sugar, salt if desired, garlic powder and pepper. Pour over skewers. Marinate for 15 minutes, turning and basting frequently. Grill, covered, over indirect heat for 10-15 minutes or until the vegetables are crisp-tender. Brush with orange juice just before serving. **Yield:** 8 kabobs. **Nutritional Analysis:** One kabob (calculated without salt) equals 111 calories, 13 mg sodium, 0 cholesterol, 12 gm carbohydrate, 2 gm protein, 7 gm fat, 3 gm fiber. **Diabetic Exchanges:** 2 vegetable, 1 fat.

S'mores Bars

(Also pictured on page 292)

Glowing campfire coals are not needed to enjoy the traditional taste of s'mores with this recipe.
—Kristine Brown, Rio Rancho, New Mexico

      8 to 10 whole graham crackers (about 5 inches
        x 2-1/2 inches)
      1 package fudge brownie mix (13-inch x 9-inch
        pan size)
      2 cups miniature marshmallows
      1 cup (6 ounces) semisweet chocolate chips
    2/3 cup chopped peanuts

Arrange graham crackers in a single layer in a greased 13-in. x 9-in. x 2-in. baking pan. Prepare the brownie batter according to package directions. Spread over crackers. Bake at 350° for 25-30 minutes or until a toothpick inserted near the center comes out clean. Sprinkle with marshmallows, chocolate chips and peanuts. Bake 5 minutes longer or until marshmallows are slightly puffed and golden brown. Cool on a wire rack before cutting. **Yield:** 2 dozen.

Dressed-Up Steak Salad

In a jar with a tight-fitting lid, combine the first six ingredients; shake well. Refrigerate until serving. In a small bowl, combine marinade ingredients. Brush on both sides of steak; let stand for 30 minutes. Broil steak 4 in. from the heat for 5-6 minutes on each side or until meat reaches desired doneness. Meanwhile, on two plates, arrange the greens, tomato, avocado and onion. Thinly slice the steak; place on top of the salads. Serve with dressing. **Yield:** 2 servings.

Glazed Ham Slice

(Pictured below)

Ready in 30 minutes or less

This pineapple-topped ham slice is a snap to cook on top of the stove. For a fast finish, serve it with two simple side dishes. Pair a long grain and wild rice mix with frozen peas, or try scalloped potatoes and frozen green beans.

> 1 fully cooked ham slice (about 3/4 pound and 1/2 inch thick)
> 1 tablespoon butter *or* margarine
> 1 can (8 ounces) sliced pineapple
> 1-1/2 teaspoons cornstarch
> 2 tablespoons honey
> 1 tablespoon steak sauce
> 1 tablespoon Dijon mustard

Cut ham slice in half. In a skillet, cook ham in butter for 3-4 minutes on each side or until heated through. Meanwhile, drain pineapple, reserving the juice. Set aside two pineapple slices; refrigerate remaining pineapple for another use. In a bowl, combine cornstarch, pineapple juice, honey, steak sauce and mustard until smooth. Remove ham and keep warm. Add honey mixture to skillet. Bring to a boil over medium-low heat; cook for 1-2 minutes. Return ham to skillet; top with the reserved pineapple slices. Spoon glaze over the top; heat through. **Yield:** 2 servings.

Dinner Duets

SPEEDY SUPPERS that feed a crowd can hit the right note for large households, family get-togethers and church potlucks. But those meals are not always in harmony with folks cooking for one or two.

So our test kitchen came up with four recipes for main dishes that serve two people. (These recipes are great for singles, too. Just wrap and refrigerate the extras so you can enjoy a homemade meal the next day.)

Dressed-Up Steak Salad

(Pictured above)

Plan ahead...needs to marinate

This sirloin salad gets its fresh taste from tomato, red onion and avocado. Steak sauce gives the light dressing its delicious difference. To complete the meal, serve soft breadsticks and lemon sherbet.

> 1/3 cup vegetable oil
> 2 tablespoons lime juice
> 1 tablespoon steak sauce
> 1 tablespoon cider *or* red wine vinegar
> 1/2 teaspoon Dijon mustard
> 1/4 teaspoon salt
> MARINADE:
> 2 tablespoons steak sauce
> 1 teaspoon vegetable oil
> 1 teaspoon lime juice
> 1/8 to 1/4 teaspoon hot pepper sauce
> SALAD:
> 1/2 pound boneless sirloin steak
> 3 cups torn mixed salad greens
> 1 medium tomato, cut into wedges
> 1 small ripe avocado, peeled and cubed
> 2 slices red onion, separated into rings

Glazed Ham Slice

Dijon Chicken

(Pictured below)

Ready in 30 minutes or less

Tender chicken breasts are browned to a golden color, then served over a rice blend. A tangy sauce complements this main dish perfectly. Add spinach salad with bacon dressing and cookies, and you have a meal.

  1/3 cup prepared ranch salad dressing
    1 tablespoon Dijon mustard
    2 boneless skinless chicken breast halves
    2 tablespoons butter *or* margarine
    3 tablespoons white wine *or* chicken broth
Hot cooked long grain and wild rice *or* pasta
Fresh parsley, optional

In a small bowl, combine salad dressing and mustard; set aside. In a skillet, cook chicken in butter over medium heat for 8-10 minutes or until juices run clear. Remove and keep warm. Add wine or broth to skillet; cook over medium heat for 2 minutes, stirring to loosen browned bits from pan. Whisk in mustard mixture; cook and stir until blended and heated through. Serve over chicken and rice. Garnish with parsley if desired. **Yield:** 2 servings.

Stuffed Pork Tenderloin

(Pictured above right)

Plan ahead…needs to marinate

These taste-tempting slices of pork tenderloin are marinated overnight, then filled with a flavorful apple stuffing. For a simple side dish, prepare steamed broccoli with lemon or garlic brussels sprouts. To complete the meal, serve pumpkin pie with whipped topping or warm apple crisp with ice cream.

  1/3 cup apple jelly
    2 tablespoons lemon juice
    2 tablespoons soy sauce
    2 tablespoons vegetable oil

Stuffed Pork Tenderloin

  1/2 teaspoon ground ginger
    2 pork tenderloins (about 1/2 pound *each*)
  1/2 cup chopped tart apple
  1/2 cup soft bread crumbs
    2 tablespoons finely chopped celery
    2 tablespoons chopped pecans
  1/2 cup apple juice

In a saucepan, combine the first five ingredients. Cook and stir until the jelly is melted; cover and refrigerate 4-1/2 teaspoons. Slice each tenderloin lengthwise to within 1/2 in. of the bottom. Place in a large resealable plastic bag. Add remaining jelly mixture. Seal and refrigerate for 4 hours or overnight. Place meat in a 9-in. square baking dish; discard marinade. In a bowl, combine apple, bread crumbs, celery, pecans and reserved jelly mixture. Spoon apple mixture down the center of tenderloins; secure with toothpicks. Drizzle with apple juice. Cover and bake at 375° for 30 minutes. Uncover; bake 10 minutes longer or until a meat thermometer reads 160°. Discard toothpicks. Let stand for 10 minutes before slicing. **Yield:** 2 servings.

Dijon Chicken

Recipes Showcase Garlic's Goodness

FOR SOME cooks, garlic isn't everything...it's the only thing! Whether you're a die-hard fan of the robust cloves or just someone looking to pep up your menu, you'll enjoy these tempting reader recipes that celebrate the goodness of garlic.

Baked Garlic Chicken

Plan ahead...needs to marinate

I serve this tender chicken with rice and green beans cooked in chicken broth. Its rich, crispy coating is golden and nicely seasoned with garlic, celery salt and paprika.
—*Suzanne Zick, Osceola, Arkansas*

        2 cups (16 ounces) sour cream
        2 tablespoons lemon juice
        4 garlic cloves, minced
        4 teaspoons celery salt
        4 teaspoons Worcestershire sauce
        2 teaspoons paprika
    1/2 teaspoon pepper
        8 boneless skinless chicken breast halves
        2 cups crushed butter-flavored crackers
           (about 50)
    1/2 cup butter *or* margarine, melted
    1/4 cup vegetable oil

In a large shallow glass dish, combine the first seven ingredients. Add chicken; turn to coat. Cover and refrigerate for 3-4 hours. Place cracker crumbs in a shallow bowl; roll chicken in crumbs until coated. Transfer to a greased 13-in. x 9-in. x 2-in. baking dish. Combine butter and oil; pour over the chicken. Bake, uncovered, at 350° for 50-60 minutes or until chicken juices run clear. **Yield:** 8 servings.

Citrus Garlic Shrimp

(Pictured at right)

Ready in 30 minutes or less

Garlic is paired with sunny citrus in this special shrimp and linguine combination. This is one of my husband's favorites.
—*Diane Jackson, Las Vegas, Nevada*

    1/2 cup olive *or* vegetable oil
    1/2 cup orange juice
    1/3 cup lemon juice
        3 to 4 garlic cloves, minced
        5 teaspoons grated lemon peel
        4 teaspoons grated orange peel
        1 teaspoon salt
    1/4 teaspoon pepper
        1 package (1 pound) linguine
        1 pound uncooked medium
           shrimp, peeled and deveined

       Shredded Parmesan cheese and minced fresh
          parsley

In a blender or food processor, combine the first eight ingredients; cover and process until blended. Pour into a large skillet; heat through. Meanwhile, cook linguine according to package directions. Add shrimp to garlic mixture; cook for 5 minutes or until shrimp turn pink. Thicken if desired. Drain linguine; top with shrimp. Sprinkle with Parmesan cheese and parsley. **Yield:** 6 servings.

Garlic Cheese Bread

(Pictured below)

Ready in 15 minutes or less

French bread is made fabulous when slices are spread with this creamy mouth-watering blend. —*Victoria Newman Antelope, California*

        1 package (8 ounces) cream cheese, softened
    1/4 cup sour cream
    1/4 cup grated Parmesan cheese
        2 tablespoons mayonnaise
        2 tablespoons minced fresh parsley
        1 tablespoon minced green onions
        6 to 8 garlic cloves, minced
        1 loaf (1 pound) French bread, cut into
           1-inch slices

In a mixing bowl, combine the first seven ingredients. Beat until blended. Spread on one side of each slice of bread and place on ungreased baking sheets. Broil 4 in. from the heat for 3 minutes or until cheese is melted and lightly browned. **Yield:** 8-10 servings.

Garlic Cheese Bread
Citrus Garlic Shrimp

Chill Out with Icebox Cookies

Neapolitan Cookies

WHEN you're making holiday plans, don't forget to add convenient slice-and-bake cookies to your list. They're a surefire time-saver during the Christmas rush.

These recipes fit into the busiest of schedules because they allow you to mix up the dough ahead of time and store it in the fridge.

Then, when you have a few free minutes, just slice the dough, fill your cookie sheets and bake. (For very thin kinds, like the Neapolitan Cookies shown at right, try freezing the dough to make slicing easier.)

Neapolitan Cookies

(Pictured at right)

These crisp cookies are fun to eat—one section at a time or with all three in one bite. —Jan Mallo
White Pigeon, Michigan

 1 cup butter (no substitutes), softened
1-1/2 cups sugar
 1 egg
 1 teaspoon vanilla extract
2-1/2 cups all-purpose flour
1-1/2 teaspoons baking powder
 1/2 teaspoon salt
 1/2 teaspoon almond extract
 6 drops red liquid food coloring
 1/2 cup chopped walnuts
 1 square (1 ounce) unsweetened baking
  chocolate, melted

Line a 9-in. x 5-in. x 3-in. loaf pan with waxed paper; set aside. In a mixing bowl, cream butter and sugar. Beat in egg and vanilla. Combine flour, baking powder and salt; gradually add to the creamed mixture. Divide the dough into thirds. Add almond extract and food coloring to one portion; spread evenly into prepared pan. Add nuts to second portion; spread evenly over first layer. Add melted chocolate to third portion; spread over second layer. Cover with waxed paper; refrigerate overnight. Unwrap; cut loaf in half lengthwise. Cut each portion into 1/8-in. slices. Place 1 in. apart on ungreased baking sheets. Bake at 350° for 10-12 minutes or until edges are firm. Remove to wire racks to cool. **Yield:** 12 dozen.

Simple Sugar Cookies

Powdered sugar takes the place of granulated sugar in this sweet recipe. —Maxine Guin, Barnhart, Missouri

 1 cup butter (no substitutes), softened
1-1/4 cups confectioners' sugar
 1 egg
 1 teaspoon vanilla extract

 2 cups all-purpose flour
 1 teaspoon baking soda
 1 teaspoon cream of tartar
1/8 teaspoon salt

In a mixing bowl, cream butter and sugar. Beat in egg and vanilla. Combine the flour, baking soda, cream of tartar and salt; gradually add to the creamed mixture. Shape into two 5-in. rolls; wrap in plastic wrap. Refrigerate for 1 hour or until firm. Unwrap; cut into 1/4-in. slices. Place 2 in. apart on ungreased baking sheets. Bake at 350° for 8-10 minutes. Remove to wire racks to cool. **Yield:** 3-1/2 dozen.

Orange Pecan Cookies

This cookie is pure heaven with a glass of milk. It has a subtle orange flavor and just a sprinkling of chopped pecans throughout. —Eleanor Henry
Derry, New Hampshire

 1 cup butter (no substitutes), softened
 1/2 cup sugar
 1/2 cup packed brown sugar
 1 egg
 2 tablespoons orange juice
 1 tablespoon grated orange peel
2-1/2 cups all-purpose flour
 1/2 teaspoon baking soda
 1/2 teaspoon salt
 1/2 cup chopped pecans

In a mixing bowl, cream butter and sugars. Beat in egg, orange juice and peel. Combine flour, baking soda and salt; gradually add to creamed mixture. Stir in pecans. Shape dough into two 11-1/2-in. rolls; wrap in plastic wrap. Chill for 4 hours or overnight. Unwrap; cut into 1/4-in. slices. Place 2 in. apart on lightly greased baking sheets. Bake at 400° for 7-8 minutes or until golden brown. Remove to wire racks to cool. **Yield:** 6 dozen.

Chapter 19

DO YOU forgo asking family and friends to dinner because you don't think you have the time? Go ahead and send out those invitations! Because even an elaborate meal can have time-saving elements that make entertaining easy.

Here, fellow hurried cooks share favorite fuss-free recipes they like to prepare for company. Our test kitchen then combined these step-shaving dishes to create no-hassle meals that will have you feeling like a guest at your own party—and that will surely impress family and friends.

For the finishing touch, try your hand at some of the easy and attractive ideas for garnishes and table decorations.

ENTERTAIN WITH EASE. Clockwise from upper left: Cranberry Brownie Torte, Hot Cider with Orange Twists, Corn-Stuffed Crown Roast and Glazed Carrots (all recipes on p. 315).

Delightful
Valentine's Day Fare

DEMONSTRATE your love to family and friends on Valentine's Day—or any time of year—with this heart-warming menu. It's perfect for a small dinner party.

The salad dressing can be made in advance, so the salad comes together in a snap. Pull the impressive souffle out of oven right after your guests arrive. Keep it warm (it may fall slightly) while you quickly broil the salmon steaks. End the meal with sundae parfaits. (See page 316 for tips on adding special touches to your table.)

Lemony Caesar Salad

Ready in 15 minutes or less

I rely on this recipe from a friend when I want to fix a fresh, tasty tossed salad. To save time, I take advantage of convenient ready-to-serve romaine in a bag as well as garlic-seasoned croutons for extra flavor.
—*Kathy Kochiss, Huntington, Connecticut*

✓ Uses less fat, sugar or salt. Includes Nutritional Analysis and Diabetic Exchanges.

  1/2 **cup olive** *or* **vegetable oil**
    3 **tablespoons lemon juice**
    2 **garlic cloves, minced**
    1 **teaspoon Dijon mustard**
  1/2 **teaspoon salt, optional**
  1/8 **teaspoon pepper**
    9 **cups torn romaine**
  1/4 **cup grated Parmesan cheese**
    1 **cup salad croutons, optional**
Sliced red onion, optional

In a small bowl, combine oil, lemon juice, garlic, mustard, salt if desired and pepper; mix well. In a salad bowl, combine romaine and cheese. Drizzle with dressing; add croutons and onion if desired. Toss to coat. Serve immediately. **Yield:** 6-8 servings. **Nutritional Analysis:** 1 cup of salad with 1 tablespoon of dressing (prepared without salt and croutons) equals 146 calories, 79 mg sodium, 2 mg cholesterol, 2 gm carbohydrate, 2 gm protein, 15 gm fat, 1 gm fiber. **Diabetic Exchanges:** 3 fat, 1 vegetable.

Seasoned Salmon Steaks

Ready in 30 minutes or less

A flavorful basting sauce adds plenty of spark to these delicious salmon steaks. The moist firm fish broils to perfection in mere minutes.
—*Cary Winright*
Medina, Texas

    6 **salmon steaks (1 inch thick)**
  1/2 **cup butter** *or* **margarine, melted**
    2 **teaspoons seasoned salt**
    2 **teaspoons Italian seasoning**
    2 **teaspoons lemon juice**
  1/2 **teaspoon garlic powder**
  1/2 **teaspoon grated lemon peel**
Dash cayenne pepper

Place salmon on a greased broiler rack. Broil for 8-10 minutes. Meanwhile, combine the remaining ingredients in a bowl; mix well. Brush some over salmon. Turn and broil 10 minutes longer or until fish flakes easily with a fork. Baste with remaining butter mixture. **Yield:** 6 servings.

Broccoli Souffle

Ready in 1 hour or less

This golden-crowned souffle puffs up elegantly into an airy treat. Guests will delight in its fluffy texture and luscious taste. It's a great way to dress up everyday broccoli.
—*Clem Hood, North Battleford, Saskatchewan*

    1 **package (10 ounces) frozen chopped broccoli, thawed and drained**
    2 **tablespoons butter** *or* **margarine**
    2 **tablespoons all-purpose flour**
  1/2 **teaspoon salt**
  1/2 **cup milk**
  1/4 **cup grated Parmesan cheese**
    4 **eggs,** *separated*

In a saucepan over medium heat, cook and stir broccoli and butter until the butter is melted. Set 2 tablespoons aside for topping. Add flour and salt to the remaining broccoli; stir until blended. Gradually add milk. Bring to a boil; cook and stir for 2 minutes or until thickened. Remove from the heat; stir in cheese. In a large mixing bowl, beat egg yolks until thick and lemon-colored, about 3 minutes. Add broccoli mixture and set aside. In a small mixing bowl, beat egg whites until stiff peaks form; fold into broccoli mixture. Pour into an ungreased 1-1/2-qt. deep round baking dish. Bake, uncovered, at 350° for 20 minutes. Sprinkle with the reserved broccoli. Bake 10 minutes longer or until a knife inserted near the center comes out clean. **Yield:** 6 servings.

Sweetheart Sundaes

Ready in 30 minutes or less

A creamy peanut butter sauce and chocolate garnishes turn plain ice cream into pretty parfaits. This tempting dessert is easy to prepare and goes with most any meal. The cute homemade chocolate hearts are a cinch to make.
—*Suzanne McKinley, Lyons, Georgia*

1-1/2 **cups packed brown sugar**
  1/2 **cup milk**
  1/3 **cup corn syrup**
    4 **teaspoons butter** *or* **margarine**
  1/3 **cup peanut butter**
Vanilla ice cream
  3/4 **cup chopped peanuts**
    6 **chocolate hearts (see page 316), optional**

In a saucepan, combine brown sugar, milk, corn syrup and butter. Cook and stir over medium heat until sugar is dissolved and mixture is smooth. Remove from the heat; stir in peanut butter until smooth. Cover and refrigerate until serving. Divide half of the peanut butter mixture between six parfait glasses; top with a scoop of ice cream. Repeat layers. Sprinkle with peanuts. Garnish with a chocolate heart if desired. **Yield:** 6 servings.

Flair with Little Fuss

ELEGANT ENTERTAINING is possible, especially when you rely on this memorable menu loaded with make-ahead convenience. (For tips on preparing artichokes and on decorating your table, see page 317.)

Plum-Glazed Cornish Hens

The plum sauce that's baked onto these tender Cornish hens is wonderful. —Annie Tompkins, Deltona, Florida

   4 large navel oranges, sliced
   4 Cornish game hens (1 to 1-1/2 pounds *each*), split lengthwise
1/4 teaspoon pepper
   1 can (16 ounces) plums, drained and pitted
1/4 cup finely chopped onion
1/4 cup butter *or* margarine
3/4 cup lemonade concentrate
1/3 cup chili sauce
1/4 cup soy sauce
1-1/2 teaspoons prepared mustard
   1 teaspoon ground ginger
   1 teaspoon Worcestershire sauce
1/4 cup flaked coconut, toasted, optional

Arrange orange slices in two greased 13-in. x 9-in. x 2-in. baking dishes. Top with game hens; sprinkle with pepper. Bake, uncovered, at 350° for 45 minutes. Meanwhile, place the plums in a food processor or blender; cover and process until smooth. Set aside. In a large skillet, saute onion in butter until tender; stir in lemonade concentrate, chili sauce, soy sauce, mustard, ginger, Worcestershire sauce and plums. Bring to a boil. Reduce heat; simmer, uncovered, for 15 minutes, stirring occasionally. Set 1 cup of sauce aside. Brush remaining sauce over hens; bake 30-45 minutes or until juices run clear and a meat thermometer reads 180°, basting occasionally with drippings. Sprinkle with coconut if desired. Serve with reserved sauce. **Yield:** 4-6 servings.

Steamed Artichokes with Lemon Sauce

(Not pictured)

Ready in 1 hour or less

My husband created this smooth, tangy sauce back in the '60s. It complements the steamed artichokes nicely.
— Lois Gelzer, Oak Bluffs, Massachusetts

✓ Uses less fat, sugar or salt. Includes Nutritional Analysis and Diabetic Exchanges.

   6 medium fresh artichokes
1-1/2 cups mayonnaise
4-1/2 teaspoons lemon juice
3/4 teaspoon seasoned salt *or* salt-free seasoning blend
   3 drops hot pepper sauce

Place the artichokes upside down in a steamer basket; place the basket in a saucepan over 1 in. of boiling water. Cover and steam for 25-35 minutes or until tender. In a small bowl, combine the mayonnaise, lemon juice, salt and hot pepper sauce. Cover and refrigerate until

serving with the steamed artichokes. **Yield:** 6 servings.
Nutritional Analysis: One serving (prepared with fat-free mayonnaise and salt-free seasoning blend) equals 102 calories, 534 mg sodium, 0 cholesterol, 22 gm carbohydrate, 4 gm protein, trace fat, 7 gm fiber. **Diabetic Exchanges:** 1 starch, 1 vegetable.

Asparagus Salad Supreme

Plan ahead…needs to chill

This salad is a unique way to present this pretty spring vegetable. —Paula Bass, Washington, North Carolina

   2 pounds fresh asparagus, trimmed
1/2 pound fresh mushrooms, sliced
   4 green onions, thinly sliced
1/2 cup chopped walnuts
1/4 cup butter *or* margarine
1/2 cup mayonnaise
1/2 cup sour cream
1/2 teaspoon salt
1/8 teaspoon ground nutmeg
Additional walnuts, optional

In a skillet, cook asparagus in a small amount of water until crisp-tender, about 6-8 minutes; drain. Cover and refrigerate for at least 1 hour. In the same skillet, saute mushrooms, onions and walnuts in butter until mushrooms are tender. In a bowl, combine the mayonnaise, sour cream, salt and nutmeg. Stir in mushroom mixture. Cover and refrigerate for at least 1 hour. Just before serving, place asparagus on a serving platter; top with dressing and walnuts if desired. **Yield:** 6 servings.

Layered Chocolate Cake

It is hard to believe this impressive dessert starts with a boxed cake mix. —Dorothy Monroe, Pocatello, Idaho

   1 package (18-1/4 ounces) German chocolate cake mix
1-1/3 cups water
   3 eggs
1/3 cup vegetable oil
   1 package (3 ounces) cook-and-serve vanilla pudding mix
   1 teaspoon unflavored gelatin
   2 cups milk
   1 package (8 ounces) cream cheese, softened
1/2 cup butter *or* margarine, softened
   1 teaspoon vanilla extract
1-1/2 cups confectioners' sugar
   3 tablespoons baking cocoa

In a mixing bowl, combine the first four ingredients; mix well. Pour into a greased 15-in. x 10-in. x 1-in. baking pan. Bake at 350° for 23-25 minutes. Cool on a wire rack. In a saucepan, combine pudding mix, gelatin and milk; cook according to package directions for pudding. Cool. Cut cake into three 10-in. x 5-in. rectangles. Place one on a serving platter. Spread with half of the pudding mixture; repeat layers. Top with third layer. In a mixing bowl, beat cream cheese and butter. Add vanilla; mix well. Add sugar and cocoa; beat until smooth. Frost top and sides of cake. Refrigerate until serving. **Yield:** 10 servings.

Sunny-Side Outdoor Dining

JUST BECAUSE you're dining outdoors doesn't mean hamburgers, baked beans and chips are your only menu options. Liven things up a bit with this sensational summertime supper. (You'll find decorating and garnishing tips on page 318.)

Southwestern Lamb Chops

Ready in 30 minutes or less

This flavorful yet not-too-spicy sauce is our family's favorite. It's tasty with any choice of grilled meat, although we like it best with tender lamb. —Margaret Pache Mesa, Arizona

✓ Uses less fat, sugar or salt. Includes Nutritional Analysis and Diabetic Exchanges.

   1 cup orange juice
   2 jalapeno peppers, seeded and finely chopped*
   1 teaspoon ground cumin
1/2 teaspoon salt, optional
Dash pepper
3/4 cup halved sliced sweet onion
   4 teaspoons cornstarch
1/4 cup cold water
   1 cup fresh orange sections
   2 tablespoons minced fresh cilantro *or* parsley
   8 lamb loin chops (1 inch thick)

In a saucepan, combine orange juice, jalapeno, cumin, salt if desired and pepper. Cook over medium-high heat until mixture begins to simmer. Stir in onion. Combine cornstarch and water until smooth; add to the sauce. Bring to a boil over medium heat; cook and stir for 1 minute or until thickened and bubbly. Remove from the heat. Stir in oranges and cilantro; keep warm. Grill the lamb chops, covered, over medium-hot heat for 12-14 minutes, turning once, or until a meat thermometer reads 140° for rare; 160°, medium-well; or 170°, well-done. Serve with orange sauce. **Yield:** 4 servings. **Nutritional Analysis:** One serving (prepared without salt) equals 274 calories, 83 mg sodium, 87 mg cholesterol, 18 gm carbohydrate, 29 gm protein, 9 gm fat, 2 gm fiber. Diabetic Exchanges: 4 lean meat, 1 fruit. ***Editor's Note:** When cutting or seeding hot peppers, use rubber or plastic gloves to protect your hands. Avoid touching your face.

Baked Onion Dip

(Pictured on page 318)

Ready in 1 hour or less

Some people like this cheesy dip so much that they can't tear themselves away from the appetizer table to eat their dinner. As the hostess, it makes me happy to see people enjoying themselves and the food I've prepared.
—Mona Zignego, Hartford, Wisconsin

   1 cup mayonnaise
   1 cup chopped sweet onion
   1 tablespoon grated Parmesan cheese
1/4 teaspoon garlic salt

   1 cup (4 ounces) shredded Swiss cheese
Minced fresh parsley, optional
Assorted crackers

In a bowl, combine mayonnaise, onion, Parmesan cheese and garlic salt; stir in Swiss cheese. Spoon into a 1-qt. baking dish. Bake, uncovered, at 325° for 40 minutes. Sprinkle with parsley if desired. Serve with crackers. **Yield:** 2 cups.

Asparagus Brie Soup

Ready in 30 minutes or less

This rich soup is wonderful when fresh asparagus is in season. It's an elegant dish to serve company.
—Melissa Petrek-Myer, Austin, Texas

1/2 pound fresh asparagus, cut into 2-inch pieces
1/2 cup butter *or* margarine
1/4 cup all-purpose flour
   3 cups chicken broth
   1 cup whipping cream
1/2 cup white wine *or* additional chicken broth
   4 to 6 ounces Brie, rind removed
Dash salt and pepper

In a large saucepan, saute asparagus in butter until tender. Stir in flour until blended. Cook and stir for 2 minutes or until golden brown. Gradually add broth, cream and wine or additional broth. Bring to a boil. Reduce heat; simmer for 10-15 minutes. Place half of the soup at a time in a blender or food processor; cover and process until smooth. Return to the pan. Cube Brie and add to soup. Simmer, uncovered, for 5 minutes or until cheese is melted. **Yield:** 4 servings.

Apricot Sorbet

(Pictured below)

Plan ahead...needs to freeze

I like to end summer meals with a refreshing treat. With only three ingredients, this sorbet is simple to blend and freeze. You can make it in winter with canned apricots.
—Ruth Kahan Brookline, Massachusetts

   1 can (15 ounces) apricot halves, undrained
   1 to 2 tablespoons sugar
   1 tablespoon lemon juice

Freeze the apricots in a freezer-proof container. Place frozen apricots in a blender or food processor; add sugar and lemon juice. Cover and process until combined. Serve immediately or freeze. **Yield:** 4 servings.

Pleasing
Menu Packed
With Produce

WHEN FRUIT and vegetable season is in full swing, fix this filling feast loaded with garden-fresh flavor.

Start with crisp veggies or crackers and a creamy dip served in a pepper cup. For the main course, bring out succulent orange-flavored chicken with dressed-up green beans on the side. A light, fruit-filled pie provides a fabulous finale. (See page 319 for inexpensive ideas on decorating your table.)

Chunky Vegetable Dip

Ready in 15 minutes or less

Chopped green onions, radishes and cucumber spark the taste of this thick dip for fresh veggies, breadsticks or crackers. You can also use it as a salad dressing.
—Emma Magielda, Amsterdam, New York

  1 cup (8 ounces) sour cream
1/2 cup finely chopped seeded cucumber
1/4 cup chopped green onions
1/4 cup finely chopped radishes
  1 to 2 tablespoons cider *or* tarragon vinegar
1-1/2 teaspoons prepared horseradish
3/4 teaspoon salt
  1 large bell pepper, cut into a cup (see page 319)
Assorted fresh vegetables

In a bowl, combine the first seven ingredients; mix well. Cover and refrigerate. Serve in a pepper cup with vegetables for dipping. **Yield:** 1-1/2 cups.

Almond Orange Chicken

Ready in 30 minutes or less

This moist tender chicken with its crunchy nut coating and smooth sauce is one of my best recipes. I sometimes cook it in my electric skillet because it holds all the chicken.
—Sharon Lebold, Bayfield, Ontario

1/2 cup plus 2 tablespoons all-purpose flour, *divided*
  2 eggs
3/4 cup ground almonds
  6 boneless skinless chicken breast halves
  4 tablespoons butter *or* margarine, *divided*
1/3 cup chopped onion
1/4 teaspoon poultry seasoning
1-1/2 cups milk
1/3 cup orange marmalade
1/4 cup orange juice
1/2 teaspoon grated orange peel
  1 teaspoon salt
1/4 teaspoon pepper
Hot cooked rice, optional

Place 1/2 cup flour in a shallow bowl. In another bowl, lightly beat the eggs. Place the almonds in a third bowl. Coat chicken with flour, then dip in eggs and roll in almonds. In a skillet over medium-high heat, cook the chicken in 2 tablespoons butter on both sides until juices run clear, about 10 minutes. Remove and keep warm. In the same skillet, saute the onion in remaining butter until tender. Stir in poultry seasoning and remaining flour until blended. Gradually stir in milk until smooth. Bring to a boil; cook and stir for 2 minutes. Remove from the heat; stir in the orange marmalade, orange juice and peel, salt and pepper. Pour over the chicken. Serve with rice if desired. **Yield:** 6 servings.

Garden Green Beans

Ready in 30 minutes or less

This recipe uses garlic and Italian seasoning to dress up green beans straight from the garden. This fast, flavorful side dish is frequently on the menu for special occasions.
—Diane Hixon, Niceville, Florida

☑ Uses less fat, sugar or salt. Includes Nutritional Analysis and Diabetic Exchanges.

  4 cups cut fresh green beans (2-inch pieces)
1/2 cup sliced fresh mushrooms
  2 tablespoons chopped onion, optional
  1 garlic clove, minced
  2 tablespoons olive *or* vegetable oil
1/3 cup sliced water chestnuts
1/4 teaspoon Italian seasoning
1/4 teaspoon salt, optional
1/8 teaspoon pepper
  2 tablespoons shredded Parmesan cheese

Place beans in a saucepan and cover with water; bring to a boil. Reduce heat; cover and simmer until crisp-tender. Meanwhile, in a skillet, saute mushrooms, onion if desired and garlic in oil until tender. Stir in water chestnuts and seasonings; heat through. Drain beans and stir into skillet. Sprinkle with Parmesan cheese. Serve immediately. **Yield:** 6 servings. **Nutritional Analysis:** One serving (prepared without salt) equals 38 calories, 40 mg sodium, 2 mg cholesterol, 6 gm carbohydrate, 2 gm protein, 1 gm fat, 3 gm fiber. **Diabetic Exchange:** 1-1/2 vegetable.

Banana Blueberry Pie

Ready in 1 hour or less

This light fruity dessert is so simple to prepare. It makes two, so you have one pie for guests and a second to enjoy the next day. —Priscilla Weaver, Hagerstown, Maryland

  1 package (8 ounces) cream cheese, softened
3/4 cup sugar
  2 cups whipped topping
  4 medium firm bananas, sliced
  2 pastry shells (9 inches), baked
  1 can (21 ounces) blueberry pie filling
Fresh blueberries and mint and additional sliced bananas, optional

In a mixing bowl, beat cream cheese and sugar until smooth. Fold in whipped topping and bananas. Pour into pastry shells. Spread with pie filling. Refrigerate for at least 30 minutes. Just before serving, garnish with blueberries, mint and bananas if desired. **Yield:** 2 pies (6-8 servings each).

Take Stock In Hearty Fare

HEARTY HOMESPUN favorites fall into place when you want to celebrate the change of seasons. The eye-catching pinwheel steak and squash casserole can be baked together, while the cake and homemade dressing for the salad can be made early in the day. (Turn to page 320 for tips on rolling the steak and on bringing color to your table.)

Spinach-Stuffed Steak

A mixture of spinach, peppers and sunflower kernels gives extra-special flavor to these steak slices.
—Jetta Kaune, Mendon, Ohio

    1 package (10 ounces) frozen chopped
       spinach, thawed and drained
    1 jar (7 ounces) roasted red peppers, drained
    1 egg white
  1/2 cup seasoned bread crumbs
  1/4 cup grated Parmesan cheese
  1/4 cup sunflower kernels, toasted
    1 garlic clove, minced
  1/2 teaspoon salt
    1 flank steak (about 1-1/2 pounds)

In a bowl, combine the first eight ingredients; mix well. Cut steak horizontally from a long edge to within 1/2 in. of opposite edge; open (like a book) and flatten to 1/2-in. thickness. (See page 320 for details.) Spread spinach mixture over the steak to within 1 in. of edges. Roll up, jelly-roll style, starting with a long side; tie with kitchen string. Place in a greased 13-in. x 9-in. x 2-in. baking dish. Cover and bake at 350° for 1 hour. Uncover; bake 30-45 minutes longer or until tender. Let stand for 10-15 minutes. Cut into 1/2-in. slices. **Yield:** 6 servings.

Summer Squash Bake

Ready in 1 hour or less

This colorful casserole makes the most of summer squash. A handful of chopped pecans adds a nutty crunch.
—Gail Smrtic, Broken Arrow, Oklahoma

    3 cups sliced yellow summer squash
    2 tablespoons water
  1/2 cup finely chopped green pepper
  1/2 cup finely chopped onion
  1/2 cup chopped pecans
  1/2 cup mayonnaise*
  2/3 cup shredded cheddar cheese, *divided*
  1/2 teaspoon sugar
  1/2 teaspoon salt
  1/4 teaspoon pepper

Place squash and water in a 1-1/2-qt. microwave-safe bowl. Cover and microwave on high for 4-5 minutes or until crisp-tender; drain well. Stir in green pepper, onion, pecans, mayonnaise, 1/3 cup of cheese, sugar, salt and pepper. Transfer to a lightly greased shallow 1-1/2-qt. baking dish. Cover and bake at 350° for 25 minutes. Sprinkle with remaining cheese. Bake, uncovered, for 5 minutes or until cheese is melted. **Yield:** 6 servings.
*Editor's Note: Light or fat-free mayonnaise may not be substituted for regular mayonnaise.

Colorful Mixed Salad

Plan ahead…needs to chill

Dried cranberries and mandarin oranges add sweetness to this green salad. It's loaded with other goodies, then tossed with a pleasant orange dressing. —Sandra Lashua
Henderson, Nevada

  1/2 cup orange juice
  1/3 cup cider *or* white wine vinegar
  1/3 cup olive *or* vegetable oil
    4 teaspoons sugar
    6 cups torn mixed salad greens
    1 can (11 ounces) mandarin oranges, drained
    1 small red onion, thinly sliced
    4 radishes, thinly sliced
    4 green onions, thinly sliced
  1/3 cup dried cranberries
  1/3 cup sunflower kernels
  3/4 cup crumbled feta *or* blue cheese
  3/4 cup cherry tomatoes, halved

In a jar with a tight-fitting lid, combine the orange juice, vinegar, oil and sugar; shake well. Cover and refrigerate for 1 hour. Just before serving, combine the remaining ingredients in a large serving bowl. Drizzle with dressing and toss gently. **Yield:** 6 servings.

Pineapple Carrot Cake

This moist cake with cream cheese frosting is the best I've ever eaten. It's so simple because it uses jars of carrot baby food instead of fresh carrots that need to be grated.
—Jeanette McKenna, Vero Beach, Florida

    2 cups all-purpose flour
    2 cups sugar
    2 teaspoons baking soda
    2 teaspoons ground cinnamon
    1 teaspoon salt
1-1/2 cups vegetable oil
    4 eggs
    2 jars (6 ounces *each*) carrot baby food
    1 can (8 ounces) crushed pineapple, drained
  1/2 cup chopped walnuts
FROSTING:
    1 package (8 ounces) cream cheese, softened
  1/2 cup butter *or* margarine, softened
    1 teaspoon vanilla extract
3-3/4 cups confectioners' sugar
Additional chopped walnuts, optional

In a mixing bowl, combine the dry ingredients. Add the oil, eggs and baby food; mix on low speed until well blended. Stir in pineapple and nuts. Pour into two greased and floured 9-in. round baking pans. Bake at 350° for 35-40 minutes or until a toothpick inserted near the center comes out clean. Cool for 10 minutes before removing from pans to wire racks to cool completely. For frosting, in a mixing bowl, beat cream cheese and butter until smooth. Beat in vanilla and confectioners' sugar until mixture reaches spreading consistency. Spread between layers and over top and sides of cake. Garnish with nuts if desired. Store in the refrigerator. **Yield:** 12 servings.

THE HOLIDAY SEASON may be hectic, but that doesn't mean entertaining needs to be! The trick is to work with recipes that are packed with convenience...like the ones featured here. (Page 321 offers tips on creating garnishes and table decorations.)

Corn-Stuffed Crown Roast

(Also pictured on page 303)

My mother always made this elegant entree for company dinners and special family celebrations.
—Dorothy Swanson, St. Louis, Missouri

   1 pork crown roast (about 7 pounds and 12 ribs)
1/2 teaspoon pepper, *divided*
   1 cup chopped celery
   1 cup chopped onion
   1 cup butter *or* margarine
   6 cups corn bread stuffing
   2 cups frozen corn, thawed
   2 jars (4-1/2 ounces *each*) sliced mushrooms, undrained
   1 teaspoon salt
   1 teaspoon poultry seasoning

Place roast on a rack in a large roasting pan. Sprinkle with 1/4 teaspoon pepper. Cover rib ends with small pieces of foil. Bake, uncovered, at 350° for 2 hours. In a Dutch oven, saute celery and onion in butter until tender. Stir in stuffing, corn, mushrooms, salt, poultry seasoning and remaining pepper. Loosely spoon 1-3 cups into the center of the roast. Place remaining stuffing in a greased 2-qt. baking dish. Bake roast 1 hour longer or until a meat thermometer reads 160° and juices run clear. Cover and bake extra stuffing for 30-40 minutes. Transfer roast to serving platter. Remove foil; cut between ribs to serve. **Yield:** 12 servings.

Hot Cider with Orange Twists

(Also pictured on page 303)

Plan ahead...uses slow cooker

A steaming mug of this comforting drink warms you up.
—Catherine Allan, Twin Falls, Idaho

✓ Uses less fat, sugar or salt. Includes Nutritional Analysis and Diabetic Exchanges.

   2 quarts unsweetened apple cider
   1 cup unsweetened pineapple juice
   1 cup unsweetened orange juice
   1 tablespoon brown sugar
   1 tablespoon lemon juice
1/8 teaspoon salt
   8 whole cloves
   4 unpeeled fresh orange slices (1/4 inch thick)
   4 cinnamon sticks (3 inches)
Additional orange slices and cinnamon sticks

In a slow cooker, combine the first six ingredients. Push two cloves through each orange slice. Push a cinnamon stick through the center of each orange slice; add to cider mixture. Cover and cook on low for 2-4 hours or

until heated through. Discard oranges, cloves and cinnamon sticks. Stir cider before serving. Use additional oranges and cinnamon sticks to make orange twist garnish (see page 321). **Yield:** 2-1/2 quarts. **Nutritional Analysis:** One serving (1 cup) equals 123 calories, 36 mg sodium, 0 cholesterol, 31 gm carbohydrate, trace protein, trace fat, trace fiber. **Diabetic Exchange:** 2 fruit.

Glazed Carrots

(Also pictured on page 302)

Ready in 30 minutes or less

Ranch salad dressing mix easily flavors these tasty baby carrots.
—Marion Reed, Omak, Washington

   2 packages (16 ounces *each*) fresh baby carrots
1/2 cup butter *or* margarine
1/2 cup packed brown sugar
   2 envelopes ranch salad dressing mix

Place carrots in a saucepan; add 1 in. of water. Bring to a boil. Reduce heat; cover and cook for 8-10 minutes or until crisp-tender. Drain and set aside. In the same pan, combine butter, brown sugar and salad dressing mix until blended. Add carrots. Cook and stir over medium heat for 5 minutes or until glazed. **Yield:** 10-12 servings.

Cranberry Brownie Torte

(Also pictured on page 302)

Plan ahead...needs to chill

Canned cranberry sauce adds a festive touch to this dessert.
—Gloria Kirchman, Eden Prairie, Minnesota

   1 package fudge brownie mix (13-inch x 9-inch pan size)
   2 eggs
1/2 cup vegetable oil
1/4 cup water
1/2 cup chopped pecans
FILLING:
   1 package (8 ounces) cream cheese, softened
1/2 cup cranberry juice
   2 tablespoons sugar
   1 carton (12 ounces) frozen whipped topping, thawed
TOPPING:
   1 can (16 ounces) whole-berry cranberry sauce
Pecan halves, optional

In a bowl, combine brownie mix, eggs, oil and water; beat until combined. Fold in pecans. Transfer to a greased 10-in. springform pan. Bake at 350° for 35-40 minutes or until a toothpick inserted near the center comes out with moist crumbs. Cool completely. For filling, in a mixing bowl, beat the cream cheese, cranberry juice and sugar until smooth. Set aside 1 cup whipped topping for garnish. Fold remaining topping into cream cheese mixture. Carefully spread over brownie. Stir cranberry sauce; carefully spread over the filling. Garnish with reserved whipped topping and pecan halves if desired. Refrigerate for at least 2 hours before serving. Store leftovers in the refrigerator. **Yield:** 12 servings.

Table Toppers

WHEN company's coming, take a little extra time to dress up your table. Our kitchen staff came up with these inexpensive ideas for attractive table toppers, fuss-free folded napkins and fancy food presentation.

Seasonal Confetti Sets the Scene

A SIMPLE sprinkling of colorful confetti can dress up your table quickly and inexpensively. It's usually packaged in small bags and sold at card and party stores, craft shops and near the gift wrap and card sections of larger discount and drug stores.

There are plenty of colors and designs available that are suited to most holidays and milestones.

For Valentine's Day, we chose tiny red hearts along with larger three-dimensional hearts.

We also found packets of multicolored hearts combined with X's and O's as well as gold and silver hearts that would be appropriate for anniversaries.

You don't need a lot of confetti to make an impression. A small bag should be more than enough.

Easy Dessert Decorations

DRESS UP any dessert with these garnishes that are simple to make ahead of time with melted chocolate.

You can tailor the designs to fit the occasion. For Valentine's Day, we chose a heart with an arrow through it. The garnishes are a lovely addition to the

Sweetheart Sundaes (recipe on page 305).

To start, trace your design several times on a piece of paper. Place the paper on a baking sheet and cover it with waxed paper. In a microwave-safe bowl, heat chocolate chips just until melted.

Transfer the melted chocolate to a heavy-duty resealable plastic bag and cut a very small hole in one corner.

The more detailed the design, the smaller the hole in the bag should be. But remember, when finished, thicker designs will be sturdier and easier to remove.

1. Following traced designs, pipe chocolate onto waxed paper. Refrigerate until the chocolate is firm, about 15 minutes.

2. Just before serving, carefully remove the hearts with a metal spatula. Store any leftovers in an airtight container in a cool dry place.

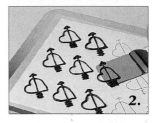

Plant Gets Heartwarming Touch

THE HEART-SHAPED "plant poke" (pictured below left) is easy to assemble with just a few supplies. You'll need two thin bendable branches that are about 26 inches long. You'll also need a 6-inch wired florist pick, additional florist wire, ribbon and a flowering plant in a 6-inch pot.

1 Trim branches to the same length. Holding them snugly side by side, wire the branches together at one end with the florist pick, making sure the pick extends a few inches below the branches.

2 About 7 inches up from the bottom of the wired branches, tie a 40-inch length of ribbon into a pretty bow. (This will become the inside top of the heart when finished.) The ribbon can be secured in place with a glue gun if necessary.

3 Bend the loose ends of branches to meet the wired ends to form a heart. We used about 18 inches of florist wire to secure the loose ends. Poke the florist pick into the plant soil, arranging the bow and ribbon ends attractively.

No Fancy Folding Required

BRIGHTEN place settings by putting one of these pretty pockets on each guest's plate. They're a snap to fold with a square napkin made from colorful fabric.

To start, fold the napkin in half to form a rectangle. Then fold it in half again to form a square.

1 Fold over the open point of the top layer until it's a short distance from the closed point. Repeat this with the next two layers, placing each open point a short distance from the previous point.

2 Now, carefully tuck one side corner under the napkin so the tip reaches the center of the napkin. Repeat with the remaining side corner so the two corners meet beneath the napkin in the middle. The pocket that results can hold a single flower, a small present or silverware.

Artichokes Are Easy Elegant Appetizers

GUESTS will be impressed when they sit down at the table to find individual artichoke appetizers at each place setting. The distinctively shaped vegetables look appealing and are easy to prepare when simply steamed on the stovetop.

To prepare a fresh artichoke for steaming, use a sharp paring knife to evenly trim the base. This will help the artichoke sit upright when served. Next, slice 3/4 inch from the top of the artichoke.

Using a kitchen shears, snip off the tip of each leaf. To prevent browning, rub all cut edges with lemon juice.

To cook the artichokes, follow the recipe on page 307 for Steamed Artichokes with Lemon Sauce. Once steamed, artichokes can be served hot, cold or at room temperature.

For those who have never sampled a whole steamed artichoke, don't be intimidated. They're actually easy to eat.

First, pull an outside leaf off the artichoke. Holding the trimmed tip in your fingers, dip the lower part of the leaf into melted butter or a savory sauce. Use your teeth to gently scrape off the tender flesh from the inside of the leaf, then discard the leaf. Repeat with remaining leaves.

After going through all the leaves, you will find a fuzzy growth in the center called the "choke". Scrape this off and discard it. Underneath you will find the tender heart of the artichoke, which you can eat with a knife and fork.

Candle Holders Furnish Warm Glow

ADD a whimsical touch and soft lighting to your table with easy candle holders made with fresh artichokes.

First, trim the stem of the artichoke to level the bottom. This will keep the artichoke flat so the candle, once in place, doesn't tip.

Cut 3/4 inch from the top of the artichoke, then rub cut edges with lemon to keep them from browning.

To make room for the candle, we used a small sharp paring knife to cut out a little of the center of the artichoke. (It's best not to remove too much...that way your candle will fit more snugly.)

Insert the candle into the center of artichoke, gently twisting it down until it's firmly in place.

To protect the surface of your table or tablecloth from melted wax, place the artichokes on tiles, trivets or glass candle bases.

Then light the candles and enjoy the glow!

thin slice off the top and bottom of the orange.

1. Place one cut side down on a cutting board. With a sharp paring knife, cut strips of peel from top to bottom until all of the peel and white rind is removed.

2. Slice between the membrane of a section and the fruit until the knife reaches the center of the orange. Turn the knife and follow the membrane so the fruit is released into a bowl. Repeat until all sections are removed.

Citrus Centerpiece Offers Sunny Touch

BRIGHT orange slices add a colorful look to your table when they become part of a fast floral centerpiece. This arrangement is easy to assemble and requires just a few blossoms.

When your entree—such as Southwestern Lamb Chops (recipe on page 309)—calls for orange sections, you can pick up a few extra oranges to use in the centerpiece.

Depending on the foods you're serving and the color of your dishes and table linens, you may want to choose lemons or limes for your centerpiece instead. Because you'll want the citrus slices to stay flat against the sides of your container, select a straight-sided bowl or vase. We used a square glass canister.

Cut your fruit into 1/4-inch slices and arrange the slices against the side of the vase or bowl. Depending on the container, you may leave the slices whole or cut them in half as we did. If you're using a shallow container, try overlapping the slices for a slightly different look.

To hold the fruit in place, drop clear marbles or pebbles into your container. (They will also help anchor your flower stems.)

Then add water and your flowers. We only needed a half dozen roses to create this pretty arrangement, then we tucked in a few sprigs of smaller flowers to fill it out (see photo above).

Simple Guide to Sectioning Citrus

FRESH citrus fruit sections add fresh flavor to many dishes. To obtain the sections without the time-consuming task of peeling the orange and removing the membrane by hand, use the method here.

First, place the orange on a cutting board. Cut a

Fold Napkin into Flowery Basket Liner

TO GIVE your dinner table a special look in mere minutes, create a unique liner for your bread or cracker basket. It's easy when you fold a bright cloth napkin into a lovely flower shape.

1 To start, place the napkin on a flat surface and bring all four corners together to meet in the center. (This will create a square.)

2 Carefully turn the napkin over, preserving the folds you just made. Again, bring opposite corners together to meet in the center, forming a smaller square.

3 With your hand holding down the center of the napkin, gently pull up the point underneath each corner to form a petal.

4 Carefully place the completed flower in basket. Fill with rolls and bread or crackers, breadsticks or rye chips when serving a spreadable appetizer like Baked Onion Dip (recipe on page 309).

Matching Napkin Is Fit to Be Tied

IF YOU get a knot in your stomach when you think about folding napkins, then you'll appreciate the ease of this napkin treatment that's as simple as tying a knot.

First, choose a bright cloth napkin that coordinates with your dishes. Fold napkin in half to create a triangle, then loosely bunch napkin in the middle.

Place two or three dry breadsticks in the center of the bunched napkin and bring the napkin's outside corners together to tie a simple half-knot that's just tight enough to hold the breadsticks in place.

Set a knotted napkin on each guest's plate as shown below right. Once they untie their napkins, they'll have something to nibble on while you put the finishing touches on dinner.

Perk Up Place Mats With Ribbons

LOOKING for an easy way to dress up everyday place mats? Add color and flair to your table by running contrasting ribbons through the edges of plain place mats.

You can border all four sides of a place mat, do only the top and bottom, just the sides, or the top and one side as we show below.

This treatment works best with rubber-coated waffle-weave place mats that you may already have in your kitchen. If you don't, you can find them at discount and department stores. (We picked up ours for less than $1 each.)

Next, you'll need a large tapestry or yarn needle and narrow ribbon. You can use more than one color of ribbon if you'd like. To coordinate with our table linens and foods, we chose orange and blue polyester ribbon that's 1/4 inch wide.

1 About 1-1/2 inches from the left edge of the place mat, use the needle to simply "sew" the ribbon up and down every third or fourth opening. Since it takes less than a minute per 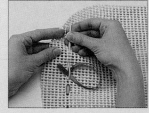 length of ribbon, you can quickly do more than one ribbon on a side. We put the second ribbon about 1/2 inch to the right of the first.

2 Choose another color ribbon to add a bright border to the top of the place mat, this time sewing the top ribbon about 1 inch from the top of the place mat.  The second ribbon was added about 3/4 of an inch below the first. Snip ribbon ends, leaving up to an inch to trail.

Once dinner's over, if you'd like to return your place mats to their original state, the ribbons can easily be pulled out.

Breadsticks work especially well when your menu includes a cheesy spread or creamy dip as an appetizer. For example, the breadsticks would be tasty with the Chunky Vegetable Dip served in a pepper cup (recipe on page 311).

Prepare a Pretty Pepper Cup

SWEET BELL PEPPERS make bright and attractive serving dishes for creamy dips, spreads or even for fresh vegetable strips. They're also charming containers for presenting individual servings of chicken, tuna, rice or pasta salads at special luncheons.

Since bell peppers are usually available in a range of colors—including green, red, orange and yellow—you can choose the hue that looks best with the rest of your menu.

To begin, use a sharp knife to cut the stem and about 1/2 inch off the top of the pepper. Carefully remove the membrane and seeds inside. If necessary, cut a thin slice off the bottom of the pepper so it sits flat.

To give this quick container a more decorative design, cut out triangles along the top edge of pepper.

Now it's easy to fill with Chunky Vegetable Dip (recipe on page 311) or your favorite dip or spread.

Apple Candles Add Appeal

IF YOU'RE looking for a warm accent to brighten your table, these cute candle holders will quickly become the apple of your eye.

First, gather your supplies. You'll need a toothpick, paring knife, melon baller and votive candles. (If you don't have a melon baller, use a small spoon, cookie scoop or apple corer.)

You'll also want several medium-sized apples. We chose bright green Granny Smiths, but other varieties can easily be substituted.

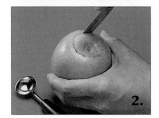

1. Position a votive candle on top of an apple, centering it over the stem. With a toothpick, poke holes around the base of the candle about 1/4 inch apart. This dotted circle indicates the area that will need to be removed to fit the candle.

2. Using a paring knife, cut along dotted circle and straight down about three-fourths of the way into the apple. Do not cut through the bottom of the apple.

Use the melon baller to scoop out the core and insides. If necessary, trim the opening with your paring knife to smooth any ragged edges. Then rub the edges with lemon juice to prevent browning.

Place a votive candle into the apple and place it next to the individual plates (see photo above).

As soon as dinner is ready, light the candles and watch your guests' faces light up, too.

Pinwheel Steak Gets Menu Rolling

YOU DON'T need a dazzling centerpiece to impress company when you serve a memorable main dish like Spinach-Stuffed Steak (recipe on page 313). It relies on an easy technique for stuffing and rolling beef.

To start, prepare the filling mixture as directed by the recipe, then set it aside.

Now you're going to slice the flank steak in half like you would butterfly a pork chop. Put the steak on a cutting board. Hold your knife so the blade is flat and carefully slice the steak in half horizontally, making sure not to cut all the way through the opposite edge.

Then open the steak like a book, so that both sides are flat. Using a mallet or meat tenderizer, pound the steak to 1/2-inch thickness. Spoon the filling mixture onto the steak and spread to about 1 inch from the edges of the meat.

Roll steak up jelly-roll-style. Secure with kitchen string and cook according to the recipe instructions. When it's done, slice into attractive swirls.

Novel Napkin Fold

SOMETIMES, it's the little things, like elegantly folded napkins, that make a meal special. To begin, choose a square cloth napkin that complements your dinnerware. Lay the napkin on a flat surface and fold it in half to form a rectangle.

1 Take hold of both layers of the two open corners and bring them together to meet at the center of the fold. (The napkin should resemble a triangle.)

2 Now, bring the two outside points of the triangle together to meet at the center of the opposite side. (Your napkin should now form a small square.)

3 Pinch the closed point of the napkin together and slide it through a napkin ring. Then peel back the top section of the napkin on each side like a petal. Fluff upper folds for a full, layered look (see photo above) or leave flat.

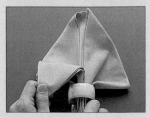

Seasonal Things Become Napkin Rings

WHEN decorating a holiday table, take a cue from your seasonal surroundings.

Dress up place settings with items you already have on hand. For instance, we found several objects that could be used as napkin rings for a special dinner.

Some tree ornaments can be used this way. Ones that work well include colorful reindeer (shown at right), rocking horses, bright wreaths, musical horns and other decorations that have open areas to pull the napkins through.

Or try other types of tree trims. A length of most any type of garland can be tied around a napkin to form an impromptu ring. We used an easy-to-shape wire garland that sparkled with gold metallic stars (shown below and also in photo above).

Cute cookie cutters, like the metal star-shaped one above right, work well as napkin rings, too. Try a variety of shapes, such as gingerbread boys and girls, angels, stockings or most any other open cookie cutter.

Use your imagination... and have fun!

Time-Easing Twists Add Spice

IF YOU'RE looking for a warm way to greet guests on a cool evening, try Hot Cider with Orange Twists (recipe on page 315). This steaming spiced beverage looks impressive with its citrusy cinnamon stirrers.

You don't need a long list of supplies to put together these gorgeous garnishes, so assembly is a snap.

First, you'll want some cinnamon sticks. You can use the regular ones from the spice aisle of your fa-

vorite grocery store. Or, depending on the depth of your mug, you may want to buy longer ones, like we did, that can be found at specialty grocery stores.

You'll also need a few oranges cut into 1/4-inch slices. You'll get about four to six full slices from an orange, depending on its size.

For each garnish, make a cut from the center of an orange slice out through the peel. Holding the edge of the peel on each side of that cut, twist slice in opposite directions to form an S.

Now insert a cinnamon stick through the S in two places near the edge of the peel to hold its curved shape. Then simply place a garnish in each mug of cider for a fancy-looking yet fuss-free touch.

Pinecone Pots Spruce Up Place Settings

BRING the outdoors inside with these pretty potted pinecones that mark individual place settings. It's like sending each of your guests home with their own personal Christmas tree. To make each miniature tree, you'll need a standard 2-1/2-inch clay flowerpot. You'll also need a pinecone, some acrylic craft paint and a 1-inch strip cut from an ordinary kitchen sponge.

To paint the pinecone, you can choose white to resemble snow or use green, like we did.

1 Pour a tiny amount of paint onto a disposable plastic or paper plate. Dip the end of the sponge strip into the paint and gently dab color onto the tips of the pinecone. Place cone on newspaper and let it dry for about 5-10 minutes.

2 To perk up the pot, cover it in colorful paper. We used gold foil floral paper, but you can choose any colorful gift wrap or tissue paper.

Place the pot in the center of a square of paper and gather the edges up around the top of the pot. Secure with a rubber band.

3 Now place a painted pinecone into the small opening in the paper. The cone should sit there nicely. But for more secure placement, use hot glue to attach the base of the pinecone to the paper. For a speedy finishing touch, add a bow to the pot and attach a gift tag labeled with each guest's name (see photo at left).

IF YOU'RE like most busy cooks these days, your weekdays are hurried and hectic with little time to spare preparing elaborate dishes.

But on those more leisurely weekends when you do have a little extra time at your disposal, you're eager to head to the kitchen to try your hand at more challenging recipes or to get a refresher on basic cooking techniques.

Whether you'd like to enhance your knowledge of purchasing pots and pans, creating gorgeous garnishes and using a pressure cooker or you're interested in making coffee cakes, basic baked goods or successful from-scratch stuffing, these helpful hints and easy-to-follow recipes will surely sharpen your culinary skills!

QUICK COFFEE CAKES. Top to bottom: Braided Coffee Cake and Coffee Cake Ring (both recipes on p. 327).

Picking Pots and Pans

MAKING MEALS on the stovetop—from stir-fries to skillet dishes—is a popular practice for time-pressed cooks. The stove allows you to fry meats, steam or saute vegetables, prepare sauces or boil noodles in mere minutes.

Stovetop Necessities

Using the right cookware can help simplify meal preparation. It's best to start out with a basic selection for everyday cooking, then add to it as needed.

Most kitchens shouldn't be without a 5-quart Dutch oven with lid, 1- and 2-quart saucepans with lids, a 10- to 12-inch skillet with lid and an 8- or 9-inch saute pan. (See the box below, which highlights this basic equipment.)

Other useful cookware includes a stockpot or soup kettle, a double boiler, a steamer insert basket, a cast-iron skillet, a griddle, and additional saucepans and skillets with covers.

Because pots and pans come in a wide range of materials and prices, buying the right ones for your needs can be a difficult task.

Good cookware should do two things: conduct heat quickly and evenly distribute that heat over the pan's surface to cook food evenly. These qualities are determined by the type of material the pan is made with and its thickness.

Materials Matter

Each material has distinct advantages as well as disadvantages.

Of all the metals used, *copper* conducts heat the best. Unfortunately, it's expensive, requires polishing to remain looking nice and must be lined with another metal to prevent it from reacting with acidic ingredients like tomatoes.

In comparison, pans made from *aluminum*—also a good heat conductor—are less expensive. But they, too, can react with acidic foods. That's why a better choice is *anodized aluminum*, which is becoming quite popular.

An electrochemical process makes the surface of aluminum smoother, harder and less reactive to acidic foods yet it still conducts heat nicely. Another bonus is that although anodized aluminum pans are not "nonstick", food is less likely to stick to their smoother surface.

Stainless steel pots and pans are poor conductors of heat, but they are very durable and remain looking new for many years. To get the best of both worlds, some manufacturers offer stainless steel pans with aluminum or copper bottoms because they're both durable and good conductors of heat.

Cast iron is also an excellent conductor of heat, will

Stock Your Kitchen with Basic Cookware

1. Dutch oven with cover: This large 4- or 5-quart pot has handles and a lid. A 12-inch-diameter pot is best and can double as a skillet or large saucepan. It's perfect for braising or frying meats as well as making soups, stews and sauces.

2. Saucepans with covers: These versatile pans come in a range of sizes from 2 cups to 4 quarts. The 1-quart and 2- or 3-quart saucepans are the most commonly used. These pans should come with lids, which are frequently interchangeable. Saucepans can be used for boiling, simmering, poaching and steaming.

3. Skillet with cover: Skillets are available with straight or sloping sides. A 10- to 12-inch straight-sided skillet is best for stir-fries, frying and recipes with a sauce or large yield. In this case, the lid for the Dutch oven shown also fits this skillet.

4. Saute pan: An 8- to 9-inch slope-sided skillet is great for sauteing because it allows a spatula to slide easily under the food. These pans are also the best choice for omelets and crepes.

1. Dutch oven

2. Saucepans

3. Skillet

4. Saute pan

last for many years and is reasonably priced. However, it must be seasoned periodically and its weight can make it hard to handle for some cooks. (Learn more about seasoning cast iron below.)

Heatproof glass is a versatile option because it can be used to cook, bake, freeze and microwave. But it has drawbacks, too; it is heavier to handle and can break, crack or chip.

Other Considerations

Once you've decided on the type of material for your cookware, consider its thickness (or gauge). Generally, the heavier a pan feels when picked up, the thicker its gauge is.

Thicker-gauge cookware offers more even heating so it is less likely to burn foods or have hot spots. Thin-gauge pans heat up quickly, but also cook very unevenly and can warp over time.

Pans with nonstick surfaces are nice because they make cleanup a breeze. This feature is handy for skillets and saute pans, but usually not necessary for saucepans, Dutch ovens and large pots.

Also look for cookware with handles that feel comfortable in your hand, stay cool while cooking and are oven-safe. Pots that have two handles make it easier to pick up when full.

Depending on the cookware you plan to use, it may be a wiser investment to purchase pieces individually rather than buy a packaged set.

While more expensive pieces are generally of superior quality, a general rule is to buy the best quality you can afford.

Take Care of Your Cookware

ROUTINE care of pots and pans will ensure you get the best performance and longest use out of them. Keep these tips in mind when using your cookware:

- Cast-iron pans should be seasoned before using to protect the surface and prevent food from sticking. One way to season a cast-iron skillet is to brush the inside with vegetable oil, then add an extra tablespoon of oil to the pan. Place the pan over low heat for 1 hour. When cool, wipe it dry with paper towels.
- Use nonmetal utensils during cooking to minimize cuts and scratches to the interior of your pans.
- To remove dark stains from an aluminum pot or pan, fill it with water, add 3 tablespoons fresh lemon juice and simmer gently until the pan brightens.
- To help remove stuck-on food from pots and pans, soak them in hot soapy water. However, if the pan has a sugary or protein-based substance (like eggs) on it, soak it in cold water.
- Stainless steel should be washed quickly after cooking salty foods because salt can pit the surface.
- Always dry aluminum or stainless steel pans immediately to prevent water spots from forming.
- To prevent nonstick linings from damage during storage, place paper towels between the pans when stacking them in your cabinet.

Common Cooking Techniques

IT'S SIMPLE to cook on the stovetop when you have the right equipment. Here we show the pots and pans needed for everyday cooking methods.

◄ **To fry:** Place food, such as chicken, in 1/2 to 1 inch of hot oil in a skillet. Fry, uncovered, until food is browned and cooked through.

►**To saute:** Place food, such as fresh vegetables, in a small amount of hot oil in a skillet or saute pan. Cook quickly and stir frequently.

◄**To steam:** Place food, such as sliced carrots, in a perforated basket (steamer insert) set just above, but not touching, the boiling water in a saucepan. Cover pan and allow food to cook in the steam given off by the boiling water.

►**To braise:** In a Dutch oven, brown meat, such as pork ribs, in a little oil, then add a small amount of liquid. Cover and simmer until cooked.

Quicker Coffee Cakes

Braided Coffee Cake
Coffee Cake Ring

STORE-BOUGHT pastries are fine for breakfast when time is tight. But for a weekend brunch or special occasion, nothing beats a warm-from-the-oven coffee cake.

Making these sweet breads from scratch can be a long and involved process. With the traditional yeast mixing method, active dry yeast is first dissolved in warm water or other liquids (110°-115°). Then the remaining ingredients are added as the recipe directs. Generally the dough rises twice before baking (once after kneading and once after shaping).

With the advent of quick-rise or rapid-rise yeast, making yeast bread is easier than ever. This finely granulated instant yeast has two time-saving advantages. It does not need to be dissolved in water first...and it requires only one rise (after shaping).

To prepare the dough, the undissolved yeast is combined with some of the flour in the recipe and other dry ingredients in a bowl. Because the yeast is coated with the dry ingredients, the liquid is added at a warmer temperature (120°-130°). Then the remaining ingredients are stirred into the yeast mixture.

In place of the first rise, the dough rests on a floured surface for 10 minutes before shaping. Generally, this cuts the rise time by about one-third.

Jenny Reece of Lowry, Minnesota shares her recipe for Basic Sweet Dough that takes advantage of this time-saving ingredient. The versatile dough can be made into the Braided Coffee Cake or the Coffee Cake Ring. "I usually use the Chocolate Lover's Filling and shape the dough into a braid," Jenny notes.

The braid and the ring also can be filled with the Cinnamon Nut Filling or Fruity Cream Cheese Filling developed in our test kitchen.

Basic Sweet Dough

    3 cups all-purpose flour, *divided*
1/4 cup sugar
    1 package (1/4 ounce) quick-rise yeast
1/2 teaspoon salt
1/2 cup milk
1/2 cup butter *or* margarine, softened
1/4 cup water
    1 egg

In a mixing bowl, combine 2 cups flour, sugar, yeast and salt. In a saucepan, heat milk, butter and water to 120°-130°. Add to dry ingredients; beat just until moistened. Add egg and remaining flour; beat until smooth. Shape into a ball. Do not knead. Cover and let rest for 10 minutes. Use for Braided Coffee Cake or Coffee Cake Ring. **Yield:** 1 recipe.

Hints for Success with Yeast Breads

Yeast Tips
- Yeast should be used before the expiration date on the package. Unopened yeast packages or jars should be stored in a cool dry place. Once opened, they should be refrigerated.
- If the yeast is dissolved in a liquid, it is important that the temperature of the liquid be 110° to 115°F. If the liquid is added to the yeast and dry ingredients, it is important that the temperature be 120° to 130°F.

Dough Tips
- 1-pound loaves of frozen white or sweet dough, thawed, may be substituted when one recipe of Basic Sweet Dough is called for on these pages. However, a basic white dough will produce a bread that is slightly less sweet, so an icing or glaze may be desired.

- Dough should not be stretched larger than the recipe states or it may become too thin and tear, causing the filling to leak out.
- For a decorative edge on the strips of braided breads, use a pastry wheel to cut each strip.

Storage Tips
- Cool yeast breads completely before placing in an airtight container or plastic bag. Breads with cream cheese filling should be refrigerated. Those without can be stored in a cool dry place for 2 to 3 days. If you want to keep the bread longer, freeze it.
- To freeze yeast breads, place cooled, unfrosted bread in an airtight container or bag, then freeze for up to 3 months. Thaw at room temperature, then frost or glaze as desired.

Cinnamon Nut Filling

1/2 cup packed brown sugar
1/2 cup chopped walnuts *or* pecans
  1 teaspoon ground cinnamon
  2 tablespoons butter *or* margarine, softened

In a bowl, combine the brown sugar, walnuts and cinnamon. Use for Braided Coffee Cake or Coffee Cake Ring. Spread butter over dough; sprinkle with sugar mixture. **Yield:** about 1 cup.

Chocolate Lover's Filling

3/4 cup semisweet chocolate chips
1/3 cup evaporated milk
  2 tablespoons sugar
1/2 cup chopped pecans
  1 teaspoon vanilla extract
1/4 teaspoon ground cinnamon

In a saucepan, combine the chocolate chips, milk and sugar. Cook and stir over low heat until chocolate is melted. Stir in pecans, vanilla and cinnamon. Use for Braided Coffee Cake or Coffee Cake Ring. **Yield:** about 1-1/4 cups.

Fruity Cream Cheese Filling

  2 packages (3 ounces *each*) cream cheese, softened
1/4 cup sugar
  1 tablespoon butter *or* margarine, softened
  1 teaspoon lemon juice
1/4 cup strawberry jam *or* preserves of your choice

In a mixing bowl, beat the cream cheese, sugar, butter and lemon juice until smooth. Use for Braided Coffee Cake or Coffee Cake Ring. Refer to each coffee cake recipe for directions on adding jam. **Yield:** about 3/4 cup.

Coffee Cake Ring

(Pictured above left and on page 322)

  1 recipe Basic Sweet Dough
  1 recipe Chocolate Lover's, Cinnamon Nut *or* Fruity Cream Cheese Filling
GLAZE:
  1 cup confectioners' sugar
  1 tablespoon butter *or* margarine, softened
1/2 teaspoon vanilla extract
  2 to 3 tablespoons milk

Turn dough onto a lightly floured surface. Roll into a 15-in. x 12-in. rectangle. Spread filling to within 1/2 in. of edges. (If using Fruity Cream Cheese Filling, spread with cream cheese mixture; set jam aside.) Roll up, jelly-roll style, starting with a long side; pinch seam to seal. Place, seam side down, on a greased 12-in. pizza pan; pinch ends together to form a ring. With scissors, cut from outside edge two-thirds of the way toward center of the ring at 1-1/2-in. intervals (see photos above right). Separate pieces; slightly twist to show filling. Cover and let rise in a warm place until doubled, about 45 minutes.

◄ **To form a braid:** Start at one end of the rectangle and fold strips alternately at an angle across the filling.

► **To form a ring (Step 1):** Using kitchen scissors, make cuts two-thirds of the way through dough at 1-1/2-inch intervals.

► **To form a ring (Step 2):** Separate the cut pieces slightly, twisting each individually to show the filling inside.

(If using Fruity Cream Cheese Filling, place 1 teaspoon of jam in the center of each slice.) Bake at 375° for 20-25 minutes or until golden brown. Remove from pan to a wire rack to cool. For glaze, combine sugar, butter, vanilla and enough milk to achieve desired consistency. Drizzle over coffee cake. **Yield:** 12 servings.

Braided Coffee Cake

(Pictured above left and on page 323)

  1 recipe Basic Sweet Dough
  1 recipe Chocolate Lover's, Cinnamon Nut *or* Fruity Cream Cheese Filling

Roll dough into a 14-in. x 11-in. rectangle on a large greased baking sheet. Spread filling down center third of rectangle. (If using Fruity Cream Cheese Filling, first spread cream cheese mixture over dough, then top with jam.) On each long side, cut 1-in. strips about 3 in. into center. Starting at one end, fold alternating strips at an angle across filling (see photo above). Pinch ends to seal. Cover and let rise in a warm place until doubled, about 45 minutes. Bake at 375° for 20-25 minutes or until golden brown. Remove from pan to a wire rack to cool. **Yield:** 12-14 servings.

Pretty Produce Garnishes

WHEN planning a menu for a special occasion, the focus is often on what foods to feature. But how the foods are garnished can really make a statement.

Vegetable garnishes can add an elegant touch to individual dinner plates at an intimate gathering to honor mom or dad or to a meat and cheese tray at a large graduation party.

In the photo above, we show how four cucumber fans and a tomato rose surrounded by a cucumber spiral really dress up a platter. Then, on the opposite page, we give step-by-step directions for making each garnish, as well as pretty zucchini asters. Since these garnishes can be made ahead of time, there's no last-minute fuss.

Choosing the Right Tools

The key to successful garnishes is a sharp knife. A sharp knife enables you to control the depth and direction of your cuts. Because you must use more force with a dull blade, you're more likely to slip and make unwanted cuts.

A small paring knife works best for most garnishes. Knives with serrated blades are not recommended because they are angled on only one side of the blade and may veer off in that direction.

A vegetable peeler with a blade that swivels is another useful tool. It's best to avoid vegetable peelers that don't swivel because they can dig too deeply into the food.

If you don't have a peeler, a cheese slicer can be used to cut some garnishes, such as zucchini asters.

Working with Vegetables

For best results, use ripe, firm, unbruised vegetables. To prevent vegetables from splitting or cracking when cutting and shaping, work with items that are at room temperature.

You can vary the color of some garnishes by substituting similar vegetables. For example, yellow squash can be used instead of cucumbers when making fancy fans or spirals.

While crisp garnishes add a fresh look to foods, the firmness of some vegetables can make it difficult to bend and shape them.

Sprinkling salt on cut surfaces of vegetables, then letting them sit for 2-3 minutes will help remove some water and make the vegetable slices softer and more pliable. Be sure to rinse the salt off before finishing the garnish.

Properly Storing Garnishes

Soaking completed garnishes in very cold water will help maintain their freshness and enhance their appearance.

For instance, soaking zucchini asters will cause them to absorb some water, swell and expand to complete their shaping.

Placing carrot ribbons and green onion strips in a bowl of cold water will make them curl.

Most garnishes can be made up 2 days in advance. Once completed, gently wrap or cover garnishes and refrigerate until ready to use.

If garnishes begin to wilt while being displayed, mist them with cold water to keep them fresh and bright.

If you would like to save a garnish to use again in a day or two, soak it in cold water for a half hour before wrapping and refrigerating it. In general, the larger and less delicate a garnish is, the longer it will stay fresh and reusable.

How to Create Great Garnishes

For cucumber fan (Step 1): Cut a 5- to 6-inch cucumber in half lengthwise. Trim off ends and discard. Then make a 2- to 3-inch diagonal cut across one of the cut ends.

(Step 2): Starting with the end that's diagonally cut, make an odd number of thin cuts to within 1/4 inch of the edge of the cucumber. On the last cut, slice all the way through.

(Step 3): Starting with the second slice of the cut section, bend and tuck every other slice toward the uncut edge. To vary fan size, increase or decrease cuts by any odd number.

For tomato rose (Step 1): Starting at the base of the tomato, use a paring knife to peel a thin continuous strip around, finishing at the stem.

(Step 2): Place the strip, skin side down, on your work surface. Beginning with the stem end of the strip, roll up the strip to form a coil.

(Step 3): When the strip is almost completely rolled up, place tomato rose on its base and tuck the end of the strip under it.

For cucumber spiral (Step 1): Carefully push a wooden skewer through the center of a 3- to 4-inch-long piece of cucumber. (If you don't have a wooden skewer, a thin wooden spoon handle also will work.) Then hold the cucumber at an angle above your work surface.

(Step 2): Place a sharp knife at a slight angle and cut through the cucumber until the knife touches the skewer. Leaving blade against the skewer, rotate cucumber away from your body and continue cutting around the cucumber so the cut remains at a constant 1/4-inch width.

(Step 3): Remove the skewer and pull the ends of the cucumber to form a spiral. If you make the spiral ahead, wrap it in its original shape, then extend it just before displaying it. You can join ends to form a circle. To make a more delicate spiral, decrease the width of the cut.

For zucchini asters (Step 1): With a cheese slicer or vegetable peeler, cut a very thin slice down the length of the zucchini. Repeat, making one slice for each flower.

(Step 2): With a small sharp knife, make cuts along one edge of the slice so it resembles a comb. Keep cuts close together and be careful not to cut through the opposite edge.

(Step 3): Gently roll up zucchini slice and secure at the base with a small toothpick piece. Stand upright for petals to open. Use chopped pimiento for the flower center if desired.

Pressure Cooker Basics

WHEN the pressure's on, Sally Williams relies on her pressure cooker to put dinner on the table in a jiffy. "I'm amazed at the tender slow-cooked taste of food prepared this way and thrilled with cooking times of only 15-30 minutes for most recipes," says the Portland, Oregon cook.

But initially, Sally approached pressure cooking with some reservations. "I remember my mom made such good meals in the pressure cooker," she recalls. "But I had a real fear of using one, because Mom always said if you didn't use it correctly, it might explode.

"After reading about the newer safer pressure cookers on the market, I decided to buy one," Sally relates. "To my delight, I find this cooking method to be quick, easy and not scary at all."

The Pressure Principle

So how does a pressure cooker cook foods so quickly? No matter what brand, style or size, they generally cook the same way—with pressurized steam.

After the pressure cooker's lid is secured, the liquid inside begins boiling and produces steam. The trapped steam causes pressure to build and the temperature in the cooker to rise above the normal boiling point.

When the cooker reaches full pressure (15 pounds pressure), the pressure regulator in the center of the lid starts to rock or jiggle. (See illustration below.) At this time, the heat should be reduced just enough to maintain a slow rocking motion.

It's also very important to set a timer for the recommended cooking time at this point, since it's impossible to lift the lid to check the doneness of the food without releasing the pressure. Precise timing will help avoid under- or over-cooking the food.

At the end of the cooking time, the pressure should be released according to the recipe or manufacturer's directions.

Like Sally, if you've never used a pressure cooker before, you may be leery about trying one. Pressure cookers are safe as long as they are used properly and according to the manufacturer's directions.

Many newer pressure cookers include the following safety features:

• If the lid is not locked securely in place, the pressure will not rise.

• A rubber gasket in the lid prevents opening the cooker until the pressure has been reduced enough to open it safely.

• Over-pressure and/or backup plugs release steam if the heat is not reduced when the cooker reaches full pressure or if the vent pipe becomes clogged.

Keep these tips in mind when using a pressure cooker:

• Not every food can be cooked in a pressure cooker. Some foods "foam" while cooking and can clog the vent pipe and over-pressure plug. Pasta, rice, oatmeal or other cereals, split peas, barley, cranberries and rhubarb should not be cooked under pressure.

• Do not fill the cooker more than two-thirds full. Foods tend to expand when cooked under pressure, and if food blocks the vent pipe or the over-pressure plug, extra pressure won't be able to be released during cooking.

• Boiling liquid creates steam, so at least 1/2 cup liquid must be used when pressure cooking.

• Using a cooking rack allows some or all of the food to be held above the liquid during cooking.

• Always make sure the vent pipe is clear. Before using, hold the lid up to the light and look through the vent pipe to be sure it's clear. If it's blocked, use a wire or toothpick to clean it.

• Never open the cooker or remove the pressure regulator when it is under pressure. When the cooker is removed from the heat, the pressure will drop gradually on its own. Pressure can be reduced more quickly by placing the cooker under running cold water. Gently push the pressure regulator and listen to make sure steam is not still escaping before removing the regulator or opening the cooker.

Barbecued Country Ribs

(Pictured above right)

Ready in 1 hour or less

These tender chunks of pork ribs served with a pleasant sauce are so tasty. —John Bell, Windber, Pennsylvania

    1/3 cup all-purpose flour
    1/4 teaspoon garlic powder
    1/4 teaspoon salt
    1/8 teaspoon pepper
1-1/2 pounds boneless country-style ribs, cut into 2-inch chunks
    1 tablespoon vegetable oil
    1 cup hot water
    1/2 cup ketchup
    1/4 teaspoon chili powder
    1/8 to 1/4 teaspoon hot pepper sauce
    1 small onion, halved and sliced

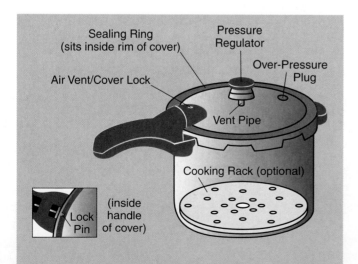

Sealing Ring (sits inside rim of cover)
Pressure Regulator
Over-Pressure Plug
Air Vent/Cover Lock
Vent Pipe
Cooking Rack (optional)
Lock Pin
(inside handle of cover)

Barbecued Country Ribs
Tender Lemon Chicken

In a large resealable plastic bag, combine the flour, garlic powder, salt and pepper. Add rib pieces; shake to coat. In a pressure cooker, brown meat on all sides in oil; drain. Combine the water, ketchup, chili powder and hot pepper sauce; pour over ribs. Add onion. Close cover securely; place pressure regulator on vent pipe. Bring cooker to full pressure over high heat. Reduce heat to medium-high and cook for 15 minutes. (Pressure regulator should maintain a slow steady rocking motion; adjust heat if needed.) Remove from the heat; allow pressure to drop on its own. Skim fat from sauce if necessary; serve sauce with ribs if desired. **Yield:** 4 servings.

Tender Lemon Chicken

(Pictured above)

Ready in 30 minutes or less

You'll love the zesty flavor of this moist delicious chicken. Using the pressure cooker cuts the cooking time in half.
—Lee Bremson, Kansas City, Missouri

✓ Uses less fat, sugar or salt. Includes Nutritional Analysis and Diabetic Exchanges.

```
    1 medium onion, chopped
    4 garlic cloves, minced
    1 to 3 tablespoons olive or vegetable oil
    4 bone-in chicken breast halves, skin removed
    1 cup chicken broth
  1/4 cup water
  1/4 cup lemon juice
  3/4 cup minced fresh parsley
  1/2 cup chopped celery with leaves
1-1/2 teaspoons Italian seasoning
  1/2 teaspoon salt, optional
  1/4 teaspoon pepper
4-1/2 teaspoons cornstarch
    3 tablespoons cold water
```

In a pressure cooker, saute onion and garlic in oil until tender; remove with a slotted spoon and set aside. Brown the chicken, a few pieces at a time, in the cooker. Return onion mixture and all chicken to pan. Add broth, water, lemon juice, parsley, celery, Italian seasoning, salt if desired and pepper. Close cover securely; place pressure regulator on vent pipe. Bring cooker to full pressure over high heat. Reduce heat to medium-high and cook for 8 minutes. (Pressure regulator should maintain a slow steady rocking motion; adjust heat if needed.) Immediately cool according to manufacturer's directions until pressure is completely reduced. Remove chicken and keep warm. Measure pan juices; return 1-1/2 cups to pan. Combine cornstarch and cold water until smooth; stir into pan juices. Bring to a boil; cook and stir for 2 minutes or until thickened. Serve over chicken. **Yield:** 4 servings. **Nutritional Analysis:** One serving (prepared with 1 tablespoon oil and low-sodium broth and without salt) equals 233 calories, 125 mg sodium, 67 mg cholesterol, 10 gm carbohydrate, 28 gm protein, 9 gm fat, 2 gm fiber. **Diabetic Exchanges:** 3-1/2 lean meat, 1 vegetable, 1/2 fat.

Pressure-Cooked Beef Stew

I like to serve this twist on traditional stew with fresh rolls or crusty bread. The roast and vegetables cook quickly and make a comforting meal.
—Joanne Wright
Niles, Michigan

```
    1 boneless chuck roast (2 pounds)
    1 tablespoon vegetable oil
    5 cups water, divided
    8 medium potatoes, peeled and quartered
    4 medium carrots, halved widthwise
    1 medium onion, quartered
    2 garlic cloves, minced
  3/4 teaspoon salt
  1/2 teaspoon pepper
  1/2 teaspoon dried thyme
    2 bay leaves
    2 to 3 tablespoons cornstarch
  1/4 cup cold water
```

In a pressure cooker, brown roast on all sides in oil. Remove roast. Add cooking rack; return roast to pan. Add 4 cups of water. Close cover securely; place pressure regulator on vent pipe. Bring cooker to full pressure over high heat. Reduce heat to medium-high; cook for 40 minutes. (Pressure regulator should maintain a slow steady rocking motion; adjust heat if needed.) Remove from the heat; allow pressure to drop on its own. Remove meat and keep warm. Pour juices into a cup or bowl; skim fat. Remove rack from cooker. Add potatoes, carrots, onion, garlic, salt, pepper, thyme, bay leaves, pan juices and remaining water to cooker. Cover securely; return cooker to full pressure. Reduce heat; cook for 8 minutes. Immediately cool according to manufacturer's directions until pressure is completely reduced. With a slotted spoon, remove vegetables and keep warm. Discard bay leaves. Combine cornstarch and cold water until smooth; stir into the pan juices. Bring to a boil; cook and stir for 2 minutes or until thickened. Serve with the meat and vegetables. **Yield:** 6 servings.

From-Scratch Baked Goods

Apricot Upside-Down Cake
Fudge Ripple Brownies

FROM CAKES and cookies to bars and brownies, homemade goodies are a winning way to show your family how much you care.

But novice cooks—and sometimes even veteran bakers—come across a term or technique in a recipe that makes them hesitate.

So we've compiled a list of common baking terms and their definitions in the box on the next page. But before you head to the kitchen, let's review some of the basics of baking.

Picking Proper Pans

Shiny metal pans made from aluminum or tin are best for baking because they reflect heat away from the baked product. If you use pans made of other materials, you may need to adjust your baking times.

For example, items baked in insulated pans require more baking time and take longer to brown while foods baked in dark-colored pans require less baking time and brown more quickly. Glass and enamel pans conduct and retain heat and result in a heavier, browner crust.

For the best results, it's important to use the correct size pan called for in the recipe. When checking the size of a pan, measure from the top inside edge to the opposite inside edge.

Operating the Oven

Once you have your equipment and ingredients on hand, preheat your oven for 10 to 15 minutes, then prepare your pan. For layer or sheet cakes, recipes call for greasing and flouring the pan before adding the batter. This makes it easier to remove the cake from the pan after it's baked.

But there are exceptions. Do not grease or flour pans for foam cakes, such as angel food, chiffon or sponge cakes. The batter must be able to cling to the sides of the pan in order to rise correctly.

Only add batter until the pan is one-half to two-thirds full. This will allow baked goods to bake evenly and prevent batter from overflowing the pan.

Place pans on the middle oven rack unless the recipe directs otherwise, allowing at least 2 inches between pans and the sides of the oven for good circulation. Overcrowding can result in uneven baking.

To avoid overbaking, start checking for doneness at the minimum baking time, then at 1- to 2-minute intervals.

Serving and Storage

Once you remove your baked goods from the oven, follow the cooling directions noted in the recipe. In general, most cakes should be cooled on a wire rack for 10 minutes before being removed from pans. (If your cake is not removed soon enough and sticks to the pan, return it to the oven and heat for 1 minute, then try removing it.)

Don't cover or store cakes until they are completely cool. They also should be cool before filling, frosting or glazing unless recipe directs otherwise.

Letting bars and brownies completely cool will help prevent them from crumbling when cut.

To freeze baked goods, use freezer bags or containers with tight-fitting lids, or wrap items securely in moisture-proof wrap, heavy-duty foil or freezer paper.

Fudge Ripple Brownies

(Pictured above left)

These brownies have a rich chocolate taste and yummy brown butter frosting. —Bobi Raab, St. Paul, Minnesota

- 1 cup butter (no substitutes), softened
- 2 cups sugar
- 4 eggs
- 2 squares (1 ounce *each*) unsweetened chocolate, melted

2 teaspoons vanilla extract
1-1/2 cups all-purpose flour
1 teaspoon baking powder
1 teaspoon salt
1 cup chopped walnuts
FROSTING:
1/3 cup butter (no substitutes)
3 cups confectioners' sugar
1-1/2 teaspoons vanilla extract
4 to 5 tablespoons whipping cream
TOPPING:
1 square (1 ounce) unsweetened chocolate
1 tablespoon butter (no substitutes)
1 tablespoon confectioners' sugar

In a mixing bowl, cream butter and sugar. Add eggs, one at a time, beating well after each addition. Add chocolate and vanilla; mix well. Combine flour, baking powder and salt; add to creamed mixture and mix well. Stir in walnuts. Spread into a greased 15-in. x 10-in. x 1-in. baking pan. Bake at 350° for 25-30 minutes or until a toothpick inserted near the center comes out clean. Cool on a wire rack. For frosting, in a saucepan, cook and stir butter over medium heat for 6-7 minutes or until golden brown. Pour into a mixing bowl; add confectioners' sugar, vanilla and enough cream to achieve spreading consistency. Frost cooled brownies. For topping, melt chocolate and butter; stir until smooth. Add confectioners' sugar; stir until smooth. Drizzle over frosting. Cut into bars. **Yield:** 4 dozen.

Apricot Upside-Down Cake

(Pictured at far left)

My Aunt Anne, who is a great cook, gave me a taste of this golden cake and I couldn't believe how delicious it was. Apricots give it an elegant twist from traditional pineapple versions. —Ruth Ann Stelfox, Raymond, Alberta

2 cans (15 ounces *each*) apricot halves
1/4 cup butter *or* margarine
1/2 cup packed brown sugar
2 eggs, *separated*

2/3 cup sugar
2/3 cup cake flour
3/4 teaspoon baking powder
1/4 teaspoon salt

Drain apricots, reserving 3 tablespoons juice (discard remaining juice or save for another use); set aside. Place butter in a greased 9-in. square baking pan; place in a 350° oven for 3-4 minutes or until melted. Stir in the brown sugar. Arrange apricot halves, cut side up, in a single layer over sugar. In a mixing bowl, beat egg yolks on high for 4 minutes or until thick and lemon-colored. Gradually beat in sugar. Stir in reserved apricot juice. Combine flour, baking powder and salt; gradually add to egg yolk mixture. In another mixing bowl, beat egg whites until stiff. Fold into yolk mixture. Carefully spread over apricots. Bake at 350° for 35-40 minutes or until a toothpick inserted near the center of cake comes out clean. Cool for 10 minutes before inverting onto a serving plate. **Yield:** 9 servings.

Mixing Methods

- **Beat:** To make a mixture smooth by rapidly mixing with an electric mixer, fork, spoon or wire whisk. (See "Batter Techniques" below for an example.)
- **Combine:** To place several ingredients in a single bowl or container and thoroughly mix.
- **Cream:** To beat butter, margarine or shortening alone or with sugar using a spoon or mixer until light and fluffy.
- **Fold:** To combine light or delicate ingredients, such as whipped cream or egg whites with heavier ingredients without beating.
- **Moisten:** To add enough liquid to dry ingredients while stirring to make a wet but not runny mixture.
- **Soft peaks:** To beat cream or egg whites until soft, rounded peaks form when the beaters are lifted.
- **Stiff peaks:** To beat egg whites until stiff, pointed peaks form when beaters are lifted.
- **Whip:** To beat rapidly by hand or with an electric mixer to add air and increase volume.

Batter Techniques

Want to make better batters? The recipe for Apricot Upside-Down Cake on this page uses two common mixing methods demonstrated below:

To beat egg yolks: Use an electric mixer on high speed to beat yolks until thick and lemon-colored.

To fold in ingredients: To fold a lighter mixture into a heavier one, use a rubber spatula to gently cut down through the middle of the ingredients. Move spatula across bottom of bowl and bring up part of heavier mixture. Repeat this circular motion just until mixture is combined.

Standout Stuffing

AT Thanksgiving time, most folks enjoy a fabulous feast featuring succulent roast turkey with all the fixings.

What time-honored dish are you likely to find alongside the creamy mashed potatoes, marshmallow-topped sweet potatoes and ruby-red cranberry sauce? Sensational stuffing, of course!

It's that perfectly seasoned blend of bread, rice, other grains or even potatoes—baked in or out of the bird—that's gobbled up year after year.

Most traditional stuffings, or dressings as they're sometimes called, start with sauteed vegetables like onion and celery. Then cubed or crumbled bread, such as corn bread, French, Italian or white bread, and seasonings are added to the vegetable mixture.

Depending on family traditions and regional tastes, other ingredients—from fruits and nuts to meats and seafoods—can be used to lend additional flavor.

Tips on Texture

When it comes to texture, there is no right or wrong way to make stuffing. Some people like it dry and crisp; some like it moist and dense.

Soft breads tend to produce a stuffing that is dense and spongy. Toasted breads produce a much drier stuffing because the bread crumbs can absorb more juices without becoming overly soggy.

To get the consistency your family prefers, follow these simple suggestions:

- For a drier stuffing, use prepackaged dry bread crumbs or cubes and limit the amount of liquid.
- For moister stuffing, use melted butter in your recipe. The butter won't evaporate when heated or make the stuffing soggy like liquids can.
- Another option for moister stuffing is to add stock, broth or juice until the mixture is just moist enough that it sticks together when pinched. But keep in mind that stuffing baked in poultry or in a tightly covered dish will not dry out as it bakes.
- For a fluffier stuffing, add a beaten egg or pasteurized egg product. It will allow the stuffing to bake to a lighter, more airy consistency.

For food safety reasons, the folks at Butterball Turkey recommend using an egg substitute in dressing that is stuffed into poultry. To be sure the stuffing is done, a meat thermometer at the center of the stuffing inside the bird should reach 165°.

For stuffing baked in a separate dish, either egg or egg substitute can be used. Refrigerate leftover stuffing promptly.

Two-Bread Stuffed Turkey

(Pictured below left)

I reach for bacon and canned corn to make this subtly sweet stuffing that combines corn bread and white bread. The moist mixture is terrific with turkey but just as good served solo.   —Fancheon Resler, Bluffton, Indiana

Two-Bread Stuffed Turkey

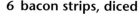

        6 bacon strips, diced
        2 cups chopped celery
        1 cup sliced green onions
        6 cups cubed corn bread
        6 cups cubed white bread
        1 can (15-1/4 ounces) whole
            kernel corn, undrained
    1-1/4 cups chicken broth
      3/4 cup egg substitute
      1/4 cup butter *or* margarine,
            melted
        2 teaspoons rubbed sage
        1 teaspoon dried thyme
      1/2 teaspoon salt
      1/4 teaspoon pepper
        1 turkey (10 to 12 pounds)
        2 tablespoons vegetable oil

In a large skillet, cook bacon over medium heat until crisp. Remove bacon to paper towels to drain. In the drippings, saute celery and onions until tender. Transfer to a large bowl. Add corn bread, bread, corn, broth, egg substitute, butter, seasonings and bacon; mix well. Just before baking, loosely stuff turkey. Skewer openings; tie drumsticks together. Place on a rack in a roasting pan. Brush with oil. Cover lightly with a tent of foil. Bake at 325° for 3-3/4 to 4 hours or until a meat thermometer reads 180° for turkey and 165° for stuffing. **Yield:** 8-10 servings (10 cups stuffing). **Editor's Note:** Stuffing may be prepared as directed and baked separately in a greased shallow 3-qt. baking dish. Cover and bake at 325° for 60 minutes. Uncover; bake 10 minutes longer or until golden brown.

Fruited Stuffing Balls

(Pictured at right)

Ready in 1 hour or less

This delightful dressing, shaped into individual servings, is a perfect addition to a traditional Thanksgiving dinner. We love the extra flavor it gets from apricots, raisins and crunchy pecans.
— Lucille Terry
Frankfort, Kentucky

Wild Rice Stuffing
Fruited Stuffing Balls

2 cups diced celery
1/2 cup chopped onion
1/3 cup butter *or* margarine, melted
4 cups seasoned stuffing cubes
1 cup dried apricots, finely chopped
3/4 to 1 cup chicken broth
1/2 cup raisins
2 eggs, lightly beaten
1/4 cup chopped pecans
1 teaspoon rubbed sage
1 teaspoon salt
1/4 teaspoon pepper

In a large skillet, saute celery and onion in butter until tender. Remove from the heat. Add remaining ingredients; mix well. Shape into 12 balls. Place in a greased 13-in. x 9-in. x 2-in. baking dish. Bake, uncovered, at 375° for 20-25 minutes or until golden brown. **Yield:** 12 servings.

Wild Rice Stuffing

(Pictured above)

Although it uses many of the same ingredients found in typical stuffings, this version is especially enjoyable because the wild rice provides a different texture.
— Edie DeSpain, Logan, Utah

✓ Uses less fat, sugar or salt. Includes Nutritional Analysis and Diabetic Exchanges.

2 cans (14-1/2 ounces *each*) chicken broth
1-1/2 cups water
2/3 cup uncooked wild rice
1/2 teaspoon salt
1/2 teaspoon dried thyme

4 medium carrots, sliced
2 celery ribs, chopped
1 medium onion, chopped
2 tablespoons vegetable oil
1/2 pound fresh mushrooms, sliced
1-1/2 cups uncooked long grain rice
1/4 cup minced fresh parsley

In a large saucepan, bring broth and water to a boil. Add the wild rice, salt and thyme. Reduce heat; cover and simmer for 30 minutes. Meanwhile, in another saucepan, saute carrots, celery and onion in oil until almost tender. Add the mushrooms; saute 5 minutes longer. Add vegetables and long grain rice to wild rice. Cover and cook for 30-35 minutes or until rice is tender. Stir in parsley. **Yield:** 7 servings. **Nutritional Analysis:** One 1-cup serving (prepared with reduced-sodium broth) equals 313 calories, 272 mg sodium, 2 mg cholesterol, 57 gm carbohydrate, 9 gm protein, 6 gm fat, 4 gm fiber. **Diabetic Exchanges:** 3 starch, 2 vegetable, 1 fat.

Bye-Bye Birdie

If you like stuffing, you don't have to limit it to Thanksgiving turkey dinners. It bakes up just as nice on its own as an accompaniment to chicken or other meats. Simply place stuffing in a greased shallow baking dish, cover with foil and bake at 325° to 350° for 1 hour or until heated through. For a crisper crust, uncover stuffing during the final 15-20 minutes of baking and dot with butter.

General Recipe Index

This handy index lists every recipe by food category, major ingredient and/or cooking method, so you can easily locate recipes to suit your needs.

✓ Recipe includes Nutritional Analysis and Diabetic Exchanges

✓ Recipe includes Nutritional Analysis and Diabetic Exchanges

✓ Recipe includes Nutritional Analysis and Diabetic Exchanges

✓ Recipe includes Nutritional Analysis and Diabetic Exchanges

✓ Recipe includes Nutritional Analysis and Diabetic Exchanges

✓ Recipe includes Nutritional Analysis and Diabetic Exchanges

✓ Recipe includes Nutritional Analysis and Diabetic Exchanges

✓ Recipe includes Nutritional Analysis and Diabetic Exchanges

✓ Recipe includes Nutritional Analysis and Diabetic Exchanges

✓ Recipe includes Nutritional Analysis and Diabetic Exchanges

✓ Recipe includes Nutritional Analysis and Diabetic Exchanges

✓ *Recipe includes Nutritional Analysis and Diabetic Exchanges*

Alphabetical Index

This handy index lists every recipe in alphabetical order so you can easily find your favorite recipes.

✓ Recipe includes Nutritional Analysis and Diabetic Exchanges

✓ Recipe includes Nutritional Analysis and Diabetic Exchanges

Golden Potato Rounds, 54
Graham Pie Crust Mix, 89
Grandma's Potato Salad, 190
Granola Raisin Bread, 167
✓Greek Garden Salad, 13
✓Green Pepper Meat Loaf, 96
Grilled Chicken Cordon Bleu, 285
Grilled Chicken Salad, 189
✓Grilled Corn and Peppers, 102
Grilled Peaches 'n' Berries, 283
Grilled Pineapple, 282
✓Ground Beef and Veggies, 149
✓Ground Beef Gyros, 190

H

Ham and Bean Chili, 107
Ham 'n' Cheese Crepes, 120
Ham and Cheese Puffs, 257
Ham 'n' Swiss Chicken, 267
Ham Potato Scallop, 73
Hard-Cooked Eggs, 98
Harvest Ham Skillet, 148
✓Hawaiian Ham Skillet, 145
Hearty Eight-Layer Salad, 179
✓Hearty Hotcakes, 132
Herbed Beef Barley Soup, 110
Herbed Chicken and Shrimp, 272
Herbed Chicken Fettuccine, 148
Herbed Gazpacho, 189
Herbed Green Beans, 290
Herbed Tomato Bread, 168
✓Herbed Vinaigrette, 181
Holly Sandwich Wreath, 45
Homemade Chocolate Cake, 217
Home-Style White Bread, 19
Honey Barbecued Ribs, 281
✓Honey-Dijon Potato Salad, 231
Honey Fruit Loaves, 157
Honey-Lime Grilled Chicken, 297
✓Honey-Mustard Chicken, 50
✓Honey Oatmeal Bread, 171
Honey-Raisin Quick Bread, 161
Horseradish Potatoes, 288
Hot 'n' Spicy Omelet, 132
✓Hot Cider with Orange Twists, 315
Hot Cranberry Punch, 271
Hot Dog Cookies, 41
Hot Dogs 'n' Beans, 269
Hot German Potato Salad, 276
Hot Ham Sandwiches, 273
Hot Italian Patties, 197
Hot Pizza Dip, 64

I

Ice Cream Dessert, 113
Ice Cream Sandwich Dessert, 118
✓Italian Beans and Pasta, 146

Italian Beef Hoagies, 277
Italian Bread Salad, 22
Italian Deli Rollers, 189
Italian Holiday Bread, 170
Italian Meatball Mix, 90
Italian Meat Loaf, 289

J

Jazzy Gelatin, 43
Jelly-Filled Muffins, 161
Jiffy Jambalaya, 146
Jumbo Molasses Cookies, 209
Jumbo Raisin Cookies, 215

K

Kool-Aid Pie, 257

L

Ladyfinger Cheesecake, 202
Lamb Ratatouille, 149
Layered Brownies, 220
Layered Chocolate Cake, 307
Layered Deli Loaf, 194
Lazy Day Cake, 246
Lemon Berry Cake, 85
Lemon Garlic Mushrooms, 280
Lemon Grape Cooler, 57
Lemon Ice, 22
✓Lemony Caesar Salad, 305
Lemony Corn Muffins, 157
✓Light Lemon Cake, 227
✓Light Lemon Mousse, 231
✓Light Tiramisu, 234
Lime Chiffon Dessert, 210
✓Lime Garlic Shrimp, 228
Lime Yogurt Pie, 32
✓Low-Fat Corn Bread, 227
✓Low-Fat Devil's Food Cake, 233

M

Make-Ahead Shortcake, 215
Make-Ahead Squash Soup, 110
✓Mandarin Chicken, 286
Mandarin Salad, 51
✓Marinated Broccoli Salad, 176
Marinated Turkey Slices, 283
Mashed Potatoes with Ham, 23
Meal-in-One Casserole, 271
✓Meat Loaf Burritos, 97
Meat Loaf Patties, 246
Meat Loaf Shepherd's Pie, 97
✓Melon Fruit Bowl, 131

Merry Berry Salad, 45
Mexicali Pork Chops, 69
Mexican Manicotti, 139
Microwave Apple Crisp, 286
Microwave Pickles, 287
✓Microwave Swiss Steak, 288
Miniature Meat Pies, 119
Mini Ham Quiches, 135
Mint Chocolate Chip Pie, 118
Minty Cocoa Mousse, 218
Mocha Punch, 61
Moist Poultry Dressing, 270
Mom's Buttermilk Cookies, 202
Mom's Coleslaw, 53
Multigrain Bread, 172
Mushroom Pork Tenderloin, 271
Mushroom Steak Hoagies, 199
Mushroom Wild Rice, 274

N

Neapolitan Cookies, 301
No-Crust Tropical Pie, 110
No-Fry Potato Doughnuts, 164
No-Fuss Meatballs, 68
✓No-Oil Salad Dressing, 226
Nutty Broccoli Slaw, 186
Nutty Fruit Medley, 132

O

Oatmeal Brownies, 17
Old Glory Dessert, 39
Onion Beef Stroganoff, 74
Onion Salisbury Steak, 30
✓Open-Faced Omelet, 230
Open-Faced Turkey Sandwiches, 195
Orange Coconut Crescents, 156
Orange Coffee Cake, 132
Orange Cream Dessert, 61
✓Orange Lettuce Salad, 25
Orange Pecan Cookies, 301
Orange Poppy Muffins, 161
Orange Toast, 157
✓Orange Vegetable Kabobs, 297
Oregano Chicken, 247
Oriental Tossed Salad, 31
Oven Denver Omelet, 128
Oven-Ready Lasagna, 115

P

Paprika Onion Bread, 164
Parmesan Broccoli Bake, 52
Parmesan Chicken, 105
✓Parmesan Muffins, 153
Parmesan Walnut Bread, 163
✓Parmesan Zucchini Strips, 236
✓Pasta Primavera, 244

✓ Recipe includes Nutritional Analysis and Diabetic Exchanges

✓ Recipe includes Nutritional Analysis and Diabetic Exchanges

✓ *Recipe includes Nutritional Analysis and Diabetic Exchanges*